THE CHURCH OF CHRIST
VOLUME TWO

OTHER SOLID GROUND TITLES

We recently celebrated our eighth anniversary of uncovering buried treasure to the glory of God. During these eight years we have produced over 225 volumes. A sample is listed below:

Biblical & Theological Studies: *Addresses on the 100th Anniversary of Princeton Theological Seminary in 1912* by Allis, Machen, Wilson, Vos, Warfield and more.
Power of the Pulpit by Gardiner Spring
Princeton Sermons by Aiken, Green, Hodge, Patton, Warfield
Thoughts on Preaching by James W. Alexander
Notes on Galatians by J. Gresham Machen
The Origin of Paul's Religion by J. Gresham Machen
A Scientific Investigation of the Old Testament by R.D. Wilson
Theology on Fire: *Sermons from Joseph A. Alexander*
Evangelical Truth: *Sermons for the Family* by Archibald Alexander
A Shepherd's Heart: *Pastoral Sermons of James W. Alexander*
Grace & Glory: *Sermons from Princeton Chapel* by Geerhardus Vos
The Lord of Glory by Benjamin B. Warfield
The Person & Work of the Holy Spirit by Benjamin B. Warfield
The Power of God unto Salvation by Benjamin B. Warfield
Calvin Memorial Addresses by Warfield, Johnson, Orr, Webb…
The Five Points of Calvinism by Robert Lewis Dabney
Annals of the American Presbyterian Pulpit by W.B. Sprague
The Word & Prayer: *Classic Devotions from the Pen of John Calvin*
A Body of Divinity: *Sum and Substance of Christian Doctrine* by Ussher
The Complete Works of Thomas Manton (in 22 volumes)
A Puritan New Testament Commentary by John Trapp
Exposition of the Epistle to the Hebrews by William Gouge
Exposition of the Epistle of Jude by William Jenkyn
Lectures on the Book of Esther by Thomas M'Crie
Lectures on the Book of Acts by John Dick

To order any of our titles please contact us in one of three ways:

Call us at **1-866-789-7423**
Email us at **sgcb@charter.net**
Visit our website at **www.solid-ground-books.com**

THE CHURCH OF CHRIST

A Treatise on the Nature, Powers,
Ordinances, Discipline & Government
of the Christian Church

VOLUME TWO

JAMES BANNERMAN

SOLID GROUND CHRISTIAN BOOKS
BIRMINGHAM, ALABAMA USA

Solid Ground Christian Books
PO Box 660132
Vestavia Hills AL 35266
205-443-0311
sgcb@charter.net
solid-ground-books.com

The Church of Christ: Volume Two
by James Bannerman (1807 – 1868)

First Solid Ground Edition October 2009

First published in 1868 by T & T Clark,
Edinburgh, Scotland.

Cover photo by Ric Ergenbright. Please view his
beautiful photographs at ricergenbright.com

Cover design by Borgo Design, Tuscaloosa, AL

ISBN: 978-159925-228-5

CONTENTS.

APPENDIX.

THE CHURCH OF CHRIST.

PART III.—MATTERS IN REGARD TO WHICH CHURCH POWER IS EXERCISED.

DIVISION II.
CHURCH POWER EXERCISED IN REGARD TO ORDINANCES.

SUBDIVISION IV.
POSITIVE DIVINE INSTITUTIONS IN ADDITION TO THE ORDINARY PUBLIC WORSHIP OF THE LORD'S DAY; OR THE SACRAMENTS.

CHAPTER I.

THE SACRAMENTS IN GENERAL.

FOR some time past we have been occupied with the subject of the ordinances of the Christian Church. We have discussed the questions connected with the public worship appointed in the Church, the special time set apart and sanctified for worship, and the ministry by means of which the worship of the Church is conducted. All these are outward ordinances which Christ has established in His Church, as parts of that external provision which He has made for the spiritual benefit and advancement of His people, and which He specially makes effectual to that end by the presence and power of His Spirit. All of these ordinances are in themselves, perhaps, and naturally adapted by their inherent character and influence to promote the edification of Christians; but above and beyond this natural or moral efficacy for that end, there is a spiritual blessing connected with them in consequence of the positive appointment of Christ, and the positive promise of His Spirit fulfilled in the right use of them. There may be a natural or moral efficacy in the ordinances of the Church considered in themselves, so that, apart from any other influence, they would, to a certain extent, be beneficial and advantageous in the case of those who used them. But in addition to this, there is a spiritual efficacy in the ordinances of the Church, distinct from the natural, and which is derived from the blessing of Christ and the working of His Spirit in them who by faith make use of them as He has appointed. What this spiritual and supernatural efficacy of outward ordinance exactly is,—what is the measure or amount of the inward benefit to the believer,—in what way and to what extent grace is connected with the external observance,—how beyond the sphere of this natural or moral influence the positive institutions of the Church have a blessing not natively their own,—these are questions which it is impossible for us distinctly to answer. The only wise and fitting reply to such questions is, that we have now reached the region of the supernatural, and that *there* we have no data to guide us beyond what has been revealed. We know, from revelation, that there is a promise of grace annexed to outward ordinances when rightly used; we know that in the external observances Christ meets with His people to bless them and to do them good;—but beyond this we do not know. The character, the measure, the amount of the blessing promised,—how it stands connected with the outward ordinance, and what is the extent and efficacy of the supernatural grace over and above the natural efficacy of the ordinance,—of all this we know nothing, because we have been told nothing. We can distinctly understand, from the analogy of other cases, how the preaching of the Word, viewed as a system of human teaching of truth, and no more, may have a natural tendency to benefit the understanding and the heart. But we do not understand the supernatural efficacy which, over and above the natural, is imparted to it by the presence and the power of the Spirit in the ordinance.

In passing, as we do at this stage, from the non-sacramental to the sacramental ordinances appointed by Christ in His Church, it is of great importance to carry this general principle along with us. A supernatural grace is not peculiar to the Sacraments, although it may be found in them in larger measure than in other ordinances. It is common to all the ordinances which Christ has appointed in His Church. Whatever mystery there may be in the connection which by the promise of Christ has

been established between the outward act and the inward blessing,
—between the external observance rightly used and the internal
grace divinely bestowed,—it is a mystery not belonging to Sacraments alone, but belonging to them in common with all Church
ordinances. *There is the supernatural element in them all.* There
is that supernatural element connected in some manner with the
outward act of the believer in the use of ordinances. There is a
mystery in respect to any ordinance, not less than in respect of
sacramental ordinances, which we cannot explain. It is, in short,
the mystery of the Spirit of God, promised to dwell in the
Church, and making every ordinance of the Church, whether
sacramental or not, the channel for the conveyance of supernatural grace. If we would rid ourselves of this mystery, we
can only do so by denying that the Spirit is present in ordinances
at all. " As the wind bloweth where it listeth, and thou hearest
the sound thereof, but canst not tell whence it cometh, and
whither it goeth,"—so is every ordinance, as well as each person,
touched and sanctified of the Holy Ghost. There can be no
natural explanation of the supernatural.[1]

What, then, is the character of those special ordinances
instituted by Christ in His Church, which are usually denomi-
nated sacramental ordinances ; and in what respect are they to be
distinguished from the other ordinances of the Christian Church,
not sacramental? In administering Sacraments, what is the
peculiar nature or character of the Church's act; and in what
manner does the administration differ from that of common
ordinances?

The term *Sacrament*, by which these peculiar ordinances are
known, is not of scriptural, but of ecclesiastical origin ; and there
is some doubt as to the manner in which it came to be applied
to these special solemnities of the Church, and to be restricted
to the peculiar meaning in which it is now almost universally
employed. In classical use, the word " *sacramentum* " is almost
always, if not invariably, employed to signify an oath,—more
especially the military oath by which a soldier bound himself to
obey the officer placed over him. And it has been conjectured
that from its classical use it was transferred into the service of
the Church, as significant of the obligation which the Christian

---

[1] [Bannerman, *Inspiration: The infallible Truth and Divine Authority of the
Holy Scriptures*, Edin. 1865, pp. 217-228, 472 f.]

comes under, in voluntarily participating in the Sacraments, to
serve Christ as the Captain of his salvation,—these Sacraments
being the characteristic badges or symbols by which the Christian
is distinguished from other men.   There is a second explanation,
advocated by not a few, of the way in which the Latin term
Sacrament came to be appropriated to its present ecclesiastical
sense.   It is the ordinary translation of the Greek word μυστηριον
among the ecclesiastical writers of the early ages, and more especially in the Vulgate and other old Latin translations of the Bible.
The term Sacrament, according to this supposition, came to be
employed to signify the "mysteries" of Christianity,—whether
"mystery" is employed to denote a doctrine unknown until it
was revealed, or a type or emblem bearing a hidden and secret
meaning.[1]   There is some reason to believe that both the Greek
term μυστηριον and the Latin translation of it—sacramentum—
came at an early period to be applied by the primitive Christians
to those special solemnities of their faith, which, although made
up of outward and sensible signs or actions, bore in them a secret
and spiritual meaning.   In one or other of these ways, or perhaps
in both, the term "Sacrament" soon came to be restricted in its
meaning and application, by ecclesiastical practice, to those outward
ordinances of Christianity which signify and seal its most precious
and momentous truths.   But as the term itself is of Church
origin, and not found in Scripture, we must look not to it, but to
the descriptions and intimations given in Scripture in regard to
the ordinances themselves, for an explanation of their true nature
and import.[2]   In what respects, then, do the Scriptures represent
the Sacraments of the Church as differing from its other ordi-

---

[1] Turrettin, *Opera*, loc. xix. qu. i. 1-6.   Halley, *The Sacraments*, Lond.
1844, pp. 7–14.
[2] ["The Apostle calleth the vocation of the Gentiles a mystery (Eph. iii.
4-6); the conjunction quhilk is begun here 'betwixt us and Christ is called
a mystery (Eph. v. 32), and the Latin Interpreters call it a Sacrament; and,
to be short, ye will not find in the Book of God a word mair frequent nor
the word mystery. . . . Alwayis, the word Sacrament is very ambiguous in
itself, and there raise about the ambiguity of this word many tragedeis quhilk
are not yet ceased, nor will cease while the warld lasts; quher otherwise,
gif they had keeped the Apostle's words, and called them, as the Apostle calls
them, signs and seals, all this digladiatioun, strife, and contention appearandly
had not fallen out.   But quher men will be wiser than God, and give names
to things beside God, upon the wit of man, quhilk is but mere folly, all this
cummer falls out. . . .   The ancient theologues took the word Sacrament in a
fourfold manner.   Sometimes they took it for the hail action, that is, for the
hail ministrie of the elements.   Sometimes they took it, not for the hail

nances which are not sacramental? What, according to Scripture, must we regard as the true nature and design of a Sacrament? To this general question we shall direct our attention in the first place, postponing for the present the special consideration of the Sacraments individually. And in endeavouring to ascertain the real nature and design of the Sacraments of the New Testament, we shall be enabled to understand at the same time, and by means of the same inquiry, in what respects they differ from other ordinances not sacramental.

SECTION I.—NATURE AND EFFICACY OF THE SACRAMENTS OF THE NEW TESTAMENT, AND DIFFERENCE BETWEEN THEM AND NON-SACRAMENTAL ORDINANCES.

I. The Sacraments of the New Testament are Divine institutions appointed by Christ.

It is the positive institution by Christ that sets these ordinances apart to the religious purpose for which they are intended, that makes them significant of spiritual things, and connects them with the virtue or blessing which they are made instrumental to impart. An express Divine appointment is necessary to constitute a Sacrament. In this respect they are similar to the other ordinances which form part of Church worship. Like them, they can claim Divine authority for their institution; and without this authority they would not be Sacraments at all. No observance not ordained by God can properly form any part of His service; far less can any observance not instituted by Him become a sign of His spiritual grace, or a pledge of a blessing which it depends upon His pleasure to give or to withhold. Hence,

action, but for the outward things that are used in the action of Baptism and of the Supper; as they took it for the water and sprinkling of it, for the bread and wine, breaking, distributing, and eating thereof. Again, they took it, not for the hail outward things that are used in the action, but only for the material and earthly things,—the elements; as for bread and wine in the Supper, and water in Baptism. After this sort sayeth Augustine: 'The wicked eats the body of our Lord concerning the Sacrament only;' that is, concerning the elements only. (Aug. in *Joann*. Tract xxvi. 18). Last of all, they took it not only for the elements, but for the things signified by the elements. And after this manner, Irenæus saith, 'that a Sacrament stands of twa things,—the ane earthly, the other heavenly.' (*Adv. Hæres*. lib. iv. cap. 18.) The ancients, then, taking the word after thir sorts, na question all thir ways they took it rightly."—ROBERT BRUCE, *Sermons on the Sacraments*, p. 6, Wodrow Soc. ed. Edin. 1843.]

that any outward institution may answer to our idea of a Sacrament, it must be a positive appointment of God, and made both a sign and a pledge of spiritual blessings, in consequence of His promise and command. Without this, it would be a mere human ordinance, not only destitute of all real religious significance and efficacy, but profanely mimicking the form and character of a Divine ordinance in the Church. This is the first element that goes to make up a Sacrament, and which it has in common with all other ordinances, really forming a lawful or proper part of Divine worship,—namely, that it be of positive appointment by Christ.

II. The Sacraments of the New Testament are sensible signs of spiritual blessings, teaching and representing by outward actions Gospel truths.

The word or promise of God is an appeal to the understanding only; the Sacraments, embodying the same word or promise in outward and sensible signs, form a twofold appeal, *first*, to the senses, and *secondly*, to the understanding. There is Christ in the Word preached; and in the preaching of the Word, Christ is presented directly to the understanding and heart, and the truth addressed singly to the spiritual nature of man. But Christ is also in the Sacrament administered; and, in the administration of the Sacrament, over and above the same truth taught to the understanding and spiritual nature of man, there is the truth taught to the senses, and impressed by sensible signs upon them. There is a striking similarity between the method God has employed in the Sacraments of the New Testament to embody the Word and promises of Christ, and of a *past* salvation, to the view of His people since His departure, and the method that He employed before Christ's coming to embody the Word and promises of a *future* salvation. Under the Old Testament Church, there were, from the very first, two lines of promise and prediction,— both pointing forward to the coming of the Redeemer, running parallel with each other, and throwing mutual light upon each other's announcements. There was the line of promise embodied in verbal revelation, and there was the line of promise embodied in outward representation or type.

These two revelations ran parallel with each other since the first hour that a revelation was given to man in Paradise concerning the future coming of a Saviour. At that time there was a promise embodied in words, that " the woman's seed should bruise the serpent's head, while His own heel was to be bruised;" and side by side with that verbal announcement, there was the same promise embodied in type through means of the ordinance of sacrifice then appointed. There was Christ in the word of promise, and Christ in the sign of promise. When the promise was renewed to Noah, the second father of the human family, we have again the revelation by word, and the revelation by sensible sign; the covenant was repeated in another form, and the bow was set in the cloud as the outward representation of it. Once more: when Abraham was selected by God to be the depositary of a new development of the promise, we have again that promise embodied in words, and also in outward action ; we have the special covenant with Abraham revealed in words, and revealed side by side with the word in the external sign of circumcision ; and—to mention no further examples of a practice which must be familiar to every reader of the Old Testament—the whole of the Jewish economy was an exemplification of the two parallel lines that run through every economy of God,—the promise in word and the promise in sign revealed together, and throwing mutual light on each other. The typology of the Old Testament shows us God embodying His promises in signs ; the revelation of the Old Testament shows us God embodying the same promises in words ; and the Sacraments of the New Testament afford, under the Gospel economy, an exemplification of the same great principle.

The connection between the outward action in the Sacraments and the spiritual blessings to which they stand related is not a mere arbitrary one, arising from positive institution : there is a natural analogy or resemblance between the external signs and the things represented ; so that, in the Sacraments of the New Testament, as in the types of the Old, our senses are made to minister to our spiritual advantage, and the outward action becomes the image of inward grace. In the Word, Christ is impressed on the understanding ; in the Sacraments, Christ is impressed both on the understanding and the senses. They become teaching signs, fitted and designed to address to the believer the very same truths as are addressed to him in the Word ; but having this peculiarity, that they speak at the same time and alike to the outward senses and to the inward thought. In this respect the Sacraments differ from other ordinances of the New Testament Church. Prayer and preaching and praise are ordinances that address themselves to the intellectual and spiritual nature of man alone. They are the expressions and utterances of his intellectual and spiritual being in holding intercourse with God; or they are the means fitted to speak to that nature, and that only, in impressing Divine truth upon men. But in those significant and teaching signs, which we call the Sacraments, Christ is embodied in the ordinance in such a manner as to appeal to the twofold being of man, as made up of body and soul, to minister both to the senses and the understanding; and to speak at once to the outward and inward nature of the believer. In addition to Christ in the Word, we have Christ also in the sign, taught as really in the latter way as in the former, and taught with the advantage of being submitted to the eye, and pictured to the outward senses. This, then, is one important difference between the sacramental ordinances of the New Testament Church and those which are not sacramental.

III. The Sacraments of the New Testament are federal acts affording a seal or confirmation of the covenant between God and His people.

This is the main and primary characteristic of sacramental ordinances. They constitute a formal testimony to an engagement entered into by two parties through means, not of words, but of speaking and significant actions,—these actions being the visible witnesses to the engagement, and the outward confirmations of its validity. In other words, they become, according to the expression of the apostle in his Epistle to the Romans, when speaking of one of the Sacraments of the Old Testament, visible " seals " of the covenant, and of the blessings contained in it.[1]

There are not a few examples to be found in the Old Testament Scriptures of covenants between man and man ratified by some outward monument, framed or chosen to attest and confirm the transaction. When Jacob parted from his father-in-law Laban, they made a covenant together, and raised a heap of stones and a pillar, to be a memorial of the transaction, and to serve as a witness on both sides to attest their fidelity to the terms of the covenant. " This heap be a witness, and this pillar be a witness, that I will not pass over this heap to thee, and that thou shalt not pass over this heap and this pillar to me, for harm." [2]

[1] Rom. iv. 11.   [2] Gen. xxxi. 52.

The outward monument or memorial of the covenant entered into between Jacob and Laban was a witness of the engagement, serving to bind the obligation of it more strongly on both parties, and to ratify and confirm, in a formal and significant manner, its validity. And what we find in patriarchal times, we also find, in one shape or other, in every stage of society, some outward sign or significant action being made use of between men to confirm and attest their plighted faith. In addition to the spoken promise or oath, there has been—if not the stone of the times of Jacob—at least the formal signature and solemn deed, and seal attached to the deed, to remain after the verbal engagement, as the witness and ratification of the transaction. Such outward monuments or significant solemnities are intended for the satisfaction of both parties, and to give additional certainty and confirmation to the agreement. And the practice in this respect, which has obtained universally among men, we find to be made use of also by God. There are repeated examples in the Old Testament Scriptures of God ratifying His engagements or covenants with men by means of appropriate signs or solemnities, and making use of these solemnities for the very same purpose that a signed and sealed deed is employed for in the present day, when it attests or confirms a previous engagement, and gives additional security to both parties for the fulfilment of it. That in such a sense the rainbow in the cloud was employed by God, when it became the sign of His covenant with Noah, is very expressly stated by Himself: " And the bow shall be in the cloud; and I will look upon it, that I may remember the everlasting covenant between God and every living creature of all flesh that is upon the earth. And God said unto Noah, This is the token of the covenant, which I have established between me and all flesh that is upon the earth." [1] In this point of view the bow was a seal, giving validity and additional security to the covenant then made, and serving as a standing witness for the truth of it. In a precisely similar manner, the rite of circumcision was appointed to Abraham for a voucher of the covenant between God and him. The terms of the institution of the rite would themselves lead us to this conclusion, even had they not been interpreted by the inspired commentary of the Apostle Paul in that sense. " And God said unto Abraham, Thou shalt keep my

[1] Gen. ix. 16, 17.

covenant therefore, thou, and thy seed after thee in their generations. This is my covenant, which ye shall keep, between me and you, and thy seed after thee. Every man-child among you shall be circumcised. And ye shall circumcise the flesh of your foreskin ; and it shall be a *token of the covenant* betwixt me and you." And in reference to this transaction, the Apostle Paul expressly says of Abraham: " And he received the sign of circumcision, *a seal of the righteousness of the faith* which he had yet being uncircumcised." [1] The outward act of circumcision, then, was a witness or a seal of the covenant transaction between God and the patriarch, and thus became a voucher to ratify and confirm the validity of it.

In exact accordance with the practice, universal in one shape or other among men, and expressly sanctioned by the example of God Himself in the Old Testament Church, we affirm that the Sacraments of the New Testament are parts of a federal transaction between the believer and Christ, and visible and outward attestations or vouchers of the covenant entered into between them. In addition to being signs to represent the blessings of the covenant of grace, they are also seals to vouch and ratify and confirm its validity. That the Sacraments of the Christian Church are thus seals of the covenant, appears to be very explicitly asserted, in so far at least as regards the Lord's Supper, in the words of the institution themselves : " *This* cup," said our Lord, " *is the new covenant in my blood, which is shed for you*," [2]— language which seems undoubtedly intended to convey the idea that the element used in the Supper was to be the witness of the new covenant,—a visible seal or security to ratify and vouch for it. No doubt that covenant in itself is sufficiently secure without any such confirmation, resting as it does on the word of God. That word alone, and without any further guarantee, is enough. But in condescension to the weakness of our faith, and adapting Himself to the feelings and customs of men, God has done more than give a promise. He has also given a guarantee for the promise,— has vouchsafed to bestow an outward confirmation of His word in the shape of a visible sign, appealing to our senses, and witnessing to the certainty and truth of the covenant. In the case of the Sacraments, God has proceeded on the same principle as is announced by the Apostle Paul in reference to His oath : " God,

---

[1] Gen. xvii. 9–11 ; Rom. iv. 11.   [2] Luke xxii. 20.

willing more abundantly to show unto the heirs of promise the immutability of His counsel, confirmed it by an oath; that by two immutable things, in which it was impossible for God to lie, we might have a strong consolation, who have fled for refuge to lay hold upon the hope set before us."[1] The word of promise was itself enough to warrant and demand the belief of God's people. But more than enough was granted : He has not only said it, but also sworn it. By two immutable things—His word and His oath —is the faith of the believer confirmed. The oath is the guarantee for His word. And more than this still : In the visible seal of the Sacraments God would add another and a third witness,—that at the mouth, not of two, but of three witnesses, His covenant may be established. He has not only given us the guarantee of His word, and confirmed that word by an oath, but also added to both the seal of visible ordinances. There is the word preached to declare the truth of the covenant to the unbelieving heart. More than that,—there is the oath sworn to guarantee it. More than that still,—there is the sign administered in order to vouch for all. Christ in the word, unseen but heard, is ours, if we will receive that word with the hearing ear and the understanding heart. Over and above this, Christ, both seen and heard in the Sacrament, is ours, if we will see with the eye or hear with the ear.[2]

The Sacraments are the outward and sensible testimony and

---

[1] Heb. vi. 17, 18.

[2] [" What mister (need) is there that thir Sacraments and seals suld be annexed to the Word ? Seeing we get na new thing in the Sacrament but the same thing quhilk we gat in the simple Word, quherefore is the Sacrament appointed to be hung to the Word ? It is true certainly, we get na new thing in the Sacrament, nor we get na other thing in the Sacrament nor we gat in the Word ; for *quhat mair walde thou crave nor to get the Son of God*, gif thou get Him weil ? Thy heart cannot wish nor imagine a greater gift nor to have the Son of God, quha is King of heaven and earth. And therefore I say, quhat new thing walde thou crave ? For gif thou get Him, thou gettest all things with Him. Quherefore, then, is the Sacrament appointed ? Not to get thee a new thing. I say it is appointed to get thee that same thing *better* nor thou gat it in the Word. The Sacrament is appointed that we may get a better grip of Christ nor we gat in the simple Word ; that we may possess Christ in our hearts and minds mair fully and largely nor we did of before in the simple Word ; that Christ might have a larger space to make residence in our narrow hearts nor we could have by the hearing of the simple Word. And to possess Christ mair fully it is a better thing ; for suppose Christ be ae thing in Himself, yet the better grip thou have of Him thou art the surer of His promise."—BRUCE, *Sermons on the Sacraments*, Wodrow Soc. ed. Edin. 1843, p. 28.]

seal of the covenant, added to the word that declares it. This is the grand peculiarity of sacramental ordinances, separating them by a very marked line from ordinances not sacramental. They are federal acts,—seals and vouchers of the covenant between God and the believer. They presuppose and imply a covenant transaction between the man who partakes of them and God; and they are the attestations to and confirmations of that transaction, pledging God by a visible act to fulfil His share of the covenant, and engaging the individual by the same visible act to perform his part in it. Other ordinances, such as the preaching of the Word, presuppose and attest no such personal engagement or federal transaction between the individual and God. Christ in the Word is preached to all, and all are called upon to receive Him; but there is no personal act on the part of the hearer that singles him out as giving or receiving a voucher of his covenant with his Saviour. But when the same individual partakes of the Sacraments, his own personal deed is an act of covenanting with God; and Christ in the ordinance is made his individually, and he is made Christ's by the very action of partaking of the ordinance. He is singled out by his own voluntary act, if he rightly partakes of the ordinance, as giving a voucher for his engagement with Christ; and Christ Himself gives a voucher of His engagement to the individual; and the visible Sacrament is the seal to the personal and mutual engagement. In this respect, as not only signs but seals of the covenant of grace to the individual who in faith partakes of them, the Sacraments are very markedly distinguished from ordinances not sacramental.

IV. The Sacraments of the New Testament are made means of grace to the individual who rightly partakes of them.

It is carefully to be noted that they presuppose or imply the possession of grace in the case of those who partake of them; but they are also made the means of adding to that grace. They are seals of a covenant already made between the soul and Christ,—attestations of a federal transaction before completed,—confirmations, visible and outward, of engagement between the sinner and his Saviour previously entered into on both sides. They presuppose the existence of grace, else they could not be called seals of it. Just as the signature and seal of some human covenant necessarily presuppose that the covenant exists before they can become vouchers for it, so the seal of God's covenant, affirmed by means of sacramental ordinances, presupposes the existence of that covenant as already subsisting between God and the rightful participator in the ordinance. But although grace exists in the soul before, the Sacraments are made to those who rightly receive them the means of increasing that grace, and communicating yet more of spiritual blessing. They serve to strengthen the faith of those who already believe, and add to the grace of those who previously possessed grace. They become effectual means of imparting saving blessings in addition to those enjoyed before.[1] In this respect they are similar to the other ordinances which Christ has appointed in His Church, and which by His power and Spirit are made instrumental in advancing the interests of His people. But from the very peculiarity that attaches to their distinctive character, as seals of a personal covenant between God and the believer, Sacraments may reasonably be supposed to be more effectual than non-sacramental ordinances in imparting spiritual blessings. The spiritual virtue of Sacraments is more and greater than other ordinances, just because, from their very nature, they imply more of a personal dealing between the sinner and his Saviour than non-sacramental ordinances necessarily involve.

---

[1] ["The Church has always seen in the Sacraments," says Mr. Liddon in his recent very valuable work on the Divinity of our Lord, "not mere outward signs addressed to the taste or imagination, nor even signs, as Calvinism asserts, which are tokens of grace received independently of them, but signs which, through the power of the promise and Word of Christ, effect what they signify." For this very defective statement of the Calvinistic doctrine of the Sacraments the only authority Mr. Liddon gives is a single secondhand quotation from Cartwright. He then proceeds to contrast with this supposed Calvinistic view the words of the 25th Article: "The Sacraments are *effectual* signs of grace and God's goodwill toward us, by which He doth work invisibly in us;" and the definition of the Church Catechism: "A Sacrament is an outward and visible sign of an inward and spiritual grace given unto us, ordained by Christ Himself as a *means whereby* we receive the same, and a pledge to assure us thereof." *Bampton Lectures*, 1866, p. 721. A very slight reference to the symbolical books or the leading theologians of some of the Calvinistic Churches would of course have shown that all these phrases have been constantly used by them with respect to the Sacraments. The isolated sentence from Cartwright adduced by Hooker, from whom Mr. Liddon takes it, refers to a particular aspect of a particular Sacrament; it was never designed to be a full definition of the efficacy of these ordinances in a typical case. Moreover, the passage in question is just a translation of Calvin, *Inst.* iv. xv. 22. It might as well, therefore, have been brought forward as expressive of *his* whole doctrine on the subject. But Mr. Liddon must surely be aware that Calvin constantly speaks of the Sacraments both of the Old and New Testaments as "*effectual* means of grace," "efficacious instruments," "signs in which God *gives* what He

What is the nature and extent of the supernatural grace imparted in Sacraments,—in what manner they work so as to
impart spiritual benefit to the soul, it is not possible for us to
define. As visible seals of God's promises and covenant, we can
understand how they are naturally fitted, in the same way as the
vouchers of any human engagement or covenant are naturally
fitted, to attest and confirm them. But beyond this, all is unknown. The blessing of Christ and the working of His Spirit in
Sacraments we cannot understand, any more than we can understand the operation of the same supernatural causes in respect
of other ordinances. They have a virtue in them beyond what
reason can discover in them, as naturally fitted to serve the purposes both of signs and seals of spiritual things. They have a
blessing to the right receiver of them, not their own to give.
" They are made effectual means of salvation, not from any virtue
in them, or in him that doth administer them, but only by the
blessing of Christ, and the working of His Spirit in them who by
faith receive them."[1] In this respect their power and virtue are
not more and not less mysterious than those of ordinances nonsacramental.

Such are the general conclusions which a consideration of the
nature of the Sacraments of the New Testament lead us to

holds out to us," etc. (" non modo salutaria exercitia, et adjumenta pietatis, sed
etiam *efficacia gratiæ instrumenta.*" " *Præstat* igitur vere Deus quicquid signis
promittit ac figurat ; nec effectu suo carent signa, ut verax et fidelis probetur
eorum Author").—*Comment. in* Gal. iv. 9, Col. ii. 17, *Inst.* iv. xiv. 17, etc. Cf. i.
Conf. Helv. c. 21, ii. c. 21. Conf. Gall. Art. 37, Catech. Gen. v. etc. Some of
the expressions in the Church Catechism, indeed, with respect to Baptism seem
to Presbyterians to require at least all the explanation which Dean Goode and
others have bestowed upon them. And the passage from Martensen about the
" communication of Christ's glorified corporeity " in the Lord's Supper, which
Mr. Liddon quotes, seemingly as supplementary of the Catechism, would of
course be disapproved of by Calvinists generally, although there are statements
in the works of Calvin himself which might perhaps be adduced in its favour.
Mr. Liddon concludes by observing that, " though there have been and are
believers in our Lord's Divinity who deny the realities of sacramental grace,
experience appears to show that their position is only a transitional one."
There is " a law of fatal declension," which will ultimately, Mr. Liddon
thinks, bring all who do not hold the High Church doctrine of the Sacraments
to the Socinian position. " Centuries," however, " may intervene between
the premisses and the conclusion;" so that the prediction is a singularly safe
one. By a precisely similar process of reasoning, Dr. Manning and others
are prepared to prove that there is an indissoluble connection between the
worship of the virgin and a belief in the Divinity of Christ.—*Engl. and
Christend.* p. civ. Faber, *Growth in Holiness,* p. 72.]
[1] Shorter Catechism, qu. 91.

acquiesce in. They are Divine institutions appointed by Christ; they are signs and significant representations of spiritual things; they are seals and vouchers of a federal transaction between God and the worthy receiver of Sacraments; they are the means for applying spiritual grace to the soul. To sum up the discussion in the language of the Shorter Catechism : " A Sacrament is an holy ordinance instituted by Christ, wherein by sensible signs Christ and the benefits of the new covenant are represented, sealed, and applied to believers." [1]

Sacraments and non-sacramental ordinances are like each other in two respects; and in two respects they differ. In the first place, sacramental and non-sacramental ordinances agree in this : first, that they are both positive institutions of Christ; and second, that they are both means of grace to believers. Without a Divine warrant and institution, neither non-sacramental ordinances nor Sacraments could have any place in the worship of God as part of His service; and both are therefore Divine appointments. They are both likewise means of grace to believers,— there being a positive promise attached to the right use of them, and that promise being fulfilled in the bestowment of spiritual blessing in connection with their use. This spiritual benefit, linked to the proper use of ordinances, whether sacramental or not, is over and above and quite distinct from the natural or moral influence such ordinances may have to benefit those who employ them. There is a benefit, for example, which the ordinance of preaching the Word is naturally fitted to impart, because the truth preached is adapted to man's moral and intellectual nature, and so naturally fitted to be of advantage to the hearers. In like manner there is a benefit which Sacraments are naturally fitted to impart, because they are symbolical ordinances or teaching signs; and the truths represented or taught by them are, upon the very same principle, naturally fitted to be of advantage to the receiver. But in both cases there is a blessing distinct

---

[1] Shorter Catechism, qu. 92. Calvin, *Inst.* lib. iv. cap. xiv. *Consensus Tigurinus* in Niemeyer's *Collectio Confess.* Lipsiæ 1840, pp. 192–217, translated in Calvin's *Tracts*, Edin. 1849, vol. ii. pp. 205–244. Turrettin, *Opera*, tom. iii. loc. xix. qu. i.–ix. Cunningham, *Works*, vol. i. pp. 225–291, vol. ii. pp. 201–207, vol. iii. pp. 121–133. Amesius, *Bellarm. Enerv.* tom. iii. lib. i. cap. i. Willison, *Works*, Hetherington's ed. pp. 456 f. Gillespie, *Aaron's Rod Blossoming*, B. iii. chap. xii.–xiv. Mastricht, *Theol. Theoretico-Pract.* tom. ii. lib. vii. cap. 3.

from and additional to the natural or moral effect of the Word preached or the Sacraments administered. There is the work of the Spirit making use of Word and Sacrament to reach the understanding and the heart, and to convey to the worthy hearer or worthy receiver a spiritual blessing. And this work of the Spirit, over and above the natural effect of the truth received, is a mystery, both in the case of the ordinance of preaching and the ordinance of the Sacraments; and not, I think, a greater mystery in the one case than in the other.

We do not plead for the Sacraments as means of grace, viewed merely as natural actions and ceremonies apart from the truths which they represent, any more than we would plead for the preaching of the Word being a means of grace, viewed as the mere letter of the Word apart from the meaning of the truth which is uttered. The case of *infant* Baptism, which is, as we shall afterwards see, in some respects exceptional, and not to be taken as completely bringing out the full and primary idea of the Sacrament,[1] we for the present put aside, postponing it for future consideration. But in the case of adult participation in the Sacraments, we do not plead for these generally as means of grace, when viewed simply as outward acts, and apart from the truths represented, any more than the sound of the Word preached would be a means of grace apart from the intelligent apprehension of it. Through the truths, however, in one case impressed on the hearer by significant words, and in the other case impressed on the participator through significant actions, the Spirit of God *does* operate upon the intellectual and moral nature of man, making both the one ordinance and the other a means of grace. How the Spirit thus operates and imparts of His gracious gifts, we cannot tell in the one instance more than in the other. What is the mode or measure of His communications of a spiritual kind, over and above the natural or outward influence of the truth, we cannot tell. It is His own secret and supernatural work, known and recognised by the believer in the effects wrought on His soul, both in the case of the Word preached and the Sacraments administered, but not to be explained or defined in the manner of working. Let it never be forgotten that there is a mystery not to be explained whenever we get beyond the natural effect of the ordinance, whether sacramental or not,

---

[1] Cunningham, *Works*, vol. iii. pp. 144-154.

necessarily resulting from the fact that it is an effect of the Spirit, and not of any natural cause. All ordinances, as means of grace, must in that character have something in them mysterious and inexplicable. We cannot rid ourselves of the mysterious by simply ridding ourselves of sacramental ordinances,—as very many in the present day seem to imagine. We can only disconnect all mystery from the ordinances of the Church when we limit their efficacy simply to their natural influence, and deny the influence of the Spirit of God as at all connected with them.

In the second place, Sacraments differ from ordinances not sacramental in the New Testament Church, in these two things : first, they are sensible signs of spiritual truths ; and second, they are seals or vouchers of a federal transaction. In respect that they are sensible exhibitions and significant actions, having a definite meaning in them, Sacraments stand out distinctly marked from other ordinances. Speaking generally, sacramental ordinances are spiritual acts of the mind or soul embodying themselves in outward and sensible actions, in so far as regards the part of the receiver in the ordinance. They are outward representations, by means of certain actions on the part of the worthy participator, of the great fact that he gives himself to Christ according to the terms of the covenant of grace. In partaking of the ordinance, he embodies in the sensible actions of the ordinance a spiritual surrender of himself to Christ, in the manner and upon the terms which Christ has appointed. This is the receiver's part in the ordinance. On the other side, Christ, through the person of the administrator of the ordinance, embodies in the actions of it a picture or representation of a spiritual communication of Himself and all the blessings of His grace to the worthy receiver. Christ, in the Sacrament, and by means of its sensible signs, gives Himself and the benefits of the new covenant, spiritually, although under an outward representation, to the believing participator. The outward signs of the Sacrament exhibit, then, a twofold action : the believer giving himself to Christ in covenant, and Christ giving Himself to the believer in the same covenant. There is a spiritual act on the part of the believer embodied in outward representation,—the act, namely, of his surrendering of himself to Christ in the way and on the terms which Christ has appointed ; and there is a spiritual act on the part of Christ embodied in outward representation also,—

the act, namely, of Christ with all His precious and unspeakable blessings communicating Himself to the soul of the worthy receiver. There is thus a double significance comprehended in the administration and in the participation of the sacramental ordinance, each of them having a definite and intelligible meaning of its own. In the administration of the Sacrament, Christ makes over Himself and all the benefits of His atonement to the believer, and accepts in return the believer as His. In the participation of the Sacrament on the part of the worthy receiver, he makes over himself to Christ; and receives, in return for his own soul, Christ and His covenant blessings. The double action of the administration and participation of the Sacrament is the embodiment in outward sign of a double spiritual act. There is a mutual intercommunication spiritually of Christ and the believer embodied and represented in action,—a covenant interchangeably exhibited in sensible signs, whereby Christ becomes the believer's, and the believer becomes Christ's. In their being signs of spiritual truths, Sacraments differ in a marked manner from non-sacramental ordinances.

Sacraments differ also from other ordinances in this, that they are seals or vouchers of a federal or covenant transaction. This, after all, is the grand and essential distinction between sacramental and non-sacramental ordinances. As a kind of types, as speaking and teaching signs, they are fitted to express, by the help of significant actions cognisable by the senses, the twofold spiritual act of Christ making over Himself and all His blessings to the believer, and of the believer making over himself with all his poverty and sins to Christ. But they are more than signs of a covenant thus entered into between the two parties,—they are seals and vouchers for the covenant, serving to give confirmation and validity to the engagement, as one never to be broken. In the Sacraments there is a twofold seal, as well as a twofold action, represented. There is a seal on the part of Christ, and there is a seal on the part of the believer. In marvellous condescension to our infirmity and unbelief, Christ has been pleased to add to the promise of His covenant an outward and visible voucher for it,—thereby, as it were, binding Himself doubly to the fulfilment of it, and pledging Himself, both by word and by sign, to implement all its terms. And in the worthy receiving of the Sacrament, the believer gives also a visible voucher for his part of the engage-

ment,—thereby placing himself under new and additional obligations to give himself to Christ, and adding the outward seal to
ratify the inward pledge of his heart. The covenant is mutual,
and the seal is mutual. Without either part of the covenant
transaction, the Sacrament would be incomplete. Withdraw
Christ from the ordinance as both entering into covenant with
the believer and giving him a seal of it,—take away Christ sealed
to the soul in the Sacrament,—and the ordinance is reduced to a
bare sign of spiritual blessing, having, perhaps, a certain natural
effect by signifying truth, but empty and destitute of all spiritual
grace. Or withdraw the believer from the ordinance in so far as
he really by means of it gives himself to Christ,—take away the
spiritual act by which the worthy participator surrenders his soul
to the Saviour through his outward participation of the Sacrament,—and the Sacrament is made to be a charm, in which Christ
and grace are communicated apart from the spiritual act or state
of the receiver. Abstract from the ordinance the act of Christ
covenanting with the believer and giving to the soul Himself and
His blessings, and the remaining portion of the ordinance may
continue,—the believer may still be accounted as giving himself
to Christ in the Sacrament; but in the absence of Christ's act
there is no spiritual blessing given in return, and the believer's
act of participating in the Sacrament becomes a mere sign of
adherence to Christ on his part, and nothing more than a sign.[1]
Again, abstract from the ordinance the act of the believer spiritually covenanting with Christ and giving his soul in faith to the
Saviour, and the remaining portion of the ordinance may continue,—Christ may be held as present in the Sacrament giving
Himself and His supernatural grace; but in the absence of the
receiver's act surrendering his soul in faith to his Saviour, the
communication of spiritual grace is degraded to the position of
being the result of a charm or talismanic formula,—something
effected, *ex opere operato*, apart from the spiritual character or
faith of the receiver. It is only when the separate spiritual acts of
both parties meet and combine in one transaction, that the covenant

---

[1] [" Quod omnes fere opinantur, hoc ritu, quem Sacramentum appellant,
confirmari saltem fidem nostram, ne id quidem verum censeri debet; cum nec
ullo sacro testimonio comprobetur, nec ulla ratio sit cur id fieri possit. Quo-
modo enim potest nos in fide confirmare id *quod nos ipsi facimus, quodque,
licet a Domino institutum, opus tamen nostrum est?* "—Faustus Socinus, *De
Cœnâ Dom. Tract. Brev.* Racovian Catechism, 1609, p. 144 f.]

is real or complete; or that the ordinance, as a seal of the mutual
engagement, is a true and proper Sacrament. As the voucher or
seal of a real covenant, spiritually entered into between Christ and
the believer through the ordinance, a Sacrament differs, in a very
marked and important way, from ordinances not sacramental.

SECTION II.—UNSCRIPTURAL OR DEFECTIVE VIEWS OF THE SACRAMENTS.

The principles which I have laid down in regard to the nature
of Sacraments, and in regard to the difference between them and
ordinances not sacramental, stand opposed to the views of two
parties holding extreme positions on either side of this question.
There is one party who deny the grand and characteristic distinction between sacramental and other ordinances already enunciated,
and hold that the Sacraments have no virtue except as badges of
a Christian profession, and signs of spiritual truths. There is
another party holding opinions on the subject admitting of various
modifications, but agreeing in this, that they ascribe a high spiritual efficacy to the Sacraments apart from the faith or spiritual
act of the receiver. By the first party the views of the Sacraments already stated by me are held to be erroneous in the way
of attributing to them a greater virtue than actually belongs to
them. By the second party these views are regarded as defective
in the way of ascribing to Sacraments a less virtue than really
belongs to them. Let us endeavour briefly and generally to estimate the merits and truth of the principles adopted by these two
parties,—reserving until a future stage in our discussions the
more particular examination of their theories, in their application to the Sacraments of the New Testament individually.

I. The Sacraments of the New Testament are regarded by
one party as signs, and no more than signs, of spiritual things,—
symbolical actions fitted to represent, and impress upon the minds
of men, Gospel truths. The Socinian party have made this
doctrine peculiarly their own. According to their views, a federal
transaction between the believer and Christ founded on His atonement is no part of the Gospel system at all; and hence the
Sacraments of the New Testament can be no seals appointed
and designed to ratify such a covenant. The Socinian doctrine
concerning the nature of the Sacraments allows to them no more

than a twofold object and design. They are not essentially distinct from other ordinances, as set apart by themselves to be the
seals of the one great covenant between the believer and Christ,
at his entrance into the Church at first, and from time to time
afterwards, as occasion justifies or demands. But in the first
place, they are signs in which something external and material is
used to express what is spiritual·and invisible,—the only virtue
belonging to them being what they are naturally calculated to
effect, as memorials, or illustrations, or exhibitions of the important
facts and truths of the Gospel; and in the second ₊place, the
Sacraments are solemn pledges of discipleship on the part of
those who receive them, discriminating them from other men, and
forming a public profession of or testimony to their faith as Christians. These are the two grand objects, which, according to the
Socinian view, the Sacraments were intended to serve; and such,
according to their theory, is the nature of the ordinance.

   The same system in substance, making, as it does, Sacraments
entirely or essentially teaching and symbolical signs, has been
adopted by many who disown the tenets of Socinianism in regard
to the Gospel system generally. The theory of the Sacraments
now described has been and is held by not a few in the Church
of England of somewhat latitudinarian views,—the representative
of such, as a class, being Bishop Hoadly. It is avowed and advocated in the present day by a very large proportion of the Independent body, who count the Sacraments to be no more than
symbolical institutions, and who are ably represented by Dr.
Halley in his work, entitled, *An Inquiry into the Nature of the
Symbolic Institutions of the Christian Religion, usually called the
Sacraments*. The single difference between the Socinian doctrine,
as maintained by Socinians in the present day, and the Independent doctrine, as maintained by Dr. Halley and others, is probably
this, that Socinians limit the efficacy of the Sacraments to the
natural or moral power that belongs to them as signs of Gospel
truth, while Independents may admit that beyond the natural
and moral power of the ordinance, as symbolical of truth, the
Spirit of God makes use of them in representing truth to the
mind. Let Dr. Halley speak his own views as they are generally
held by English Independents. " The opinion we propose is, that
the Sacraments are significant rites,—emblems of Divine truth,—
sacred signs of the evangelical doctrine,—designed to illustrate, to

enforce, or to commemorate the great and most important truths of the Gospel. Baptism, we believe, is the sign of purification, on being admitted into the kingdom of Christ, but neither the cause nor the seal of it; the Lord's Supper the commemoration of the death of Christ, the symbol of its propitiatory character, but not the assurance of our personal interest in its saving benefits. The truth exhibited in the Sacraments, just as when it is propounded in words, may be the means of the communication of Divine grace; but then the evangelical doctrine and not the Sacrament, the truth and not the symbol, the spirit and not the letter, gives life and sanctity to the recipient, as it may even to a spectator."[1] According to this theory, it is the truth signified in the Sacrament— and not, over and above that, the Sacrament itself as a seal—that possesses any spiritual virtue; and that virtue may be, according to Socinians, the natural influence of the truth on the mind,— or, according to Independents, that natural influence, with the addition of the power communicated through the truth by the Spirit.

Now, in reference to this view of the Sacraments, it is necessary to bear in mind that there is no dispute as to the fact that sacramental ordinances are symbolical,—signs fitted to represent and to teach Gospel truths. Further, there is no dispute as to the fact, acknowledged by some of the advocates of this theory, that in so far as they teach or convey truth to the mind, they may be made the means of the communication of Divine grace, in the same manner very much as when the truth is propounded in words.[2] But the point in debate is, whether the Sacraments are not more than signs, and more than merely symbolical representations of truth. We hold that they are. We contend that,

---

[1] Halley, *The Sacraments: an Inquiry*, etc. Lond. 1844, vol. i. p. 94 f.

[2] ["Es geschah in dem Zeitpunkte der Reformation, aber nicht zum ersten Male, dass die hypermystische oder zauberische Vorstellung den entgegengesetzten Fehler, die Behauptung des *signum nudum* oder des blossen Bekenntnisszeichens, hervorrief. Gegen diejenige Kirche, die im Dienste der Verwandlungslehre und des *opus operatum* die symbolische Natur des Sacraments verleugnete und zerstörte, hatte die sogenannte Ketzerei allezeit Recht, zunächst nur wieder das Daseyn des Symbols und die Bedeutung zu behaupten. Diejenige Kirche, die des Sacramentes Wirkung und Wesen vom lebendigen Worte und Glauben, den Sohn vom Geiste losgerissen hatte, durfte einen Gegner nie Lügen strafen oder des Unchristenthums zeihen, der der Gemeinschaft des Erlösers durch die Speise des Wortes als durch die rechte Assimilation mit seinem Leben theilhaft zu werden hoffte, und sich des Sacramentes nur noch als eines Zeichens dieser Gemeinschaft, oder auch dieses Zeichens nicht mehr bediente weil es so sehr vom Wesen abgelenkt und etwa nur habe bei noch nicht ganz befestigter Wirksamkeit des Wortes einem anfänglichen

in addition to being signs, they are also seals,—the visible vouchers
of a federal transaction between Christ and the believer who partakes of His Sacraments,—the outward pledges speaking to the
eye and the senses of the completed covenant by which Christ
becomes the believer's, and the believer becomes Christ's. And
further, we contend that, as seals, they are made a means of grace
more powerful and efficacious than simply as signs of truth.

The arguments urged by Dr. Halley against this additional
office and virtue attributed to Sacraments as more than signs, and
as the seals of a federal engagement between the worthy recipient
and Christ, are the two following, as stated in his own words:
" First, The ceremonial institutes of preceding dispensations, the
Sacraments of the patriarchal and Jewish Church, correspond only
with the view which we take of the Christian Sacraments as sacred
signs of Divine truth. Second, The Sacraments considered as the
causes or the means, or even the seals of converting or regenerating grace, stand opposed to the great Protestant doctrine of justification by faith without works."[1]   We shall very briefly examine
each of these two objections to the view which we have announced.
And we do this all the more readily, as it will afford us the better
opportunity of bringing out our own principles in contrast with
those embodied in the Independent theory of the Sacraments.

1st, Dr. Halley alleges, against the ascription to the New
Testament Sacraments of the character of seals, that the ceremonial institutes of preceding dispensations, the Sacraments of
the patriarchal and Jewish Church, correspond only with the
views which he advocates of the Christian Sacraments as exclusively signs of Divine truth.   Perhaps there never was a more
unfortunate or unfounded assertion.   " One passage of St. Paul,"
says Dr. Halley, " will establish this proposition."[2]   And the
single passage which is to bear the weight of the whole argument
is the following one from the Epistle to the Romans : " He is
not a Jew which is one outwardly ; neither is that circumcision

---

Bedürfnisse dienen sollen." (This is still the position of the Quakers as
expounded by Barclay in his *Apology*.)   " *Blosse Gebetschristen*, Messalianer
und dergleichen, *sind nicht weniger Christen als blosse Sacramentschristen ;
blosse Symboliker stehen sich nicht schlechter mit der Quelle des Lebens als die
Hierurgen die den Leib Christi conficiren*.   Diese sind am Ende des verschwin-
denden Christenthums angelangt, jene stehen am Wiederanfange der Ent-
wickelung."—Nitzsch, *prot. Beant. der Symb. Möhlers*, Hamburg 1835, p. 162.]
    [1] Halley, p. 95.   [2] *Ibid.* p. 96.

which is outward in the flesh. But he is a Jew which is one inwardly; and circumcision is that of the heart, in the spirit, and not in the letter; whose praise is not of men, but of God."[1] This is the solitary passage quoted to prove the broad and general assertion, that the Sacraments of the patriarchal and Jewish Church afford no precedent or example of Sacraments as seals, but only of Sacraments as signs. The verses quoted plainly amount to nothing more than a statement of the difference between what the apostle calls circumcision outwardly and circumcision inwardly, the external rite and the internal grace, and a declaration that a man might have the outward rite, and not the inward grace. The apostle does not say, and cannot, except by a violent misapplication of his words, be made to say, that *in the case of the man who has both the outward and inward circumcision,* the external rite may not be the visible seal of the spiritual grace. The very opposite of this the same apostle in the very same Epistle undeniably asserts. In language as plain as he could possibly select or employ, Paul affirms that in the case of Abraham, who had the inward grace, the outward rite of circumcision was a seal to him of that grace. "Abraham," says the apostle, "received the sign of circumcision, a *seal* of the righteousness of the faith which he had yet being uncircumcised."[2] And how is it that Dr. Halley gets rid of this express assertion of the apostle, standing as it does in explicit contradiction to his general averment that the Sacraments of the Jewish Church were signs and not seals? He admits that to Abraham personally and individually circumcision was a seal, and not merely a sign. But by a strange misapprehension of the doctrine of his opponents, he argues that it could not be a seal of faith to others of Abraham's family or countrymen who had not his faith. "Although," says Dr. Halley, "to him circumcision was the seal of faith, it could not have been so to his posterity." "Was it," he asks, "was it, in this sense, a seal of the righteousness which they had, an approval of their faith, to the men of his clan, or to Ishmael, or to the infants of his household, or to any of his posterity in subsequent ages?"[3] The answer to such a question is abundantly obvious. If the men of Abraham's clan had not faith, if Ishmael had not faith, circumcision could have been no seal of faith to them. The outward rite could not be a

---

[1] Rom. ii. 28, 29.   [2] Rom. iv. 11.   [3] Halley, p. 100.

seal of the inward grace, when the latter did not exist. It could not be a seal of a spiritual covenant between them and God which had not been entered into. I do not stop to consider the question of whether or not circumcision is to be accounted, even in such a case, the seal to such individuals of the outward blessings promised to them, as Jews, by God, as the rightful King of Israel as a nation ; but, as a seal of a spiritual covenant, it of course could not be a seal at all to those who were not parties to the covenant,—while it was a seal, according to the explicit assertion of the apostle, to those who were. The very express statement of Paul cannot be evaded, but fully bears out the assertion that the Sacraments of the Jewish Church were not signs alone, but seals of a spiritual covenant to those who were really parties to the covenant. "Abraham received the sign of circumcision, a *seal* of the righteousness of the faith which he *had*."

2*d*, Dr. Halley alleges that the Sacraments, if they are considered as the cause or the means, or even the seals of spiritual and saving grace, would be opposed to the great Protestant doctrine of justification by faith without works. Now it is readily admitted, that if Sacraments are regarded as the causes or means of justification, they are utterly inconsistent with the Protestant doctrine of justification by faith alone ; and in this point of view the objection is true and unanswerable when directed against some of those theories of the Sacraments which we may be called upon to consider by and by. But it is denied that the objection is true when directed against the theory of the Sacraments which maintains that they are not causes and not means of justification, but seals of it and of other blessings of the new covenant. The Sacraments as seals, not causes of justification, cannot interfere with the doctrine of justification by faith, for this plain reason, that before the seal is added, the justification is completed. The seal implied in the Sacrament presupposes justification, and does not directly or instrumentally cause it ; the seal is a voucher given to the believer that he is justified already, and not a means or a cause of procuring justification for him. Justification exists before the seal that attests it is bestowed. The believer has previously been " justified by faith without the works of the law," ere the Sacrament of which he partakes can affix the visible seal to his justification. All this is abundantly obvious ; and the objection of Independents, that the doctrine of the Sacraments as personal seals is opposed to the principle of justification by faith, is wholly without foundation. That the Sacraments are a means of grace additional to what the believer possessed before his participation in them, it is not necessary to deny, but rather proper strongly to assert.[1] In entering into a personal covenant with Christ through particiption in the Sacraments, or in renewing that covenant from time to time, the faith of the believer is called forth and brought into exercise in the very act of participation, and by the aids to faith which the ordinance affords. And in answer to this faith so exercised and elicited, there is an increase of grace given to the worthy recipient above and beyond what he had before. The faith of the believer, called into exercise in partaking of the ordinance and by means of it, is met by the bestowment of corresponding grace. But it is never to be forgotten that the Sacraments presuppose the existence of grace, however they may give to him that already has it more abundantly. They presuppose, and beforehand require, that a man is justified by faith before they give their seal to his justification.

There is no ground, then, in Scripture, but the very opposite, for asserting that the Sacraments are no more than signs or symbolical actions, as held by Dr. Halley and those whom on this question he represents. The fundamental error involved in the views now adverted to is, the denial of Christ's part in the federal transaction involved in a Sacrament. Independents overlook *His* department of the work in the engagement entered into through means of the act of receiving the Sacraments; and in the absence of the act of Christ giving Himself and all His spiritual blessings to the believer in the ordinance, the act of the recipient

---

[1] ["Das Gläubigste, so zu sagen, am sacramentlichen christlichen Gemeinglauben ist doch wohl dieses : je mehr das Sacrament mit voller Empfänglichkeit genossen wird, desto weniger ist es blosses Zeichen, oder blosses Unterpfand der Lebensmittheilung Christi, desto mehr diese Mittheilung selbst. Das Sacrament ist Leiter, Kanal der Gnade, wie der römische Katechismus sich ausdrückt. Bis auf diesen Punkt wird der Sacramentsbegriff— ich will zugeben unter sehr verschiedenen Bedingungen (from those of the Romanist theory)—durch das in dieser Hinsicht ganz ungetheilte Bekenntniss der Protestanten gesteigert. . . . Der protestantische Begriff des Siegels oder Pfandes ist weit entfernt die *collative* Kraft des Sacraments zu schwächen ; er gestattet sogar die mystische Verknüpfung der Elemente des Sacraments mit der *res signata et exhibenda ; signa et res significatæ sacramentaliter conjunguntur* (*Conf. Helv. post.* xix.). *Bezeichnung, Besiegelung, Darreichung* der Gnade Christi vereinigen sich im Sacramente. (*Decl. Thorun. De Sacr.* 1, 7)."—Nitzsch, *prot. Beant. der Symb. Möhlers,* Hamburg 1835, p. 151 f.]

is not met by the grace that Christ confers, but is reduced to a mere significant dedication of himself to the Saviour unconnected with any grace at all. Take away Christ from the ordinance as present there, to covenant with the believer, actually giving Himself and His blessings spiritually through means of the outward ordinance, in answer to the faith of the believer giving himself to Christ through the same ordinance, and the Sacrament is evacuated of all spiritual grace; the act of the receiver becomes a mere expressive sign of what he is willing to do in the way of dedicating himself to Christ; but not an actual dedication, accomplished through means of a covenant *then* and *there* renewed, by which the believer becomes Christ's, and Christ becomes the believer's. The principle of the Independents in regard to the Sacraments cuts the Sacrament, as it were, in twain, and puts asunder what God has joined. It leaves to the believer his part in the transaction, in so far as he employs the Sacrament as a sign of his dedication to Christ; but it takes away Christ's part in the transaction, in so far as He meets with the believer and enters into covenant with him,—accepting the believer as His, and giving Himself to the soul in return. Severed from Christ in the ordinance, and from the covenant with His people into which Christ there enters, the act of the recipient can be no more than an expressive sign, or convenient profession of faith, unconnected with true and proper sacramental grace.

II. The Sacraments of the New Testament are regarded by another party as in themselves, and by reason of the virtue that belongs to them, and not through the instrumentality of the faith or the Spirit in the heart of the recipient, effectual to impart justifying and saving grace directly, in all cases where it is not resisted by an unworthy reception of the ordinance. This general opinion may be held under various modifications; but all of them are opposed to the doctrine I have already laid down, that the Sacraments are seals of a justifying and saving grace already enjoyed by the recipient, and not intended for the conversion of sinners; and that they become means of grace only in so far as the Spirit of God, by the aid of the ordinance, calls forth the faith of the recipient, and no further.

The doctrine of the efficacy of Sacraments, directly and immediately of themselves, and not indirectly and mediately through the faith of the receiver, and through the Spirit in the receiver, is advocated in its extreme and unmodified form by the Church of Rome. According to that Church, these ordinances, as outward and material rites, become, after certain words of institution pronounced by the priest, possessed of a sacramental virtue, which is conveyed infallibly to the soul of the person who receives them, on *two* conditions, which are necessary to justifying and spiritual grace being really imparted. *First,* on the side of the priest who pronounces the words of institution, there is required, as a condition of the supernatural grace being imparted, that he have the intention to make the Sacrament and confer it; for without this, the outward matter of the ordinance would remain mere matter, and have no sacramental character or virtue. And *second,* on the side of the recipient of the ordinance, it is required that he be free from any of those sins which, in the language of Popery, are called " mortal, " and which, when contracted and not removed, would resist the operation of the sacramental virtue, and prevent his soul receiving spiritual grace. But when these two conditions are present,—when the priest intends to consecrate and dispense the ordinance, and the recipient is not barred from the reception of its virtue by mortal sin,—such is the efficacy of the Sacrament in itself, and directly, that it infallibly communicates to the partaker of it justifying and saving grace. The doctrine of the Church of Rome is very distinctly brought out in the canons of the Council of Trent, and also in her Catechism. " If any," says the 11th canon concerning the Sacraments in general, " if any shall say that there is not required in the ministers, when they make and confer the Sacraments, at least the intention of doing what the Church does, let him be accursed." " If any shall say that the Sacraments of the New Law do not contain the grace of which they are the signs, or that they do not confer that grace on those who place no obstacle in the way, as if they were only outward signs of grace or justification already received by faith, and certain badges of the Christian profession, by which believers are distinguished from infidels, let him be accursed." " If any shall say that grace is not conferred by the Sacraments of the New Law, *ex opere operato,* but that faith in the Divine promise alone avails to secure grace, let him be accursed." [1] According

---

[1] *Concil. Trident. Canones et Decreta,* Sess. vii. *De Sacr. in Gen.,* Can. vi. viii. xi. [Compare Möhler's statement of the Roman Catholic theory of the Sacraments (*Symb.* 6te Aufl. pp. 253–258). It is worthy of remark, that that

to this doctrine, then, Sacraments impart grace, not through the channel of the faith of the receiver, and not in dependence in any way on his spiritual act, but immediately and directly from themselves, " *ex opere operato.*" This last expression is to be interpreted in connection with the distinction drawn by the Church of Rome between the Sacraments of the Old and New Testament Churches. The Sacraments of the Gospel Church are superior in efficacy to those under the law, in the Popish theory, because the former, or the New Testament Sacraments, work grace independently of the spiritual disposition or act of the

acute and dexterous controversialist, in his own exposition of the doctrine, passes over in utter silence the very remarkable and important element of the priest's intention, as defined at Trent,—the sole reference to it being in a quotation from Bellarmine given in a note (p. 256). Nitzsch's remarks on the significance of the point thus ignored, are worth quoting: " The demand of an *intention* on the part of the priest in order to the Sacrament being savingly effectual, or effectual at all, met opposition among the Romish theologians, both at and before the Council of Trent. At one time the danger was pleaded incurred by the baptized or the absolved, who might now so easily miss obtaining grace, or be left in uncertainty about it ; at another, the much greater concession already made, that unbelief, or even mortal sin on the part of the priest, did not destroy the efficacy of the priestly act. On these grounds, the Council saw themselves compelled to restrict the demand as much as possible ; it asserted itself, notwithstanding. Sess. vii. Can. 11 : ' Si quis dixerit in ministris, dum Sacramenta conficiunt et conferunt, non requiri intentionem saltem faciendi quod facit Ecclesia, anathema sit,' with good reason, as is easily to be seen. For if, as Can. x. decided, the private Christian cannot make or confer most of the Sacraments,—if the supernatural qualification of the priest, although a ' *gratia gratis data*,' and not ' *gratum faciens*,' still was of the essence of the sacramental dispensation,—while, on the other hand, no ' *bonus motus* ' of the recipient was necessary for the reception of the grace, nay, in the case of private mass, no recipient at all, in the case of infant Baptism, no conscious recipient, was needed,—then, should there be an *entire* absence of harmony between the mental state of the priest and the design of the transaction, there would be absolutely nothing left but the bare, mechanical, accidental, external act; and from this hardly a single believer would have expected any blessing whatsoever. The worth of the words of institution and promise, as appropriated by faith, had already been sacrificed to the worth of the ' *opus;* ' so had the dignity of the congregation to the dignity of the priest: hence arose great perils and perplexities, if now, after all, the worth of the words should be allowed to stand without moral desert on the part of the priest. The morally indifferent supernatural qualification of the priest must therefore now receive at least a psychological quickening, and the co-operation of the mental state of the priest be thus brought in to give the requisite support to a transaction otherwise bereft of all substance and security. They resigned themselves, accordingly, to the lesser perplexity. The doctrine of the ' *intentio ministri* ' is a reinforcement to the doctrine of the ' *opus operatum*,' which yields at the same time various advantages of another sort ; and the latter dogma is again explained and supported by the notion of the ' not interposed hindrance.' "—*Prot. Beant.* Hamburg 1835, p. 154. Gerhard, *Loci*, xviii. 31-38, ed. Preuss. tom. iv. pp. 151-158.]

recipient; whereas the latter, or Old Testament Sacraments, were dependent on the spiritual disposition or act of the receiver of them. The "*opus operatum*" of the New Testament Sacraments, or the virtue they have by their own act, apart from the spiritual state of the recipient, is contrasted with the "*opus operantis*" in the Old Testament Sacraments, or the virtue which they had, not in themselves, or in their own operation, but only in connection with the spiritual act of the partaker. According to the proper theory of the Church of Rome, the Sacraments of the New Testament impart grace *ex opere operato*, or from their own intrinsic virtue and direct act on the soul of him who receives them.[1]

This doctrine of the inherent power of Sacraments in themselves to impart grace, held by the Church of Rome, is also the system maintained, although with some important modifications, by another party beyond the pale of that Church, the representatives of which, at the present day, are to be found in the High Churchmen of the English Establishment. The doctrine of the High Church party in the English Establishment in regard to the Sacraments differs indeed in *two* important particulars from the full and unmodified development of it found in the Popish system; but in other respects it is substantially the same,— equally implying the inherent power of Sacraments to impart grace, not through the spiritual act of the recipient, but apart from and independently of it. The advocates of High Church principles in the Church of England generally—although there is a numerous and increasing section of them who in this respect

---

[1] The statement that Papists hold the Sacraments to be efficacious of themselves, apart from the spiritual condition of the recipient, is often met— especially by English Romanists—with a flat denial. And on this ground. They hold that many elements are, in point of fact, present in every case in which the Sacraments are efficacious ; some of these elements are connected with the state of the recipient,—such as a desire to receive the ordinance,— and others with the working of God. Thus Bellarmine objects to Calvin's stating the point in debate to be, not as to grace being conferred in the Sacraments, but only "whether God works in them by His own proper, and, so to speak, intrinsic virtue, or whether He resigns His place to the external signs."—*Inst.* lib. iv. c. xiv. 17. (See next note.) Any Romanist, however, who has the slightest regard for the authoritative declarations of his Church, can be fixed down conclusively to this position, that, whatever other elements may, in point of fact, be present, the immediate, efficient, instrumental cause of the grace invariably conveyed to all "qui non ponunt obicem" is "the outward action called a Sacrament," and nothing else. See Turrettin's masterly treatment of this point, *Opera*, loc. xix. Qu. viii. 2-6. Cunningham, *Works*, vol. iii. pp. 124-139. Hodge, *Princeton Essays and Reviews*, New York 1857, pp. 370 f., 388.

approximate more nearly to Rome—generally reject the Popish doctrines,—*first*, of the *opus operatum*, and *second*, of the necessity for the intention of the priest in the Sacrament. They deny that the Sacraments have any immediate physical influence upon the soul, by the very act of outwardly participating in them,—such as is implied in the *opus operatum* of the Church of Rome; and they deny, further, that the intention of the priest to make and confer the Sacrament is a necessary condition of it, without which it could impart no grace. These two elements in the Popish theory of sacramental ordinances are rejected, generally speaking, by the High Church disciples of the English Establishment, although instances are not awanting—and they seem to be multiplying of late—of both these monstrous pretensions being, in a certain sense, maintained by them. But they agree with the Romish Church in the grand and fundamental principle which belongs to its doctrine of the Sacraments,—namely, that they communicate grace from the sacramental virtue that resides in themselves,—or, as some prefer to put it, that invariably accompanies them by Christ's appointment,[1]—and by their own immediate influence on the soul, and not instrumentally by the operation of the Spirit of God on the worthy recipient and through the medium of his faith. This is the characteristic principle that is common both to the Popish and the High Church theories of Sacraments. Both these parties hold that there is something in or connected with the ordinance which directly and immediately does the work of grace upon the soul; and not merely indirectly and mediately through the Spirit of God working on the soul, and the faith of the soul working in return. The Church of Rome ascribes this efficacy of the ordinances to the *opus operatum* of the Sacraments, and the act and intention of the priest in consecrating them. The High Churchmen of the English Establishment usually reject both of these doctrines as laid down by the Council of Trent, and ascribe this efficacy of the ordinances to the deposit of spiritual grace which Christ has communicated

---

[1] In, cum, or sub Sacramento. [" It is to be observed," says Bellarmine, " that the dispute is not about the *mode* in which Sacraments are causes of justification, *i.e.* whether the effect is produced by physical or moral means; and again, if the influence be of a physical sort, whether it be by some inherent quality, or by the simple will of God; for these points do not belong to the question of faith; but only in general, whether the Sacraments are true and proper causes of justification; so that it truly follows, from a man's being baptized, that he is justified."—*Disputationes*, tom. iii. lib. ii. cap. i.]

to the Church, and connected with the Sacraments, and given them the power to impart. But the High Churchmen of Rome and the High Churchmen of England agree equally in this, that there are in the Sacraments an efficacy and power to impart grace of themselves, directly and immediately, to the soul of the recipient; and that they are not merely aids or instruments for bringing the recipient into direct and immediate communication with Christ to receive grace from Him.[1]

Although both the Canons and Catechism of the Council of Trent lay down, to all appearance, expressly and undeniably the doctrine that there is a physical virtue in Sacraments, whereby they operate upon the recipient, yet there are not awanting doctors of the Romish Church who are anxious to soften down the dogma of the *opus operatum*, and to explain it in the sense of a moral and spiritual, and not a physical virtue, residing in the ordinance. And in this modified form of it, the Romish doctrine of the Sacraments—apart from the necessity of the priest's intention—approximates very closely to the High Church theory entertained by many in the Church of England. That theory maintains the doctrine of not a physical but a spiritual virtue deposited and residing in the Sacrament, which operates universally, not through the faith or spiritual act of the recipient, but directly and immediately through the act of participation in the outward ordinance. This, in fact, is no more than part of the general doctrine that the Church is the grand storehouse of grace to man, and not Christ Himself; and that it is by communication with the Church, and not by direct communication with Christ, that the soul is made partaker of that grace. The Sacraments, as the chief medium through which the Church communicates of its stores of spiritual blessings, are the efficient instruments for imparting grace directly to the recipient.

Now, there is one preliminary remark which, in proceeding to estimate the value and truth of such principles in regard to the Sacraments, it is necessary to bear in mind. It is not denied, but, on the contrary, strongly maintained and asserted, that the Sacraments are means of grace. To the believer who uses them aright, they are made the means of conveying spiritual blessings. In regard to this, there is no controversy between the opponents and

---

[1] [Goode, *Nature of Christ's Presence in the Eucharist*, Lond. 1856, vol. i. pp. vi. 11–55. Cunningham, *Works*, vol. i. pp. 233–237.]

the advocates of High Church views of the Sacraments, whether Popish or Tractarian. But the question in dispute is, whether the Sacraments become effectual, from a virtue in themselves, or in the priest that consecrates them, or only by the work of the Spirit and the faith of the recipient? That the faith of the believer is called forth and exercised in the ordinance, and that through this faith he receives grace additional to what he enjoyed before, we do not dispute, but, on the contrary, strenuously maintain. That the spiritual act of the believer in the ordinance, when in faith he gives himself to his Saviour, is met by the spiritual act of Christ in the ordinance, when in return He gives Himself and His grace to the believer, is a doctrine at all times to be asserted and vindicated. That the faith of the recipient, in the act of committing and engaging himself to Christ, through means of the ordinance, is a faith unto which Christ is given in return, we would constantly affirm; and in this sense, and in this way, the Sacraments become means or channels or instruments whereby grace is given and conveyed. But they are no means of grace except through the faith of the recipient, and in consequence of his own spiritual state and act. There is no inherent power in the ordinance itself to confer blessing, apart from the faith of the participator, and except through the channel of that faith. There is no deposit of power —whether, with the Church of Rome, we deem it physical and *ex opere operato*, or whether, with Tractarians and High Churchmen, we call it spiritual—in the Sacraments themselves to influence the mind of him who receives them. They have no virtue of themselves, apart from the work of Christ through His Spirit on the one side, and the spiritual act of the recipient through his faith on the other side. In the language of Amesius, in his admirable reply to Bellarmine, Sacraments have no power " efficere gratiam immediate, sed mediante Spiritu Dei et fide." [1]

---

[1] Amesius, *Bellarm. Enerv.* Amsterdam 1658, tom. iii. lib. i. cap. v. p. 22. [" In the following sentences of the *Declaration of Thorn*," observes Nitzsch, " all Protestants agree : ' Sacraments are outward and visible signs, seals, and testimonials of the Divine will, instituted by God Himself, by the combination of Word and element, in order to seal and exhibit, through means of these signs, the invisible grace which is promised in the Word of the covenant. It is obvious that we by no means make them bare signs, empty and inefficacious, or mere badges of outward profession, since, besides their mystical significance, according to the Divine institution, we attribute to the Sacraments a sure sealing of God's promises, and at the same time a true and infallible exhibi-

Has the Church, then, ordinances for its administration and use which, either by the original appointment of Christ, or by deposit of grace from Christ, have in themselves virtue to impart spiritual blessing through the administration of them alone? Or has the Church ordinances for its administration and use which have no virtue in themselves to communicate grace, except in connection with the faith of the receiver, and the blessing imparted by the Spirit? Are the Sacraments of the New Testament themselves a quickening power in the soul, apart from the faith or spiritual act of the participator,—the original deposit of grace committed to them being still retained, and still communicable through their administration, and that alone? Or are these Sacraments effectual to impart grace only in connection with the faith and spiritual disposition of the recipient,—there being necessary to their efficacy, both the act of the believer, in the use of them, giving himself to Christ, and the act of Christ, through the same ordinance, giving Himself to the believer. It matters little whether, as with the Popish Church, the Sacraments are invested with a *physical* virtue, in consequence of which they impart grace ; or whether, as with the High Churchmen of other denominations, they are invested with a *spiritual* virtue in consequence of which they impart grace,—if in both cases the grace is given by the Sacrament itself, and not given through the Spirit and the faith in the heart of the recipient. It matters little whether a physical or a spiritual explanation is given of sacramental efficacy, if it be efficacy exerted apart from Christ in the ordinance giving Himself to the believer, and experienced apart from the believer in the ordinance giving himself to Christ. Whatever be the efficacy and virtue, physical or moral, if it is independent of and separate from the faith of the recipient covenanting in the ordinance with Christ, and the act in answer to that faith of Christ covenanting with the recipient, it is not the sacramental grace which the Scripture recognises. It becomes, when thus separated and drawn apart, a mere charm, a trick of magic, whether physical or spiritual, utterly unknown to the Gospel economy. Let us endeavour to apply to this theory those tests which may serve to

tion of the things promised, in the way suited and proper to them, to be received by a living faith.'" (Niemeyer, p. 680.) *Prot. Beant. der Symb. Möhler's*, Hamburg 1835, p. 175. Bruce, *Serm. on the Sacr.* Wodrow Soc. ed. Edin. 1843, p. 10 f. Calvin, *Antidote to Council of Trent*, Sess. vii. Can. ii. iv.–vi. *Tracts*, vol. iii. Calvin Transl. Soc. Edin. 1851, pp. 172-175.]

try its merits and its truth. There are four different tests by
which we may try the merits of this sacramental theory, whether
held in its extreme form by Papists, or in its more modified form
by High Churchmen of other communions.

1st, Tested by Scripture, which constitutes the rule for the
exercise of Church power, there is no warrant for asserting that
there is an inherent and independent virtue in Sacraments to
impart justifying or saving grace.

The truth of this general proposition may be established by a
very wide and ample deduction of evidence from Scripture. It
is impossible for us to do more than advert to the leading heads
of proof in connection with this question. *In the first place*,
those multiplied and various declarations of Scripture, which
state that we are justified by faith alone without works on our
part, very distinctly prove that the Sacraments cannot have an independent and inherent power in themselves of conveying justifying and saving grace. Such passages expressly assert that faith
is the immediate instrumental cause of justification. They are inconsistent, therefore, with the theory that the Sacraments directly
and immediately of themselves impart grace, although they are
quite consistent with the doctrine that the Sacraments indirectly,
and through the faith of the worthy receiver, may impart grace.
In the second place, the doctrine that the Sacraments have an
inherent virtue to confer grace, is opposed to the whole tenor
of Scripture, which sets forth Christ as the one and the immediate
object of faith and hope to the believer, in the matter of his
justification and salvation. The Word of God, from its commencement to its close, clearly and constantly and invariably
points to Christ, and to nothing but Christ, as the only source to
which a sinner must look for forgiveness and acceptance with
God. The theory of the Sacraments held by High Churchmen
presents another and a different object for his faith, and teaches
him to rest in an outward observance as sufficient. It is part of
that most destructive system which places the Church and the
ordinances of the Church between the sinner and his Saviour.
In the third place, the very express testimony of the Apostle
Paul, in regard to the insufficiency of the Sacraments under the
Old Testament Church to communicate grace of themselves, is
an argument equally effectual to show that the New Testament

Sacraments are insufficient likewise. Abraham was not justified by circumcision, but by the faith of which his circumcision was the seal.[1] *In the fourth place*, the statements of Scripture which at first sight might be construed as if they ascribed a gracious influence to the Sacraments of the New Testament in themselves, and which seem to connect saving benefits with the observance of them, are not stronger or more numerous, but less so, than those which ascribe justifying and saving blessings to the ordinance of the Word, or truth received by the reader or hearer of it. We know that the Word or the truth justifies, not of itself, but through the faith of him that receives it; and that, apart from this faith, it has no virtue or power of a gracious kind at all. In the same manner, Sacraments impart grace, not of themselves, but through the faith of those who receive them; and, apart from that faith, they have no life or blessing whatsoever. *In the fifth place*, the theory of an inherent virtue or power in the administration of the outward ordinance is utterly opposed to those numerous passages of Scripture which assert that the power of the Gospel is altogether of a spiritual kind, and is in no respect akin to a mere external and material influence, as if such could impart a supernatural grace. It is "not meat and drink, but righteousness, and peace, and joy in the Holy Ghost." And instead of pointing to any outward source of power or efficacy, and exclaiming, "Lo here, or Lo there!" the Christian has been taught to think that "the kingdom of God" has its source and presence "within him."[2] The theory which ascribes to the Sacraments an infallible virtue which, unless counteracted by some obstacle, such as infidelity or open vice, must operate to impart grace, is inconsistent with those numerous statements of Scripture which represent the Gospel as a spiritual power, adapted to the spiritual nature of man.[3]

In estimating the bearing of Scripture testimony on this question, there is one consideration of a general kind which it is of great importance to the argument to bear in mind. In every theory of the Sacraments that can be held,—from the lowest to

---

[1] Rom. ii. 25–29, iii. 20, 30, iv. 3–11; Heb. ix. 11 f., x. 1–11. [Comp. the Apology for the Confession of Augsburg, vii. 18, p. 203, in Hase, *Libri Symbolici Eccles. Evang.* Lipsiæ 1827.]

[2] Rom. xiv. 17; Luke xvii. 21.

[3] Gillespie, *Aaron's Rod Blossoming*, B. iii. chap. xii.-xiv.

the highest, from the Socinian up to the Popish,—the Sacraments are regarded as at least signs of spiritual things, representing and exhibiting the blessing in outward resemblance. The union thus established, according to any theory that can be held of them, between the sign and the thing signified by it, has introduced into Scripture a kind of phraseology which at first sight appears to give some sanction to the High Church system in regard to sacramental ordinances. There is often an exchange of names between the sign and the thing signified in Scripture, in consequence of which what may be predicated of the one is often asserted of the other, and *vice versâ*. This usage of language, so frequently exemplified in Scripture in connection with this matter, is a usage found commonly in other writings and in regard to other matters, and gives rise to no sort of misapprehension in our interpretation of it. It is the great foundation indeed of all figurative language.[1] Thus, when Christ is said to be " the Passover sacrificed for us," there is an exchange of this kind, in which the name of the sign is given to the thing signified; and when Christ says of the bread, " This is my body," there is an exchange in the opposite way, and the name of the thing signified is attributed to the sign. And in perfect accordance with this usage of language, there are several passages in Scripture in which the mere outward observance in the case of the New Testament Sacraments, the external sign, has a virtue attributed to it which in reality belongs, not to the sign, but to the grace represented in the observance, or to the thing signified. Thus, for example, " *Baptism* " is said in one passage " *to save us ;*" although, from the further explanation contained in the passage itself, it is plain that it is not the outward sign but the thing signified that is spoken of under the name of the sign ; for the apostle adds immediately, " not the putting away of the filth of the flesh, but the answer of a good conscience towards God."[2] In the same manner the Apostle Paul speaks of " the cup of blessing" as "the communion of the blood of Christ,"[3] —language in which that is predicated of the sign which is truly predicated only of the thing signified. In short, the sacramental

---

[1] [" Omnia significantia videntur quodam modo earum rerum quas significant sustinere personas: sicut dictum est ab Apostolo, ' Petra erat Christus,' quoniam petra illa, de quâ hoc dictum est, significabat utique Christum."— Aug. *De Civitate Dei*, lib. xviii. cap. 48.]
[2] 1 Pet. iii. 21.　　　　[3] 1 Cor. x. 16.

union between the outward sign and the inward grace gives
occasion to not a few examples in Scripture in which what is
true of the one only, or the inward grace, is attributed to the
other, or the outward sign. Almost the whole plausibility of
the argument from Scripture in favour of the High Church theory
of the Sacraments comes from this source; and it is completely
removed when the familiar canon of criticism, applicable to Scripture in common with other writings, is attended to,—namely,
that what truly belongs to the thing signified is often predicated
figuratively of the sign, and so ought to be interpreted and understood.[1]

2d, The theory of an inherent power, physical or spiritual,
in the Sacraments, is inconsistent with the supreme authority of
Christ, from whom all Church power is derived.

The doctrine that would deposit in sacramental ordinances a
grace communicable to the participator, apart from his communion
with Christ, directly and immediately, is inconsistent with the
office and right of Christ to hold in His own hand all blessing,
and to dispense from His own hand, not mediately through another,
but at once from Himself, the grace which His people receive.
Such a theory takes the administration of grace out of the hands
of Christ, ever present to dispense it, and transfers it to a priest
standing in His room. There can be no participation in heavenly
blessing except what comes from direct communication with
Christ on the part of the soul that receives it; and it is a dishonour to Him, who is the ever-living and ever-present administrator of all grace to His people, to put the mute and conscious
ordinance in the place of Christ, and to transfer the dependence
of the soul for spiritual blessing from the Divine Head in heaven
to the outward ministry of Sacraments on earth. That Christ
might by His original appointment have made the Sacraments the
receptacle of a physical influence, fitted and able to work a supernatural blessing on the soul, it would perhaps be presumptuous to
deny. That Christ *might* at the first institution of the ordinances
have made them a reservoir or storehouse of grace enough for all
ages of the Church, and imparted to them a spiritual blessing
out of which every subsequent generation of His people might
draw their supply, we need not be anxious to dispute. Or that

---

[1] [Westminst. Conf. chap. xxvii. 2, xxix. 5. Goode, *Nature of Christ's
Presence in the Eucharist*, Lond. 1856, vol. i. pp. 241-250, 598.]

Christ, without communicating at the beginning to Sacraments a store either of physical or spiritual grace sufficient for all generations, might have tied Himself up to the indiscriminate and invariable communication of His Spirit along with the administration of outward Sacraments, and bound Himself down, without any choice or discretion, to link spiritual grace to material rites, apart from the faith of the person observing them,—this, too, is perhaps a *possible* imagination.   But had Christ, as the Head of ordinances in His Church, done either the one or the other of these things, He must to that extent have divested Himself of His office as Mediator, or resigned the exercise of it; He must in so far have abdicated His functions as the sole and living and ever-present administrator of grace to His Church; and been shut out from that exclusive and supreme agency which He maintains as the dispenser as well as author of every blessing by which the soul is to be saved.

3d, The theory of the Sacraments which ascribes to them an independent virtue or power, is inconsistent with the spiritual liberties of Christ's people.

Such a system brings the soul itself into bondage.   It keeps the spirit, which Christ has Himself redeemed, waiting upon man for the communication of the blessings of its redemption; it makes the soul which Christ has ransomed dependent for its freedom on the ministry of a fellow-creature.   There cannot be a worse or more abject thraldom than that which subordinates the flock of the Saviour's purchase to any one but Himself, and causes them to hang upon the intention entertained or not entertained by a priest for the enjoyment or forfeiture of spiritual blessing.   But even apart from the monstrous doctrine of the Romish Church as to the intention of the priest being necessary to the efficacy of the ordinance, the sacramental theory we have been considering, whether Popish or Tractarian, is inconsistent with the spiritual freedom of those whom Christ has redeemed.   That freedom consists in subjection to and dependence on Christ, and none but Christ,—in being emancipated from all dependence on any other except their Saviour,—in being kept waiting, not at the footstool of man for saving blessings, but at the footstool of Christ,—and in being taught to look for all the grace they need day by day, not to the ministry of man's hand, but to the hand of Christ.   Spiritual freedom for the believer is bound up with a dependence on Christ immediately and directly, and on Him alone, for every blessing that he needs.[1]

4th, The sacramental theory we have been considering is inconsistent with the spirituality of the Church, and of the power exercised by the Church for the spiritual good of men.

When, according to that theory, the Sacraments become the instruments of justification and the source of faith, instead of the seal of a justification already possessed, and the exercise and aid of a faith already in existence,—when they are made to come between the soul, in its approach to Christ, and Christ Himself, and communion in the external ordinance is substituted for the fellowship of the Spirit, it is a fatal evidence that the Church, which so teaches and so practises her teaching, although she has "begun in the Spirit," has "sought to be made perfect by the flesh."[2] If the external ordinance be made to occupy that place which belongs to the Spirit, and participation in the ordinance be the substitute for faith, the sacramental theory thus reduced to practice will be but the commencement of worse and deeper degradation. It is but the beginning of a course which, consistently followed, must lead to a religion of form and self-righteousness, of sense and sensuous observances, of carnal ordinances and a ceremonial holiness, of outward satisfaction and penances and merit. There will be the priest and the bloodless but efficacious sacrifice, grace conferred by the tricks of a physical or spiritual magic, a religion that manifests itself outwardly and not inwardly, the holiness of houses, and altars, and sacred wood and stone, but not the holiness of the Spirit; the atonement of Sacraments and penances and creature merits, but not the atonement of the Saviour received by faith; a righteousness of bodily discipline and fleshly mortification, but not the righteousness of God imputed to the believer; a justification made out of pains and merits, of sufferings and works, but not a justification freely given by Divine grace and freely accepted by faith; an outward baptism to regenerate the sinner with water at first,—the food of the communion table, made flesh and blood by the consecration of a priest, to sustain the life so begun, and the anointing with oil at last to prepare the soul for the burial. Such are the inevitable

---

[1] [Goode, *Letter to a Lay Friend*, Lond. 1845, pp. 18-24. Litton, *Church of Christ*, Lond. 1851, pp. 11-13, 202-232, 240 f.]

[2] Gal. iii. 3.

fruits of the sacramental theory, consistently carried out in the Church of Christ, making the very temple of God to be the habitation of every carnal and unclean thing.[1]

<hr>

[1] Bellarm. *Disputationes*, tom. iii. lib. ii. cap. i.–xxii. Perrone, *Prælectiones Theologicæ*, Parisiis 1842, tom. ii. pp. 5–66. Amesius, *Bellarm. Enerv.* tom. iii. lib. i. cap. i.–v. Turrettin, *Opera*, tom. iii. loc. xix. qu. i.–ix. Cunningham, *Works*, vol. iii. pp, 121-133. [Bruce, *Sermons on the Sacraments*, Wodrow Soc. ed. Edin. 1843, pp. 11-33. Newman, *Lectures on Justification*, pp. 316, etc.; Tract No. 90, 2d ed. p. 13. Wilberforce, *Doctrine of the Holy Eucharist*, 3d ed. Lond. 1854, pp. 17-38, 97-130. Goode, *Doctrine of the Church of England as to the Effects of Baptism in the case of Infants*, 2d ed. Lond. 1850, pp. 3-10. *Vind. of the ' Defence of the XXXIX. Art.'* etc., 2d ed. p. 38 f. *Unpublished Letter of Martyr to Bullinger*, Lond. 1850, pp. 11-13. Martensen, *Dogmatik*, 4te Aufl. Kiel 1858, pp. 361, 364. Matthes, *Comparative Symbolik*, Leipzig 1854, pp. 492-510. Thomasius, *Dogmatik*, 3ter Theil, 2te Abth. Erlangen 1861, pp. 113-135.]

CHAPTER II.

THE SACRAMENT OF BAPTISM.

SECTION I.—NATURE OF THE ORDINANCE.

PASSING now from the doctrine of the Sacraments in general, or viewed in respect of what belongs to them in common, I proceed to consider them more in detail and individually; and for this purpose I commence with the Sacrament of Baptism, as the initiatory rite. Upon what grounds are we justified in attributing to Baptism the name and character of a Sacrament? What is the nature of the ordinance, the place which it occupies, and the office it is intended to serve in the Christian Church? The general principles which we have already laid down in regard to Sacraments as such, when applied more particularly to Baptism, will enable us to bring out distinctly the character, authority, and meaning of the ordinance. There were four elements which we found to enter into the idea of a Sacrament. Let us proceed to apply these to the ordinance of Baptism, in order that we may ascertain its true nature and import. And in doing so, we shall have an opportunity, at the same time, of noticing some of the opinions in regard to Baptism which we hold to be unscriptural and erroneous.

I. The first characteristic of a Sacrament is, that it must be a positive institution of Christ in His Church; and this mark applies to Baptism.

The doctrine of the Quakers is opposed to this first position. They contend that Baptism, and the Lord's Supper also, were Jewish practices, neither suited to the Gospel economy nor appointed for the Gospel Church, but destined to be done away with under the dispensation of the Spirit.[1] Now, in reference to Baptism, it cannot be doubted that it was a Jewish observance

---

[1] [Barclay, *Apology*, 10th ed. Lond. 1841, pp. 387–421.]

before it became a Christian one, and that it was administered by the Jews to proselytes joining them from amóng the Gentiles, previously to the time when it was adopted by our Lord as one of the Sacraments of His Church. This is sufficiently attested by the statements of Jewish writers; it may be inferred, indeed, from the narratives of the Evangelists. Baptism, as an initiatory rite and token of discipleship, connected with a sect or school of religion, was familiarly known among the Jews; and it is on the ground of their previous acquaintance with and practice of it amongst themselves, that we can understand the question addressed to John the Baptist: "Why baptizest thou then, if thou be not that Christ, nor Elias, neither that Prophet?"[1] Had John been any of those personages come into the country as a teacher or founder of a new school of religion, the Jews would have felt no surprise, and expressed no objection to his practice of baptizing with water; and it was only because he denied that he was either Christ or Elias, that they were led to demand the authority by which he baptized. Although, then, there is no mention of any such ordinance in the law of Moses, yet there seems to be no doubt that it was a ceremony that had found its way into the practice of the Jews.[2] But we are not on this account to imagine that Christian Baptism was one of those temporary ordinances destined to be done away with, or that it is not a positive institution of Christ in His Church. During His own personal ministry on earth, we are given to understand that, acting on our Lord's direct authority, His Apostles adopted the rite, and administered it to the Jews who professed their desire to become Christ's disciples. Side by side with the commission to preach the Gospel given to the Apostles, when the Church was set up by our Lord after His own resurrection, we find the command to baptize those whom they taught; and the ordinances of the Word and of Baptism are spoken of in terms significant equally of the authority and standing obligation of both. "Go ye therefore, and make disciples of all nations, baptizing them in the name of the Father, and of the Son, and of the Holy Ghost; teaching them to observe all things whatsoever I have com-

---

[1] John i. 25.

[2] The question of Jewish Baptism is ably discussed by Dr. Halley; and the conclusions at which he arrives on this subject are, I believe, substantially correct. *The Sacraments*, Lond. 1844, pp. 111–160. Wall, *Hist. of Infant Baptism*, Lond. 1720, vol. i. pp. lxvi.-cx.

manded you: and, lo, I am with you alway, even unto the end of the world."[1]

The natural and indeed unavoidable interpretation of the apostolic commission seems to establish these two things: first, that a literal Baptism, or washing, with water, was to accompany the discipleship brought about by the preaching of the Apostles; and second, that both the ordinance of Baptism and that of preaching were to be continued unto the end of the world. Added to this, we have the evidence for the Divine authority and permanent obligation of Baptism in the Church of Christ, from the unvarying practice of the Apostles in regard to their converts, whether Jewish or Gentile, down to the latest period in the history of the Church to which the inspired narrative refers. Such considerations as these go to prove that Baptism was not a mere Jewish practice, suffered for a time in the Christian Church, and destined to be cast off with other Jewish customs and observances. On the contrary, the positive appointment of our Lord expressed in the commission He addressed to the Apostles as founders of the Christian society,—the apostolic example itself as regards Baptism equally of Gentile and Jewish converts,—and the entire absence of any intimation, either express or implied, that the practice was only temporary and designed to be discontinued, go undeniably to prove that Christian Baptism is a permanent institution of Christ in His Church.

II. Another characteristic of a Sacrament is, that it be an external and sensible sign of an internal grace,—a spiritual truth embodied in an outward action; and this mark is applicable to Christian Baptism.

That Baptism is symbolical of unseen and spiritual blessings, is admitted by all parties who hold the ordinance itself to be an appointment of Christ, whatever theory they may entertain as to its sacramental character or virtue. Adopted as it was by Christ from Jewish customs and practices, it could hardly fail, indeed, at its original institution in the Christian Church, to appear to those who used it to be of a symbolical character. They had been accustomed to the washings and sprinklings practised under the law as symbolical observances, expressive of the removal of ceremonial uncleanness, and of such a ceremonial purification as secured acceptance with God,—at least outwardly. And when

[1] Matt. xxviii. 19, 20.

Baptism was appointed by our Lord, the washing with water included in it must have been interpreted, in accordance with the previous use and meaning of the Jewish observances, as a purification, or a putting away of defilement of sin, so that the person baptized was accounted clean, and fitted for acceptance with God. Hence the language of Scripture everywhere in connection with Baptism conveys the idea of its being a symbolical ordinance like the ancient washings and sprinklings customary among the Jews, and indeed among other nations, as expressive of religious purification or cleansing. The body washed with pure water was an emblem of the soul purified and cleansed through the blood and Spirit of Christ. The "Baptism for the remission of sin" was expressive of the cleansing by which sin is removed. The action by which water was applied by the administrator to the person, was representative of the application of the blood of Christ to the guilt of the soul. The action by which the washing of Baptism was submitted to by the recipient, was expressive of his passing under the washing of regeneration and the renewing of the Holy Ghost. And the distinguishing practice in Christian Baptism, that the person who received the ordinance was baptized "into the name of the Father, and the Son, and the Holy Ghost," was symbolical of his dedicating himself to the Father, through his justification by the blood of the Son, and his sanctification by the grace of the Spirit.

There was the twofold representation, exhibited in the ordinance of Baptism, of Christ giving Himself to the believer in the two great initial blessings of the covenant,—justification and sanctification,—and of the believer dedicating himself to Christ as one of His justified and sanctified people. Christ united to the believer, and the believer united to Christ, in consequence of the removal both of the guilt and pollution of sin which had separated between them, is the great lesson exhibited in the ordinance of Baptism as a symbol. Hence Baptism, rather than the Lord's Supper, forms the great initiatory rite of the Church. The former ordinance is more especially fitted symbolically to represent the union of the believer to Christ; the latter to set forth the communion of the believer with Christ. Baptism meets us at our entrance into the Church, and by the purification from the guilt and defilement of sin, which it more particularly represents, it exhibits us as entering into union with a Saviour in the only way in which that union can be effected,—in the way, namely, of free justification by the blood of Christ sprinkled upon the soul, and full sanctification by the Spirit of Christ cleansing and renewing our nature.[1] In regard to this office which we assign to Baptism, of being a sign of the spiritual blessings of the covenant by which the believer is united to Christ, all parties who hold Baptism to be an ordinance of Christ at all, agree, whatever additional views they may hold as to its sacramental character or virtue.

III. Another characteristic of a Sacrament, as we have already seen, is, that it is a seal of a federal transaction between two parties in the ordinance; and this third mark also belongs to Christian Baptism.

It is more than a sign of spiritual blessings; it is a visible seal and voucher of these to those who rightly partake of the ordinance. At this point the theory of Baptism laid down in the standards of our Church differs from the views held in regard to it by Socinians, and by many of the English Independents. They contend that Baptism is a symbol, and nothing more than a symbol, of spiritual blessings. We maintain that the statements of Scripture warrant us in asserting that, in addition to its being a symbol, it is also a seal of the covenant entered into between Christ and the believer through the ordinance. That in the administration and participation of Baptism there is a federal transaction between Christ and the believer who rightly receives it, and that the outward ordinance is a seal of the covenant engagement, may be established by abundant evidence from Scripture.

1st, There are a number of statements of Scripture connected with the ordinance which cannot be understood except upon the supposition that Baptism is not only a sign, but also a seal of a

---

[1] ["Baptisma nobis quod purgati et abluti simus testificatur; Cœna Eucharistiæ, quod redempti. In aqua figuratur ablutio; in sanguine satisfactio. Hæc duo in Christo reperiuntur, qui, ut ait Joannes (i. v. 6), 'venit in aquâ et sanguine,' hoc est, ut purgaret et redimeret. . . . . Sic autem cogitandum est quocunque baptizemur tempore, nos semel in omnem vitam ablui et purgari. Itaque quoties lapsi fuerimus repetenda erit Baptismi memoria, et hâc armandus animus, ut de peccatorum remissione semper certus securusque sit. [Comp. Luther's Sermon on Absolution and the Sacraments in the *Kirchen Postill.*] Nam etsi semel administratus præteriisse visus est posterioribus tamen peccatis non est abolitus. *Puritas enim Christi in eo nobis oblata est;* ea semper viget, nullis maculis opprimitur, sed omnes nostras sordes abluit et extergit."—Calvin, *Inst.* lib. iv. cap. xiv. 22, xv. 3. Bruce, *Sermons on the Sacraments*, Wodrow Soc. ed. Edin. 1843, pp. 38–40.]

covenant transaction between Christ and the believer. The very
words of the institution seem to point to this. Baptism " *into* the
name (εἰς τὸ ὄνομα) of the Father, and the Son, and the Holy
Ghost " means more than Baptism by their authority, or an expression of our submission to them. It plainly implies, on the part of
the baptized person, an act of dedication of himself to the Three
Persons of the blessed Godhead, under the separate characters
which they bear in the work of redemption,—an act of engagement by the recipient of the ordinance unto the Father, through
the Son, and by the Spirit; or, in other words, a dedication of himself to God through the medium of justification and sanctification.
In exact accordance with this view, we find in Scripture that
Baptism is connected with " remission of sins," obtained through
Christ, and with " the washing of regeneration," performed by
the Spirit,—expressions which go much farther than merely to
represent the ordinance as symbolical of these blessings, and which
appear to imply that there is an intimate connection between the
right reception of Baptism and the privilege of forgiveness of sins
through the blood of Christ, and of sanctification of our nature
by the Spirit. What that sort of connection is which is more
than a mere sign to represent, and less than an outward charm to
impart these blessings, is illustrated by the Apostle Paul in a
remarkable passage of his Epistle to the Romans : " Know ye
not," says the Apostle, " that so many of us as were baptized into
Jesus Christ were baptized into His death? Therefore we are
buried with Him by baptism into death ; that like as Christ was
raised up from the dead by the glory of the Father, even so we
also should walk in newness of life. For if we have been planted
together in the likeness of His death, we shall be also in the likeness of His resurrection."[1] Of course in this passage the Apostle
must be held as referring to the Baptism of a believer, in whose
case it was a spiritual act of faith embodying itself in the outward
ordinance. There are two things which seem plainly enough to
be included in this remarkable statement. *In the first place*, the
immersion in water of the persons of those who are baptized is
set forth as their burial with Christ in His grave because of sin ;
and their being raised again out of the water is their resurrection
with Christ in His rising again from the dead because of their
justification. Their death with Christ was their bearing the

[1] Rom. vi. 3-5.

penalty of sin, and their resurrection with Christ was their being freed from it, or justified. And *in the second place*, their burial in water, when dying with Christ, was the washing away of the corruptness of the old man beneath the water; and their coming forth from the water in the image of His resurrection was their leaving behind them the old man with his sins, and emerging into newness of life. Their immersion beneath the water, and their emerging again, were the putting off the corruption of nature and rising again into holiness, or their sanctification.[1] All this seems to be implied in this statement of the Apostle in regard to a believer's Baptism; and it cannot be doubted that, in accordance with many other passages of Scripture, it makes Baptism in the case of a believer far more than a sign of the initial blessings of justification and regeneration. The Apostle undoubtedly represents the act as a federal one, in which the believer gives himself to God in the way that God has appointed, through faith in Christ for pardon, and through submission to the Spirit for regeneration; and in which these blessings are communicated and confirmed to him. Such statements of Scripture seem to bear out the assertion, that in the Baptism of a believer there is a federal transaction, and that the outward ordinance is the seal of the spiritual covenant.

2d, The same conclusion, that Baptism is not only a sign but also a seal of the covenant, may be supported by the consideration, that Baptism has come in the room of the Old Testament Sacrament of circumcision. That the ordinance of Baptism under the New Testament has taken the place of circumcision in the ancient Church, is apparent from the statements of the Apostle Paul in his Epistle to the Colossians, in which he argues against the necessity of circumcision under the Gospel, on the ground that Baptism was all to believers now that circumcision had been to believers in former times ; and where he actually calls Baptism by the name of " *the circumcision of Christ.*" " In whom also ye are circumcised with the circumcision made without hands, in putting off the body of the sins of the flesh by the circumcision of Christ: buried with Him in Baptism, wherein also ye are risen with Him, through the faith of the operation of God, who hath

---

[1] [For a very able exposition of this passage and Col. ii. 11 f., agreeing in substance with that given above, but not finding in either case any allusion to a particular mode of Baptism, see Beecher, *Baptism with reference to its Import and Modes*, New York 1849, pp. 83-114 ; also Williams, *Antipæd. Exam.* vol. i. pp. 189-195. Wardlaw, *Disert. on Inf. Baptism*, 3d ed. pp. 155-164.]

raised Him from the dead." [1] This assertion, that Baptism is now the circumcision of the Christian Church, leads very directly to the inference that we must regard Baptism as being as much a seal of the covenant of grace, as circumcision was a seal of the Abrahamic covenant; and it goes very clearly to establish the position, that Baptism is far more than the simple symbolical institution which many Independents would make it,—that it has more in it than the character of a mere empty sign; that there belongs to it the grand characteristic of a sacramental ordinance, namely, the character of a seal, confirming and attesting a federal transaction between God and the believer.

IV. Another characteristic of a Sacrament is, that it is a means of grace; and this fourth mark, like the former ones, belongs to Christian Baptism.

Baptism is a means for confirming the faith of the believer, and adding to the grace which he possessed before. It is not intended for the benefit or conversion of unconverted men ; it is not designed or fitted to impart justification or spiritual grace to those who were previously strangers to these; but it is made a means of grace by the Spirit to those who are believers already, and fitted and intended to promote their spiritual good. I do not at present speak of the case of infants baptized, or of the benefits which they may be supposed to receive from the administration of the ordinance. Their case, as peculiar and exceptional, I shall reserve for separate and more detailed consideration. But, putting aside the case of infant Baptism for the present, the position that I lay down is, that Baptism is a means of grace fitted and blessed by God for the spiritual good of the believer. And that it is so, the considerations already stated in regard to the nature of the ordinance, if they are correct and scriptural, will sufficiently enable us to understand. If the act of the adult believer in receiving Baptism be an act of making or renewing his covenant with God through the ordinance,—if his part of the transaction be the embodiment in outward sign of the spiritual act whereby he dedicates himself to Christ,—and if Christ's part of the transaction be the giving of Himself and His grace to the believer in return, then it is plain that the ordinance, so understood, must be a divinely instituted means of grace to the parties who rightly partake of it. Christ given to the believer in the Sacrament is

[1] Col. ii. 11, 12.

not less precious and blessed, but more so, than Christ given to
the believer in the Word; and for this reason, that in the Sacrament Christ is not only in the Word, but in the sign also. In
both cases, it is, however, only in connection with the faith of the
believer that the blessing is received and enjoyed; and apart
from that faith, there is no blessing either in Word or Sacrament.
Christ in the Word, received into the soul by faith, is the source
of saving grace to the soul. Christ in the Sacrament, received
into the soul by faith, is not less, but more, a blessing likewise.
But in neither case can the grace and blessing be enjoyed except
in connection with the exercise of faith on the part of the hearer
or receiver. There is no promise connected with Word or Sacrament over and above the promise that " the just shall live by
faith." It is only in connection with faith, indeed, that grace
can be imparted in a manner consistent with the nature of man
as a moral and intelligent being, and without a subversion of its
ordinary laws. The case of infants is an exceptional case, to be
dealt with apart, and by itself. But in the case of adults, the
communication of supernatural grace, whether through Word or
Baptism, must be in connection with, and not apart from, the
exercise of their own spiritual and intelligent nature, and in
connection with that act of the spiritual nature which we call faith.
Baptism is no exception to the ordinary principle that represents
all the blessings of God's salvation as associated with faith on the
part of the receiver of them. It becomes a means of grace in
connection with the faith of the believer, which it calls into life
and exercise.

The views now stated are of course opposed to the doctrine
of what has been called " baptismal regeneration," whether held
by Romanists or Romanizing Protestants. The Church of Rome
considers Baptism, like the other Sacraments, to be a means of
imparting grace *ex opere operato*, and to carry with it the virtue of
so applying to the person baptized, whether infant or adult, the
merits of Christ, as that both original and actual transgression
are completely removed by the administration of it, in every case,
apart altogether from the faith of the recipient. The authorized
formularies of the Church of England seem to maintain the
doctrine of baptismal regeneration in a sense at least approximating to that of the Church of Rome. The Thirty-nine Articles,
indeed, give no countenance to such a theory; but both her

Liturgy and her Catechism appear to speak differently on the subject; and the doctrine, under various modifications, is held and asserted by a large number of her ablest divines. It is extremely difficult, in investigating this question, to ascertain the exact sense in which regeneration is understood to be imparted through the ordinance of Baptism, or the precise nature and amount of change which, according to the advocates of this doctrine, actually takes place on the person baptized. In some instances, I believe that the doctrine of baptismal regeneration is held in words, whilst it is not held in reality; the advantage conferred by Baptism on all equally and indiscriminately being nothing more than admission to the outward privileges of the visible Church, in consequence of the reception of it. But although, in the case of a few, the doctrine, as held by them, may be regarded as more nominal than real, yet it cannot be doubted that very many in the Church of England approximate, on this question, more or less closely to the views asserted in the standards of the Church of Rome.

There are at least three different modifications of the doctrine of baptismal regeneration held by divines of the Church of England, which can be readily enough distinguished from each other. *First*, there is one party who assert that Baptism, by the administration of it, gives the person baptized a place within the covenant of grace, in such a sense that he has a right to all its outward privileges and means of grace, and by a diligent and right use of them, may secure to himself salvation. This is the lowest view of the efficacy of Baptism held by those who assert the doctrine of baptismal regeneration, and amounts apparently to this, that Baptism is necessary in order to the salvability of a man,—all unbaptized persons having no right to the privileges of the covenant, and being left to " the uncovenanted mercies of God." In answer to such a theory, it is enough to assert, with the Word of God, that the Gospel is free to all; that all, without exception of class or character, are invited to avail themselves of it; and that " the free gift unto justification of life " is not restricted to any limited number of men, baptized or unbaptized, but is co-extensive in its promises and invitations with " the judgment that has come upon all unto condemnation." [1] *Second*, there is another party

---

[1] Rom. v. 18. [" Atqui jam visum est fieri non levem injuriam Dei fœderi nisi in eo acquiescimus, acsi per se infirmum esset; quum ejus effectus neque

who assert that Baptism conveys to the soul, by the administration of it, regenerating grace—a true spiritual life; which may continue with the baptized person, so as to avail at last to his everlasting salvation, but which may also be forfeited in after years by means of sin. This second form of the doctrine of baptismal regeneration proceeds upon an alleged distinction—held apparently by Augustine,[1] and after him maintained by many Lutheran divines—between those who are predestinated unto life, and those who are regenerated. It is affirmed that the two classes do not coincide, and that regeneration, though once imparted to the soul, may be subsequently lost. *Third*, there is another party who admit that Baptism imparts saving grace and regeneration to the soul, which under no circumstance can be entirely forfeited, but which entitle the person baptized to everlasting life.

These three different forms of the theory of baptismal regeneration it is not necessary to reply to separately. The only plausible arguments which can be brought in defence of such a doctrine are derived from a few passages of Scripture which apparently, at first sight, connect the inward and spiritual grace with the outward action in Baptism which is its sign. These passages it is not difficult to explain by the help of the canon of interpretation, to which I formerly had occasion to refer, founded on the practice of Scripture, and the practice of every other book, of predicating of the sign figuratively what can only be truly and literally predicated of the thing signified.[2] The sacra-

---

a Baptismo neque ab ullis accessionibus pendeat. Accedit postea Sacramentum sigilli instar, non quod efficaciam Dei promissioni, quasi per se invalidæ, conferat, sed eam duntaxat nobis confirmet. Unde sequitur, non ideo baptizari fidelium liberos ut filii Dei tunc primum fiant qui ante alieni fuerint ab Ecclesiâ, sed solenni potius signo ideo recipi in Ecclesiam, quia promissionis beneficio jam ante ad Christi corpus pertinebant."—Calvin, *Inst.* lib. iv. cap. xv. 22.]

[1] [Cunningham, *Works*, vol. ii. pp. 356-358.]

[2] This principle applies to the famous text, John iii. 5, on which Dr. Pusey says he " would gladly rest the whole question of baptismal regeneration " (*Tracts for the Times*, No. 67). In this passage the second clause is epexegetical of the first,—" born of water, even of the Spirit,"—the one being the sign, the other the thing signified. This is shown mainly by two considerations : 1. Christian Baptism was not yet instituted,—the proper baptismal commission being only given after our Lord's resurrection. This is perfectly clear from Scripture ; and the Fathers, on whose statements in this matter Romanists and High Churchmen mainly rely, declare with one voice that baptismal regeneration was unknown till the promised Spirit was poured out freely by the ascended Saviour. To quote Dr. Halley's words : " The spring of living water had not then issued from the foot of the Cross to fill the regenerating font ; the angel of Baptism had not then descended to trouble the

mental relation between Baptism and regeneration, which it represents, easily explains the application to Baptism, figuratively, of language that belongs literally to regeneration. And while this principle, rightly understood and applied, is sufficient to explain the statements of Scripture that apparently, at first sight, give countenance to the doctrine of baptismal regeneration, the whole tenor of the Word of God clearly and decisively contradicts the theory. It is inconsistent with the fundamental principle which regulates the matter of a sinner's salvation,—the principle that he is saved and lives by faith; and that it is by faith, and not through any other channel, that he receives from God all that is necessary to his present and his everlasting well-being.[1]

holy waters, and impart to them their sanative virtue; the sacramental gifts were not conferred upon men; the priesthood was not consecrated; St. Peter had not been invested with the keys; the life-inspiring baptistry was not erected in the porch of the Church; the initiation into the greater mysteries of the faith had not commenced. Did our Lord, then, speak to Nicodemus of what it was impossible for him or any one else to experience or understand until the day of Pentecost,—the date of the great gift of baptismal regeneration? If He did, how could He say, ' Art thou a master in Israel, and knowest not these things?' Can any one seriously expound the passage, as though it were to Nicodemus, not a declaration of what then actually was, but a dark prophecy of what was afterwards to take place?"—*The Sacraments*, vol. i. p. 230. 2. The precise meaning of the phrase "born of water" is fixed, beyond reasonable doubt, by a reference to the Jewish ideas and modes of expression. Nicodemus *must* have understood the words addressed to him—our Lord must have intended him to understand them—in the sense in which any Jew of that day conversant with the Old Testament Scriptures, and with the habits of speech and action of his nation, must infallibly have regarded them, in the sense in which psalmists and prophets had said : " Wash me, and I shall be whiter than snow." " Wash you, make you clean, put away the evil of your doings from you." " Then will I sprinkle clean water upon you, and ye shall be clean ; from all your filthiness, and from all your idols, will I cleanse you." (Ps. li. 2, 7 ; Isa. i. 16 ; Ezek. xxxvi. 25.) The passage, in short, does not refer—at least in any direct sense—to Christian Baptism at all. It points to the purification of heart and renewal of nature by the Holy Spirit, for which " washing," or being " born of water," was the familiar sign and figurative expression among the Jews. Comp. John vii. 37 ; Titus iii. 5. [Cf. Calvin, *in loc.* and *Inst.* iv. xvi. 25. " Postquam naturæ corruptionem Nicodemo exposuit Christus, ac renasci oportere docuit ; quia ille renascentiam corporalem somniabat, modum hic indicat quo regenerat nos Deus, nempe per aquam et Spiritum ; quasi diceret, per Spiritum, qui purgando et irrigando fideles animas vice aquæ fungitur. Neque hæc nova est locutio ; prorsus enim cum illâ quæ Matth. iii. 11, habetur convenit : ' Ille est qui baptizat in Spiritu sancto et igni.' Quemadmodum ergo Spiritu sancto et igni baptizare est Spiritum sanctum conferre, qui in regeneratione ignis officium naturamque habet : ita renasci aquâ et Spiritu nihil aliud est quam vim illam Spiritûs recipere, quæ in animâ id facit quod aqua in corpore."]

[1] Williams, *Antipædobaptism Examined*, Shrewsbury 1789, vol. i. pp. 102-111, 121-171, 180-197. Halley, *The Sacraments*, Lond. 1844, vol. i. pp. 213-283. Goode, *Doct. of the Church of Engl. as to the Effects of Baptism in*

SECTION II.—THE SUBJECTS OF BAPTISM AS REGARDS ADULTS.

Having discussed the general nature of Baptism, the question that next awaits our consideration is, as to the subjects of Christian Baptism, 'or the parties to whom this ordinance ought to be administered. There are three opinions that may be maintained in regard to this matter. There is one party who affirm that Baptism ought to be administered to all, not infants, who are qualified to become members of the Christian Church in virtue of a credible profession of faith in Christ and a corresponding conduct. There is a second party who assert that Baptism rightfully belongs not only to such persons, but also, in virtue of a representative relation between parents and their offspring, to their children. And there is a third party who hold that Baptism ought to be administered without restriction to parents and children, without demanding, as a prerequisite from the applicant, any profession of faith or corresponding conduct. These three classes, holding principles markedly different from each other, probably exhaust the answers to the question : To whom is Baptism to be administered? The first, or the Antipædobaptists, administer the ordinance only to adults, who, by their faith and obedience, appear to be possessed personally of a title to be regarded as members of the Christian Church, and exclude infants, who cannot, by their own faith and profession, make good their claim to be regarded as proper subjects of the ordinance. The second, or the Pædobaptists, administer the ordinance not only to adults, who personally possess a right to be regarded as members of the Christian Church, but also to their infants, who can have no right except what they derive from their parents. And the third class, or the advocates of indiscriminate Baptism, administer the ordinance to all applicants without any restriction, and without demanding, in the case of adults, that they establish their claim to the ordinance by exhibiting a credible profession of faith in their own persons, or, in the case of infants, in the persons of their parents or guardians.

the case of Infants, 2d ed. Lond. 1850, pp. 9–37, 143–178. [Calvin, Inst. lib. iv. cap. xv. Turrettin, Op. tom. iii. loc. xix. qu. 11-13, 19. Bp. E. H. Browne, Expos. of the Thirty-nine Art. 8th ed. Lond. 1868, pp. 612–671. Martensen, Dogmatik, 4te Aufl. pp. 367–370. Thomasius, Dogmatik, 3te Th. 2te Abth. Erlangen 1861, pp. 6–10, 22–25. Cunningham, Works, vol. iii. pp. 133–142. Goode, Vind. of the ' Def. of the XXXIX Art., etc.,' in reply to the Bishop of Exeter, 2d ed. pp. 8–22.]

In proceeding to examine these different systems, it will not be
necessary for me to discuss over again what occupied our attention at an early period of the course,—the question of what are
the qualifications that give a person a title to be regarded as a
member of the Christian Church,—or to enter into the controversy
between Independents and Presbyterians as to the necessity in
order to membership of a true and saving faith, or simply an outward profession and consistent practice.[1] Without entering upon
that subject a second time, the three systems of opinion as to the
proper subjects of Baptism now mentioned may be conveniently
discussed under the head of these two questions. *First:* Are we
warranted by the Word of God to administer the ordinance of
Baptism to *all* applicants for themselves or their children, without
any restriction as to religious profession and character in the case
of the applicant? And *second:* Are we warranted by the Word
of God to administer the ordinance of Baptism to the children of
a parent who would himself be a proper subject for Baptism, and
is a member of the Church? The first question, or the point in
debate between our Church and the advocates of indiscriminate
Baptism, we shall now proceed to deal with, reserving the second,
or the question of infant Baptism, for after consideration.

The doctrine of Baptism without restriction, and apart from
the religious character and profession of the applicant, has assumed
an aspect of more than ordinary importance recently, in consequence of the extent to which it has prevailed and the manner
in which it has been advocated among Independents. Dr. Wardlaw,—who was no friend of such a doctrine, but the reverse,—
when speaking in reference to a former statement of opinion, to
the effect that all parties were of one mind as to the necessity for
a religious profession as a prerequisite to Baptism, says : " Until
of late, I had no idea of the degree or of the extent of this laxity,
both as to the requisites in adults to their own baptism, and in
parents, to the baptism of their children. It has been a cause of
equal surprise and concern to me to find, from the publications of
more than one of my brethren which have recently appeared, that
in my first statement I have been so very wide of the truth. The
lax views to which I now refer have been propounded and argued
at length in the Congregational Lecture for 1844, by my esteemed
friend, Dr. Halley of Manchester." The surprise expressed by

[¹ See above, vol. i. pp. 68-80.]

Dr. Wardlaw at the acceptance which the doctrine of indiscriminate Baptism has received, and the prevalence which the practice has obtained among English Independents, is not without foundation. Dr. Halley may, I believe, be fairly regarded as the representative of the views of Independents, at least in England, on the subject; and he is perhaps the ablest defender of the practice which prevails, very nearly universally, among them. The doctrine of the class to which he belongs, and whose views he advocates, is expressed by Halley as follows. After stating the principles held by other and opposite parties, he says: "There are, lastly, those who baptize all applicants whatsoever, provided the application does not appear to be made scoffingly and profanely,—for that would be a manifest desecration of the service,—and all children offered by their parents, guardians, or others who may have the care of them." "The third class maintain that, as no restriction is imposed upon baptism in the New Testament, none ought to be imposed by the ministers of the Gospel."[1] "These views,"—I quote again from Dr. Wardlaw,—"these views, which he broaches and defends, are characterized by a latitudinarian laxity, which in my eyes is as mischievous as unscriptural,—the former, because the latter."[2] The question, then, of indiscriminate Baptism is one of very great interest and importance,—more especially in the present day,—and amply deserves discussion. In that discussion we must of course appeal for the only arguments which can decide the controversy to the Scriptures themselves. We learn from them that Baptism is a positive institution of Christ in the worship of the Christian Church; and from them also we must learn the terms on which the ordinance is to be dispensed, and the parties entitled to receive it. Is the ordinance, then, to be administered to all applicants indiscriminately without regard to religious profession or character,—to believers and unbelievers alike,—without any restriction, except, according to Dr. Halley, that they do not apply for it "scoffingly and profanely?" Or, on the contrary, does a title to participation in the ordinance of Baptism imply, as a prerequisite, a religious profession and corresponding conduct on the part of the applicant?

Now, in examining into the doctrine and practice of Scripture

---

[1] Halley, *The Sacraments*, Lond. 1844, vol. i. p. 496.
[2] Wardlaw, *Dissertation on the Scriptural Authority, Nature, and Uses of Infant Baptism*, 3d. ed. Glasg. 1846, pp. 221-223.

bearing upon this question, it is important to understand distinctly at the outset the real point in debate. There are two preliminary remarks which may help to place it in its true light.

1st, The question in debate between the advocates and opponents of indiscriminate Baptism is *not*, as Dr. Halley has stated it to be: " Whether the Apostles and their assistants baptized indiscriminately all applicants, leaving their characters to be formed and tested by subsequent events."[1] The question rather is: Whether, in such application made to the Apostles for Baptism, there was not included or implied a religious profession of faith in Christ, such as to warrant them to administer the ordinance because of the profession. It is manifest that, in apostolic times, when men were called upon in consequence of a Christian Baptism to forsake all that was dear to them on earth, and to incur the hazard of persecution and death, almost any such application necessarily involved or implied at least a credible profession of faith in Christ; inasmuch as hardly any conceivable motive except a belief in Christ would have induced any one to make the application, except, it may be, in rare and exceptional cases. Generally speaking, the fact of a man's applying for Baptism in apostolic times was itself the evidence of a credible profession, and enough to warrant the administration of the ordinance, not on the principle of baptizing all, believers and unbelievers alike, with a profession or without it; but rather on the principle that the applicant, by the very act of application, in the circumstances of the early Church, professed his faith in Christ. Upon this principle we can easily explain why, in the Scripture narrative of the practice of baptizing in the early Church, we find no example of the applicant being kept for a length of time in the position of candidate for Baptism, so as thereby to test his character and profession.

2d, The question in debate between the advocates and opponents of indiscriminate Baptism is *not*, whether the Apostles, in their administration of the ordinance, baptized, as Dr. Halley asserts, " bad men as well as good."[2] That the Apostles did so in particular instances, the case of Simon Magus plainly attests. But that case no less plainly attests that the Baptism was administered, not in the absence of any religious profession, but in consequence of such a profession. Nothing can be more undeniable than that it was upon the ground of his professed belief in

[1] Halley, *The Sacraments*, Lond. 1844, vol. i. p. 505.   [2] *Ibid.* p. 505.

the Gospel preached by Philip that Simon Magus was baptized. "Then Simon," says the inspired account of the transaction, "then Simon himself *believed also:* and when he was baptized," etc.[1] Like the other hearers who were baptized in consequence of their profession of faith in Philip's doctrine, Simon professed to believe, and, on the credit of that profession, was baptized as they were. But although among the number of those who received apostolic Baptism there were good men and bad men, as there must be among the members of the Church in all ages, this is not the real question at issue between the friends and opponents of indiscriminate Baptism. The real question in controversy between them is, whether Baptism was generally, or was ever, administered without a religious profession at all on the part of the applicant; or whether such a profession was invariably present as a prerequisite to Baptism. "Baptism," says the Shorter Catechism, "is not to be administered to any that are out of the visible Church, till they profess their faith in Christ and obedience to Him."[2]

Bearing in mind these preliminary remarks, it is not difficult, I think, from an examination of Scripture doctrine and practice in regard to Baptism, to establish the conclusion, that it is a sacramental ordinance not to be administered indiscriminately and without restriction to all applying for it, but, on the contrary, limited to those maintaining an outward character and profession of Christianity.

I. The nature and import of the ordinance of Baptism are inconsistent with the idea of an indiscriminate administration of it to all, without respect to religious character and profession.

The doctrine and practice of the advocates of indiscriminate Baptism very naturally arise out of the system maintained by them as to the nature of the ordinance. With Dr. Halley and the Independents, whom he represents, Baptism is not, in the proper and peculiar sense of the term, a Sacrament, but only a sign; and a sign, too, of a very restricted meaning indeed. It is a sign that the person holds certain Christian truths, or is willing to learn them; which truths may be held in the way of a mere intellectual apprehension, without the man who so holds them being a Christian, or even seriously professing to be one. Upon this theory,—that Baptism is no more than a sign, expressive of

---

[1] Acts viii. 13.   [2] Shorter Catechism, qu. 95.

certain truths of Christianity,—it is quite possible to engraft the doctrine of an indiscriminate administration of the ordinance in every instance where those truths, as is usually the case in a Christian country, are not openly renounced or publicly denied. To affix the sign of allegiance to those truths in the case of every man who merely does not deny them, and must be held by the very act of applying for the sign, as at least in some tolerable degree acquainted with them, is consistent enough. To affix the sign to all infants proposed for Baptism, is also consistent; for they are capable of being instructed in the truths represented, and the act of their parents in bringing them to receive the ordinance may be regarded as an acknowledgment that they are willing that their children be so instructed. Restrict the import of Baptism to that of a mere sign of certain Gospel truths, and it is quite in accordance with the theory of indiscriminate administration. " Practically, " says Dr. Halley, " those who baptize indiscriminately all applicants and all children proposed for baptism, and those who reckon upon the prospect of teaching the baptized, will be found seldom at variance; for scarcely ever is any one proposed whose religious instruction might not be secured by proper care." [1]   As a sign expressive of acquaintance with certain Christian truths, or of a capacity and willingness to receive them, Baptism may consistently enough be administered without restriction to all applicants, whether adults or infants.

But the very opposite doctrine and practice must be maintained, on the supposition that the Sacrament of Baptism is not a sign merely, and that in a very restricted sense, of Christian truth, but a seal of a federal transaction between two parties in the ordinance, whereby the recipient gives himself in Baptism to Christ, and Christ in Baptism gives Himself and His grace to the recipient. A seal of a covenant which the party baptized does not even profess to make, and has avowedly no intention of entering into,—a voucher to a federal transaction, in which there is no person in the least professing to be a party,—an attestation to a mutual engagement never pretended by the individual who is supposed to give the attestation,—this is a contradiction and inconsistency not to be got over. There is a manifest incongruity in administering equally to those who avow that they are believers, and to unbelievers with no such avowal, the same

[1] Halley, *ut supra*, p. 479.

Christian ordinance,—in dispensing a Gospel Sacrament indiscriminately to those who profess to have received the Gospel, and to those who do not,—in giving a religious privilege to those who make no religious profession, not less than to those who do. If Baptism be no more than a sign of certain religious truths known, or at least that may be learned, by the party baptized, then indeed there is no such incongruity between the nature of the rite and its unrestricted administration. But if Baptism be the outward seal of a federal engagement, distinctively marking the true Christian, then the very nature of the ordinance forbids it to be administered to men with no profession of Christianity. If it be the Sacrament of union to the Saviour and admission into the Christian Church, the ordinance itself points out the necessity of its restriction to those who " name the name of Christ," and whose life and conduct are not outwardly inconsistent with their claim to be numbered among His people.

II. The administration of Baptism by John, the forerunner of our Lord, has been very generally appealed to in favour of an indiscriminate dispensation of the ordinance,[1] but in point of fact may be regarded as affording evidence of a contrary practice.

The Baptism of John, when we are told that multitudes of the Jews flocked to him in the wilderness to be baptized, has been quoted in favour of the doctrine and practice of English Independents. There are two things which it is necessary to establish before any argument for indiscriminate Baptism in the Christian Church could be drawn from the preaching of John ; and both these things, so far from being proved, may with good reason be denied. In the first place, it were necessary to prove that the Baptism of John was identical with Christian Baptism, before any countenance could be derived from his practice,—even if it were, as is alleged, that of indiscriminate Baptism,—in favour of the same custom in the Christian Church. And in the second place, it were necessary to establish the assumption that John really baptized all equally who came to him, without regard to their religious profession. I believe that neither the one nor the other of these positions can be established from Scripture, but the reverse.

With regard to the first position, there seems to be warrant from Scripture to say that John's Baptism was not identical with

[1] Halley, *ut supra*, pp. 163–167, 194–201.

that of Christ. His doctrine and his office occupied an intermediate place between those of the Old Testament teachers and
those of the Gospel Church; and his Baptism corresponded with
his doctrine. He taught the doctrine of repentance and of pre-
paration for Him that should come after him; he pointed to the
future Saviour, rather than preached a present one; and his
Baptism was the same in character. We have no reason to
believe that he baptized in the name of Christ; and we have
ground for asserting that the Baptism of John, in the case of
those who received it, was afterwards replaced by Christian
Baptism, when they were received into the Christian Church.
That such was the case, the instance of the disciples at Ephesus
proves; whom Paul rebaptized, as is recorded in the nineteenth
chapter of the Acts of the Apostles: " And he said unto them,
Unto what then were ye baptized? And they said, Unto John's
baptism. Then said Paul, John verily baptized with the baptism
of repentance, saying unto the people, that they should believe on
Him which should come after him, that is, on Christ Jesus. When
they heard this, they were baptized in the name of the Lord
Jesus." [1]

With regard to the second point, or the assumption that the
Baptism of John was really given to all applicants indiscriminately,
without respect to religious character, there seems to be no evidence for it in Scripture, but the reverse. We seem to have as
good evidence, that John demanded a profession of a religious
kind from those whom he baptized, as the character of the very
brief and scanty narrative which has come down to us of the
transaction would naturally lead us to expect. That vast multitudes of the Jews enrolled themselves by Baptism in the number
of John's disciples, would appear to admit of no doubt; for we
are expressly told that " there went out unto him into the wilderness all the land of Judea, and they of Jerusalem, and were all
baptized of him in the river Jordan." That of this great multitude all were truly brought to repentance, and turned from sin,
and savingly taught to look forward to the Messiah who was to
come, may, from many circumstances, appear improbable. But
that they were all admitted to the ordinance of John's Baptism,

[1] Acts xix. 3-5. Williams, *Antipædobaptism Examined*, Shrewsbury 1789,
vol. i. pp. 113-120. Wardlaw, *Dissert. on Infant Baptism*, 3d ed. Glasg. 1846,
pp. 223-269.

without any regard to the religious profession that they made, is undeniably contradicted by the express language of the sacred historian ; for it is added: " They were all baptized of him in the river Jordan, *confessing their sins*." [1] The Baptism and the confession of sins went together,—the one being the accompanying condition of the other. So far is it from being true that the practice of John gives countenance to the theory of indiscriminate Baptism, that the very opposite may be proved from the inspired narrative, brief though it be.

III. The terms of the commission given by our Lord after His resurrection to His Apostles in regard to founding and establishing the Christian Church, seem very clearly to forbid the practice of indiscriminate Baptism, and to require a profession of faith in Christ as a prerequisite to Baptism in His name.

The terms of the commission, as recorded in the Gospel by Matthew, are these : " Go ye therefore, and disciple—$\mu\alpha\theta\eta\tau\epsilon\upsilon$-$\sigma\alpha\tau\epsilon$—all nations, baptizing them into the name of the Father, and of the Son, and of the Holy Ghost; teaching them to observe all things whatsoever I have commanded you." [2] Such is the language employed by our Lord in what must be regarded, I think, as the original institution of Christian Baptism. The commentary of Dr. Halley on these words brings out his argument in favour of indiscriminate Baptism. " The question," says he, " respecting the subject of Baptism is here resolved into one of grammar and criticism. It is simply what is the antecedent to the word *them*, or for what noun is that pronoun substituted. 'Going forth, disciple all the nations—$\pi\alpha\nu\tau\alpha$ $\tau\alpha$ $\epsilon\theta\nu\eta$—baptizing *them*—$\alpha\upsilon\tau\sigma\upsilon\varsigma$—all the nations, into the name of the Father, and the Son, and the Holy Ghost; teaching *them*—all the nations—to observe all things whatsoever I have commanded you.' So far as the grammatical construction is concerned, the meaning of the terms is precisely the same, as it would be if the words of the commission were, ' baptize all the nations.' Adhering, therefore, to the grammar of the words, we say, the commission, which no man has a right to alter, is, 'baptize all the nations.'" [3] Now, this somewhat summary and confident mode of reasoning may be satisfactorily set aside in two ways.

1. There is some weight due to the order in which the terms of the commission run, as indicating the order in which the dis-

---

[1] Matt. iii. 5, 6.   [2] Matt. xxviii. 19.   [3] Halley, *ut supra*, p. 489.

cipling, the baptizing, and the teaching of all the nations were
to take place, and were to be accounted necessary parts of the
Apostles' or the Church's obedience to the commission of Christ.
There are three particulars embraced in the authoritative commission addressed to the Apostles, and, through them, binding
upon the Church in every age. *First*, the command is to make
disciples of all nations, turning them to the profession and belief
of the faith of Christ. *Second*, there is the command to baptize
all nations, granting them the formal and public rite by which
their admission into the Church was to be attested and ratified.
And *third*, there is the command to teach all nations to observe
all things whatsoever Christ had appointed for His Church collectively, or His people individually. This is the order in which,
according to the nature of the various particulars embraced in the
commission, they were to be accomplished. That the order of
procedure here indicated is in harmony with the nature of the
work to be done by the Church in reference to the world, is
abundantly plain from the scriptural account given of it in many
other passages of the Bible. First of all is the preaching of the
Gospel, as the grand instrument employed by the Church to
gather in the disciples of Christ within its pale. Next there is
the affixing to the disciples thus gathered the characteristic badge
of discipleship, and granting them, by the initiatory rite of Baptism, formal admission into the Christian Church. And lastly,
there is the instructing those thus admitted in the observance of
all their appointed duties as disciples of Christ and members of
His Church. This is plainly, I think, the order of procedure
indicated in the apostolic commission; and it is an order which
implies that a knowledge and profession of the faith as disciples
preceded the administration of Baptism to them. The expression,
" *all nations* "—παντα τα ἐθνη—upon which Dr. Halley builds his
argument for universal and indiscriminate Baptism, is not to be
regarded so much as declaring the duty of the Apostles to teach
and baptize every individual of the world, or as denoting the
absolute extent of the commission, as asserting that individuals of
every nation were to be discipled and baptized, and marking out
that no nation or class were excluded from the range of the commission. The terms, " disciple," " baptizing," must be taken together, and not separately; and in the order of the inspired
declaration, and not in the reverse of that order.

2. The words of institution in the baptismal service seem to imply that a knowledge and profession of the faith of Christ are necessary as a prerequisite to Baptism. The recipients of the ordinance are to be baptized " into the name, εἰς τὸ ὄνομα, of the Father, the Son, and the Holy Ghost,"—language which obviously refers to the peculiar character the Three Persons of the Godhead sustain, and the offices they discharge in the work of man's redemption. Unless Christian Baptism, then, be a mere heathen mystery, to suffice as a sign or to work as a charm, it necessarily implies previous knowledge and instruction in the fundamental truths of the Gospel system; and this, again, implies that the Church, in administering the ordinance, has a right to require some evidence, such as an intelligent profession of the faith, that such knowledge has been obtained. All this points very distinctly to a profession of faith in Christ as a necessary prerequisite to the administration of the ordinance in the case of candidates for Baptism.

IV. An examination in detail of Scripture practice, as bearing upon the doctrine of indiscriminate Baptism as contradistinguished from Baptism restricted to professing Christians, will sufficiently bear out the conclusion to be drawn from the previous considerations, that at least a profession of faith is necessary as a prerequisite to the scriptural administration of the ordinance.

It is impossible, and indeed unnecessary, for us to enter at length into this field of argument. Nothing but the most violent injustice done to the language of Scripture by a bold and unscrupulous system of interpretation can suffice to get rid of the evidence which, in the case of the Baptism of converts mentioned in Scripture, connects the administration of the rite with a profession of faith in Christ on the part of the person who was the recipient of it. The association of the person's profession, faith, repentance, or believing, with Baptism, appears in a multitude of passages; while not one passage or example can be quoted in favour of the connection of Baptism with an *absence* of profession. " He that believeth, and is baptized, shall be saved;" "repent every one of you, and be baptized;" " many having believed, and been baptized,"[1]—these and many other passages of a like import connect together, as inseparable in the process by which under the eye

---

[1] Mark xvi. 16; Acts ii. 38, 41, viii. 12, 13, 36-38, xvi. 14, 15, 30-34, xviii. 8.

of the Apostles many in their days were added to the Christian Church, the two facts of the religious profession of the candidate, and the administration of the religious ordinance by which formally he became a member of the Church of Christ. In the history, although brief and incomplete, of the Baptism of the early converts to the Christian faith, there is almost invariably some statement by which is attested the distinctive Christian profession that stands connected with the administration of the outward rite; while in no instances are there any statements from which it could be proved that Baptism ever stood connected with the absence of such a profession. Connected with the Baptism of the three thousand on the day of Pentecost, there stands the statement, " Then they that gladly received the Word were baptized." Connected with the Baptism of the people of Samaria in consequence of the preaching of Philip, there stands the assertion, " When they believed Philip preaching the things concerning the kingdom of God, and the name of Jesus Christ, they were baptized, both men and women." In regard to the Baptism of the Ethiopian treasurer, we are told that, after the Gospel was preached to him by the same evangelist, "the eunuch said, See, here is water; what doth hinder me to be baptized? And Philip said, If thou believest with all thine heart, thou mayest. And he answered and said, I believe that Jesus Christ is the Son of God. And he commanded the chariot to stand still : and they went down both into the water, both Philip and the eunuch, and he baptized him." In connection with the Baptism of Lydia, and as preceding the administration of the rite, we have the statement: " whose heart the Lord opened, that she attended unto the things that were spoken of Paul." Connected with the Baptism of the Philippian jailer, there stands the statement : " And he rejoiced, believing in God, with all his house." In short, in almost every example of Baptism which the New Testament records, there is enough in the narrative, however scanty and compressed it be, to bring out the fact, that in close association with the administration of the rite appears the religious profession of the recipient. And, on the other hand, it may be safely asserted, that in no example of Baptism recorded in the New Testament can it be distinctly proved that no such profession was made.

What, then, is the answer given to this abundant and apparently satisfactory evidence for a Baptism restricted to and connected with a religious profession by the advocates of its indiscriminate administration ?   The answer given by them is twofold : first, that there are examples of bad men as well as good baptized by the Apostles; and second, that many or most of these Baptisms were administered so immediately in point of time after the profession made, that there was no opportunity to test by any satisfactory process the sincerity of it.   Neither of these replies to the Scripture evidence is satisfactory.   With regard to the first, or the fact that unbelievers and hypocrites were baptized, it is enough to say that we do not hold the Independent doctrine that a saving belief is necessary to entitle a man to Church membership; but, on the contrary, maintain that a profession of faith is enough,[1] and that we have no security beyond the mere circumstance of an outwardly decent life against such profession being insincere.   With regard to the second, or the fact that the profession on which the apostolic Baptisms in many instances proceeded could have been of no more than a few hours' standing, and therefore not proved by the lapse of time to be true, it is enough to say that there may be, and in apostolic times were, circumstances apart altogether from its duration sufficient to give credibility to the profession.[2]

SECTION III.—INFANT BAPTISM.

We have now considered the question, To whom ought Baptism to be administered, in so far as it regards adults?   The conclusion to which we were conducted was, that the ordinance ought to be dispensed to those alone who " profess their faith in Christ, and their obedience to Him."   The theory of indiscriminate Baptism we set aside as inconsistent with the nature and meaning of the Sacrament,—as destitute of any countenance from the practice of John the Baptist,—as contrary to the terms of the apostolical commission, and opposed to the practice of the apostles and the New Testament Church.   There still remains for our consideration the question as to the connection of infants with Baptism, and as to the lawfulness or duty of administering the ordinance

---

[1] [See above, vol. i. pp. 73–80.]
[2] Halley, *The Sacraments*, Lond. 1844, vol. i. pp. 488–527, 580–585. Wardlaw, *Dissert. on Infant Baptism*, 3d ed. pp. 291–346.   Wilson, *Infant Baptism a Scriptural Service*, Lond. 1848, pp. 338–381.

to them. The subject is a delicate and a difficult one, and demands a more than usually earnest investigation. The practice of baptizing infants may be regarded at first sight as running counter to all those views which we have already asserted in regard to the nature of Sacraments in general, and of Baptism in particular. Add to this, that it seems at first view directly to traverse the principles we have so lately laid down on the question of indiscriminate Baptism. The advocates of the doctrine of baptismal regeneration, who hold that Baptism is a charm with an inherent and independent power to confer grace in all circumstances and on all parties, can readily defend the practice of administering it to infants, as efficacious in the case of unconscious children, not less than in the case of intelligent adults. The advocates of the doctrine that Baptism is no more than a sign, have also an obvious ground on which they may defend the practice of infant Baptism, — the parents' professional badge being, not without reason or precedent in other matters, affixed to the child. And once more, the party who hold the doctrine of indiscriminate Baptism, and regard themselves as authorized to dispense the rite without regard to religious character or profession, can have no sufficient reason for excluding infants from this comprehensive commission. But if Baptism be the seal of a federal transaction between the party baptized and Christ; if *this* be the main and characteristic feature of the ordinance; and if a religious profession be a prerequisite to its reception; it would appear as if there were no small difficulty in the way of admitting to the participation of it those who, by reason of nonage, can be no parties to the engagement in virtue of their own act or will. The difficulty that stands in the way of infant Baptism lies on the very surface of the question; and Antipædobaptists have the advantage of an argument on their side which is both popular and plausible.

But in this case, as in all others connected with matters of positive institution in the Church of Christ, the primary and ruling consideration in the controversy must be the express Divine appointment on the subject. In those positive, and in a sense arbitrary, institutions, set up by God in the worship of His Church, mere inferential considerations drawn from reason must be of secondary authority and subordinate force to determine their nature and use, as compared with express intimations of the

Divine will. Positive observances, from their very nature, must be regulated by positive institution; and it is only as secondary to such positive institution, that we can listen to arguments drawn from our views of the moral character or meaning of the ordinance. Our first appeal in the case of infant Baptism must, therefore, be to the express statements of the Word of God, and to the view of the ordinance as a positive institution which is there presented. We shall consider, then, in the first place, the scriptural principles which bear upon the question of the lawfulness or duty of infant Baptism. Thereafter we shall examine into the objections, from reason or Scripture, that have been brought against the practice; and also discuss the subject of the efficacy of the ordinance in the case of infants; and lastly, the scriptural mode of administering it.

What, then, is the bearing of Scripture doctrine and practice on the question of the lawfulness or unlawfulness of infant Baptism? The following five propositions I shall endeavour to establish in connection with this subject; and the discussion of these will very nearly exhaust the question. First, the covenant of grace, as revealed by God at different periods for the salvation of His people, has been essentially the same in former and in later times, and has always comprehended infants within it. Second, the Church of God, made up of His professing people, has been essentially the same in character in former and in later times, and has always included infants among its members. Third, the ordinance of outward admission into the Church has, in its essential character and meaning, been the same in former and in later times, and has always been administered to infants. Fourth, the principle on which the initiatory ordinance of admission into the Church has been administered has been the same in former and in later times, and has always applied to the case of infants. And fifth, the practice in regard to the administration of the initiatory rite has been the same in former and in later times, and has always included the case of infants. The illustration of these five propositions must, in consequence of the limits prescribed to us, be very brief, and more in the way of giving the heads of the argument than the argument itself. But taken under consideration even in the briefest way, they will embrace the prominent points of the controversy in regard to infant Baptism. One or more of them separately, if sufficiently established by an appeal to Scripture, would suffice to demonstrate that " the infants of such as are members of the visible Church are to be baptized;" [1] while all taken together afford a very full and cumulative proof of the lawfulness of the practice.

I. The covenant of grace, as revealed by God at different periods for the salvation of His people, has been essentially the same in former and in later times, and has always comprehended infants within it.

This proposition is, properly speaking, made up of two: first, that the covenant was essentially the same in all ages; and second, that within the covenant, infants were always included. Neither of these two assertions ought to be very difficult of proof. In regard to the first, it is undeniable that God has had a people on the earth since the fall, chosen from the rest of mankind, who called upon His name, and were themselves called by it. The faith and hope of that chosen people, through every generation, have been sustained by a revelation of a Saviour, who either was to come or had come, expressed in promise and in type, in prediction and in symbol before His coming, and in plainer and ampler narrative of actual fact after His appearance. In whatever outward form it was revealed, this was God's covenant—His free promise of grace—His Gospel of glad tidings for the salvation of His people, identical in character and in substance, one in its announcements and its terms in every age from the first revelation in Paradise down to the last in Patmos. It was one and the same covenant of grace which was revealed to Adam in the first promise given to him, and the first ordinance of sacrifice appointed for him ; revealed in other terms and form to Noah ; repeated to Abraham in the word of promise and type ; embodied in history, and prophecy, and symbolic institutions to the Church under the Mosaic economy ; and fully brought to light under the Gospel dispensation. That the covenant of grace established under the Gospel was not then for the first time made known, but had been announced long before,—that although in the latter times it was more fully revealed, it had been revealed all along in substance, and proved to be the same at first as at the last,—the plain statements of Scripture very expressly affirm. The Apostle Paul tells us in the Epistle to the Galatians, that " the Gospel was preached before unto Abraham." And in the same

---

[1] Shorter Catech. qu. 95.

Epistle he tells us that " the covenant confirmed of God in Christ was given to Abraham four hundred and thirty years before the giving of the law " of Moses,[1]—language fitted to mark both the identity of the covenant of Abraham with the Gospel covenant, and its independence of the Mosaic ceremonial institutions. If we turn to the book of Genesis, we shall find the account of the revelation of the covenant of grace given to Abraham, and referred to by Paul,—a covenant which, as then revealed, comprehended in it temporal blessings, such as the promise of Canaan to the patriarch and his seed, but was in itself independent of these ; which preceded the law by more than four hundred years, and was not disannulled by the giving of the law ; which was founded on the free grace and unchangeable promise of God, and thus was not bound up with any temporary institution ; and which was the very Gospel afterwards " confirmed in Christ."[2] So clear and abundant is the evidence for the first part of our proposition, that the covenant of grace, revealed under various forms in former and in latter times, was in substance one and the same.

The proof of the second part of our proposition is not less full and satisfactory, that this covenant has always comprehended infants within it. The infants of the parents with whom God's covenant was made, were not left outside that covenant. The promises of grace were not given to the parents, to the exclusion of the children. Infants were not left to their chance of un-covenanted mercies, while to adults the blessings were insured by covenant. On the contrary, that infants were comprehended within the covenant as well as their parents, is a fact that the plainest statements of Scripture demonstrate. In what sense or to what effect infants were so included, may come to be inquired into when we afterwards consider the *efficacy* of Baptism in their case, or the seal of the covenant as regards infants. But that the covenant made with the parents did not exclude but included their infant children also, the plain assertions of Scripture leave no room to doubt. In the inspired account of the various announce-ments made by God of His covenant from time to time, the terms of the announcement are almost invariably "*you and your seed.*" In the case of Abraham, as referred to by the Apostle Paul, this is very expressly stated : "And God said unto Abraham, Thou shalt keep my covenant therefore, thou, and thy seed after thee

[1] Gal. iii. 8, 17, 18.   [2] Gen. xii. 1–3, xiii. 14–17, xv. 1–18, xvii. 1–14.

in their generations. This is my covenant, which ye shall keep, between me and you, and thy seed after thee; Every man-child among you shall be circumcised."[1] The covenant of grace, as then revealed to Abraham, included infant children of eight days old; and it has at all times been equally comprehensive and the same. The seal of the covenant, as affixed to the child when eight days old, was the standing evidence and memorial for two thousand years, that infants were included in God's federal promises."[2]

And in what manner is this argument from the example of Abraham, in favour of the fact that infants are comprehended within the covenant, met by the advocates of Antipædobaptist doctrines. The ordinary reply given by the opponents of infant Baptism is this: They affirm that there were two covenants, distinct and separate from each other, made by God with the patriarch at that time; the one a covenant of temporal, and the other of spiritual blessing. They assert that the "seed" mentioned in the history of the transaction, were the natural seed of Abraham, including adults and infants, in so far as regards the *temporal* covenant; and the spiritual seed of Abraham, or adult believers alone, in so far as regards the *spiritual;* and that the seal of circumcision administered to his children was the token of a temporal, and not a spiritual blessing. And lastly, they argue that under the Gospel the natural relationship of children to their parents, which under a former economy warranted their admission to the sign and seal of a temporal covenant, does not warrant their admission to the sign and seal of a spiritual one.[3]

Now in regard to this attempted reply to the Scripture evidence for infants being included in the covenant of grace as revealed to Abraham, it is unnecessary to do more than make the following observations.

1*st*, Even although it were capable of being proved that there were two covenants made with Abraham, and not one simply,—a covenant of temporal blessing separated from the covenant of grace,—and that infants were included in the one but not in the other, this would not do away with the whole tenor of Scrip-

---

[1] Gen. xvii. 9, 10.

[2] Williams, *Antipædobaptism Examined*, Shrewsbury 1789, vol. i. pp. 172-180.

[3] [Carson, *Baptism in its Modes and Subjects*, Lond. 1844, pp. 214-231. Booth, *Pædobaptism Examined*, Lond. 1829, vol. ii. pp. 55-68.]

ture declaration in many other passages which evinces that the covenant of grace, under whatever shape and to whatever parties it was revealed, included not only the parties themselves, but also their infant offspring. The covenant of grace, as revealed to Abraham, and recorded in Genesis, has been very generally appealed to by the advocates of infant Baptism in demonstration of the interest infants had in it; and it has been so appealed to because it contains a more detailed and distinct evidence of the fact than most other passages of Scripture. But even were the record of the Abrahamic covenant expunged from the Bible, the interest of infants jointly with their parents in the covenant of grace could be satisfactorily established without it. The whole tenor of Scripture justifies us in saying, that it was a covenant which, at whatever time or in whatever form it was revealed to men, embraced both them and their infant seed.

2d, There is certainly no countenance in the narrative in Genesis given to the notion of two covenants, separate and distinct from each other; in the one of which the children of Abraham, being infants, were to have an interest, and in the other of which the descendants of Abraham, not being infants, but adult believers, were alone comprehended. The terms employed very expressly refer to one covenant, and not to two. "Thou shalt keep my *covenant*. *This is* my *covenant*, which ye shall keep, betwixt me and you, and thy seed after thee." Such is the language emphatically reiterated in the original narrative of the transaction, marking a single covenant and not many. It is true, indeed, that there was a twofold blessing, the temporal and the spiritual,—the inheritance of Canaan, and the inheritance of the heavenly Canaan,—embodied in that one covenant. But these two orders of blessing were promised by the same covenant, and referred to the same end. There is no mention of one covenant intended for the natural posterity of the patriarch, and a second intended for his spiritual posterity. The temporal blessings might, indeed, be enjoyed by the descendants of Abraham after the flesh, while they had no interest in the spiritual; just in the same manner as a man under the Gospel may enjoy the outward privileges of a Church state without participation in the inward and saving blessings. But there is nothing whatever in the book of Genesis to warrant the distinction which the opponents of infant Baptism draw between a temporal covenant made with Abraham including infants, and a second and a spiritual one made at the same time and excluding them.

3d, The rite of circumcision, appointed for every man-child when eight days old, in the Abrahamic covenant as the token of it, excludes the theory of the Antipædobaptists, that the covenant in which infants were interested was a temporal covenant only. The fact that circumcision was ordained in connection with the covenant proves that it was not a mere temporal covenant, as Antipædobaptists allege, but a spiritual one,—the very covenant of grace which was the same through all times and dispensations of the Church. It does so in two ways. *First*, circumcision, as the token of the Abrahamic covenant, was a sign not of temporal, but of spiritual blessings. That this is the case is very expressly asserted by the Apostle Paul in his Epistle to the Romans. "He is not a Jew," says Paul, "which is one outwardly; neither is that circumcision which is outward in the flesh: but he is a Jew which is one inwardly: and circumcision is that of the heart, in the spirit, and not in the letter; whose praise is not of men, but of God."[1] The ordinance of circumcision, then, had a spiritual import; it was expressive of Gospel blessings. And when it was appointed by God as the token of His covenant with Abraham, and administered in that capacity to children, it very plainly declared that the covenant, of which it was the token, and into which it introduced infants, was spiritual too. Circumcision, as the sign of the Gospel blessings, when it was appended to the covenant, demonstrated that the covenant itself was the covenant of grace. *Second*, circumcision is declared by the Apostle Paul to be more than a sign of grace; it is asserted to be a seal of grace. It is declared to be so, when he tells us, in reference to this very matter of the covenant established with Abraham, that "he received the sign of circumcision, a *seal* of the righteousness of the faith which he had being yet uncircumcised."[2] As the seal, then, of the covenant according to which Abraham was justified, the ordinance plainly testified that it was the covenant of grace; and, when administered to infants eight days old, it no less plainly indicated that they were interested in that covenant.[3]

The objections, then, brought by Antipædobaptists against the

---

[1] Rom. ii. 28, 29.   [2] Rom. iv. 11.
[3] [Calvin, *Inst.* lib. iv. cap. xvi. 3-6, 13-16.]

evidence from Scripture,—more especially derived from the covenant of grace as revealed to Abraham, but by no means confined
to that source,—to the fact that infants are interested in that
covenant, are of no great force. Our first position seems to be
fairly established by Scripture evidence, namely, that the covenant of grace has been, under all the different forms in which
from time to time it has been revealed, identical in substance and
essentially unchanged; and that it has ever included infants
within its provisions. The denial of infant Baptism cannot very
well be maintained in the face of this proposition. If included
in the provisions of the covenant of grace under the Gospel,
infants must have a right to Baptism as one of them. They cannot be excluded from the initiatory ordinance which signifies and
seals its blessings, unless the covenant of grace under the New
Testament is different essentially both in its extent and in its
terms from what it was before. The covenant of grace under
former dispensations comprehended within its limits the infants
of parties interested in it, as well as the parties themselves. This
is undeniable. And the covenant must be altered essentially as
to its extent,—it must be a *different* covenant as to the parties
with whom it is made,—if so large a portion of the members
included in it formerly, as infants were, should appear under the
New Testament Church to be excluded. Further, it must be
altered essentially as to the terms of it, and as to its free and gracious character,—it must be a *different* covenant as to the conditions of it,—if by these conditions one important class, made up
of irresponsible parties such as infants, are now cast out when
they were formerly comprehended. Unless the covenant of grace,
in short, under the New Testament Church is *another* covenant
from what it was under the Old Testament, infants must have
a place in it now as much as then. But it is not so altered or
restricted. Neither its extent nor its terms are altered. It is
God's covenant of grace still; and as it was gracious enough and
wide enough to comprehend within its limits infants under a
former economy, it does so still.[1]

There are manifold intimations in the New Testament that
the covenant of grace is not less comprehensive in latter times
than in former. At the first planting of the Christian Church
the Apostle Peter assured the Jews that there was no change in

[1] Wilson, *Infant Baptism a Script. Service*, Lond. 1848, pp. 388–437.

this respect of the covenant under the Gospel economy as compared with its comprehensiveness under the Old Testament: " For," said he, " the promise is unto you, *and to your children*, and to all that are afar off, even to as many as the Lord our God shall call."[1] To the Philippian jailer Paul declared in the very form of the Old Testament promises : " Believe on the Lord Jesus Christ, and thou shalt be saved, *and thy house*."[2] In these, and a multitude of other expressions of similar force and import, we recognise the great and important truth, that the covenant of grace was the same under the Gospel as under the law; that it was not limited or straitened in latter times in comparison with former; but that in its grace and comprehensiveness it embraces infants under the New Testament dispensation as well as under previous economies. We conclude, then, that the covenant of grace, revealed by God at different periods for the salvation of His people, has been essentially the same in former as in latter times; and has always comprehended infants within it.[3]

II. My next proposition is, that the Church of God, made up of His professing people, has been essentially the same in character in former and in latter times, and has always included infants among its members. This second proposition, like the first, consists of two parts, each of which admits of being established separately; the first part of the statement being, that the Church of God, under whatever outward form it has appeared, has been identical in substance throughout every dispensation; and the second part of it being, that it has always included infants among its members.

The first part of the proposition, which affirms the identity of the Church of God under all its outward forms, in Old Testament times and in New, may be readily demonstrated from two general considerations, independent of other arguments.

1. The oneness of the covenant of grace in every age necessarily implies the oneness of the Church of God in every age. It was on the foundation of that covenant that the Church of God was built at first, and has ever since been maintained. It is that covenant that gives to its members every privilege which, as belonging to the Church of God, they possess; it defines the

---

[1] Acts ii. 39.   [2] Acts xvi. 31.
[3] Williams, *Antipædobapt. Exam.* vol. i. pp. 234-249. Wardlaw, *Dissert. on Inf. Baptism*, pp. 20-89, 102-117.

nature and limits the extent of their rights; it is the title by which they hold their standing and place as members of the Church; it constitutes the badge that distinguishes between a Church state and character, and the absence of them. The covenant is the charter of the Church of God in every age; and that charter remaining unchanged and identical from age to age, the Church that is built upon it must, in all its essential features, be one and the same also,—whatever may be the outward form it may bear, or the circumstantial and accidental changes that may be superinduced upon it. The Church of God in the days of Abraham,—the Church in the days of Moses,—the Church under the Gospel,—are in all vital respects the same; *one* Church, founded on the same covenant of grace, having the same essential character, and the same chartered rights, although different in outward things, according to the different stages and periods in the development of the Divine dispensations. The reason of this is obvious. The charter that constituted the society was the same in the earlier as in the later times. The covenant that called into existence and defined the character of the Church was essentially identical in the age of Abraham, and in the present age. We are not to confound with the unchanged and unchanging covenant of grace, on which the Church of God was and is built, the covenant made with Israel at Sinai, and destined to be a mere local and temporary ordinance. That subsequent and secondary covenant could neither disannul nor alter the former. It superinduced, indeed, upon the former certain local and temporary ordinances; but nowise enlarged, or contracted, or changed the original charter of the Church's existence and rights. The Church of Israel under the former economy, and the Church of Christ now under the Gospel, are constituted and defined as to their character, their extent, and their membership, by the same covenant of grace. They form the same society in their nature, their essential privileges, and their real members.

2. The identity of the Church of God in every age and under every dispensation, might be evinced by the relation which the Church ever bears to Christ as Mediator, and the relation which Christ as Mediator ever bears to the Church. Since the beginning He has been the Prophet, Priest, and King of the Church, immediately discharging all His offices as Mediator towards it, and sustaining it in existence by His continual presence in the

midst of it. At different periods, indeed, He has been differently
related to the Church, in so far as regards the extent of His
manifestations of Himself, and the extent of His communications of spiritual gifts and blessings. But at no period has the
Church existed, except through the same presence and power of
Christ, as Mediator, that the Christian Church now enjoys,—the
same in nature, although different in amount. The Church has
ever been the Church *of Christ;* and this spiritual relationship, the
same and unaltered from age to age, has caused the Church itself
to be identical as a society throughout all times in its essential
character, and privileges, and membership. Such considerations
as these very clearly and abundantly attest the truth of the
first part of our proposition, namely, that the Church of God,
made up of His professing people, has been essentially the same
in character in former and in later times.

As regards the second part of the proposition, namely, that
the Church has always included infants among its members, the
proof, after what has already been said, need not demand a
lengthened illustration. If the Church of God, made up of His
professing people, be one and the same society at all times, and
under all its different dispensations, then the proof that infants
were members of it at one period must be a proof that they are
competent to be members of it at any subsequent period; unless,
indeed, some express and positive enactment can be produced,
altering the charter of the society, and excluding, as incompetent
to be admitted by the new and altered terms of the deed, those
formerly comprehended within it. If no such proof of alteration in
the charter or constitution of the society can be produced,—if the
society itself remains the same in character and terms of admission as before,—then the proof that infants were once its members
may suffice for proof that they are still competent to be so. We
know that under the Abrahamic Church infants, as well as their
parents, were admitted to the place of members. We have
already proved that they were interested and comprehended in
the covenant that constituted the Church in those days. The
sign and seal of the covenant marked them out at eight days
old, as embraced within it. The initiatory ordinance of the
Church, which was the formal evidence of admission to its membership, was administered to the infants of such as were themselves members of the Church ; and with that token in their flesh

they grew up within the pale of the Church in Old Testament times. Circumcision was not part and parcel of the Sinaitic covenant, revealed afterwards through Moses. Our Lord Himself testifies that the ordinance was " not of Moses, but of the fathers." [1] It constituted the door of admission, not into the Sinaitic Church as distinct from the Abrahamic, but into that Church of which Abraham was a member, and of which all in every age are members who have like faith with Abraham. It constituted the door of admission, in the days of Abraham, into that very Church of which Christians are members now. And turning to Gospel times, we have a right to say that infants are competent to be members of the Christian Church now, unless it can be demonstrated that the Church of God is not the same now as in former times ; that it is different in character and extent ; and that those capable of admission before are, through an express alteration in the fundamental principles of the society, excluded now. Falling back upon our general proposition, already demonstrated, that the Church of God, as the society of His professing people, is one and the same in its essential nature in every age, we are entitled to affirm that infants once competent members of it are competent members of it still.

This proof is sufficient in the absence of any statute of limitation alleged to have been enacted in New Testament times, altering the character of the Church of God, and restricting it to the reception into its membership of adults, and adults alone. But there are very plain intimations in the New Testament, not only that no statute of limitation has been passed excluding infants, but that the privilege they once undeniably enjoyed under the Old Testament economy has been continued to them under the New. I do not dwell again upon the very express declaration of Peter to the Jews, when explaining to them the Gospel privilege : " the promise is unto you and to your children," —language which, in the case of a Jewish parent, *could* have only one meaning. I would refer to the language of our Lord Himself, when the Jewish parents brought their little ones to Christ, and He took them up in His arms and blessed them, accompanying the blessing with the words: " Suffer little children to come unto me, and forbid them not; for of such is the kingdom of heaven." [2] There can be no plausible interpretation of this

[1] John vii. 22.   [2] Matt. xix. 14 ; Mark x. 14 ; Luke xviii. 16.

passage given which proceeds upon the idea that those very
infants blessed of Christ, and said by Him to belong to His
kingdom, were actually excluded from it as its members. That
they were not persons grown up, as one party of Antipædobaptists
allege, but infants, who could by no act of their own profess their
faith in Christ, is clear from the act of Christ taking them up
in His arms when He blessed them. That the expression, " of
such is the kingdom of heaven," means no more than that persons
of the like dispositions with children belonged to the kingdom
of heaven,[1] and that those very children were actually excluded
from it, as another class of opponents of infant Baptism affirm,
may be safely denied ; inasmuch as the act of Christ in blessing
them, in connection with the words He used, cannot be explained
on the supposition that they were shut out beyond the pale of
His covenant, and actually cut off from His Church. In short,
the words of our Lord, taken in conjunction with His action, very
distinctly demonstrate that the right of infants to be members
of His Church, formerly recognised under the Old Testament,
was not cancelled, but rather confirmed and continued under the
New.[2] We are entitled thus far to hold as proved our second
grand proposition in all its parts, namely, that the Church of God,
made up of all His professing people, has been essentially one in
character in former and in latter times ; and has always included
infants among its members.[3]

The two propositions, which we have already had under
consideration, established as we believe them to be by Scripture
evidence, go very far indeed, taken by themselves, to decide the
question as to the lawfulness of infant Baptism. If infants as
well as their parents have an interest in God's covenant,—if
infants as well as their parents have a place in the Church as
members,—it were difficult to affirm that they have no right to
share in the privilege of Baptism, as the seal of the covenant,
and the ordinance appointed for the formal admission into the
Church of its members. An express prohibition forbidding the
administration of the ordinance to them, or an incompatibility
no less distinct between the nature of the Sacrament and their

---

[1] [Carson, *Baptism in its Mode and Subjects*, Lond. 1844, pp. 199-202.]
[2] [*Vide* Calvin, *in loc.*]
[3] Williams, *Antipæd. Exam.* vol. i. pp. 272-321, 334-356. Wardlaw,
Dissert. on Inf. Baptism, 3d ed. pp. 117-120.

condition as infants, might, indeed, force upon us the conclusion that they are excepted. But in the absence of any such exception forced upon us by explicit prohibition or explicit incompatibility, we seem to be warranted in saying that the covenant state of infants and the Church state of infants, fairly demonstrated, unavoidably carry with them the inference that infants are entitled to the administration of Baptism as the seal of the one, and the door of formal admission into the other. The opponents of infant Baptism feel considerable difficulty in giving any explicit or consistent explanation of the relation sustained by infants either to the covenant or to the Church. Some of them deny absolutely that infants have any place either in the covenant or in the visible Church as members; while others of them hesitate about such a sweeping denial in the face of the strong Scripture evidence available to establish the fact, and rather consider infants as possessed of an inchoate and undeveloped right to be members, and as put under the care of the Church in order to be prepared for claiming and exercising the full right afterwards. But the covenant state and the Church state of infants, once fairly established, as they can readily be from Scripture, and the absence of any express bar interposed by Divine authority to the contrary, seem unquestionably to lead to a conclusion in favour of infant Baptism, even were there no further evidence that could be adduced in support of it. But there is much additional evidence at hand. The three propositions which still remain to be discussed and illustrated afford strong additional confirmation of the same conclusion; and, taken along with the positions already established, furnish a complete proof of the lawfulness and duty of baptizing infants.

III. The ordinance of outward admission into the Church has, in its essential character and meaning, been the same in former and in later times; and has always been administered to infants.

The main object of this third general proposition, as forming part of the argument for infant Baptism, is to identify, as essentially one and the same in their use and import and character, the Old Testament rite of circumcision with the New Testament rite of Baptism. If we can prove that they meant the same thing, and held the same place, and performed the same office in the Church of God in former and in later times, it were difficult to object to the conclusion that the one ought to be administered to the same infant members of the Church as was the other. To establish this general proposition we may make use of these three steps. First, circumcision and Baptism are both to be regarded as the appointed ordinance for the formal and public admission of its members into the Church. Second, both circumcision and Baptism have essentially the same meaning as the signs and seals of the same Divine truths and the same spiritual grace. Third, Baptism has been appointed to occupy the place and come in the room of circumcision, which has been done away.

In the first place, then, circumcision and Baptism are both to be regarded as the authorized ordinances for the formal admission of members into the Church.

That circumcision was the initiatory ordinance for the Old Testament Church, an appeal to the history of its institution and administration in ancient times will sufficiently evince. Without it no Israelite was accounted a member of the Old Testament Church; with it he could establish a right of membership, and a title to its ordinances. From the days of Abraham down to the date of the discontinuance of the ordinance in Gospel times, circumcision was the only thing that gave a right of admission to the privileges of the Old Testament Church; and apart from circumcision no one had a right to these. There was no access to the membership or ordinances of the ancient Church, except through the door of circumcision. That this was the case, is proved both from the case of infants and the case of adults. In the case of infants, the ordinance was universally administered; and in virtue of it alone, the circumcised infant, as it grew to manhood, was regarded as a member of the visible Church, and ceremonially qualified to receive its privileges without any other initiation or admission. In the case of adults, the administration of the rite to those who had not received it before,—as, for example, in the instance of Gentile proselytes,—was necessary as the door of admission into the fellowship of the Church. Without circumcision they were not admitted. By Divine appointment, circumcision bestowed on "the stranger, who joined himself to the Lord," a right, the same as that of the Israelites themselves, to Church privileges and to partake of the passover. "When a stranger shall sojourn with thee, and will keep the passover to the Lord,"—such were the terms of the enactment,—

"let all his males be circumcised, and then let him come near and keep it; for no uncircumcised person shall eat thereof." [1] Both in the case of infants, then, and of adults, circumcision constituted the initiatory ordinance of admission into the ancient Church from the days of Abraham downwards.

Against this fact, so very plainly attested in Scripture, it has been objected on the part of the opponents of infant Baptism, that it was not circumcision, but birth and natural descent, that gave admission into the ancient Church; and that every one born an Israelite became a member of the Israelitish Church. And in confirmation of this view, the fact of the circumcision of the descendants of Ishmael and Esau, without the observance giving them a title to admission to Church membership among the Israelites, is appealed to.[2] The objection has not the least force in it. The tribes that sprang from Ishmael and Esau were divinely separated from the descendants of Abraham in the line of the covenant; and had not, like the other children of the patriarch, any interest in the federal promise. With these, therefore, circumcision could avail nothing to give them admission into the Church. Although practised by them, it was not with them a Church ordinance in connection with the covenant Church; and could not, therefore, admit them among its members. And on the other hand, mere birth did not give to the Israelite a right of admission into the Church, unless when connected with circumcision administered and submitted to. No Israelite was born a Church member. Unless, in addition to his birth as an Israelite, he was also circumcised, he had no right to the privileges of the ancient Church. So very far is it from being true, as some Antipædobaptists affirm, that his birth as an Israelite gave him a right to be considered a member of the Church, without circumcision, that it only placed him under the certainty of a heavy judicial sentence. To be born an Israelite, without circumcision being added to birth, only brought upon his head the sentence of God : "He shall be cut off from his people." [3]

There is quite as little foundation for another objection brought by other opponents of infant Baptism against our position, when they allege that circumcision was no more than a door

---

[1] Exod. xii. 48.
[2] Carson, *Baptism in its Mode and Subjects*, Lond. 1844, pp. 223–227.
[3] Gen. xvii. 14 ; Exod. iv. 24–26.

of entrance to the Mosaic Church, and a token of admission to
its outward and ceremonial privileges; and not the initiatory
ordinance of the spiritual Church of God in Old Testament
times.   In answer to this objection, it is enough to say, that circumcision was instituted more than four hundred years before
the legal economy was set up ; and although it afterwards came
to be associated with the law of Moses, yet it never lost its
original meaning and use as the initiatory ordinance through
which members entered into the Old Testament Church.   It was
in that character that we are to regard it when first instituted
and administered in Abraham's family ; and although four
hundred years later there was superinduced upon the Church, to
which circumcision was the door, a number of outward and ceremonial observances, yet it never ceased to be the initiatory rite
of that Church of which Abraham was a member, and of which
believers in every age, who have Abraham's faith, are members
also.   Under the Mosaic law, circumcision used and owned as an
outward badge or privilege, admitted a man to an interest in an
outward ceremonial institute ; but not the less under the Mosaic
law circumcision used and owned as a spiritual ordinance, and connected with the faith of the recipient, admitted also to an interest
in that inner and spiritual Church, which was one and the same
in the days of Abraham, in the time of Moses, and at the present
time.   Circumcision, although when associated with the Mosaic
economy it was an outward badge of an outward Church, never
ceased to be what it was at the first hour of its administration to
Abraham himself, the ordinance of admission into the true
Gospel Church.

The argument from Scripture, then, to prove that circumcision was the authorized ordinance for the admission of members
into the Old Testament Church, is clear and satisfactory.   It is
hardly necessary to prove that Baptism is the authorized ordinance for the admission of members into the New Testament
Church.   That it is so, is admitted well nigh on all hands.   The
terms of the apostolic commission prove it to be so.   The practice
of Apostles and apostolic men in admitting converts to the
Christian Church by Baptism, proves it to be so.   The meaning
of the ordinance as the Sacrament of union to Christ, proves it
to be so.   In this respect, the two ordinances occupy the same
ground, and stand at the entrance of the Church publicly to

mark and define its members ; being the rites respectively belonging to the Old Testament Church and the New, for accomplishing the same object. To this extent, as the ordinance of admission into the Church of God, circumcision and Baptism are identical.

In the second place, circumcision and' Baptism are expressive of the same spiritual truths, and are to be identified as signs and seals of the same covenant blessings.

With reference to circumcision, it is important to bear in mind that it was the sign and seal of a spiritual covenant, and not merely, as has been alleged, of the Sinai covenant, with its outward and ceremonial privileges. It was the covenant of grace as revealed to Abraham of which circumcision was primarily the token ; and hence we have distinct evidence in Scripture that the spiritual blessings conveyed in that covenant to the believer were precisely the blessings which the ordinance of circumcision represents. The two cardinal blessings given by the covenant of grace are justification from guilt by faith in the righteousness of Christ, and sanctification from sin by the renewal of the heart through the work of the Holy Spirit; and these two blessings, we have express Scripture warrant to say, circumcision was intended to signify and seal. That circumcision was expressive of justification by faith in the righteousness of Christ, we are distinctly taught by the Apostle Paul to believe, in that passage of the Epistle to the Romans already more than once referred to : " And Abraham," says the Apostle, " received the sign of circumcision, a seal of the righteousness of the faith which he had, being yet uncircumcised." [1] And again, that circumcision was a token of the sanctification of the heart and renewal from sin by the Spirit, is proved by several passages of Scripture which speak of " the circumcision of the heart " as the true meaning of the ordinance. " He is not a Jew," says the same Apostle, " which is one outwardly ; neither is that circumcision which is outward in the flesh : but he is a Jew which is one inwardly ; and circumcision is that of the heart, in the spirit, and not in the letter; whose praise is not of men, but of God." [2] These passages, and others which might easily be adduced, abundantly demonstrate that circumcision, as a sign and seal, represented and attested those two spiritual blessings of the covenant of grace, which are introductory to all the rest,—the blessings of justification and sancti-

[1] Rom. iv. 11.   [2] Rom. ii. 28, 29 ; Phil. iii. 3 ; Col. ii. 11 ; Deut. xxx. 6.

fication. And it is hardly necessary to add, that these are the two very blessings mainly and emphatically represented in the ordinance of Baptism under the New Testament Church. The very words of the Baptismal service tell us, that the member formally admitted into the Church is baptized "into the name of the Father" through means of justification by the Son, and sanctification through the Spirit. That is to say, the very same spiritual blessings represented and attested of old time by circumcision, are now represented and attested by Baptism. In this respect, as the signs and seals of the very same covenant blessings, circumcision and Baptism are one and the same.[1]

In the third place, the oneness of circumcision and Baptism is yet further established by the fact that Baptism has come in the room of circumcision.

They are not only both initiatory ordinances for the admission of members into the Church, the one under the Old, and the other under the New Testament. They are not only appointed to be expressions of exactly the same spiritual truths, which stand permanently connected with the admission of a sinner into an interest in the covenant of grace. There is distinct enough evidence to show, that when circumcision was done away with at the establishment of the Gospel Church, Baptism was appointed to stand in its stead and fulfil its office. This appears, among other proofs, from the statement of the Apostle Paul in the Epistle to the Colossians. "And ye are complete in Him," says the Apostle, referring to the unspeakable fulness of blessing laid up in Christ,—"and ye are complete in Him, who is the head of all principality and power; in whom also ye are circumcised with the circumcision made without hands, in putting off the body of the sins of the flesh by the circumcision of Christ: buried with Him in Baptism, wherein also ye are risen with Him."[2] Such language seems plainly enough to imply that Baptism comes to Christians now in the room of circumcision to believers under the former dispensation; and that it is both fitted and intended

---

[1] [Calvin, *Inst.* lib. iv. cap. xvi. 2, 3. Edwards, *Works*, Lond. 1834, vol. i. pp. 441 ff. Thomasius, *Dogmatik,* 3ter Th. 2te Abth. p. 12.]

[2] ["Declarat etiamnum apertius modum spiritualis circumcisionis: nempe quia, Christo consepulti, consortes sumus mortis ejus. Id nominatio nos consequi per Baptismum docet: quo melius pateat nullum esse usum circumcisionis sub regno Christi. Poterat enim alioqui objicere quispiam: Cur circumcisionem aboles hoc prætextu, quia effectus ejus sit in Christo? An

to supply its place as a sign and seal of the blessings of the covenant. The reasoning of the Apostle appears very distinctly to intimate, that all which circumcision could do under the former dispensation, Baptism does now.[1]

Upon these grounds, then, we are warranted to say that our third proposition is established,—namely, that the ordinance of admission into the Church has, in its essential character and meaning, been the same in former and in latter times, and has always been administered to infants.

IV. The next general proposition which I laid down at the outset of the discussion was this, that the principle on which the initiatory ordinance of admission into the Church of God has been administered, has been the same in former and in latter times, and has always applied to the case of infants.

This is a proposition of much interest and importance as forming part of the argument for infant Baptism. What was the principle on which circumcision, recognising a title to membership in the Church under the Old Testament, was administered, and in accordance with which parties had a right to participate in the ordinance? This is the first question. What is the principle on which Baptism, recognising a title to membership in the Church under the Gospel, is administered, and in accordance with which parties have a right to participation in the ordinance? This is the second question. These questions in our present discussion must, of course, be restricted to the case of infants under both economies. The case of adults does not so directly concern our argument; and indeed in itself admits of little dispute. The personal act of the adult professing his religious faith is the ground on which, under the Old Testament in the case of proselytes, and under the Gospel in the case of converts, their right to be admitted as members of the Church, and to receive its initiatory ordinance, as the formal recognition of their admission, is obviously founded. But setting aside the case of adult proselytes or converts, upon what principle were infants entitled to circum-

non etiam spiritualiter circumcisus fuit Abraham? Atqui hoc minime obstitit quo minus signum rei adderet. Non est igitur supervacua externa circumcisio, etiamsi interior per Christum conferatur. Ejusmodi objectionem antipat Paulus, factâ Baptismi mentione. Circumcisionem, inquit, spiritualem peragit in nobis Christus, non intercedente veteri illo signo quod sub Mose valuit, sed Baptismo."—CALVIN, in loc.]

[1] Wardlaw, Dissert. on Infant Baptism, 3d ed. pp. 42-66.

cision in ancient times, and are infants entitled to Baptism in these latter days? Can it be established that the principle on which the ordinance is administered is one and the same in both cases?

1*st*, Upon what principle was the right of infants to circumcision founded under the Old Testament Church?

The analogy of the proceedings of God in providence and in grace not indistinctly points to the principle on which infants in the ancient Church were admitted to the same ordinance and to the membership of the same Church as their parents. By no personal act of theirs could infants become entitled, in the same manner as adults become entitled, to the privileges of the Church. But there is a familiar principle of representation, illustrated in the case of civil society, of providence, and of God's spiritual dispensations, in consequence of which infants, in certain cases and to certain effects, are held to be one with their parents, and through this relationship become entitled to the privileges of their parents. We see this representative principle in civil society, when, in consequence of no personal act of theirs, but simply in consequence of being accounted one with their father, infants become members of the civil society in which their father is a member, and their civil character and standing are the same as his. We see the representative principle, again, in the constitution of God's providence, when, in virtue of no deed of their own, but because of their relationship to their father, his place in society, his moral and intellectual character, his very bodily constitution for good or evil, to a certain extent become theirs. We see the representative principle, once more, in God's spiritual dispensation, where infants, in consequence of no personal act of theirs, but in accordance with that prevailing and universal constitution of things which is found in this world, become, in consequence of their filial relationship and the inheritance of the same flesh and blood as their father, concluded under his sin, and made one with him in original transgression and liability to punishment. In all these cases the representative principle is familiar to us, and infants are seen to partake for good or evil of the relations of their father. In most cases,—perhaps, if we were capable of understanding it, in *all* cases,—in which God deals with infants so as to show His method or law of dealing, He does so on the representative principle when He cannot deal with them on the principle of personal action and responsibility ; and He acts with respect to them as if to a certain extent they were one with their parents.

That God may act towards infants in a way of sovereignty, without regard to their connection with their parents, may be true. But when He deals with them, and desires at the same time to manifest to us His rule or method of dealing, He does so on the principle of representation ; a principle revealed to us both in His providential and spiritual economies. And such is unquestionably the principle according to which, in the constitution of the Old Testament Church, infants were dealt with. God made His covenant with infants as well as with adults ; and the way in which He did so was never in connection with any personal act of theirs, which was impossible, but in connection with their filial relationship. God made His Church to include infants among its members as well as adult believers; and this too He did not in connection with their personal act, which was impossible, but in connection with the act of their parents. The membership of the father was counted to the infant; and the circumcision of the father gave a right to the infant to be circumcised also.

There are two views somewhat different from each other, that may be held on this point, which it is of considerable importance to discriminate between. The right of the child to circumcision and to the privileges of the Jewish Church, may be viewed as depending on his immediate father ; or it may be regarded as depending on his remote progenitor, Abraham. In the one case, his title to be circumcised is counted good because of his relationship to his immediate parent, who was a member of the Jewish Church, and interested in the covenant. In the other case, his title to be circumcised is counted good because of his relationship to Abraham, his remote progenitor, with whom the covenant was made, and independently of his connection with his immediate parent, and without regard to the circumstance of his parent being or not being a member of the Jewish Church. The evidence of Scripture seems not indistinctly to point to the first view as the correct one, or to the view that connects the right of the infant directly with his immediate father's interest in the Church and covenant, and not the view that connects it indirectly with Abraham's. Dr. Halley advocates the view that connects the infant's right not with the parent's, but with Abraham's interest in the covenant, making that right independent of the parent's connection or non-connection with the Church; and he does so apparently with the view of founding upon it the doctrine of indiscriminate Baptism to all infants alike, whatever be the father's Church state, and whether he be a member of the Church or not.[1] The two following considerations, however, seem very decisively to prove that the right of the infant to circumcision in the Jewish Church was valid in consequence of the Church membership of the father, and not in consequence of his remoter connection with Abraham. *First,* mere connection with Abraham did not in all cases give a right to the privileges of the Jewish Church, as we see exemplified in the instance of the descendants of Abraham in the lines of Ishmael and Esau. They were directly connected with Abraham as their ancestor, and yet were separated from the communion of the Jewish Church. *Second,* the case of the infants of Gentile proselytes demonstrates that not remote connection with Abraham, but immediate connection with the parent, is the ground of the infant's right to circumcision. The infants of such Gentile proselytes as were circumcised and members of the Jewish Church, had no connection with Abraham through ordinary descent; and yet in virtue of their father's circumcision they had a right to be circumcised also. These two considerations seem sufficient to prove that the right of the infant to circumcision was not derived remotely from Abraham, passing over his immediate parent, but came directly from the parent. In other words, the case of circumcision under the Old Testament presents to us a complete and perfect illustration of the representative principle, and of the privileges of the child being held to be the same as those of the parent. By no personal act of their own did children become entitled to circumcision; but they were so entitled, in consequence of the right of their father to the ordinance.

2d, Now, what is the principle on which infants under the New Testament Church become entitled to Baptism? Are we warranted by Scripture in identifying the principle on which Baptism is administered now with the principle on which circumcision was administered before? I think that we are. The identity in meaning, and character, and use, already proved between circumcision and Baptism, would afford a strong presumption in favour

[1] Halley, *The Sacraments*, Lond. 1844, vol. i. pp. 535–545.

of the conclusion, even had we no further evidence for it. The strong and close analogy between the two cases would go very far of itself to establish it. But there is one passage of Scripture more especially, which seems of itself explicitly to announce that the very principle of representation found under the Old Testament in the case of parent and child, is not cancelled, but continued under the New, and must be held as a permanent principle in the dealings of God with infants. The passage to which I refer is in the First Epistle to the Corinthians, and is to the following effect. Speaking of the case of husband and wife, when one of the parties is not a Christian but an unbeliever, the Apostle says: " For the unbelieving husband is sanctified (ἡγίασται) by the wife, and the unbelieving wife is sanctified by the husband : else were your children unclean; but now are they holy (ἅγια)."[1] The principle of representation found under the Old Testament is the very principle introduced by the Apostle to explain the position and character of children in the case where no more than one parent is a believer and member of the Church.[2] That the contrasted terms, " unclean" and " holy," are to be understood in the Old Testament sense of *not set apart* and *set apart* to the service or fellowship of God, seems to be undoubted. And the assertion of the Apostle is, that one of the parents being a believer, although the other is not, avails, so that the infants are to be accounted clean, or fit for the service of God and the fellowship of His Church. The holiness of the one parent that is a member of the Christian Church, communicates a relative holiness to the infant, so that the child also is fitted to be a member of the Church, and to be baptized. The forced and unnatural interpretation put

---

[1] 1 Cor. vii. 14.

[2] [" Insignis ergo est hic locus, et ex intimâ theologiâ ductus : docet enim segregari piorum liberos ab aliis quâdam prærogativâ, ut sancti in Ecclesiâ reputentur." " Æqualis est in omnibus naturæ conditio, ut sint tam peccato quam æternæ morti obnoxii. Quod autem hic tribuit liberis fidelium speciale privilegium Apostolus id fluit ex beneficio fœderis, quo superveniente deletur naturæ maledictio, et Deo per gratiam consecrantur qui naturâ profani erant. Hinc argumentatur Paulus (Rom. xi. 16) totam Abrahæ progeniem esse sanctam, quia fœdus vitæ Deus cum illo pepigerat. 'Si radix sancta,' inquit, ' ergo et rami sancti.' Et Deus filios suos vocat omnes qui ex Israele sunt progeniti : nunc dirutâ maceriâ, idem salutis fœdus quod initum fuerat cum semine Abrahæ nobis est communicatum. Quodsi communi generis humani sorte eximuntur fidelium liberi, ut Domino segregentur, cur eos a signo arceamus? Si Dominus in Ecclesiam suam eos verbo admittit, cur signum illis negabimus?"—Calvin in *Nov. Test.* ed. Tholuck, vol. v. p. 335 f]

upon this passage by Antipædobaptists cannot stand a moment's investigation. They interpret the "cleanness" of the infant as the *legitimacy* of the infant,[1]—a construction plainly forbidden by the consideration that marriages are lawful, and the children legitimate, whether the parents be believers or unbelievers. In this passage, then, we have a very express avowal of the principle of representation, proved to obtain in the case of circumcision under the Old Testament. The child is accounted clean because the parent is clean; or, to translate the phrase into ecclesiastical language, the child is entitled to Church membership because the parent is a Church member.[2] We recognise at once the identity of the principle under the former economy and the present; and we are entitled to hold as proved the fourth of our general propositions, namely, that the principle on which the initiatory ordinance of admission into the Church of God has been administered, has

---

[1] Booth, *Pædobapt. Exam.* Lond. 1829, vol. ii. p. 196. Carson, *Baptism in its Mode and Subjects*, Lond. 1844, p. 208.

[2] " The third meaning of the word ἁγιαζειν in Scripture, is ' to consecrate,' ' to regard as sacred,' and hence ' to reverence or to hallow.' . . . . Any person or thing consecrated to God, or employed in His service, is said to be sanctified. Thus, particular days appropriated to His service, the temple, its utensils, the sacrifices, the priests, the whole theocratical people, are called holy. Persons or things not thus consecrated are called profane, common, or unclean. To transfer any person or thing from this latter class to the former, is to sanctify him or it (Acts x. 15; 1 Tim. iv. 5). . . . . Any child, the circumstances of whose birth secured it a place within the theocracy or commonwealth of Israel, was, according to the constant usage of Scripture, said to be holy. In none of these cases does the word express any subjective or inward change. A lamb consecrated as a sacrifice, and therefore holy, did not differ in its nature from any other lamb. The priests or people, holy in the sense of set apart to the service of God, were in their inward state the same as other men. . . . . The children of believers are holy in the same sense in which the Jews were holy. They are included in the Church, and have a right to be so regarded. The child of a Jewish parent had a right to circumcision, and to all the privileges of the theocracy. So the child of a Christian parent has a right to Baptism and to all the privileges of the Church, so long as he is represented by his parent; that is, until he arrives at the period of life when he is entitled and bound to act for himself. Then his relation to the Church depends upon his own act. The Church is the same in all ages. And it is most instructive to observe how the writers of the New Testament quietly take for granted that the great principles which underlie the old dispensation are still in force under the new. The children of Jews were treated as Jews; and the children of Christians, Paul assumes as a thing no one could dispute, are to be treated as Christians. . . . . To be born in holiness (*i.e.* within the Church) was necessary in order to the child being regarded as an Israelite. So Christian children are not made holy by Baptism, but they are baptized because they are holy." —Hodge, *Expos. of First Cor.* Lond. 1857, pp. 115–118. [Meyer, *Krit. exeget. Handbuch über den 1ten Korintherbrief*, 4te Aufl. p. 166 f. Wilson, *Infant Baptism*, Lond. 1848, pp. 512–517.]

been the same in former and in latter times, and has always applied to the case of infants.

·V. The practice in regard to the administration of the initiatory ordinance has been the same in former and in latter times, and has always included the case of infants.

This is the fifth and last of the general propositions which I laid down at the outset; and after what has already been established, it requires no more than the briefest notice. Of course in regard to the practice of the Old Testament Church the proposition may be regarded as proved; the circumcision of the infant eight days old being the standing proof of the practice of the Church in former times. With regard to the practice of the Church under the Gospel, there are two preliminary remarks which it is important to carry along with us. *First*, the uniform practice of the ancient Church down to the epoch of the Gospel, taken in connection with the total silence of Scripture as to any change of ·practice when the Jewish passed into the Christian Church, is itself very nearly conclusive as to the practice of the early Christians in regard to infant Baptism. *Second*, there is not a single instance among all the Baptisms recorded in Scripture in which we find a person, who had grown up a Christian and without Baptism, receiving the ordinance when he became an adult. We have many examples of adult Baptism in Scripture, but none of adults who for years had been Christians before they received the ordinance.[1]

Carrying these remarks along with us, nothing more is necessary, in regard to the practice of the Primitive Church in the matter of infant Baptism, than to refer to the frequent and almost constant mention of the Baptism of "households" and "families," in which it is morally certain that there must have been infant members. "I baptized the household of Stephanas." "He was baptized, and all his, straightway." "She was baptized, and her household,"[2] etc. Such expressions as these, interpreted in the light of the previous undoubted practice of the Jewish Church, can admit of only one meaning. Infants are not mentioned specifically as baptized along with the parents, because it is taken for granted that everybody understood that they were. Had they

---

[1] Wardlaw, *Dissert. on Inf. Baptism*, 3d ed. pp. 130–132. Wilson, *ut supra*, pp. 500–503.

[2] 1 Cor. i. 16; Acts ii. 38, 39, xvii. 15–33.

been pointedly and separately mentioned in such cases, it would very fairly and reasonably have given rise to the suspicion or inference that infant Baptism was in principle an entire novelty, that it was a new thing for the Church to have infant members. The notices of household and family Baptisms, that occur in the New Testament so repeatedly, cannot be explained on the theory of the Antipædobaptists, that the family or household were adults. In the case of Lydia, for example, it is said: "She was baptized, and her household." [1] If, according to the theory of the opponents of infant Baptism, the household of Lydia consisted of adults, who separately and personally were converted like herself, and on a personal profession of faith like hers were separately baptized, it is very difficult to understand why their conversion and Baptism were not, like hers, separately mentioned, or on what principle they are all merged under her single name. Upon the theory of infant Baptism, on the contrary, it is easy to understand how infants, with no personal profession of faith, and no conversion like her own, were merged under her name as "her household." Under the circumstances of the Apostolic Church, the repeated mention of household or family Baptism is of itself decisive evidence of the practice by which infants were baptized. We are justified in saying that our fifth and last proposition, like the former, is sufficiently established, namely, that the practice in regard to the administration of the initiatory ordinance of the Church has been the same in former and in latter times, and has always included the case of infants.[2]

SECTION IV.—OBJECTIONS TO INFANT BAPTISM.

We have been occupied of late with the consideration of the general principles laid down in Scripture, upon which the lawfulness and duty of the Baptism of infants may be argued. I have endeavoured to establish and explain five general propositions, from any of which singly, but more especially from all taken to-

---

[1] Acts xvi. 15.
[2] Williams, *Antipæd. Exam.* Shrewsb. 1789, vol. i. pp. 199–232. Wilson, *Inf. Baptism*, Lond. 1848, pp. 517–523. Wardlaw, *Dissert. on Inf. Baptism*, 3d ed. pp. 102–130. [Apollonii, *Consideratio*, Lond. 1644, pp. 99–105. Hoornbeek, *Epistola de Independentismo*, Lugdun. Batav. 1660, pp. 313–350. Owen, *Works*, Goold's ed., vol. xvi. pp. 258–268. Gillespie, *Miscell. Quest.* chap. xvii.]

gether, may be drawn a proof in favour of infant Baptism. In doing this I adopted, as upon the whole the best, the plan of following the natural order of the argument, without caring to turn aside at every step to answer the objections which Antipædobaptists have urged against it, except when these lay directly in the line of my own illustration of it. In the right understanding of the argument itself, there is contained an answer to these objections, so that they may be considered as in a good degree met by anticipation. But still, as the subject is an important one, and as it may better help to develop the principles of the argument, I shall now proceed to consider some of the most common and plausible of the objections brought by Antipædobaptists against the relevancy or conclusiveness of our reasonings.

That in the case of infants baptized, there are difficulties connected with their condition as infants, which it may be hard to solve, it would be useless to deny. But that those difficulties, in one form or other, are peculiar to infant Baptism, and nowhere else to be met with, may reasonably be questioned. Above all, that those difficulties should be permitted to overbear the very strong and cumulative evidence from Scripture in favour of the doctrine and practice, it is not the part of truth or wisdom to assert. And yet I believe that it is mainly those difficulties which have led many to scruple to accept as valid or conclusive the Scripture evidence for infant Baptism. In what sense, or to what effect, infants are interested in the ordinance of Baptism, or benefited by it; what explanation is to be given of the use and efficacy of the Sacrament in their case; in what manner we are to reconcile infant participation in the sign and seal of the covenant of grace with the absence of intelligence and responsibility in infants: these are difficulties which have had more to do in bringing about that state of mind which has led many to declare infant Baptism to be unscriptural, than the force of Scripture argument against it. I believe that these difficulties which have influenced so many against the practice of infant Baptism, and which at first sight appear to be peculiar to it, are not really peculiar to it. In one shape or other, and to a greater or less extent, these difficulties are to be encountered in the case of adult Baptism as much as in the case of infant; and, indeed, are common to the supernatural grace or virtue connected with all Divine ordinances. Such difficulties may appear more palpably and prominently in their association with infant Baptism, and by many have been regarded as connected with it alone ; but in reality they will be found in greater or less measure present, wherever we admit that the work of the Spirit of God in His own ordinances is present, making them the means or instruments of supernatural grace.

This matter will come on for consideration at a subsequent stage, when I proceed to deal with the question of the efficacy of Baptism in the case of infants. I advert to it at present for the purpose of indicating my conviction that the source of not a few of the objections to infant Baptism is to be found, not in the Scripture evidence against it, but rather in those difficulties which are thought to embarrass the theory or explanation of its efficacy. It is plain that, in the first instance, our duty is to examine and weigh the Scripture evidence on the subject, and to be guided in our belief and practice by its force and conclusiveness. It is only in the second instance that it is lawful for us to inquire as to what explanation is to be given of the difficulties which stand connected with the Scripture ordinance. Objections drawn from the mere difficulty of framing a theological theory of the Sacrament, in its application to infants, are not for one instant to be allowed to contradict Scripture evidence, where it is clear and conclusive on the subject. That such evidence we have in support of infant Baptism, the heads of argument already given may be enough to evince. Postponing, then, for after consideration, the question of the efficacy of the ordinance in the case of infants, and the difficulties alleged to be connected with that point, because that question ought not to be allowed to interfere with the Scripture evidence to be weighed and examined in the first place, I now go on to consider some of the common and most plausible objections to that evidence as it has been already laid down.

The objections generally urged against the Scripture argument for infant Baptism, may be ranged under two heads : those which deny the relevancy of a large portion of our reasoning ; and those which controvert the conclusiveness of it. There are two general objections which I shall examine, as commonly urged against the relevancy of the argument ; and there are two objections also which I shall notice, directed against the conclusiveness of our reasoning. Under these heads we shall probably be able to discuss all that is of much weight or plausibility in the objections of Antipædobaptists.

I. Under the head of objections to the relevancy of our reasoning in favour of infant Baptism, I remark in the first place, that not a few object to our argument as one based upon, as they allege, an outward and ceremonial dispensation that was to be done away, and which has no place under the Gospel. They regard our reasoning from the Abrahamic covenant as irrelevant to our duty or practice under the Gospel economy; and hold that, in transplanting the custom of affixing to infants the outward seal of the covenant from the ancient to the present dispensation, we are borrowing the carnal ordinances of a bygone time, and giving them, without warrant and unlawfully, a place in the spiritual Church of Christ.[1]

Now in reference to this objection, it is at once admitted, that the argument for infant Baptism rests partly, although not by any means exclusively, upon a consideration of the Abrahamic covenant and Church. But it rests upon nothing peculiar to that Church, or that has been done away with. It is not unfrequently demanded of the advocates of infant Baptism, why they so often begin their argument in favour of a New Testament ordinance, such as Baptism, from the days of Abraham and from the nature of the covenant made with him. The answer to such a question is very plain. We not unfrequently begin with the Abrahamic covenant in the argument for infant Baptism, because with Abraham the Gospel Church was first formally established, and endowed with that ordinance which we believe to be in its character and use identical with Baptism. No doubt the Church of God had existed from the days of the first promise made to Adam of a Saviour, and of the first believer in that promise; and downward to the present time, under all its different forms, a Church has existed in this world. But with Abraham, and not before, began that outward provision in the Church for the admission of infants by means of an initiatory rite which was to signify and seal their interest in the covenant of grace; and therefore, in seeking to ascertain the meaning and nature and use of that initiatory rite, whether you view it under the form of circumcision in other days, or of Baptism now, it is both natural and lawful to go back to its origin and first institution the better to understand it. Circumcision was, in short, the Baptism of the

---

[1] Booth, *Pædobapt. Exam.* Lond. 1829, vol. ii. p. 140. Carson, *Baptism in its Mode and Subjects*, Lond. 1844, pp. 214, 233.

Church of God in former days; and in arguing in respect to its use and administration, it is both justifiable and reasonable to inquire into its origin, and into the terms on which it was originally enforced. Nor is there the slightest ground for alleging that in doing this we are guilty of transplanting an Old Testament, carnal, and temporary practice into the New Testament and spiritual Church without warrant, and against the meaning and nature of Gospel ordinances. It is granted, that there is a vast and unspeakable difference between the spirituality of the Gospel dispensation and the outward and ceremonial nature of the Jewish economy. But it is carefully to be remarked,—and if marked, would prevent much confusion in the argument,—that although in popular and common language we are wont to speak of the Jewish and Christian Churches as if they were two separate and contrasted Churches, and not one Church under two dispensations, yet strictly speaking the expression is not correct, and has led to much confusion both of thought and argument on this question as well as on others. There were two dispensations, the Jewish and the Christian; a carnal and outward dispensation, and a spiritual and more inward one. But it was the same Church of God under both, identical in character and essence, and all that is fundamental to a Church; although in the one case, under the Mosaic dispensation, it was the Church encircled by and subsisting in a carnal and outward economy, and in the other case, under the Gospel dispensation, it was the same Church encircled by and subsisting in a less outward and more spiritual economy. What belonged to the mere dispensation within which the Church of God was at any time encircled might be done away; what belonged to the Church itself was not to be done away.[1]

There are two brief considerations that will be sufficient to remove the objection to the relevancy of our argument for infant Baptism, from the alleged fact that it is built upon the practice of a former and temporary dispensation.

1. As already indicated, the objection is founded on the fallacy that the Old Testament Church and the New Testament Church were not one but different Churches; the one being carnal and the other spiritual,—the one being outward and ceremonial, as contrasted with the other, which is not so. It is hardly

[1] Wilson, *Infant Baptism*, Lond. 1848, pp. 384–387.

necessary to repeat what has already been largely established, that the Church of God has been one and the same in all ages, whether it is made up of "the household of Abraham" whom the patriarch circumcised, or "the household of Stephanas" whom Paul baptized; whether it numbers as its members Jews as in the days of Moses, or Gentiles as in our own. The outward dispensation superinduced upon the Church was changed from time to time; but the Church itself remained the same. Circumcision did not belong to the dispensation; it belonged to the Church. The initiatory ordinance by which infants were admitted as its members, was appointed more than four hundred years before the Jewish dispensation, and was administered before as well as during the period of the ceremonial economy. That economy, with its legal observances and symbolic ritual, might have been removed, as indeed it was removed, at the introduction of the Gospel dispensation; and yet, had God not intended to introduce Baptism in the place of circumcision in these latter times, circumcision might have still remained in force as the initiatory rite of His Church, in virtue of the place which it had in the Abrahamic covenant. Circumcision was independent either of the introduction or abolition of the law of Moses; and would have continued the standing ordinance for admission into the Church of God, as the seal of the covenant of grace, had not Baptism been expressly appointed as a substitute for it.[1]

2. The objection to our reasoning, that it is founded on the practice of a bygone and temporary dispensation, arises partly out of a misapprehension in regard to the typical nature of the ordinance. Under the general and comprehensive formula that all types are now merged in their antitypes, and that all that was symbolic in other days is abolished in the New Testament Church, Antipædobaptists have argued in support of the conclusion that

---

[1] Wardlaw, *Dissert. on Inf. Baptism*, 3d ed. pp. 96–102. [" In asserendâ fœderis differentiâ," says Calvin, arguing against the Anabaptists of his day, "quam barbarâ audaciâ Scripturam dissipant et corrumpunt! neque uno in loco, sed ita ut nihil salvum aut integrum relinquant. Judæos enim adeo carnales nobis depingunt ut pecudum similiores sint quam hominum. Quibuscum scilicet percussum fœdus ultra temporariam vitam non procedat, quibus datæ promissiones in bonis præsentibus ac corporeis subsidant. Quod dogma si obtineat, quid restat nisi gentem Judaicam fuisse ad tempus Dei beneficio saturatum (non secus ac porcorum gregem in harâ saginant) ut æterno demum exitio periret? Simul enim ac circumcisionem eique annexas promissiones citamus, circumcisionem literale signum promissionis ejus carnales fuisse respondent."—*Inst.* lib. iv. cap. xvi. 10.]

circumcision belonged to a temporary economy, which can be no precedent under the Gospel. Now circumcision may, it is frankly admitted, have served the purpose of a type of Christian sanctification under the ancient economy; and *as* a type, it had place no longer than until the antitype was realized. But it cannot be denied that it served another purpose also. It cannot be denied that it was instituted and used as a sacramental ordinance in the Church of God, altogether apart from its typical character as expressive of Christian regeneration; that it was, in short, a sign and seal of the covenant of grace. And in this character, which it unquestionably sustained, over and above its typical one, we cannot regard it as part and parcel of the Mosaic institute; nor is there any ground for alleging that, in appealing to the authority of circumcision in favour of infant Baptism, we are appealing to a carnal dispensation as a precedent for the practice of the Gospel Church.

II. But under the head of objections to the relevancy of our reasoning for infant Baptism, I remark, in the second place, that not a few object to our argument, because, as they allege, it is applicable to an outward, but not applicable to a spiritual, Church. This second objection is no more than a modification of the preceding one. It is allied to the fallacy that circumcision was the badge of a temporary and typical dispensation, opposed to the spirit of the Gospel, and not to be represented under the Gospel by any parallel or identical ordinance, equally binding, and equally administered to infants.

In many cases, the source of the feeling which regards infant Baptism as akin to an outward but unsuited to the character of a spiritual Church, is to be found in the denial of the Scripture distinction, so important to be kept in mind, between the visible and invisible Church. When the character of the Church as a visible corporate society is ignored or denied,—when the Church on earth is identified with the invisible Church made up of true believers alone,—when the title to membership in the Church here below is restricted to a saving faith in Christ and regeneration by His Spirit, and none but those possessed of saving faith are considered to have a right to entrance,—when such views as to the nature of the Church and its membership are held, it is not unnatural, but the reverse, that infants should be regarded as not members of the Church, and that infant Baptism should be accounted a misapplication of the ordinance. And hence, historically, it is a fact of great significance and interest, that among Independents, who deny the distinction between the visible and invisible Church, mainly, if not entirely, have been found also that religious party who deny infant Baptism; while among Presbyterians, whose principles lead them to mark distinctly and maintain strongly the difference between the visible and invisible Church, few or no deniers of the lawfulness of infant Baptism have been found. I feel myself exempted from the necessity of falling back upon the question of the grounds on which the important distinction between the visible and invisible Church of Christ rests, inasmuch as these have been fully argued at a previous stage in our discussions.[1] It is enough for me to remind you that the Church of Christ, as exhibited in this world, has, as we have already established, a visible and corporate character, and is possessed of certain outward privileges and certain outward ordinances, by which it is known in the eyes of men, as well as an inward and spiritual character, by which it is known in the eyes of God; that the tares grow side by side with the wheat in the enclosure of the Christian Church; and that even the external provision of ordinances and Sacraments, administered, although they may be, in numberless instances, to merely nominal Christians, is not to be undervalued or set aside, but rather esteemed a gift of God to His Church exceedingly great and precious. The ordinance of Baptism, administered to infants as well as to adults, forms part of the outward provision of ordinance which God has made for the visible Church. And it is an unscriptural theory, which, by denying the existence of such a Church, and assuming one purely and exclusively spiritual, would bear with an unfriendly influence on the doctrine and practice of infant Baptism.

But passing from the objections to the relevancy of our argument in favour of infant Baptism, I go on to consider some of the more common objections to the conclusiveness of our reasonings.

1st, Under the head of the objections to the conclusiveness of the reasoning in favour of infant Baptism, I remark, in the first place, that it has been objected against infant Baptism that there is no express or explicit command in the New Testament to administer the ordinance to infants.[2]

---

[1] [See above, vol. i. pp. 6-11, 29-40, 73-80.]
[2] Booth, *Pædobapt. Exam.* Lond. 1829, vol. i. pp. 19-23, 303-367. *Catech. Racov. De Baptismo,* qu. 2.

It is readily admitted that Baptism is a positive institution; and that in regard to the nature and use of positive institutions in the Church of Christ we must be guided solely by the communications of the Word of God in regard to them. But that the objection to infant Baptism from the absence of a positive and articulate formula, enjoining the administration of the Sacrament to infants, is of no real force, can be readily evinced.

First, the absence in Scripture of an express formula enjoining any duty, is no proof that the duty is not required; and the absence of any express formula imposing the duty of infant Baptism in particular, is no argument against the practice, but the reverse. Looking at the proposition as a general one applicable to all cases, it is evidently both unwarrantable and perilous to lay down as a canon of Scripture interpretation, that whenever there is no express and explicit injunction, in so many words, requiring a duty to be performed, there the deed is unlawful, or at least not commanded. It is unwarrantable; because we have no right to limit God as to the form in which He may be pleased to make known to us His will, if, in one form or other, it is made known. It is perilous as regards ourselves; because there can be no more dangerous position than to assume the attitude of refusing to regard the will of God intimated to us, because it is not intimated in the manner which we may consider the plainest and the best. Whatever is laid upon us in Scripture, whether it be in the way of direct and explicit commandment, or in the way of indirect but necessary inference from what is commanded, is equally binding and of Divine obligation.[1]

But the absence of any express formula enforcing the Baptism of infants in Scripture is more especially and emphatically to be regarded as no argument against the practice, but rather an argument on its side. A positive formula for infant Baptism, parallel to that which was given to the Apostles, to preach the Gospel, and to baptize all nations, would have looked very much as if infant Baptism was a novelty in the Church, unknown in principle and substance before. To preach the Gospel to the Gentiles, to baptize the Gentiles, were duties unknown to the exclusiveness of the Jewish Church; and hence a new and express formula

---

[1] Cumming, *Grounds of present Differences among the London Ministers*, Part i. *On the Authority of Scripture Consequences in Matters of Faith*, Lond. 1720. [See also Append. F.]

enjoining them was necessary at the outset of the new economy. Had the admission of infants as members been equally unknown to the Church, there would have been a no less urgent necessity for an express and explicit command in regard to it. But infants had been accounted and treated as members of the Church of God for well nigh four thousand years; and at the era of the Gospel dispensation there was no need for the proclamation of any new law in regard to their admission. Any such new law formally enjoining it might well have given rise to the idea that the practice had never been heard of before; that it was as much a new thing in the Church as seeking to proselytize and baptize the Gentile nations was. All that was necessary was a positive intimation that the outward manner of admitting infants into the Church was to be different under the Gospel from what it was before,—that the ordinance of Baptism was to be used instead of circumcision; and such an intimation is very expressly given both in the way of precept and example in the New Testament. Anything beyond this in the shape of an express formula to admit infants into the Church would reasonably have led to the belief that they had been excluded before.

Second, in reply to the objection to infant Baptism taken from the absence of any explicit injunction of the practice, it may be remarked that exactly the same objection may be brought against other Christian duties, which notwithstanding are generally or universally acknowledged to be duties, because, in the absence of an express command, the authority of Scripture imposing them can be certainly learned by " good and necessary inference." For example, the duty of females to commemorate the Lord's death at His table, and the duty of keeping the Sabbath under the Gospel, are not, it has often been remarked, expressly enjoined by any separate formula in the New Testament Scriptures. The duty of females to join in the Lord's Supper is only to be gathered inferentially by a process of reasoning not more direct than that which establishes the lawfulness and duty of infant Baptism. In like manner, the duty of keeping the first day of the week holy unto the Lord can claim no express or separate injunction in the New Testament any more than the practice of infant Baptism can.

There is a marked resemblance, indeed, between the sanctification of the first day of the week and the practice of baptizing infants, in regard both to what is enjoined and what is left to be inferred in respect of each, in the New Testament. The sanctification of one day in seven was not a new appointment in the Christian Church, but rested on the practice and authority of the more ancient dispensation of God; and hence there is no re-enactment in the New Testament of the general Sabbath law. But the change in the *circumstance* of the time when the Sabbath was to be kept, was a new appointment under the Gospel; and hence, by explicit examples of an authoritative kind, the change of the day is intimated and fixed in the New Testament. Exactly parallel to this, the admission of infants as members of the Church was no new appointment in the Church of God at the introduction of the Gospel dispensation; and hence it was left very much to rest for its authority on the previous law and practice of the Church, without any re-enactment of what was binding before. But the change in the *form* of admitting infants into the Church,—the change from circumcision to Baptism,—was a new appointment; and hence, by explicit command and example in the New Testament, we have authority for the change.[1]

Third, in reply to the objection against infant Baptism, drawn from the absence of any separate authority for the practice, it might be enough to challenge the Antipædobaptist upon his own principles to prove his own practice to be scriptural; and show an explicit precept or explicit precedent for baptizing the child of a Church member not along with the parent in his infancy, but afterwards when the child has grown to manhood. The inspired history of the Christian Church contained in the Acts of the Apostles embraces a period of more than twice the number of years required to allow the infants of a baptized convert themselves to grow up to the years of discretion, when they might have been accounted able to make a personal profession of their faith, as their parents had done before; and yet there is neither precept nor example in Scripture giving express authority for baptizing the children of Christian parents, after they had grown up to years of maturity, apart from the case of adult converts, which forms common ground to both parties in this controversy. Tried by their own principles, the practice of Antipædobaptists would be found wanting in Scripture authority.

---

[1] Williams, *Antipæd. Exam.* Shrewsb. 1789, vol. i. pp. 70–96, vol. ii. 193–200. Wardlaw, *Dissert. on Inf. Baptism*, 3d ed. pp. 109–117, 127–134.

2d, Under the head of objections to the conclusiveness of our reasoning for infant Baptism, I remark further, that it is commonly or universally objected by Antipædobaptists against the practice of infant Baptism, that faith, or at least a profession of faith, in Christ, is positively demanded as a prerequisite to Baptism in all cases; and that as infants cannot have such faith, or make such a profession, they cannot be admitted to the ordinance.[1] Of the fact asserted in this objection, namely, that a profession of faith is required, both by the scriptural commission given to the Apostles to baptize, and by the apostolic examples in this matter, on the part of the person to be baptized in all ordinary cases, there is no room for doubt. We have already had occasion to illustrate and assert the fact against the doctrine and practice of indiscriminate Baptism. But the fact there asserted is too narrow a foundation to build an objection on against infant Baptism.

In the first place, the demand of Scripture for faith or a profession of faith, as a prerequisite for Baptism, is a demand that has respect to adults, and is not addressed to infants; and not being addressed to infants, it cannot be regarded as laying down the conditions or terms on which infants are to be made partakers of the ordinance. It is quite plain that those passages of Scripture in which a profession of faith is connected with Baptism, like the Scriptures at large, are intended for adults and not for infants,—for the common and general case of men in the full possession of their intellectual and moral powers, and not for the exceptional case of infants not in full possession of those powers. That this is the case, the single consideration that the Bible is God's message to men and not to infants, is enough to prove; unless it could be shown, which it cannot, that in those passages, not men but infants are specifically referred to. The passages usually quoted by Antipædobaptists in support of their objection, are the commission to the Apostles, as recorded in Mark, and the saying of Philip to the Ethiopian eunuch, recorded in the Acts of the Apostles. The apostolic commission in Mark is to this effect: "Go ye into all the world, and preach the Gospel to every creature. He that believeth, and is baptized, shall be saved; he that believeth not shall be condemned."[2] It is abundantly obvious that this language applies primarily to the ordinary case of adults,

[1] Carson, *Baptism in its Mode and Subjects*, Lond. 1844, pp. 169, 253–261.
[2] Mark xvi. 16.

and not to the exceptional case of infants ; and while the order—
first belief, and then Baptism—refers to adults, it cannot apply to
infants, to whom the Gospel cannot be preached, and who cannot
be expected to believe it. Are infants, then, in virtue of this
passage, to be excluded from Baptism, because in consequence of
their infancy they are excluded from believing ? Certainly not ;
for by the very same argument they would be excluded also from
salvation. The order of the passage is, first, belief ; second, Baptism ; third, salvation. And if, on the strength of this passage,
infants, as Antipædobaptists assert, are to be excluded from Baptism because they are excluded from believing, they must, in like
manner, be excluded from salvation too.

The saying of Philip addressed to the Ethiopian eunuch, is
quite as little available for the Antipædobaptist objection. " If,"
said Philip, addressing the man upon whose understanding and
heart there had dawned, through the evangelist's preaching, a
saving knowledge of Christ,—" if thou believest with all thine
heart, thou mayest be baptized."[1] The language was addressed
to an adult in the full possession of all his powers of mind, and
laid down for him the order of faith as preceding Baptism. But
Philip never applied the same language, nor laid down the same
order, in the extraordinary case of infants, whose salvation must
be according to a different order and a different method. The
announcements of Scripture which imply the necessity of faith
or a profession of faith in order to Baptism, are framed upon the
principle of adult Baptism, not upon the exceptional case of infant
Baptism.

In the second place, the objection of Antipædobaptists,
grounded on the impossibility of infants complying with the conditions on which Baptism ought to be administered, may be proved
to be fallacious by a consideration of the case of circumcised infants. That infants were circumcised, and had a title to be so,
will not by any party be denied. And yet circumcision involved
in it the very same profession of faith, in all its essential respects,
that Baptism now does. Substantially, it is the same ordinance
as Baptism. It expressed the same truths. It implied on the
part of the worthy recipient essentially the same spiritual qualifications. That this was the case is very expressly asserted by
the Apostle Paul in his Epistle to the Galatians. " Every man,"

[1] Acts viii. 37.

says he, "that is circumcised is a debtor to do the whole law." [1] In other words, circumcision in the case of the person circumcised involved a profession of his obligation to keep God's law, very much in the same manner as Baptism involves such a profession now. And yet infants, incapable of making such a profession, were circumcised. And exactly on the same principle, infants incapable now of making such a profession are to be baptized.

In the third place, the objection of Antipædobaptists may be proved to be groundless by a consideration of the case of infants saved. The very same difficulty, if difficulty it can be called, alleged to stand in the way of the doctrine of infant Baptism, applies with undiminished force to the case of infant salvation. "He that believeth shall be saved; he that believeth not shall be condemned." [2] Such is the simple and unchangeable formula that declares in Scripture the order and connection of faith and salvation. It is a formula adopted and intended to apply to the case of adults, responsible for their belief; and it makes the salvation of their souls to be suspended on the existence of their faith. Interpreted in the same manner, and applied in the same unlimited extent to infants, it would close against them the door of the kingdom of heaven, and exclude the possibility of their salvation; for they are incapable, by reason of their infancy, of that faith which stands connected with the justification of the sinner before God. Shall we, in virtue of the Antipædobaptist canon of criticism, proceed to reverse the Saviour's words, and turn His blessing into a curse, and say in regard to infants, that of such is *not* the kingdom of heaven? Or shall we not, on the contrary, reject a canon of interpretation that would lead to such results, and rather say that infants are subjects both of Baptism and salvation? [3]

SECTION V.—THE EFFICACY OF INFANT BAPTISM.

The efficacy of Baptism in the case of adults may be understood from what has been already said of the nature of the Sacra-

---

[1] Gal. v. 3. [2] Mark xvi. 16; John iii. 36.
[3] Williams, *Antipæd. Exam.* Shrewsb. 1789, vol. i. pp. 214–224, 303–311. Wilson, *Inf. Baptism*, Lond. 1848, pp. 415–498. Wardlaw, *Dissert. on Inf. Baptism*, 3d ed. 186–188.

ments in general. Baptism, like the Lord's Supper, is a sign and seal of a federal engagement between the receiver and Christ. It presupposes the existence of justifying and saving grace in the person baptized; and it seals or attests that grace to the soul, in this manner becoming the means of further grace.

There is a meaning in the fact that the person receiving the Sacrament has a part to perform in the ordinance,—that in the Lord's Supper he personally takes and partakes of the elements of bread and wine, and that in Baptism he personally submits himself to and receives the sprinkling of water. In both Sacraments there is a personal act on the part of the participator, which has its spiritual meaning, which cannot and ought not to be overlooked in the transaction. That act forms the link that connects the receiver of the ordinance with the ordinance itself; and the spiritual faith embodied in the act forms the link which connects his soul with the covenant blessings which the ordinance represents. The Sacrament is a seal, then, of more than the covenant generally; it is a seal of the covenant in its appropriation by the believer to himself personally in the ordinance.

There are some theologians indeed who in their explanation of the Sacraments make them seals of the covenant in general, and not seals of the believer's own personal interest in the covenant. They make the Sacraments attestations vouching for God's promises of grace at large, but not vouching for those promises as appropriated by the believer and realized in the experience of the worthy receiver of the Sacrament. This explanation of the Sacraments, however, is, I think, much too narrow and limited. It overlooks the personal act of the receiver in the Sacrament, and the spiritual meaning of that act. It disowns or neglects as not essential to the ordinance, the part which the participator has to perform, when in the case of the Lord's Supper he personally takes of the bread and wine, or when in the case of Baptism he personally presents himself to be sprinkled with water in the name of the Trinity. There is a spiritual meaning in these personal acts not to be overlooked in our explanation of the Sacraments, and essential to a right understanding of them. These personal acts constitute the part performed by the believer in the covenant transaction between him and Christ in the ordinance, and are necessary to make up the covenant. And the Sacrament, as a seal, is applicable to that part of the covenant transaction by which the believer appropriated the blessing to himself, not less than to that other part of the covenant transaction by which Christ exhibits or makes offer of the promise of grace to the believer. In other words, the Sacrament is not merely a seal of the covenant offered, or exhibited, or declared in general, but a seal of the covenant appropriated by the believer in particular, and, through means of his own spiritual act in the ordinance as well as Christ's, received in his personal experience.

In the case of Baptism administered to a believing adult, his own personal part in the ordinance, when he presents himself to the sprinkling of water, is the sign of that spiritual act of his through which the blessings of justification and regeneration, represented in the Sacrament, have previously become his; and Baptism is to him a seal not merely of these blessings as exhibited and promised in the covenant generally, but of these blessings realized and enjoyed by himself. Through the channel of his faith, and by means of the Spirit in the ordinance, Baptism becomes a seal in his justification and regeneration, and so a means of grace and spiritual blessing to his soul.[1]

Such is the efficacy of Baptism administered to an adult believer. What is the virtue or efficacy of the ordinance when administered to infants incapable of faith, although not incapable of being made partakers in the grace which the Spirit confers? In entering on the consideration of this delicate and difficult subject, it is necessary, in order to clear our way to it, to lay down one or two preliminary propositions of much importance in the discussion.

First, The proper and true type of Baptism, as a Sacrament in the Church of Christ, is the Baptism of adults, and not the Baptism of infants. In consequence of the altered circumstances of the Christian Church at present, as compared with the era when Baptism was first appointed, we are apt to overlook this truth. The growth and prevalence of the visible Church, and the comparative fewness of the instances of adult conversion to an outward profession of Christianity amongst us, have led to the Baptism of infants being almost the only Baptism with which we are familiar. The very opposite of this was witnessed in the Church of Christ at first. And the true type of Baptism, from examining which we are to gather our notions

---

[1] Turrettin, *Op.* tom. iii. loc. xix. qu. xix.

of its nature and efficacy, is to be found in the adult Baptisms
of the early days of Christianity, and not in the only Baptism
commonly practised now in the professing Church, the Baptism
of infants. It is of very great importance, in dealing with
the question of the nature and efficacy of Baptism, to remember this. Both among the enemies and the friends of infant
Baptism the neglect of this distinction has been the occasion of
numberless errors in regard to the import and effects of the
Sacrament. Men have judged of the nature and efficacy of Baptism from the type of the ordinance, as exhibited in the case of
baptized adults. They have reversed the legitimate order of the
argument, and argued from the case of infants to that of adults,
and not from the case of adults to that of infants. It is abundantly obvious that adult Baptism is the rule, and infant Baptism
the exceptional case ; and we must take our idea of the ordinance
in its nature and effects not from the exception, but from the
rule. The ordinance of Baptism is no more to be judged of from
its ministration to children, than is the ordinance of preaching to
be judged of from its ministration to children. The Sacrament in
its complete features and perfect character is to be witnessed in
the case of those subjects of it whose moral and intellectual nature
has been fully developed and is entire, and not in the case of
those subjects of it whose moral and intellectual being is no more
than rudimental and in embryo. Infants are subjects of Baptism
in so far as, and no farther than their spiritual and intellectual
nature permits of it. And it is an error, abundant illustration of
which could be given from the writings both of the advocates and
opponents of infant Baptism, to make Baptism applicable in the
same sense and to the same extent to infants and to adults, and
to form our notions and frame our theory of the Sacrament from
its character as exhibited in the case of infants. It is very plain,
and very important to remember, that the only true and complete
type of Baptism is found in the instance of those subjects of it
who are capable both of faith and repentance, not in the instance
of those subjects of it who are not capable of either. The Bible
model of Baptism is adult Baptism, and not infant.

Second, The virtue of infant Baptism, whatever that may be,
is not more mysterious than the virtue ascribed to adult Baptism,
although it may have the appearance of being so. It is a very
common idea, that the difficulty in framing an explanation of the

efficacy of Baptism in the case of infants, is peculiar to the ordinance in its administration to them, and does not attach to it in its administration to adults. I believe that this is not the case. There may be greater difficulty in gathering from the statements of Scripture what the virtue of Baptism really is in its application to infants, than in ascertaining what it is in its application to adults. But to explain the supernatural virtue itself is just as difficult in the one case as in the other, and simply from this reason, that it is supernatural. Up to a certain point it is easy enough to explain the efficacy of adult Baptism, but beyond that fixed point it is impossible to explain it. That point is where the natural efficacy of the ordinance passes into the supernatural efficacy. There is a certain natural influence which Baptism, as expressive of certain spiritual truths, and through means of these truths, is fitted to exert upon the adult, because he is a moral and intelligent being, with his faculties developed and complete. And this natural influence of Baptism, through means of the truths expressed by it, cannot be exerted upon the infant, because, although he is a moral and intelligent being, his faculties are not developed or complete. As a sign of spiritual truths understood by the adult, and not understood by the infant, Baptism has a certain natural effect on the one and not on the other, which it is not difficult to explain. But this effect is moral or natural, and not, properly speaking, the sacramental efficacy that is peculiar to the ordinance. The sacramental efficacy peculiar to the ordinance is not natural, but supernatural,—an efficacy not belonging to it from its moral character, but belonging to it in consequence of the presence and power of the Spirit of God in the ordinance. This distinctive efficacy of Baptism as a Sacrament, we cannot understand or explain, either in the case of adults or the case of infants. It is a supernatural effect of a gracious kind, wrought by the Spirit of God in connection with the ordinance; and because it is supernatural, it is not more and not less a mystery in the case of infants than in the case of adults.

The supernatural efficacy connected with Baptism, and owing to the presence of the Spirit of God with the ordinance, is an efficacy competent to infants as much as to adults. Even upon their unconscious natures the Spirit is free to work His work of grace, not less than upon the natures of adults whose understandings and hearts are consciously consenting to the work. The work of regeneration by the Holy Ghost is a work which it is as easy for Him to accomplish upon the infant of days as upon the man of mature age,—upon the child who enjoys but the rudiments of his moral and intellectual life, as upon the adult whose moral and intellectual powers are co-operating in and consenting to the gracious change. But broadly marked although the regeneration of the infant and the regeneration of the adult be, by the absence in the one instance, and the presence in the other, of a capacity moral and intellectual for faith and repentance, yet it is never to be lost sight of or forgotten that the work is the work of the Spirit of God, and not to be explained on any natural principle either in the former case or in the latter. The presence of his complete and perfect intellectual and moral powers in the case of the baptized adult, and the exercise of those powers in connection with the truths represented and signified in the Sacrament, afford no adequate explanation of the sacramental grace or efficacy connected with the ordinance in consequence of the power of the Spirit in it. At this point we have got beyond the limits of the natural, and into the region of the supernatural; and it is not more and not less supernatural in the case of infants than in the case of adults. Sacramental grace, properly so called, is a mystery of which there is no explanation, except that it is the grace of the Spirit of God. Admit that this grace is conveyed in any given case through the channel of Baptism to the believing adult, and you admit a mystery, which the presence and active exercise of his moral and intellectual powers do not in the least explain. Admit that this grace is conveyed in any given case through the channel of Baptism to the infant incapable of believing, and you admit a mystery too, but one not more mysterious than the former, and not more difficult to explain, from the absence or incapacity of his moral and intellectual faculties. In one word, the efficacy of infant Baptism, whatever that may be shown from Scripture to be, is not more mysterious than the sacramental virtue ascribed to adult Baptism.

Bearing in mind these preliminary remarks, what, I ask, are the effects of Baptism in so far as regards infants baptized? I do not pause at present in order to examine into the nature and benefit of the ordinance in so far as regards parents, who, in the exercise of a parent's right to represent their unconscious children, claim the administration of the ordinance for their offspring. In acting as the substitute for the infant, who cannot act for itself, in the solemn federal transaction between it and Christ,—in becoming a party in its name to the covenant made between the baptized infant and its Saviour through the ordinance,—the parent comes under a very great and solemn obligation on behalf of the child, thus pledged and given to the Redeemer through the parent's deed and not its own. But passing by this, let us confine our attention to the case of the infant, and proceed to inquire what are the benefits and efficacy of Baptism to the infant participators in the ordinance? In the case of adults, we know that Baptism is fitted and designed not to confer faith, but rather to confirm it,—not to originate grace, but to increase it,—not to effect that inward change of regeneration by which we are numbered with the children of God, or that outward change of justification by which we are accepted of Him, but to seal these blessings before bestowed. With adults, Baptism is not regeneration or justification, but the seal of both to the regenerated and justified man. And in the case of infants, the Sacrament cannot be regarded as accomplishing *without their faith*, what in the case of adults *with their faith*, it fails to accomplish. In other words, infant Baptism is not infant regeneration or justification, any more than in the instance of adults. The Baptism with water to a child is not the same thing as the birth by the Spirit. It is not a supernatural charm. It is not a magic spell to confer the washing of regeneration and the renewal of the Holy Ghost. Sacraments in the case of infants, as in the case of adults, have no mysterious and supernatural power of their own to impart, by the bare administration of them, spiritual life. Let us endeavour to understand what *are* the effects of Baptism in the case of infants.

I. Baptism, in the case of all infants baptized, gives to them an interest in the Church of Christ, as its members.

Circumcision gave to infants in other days a place in the ancient Church as its members; and they grew up within its pale entitled to all its outward privileges and rights, needing no other admission in after life. And what circumcision did during the time when it was in force, that Baptism does now in regard to infants baptized. It constitutes the door of admission into that visible Church of God on earth of which the parent himself is a member; and the baptized one grows up within the pale of its distinctive communion, needing no other admission, marked off at least outwardly from a world that has no interest in God, and having a right to the enjoyment of privileges which, as an outward provision for His own in this earth, God has given to them and not to the world. And this of itself is no small privilege, outward and temporal though it be, and not inward and spiritual. That outward provision of the means of grace, which has been given to the visible Church in this world for its establishment and benefit, is always represented in Scripture as a gift of Christ to His people, not to be undervalued or despised because it comes short, in those who enjoy it, of a saving blessing, but rather to be accounted exceeding great and precious. It is a gift of Christ to His Church which is of such worth and moment that the giving of it is spoken of in the Word of God as one of the great purposes for which the Saviour ascended up on high. " When He ascended up on high," says the Apostle Paul in his Epistle to the Ephesians,—" when He ascended up on high, He led captivity captive, and gave gifts unto men. And He gave some, apostles; and some, prophets; and some, evangelists; and some, pastors and teachers; for the perfecting of the saints, for the work of the ministry, for the edifying of the body of Christ." [1] That outward provision of ordinances and means of grace for the visible Church, the bestowment of which is thus represented as one of the grand objects for which Christ left this world and ascended to the Father, must be to that Church of no ordinary importance and value. It is a right to this provision of outward ordinances and means of grace which the baptized infant receives, when by his Baptism he becomes formally a member of the visible Church; and growing up in the use and enjoyment of them, the benefit to him, although short of a saving benefit, is beyond all price. Baptism as the sign of membership and the passport to the infant into the sanctuary of the visible Church, does not bestow the saving blessing, but brings him in after life into contact with the blessing; it does not constitute him a member of the kingdom of heaven, but it brings him to the very door, and bids him there knock and it shall be opened unto him.

II. Baptism, in the case of all infants baptized, gives them a right of property in the covenant of grace; which may in after

[1] Eph. iv. 9, 11, 12.

life, by means of their personal faith, be supplemented by a right of possession.

In regard to this matter, I would have recourse again to a distinction, which in other discussions we have found it necessary to adopt, and which has more than once helped us to clear our way to a right understanding of the question in debate. A man may have a right of property in an estate, and yet a stranger may be in possession of it; and he may require to add to his right of property a right of possession, acquired by making good the former in a court of law, before the stranger is extruded, and he himself introduced into the enjoyment of the inheritance. Now, to apply this distinction to the case in hand, a right of property in the blessings of the covenant of grace is conferred by the gift and promise of God, made over to every man who hears the Gospel message addressed to him. "And this is the record, that God has given to us eternal life, and this life is in His Son."[1] This right of property in the blessings of the covenant of grace, belonging to every man, is written down in these words. The charter which every man has, bearing in it inscribed his right of property to these blessings, is the revealed Word of God. This is the first and superior title. But in itself it is incomplete, and inadequate to put him into the personal possession of his heritage. It requires to be supplemented by another title, before he can actually enjoy the salvation so made over to him by right of property, and certified by God's word and promise. To his right of property there must be added a right of possession; and this latter is obtained by means of his own personal act of faith, appropriating to himself the salvation before made over to him. The Word of God addressed to him, giving him a right of property in the blessings of the covenant, and his faith receiving that Word, giving him a right of possession, complete the full and perfect title to the blessing; and both together admit him to the enjoyment of it. There are many, who have the right of property in the covenant of grace, who never complete their title by seeking for themselves a right of possession in it. The Word of God giving the one, is not supplemented by the faith in that Word which would confer the other; and hence they are never put in actual possession of the salvation of which they are invited to partake.

[1] 1 John v. 11.

Now, what the Word of God addressed to the intelligent and responsible adult is, that Baptism is when administered to the unconscious and irresponsible infant. The word of God's promise, giving a right of property in His covenant to all who hear it, cannot penetrate the silent ear, nor reach the unconscious spirit of the little child. That word cannot convey to its mind the glad tidings of its covenant right to God's grace. But is it therefore denied that right, which adults have by the hearing of the ear and the perception of the understanding, in connection with the word of promise addressed to them? Not so. If the outward word that speaks the promise of God cannot pierce to its dormant spirit,—sleeping in the germ of its moral and intellectual being, —the outward sign, that represents the promises of God, can be impressed upon it, giving to the unconscious infant, as the word gives to the intelligent adult, a right of property in the blessing of the covenant. And that is much. The infant, sprinkled with the water of that Baptism which is a sign of the covenant, has— even as the adult addressed with the word of the covenant has— a right of property in the blessings which the covenant contains ; and in after life he may, by his own personal act, supplement his right of property by a right of possession obtained through faith. When the period of infancy is passed and he is a child no longer, he bears about with him, in virtue of his Baptism, a right of property in the promise of his God ; and laying his hand upon that right, and pleading it with God in faith, he may add to it the right of possession, and so enter into the full enjoyment of the salvation that he requires for his soul. The written or preached Word cannot speak to the mute and insensible infant, as it speaks to the hearing ear and understanding mind of the adult, making over to him in conscious possession a right of property in the blessings of the everlasting covenant. But the little one is not thereby shut out from all interest in the covenant. The outward sign suited to his state of infancy, the outward mark impressed upon his outward person, when the significant Word were in vain addressed to his ear, have been given by God in gracious condescension to supply to him the want of that Word heard and understood. By the act of Baptism, suited and appropriate to his wholly sensitive condition of being and life, his name is put into the covenant with his God. And after years may witness the infant,—then an infant no more,—reading in faith his name there, and with the charter of his right in his hand making good his right, not of property merely, but of personal possession in all the blessings which are written in it.

Baptism, then, in the case of all baptized infants, gives them a right of property in the covenant of grace; which may in after life, by means of their personal faith, be supplemented by a right of possession, so that they shall enter into the full enjoyment of all the blessings of the covenant. The benefits of Baptism in the case of infants are not fully experienced by them until in after years they add to Baptism their personal faith, thereby really making out a complete title, not only to the property, but also to the possession of salvation. In this respect there is an obvious distinction between the Baptism of infants and the Baptism of adults. Infants are not capable of faith and repentance; and Baptism can be to infants no seal of the blessings which these stand connected with, at the time of its administration. But it may become a seal of such blessings afterwards, when the child has grown to years of intelligence, and has superinduced upon his Baptism a personal act of faith, and thereby become possessed of the salvation which he had not before. In such a case, he can look back upon his Baptism with water, administered in the days of his unconscious infancy; and through the faith that he has subsequently received, that Baptism which his own memory cannot recall, and to which his own consciousness at the time was a stranger, becomes to him a seal of his now found salvation. In adults it is otherwise; and the difference is appropriate to their condition as adults. Baptism to the believing adult is a seal at the moment of his interest in the covenant of grace; a sensible attestation of the blessings of justification and regeneration, of which at the time he is in possession, through the exercise of his faith contemporaneously with his Baptism. In the case of the adult, Baptism is a *present* seal in connection with the faith which he presently has. In the case of the infant, it is a *prospective* seal in connection with the faith which he has not at the moment, but which he may have afterwards. The full enjoyment of the benefits of the ordinance the adult experiences at the moment of its administration, in virtue of the faith which at the moment makes him a partaker in the blessings of the covenant. The full enjoyment of the benefits of the ordinance the infant cannot experience at the moment of its administration, in virtue of his incapacity of faith; but it may be experienced afterwards, when, in consequence of his newly formed faith in Christ, he too is made partaker of the covenant, and can look back in believing confidence on his former Baptism as a seal. "The efficacy of Baptism," says the Confession of Faith, "is not tied to that moment of time wherein it is administered; yet notwithstanding, by the right use of this ordinance, the grace promised is not only offered, but really exhibited and conferred by the Holy Ghost, to such (whether of age or infants) as that grace belongeth unto, according to the counsel of God's own will in His appointed time." [1]

III. There seems to be reason for inferring that, in the case of infants regenerated in infancy, Baptism is ordinarily connected with that regeneration.

To all infants without exception, Baptism, as we have already asserted, gives an interest in the Church of Christ as its members. To all infants without exception, Baptism, as we have also already asserted, gives a right of property in the covenant of grace, which may, by their personal faith in after life, be completed by a right of possession, so that they shall enter on the full enjoyment of all the blessings sealed to them by their previous Baptism. And beyond these two positions, in so far as infants are concerned, it is perhaps hazardous to go, in the absence of any very explicit Scripture evidence; and certainly, in going further, it were the reverse of wisdom to dogmatize. But I think that there is some reason to add to these positions the third one, which I have just announced, namely, that in the case of infants regenerated in infancy, Baptism is ordinarily connected with such regeneration. I would limit myself to the case of baptized infants regenerated in infancy,—a class of course to be distinguished broadly from baptized infants who never at any time in their lives experience a saving change; and also to be distinguished from baptized infants who experience that change, not in infancy, but in maturer years. There are these three cases, plainly to be dis-

---

[1] Conf. chap. xxviii. 6. Williams, *Antipæd. Exam.* vol. i. pp. 208–214, 220–224. Goode, *Doct. of the Church of Engl. as to the Effects of Baptism in the case of Infants*, 2d ed. pp. 9–26, 143–162, etc. [Goode, *Vind. of Defence of the XXXIX Articles*, etc., in reply to the Bishop of Exeter, 2d ed. pp. 19–21. *Letter to the Bishop of Exeter*, Lond. 1850, pp. 11, 23–44, 72–78. *Review of Sir H. J. Fust's Judgment in the Gorham Case*, Lond. 1850, pp. 23–31, 34.]

tinguished from one another. There are, *first,* those infants baptized with an outward Baptism who never at any period come to know a saving change of state or nature. To such Baptism may be an ordinance giving them a place in the visible Church, and giving them also a right of property in the covenant of grace, never completed by a right of possession, and therefore given to them in vain ; but it can be nothing more. There are, *secondly,* those infants baptized with water in infancy, but not regenerated in infancy by the Spirit of God, whose saving change of state and nature is experienced by them in after life. To such Baptism is an ordinance giving them a place in the visible Church, and giving them also a right of property in the covenant, at the moment of its administration ; and in after years, when born again by the Spirit through faith, Baptism becomes to them, in addition, the seal, as it had previously been the sign, of the covenant,—their right of property having been completed by the right of possession, and the Sacrament, although long past, having become in consequence a present grace to their souls. But there are, *thirdly,* those infants baptized with water in infancy and also regenerated in infancy ; and with regard to them I think there is reason to believe that this Baptism with water stands connected ordinarily with the Baptism of the Spirit.

That many an infant is sanctified and called by God even from its mother's womb, and undergoes, while yet incapable of faith or repentance, that blessed change of nature which is wrought by the Spirit of God, there can be no reason to doubt. There are multitudes born into this world who die ere their infancy is past,—who open their unconscious eyes upon the light only to shut them again ere they have gazed their fill,—and who, in the brief moment of their earthly being, know nothing of life save the sorrow which marks both its beginning and its close. And with regard to such infants dying in infancy, there is a blessed hope, which the Scriptures give us to entertain, that they are not lost but saved,—that they suffer, and sorrow, and die here from their interest in Adam's sin, but that, not knowing sin by their own personal act or thought, they are redeemed through their interest in Christ's righteousness.[1] But saved though infants dying in infancy may be, yet there is no exemp-

---

[1] [Du kamst, du giengst mit leiser Spur,
  Ein flücht'ger Gast im Erdenland ;

tion, even in their case, from the universal law of God's spiritual dispensation towards men, that "except a man be born again, he cannot see the kingdom of God." Within the brief hour of an infant's life, and ere the unconscious babe passes through the avenue of death into the Divine presence, must that mighty change of regeneration be undergone, which none but the Spirit of God can work; and among the rudiments of its intellectual and moral life, sleeping in the germ, there must be planted the seed of that higher life, which in heaven is destined to expand and endure through all eternity. And where, in the brief history of the young life and early death of these baptized little ones, shall we say that this mysterious work is wrought? At what moment, rather than another, is this regeneration by the Spirit accomplished? We dare not limit the free Spirit of God. The beginning of the life that comes from Him may be contemporaneous with the commencement of natural life in the infant, or it may be contemporaneous with its close. The Spirit of God is *free* to do His own work at His own time. But in the appointment of an ordinance to signify and represent that very work,—in the command to administer that ordinance as a sign to the little infant during the brief hour of its earthly life and ere it passes into eternity, there does seem to me some ground to believe that in such a case, of infants regenerated in infancy, the sign is meant to be connected with the thing signified,—that the moment of its Baptism is the appointed moment of its regeneration too,—and that, ordinarily, its birth by water and its birth by the Spirit of God are bound in one. It is Baptism which gives the baptized infant a right of property in the blessings of the covenant of grace; and when the infant is placed,—not from its own fault,—in such circumstances as to bar the possibility of its completing its title to those blessings by seeking through its personal faith a right of possession in them also, then it is consistent with the analogy of God's appointments in other departments of His Church, that in such extraordinary cases the absence of a right of possession should not exclude from the blessings, but that the right of property alone should avail to secure them ; or in other words, that in the case of infants regenerated and dying

Woher ? Wohin ? wir wissen nur :
Aus Gottes Hand in Gottes Hand.
—Uhland, *Auf den Tod eines Kindes.*]

in infancy, their Baptism should coincide with their regeneration.[1]

I do not wish to speak dogmatically on such a question as this, when Scripture has given us so little light to enable us to read the truth with certainty. But in the particular case of infants regenerated in infancy, there does seem to be some reason to believe, that the washing with water in virtue of God's own appointment stands ordinarily connected with the renewing of nature by God's own Spirit. In the instance of believing adults, regeneration is linked inseparably with *the Word believed.* In connection with the *Word,*—although the Spirit of God is free to work without it,—He does His mysterious work of regeneration upon the adult's nature. But that Word cannot profit the little infant who is to die ere his eyes can look upon it. The Spirit of God cannot, therefore, do His gracious work of spiritual renewal and cleansing on the unconscious babe in connection with the Word believed. But there is another ordinance adapted to the infant nature, which needs to be regenerated ere it passes into another state of being. There is another ordinance, not the Word, which we are commanded to administer to the babe, incapable of receiving or profiting by the Word. There is the Baptism with water, expressive of that very regeneration which, before the little one shall pass from us to eternity, its unconscious nature must undergo. And when the infant carries with it to the tomb the sign of the covenant, administered in faith, shall we not say that with the sign, and mysteriously linked to it, there was also the thing that was signified ; and that in such a case of a dying babe regenerated in infancy, the laver of Baptism was the laver of regeneration too ? In the sign of the covenant thus

---

[1] [" Quos electione suâ dignatus est Dominus, si, accepto regenerationis signo, præsenti vitâ ante demigrent quam adoleverint, eos virtute sui Spiritûs nobis incomprehensâ renovat, quo modo expedire solus Ipse providet." " Quoniam autem valde absurdum fore putant si infantibus tribuatur ulla cognitio Dei, quos boni et mali intelligentiâ Moses (Deut. i. 39) privat: respondeant quæso mihi, quid periculi sit si aliquam Ejus gratiæ partem nunc accipere dicantur cujus plenâ largitate paulo post perfruentur? Nam si vitæ plenitudo perfectâ Dei cognitione constat, quum eorum nonnulli, quos primâ statim infantiâ hinc mors abripit, in vitam æternam transeant, ad contemplandam certe Dei faciem præsentissimam recipiuntur. Quos ergo pleno lucis Suæ fulgore illustraturus est Dominus, cur non iis quoque in præsens, si ita libuerit, exigua scintilla irradiaret : præsertim si non ante exuit ipsos ignorantiâ quam eripit ex carnis ergastulo ? "—Calvin, *Inst.* lib. iv. cap. xvi. 19, 21. Turrettin, *Op.* loc. xix. qu. xx. 15-20. Witsius, *Miscell. Sacr.* tom. ii. Exercit. xix. 1.]

administered to the child, and linked, as we believe, in such a case to a new and spiritual life, there is a ground of hope and consolation to a bereaved but Christian parent beyond all price. There is a joy at its birth, which none but a mother can feel, when it is said unto her that a man-child is born into the world ; and there is a bitter sorrow at its early death, which none but a mother can know, when she is called upon to resign the little one whom she brought forth in sorrow, and to give it to the dust in sorrow deeper still. And when a Christian mother has been called upon thus to weep at the open grave of many of her infants, ere it close in peace upon herself, it is an unspeakable consolation for her to know, that the little one, whom she took from off her bosom to lay in the tomb, was indeed signed with the sign of a Christian Baptism ; and that in its case the Baptism with water and the Baptism with the Spirit were bound up in one.

> " Oh when a mother meets on high
> The babe she lost in infancy,
> Hath she not then for pains and fears,
> The day of woe, the watchful night,
> For all her sorrows, all her tears,
> An over-payment of delight? "[1]

SECTION VI.—THE MODES OF BAPTISM.

Before passing altogether from the subject of Baptism, it may be desirable briefly to consider the mode or modes in which the ordinance may lawfully be administered. It may seem, indeed, at first sight, a question of no great importance whether we baptize by sprinkling or by immersion,—the former being the method adopted by almost all Protestant Churches and by Western Christendom generally, the latter prevailing to a great extent in the early centuries, and still practised largely in the East. The almost unanimous opinion of orthodox theologians has always been, that Baptism in the name of the Trinity was equally valid in whichever of the two ways referred to it was administered. The position, however, taken up in our own day by many of the advocates of Baptism by immersion has given to the question an importance not properly belonging to it.[2]   The Evangelical

---

[1] Southey, *Curse of Kehama.*
[2] [" How abundant and copious in the faculty of lying and inventing of errors the spirit of Anabaptism was of old,—how much superior in an ex-

Baptists in America, for example,—a numerous and energetic denomination,—deny the validity of Baptism by sprinkling, and declare that all persons thus baptized are living in open sin, should not be regarded as members of the Church of Christ, nor be admitted to the Lord's table. Further, they aver that the English authorized version of the Scriptures is false and unfaithful on the subject of Baptism,—purposely so, many of them add. They have issued accordingly a translation of their own with the requisite changes, and consider,—to use the words of a resolution of the Baptist American and Foreign Bible Society,—" That the nations of the earth must now look to the Baptist denomination *alone* for faithful translations of the Word of God."[1]

Our translators, in point of fact, seeing that they had to frame their version of the Bible in the very heat of a controversy about Baptism, strove carefully to stand neutral on the subject. They simply gave the Greek word an English dress; instead of $\beta \alpha \pi \tau \iota \zeta \omega$ and $\beta \alpha \pi \tau \iota \sigma \mu \alpha$, they wrote " baptize" and " baptism," thereby deciding nothing either way.

The real question at issue has been very clearly stated by President Beecher, to whose valuable work on the Mode of Baptism I would refer you for an exceedingly able and exhaustive discussion of this whole subject. " The case," he says, " is this :

tremely malignant fruitfulness he hath been to any evil spirit that ever appeared in the Christian Church before him,—we have, I hope, demonstrated in our first two chapters (which contain a formidable catalogue of the errors and heresies prompted by the said spirit). That the younger Anabaptists who now trouble the Church of England are nothing inferior to their fathers in the art of erring, being sure, wherever they are ashamed of any one of their predecessors' tenets, to give us two much worse in the place thereof, we have endeavoured to make appear in our third and fourth chapters. Among the new inventions of the late Anabaptists, there is none which with greater animosity they set on foot than the necessity of dipping over head and ears— than the nullity of affusion and sprinkling in the administration of Baptism. Among the old Anabaptists, or these over sea to this day, so far as I can learn, by their writs, or any relation that has yet come to my ears, the question of dipping and sprinkling came never upon the table. . . . The question about the necessity of dipping seems to be taken up only the other year by the Anabaptists in England, as a point which alone, as they conceive, is able to carry their desire of exterminating infant Baptism ; for they know that parents upon no consideration will be content to hazard the life of their tender infants by plunging them over head and ears in a cold river. Let us, therefore, consider if this sparkle of new light have any derivation from the lamp of the Sanctuary, or the Sun of righteousness,—if it be according to scriptural truth, or any good reason."—Baillie, *Anabaptism*, Lond. 1647, p. 163.]

[1] Beecher, *Baptism with ref. to its Import and Modes*, New York 1849, pp. 117–120.

Christ has enjoined the performance of a duty in the command to baptize. What is the duty enjoined? or, in other words, What does the word '*baptize*,' in which the command is given, mean? One of two things must be true: Either it is, as to mode, *generic*, denoting merely the production of an effect (as purity), so that the command may be fulfilled in many ways; or it is so *specific*, denoting a definite mode, that it can be fulfilled in but one. To illustrate by an analogous case, Christ said: 'Go, teach all nations.' Here the word *go* is so generic as to include all modes of going which any one may choose to adopt. If a man walks, or runs, or rides, or sails, he equally fulfils the command. On the other hand, some king or ruler, for particular reasons, might command motion by a word entirely specific, as, for example, that certain mourners should *walk* in a funeral procession. Now it is plain that such a command could not be fulfilled by riding or by running, for, though these are modes of going, they are not modes of walking, and the command is not to go in general, but specifically to walk. . . . So likewise, when Christ said, '*baptize*,' He either used a word which had a generic sense, denoting the production of an effect, in any mode, such as 'purify,' 'cleanse;' or a specific sense, denoting a particular mode, such as 'immerse,' 'sprinkle,' 'pour.'"[1]

Now the scriptural meaning of the term βαπτίζω, I believe there is abundant evidence to show, is generic and not specific; it denotes the production of an effect which can be brought about equally well in more ways than one. The adherents of Baptist views, on the other hand, consider that the word is so specific in its signification as to fix down the lawful performance of the duty enjoined to one method only; they hold that " in Baptism the mode is the ordinance; and if the mode is altered, the ordinance is abolished."[2]

The word βάπτω, from which βαπτίζω is derived, was long maintained by Dr. Gale and other advocates of the Baptist theory to have one meaning, and only one, alike in classic, Hellenistic, and ecclesiastical Greek. It meant, they held, to immerse or dip; and it never meant anything else. This view, however, was with good reason abandoned by Dr. Carson, probably the ablest defender of the Baptist theory in our own days. It is now very

[1] Beecher, p. 3.
[2] *Prim. Church Magazine*, Oct. 1844, quoted by Wilson, *Inf. Bapt.* p. 4.

generally admitted by our opponents on this question that βαπτω has at least two meanings; *first*, to immerse, and *second*, to dye or colour. The same is true of the Latin "tingo," and various similar words in other languages. It will not therefore be thought improbable that the derivative βαπτιζω should also have a primary and a secondary meaning. In point of fact, we find that, especially in later Greek, while often denoting to immerse or overwhelm, it means also, in many cases, to wash, sprinkle, cleanse.[1] It is natural, however, to suppose that when transferred from common to ecclesiastical use, and applied in Scripture to a religious ordinance which is confessed by all parties to symbolize regeneration or spiritual purification, the meaning of the word might undergo some change. The question therefore comes to be, What is the *usus loquendi* of the New Testament as regards the term βαπτιζω? Looking, then, to all the passages in which the word occurs, it becomes plain, I think, that the only meaning which will carry us consistently through *all* of them is that of purification or cleansing. It is perfectly clear that whatever signification of the word we adopt, we must adhere to it throughout. It is quite true that βαπτιζω may have, and has, more meanings than one in ordinary Greek; but that is when it is applied to different things, and used under different circumstances. It can have but one meaning when used with respect to one definite appointment or rite, and under the same circumstances. This test can be easily applied to the various interpretations of the word in question. Take, for example, the first passage in the New Testament in which the term baptize occurs, the third chapter of Matthew, and substitute for it first the rendering which I have adopted, and then that of our Baptist brethren. It is not difficult, I think, to see which of the two best suits the whole scope of the passage: "Then went out unto John Jerusalem, and all Judæa, and all the region round about Jordan, and were purified (immersed, or plunged) of him in Jordan, confessing their sins. But when he saw many of the Pharisees and Sadducees come to his purification (immersion, or plunging), he said, . . . I indeed purify (immerse or plunge) you with water unto repentance: but He that cometh after me is mightier than I, whose shoes I am not worthy to bear: He shall purify (immerse or plunge) you with the Holy Ghost, and with fire. . . . Then cometh

[1] Beecher, 40-47, 158–176, 185–202, etc.

Jesus from Galilee to Jordan unto John, to be purified (immersed or plunged) of him. But John forbade Him, saying, I have need to be purified (immersed or plunged) of Thee, and comest Thou to me? And Jesus answering said unto him, Suffer it to be so now: for thus it becometh us to fulfil all righteousness."[1]

That such a transition of meaning should have taken place in the case of the word βαπτίζω, appears very natural when we consider the historical circumstances connected with it. It is repeatedly used in the Septuagint, and in the works of Jewish writers who employed the Hellenistic or Alexandrian dialect, to denote the ceremonial immersions, washings, and sprinklings with water, blood, or ashes, common among the Jews. These "divers baptisms," as the Apostle Paul calls them,[2] were all practised for the sake of purification, legal or ceremonial. The two ideas, of " baptizing " and of "purifying," were therefore constantly associated in the minds of the Jewish people; and nothing seems more natural than that in the course of time the one should pass into the other, and the words come to be used as synonymous. To recur to the history of the kindred word already alluded to: Men dipped objects in liquid in order to impart colour to them; and βάπτω came to signify " to dye." The Jews immersed, or washed, or sprinkled, in order to attain purity; and so βαπτίζω came to mean "to purify." In Jewish ecclesiastical language, considerably before our Lord's time, βαπτίζω seems to have dropped all reference to mode, and to have become a general term for purifying, practically equivalent to καθαρίζω. A remarkable confirmation of this may be found in the third chapter of John. We are there told that a dispute had arisen between the disciples of John the Baptist and a Jew (as the true reading seems to be; not Jews as in the A. V.) "about purifying" (περὶ καθαρισμοῦ). Now this dispute, as is shown by the context, was simply about the respective Baptisms of John and of Christ. The followers of the former were jealous on their master's behalf of the seemingly rival claims of our Lord, which had apparently been urged against them by this Jew. " They came unto John, and said, Rabbi, He that was with thee beyond Jordan, to whom thou barest witness, behold, the same baptizeth, and all men come unto Him."[3] The " question about purifying " was just a " ques-

[1] Matt. iii. 5-15.   [2] Heb. ix. 10, διαφοροι βαπτισμοι.
[3] John iii. 23-26.

tion about baptizing;" and the Evangelist uses the words inter-changeably, just because in the ecclesiastical language of his day the two meant the same thing.[1]

The evidence by which the position which I have laid down on this subject can be still further established and strengthened, is of a cumulative sort, and for the details of it I must refer you to such works as that by Dr. Beecher, already referred to.[2] With respect to the apostolic practice in this matter, I am disposed to agree with the author last named, that " it is not possible *decisively* to prove the mode used by the Apostles; for if going to rivers, going down to the water and up from it, etc., create a presumption in favour of immersion ; so does the Baptism of three thousand on the day of Pentecost in a city where water was scarce, and of the jailor (and his household) in a prison, create a presumption in favour of sprinkling. And if a possibility of immersion can be shown in the latter cases, so can a possibility of sprinkling or pouring be shown in the former. The command being to purify, and the facts being as stated, the decided probability is, that either sprinkling, pouring, or immersion, was allowed, and Chris-tian liberty was everywhere enjoyed. A tendency to formalism led to a misinterpretation of Paul in Rom. vi. 3, 4, and Col. ii. 12; and this gave the ascendency to immersion, which increased (in the postapostolic Church) until it became general, though it was not insisted on as absolutely essential on philological grounds."[3]

In conclusion, I remark, that many take up what appears to me a wrong ground on this question, in seeking first to prove that the word βαπτιζω, in the whole wide field in which it occurs, some-times means to immerse, sometimes to wash, sometimes to sprinkle or pour; and then drawing from that the inference that we may lawfully baptize in any of these ways. It may be perfectly true that in profane literature the word has several meanings, but it by no means follows from that fact that, when used ecclesiastically, and applied definitely to one thing, it has more meanings than one. As employed to denote a definite religious rite, the term *Baptism* must have but one definite signification. And whatever we hold that to be, we must adhere to it throughout, and in all cases in which the word occurs. The true meaning of Baptism in the New Testament I believe to be purification or cleansing.

[1] Beecher, pp. 22-25, 213 ff.   [2] Ibid. pp. 211-224, etc.   [3] Ibid. p. 114.

That purification may be effected either by sprinkling or by immersion, according to the dictates of Christian expediency. The command to baptize is a generic command, which may be carried out in either way with equal lawfulness.[1]

[1] Beecher, *Baptism with reference to its Import and Modes*, New York 1849. Williams, *Antipæd. Exam.* vol. ii. pp. 2-189. Wardlaw, *Dissert. on Inf. Baptism*, 3d ed. pp. 163-182. Wilson, *Inf. Baptism*, pp. 9-186. With respect to the evidence of the Fathers as to the matter of fact of infants being baptized in the early Church in postapostolic times, I may refer to Wall's *History of Inf. Baptism*, 3d ed., Lond. 1720, a very complete and reliable work ; Williams, vol. ii. pp. 200-228. Neander was the first theologian of any eminence to maintain, though not very confidently, that infant Baptism was a novelty of the third century. (*Hist.* Torrey's Transl., Edin. 1847, vol. i. pp. 424-429; *Planting of the Christian Church*, Ryland's Transl., Edin. 1842, vol. i. pp. 189-194.) He has been followed in this to some extent by Gieseler, by Hagenbach, and others in Germany ; and by some English Churchmen. What Neander chiefly builds upon to establish his view of the matter is the well-known statement of Tertullian, which has been usually held, and, I think, with good reason, to prove the very contrary. Tertullian,—speaking, be it observed, of the practice of the Church at the end of the second century and the very beginning of the third,—advises that with respect to several classes Baptism should be deferred : so of unmarried persons and widows; so in particular of infants. He urges this, not on the ground of its being unscriptural or a novelty, but on the ground of reason and expediency. " It would be *more useful* to delay." (Cunctatio Baptismi utilior est.) " Why does that innocent age hasten to the remission of sins ? Men act more prudently in worldly matters. Why should the Divine heritage be intrusted to those to whom we would not commit the keeping of their earthly goods ? " etc.—*De Baptismo*, cap. 18. It is surely very plain that we have here just a specimen of that tendency to exaggerated and unscriptural views of the Sacraments which so soon and so fatally prevailed in the Christian Church. When Baptism came to be regarded as a magic charm to wash away guilt whenever it was applied, the idea was a very natural one that the wisest course was to reserve it as long as possible. Hence the frequency of deathbed Baptisms, as in the case of Constantine ; and hence Tertullian's argument, that children in " the guiltless age" of infancy had less need of the ordinance than in after years.

CHAPTER III.

THE SACRAMENT OF THE LORD'S SUPPER.

SECTION I.—NATURE OF THE ORDINANCE.

CHRIST, as Head of His Church, has dealt out to it with a guarded hand merely outward and visible rites. In the provision which He has made for it there is enough in the way of outward and sensible ordinances for creatures made up of flesh as well as spirit to repose upon for the strengthening and confirmation of their faith; and yet not enough to convert their religion from a spiritual to a bodily service, and to transmute their faith into sight. There are but two ordinances, properly speaking, that link the Spirit with the flesh in the Christian Church; and lend the aid of a seen and sensible confirmation to an unseen and saving faith. There is one ordinance adapted to, and, it may be, specially designed for the case of infants, whose moral and intellectual life, still in the germ, lies hidden in a merely sensitive nature; and Baptism administered to the unconscious babe, whose ear cannot hear the word of salvation, becomes a visible and sensible token and seal impressed upon its flesh, of its interest in the covenant of its God. There is a second ordinance in a similar manner adapted for adults, in which an outward and sensible seal gives witness to their inward and unseen faith; and the Lord's Supper, preaching Christ by sign as well as word, is a fleshly witness, speaking to the flesh as well as to the spirit of the believer, of the blessings of the covenant of grace. There are these two, but no more than these two, outward and visible ordinances in the Church of Christ, like material buttresses, to strengthen and confirm a spiritual and immaterial faith,—the guarded and sparing acknowledgments of the fleshly nature, as well as the spiritual, which in the person of the Christian has shared in the sin, and shared also in the salvation from sin, which he knows.

We cannot doubt that a religion with these two, and neither more nor less than these two, outward rites is divinely proportioned and adapted to the need and benefit of our twofold nature, made up as it is of the fleshly and the spiritual, and both partners in the redemption, as they were formerly partners in the ruin, that belong to us. More than this in the way of the outward and sensible in the religion of Christ would have ministered all too strongly to the carnal and sensuous propensities of our nature, and would have tended towards a system which would have been " meat and drink," and not " righteousness, and peace, and joy in the Holy Ghost." Less than this in the way of outward and sensible ordinance would have left no room in the provision made in the Church for the adequate acknowledgment of our fleshly nature; and denied to our spiritual faith the benefit and support which it derives from some visible witness and confirmation of what it surely believes. Again, Baptism, as commonly administered to entrants into the Church, takes infeftment, so to speak, of our flesh when we enter into covenant with Christ, that not even the lower part of our being may be left without the attestation that He has redeemed it. The Lord's Supper, as administered from time to time to those who have been admitted into the Church before, renews this infeftment at intervals, and attests that the covenant by which we are Christ's still holds good both for the body and spirit which He has ransomed to Himself. The Sacrament of union to and the Sacrament of communion with Christ, tell that our very dust is precious in His sight, and has shared with the spirit in His glorious redemption. Other ordinances address themselves to the intellectual and moral nature exclusively, and speak of the care of Christ and the provision He has made for the growth and advancement of the spirit in all spiritual strength and life. The two ordinances of Baptism and the Lord's Supper, at different periods of our natural existence, and commonly in infancy and age, address themselves to both our outward and inward nature; and speak to us the testimony that both body and soul are cared for and redeemed by Christ, and that both in body and in soul we are His.

In formerly dealing with the case of Baptism as a sacramental ordinance, I endeavoured to ascertain its nature by an appeal to those marks or characteristics, in their application to Baptism, which we have found to define a Sacrament generally. Let us endeavour, by the same process, to make out the true nature and import of the Lord's Supper as a sacramental ordinance.

I. The first mark or characteristic of a Sacrament which we laid down is, that it be a Divine institute appointed by Christ for His Church. There is no religious party, whatever be their opinions in regard to the meaning of the ordinance, who do not hold the Divine appointment of the Lord's Supper as a permanent institution in the Christian Church, with the single exception of the Quakers. According to their view, the Lord's Supper, like Baptism, is to be regarded as a Jewish ordinance, and the practice of it in early times as an accommodation to Jewish prejudices and customs, but an ordinance really opposed in its nature to the spirituality of the Gospel dispensation, and not intended for continuance in the Gospel Church.

Now, in reference to this averment by the Quakers, it cannot be denied that, in the case of the Lord's Supper, as in the case of Baptism formerly noticed, our Lord adopted a Jewish practice or observance, and consecrated it as an ordinance in the Christian Church. The parts and ritual of the Supper are evidently derived from the observances connected with the passover as practised among the Jews. The Christian ordinance seems to be grafted upon the Jewish. We know from the Jewish accounts that we have of the passover service, that the master of the family or priest took unleavened bread, and broke it, and gave thanks to God, in much the same manner as we find it recorded of our Lord at the institution of the Supper. We know also from the same quarter, that there was one particular cup called "the cup of blessing," or of "thanksgiving," used at the paschal feast, of which the guests partook; and this was followed by the singing of psalms. These usages, connected with the Jewish passover, Christ adopted and accommodated to the ritual of that ordinance which we regard as the commemoration of His own death,—very much in the same manner as the washing with water employed in the Jewish baptisms or purifications was adopted and accommodated by Him to the other Sacrament which He established in the Christian Church.[1] All this must be conceded to the Quaker

[1] [Waterland, *Review of the Doctrine of the Eucharist*, Cambridge 1737, pp. 58–71.]

theory in regard to the origin of the Christian Sacrament of the Supper. But all this, so far from making the ordinance a Jewish one, or justifying the explanation given by Quakers of the apostolic practice of administering it, as a mere accommodation to Jewish customs or feelings, is very evidently calculated to demonstrate the reverse. The adoption of some parts of the paschal feast without the rest,—the eating bread and drinking wine as at the passover by Christians, without the slaying of the paschal lamb,—the observance of the practice at other times than once a year on the return of the anniversary of its first institution,—must, so far from being an accommodation or concession to Jewish feeling or prejudice on the part of the Apostles and first Christians, have been in reality a usage most repugnant to all the habits and prepossessions of the Israelites. The withdrawment of the outward ritual of the paschal service from the object of its original institution, and its destination to the purposes of a feast in commemoration of an event by which that service was abolished, were the very circumstances, above all others, calculated to make the ordinance not acceptable, but revolting, to Jewish feeling.

There is no truth, therefore, but the reverse, in the Quaker assumption, that the temporary continuance of the Lord's Supper in the Christian Church is to be accounted for on the theory of a concession to prejudices on the part of the Jewish converts. Add to this, that both in the statements of Scripture, and in the practice of apostolic men as recorded in Scripture, there is abundant evidence to prove that the Lord's Supper was no temporary ordinance, destined to pass away with the first merging of the Jewish into the Christian Church ; but, on the contrary, was intended to be an abiding appointment for the use of its members. The command of our Lord to the disciples at the moment of the institution of the ordinance, spoke of its standing and permanent observance : " This do in remembrance of me."[1] The connection intimated by the Apostle Paul, in his account of the Supper, between the keeping of it and the second coming of Christ, evinces his opinion of the perpetual duration of the ordinance : " As often as ye eat this bread, and drink this cup, ye do show forth the Lord's death *till He come*."[2] The practice in the primitive Church, while under inspired direction in regard to the Lord's

[1] Luke xxii. 19.   [2] 1 Cor. xi. 26.

Supper, taken in connection with the absence of the faintest indication that it was meant for no more than a temporary purpose, is decisive evidence of the same conclusion. In short, the nature of the ordinance, as a memorial of Christ until that memorial shall be no more required on earth, in consequence of His second appearing,—the command to Jew and Gentile alike to keep the feast,—the universal practice of the Church under apostolic guidance,—and the absence of any statement express or implied in regard to the temporary character of the ordinance,—very clearly and abundantly demonstrate that the Supper of our Lord was a Divine and permanent appointment for the Church.[1]

II. The next mark laid down by us as characteristic of sacramental ordinances, was, that they be sensible and outward signs of spiritual truths; and this mark applies to the ordinance of the Lord's Supper.

Simple and obvious although the idea be, that in the Lord's Supper we are commemorating, by appropriate and sensible images and actions, the grand spiritual truths characteristic of the Gospel, yet it is the omission or denial of this that has been the primary cause of numberless errors in regard to the nature of the ordinance. The Lord's Supper is not *merely* a commemoration; it is much more. But the fundamental idea which must be carried along with us in all our explanations of its nature and meaning is, that it is in the first instance a commemoration of the great truths connected with the death of Christ, as the sacrifice for the sins of His people. Nothing is easier, indeed, than to confound the sign with the thing signified; and nothing is more common in theological argument in reference to this matter. The nature and necessities of language lead us to attribute to the type what is only actually and literally true of the thing imaged or represented by the type; and in the frequent or common identification of the one with the other, we may be led not unnaturally to one or other extreme,—that of sinking the sign in the thing signified, or that of sinking the thing signified in the sign. The result is, either that we make the Sacrament to be nothing more than a sign, with no spiritual reality; or that we make it a mysterious spiritual reality, without being a sign at all. The identifying of the sign with the supernatural grace, and making them one and the same thing, must either lead to the Socinian notion that the Sacraments

[1] Halley, *The Sacraments*, Lond. 1844, vol. i. pp. 66–74, 86–92.

are nothing but symbols,—thereby evacuating the ordinance of all sacramental grace ; or must lead to the Romanist or semi-Romanist notion that they are charms embodying and conveying spiritual grace, without regard to the spiritual meaning realized and appropriated by the believer in the ordinance. Hence the necessity and importance of bringing out distinctly, and laying down broadly, the character which Sacraments possess as signs of spiritual truths.

In regard to the Lord's Supper, nothing can be more distinct or conclusive than the commemorative character which is impressed upon the original institution of the ordinance by our Lord. With regard to the bread, the commandment was : " Take, eat : this is my body broken for you : this do in remembrance of me." With regard to the second element in the ordinance—the cup—the appointment was no less explicit : " This is the New Testament in my blood : this do ye, as oft as ye drink it, in remembrance of me." [1]   And in entire accordance with these declarations of our Lord as to the grand object of the Supper as commemorative, we have the further statement by the Apostle Paul, received by immediate revelation, as to the nature of the institution : " For as often as ye eat this bread and drink this cup, ye do show forth the Lord's death till He come." In addition to all this, which very clearly exhibits the Sacrament of the Supper as in its first and most obvious character commemorative, we have the natural significance or pictorial meaning of the elements and actions in the ordinance.   A rite may be in its sole or primary character commemorative in consequence of arbitrary appointment, although it may have nothing in itself naturally representative of the event commemorated. But this is not the case with the ordinance of the Communion Table. Over and above its positive institution in remembrance of the death and crucifixion of our Lord, there is a pictorial significance in the actions and elements of the Sacrament, fitted to keep constantly in view the grand and essential idea of the rite, as a rite of commemoration.   The broken bread representing the broken and crucified body,—the wine poured out, the shed blood,—the eating and drinking of them, the participation in Christ's blessings to nourish the soul and make it glad,— the " one bread " and " one cup," the communion of Christ with His people, and of them with each other,[2]—all these are no

---

[1] Luke xxii. 19 ; 1 Cor. xi. 22-26.   [2] 1 Cor. x. 17.

dumb or dark signs, but speaking and expressive of what it is intended to commemorate. This obvious characteristic of a sacramental ordinance, then, is most clearly seen in the Lord's Supper, that it is an outward and sensible sign of an inward and spiritual truth. It is the primary idea of the institution, never to be forgotten without infinite damage done to our understanding of its meaning, that, both naturally and by express Divine appointment, it is a symbolical and commemorative observance.[1]

That the Sacrament of the Lord's Supper is an outward and sensible sign expressive of the grand and central truths connected with His death and sacrifice, is professedly held by all parties who hold that it is a Christian ordinance at all, and consider it to be binding upon Christians. And yet, notwithstanding of this professed and apparent unanimity upon the point, there is one religious denomination whose principles amount to a denial of this simple truth ; and who virtually and really make the Lord's Supper to be not a sign, and not a commemorative ordinance at all,—thereby denying to it the proper character of a Sacrament. I allude to the Church of Rome. I do not mean to enter upon a consideration of the doctrine of that Church with regard to the Lord's Supper at present—for I intend to take up that subject afterwards,—but it may be not unsuitable or unimportant, meanwhile, to remark, that many of the errors of the Church of Rome in regard to this Sacrament are to be traced back to the neglect or denial of the simple but fundamental truth, that in its primary and essential character the Lord's Supper is a commemorative ordinance,—a remembrance of a sacrifice, and not a sacrifice itself,—a memorial of the great atonement and offering up of Christ on the Cross, and not a repetition of that atonement. By the doctrine of transubstantiation held by the Church of Rome, the elements of bread and wine are asserted to be changed into the actual body and blood of Christ, the Son of God ; so that the use of these elements in the Sacrament is not to represent, but to repeat or continue the offering once made for sinners upon the Cross. The sign is identified with the thing signified ; the symbol, instead of remaining a symbol, becomes one and the same with what was symbolized ; the image and the reality are not two separate and independent things, but are confounded together. This is the unavoidable consequence of the doctrine of transub-

1 [Waterland, *Review of the Doctrine of the Eucharist*, pp. 71–112.]

stantiation held in regard to the communion elements. The bread in the ordinance ceases to be the sensible sign of the Lord's body, and actually becomes that body ; the wine in the cup ceases to be the representation symbolically of the blood of the Lord, and is transmuted into that very blood. There is no separating idea which continues to divide the symbol from the reality represented. The two are lost in one. The grand and fundamental characteristic of a Sacrament—that it is the outward and sensible sign of an inward and spiritual truth—is utterly forgotten or denied ; and the consequence is the subversion of every idea essential to a Sacrament. While professedly, in some sort of way not easily understood, the Church of Rome holds that the Lord's Supper is a commemorative Sacrament,[1] it in reality does away with the fundamental characteristic of a Sacrament as a sensible sign of spiritual truth.[2]

III. The third mark laid down by us as characteristic of sacramental ordinances, is, that they are the seals of a federal transaction between the believer and Christ through means of the ordinance ; and this mark is applicable to the Lord's Supper.

There are not a few who rest contented with the position already laid down in regard to the Lord's Supper, and restrict themselves to the view which makes it a sensible sign of spiritual truth. At the date of the Reformation the subject of the Lord's Supper was very keenly canvassed amongst the Protestant Churches ; and the Sacramentarian controversy, or the dispute as to the true meaning and nature of the Lord's Supper, went further than any other to divide the opinions of the early Reformers.[3] While Luther held views approximating to those of the Church of Rome on this subject, although denying the doctrine of transubstantiation, there was another party among the first Reformers, especially in Switzerland, headed by Zwingli, who advocated principles differing very widely from those of Luther. Zwingli, the chief founder of the Protestant Churches in Switzerland, and the predecessor of Calvin in the Swiss Reformation, is not uncommonly regarded as the originator of those views of the Lord's Supper which represent it as a symbolical

---

[1] *Concil. Trident. Canones et Decreta,* Sess. xiii. cap. ii. Sess. xxii. cap. i.

[2] [Bruce, *Sermons on the Sacraments,* Wodrow Soc. ed. p. 84 f.]

[3] Beveridge, Pref. to vol. ii. of Calvin's *Tracts,* Edin. 1849, pp. xviii.-xxx. [Hospinian, *Historia Sacramentaria,* Tiguri 1602, Pars ii. pp. 5-18, etc.]

action commemorative of the death of Christ, and as nothing more than this. There seems to be good ground to question this opinion, and to doubt whether Zwingli ever really meant to deny that the Lord's Supper is a seal, as well as a sign of spiritual grace,—the outward voucher as well as representation of a spiritual and federal transaction between the believer and Christ through means of the ordinance. Under the strong reaction then felt from the views of the Lord's Supper entertained by the Church of Rome, which virtually set aside and denied the symbolical character of the ordinance, and superseded the outward sign by the thing signified, Zwingli and others felt that the true source of the doctrine of transubstantiation was the denial of the primary character of the ordinance as a commemorative sign, and the making the symbol give place to the reality symbolized under it. In other words, Zwingli and his associates in Switzerland held that the root of the evil lay in denying that the bread and wine in the Lord's Supper were signs, and constituting them the thing signified,—the very body and blood of the Lord. And in bringing out this principle as against the dogma of transubstantiation, they were led in their argument to speak somewhat unguardedly, as if, while Scripture represented the Sacrament as symbolical, it did not represent it as anything more than symbolical. Notwithstanding the violent controversy which the opinions of Zwingli and his followers excited, and the opposition they encountered from Luther and others of the German section of the Reformation, it is very doubtful indeed whether their opinion really excluded or denied the idea of a seal of a federal transaction, as well as a sign, as really belonging to the character of the Lord's Supper.[1] However this may be, it was reserved for the successor of Zwingli, as the leader in the Swiss Reformation, to bring out from Scripture, and to establish on its true foundation, the proper notion of the Lord's Supper as more generally entertained by Protestant Churches since his time; and it is not the least of the many debts due by the Church to the illustrious Calvin, that we owe to him the first full and accurate development and decided maintenance of the true doctrine of the ordinance, as neither a sign alone, nor yet the thing signified alone, —as neither an empty symbol, nor yet the transubstantiated body

[1] Cunningham, *Works*, vol. i. pp. 225-231. [Nitzsch, *prot. Beant.* Hamburg 1835, pp. 162-166.]

and blood of Christ,—but as a sign and, at the same time, a seal
of spiritual and covenant blessings, made over in the ordinance
to the believer. The doctrine of the Sacrament of the Lord's
Supper as a sign or symbol, and nothing more, has become the
characteristic system of the Socinian party. More recently still,
it has become the theory of not a few of the Independent body in
England, as represented by Dr. Halley.[1]

That the Lord's Supper, in addition to being a sign, is also a
seal of a federal transaction, in which the believer through the
ordinance makes himself over to Christ, and Christ makes Himself over with His blessings to the believer, may be satisfactorily
evinced from a brief review of the statements of Scripture on the
subject. There are four different occasions on which the Lord's
Supper is more especially referred to in Scripture ; and from the
statements made in regard to it on these occasions, it may be
conclusively proved that much more is attributed to the ordinance than merely the character of a sign.

1st, There is the description given of the nature and meaning
of the ordinance in connection with the history of its institution,
as given by the different evangelists, and educed from a comparison of them, which seems not indistinctly to intimate that the
Lord's Supper is more than a commemorative sign. In the
words of the institution, our Lord calls the cup " the New Testament or covenant in His blood,"[2]—language which *can* be interpreted, and apparently *requires* to be interpreted, so as to assert
a more intimate connection than any between a symbol and the
thing signified, between the cup drunk in the Supper and the
covenant of grace which secures the blessings represented. Add
to this, that our Lord asserts the bread to be His body, and the
wine to be His blood,[3] in such terms as certainly imply that the
one was a sign of the other, but apparently imply more than this,
—the words seeming to intimate a sacredness in the symbols more
than could belong to mere outward signs, and unavoidably suggesting a more intimate relationship between the elements of the
ordinance and the spiritual blessings represented,—even such a

---

[1] *Catech. Racov. de Prophet. Jesu Christi Mun.* cap. iii. Hoadly, *Plain
Account of the Nature and End of the Sacrament of the Lord's Supper*, 2d ed.
pp. 24, 58, 164-177. Halley, *The Sacraments*, Lond. 1844, vol. i. pp. 94-
110 ; vol. ii. pp. 63 f. 227-239.

[2] Matt. xxvi. 28 ; Luke xxii. 20.

[3] Matt. xxvi. 26, 28 ; Mark xiv. 22-24 ; Luke xxii. 19 f.

connection as that which would make the use of the one by the worthy receiver stand connected with the actual enjoyment spiritually of the other.[1]

2d, There is a separate account of the institution of the Lord's Supper given by the Apostle Paul in the 11th chapter of 1st Corinthians, in which the intimacy and sacredness of the connection between the symbols of the ordinance and the blessings represented are still more strongly brought out. The "eating and drinking unworthily" is represented as the sin of being "guilty of the body and blood of the Lord;" a second time it is spoken of by the apostle as the guilt on the part of the unworthy participator of "eating and drinking judgment to himself,"—the reason assigned for the heinousness of the offence being, that he "has not *discerned* the Lord's body;" and, as a precaution against the danger of such transgression, a man is commanded to "examine himself" before he partake of the Supper.[2] It seems impossible, with any show of reason, to assert that the "discernment" (διακρισις) here spoken of is the mere power of interpreting the signs as representative of Christ's death; or that the "guilt" incurred is nothing more than the danger of abusing certain outward symbols; or that the "examination" enjoined is no more than an inquiry into one's knowledge of the meaning of the commemorative rite. All these expressions evidently point to a spiritual discernment and participation by the believer, not of the sign, but of the blessing signified; and to a spiritual and awful sin, not of misusing and profaning outward symbols, but of misusing and profaning Christ actually present in them.[3]

3d, There is a brief but most emphatic reference to the Lord's Supper in the 10th chapter of 1st Corinthians, which can be interpreted upon no principle which limits the meaning of the ordinance to a mere sign, but which very plainly asserts a federal transaction between the believer and Christ in the ordinance, and the communication through the ordinance of spiritual blessings. "I speak as to wise men," says the apostle; "judge ye what I say. The cup of blessing which we bless, is it not the communion of the blood of Christ? The bread which we break, is it not the

---

[1] [Cf. Calvin *in loc.*]   [2] 1 Cor. xi. 27–29.
[3] Hodge, *Expos. of 1st Cor.* Lond. 1857, pp. 214–236. [Calvin, *In Nov. Test.* ed. Tholuck, vol. v. pp. 379–381, 397–406. Meyer, *krit. exeget. Handbuch über den erst. Korintherbrief*, 4te Aufl. pp. 267–280.]

communion of the body of Christ?"[1] The κοινωνια—the communion, or participation, or interchange, or mutual fellowship of the blood of Christ and the body of Christ—cannot possibly be understood of the mere signs of the body and blood, without a very violent experiment practised on the language of the apostle. And if "the fellowship" does not refer to the outward symbol, it can only refer to the spiritual blessings represented in the ordinance,—to Christ Himself present after a spiritual manner in the Sacrament, and giving Himself to the believer, while the believer gives himself to Christ, so as to establish a true κοινωνια, or fellowship, or communion between them. It is hardly possible with any plausibility to interpret the language of the apostle in any other way than as expressive of a federal transaction between the believer and Christ in the ordinance.[2]

4th, There is a lengthened discourse in the 6th chapter of the Gospel by John, in which our Lord indeed makes no express reference to the Supper by name, but which it is hardly possible, I think, to avoid applying in its spiritual meaning to the ordinance.   In that discourse our Saviour declares Himself to the Jews to be "the bread of life which came down from heaven;" He tells them that "except they eat the flesh and drink the blood of the Son of man, they have no life in them;" He asserts that "His flesh is meat indeed, and His blood drink indeed;" and He affirms that "He that eateth my flesh, and drinketh my blood, dwelleth in me, and I in him."[3] Whether this discourse refers directly and expressly to the ordinance of the Lord's Supper or not, it is quite plain that it affords, by the parallelism of the language employed to that used in connection with the ordinance, a key to interpret the sacramental phraseology applied to the Supper. It very plainly points to a spiritual eating and drinking of the flesh and blood of the Son of God, and a spiritual participation, far beyond a mere fellowship in an outward and empty symbol.[4]

On such grounds as these, we hold that the theory which explains the Sacrament of the Supper to be no more than a commemorative sign comes very far short of the Scripture represen-

---

[1] 1 Cor. x. 15 f.
[2] Hodge, *Expos. of 1st Cor.* pp. 185–195. [Meyer, *ut supra*, pp. 237–243.]
[3] John vi. 32–63.
[4] Goode, *Nature of Christ's Presence in the Eucharist*, Lond. 1856, vol. i. pp. 91–120.

tations of the ordinance; and that nothing but the idea of a seal of a federal transaction between the believer and Christ in the Sacrament will come up to the full import of the observance.[1]

IV. The fourth and last mark laid down by us as characteristic of a sacramental ordinance, is, that it is a means of grace; and this mark also applies to the ordinance of the Lord's Supper. After what has been said, it is not necessary to do more than lay down this position. As the sign and seal of a federal transaction between the believer and Christ, it is plain that it must be the means of grace to his soul. It presupposes, indeed, the existence of saving grace on the part of the participator in the ordinance; it is a seal to him of the covenant actually and previously realized and appropriated by him; but, as a seal, it is fitted to add to the grace previously enjoyed, and to impart yet higher and further blessing.[2] What is the manner in which this grace is imparted; how the Sacrament of the Supper becomes a living virtue in the heart of the participator; what is the efficacy of the ordinance,—these are questions the consideration of which opens up to us those further discussions to which we have next to address ourselves. While we believe that the Sacrament of the Supper is an eminent and effectual means of grace, as a seal of the covenant transaction represented in the ordinance, and through the faith of the participator, Romanists and semi-Romanists attribute to the ordinance a character and an efficacy which we believe that Scripture does not sanction, but, on the contrary, disowns. To the unscriptural views of the Supper held by the Church of Rome we shall now turn our attention.

[1] [Gillespie, *Aaron's Rod Blossoming*, B. iii. ch. xii. xiii.; *CXI. Propositions*, 15-19; *Miscell. Quest.* ch. xviii. Rutherford, *Due Right of Presbyteries*, Lond. 1644, pp. 525 ff. Willison, *Works*, Hetherington's ed. pp. 466–488, 518–522, 578–586. Waterland, *Review of the Doct. of the Euch.* pp. 197–214, 424–466.]

[2] Calvin, *Inst.* lib. iv. cap. xvii.; *Short Treatise on the Lord's Supper*, 1540, Consensus Tigurinus, 1554, with the Exposition of it. *Second Def. of the Orthod. Faith concerning the Sacr. against Westphal.* 1556. *Last Admon. against Westphal. True Partaking of the Flesh and Blood of Christ in the Holy Supper*, in Calvin's *Tracts*, Edin. 1849, vol. ii. pp. 164–579. Turrettin, *Op.* tom. iii. loc. xix. qu. xxi. xxii. Compare with these works Dr. Hodge's very masterly discussion of the "Doctrine of the Reformed Church on the Lord's Supper," *Princeton Essays and Reviews*, New York 1857, pp. 342–392. Goode, *Nat. of Christ's Pres. in the Euch.* vol. i. pp. 56–129, etc. [Owen, *Works*, Goold's ed. vol. viii. pp. 560–564. Bruce, *Serm. on the Sacr.* Wodr. Soc. ed. pp. 34–80. Edwards, *Qualifications for Communion*, P. ii. sec. ix. and obj. iii.–xx.; *Works*, Lond. 1834, pp. 458 ff. 464–478.]

SECTION II.—TRANSUBSTANTIATION.

Both the Lord's Supper and Baptism are Divine appointments of perpetual authority in the Christian Church. Both are outward and sensible signs, expressive of spiritual truths; both are seals of a federal transaction between Christ and the believer in the ordinance; and both, while they presuppose the existence of grace on the part of the receiver, are at the same time the means, by the Spirit, and through the believer's faith, of adding to that grace, and imparting a fresh spiritual blessing. And thus, parallel as the Sacraments of the Christian Church are in their nature and efficacy, they are alike also in the misapprehensions to which they have been exposed. Baptism has been misrepresented as an ordinance possessed in itself of an independent and supernatural virtue, apart from the spiritual state or disposition of the participator, so that, *ex opere operato*, it infallibly communicates saving grace to the soul. And, in like manner, the Sacrament of the Lord's Supper has been misrepresented as an ordinance embodying in itself a spiritual power, and efficacious of itself to impart saving grace. The full-grown and legitimate development of these views in regard to the Lord's Supper is to be found in the principles of the Church of Rome, and in the doctrine which she propounds under the name of transubstantiation.

The Romish system of belief and instruction in regard to the ordinance of the Supper is briefly this. At the original institution of the ordinance, it is believed by the Church of Rome that our Lord, by an exertion of His almighty power, changed miraculously the bread and wine into His body and blood, His human soul and His Divine Godhead; that this supernatural change was effected in connection with the words of institution uttered by Him: "This is my body; this is my blood;" that in giving the appearance of ordinary elements into the hands of His Apostles, He actually gave Himself, including both His humanity and His Divinity; and that they really received and ate His flesh, and drank His blood, with all their accompanying blessings to their souls. And what was thus done in a supernatural manner by Christ Himself at the first institution of the ordinance, is repeated in a manner no less supernatural every time the Lord's Supper is administered by a priest of Rome with a good intention.[1] The

---

[1] [In what is called the "Scotch Communion Office" the words of "Invo-

priest stands in the place of Christ, with an office and power similar to Christ's, in every case in which he dispenses the Supper; the words of institution repeated by the lips of the priest are accompanied or followed by the same supernatural change as took place at first; the substance of the bread and wine used in the ordinance is annihilated, while the properties of bread and wine remain. In place of the substance of the natural elements, the substance of Christ in His human and Divine nature is truly present, although under all the outward attributes of bread and wine; and those who receive what the priest has thus miraculously transubstantiated are actual partakers of whole Christ, under the appearance of the ordinary sacramental elements.

Under this fearful and blasphemous system there are properly two grand and fundamental errors from which the rest flow; and which it is important to mark and deal with separately, although they are intimately connected, and form part of the same revolting theory of the Sacrament. There is, first of all, that supernatural change alleged to be wrought upon the elements by the authority of the priest in uttering the words of institution,—the transubstantiation properly so called,—by which the bread and wine become not a sign or symbol, but the actual substance of the crucified Saviour; and there is, secondly, and in consequence of such transubstantiation, the making of the elements not the signs of Christ's sacrifice, but the reality of it,—the bread and wine having become Christ Himself, and the priest having, in so transubstantiating them, actually made the

---

cation" are: " We most humbly beseech Thee, merciful Father, to bless and sanctify with Thy Word and Holy Spirit these Thy gifts and creatures of bread and wine, *that they may become* the body and blood of Thy most dearly beloved Son." The corresponding words in the Romish missal are: " *that they may become to us* the body and blood of Thy most dearly beloved Son " (ut nobis corpus et sanguis fiant dilectissimi Filii Tui). The words of the Scotch Office, therefore—as has often been pointed out—seem to make an even more unqualified assertion of transubstantiation than those of the Romish service,—the subjective element, which may be thought to be introduced by the " nobis," being in the former case entirely thrown out. By the 21st canon of the Scotch Episcopal Church, it is enacted " that the Scotch Communion Office continue to be held of primary authority in this Church." Compare some of the recent utterances of English High Churchmen : " We are teaching men to believe *that God is to be worshipped under the form of bread ;* and they are learning the lesson from us, which they have refused to learn from the Roman teachers who have been among us for the last three hundred years," etc. *Essays on the Re-union of Christendom,* edited by Rev. F. G. Lee (Secretary to the A. P. U. C.) ; with Preface by Dr. Pusey, 1867, pp. 179 f.]

sacrifice of the Cross once more, and offered it to God. These two doctrines of real transubstantiation, and a real sacrifice in the ordinance of the Supper, are both avowed as fundamental in the theory of the Church of Rome; and from these two doctrines all the others connected with the subject are derived. *First*, From the doctrine of the transubstantiation of the elements into the actual humanity and Divinity of the Lord Jesus Christ, there very obviously, and perhaps not unnaturally, follows that other doctrine, which declares that the elements are proper objects for the worship of Christians; and hence we have the elevation and adoration of the Host in connection with the Romanist doctrine of the Supper.[1] *Second*, From the doctrine that the elements, transubstantiated into a crucified Saviour, become a real sacrifice, and a true repetition or continuation of the offering made upon the Cross, there very obviously and naturally follows that other doctrine, which teaches that the ordinance procures for the participator in it atonement and forgiveness of sin; and hence we have the saving grace infallibly communicated by the Sacrament wherever there is a priest to dispense it, or a soul to be saved by the participation of it. We shall consider, then, the doctrine of the Church of Rome in connection with the Supper, under the twofold aspect of the real transubstantiation alleged to pass upon the elements, and the real sacrifice alleged to be offered in the ordinance. These two points form the grand and essential features of the Romanist theory of this Sacrament; and, separately discussed, will enable us to review all that is of chief importance connected with it.

The doctrine of transubstantiation is thus laid down in the Canons of the Council of Trent: "If any shall deny that in the Sacrament of the most holy Eucharist there is contained truly, really, and substantially the body and blood, together with the soul and Divinity of our Lord Jesus Christ, and so whole Christ, but shall say that He is only in it in sign, or figure, or virtue, let him be accursed." "If any shall say that in the Holy Sacra-

---

[1] [An interesting fact regarding John Knox's influence in effecting the change of doctrine as to transubstantiation and adoration of the elements in the English Prayer Book of 1552, as contrasted with that of 1549, is brought out by Laing in his ed. of Knox's Works, vol. iii. pp. 79 f. The Scottish Reformer, however, counselled the abandonment of kneeling at the Communion altogether, instead of a mere disavowal of the Popish interpretation of the attitude, p. 279. Cf. Proctor, *Hist. of Book of Com. Prayer*, pp. 30 ff.]

ment of the Eucharist there remains the substance of bread and wine, together with the body and blood of our Lord Jesus Christ, and shall deny that wonderful and singular conversion of the whole substance of the bread into the body, and of the whole substance of the wine into the blood, while only the appearances (species) of bread and wine remain—which conversion the Catholic Church most aptly styles transubstantiation,—let him be accursed." "If any shall say that Christ, as exhibited in the Eucharist, is only spiritually eaten, and not also sacramentally and really, let him be accursed."[1]

This monstrous and audacious perversion of the doctrine of Scripture by the Church of Rome is founded upon and defended by an appeal to the literal meaning of the words of Scripture in speaking of the ordinance, in contradistinction to the figurative meaning of them. It is on this literal sense of the Scripture language that the only argument of Romanists in support of their system is built; and, over and above an appeal to the bare literalities of the expressions employed, there is not the shadow of a reason that can be alleged in defence of it. "It is impossible for me," says Cardinal Wiseman in his *Lectures on the Principal Doctrines and Practices of the Catholic Church,*—"it is impossible for me, by any commentary or paraphrase that I can make, to render our Saviour's words more explicit, or reduce them to a form more completely expressing the Catholic doctrine than they do themselves: 'This is my body; this is my blood.' The Catholic doctrine teaches that it *was* Christ's body, that it *was* Christ's blood. It would consequently appear as though all we had here to do were simply and exclusively to rest at once on these words, and leave to others to show reason why we should depart from the literal interpretation which we give them."[2] Since Romanists, then, take up their position in defence of tran-

---

[1] *Concilii Trident. Canones et Decreta,* Sess. xiii. can. i. ii. viii. [Compare *Lateran,* iv. can. i.; *Creed of Pius IV. Super form. jurament.* Percival, *The Roman Schism,* Lond. 1836, pp. 132 f. xlviii.]

[2] Wiseman, *Lect. on the prin. Doct. and Pract. of the Cath. Church,* Lond. 1847, vol. ii. p. 174. *Reply to Turton,* Lond. 1839, p. 125. [The position of the advocates of consubstantiation since the days of the Conference of Marburg, has been in this respect precisely identical with the Romanist one. "Das Subject," says Thomasius in reference to the words of institution, "ist natürliches Brod und Wein, das Prädikat aber der natürliche, substantielle Leib, das natürliche, wesenhafte Blut des Herrn, der Leib in dem er leibhaftig vor ihnen sitzt, das Blut welches das Leben dieses seines Leibes ist, und das er zu vergiessen im Begriff steht. .... Die Einsetzungsworte sagen nichts

substantiation on the literal construction of the words employed in reference to the ordinance, and on that alone, what is material or essential to the argument is brought within a very narrow compass indeed. That argument may be, and indeed often is, encumbered with much irrelevant matter. But the main and only essential point to be discussed is simply this : Are we bound to interpret the Scripture phraseology employed in connection with the Lord's Supper in a literal sense, as affirming that the true body and blood of Christ are given in the ordinance; or, do the very terms of that phraseology, and the nature of the thing spoken of, compel us to adopt not a literal, but a figurative interpretation? This is evidently the *status quæstionis* between the Romanists and their adversaries in reference to the debate about transubstantiation. Romanists never pretend to bring any argument in aid of their theory of the Supper, except the argument of the literal meaning of the sacramental words. This disposed of, there is no other in the least available to defend their position. Is it, then, *possible* to adopt a literal interpretation of the words which Scripture employs to describe the sacramental elements ? Is it *competent* to adopt a figurative interpretation ? Is it *necessary* to adopt a figurative interpretation ? These three questions, fairly answered, will embrace the whole controversy necessary to the discussion of the Romanist dogma of transubstantiation.

I. It is impossible to adopt a literal interpretation of the sacramental phraseology ; and this is evinced by Romanists themselves, in their own departure from it in the very matter under discussion.

The principle of a strictly literal interpretation of the sacramental language of Scripture is the only principle which furnishes a single plea in favour of the dogma of transubstantiation ; and yet the necessities of the language employed compel Romanists

davon, dass Brod und Wein Zeichen oder Unterpfänder des Leibes und Blutes Christi seien, sie gestatten auch nicht den Begriff beider umzusetzen in den der Lebenshingabe und Blutvergiessung, und eben so wenig ihn aufzulösen in den des Personlebens des Erlösers, oder des *Christus cum omnibus suis bonis*, sie sagen endlich auch nichts von einer *manducatio spiritualis ;* das Alles sind willkürliche Ausdeutungen oder Eintragungen ; sondern einfach und bestimmt bezeichnen sie als die *res*, die im heiligen Mahle mitgetheilt und empfangen wird, den Leib und das Blut, und zwar den wesenhaften, stofflichen, natürlichen Leib und das leibliche Blut des Herrn, womit selbstverständlich der münliche Genuss mitausgesagt ist."—*Dogmatik*, 3ter Th. 2te Abth. Erlangen 1861, pp. 58, 60. Cf. *Form. Concord.* vii. 2–40, in Hase, *Lib. Symb.* pp. 597–604.]

to surrender that principle in its application to the very case in which they demand that we shall observe it. The advocate of transubstantiation, by his own practice in the very matter in hand, nullifies his own solitary argument. He demands from us a literal rendering of the Scripture language; and yet in the very same passage of Scripture he is·himself forced to adopt a non-literal. Take the words of Luke as he records the first institution of the Supper, and we see at once that in these the Romanist is forced again and again to abandon a literal, and have recourse to a figurative interpretation. "And He took the cup," says the evangelist, describing our Lord's action, " and gave thanks, and said, Take this, and divide it among yourselves." According to the strictly literal method of interpretation advocated and demanded by the Romanist, it was the cup, and not the wine in the cup, that was to be taken and shared by the disciples; and the Romanist is obliged to adopt the non-literal rendering in this case to suit his views of what occurred. Again, we find the inspired historian saying, in reference to what our Lord did, " Likewise also the cup after supper, saying, This cup is the New Testament in my blood,"—language which once more demands that the Romanist shall surrender his literal, and have recourse to a non-literal interpretation, so that he may not identify the vessel in which the wine was contained with the New Covenant, nor transubstantiate the cup into a covenant, but make the one merely a sign or symbol of the other by a figurative use of the language. Once more, the Romanist departs from his principle of a literal interpretation, when the evangelist tells us that Christ spoke of His blood " which is shed for you."[1] At the moment of the utterance of these words, the shedding of His blood was a future event, to happen some hours afterwards, and not a present one, as the words literally rendered would assert ; and, accordingly, the Romanist has no scruple in interpreting it in a non-literal sense, as indeed he is forced to do by the very necessity.of the language. Or, take the words of the Apostle Paul in his account of the ordinance of the Supper, which he had, separately from the evangelists, himself received of the Lord. Here, again, we have the same use of terms which no literal interpretation will enable even the Romanist to explain. The apostle, like the evangelist, tells us that the words of our Lord were expressly, "This cup is

[1] Luke xxii. 17–20.

the New Testament in my blood,"—language which, interpreted upon the principle of strict literality, would identify the vessel containing the wine with the Divine covenant, and which requires, therefore, even in the opinion of the Romanist, to be understood figuratively.[1] And, further still, the apostle, *after* the giving of thanks by our Lord, still speaks·of the elements, not in language which denotes their transubstantiation, but in terms which plainly declare that they were bread and wine still. "For as often as ye eat *this bread*, and drink *this cup*, ye do shew the Lord's death till He come."[2] In this case no literal rendering of these words will be sufficient to reconcile them with the dogma of transubstantiation; and even in supporting that dogma, the Romanist is compelled in this passage to fall back upon an interpretation not literal. We are warranted, then, by the practice of Romanists themselves, in the very case of the sacramental language employed in Scripture, to say that it is not possible to adhere to, or consistently to carry out, a strictly literal interpretation.[3]

II. A figurative interpretation of the sacramental language is perfectly competent and possible.

It cannot be denied—and we have no occasion or wish to deny it—that, as a general canon of interpretation, it is true that the literal rendering of any statement made by a writer ought, in the first instance, to be tried and to be adopted, if it be in ac-

---

[1] Wiseman, *Lectures on the Real Presence*, Lond. 1836, pp. 179 f. *Reply to Dr. Turton*, etc. Lond. 1839, pp. 239 f. 262.

[2] 1 Cor. xi. 25 f.

[3] Turton, *Rom. Cath. Doct. of the Eucharist Considered*, Camb. 1837, pp. 323-326. ["Twa things are necessaire and maun concur to the nature and constitution of a Sacrament, to wit, there maun be *a word*, and there maun be *an element* concurrand—(referring to Augustin's 'accedit verbum ad elementum et fit Sacramentum,' in *Joann*. Tract. lxxx. 3) ;—there is not a sect but they grant this. . . . . We by the 'word,' as I have said, understand the hail institution of Christ Jesus,—quhatsoever He said, quhatsoever He did, or commanded to be done,—without eiking, without pairing, without alteration of the meaning or sense of the word. Quhat understandis the Papists by the 'word?' They preach not the institution of Christ, nor takis not the hail institution as He left it; but instead thereof they select and pykis out of His institution four or five words, and they make the hail vertu of the institution to stand in the four or five words ; and it maid nocht gif they contented them with thae words, because they are the words of the institution, but they eike to these words, they paire frae the words, and alteris the meaning of these same words quhilk they keep as they please."—Bruce, *Serm. on the Sacr.* Wodrow Soc. ed. p. 74. Stillingfleet, *Doct. and Pract. of the Church of Rome*, Cunningham's ed. pp. 59-61. 70 f. Goode, *Nat. of Christ's Pres. in the Euch.* vol. i. pp. 66, 71-80.]

cordance with the use of words and the import and object of the statement. But the necessities and use of language justify and demand a figurative interpretation of terms, rather than a literal, in manifold instances; and those instances in which words are to be rendered not literally, but figuratively, must plainly be determined by the nature, connection, and object of the words. Now, in reference to the use of the sacramental language found in the Bible, it has often been argued, and has never yet been fairly met by the advocates of a literal meaning, that many similar passages are to be found in Scripture in which the same words admit of, and indeed require, not a literal, but a figurative interpretation, by the confession of all parties; and the conclusion is drawn from this, and fairly drawn, that the terms used in regard to the ordinance of the Supper may be figurative too. The occurrence of such texts, demanding, as all parties allow, a figurative or non-literal rendering, is valid and relevant evidence in regard to the nature of Scripture language, and proves at least this, that the words employed in reference to the Supper *may* admit of a figurative rendering also. This citation of parallel language does not in itself, indeed, demonstrate that the sacramental terms *must* be figurative; but it unquestionably proves that they *may* be figurative. Cardinal Wiseman, in his discussion of the doctrine of transubstantiation, gives a list of some texts bearing on the question, which have been referred to by Protestants as evidence in their favour, to the effect that the language, "This is my body," "this is my blood," may be understood, not literally, but figuratively. They are to the following effect:

"The seven good kine are seven years."

"The ten horns are ten kings."

"The field is the world."

"And that rock was Christ."

"For these are the two covenants."

"The seven stars are the angels of the seven churches."

"I am the door."

"I am the true vine."

"This is my covenant between me and you."

"It is the Lord's passover." [1]

In these instances, and many similar ones, it is admitted by all

[1] Gen. xli. 26 f.; Dan. vii. 24; Matt. xiii. 38 f.; 1 Cor. x. 4; Gal. iv. 24; Rev. i. 20; John x. 7, xv. 1; Gen. xvii. 10; Exod. xii. 11.

parties, Romanists as well as Protestants, that the verb *to be* must be understood in its non-literal signification, and cannot by any possibility be understood literally. From the nature of the assertion made, from the context, and from the manner in which the terms are made use of, there is no possibility of denying that these texts are to be understood not literally, but figuratively; and they seem, therefore, by this parallelism to the words employed in connection with the Supper, to prove all that they were ever quoted to prove, namely, that the expressions, "This is my body," "this is my blood," *may* be understood in a figurative sense too. Such texts are not quoted to demonstrate that the sacramental phraseology of Scripture *must* be figurative; they are only quoted to prove that there is nothing in the nature of Scripture language, judging by its use in similar cases, to prevent us, if the nature of the statement and the context should require it, from interpreting the language concerning the Supper in a non-literal or figurative sense also. The multitude of texts closely analogous in form to the phrases, "This is my body," "this is my blood," and which, as all parties allow, *must* be understood figuratively, may not indeed, taken singly, necessitate a non-literal rendering in the latter case also; but they, at the very least, authorize it, should the import and connection of the passage make the demand, if they do not go a step further, and of themselves recommend a figurative interpretation.

Now, how is it that Cardinal Wiseman in his *Lectures* deals with these passages, and disposes of the argument drawn from them? He bestows a vast deal of minute criticism upon them, in order to show that these passages must, either from the meaning of the statement made in each, or the sense of the context, or the express assertion of the sacred writer, be accounted figurative and symbolical; and that, therefore, the verb *to be* in each of these cases must be reckoned equivalent to the verb *to signify*. And having done this, he considers he has done enough to prove that the cases referred to are not parallel to the sacramental language, "This is my body," "this is my blood." Now, it is enough, in reference to such an argument, to say that we willingly adopt his explanation of these passages, accounting them, as he does, to be figurative, and reckoning, as he does, the verb *to be*, when employed in such texts, as equivalent to the verb *to signify*. And it is for this very reason that we quote them as a justification of our assertion, that the same verb, when employed in reference to the Lord's Supper, *may* be equivalent there also to the verb *to signify.* If these texts did not admit of a figurative interpretation, and if the verb *to be* did not in them appear equivalent to the verb *to signify,* we should not have quoted them, because they would not have served our purpose. The reasoning of the Cardinal is certainly a singular specimen of an attempt at logical argument. I shall give it in his own words : " Suppose," says he in his *Lectures,* " suppose I wish to illustrate one of these passages by another, I should say this text, ' The seven kine are seven years,' is parallel with ' The field is the world,' and both of them with the phrase, ' These are the two covenants ; ' and I can illustrate them by one another. And why ? Because in every one of them the *same thing* exists ; that is to say, in every one of these passages there is the interpretation of an allegorical teaching, —a vision in the one, a parable in the second, and an allegory in the third. I do not put them into one class because they all contain the verb *to be,* but because they all contain the same thing. They speak of something mystical and typical,—the interpretation of a dream, an allegory, and a parable. Therefore, having ascertained that in one of these the verb *to be* means *to represent,* I conclude that it has the same sense in the others ; and I frame a general rule, that wherever such symbolical teaching occurs, these verbs are synonymous. When, therefore, you tell me that ' this is my body' may mean ' this represents my body,' because in those passages the same word occurs with this sense, I must, in like manner, ascertain not only that the word *to be* is common to the text, but that the same thing is to be found in it as in them ; in other words, that in the forms of institution there was given the *explanation of some symbol,* such as the interpretation of a vision, a parable, or a prophecy . . . Until you have done this, you have no right to consider them all as parallel, or to interpret it by them." [1]

The objection here urged by Cardinal Wiseman seems to amount to this, that we have quoted passages which, by the nature of the statement they contain, or by the context, or by the direct assertion of the writer, are plainly demonstrated to be figurative, while the sacramental expressions, " This is my body," " this is my blood," are not so demonstrated to be figurative. The answer

[1] Wiseman, vol. ii. p. 186.

is obvious. We do not quote such texts to prove that the terms
of the sacramental institution *must* be understood figuratively,
but to prove that they *may* be understood figuratively ; to demonstrate that there is no bar in the shape of Scripture usage in the
way to prevent us from interpreting them figuratively, if it is
necessary. We are prepared to prove, by the very same means
as the Cardinal employs,—by the nature of the statement itself,
by the context, and such like considerations,—that the sacramental
terms are figurative, just as Cardinal Wiseman proves that the
words, " This cup is the New Testament," are to be understood
figuratively, or as these other terms, " The seven kine are seven
years," must be interpreted figuratively. The very nature of the
statement itself proves it to be a statement to be understood, not
in a literal, but a figurative sense. We interpret the expression,
" The seven kine are seven years," in a figurative sense, not because these words occur in the interpretation of a dream,—for
both the dream and the interpretation may be embodied in words,
literal, and not figurative,—but because the very nature of the
proposition and the sense of the context necessitate it, it being
impossible that the seven kine can be literally seven years. Again,
we interpret, and so does Cardinal Wiseman, the expression,
" This cup is the New Testament," not literally, but figuratively,
for a similar reason,—that the very nature of the proposition, and
the sense of the context, demand a non-literal rendering ; and in
like manner we interpret the expression, " This is my body,"
" this is my blood," not literally, but figuratively, for the very
same reason, because the very nature of the proposition, and the
sense of the context, necessitate such an interpretation.[1] The
citation of other passages of Scripture in which the verb *to be* is
used for the verb *to represent* or *signify*, is had recourse to in the
argument simply to prove that the usage of Scripture language

---

[1] [" Diess τουτο," says Meyer, commenting on 1 Cor. xi. 24, " kann gar
nichts anderes heissen als ; *diess gebrochene Brod da*, und damit ist εστι als die
Copula des symbolischen Seins zu fassen *geboten*." So too, Martensen, representing though he does the High Church Lutheran doctrine of the Sacraments :
" Gegen diese Verwandlungslehre, welche die natürlichen Elemente zu einem
leeren Schein verflüchtigt und dem Reiche der Natur zu nahe tritt um das der
Gnade zu verherrlichen, protestirt die ganze evangelische Kirche, und behauptet
die natürliche Selbstständigkeit der sinnlichen Zeichen. ' Brot ist Brot, und
Wein ist Wein,' ist nur Sinnbild vom Leibe und Blute Christi. In diesem Sinne
als Verwerfung der Transsubstantiation bekennt sich die ganze evangelische
Kirche zu Zwingli's ' diess bedeutet.' "—*Dogmatik*, 4te Aufl. p. 376.]

does not forbid, but countenances such a kind of interpretation. And the numerous texts already referred to are both relevant and sufficient to accomplish that object.[1]

III. A figurative interpretation of the sacramental language, "This is my body," "this is my blood," is not only possible and competent, but necessary.

In no other way can we ever discriminate between figurative and literal terms, whether scriptural or non-scriptural, whether used by inspired or uninspired men, than by a reference to the nature of the proposition which the language embodies, to the sense of the context, and to the object of the speaker or writer; unless in those exceptional cases in which he directly tells us that he is to be understood in the one way or in the other. Very seldom indeed, in regard to language not meant to deceive, is it difficult to understand, from a consideration of these points, whether it is to be interpreted figuratively or not. In the case of the Lord's Supper, the words employed in reference to the elements could have presented to the disciples who heard them no difficulty at all. The ordinance was grafted upon the passover, with the figurative language and actions of which the Apostles, as Jews, were abundantly familiar; and this circumstance alone must have familiarized their minds with, and prepared them for the figurative meaning of the words and elements in the Supper. Above all, the nature of the proposition, "This is my body," "this is my blood," interpreted by the commentary of our Lord, "This do in remembrance of me," and understood in the light of His accompanying actions and words, renders it nearly impossible that they could believe that a miracle had been wrought on the bread and wine, and that the body and blood, soul and Divinity of the Lord Jesus Christ, then present to their eyes, could be at the same instant contained under the appearance of the morsel of bread and the mouthful of wine that they ate and drank. Nothing but the "strong delusion that believes a lie" can lead any man who reads and understands the simple narrative of Scripture, to deny that the interpretation of the sacramental phraseology employed must be figurative, and not literal.[2]

There are two attempts commonly made by Romanists to explain away the impossibility of the Apostles,—or indeed any

---

[1] Turton, *Rom. Cath. Doct. of the Euch. Considered*, pp. 259-288.
[2] Turton, *ut supra*, pp. 289-308.

other man not wholly blinded by spiritual delusion,—believing in the literal interpretation of the sacramental words that refer to the Supper.

1st, The power of Christ to work a miracle, like that which is alleged to have been wrought in the case of the bread and wine, is asserted; and it is averred that the Apostles could not doubt the supernatural ability of their Lord and Master, so often in other days exerted before their eyes. "What," asks Dr. Wiseman, "is possible or impossible to God? What is contradictory to His power? Who shall venture to define it further than what may be the obvious, the first, and simplest principle of contradiction,—the existence and simultaneous non-existence of a thing? But who will pretend to say that any ordinary mind would be able to measure this perplexed subject, and to reason thus: 'The Almighty may indeed, for instance, change water into wine, but He cannot change bread into a body?' Who that looks on these two propositions with the eye of an uneducated man, could say that in his mind there was a broad distinction between them, that while he saw one effected by the power of a Being believed by him to be omnipotent, he still held the other to be of a class so widely different as to venture to pronounce it absolutely impossible? . . . . Now, such as I have described were the minds of the Apostles,—those of illiterate, uncultivated men. They had been accustomed to see Christ perform the most extraordinary works. They had seen Him walking on the water, His body consequently deprived for a time of the usual properties of matter, —of that gravity which, according to the laws of nature, should have caused it to sink. They had seen Him, by His simple word, command the elements and raise the dead to life, etc. Can we, then, believe that with such minds as these, and with such evidences, the Apostles were likely to have words addressed to them by our Saviour, which they were to interpret rightly, only by the reasoning of our opponents,—that is, on the ground of what He asserted being philosophically impossible?"[1]

It is hardly necessary to reply to such an argument as this. *In the first place*, the miracles with which the Apostles were familiar had no analogy whatsoever to the stupendous wonder of transubstantiation. Those miracles were appeals to the senses in

---

[1] Wiseman, *Lectures*, vol. ii. pp. 205 f. [Thomasius, *Dogmatik*, 3ter Th. 2te Abth. p. 61 f.]

proof of truths not seen; and they were tested by the senses, as things to be judged of by them all. The so-called miracle of transubstantiation is no appeal to the senses, but the reverse,—a thing not to be tested by the exercise of any one of them, if it were possible, and a thing denied by any one of them, because impossible.[1] If it were a possible thing, it would subvert the very principle on which our perceptions are made to us by God the primary source of our beliefs, and the foundation of truth to us; and it would cause the very instincts which His hand has laid deep within our inmost being to be to us a lie. The conversion of water into wine at that marriage supper in Cana of Galilee of old was a wonder seen by the eye, and in agreement with the evidence of the senses, because the properties, first of the water, and afterwards of the wine, were seen and judged of by all. The conversion of the bread into the body of the Lord, while yet the properties of bread remain, is a wonder that contradicts the evidence of our senses, and involves an impossibility.

In the second place, even Cardinal Wiseman himself admits that there are impossibilities in the nature of things, not competent even for Almighty power to accomplish. Such an impossibility, according to his own statement, is the " existence and simultaneous non-existence of a thing; " and side by side with this one limitation, which, upon the authority of Dr. Wiseman, is to be put even upon the power of God, we may put another limitation, and that upon higher authority than his: " God cannot deny Himself."[2] In that revelation which He has given to us in our instinctive and primary perceptions of sensible things, and in that other revelation which He has given to us in His Word, God, who is the Truth, cannot contradict Himself.[3]

---

[1] [Compare Tillotson's famous sermon on the subject.]

[2] 2 Tim. ii. 13.

[3] [" Now quhen the Papists are dung out of this fortress (the impossibility of a figurative interpretation), they flee as unhappily to a second, to wit, that God, by His omnipotency, may make the body of Christ baith to be in heaven and in the bread, baith at ae time; *ergo,* say they, it is so. Gif I denied their consequent, they would be weil fashed to prove it; but the question stands not here, quhether God *may do* it or not, but the question stands quhether God *will* it or not, or *may* will it or not. And we say, reverently, His majesty may not will it; for suppose it be true that He *may* monie things quhether He will or not, yet it is as true that there are monie things that He may not will: of the quhilk sort this is; and thir are reduced to twa sorts. *First,* He may not will these things that are contrare to His nature, as to be changeable, to decay, and sic others. . . . *Secondly,* God may not

2*d*, An attempt is made by Romanists to identify, as one and the same in principle, the dogma of transubstantiation and what are called the mysteries of revelation. " What," says Cardinal Wiseman, " becomes of the Trinity? What becomes of the incarnation of our Saviour? What of His birth from a virgin? And, in short, what of every mystery of the Christian religion?"[1] It will be time enough to answer such questions as these when it is proved that such mysteries contradict our rational nature, in the same manner as the dogma of transubstantiation contradicts our perceptive nature. Such mysteries as those referred to are *above* our reason, but not *against* it. They are *beyond* the powers of our rational nature fully to understand, but not contradictory to our rational nature so as to be inconsistent with it. The argument in defence of transubstantiation, drawn from such a source, is but one example out of many that could be quoted, of the common tactics of Romish controversialists, who are but too often prepared to hand over to the unbeliever the most sacred truths which the Scripture has recorded, rather than not make out a plea for their own superstitions.[2]

will some things by reason of a presupponed condition, as sic things quhereof He has concluded their contrair of before : of the quhilk sort is this, quhilk is now controverted. For seeing that God has concluded that all human bodies suld consist of organical parts, and therefore to be comprehended and circumscrived within ae and the awin proper place, and also seeing He has appointed Christ Jesus to have the like body, and that not for ane time, but eternallie, in respect of this determined will, I say, God may not will the contrair now, either to abolish this body quhilk He has appointed to be eternal, either yet to make it at ae time, in respect of ae thing, a body and not a body, quantified and not quantified, finite and infinite, local and not local. For to will thir things quhilk are plain contradicent in themselves He may not, na mair nor it is possible to Him to will a lie." See the remarks which follow on the nature of the miraculous, embodying very much Bishop Butler's view of the question as given in his *Analogy.*—Bruce, *Serm. on the Sacr.* p. 86 f.]

[1] Wiseman, *Lectures*, vol. ii. p. 209.

[2] Calvin, *Inst.* lib. iv. cap. xvii. 12–23. Turrettin, *Op.* loc. xix. qu. xxvii. Jewel, *A Replie unto M. Hardinge's Answeare*, Lond. 1565, Art. v.-xii. pp. 316–477. Cosin, *Hist. of Popish Transubstantiation*, Lond. 1676. Faber, *Christ's Discourse at Capernaum fatal to the Doct. of Transubst.* Lond. 1840. Goode, *Nat. of Christ's Pres. in the Euch.* Lond. 1856, vol. i. pp. 130–224. [Stillingfleet, *Doct. and Pract. of the Church of Rome*, Edin. 1837, pp. 55–77. See especially the full references to the literature of this subject given by Dr. Cunningham in his notes to the above work. *Essay on Transubstantiation* in the *Princeton Essays*, 1st Series, Edin. 1856, pp. 366–385. Bruce, *Serm. on the Sacr.* Wodrow Soc. ed. pp. 74–96. Reuss, *Histoire de la Theologie Chrétienne au Siècle Apostolique*, 3me ed. Strasbourg 1864, tom. i. pp. 244–246, tom. ii. 191 f.]

SECTION III.—THE DOCTRINE OF THE "REAL PRESENCE" AND
THE PRIESTLY THEORY.

With the dogma of transubstantiation, as held by the Church of
Rome, stands very closely connected the question as to the manner
in which Christ is present in the ordinance of the Supper. The
doctrine of the "real presence" of Christ in the Sacrament has,
more almost than any other in theology, been made the subject
of prolonged and bitter controversy. By the Church of Rome,
as we have seen, the real presence of Christ is explained to be
the true and actual existence of the body and blood, the soul and
Divinity of the Saviour, under the sensible appearances of bread
and wine ; so that in the elements Christ is as much present after
a bodily sort, in consequence of their transubstantiation, as He
ever was present to His disciples of old in the days of His flesh.
By the Lutheran Church, the real presence of Christ in the
ordinance is maintained, not upon the principle of such a change
in the substance of the elements into Christ's body and blood as
contradicts the testimony of our senses, but, rather upon the supposition that the bread and wine remaining the same, the real
body and blood of Christ are nevertheless united to them in some
mysterious manner, so as to be actually present with them, and
actually received along with them, when they are partaken of by
the communicant. By our own Church, as well as by many
other Protestant communions, the real presence of Christ in the
Sacrament is asserted on the ground that He is not in a bodily
manner present *in* the substance of the elements, nor yet in a
bodily manner mysteriously present *with* the elements, but only
spiritually present to the faith of him who receives the ordinance
in faith.[1]

---

[1] [" In defending the monstrous doctrine of transubstantiation, Papists
commonly begin with proving the *real presence* of Christ in the Sacrament,
which no Protestant Church ever denied,—the dispute being, not as to the
reality, but the *mode* of the presence of Christ ; Papists holding that He is
present in a corporal and carnal manner to the senses of all communicants,
and Protestants, that He is present in a spiritual manner to the faith of worthy
receivers. Having established the real presence, they then either assert, as
Dr. Milner does, that Protestants do not hold it, and of course are in error
upon this point ; or acknowledging, as Bossuet does, that they do hold it, try
to show that this requires them, in consistency, to admit the Popish doctrine
of transubstantiation. The latter is the course commonly adopted by Popish
controversialists."—Cunningham, *Notes on Stillingfleet's Doct. and Pract. of
the Church of Rome*, p. 69.]

The influence of the fierce and frequent controversies waged
in connection with the nature and efficacy of the Lord's Supper
shortly after the date of the Reformation, and the disposition on
the part of Luther, and the Churches affected by his influence,
to depart as little as possible from the established phraseology of
the ancient Church on the subject of the Sacrament, served to
introduce, or to continue in theological discussions, a language
somewhat exaggerated, and occasionally almost unintelligible, in
regard to this question. Such, undoubtedly, was the phrase " consubstantiation," used by some of the Lutherans to express the
mysterious corporeal presence of Christ, not *in*, but *with*, or *under*,
or somehow *in connection with* the elements; and such also was the
phrase " impanation," employed by others to elucidate, or rather
to obscure, the doctrine of the manner in which Christ's bodily
presence is connected with the sacramental bread. And I cannot
help thinking that, under the power of very much the same influences, the term " real presence" has not unfrequently been
employed and explained, even by orthodox divines, in such a way
as to give a somewhat exaggerated and mysterious aspect to
the connection subsisting between Christ and the Sacrament.
That phrase has occasionally been employed in association with
such language as to leave the impression that Christ was present
in the Supper, not spiritually to the faith of the believer, and not
corporeally to the senses of the communicant, but in some indefinite manner between the two, and after a sort mysterious and
peculiar to the Sacrament of the Supper. Such language seems
to have no warrant in the Word of God.

The Scriptures give us no ground to assert that Christ is
present in the Sacrament of the Supper in a manner different
from that in which He is present in the Sacrament of Baptism.
I do not speak at present of the *extent* of the blessing or of the
grace which He may impart in the one or the other Sacrament
by His presence ; I speak only of the *manner* of His presence.
There is nothing, I think, in Scripture to warrant us in affirming
that the *manner* of Christ's presence in the Supper is in itself unique
or peculiar, or indeed in any respect different from the manner of
His presence in Baptism, or any other of His own ordinances.
In all of these He is present, after a spiritual manner, to the faith
of the participator in the ordinance, and in no other way.[1] The

[1] " Romanists, Lutherans, and Reformed," says Dr. Hodge, in comment-

blessings which that presence may impart may be different in different ordinances, and may be more or less in one than in another. But there is nothing in the Word of God which would lead us to say that the real presence of Christ in any of His ordinances, whether sacramental or not, is anything else than Christ present, through his Spirit and power, to the faith of the believer. Such promises as these—" Lo, I am with you alway, even unto the end of the world; " " Where two or three are met together in my name, there am I in the midst of you;" " Behold, I stand at the door and knock : if any man hear my voice, and open the door, I will come in to him, and will sup with him, and he with me;"[1] and such like—plainly give us ground to affirm that Christ, through His Spirit, is *present* in His ordinances to the faith of the believer, imparting spiritual blessing and grace. But there is nothing that would lead us to make a difference or distinction between the presence of Christ in the Supper and the presence of Christ in His other ordinances, in so far as the *manner* of that presence is concerned. The efficacy of the Saviour's presence may be different in the way of imparting more or less of saving grace, according to the nature of the ordinance, and the

ing on 1 Cor. x. 16, " all agree that a participation of the cup is a participation of the blood of Christ; and that a participation of the bread is a participation of the body of Christ. But when it is asked, what is the nature of this participation, the answers given are radically different. The Reformed answer negatively, that it is " not after a corporal or carnal manner ;" that is, it is not by the mouth, or as ordinary food is received. Affirmatively they answer, that it is " by faith," and therefore by the soul. This of course determines the nature of the thing partaken of, or the sense in which the body and blood of Christ are received. If the reception is not by the mouth, but by faith, then the thing received is not the material body and blood, but the body and blood as a sacrifice, *i.e.* their sacrificial virtue. Hence all Reformed Churches teach (and even the rubrics of the Church of England) that the body and blood of Christ are received elsewhere than at the Lord's Table, and without the reception of the bread and wine, which in the Sacrament are their symbols and the organs of communication, as elsewhere the Word is that organ. Another point, no less clear as to the Reformed doctrine, is, that since the body and blood of Christ are received by faith, they are not received by unbelievers." [It is remarkable, as the same author has pointed out in his *Essays*, p. 350, that the Anglican Confessions, the Articles of 1552 and 1562, are decidedly more Zwinglian in tone and expression with regard to the Lord's Supper than the standards of any other of the Reformed, as distinguished from the Lutheran Churches. This comes out unmistakeably on contrasting the articles with the other Calvinistic confessions, among which they stand in Niemeyer's collection. In whatever way it is to be accounted for, the fact is at least a curious one, especially considering the numerous High Church expositions, to which the formularies in question have been subjected.]

[1] Matt. xviii. 20, xxviii. 20 ; Rev. iii. 20.

degree of the believer's faith. But the manner of that presence is the same, being realized through the Spirit of Christ, and to the faith of the believer. The Sacramentarian controversy has tended in no small measure to introduce into the language of theology, in connection with the " real presence," an ambiguity of thought and statement, not confined to Romanist, or even semi-Romanist divines.[1]

But, passing from that part of the Popish theory of the Supper which refers to the alleged change produced on the elements by transubstantiation, and to the manner of Christ's presence in the ordinance, I go on to consider the other part of the Popish theory of the Supper which refers to the office of the ministering priest in the Sacrament, or his power to offer the body and blood of Christ, actually present, as a true sacrifice for

---

[1] " Archdeacon Denison," observes Dean Goode, in his very able and valuable work on the *Nature of Christ's Presence in the Eucharist*, "supposes that, by calling the presence he holds a *spiritual* presence, he distinguishes it from the presence implied both by the doctrine of transubstantiation and consubstantiation. But they who hold these doctrines maintain as much as he does, that the presence is a *spiritual* presence ; meaning that Christ's body is really present in the form of a spirit (see pp. 593 f.) This interpretation of the phrase Archdeacon Denison adopts, and seems in fact acquainted with no other. He has thus turned *the spiritual eating of Christ's flesh*, which our divines maintain, meaning an act of the soul, into the *bodily eating of Christ's flesh, present in the form of a spirit*, and thus involved himself in all the absurdities pointed out by all our divines, who have treated dogmatically on the point, as attending such a notion. The controversy might perhaps be almost wholly summed up in one brief question : Is the reception of the true body and blood of Christ an act of the body or of the soul, of the mouth, or of faith ? On one side, those who hold the doctrine of the presence of that body and blood in, with, or under the forms of the elements, maintain that the *reception* is an act of the body, the soul of the believer feeding upon them by faith, *after* that reception. On the other side it is maintained that there is no such presence in the consecrated substances themselves, and that the reception is an act of the soul, an act of faith. The term " real presence" is used by both parties. By the former it is used to describe their doctrine as denoting an actual presence of the body of Christ, though in an invisible and immaterial form to the bodies of men, in the consecrated substances received into the mouth. The latter also use the phrase, inasmuch as they maintain that the presence of that body to the soul, to influence and invigorate it, is as real, spiritually considered, as a local presence of it to our bodies,—just as Augustin says that the woman that only touched the border of Christ's garment, touched Him by faith more than the crowd that pressed upon Him ; and as Bishop Jewel says, ' The thing that is inwardly received in faith and in spirit is received verily and indeed.'"—*Nat. of Christ's Pres. in the Euch.* Lond. 1856, vol. i. pp. vi. ix. 11-55, etc., vol. ii. 641-749, etc. Wilberforce, *Doct. of the Holy Euch.* 3d ed. pp. 76-95, 130-152, 221-231. Hodge, *Princeton Ess. and Rev.* New York 1857, pp. 358-370. [Turrettin, *Op.* loc. xix. qu. xxviii. Thomasius, *Dogmatik,* 3ter Th. 2te Abth. pp. 50 ff. 87-107. Bp. E. H. Browne, *Expos. of the Thirty-nine Art.* 8th ed. p. 680.]

sin. The first grand error in the Popish doctrine of the Lord's Supper is the monstrous figment of the transubstantiation of the elements; the second, intimately connected with the first, and perhaps yet more extensive and mischievous as an error in its practical bearings, is the doctrine of the power of the Church, in the ordinance of bread and wine, to offer a true and efficacious propitiation to God, both for the living and the dead. The sacrifice of the mass is founded upon, and very closely connected with, the dogma of transubstantiation,—in some sort following as an inference from the assumption that the priest stands in Christ's stead at the Communion Table, and, by a supernatural power not inferior to Christ's, changes, by the utterance of the words of institution, the elements of bread and wine into the actual body and blood, soul and Divinity, which were once the sacrifice offered up for this world upon the Cross. In the performance of this supernatural and mysterious office, which, according to its own theory, it is given to the Church of Rome to discharge, we see both the priest and the sacrifice,—the *priest*, acting as mediator between God and the people, offering a true satisfaction to God for sin, and promising remission and reconciliation; and the *sacrifice* presented to God, real and efficacious, because in fact the very same sacrifice, in its substance, of the flesh and blood of Christ, as He Himself once made and presented, and not less availing in its mighty virtue to propitiate God, and procure salvation for the sinner. A real office of priesthood, and a real offering of sacrifice, are the two features that characterize this second portion of the Popish theory of the Sacraments. Both are asserted, and both are essential in the sacrifice of the mass, which has been grafted on the dogma of transubstantiation, and both form integral parts of that monstrous system of sacerdotal usurpation by which the Church of Rome seeks to build up her spiritual tyranny. The position, then, laid down by the Church of Rome in connection with the subject of the mass, may be conveniently discussed under these two heads : first, the claim which she makes to possess and exercise the office of a true priesthood ; and second, the power that she arrogates to make and offer a true sacrifice to God. Reserving the second of these points for future consideration, we shall now proceed to deal with the claim put forth by the Church of Rome to hold and exercise the office of a real priesthood.

This claim runs through the doctrine and practice of the Popish Church in all its departments, and is not restricted to the case of its views in connection with the Supper. The priestly office and sacerdotal pretensions are recognised in almost every branch of its administration as a Church, and, indeed, are fundamental to the system. But the priesthood which it pretends to exercise towards God and on behalf of man is perhaps developed most prominently and conspicuously in connection with its doctrine of the Lord's Supper. The question is one that lies at the very root of the difference between the Popish and Protestant systems, and on that account is of more than ordinary interest and importance.

The doctrine of a real priesthood residing in the Christian ministry, more especially in connection with its chief function of offering the sacrifice of the mass, is thus stated by the Council of Trent: " Sacrifice and priesthood are so joined together by the ordinance of God that they existed under every dispensation. Since, therefore, under the New Testament the Catholic Church has received the holy visible sacrifice of the Eucharist by the institution of the Lord, it is necessary also to confess that there is in it a new, visible, and outward priesthood into which the old has been transferred. Now the sacred writings show, and the tradition of the Catholic Church has always taught, that this was instituted by the same Lord our Saviour, and that a power was given to the Apostles, and their successors in the priesthood, of consecrating, offering, and administering His body and blood, and also of remitting and retaining sins." " If any shall say that by these words, ' Do this in remembrance of me,' Christ did not appoint the Apostles to be priests, or did not ordain that they and other priests should offer His body and blood, let him be accursed." " If any shall say that the sacrifice of the mass is only one of praise and thanksgiving, or a bare commemoration of the sacrifice accomplished upon the Cross, but not propitiatory ; or that it only profits him who receives it, and ought not to be offered for the living and dead, for sins, pains, satisfactions, and other necessities, —let him be accursed." [1]

---

[1] *Concilii Trident. Canones et Decreta*, Sess. xxiii. cap. i.; *De Instit. Sacerdot. Nov. Leg.* Sess. xxii.; *De Sacrificio Missæ.* can. ii. iii. Cf. Bellarm. *Disput.* tom. iii. Pars 2 ; *De Eucharistiâ*, lib. i. cap. ii., lib. iii. cap. i.–xi., lib. v. cap. xvii. xx ; Amesius, *Bellarm. Enerv.* tom. iii. lib. iv. cap. i.–iii. ix. 16, 21.

Amid the other errors contained in these statements by the Council of Trent, what we have chiefly to do with at present is the claim which is put forth on behalf of the Church of Rome and her ministers to hold and exercise the office of priesthood in the same sense as, ceremonially, the priests of a former dispensation did so; with power now, not ceremonially, but really, to act as priests in the absence of Christ in heaven, and truly to offer sacrifice to God for sin. The question in regard to such a claim is this : Have we any warrant to believe that a visible and external priesthood has been established in the New Testament Church, with powers to act as mediators between God and man, and offer the propitiatory sacrifice for the living and the dead ; or has the office of priesthood which existed under a former economy no longer an existence now in the Gospel Church, there being none on earth authorized or qualified to undertake it,—the one Priesthood, in the end of the world for sin, having completed its work on earth, and the Priest who held the office having returned to heaven to continue it there ? This is a vital and fundamental question, not only in order to enable us to form an estimate of the real character of the system of Romanists, but also because it enters so essentially into the principles held by High Churchmen of other denominations.

I. The existence of a priesthood as a standing ordinance in the Christian Church is inconsistent with the fact that such an office was abrogated with the Jewish economy, and necessarily came to an end when that dispensation gave place to the Gospel economy.

An earthly priesthood was an ordinance appointed for a special purpose and a special time ; and the purpose having been served, and the time past, it is necessarily at an end. The priestly office, and the institution of sacrifice with which it stands inseparably connected, formed part of that instrumentality by which, for thousands of years, God prepared this world for the coming and the death of His own Son as its Saviour. First of all, it was the father of the family who was ordained the priest to offer the sacrifice for the rest, and to approach unto God on behalf of his household ; the members of which drew near to God, and worshipped, and were accepted only through him. Such seems to have been the practice in patriarchal times, and apparently not without the appointment, or at least the sanction, of

God.   The father of the family, as well as the divinely appointed sacrifice he offered, thus in a general and distant way
represented Christ as the medium whereby sinners might approach
to God in worship.   But the patriarchal institute was too general
and vague a type of the One Mediator through whom alone,
when fully revealed, men were to find access to God.   Accordingly it was done away with, and another institute was ordained
in its place, with priests specially set apart to the office of mediators between God and the people, and with more special authority
given, and more distinct provision made for them to be the
media through whom the rest were to present their worship and
sacrifices, and themselves to make their approach to God and find
acceptance.   Under the Mosaic ritual, it was no longer lawful for
the sinner himself directly to approach to God with his own
offering of worship or sacrifice ; it was no longer lawful for the
sinner even to draw near with his sacrifice unto God through the
head of the family, as under the patriarchal institute.   The
avenue of approach to God was, step by step, narrowed and
restricted.   First, the father of the family was marked out and
selected as the recognised priest and mediator for the rest.   Next,
a further limitation took place, and the priest of Aaron's line was
specially appointed to stand in the stead of the whole families of
the nation in their approach to God ; and strict provision was
made—and guarded by the most solemn penalties—that no man
should venture to present the sacrifice himself, or to worship
except through the media of this one commissioned priesthood.
The thousands of Israel were restricted in their legal worship
to the one avenue, and forbidden to draw near to the Holy One
of Israel except through the one mediation of the earthly priest
of Aaron's lineage.

And why was it that this earthly priesthood was thus marked
off from all the rest, and the other worshippers made dependent on
the one appointed priest of Aaron's house ?   And why were men
forbidden to approach to God directly and immediately themselves, or even indirectly through any other but this one mediator?
The answer is obvious.   The priesthood was so restricted, and so
fenced about with solemn limitations, in order that it might be a
type of Christ, " the one Mediator between God and man."
From age to age, and from step to step, the worshippers of God
under the old economies were more and more shut up to the idea

and the practice of approaching the Most High God only through the channel of one Priesthood and the person of one High Priest. The typical priests and priesthoods of former dispensations led men's hearts and habits to fix upon the *one* Mediator through whom alone we now draw near to God. They taught the worshippers to anticipate and to hope in that *one* Man, who is now the Priest, not of one family, as in patriarchal times, nor of one nation, as in Jewish times, but the Priest through whom all the families and all the nations of the world draw nigh to God. The earthly priesthoods of the former days of the Church all converged upon and pointed to and centred in Christ. With Christ, therefore, those priesthoods came to an end. The type was merged in the Antitype, and then was done away. The priests of other days, together with the sacrifices which they offered, have served the object designed by them, and are abolished. They can, from the very nature of their office, have no use, and no meaning, and no place in a Church to which another and a higher priesthood has been given, and when the sign has given place to the thing that was signified. The office of the priesthood on earth ceased with the former dispensation ; and not only is there no re-appointment under the Gospel of such an order of men in the Church, but they would, from the very place and office that they occupied, be inconsistent with the Gospel economy. They formed part and parcel of a typical system which has been abolished.

II. The existence of a priesthood as a standing ordinance in the Christian Church is inconsistent with the privileges of believers under the Gospel.

It is not unfrequently argued by the advocates of Romanist or semi-Romanist principles on this subject, that the privilege of a human priesthood and a human mediatorship is one so great and precious that it cannot be conceived to exist, as we know it did, under the earlier and far inferior dispensation, and yet to be awanting under the later and far better dispensation of the Gospel. The presence of an earthly priesthood, it is urged, must be enjoyed by the Church now, inasmuch as it cannot be supposed to be deprived of one of the highest privileges which belonged to the former and less richly endowed Church of the Old Testament.[1]

[1] ["The inspired prophets," says Bishop Jolly (Scotch Episcopal), "foretell the happy accession of the Gentiles to the fold of Christ, and to the

A comparison between the superior advantages of the Gospel Church, as measured by those of the Jewish, is the very consideration which, instead of proving that a human priesthood is continued to us now, most emphatically demonstrates that it is abrogated. The presence and office of a human priesthood, enjoyed by worshippers under the law, are far surpassed by the higher and more glorious privileges enjoyed by believers under the Gospel. No doubt it was an act of grace and condescension on the part of God, to permit sinners to approach His presence through the avenue of a visible priesthood and a visible sacrifice in former times, even although that boon was granted to them under solemn and jealous restrictions; and it was a great and precious privilege for the worshipper to be allowed to draw near to the mercy-seat through means of a human mediator, and by the intervention of a material offering. But the privilege of Christians in the New Testament Church is better and more glorious still. Through Christ a new and living way has been opened up for all to draw nigh to God, not indirectly through a human mediator, but directly, each man for himself. The whole brotherhood of believers are no longer dependent upon one of themselves for the liberty or opportunity of access to the common Father; and without distinction of special office, it is the freedom purchased for all, without earthly priest or earthly intercessor interposed, to go with boldness into the very holiest. The presence of an earthly and external priesthood is no evidence of superior privilege, but the reverse. It is the mark of an imperfect and carnal dispensation.

That it was necessary for the worshipper to employ the intervention of another than himself in order that he might approach to his Creator,—that a sinner should be dependent on another sinner for pardon or access to heaven,—that he should not dare to engage his heart to draw near to God except through the medium of a human priesthood,—were strong arguments to prove

benefits of His sacrifice for the sins of the world, by means of a sacrifice and altar similar to what had prevailed among the Israelites, but of more extensive compass and reach." (In proof of this, the author cites the usual texts —Isa. xix. 19-23, lxvi. 21, Jer. xxxiii. 18, and Mal. i. 11.) "Levi still continues, and is perpetuated in his sacerdotal ministry; the high priest, priests and Levites of the law still in effect subsisting in the Bishops—all considered as only *one* (!)—with the priests and deacons."—*Christian Sacrifice in the Eucharist*, 2d ed. pp. 24, 26. Wilberforce, *On the Incarnation*, p. 386, etc.]

the essential imperfection of that dispensation which witnessed such things, and constituted a yoke of bondage which it was hard to bear. And what it was when the sons of Aaron by God's own appointment were the human priests and mediators, that it is now in the case of those Churches who bind upon their own necks the institute of a human priesthood, and then boast of it as their exclusive distinction and privilege. It is a spiritual yoke that is too heavy to bear; it is a retrogression from the freedom wherewith under the Gospel Christ has made His people free; it is a badge of the voluntary thraldom and debasement of a Church that has itself gone into bondage to men, instead of maintaining the liberty of Christ the Lord. The restriction of approaching God only through the earthly priest in the local temple at Jerusalem, and by the blood of bulls and goats,—the prohibition forbidding the sinner to draw near to the mercy-seat directly himself, or through any other medium,—those were evidences of essential imperfection in the Church state of the worshippers under a former economy. And the human priest-hood of the Church of Rome,—the material sacrifice made and offered for the worshippers,—the priest standing between the sinner and God, and barring or opening the way of approach,—the mediator acting as the medium of communication between the Most High and His creatures, and retaining or remitting their sin,—these, too, are restrictions, and, because human and unauthorized, daring and impious restrictions, upon the freeness of God's grace and the liberties of His redeemed people.

It is a fact of much significance, and indeed of decisive force in this argument, that throughout the whole of the New Testament Scriptures there is no instance in which either the name of priest, or the functions belonging to the office of priesthood, are ascribed to the ministers of the Christian Church; that the only examples of the use of the term are those in which it is given, not to the minister, but to the people; and that the ascription of the privileges of the office is uniformly made to the members at large. On the one hand, the term ἱερεύς, or "priest," is never in any single instance in the New Testament applied to a minister of the Christian Church, although always made use of to designate the priest of the Aaronic dispensation. The usual name given to the minister of the New Testament Church is πρεσβύτερος,—the change of designation marking very decisively the change in the nature of the office.[1] On the other hand, on the only occasions on which the word ἱερεύς is used in the New Testament in reference to any except a Jewish priest, it is given to the members of the Christian Church at large, and not to the ministers of that Church. In the Book of Revelation, believers are spoken of as "kings and priests to God;" and in the first Epistle of Peter they are described as a "royal priesthood."[2] The name formerly appropriated to the sons of Aaron, selected and anointed from among the rest of the congregation to be priests to God, is not inherited by the ministers of the Christian Church in the same exclusive manner, but, on the contrary, is applied in an enlarged and extended sense to the whole body of believers. More than this: the privilege enjoyed by the priests of old, of alone of all the worshipping assembly drawing near to God without the intervention of any other, is a privilege uniformly represented in the New Testament as not peculiar to the ministers of the Church, but extended now to all its members, and common to all believers. The office peculiar to the minister of the Christian Church is described at large in the New Testament Scriptures, and is a "ministry" or "service" unto others (διακονια, λειτουργια), not a mediatorship on behalf of others. It is spoken of as an office of "ministering," "preaching," "exhorting," "ruling," amid the flock of Christ, not an office of sacrificing, and making reconciliation, and approaching to God as the mediator on behalf of the rest, and becoming the avenue for the access of their persons or worship to the Divine presence. On the contrary, this privilege of approaching directly to God without the intervention of any substitute or proxy on earth, is a privilege which is expressly attributed to all believers as their personal right: so that, if in any sense there are priests now on earth, those priests are the believing people of God at large; and if in any sense there are priestly sacrifices now offered up, they are the spiritual sacrifices of the prayer and praise of Christians, without distinction of office or place in the Church. The sacerdotal theory on which the Church system of Rome is built, and the priestly office which is so conspicuously developed in her practice as regards the Lord's

---

[1] ["In truth, the word *Presbyter* doth seem more fit, and, in propriety of speech, more agreeable than *Priest* with the drift of the whole Gospel of Jesus Christ."—Hooker, *Eccles. Pol.* B. v. ch. lxxviii. 4.]

[2] Rev. i. 6; 1 Pet. ii. 5–9.

Supper, are utterly repugnant to the spirit of the New Testament
Church, and to the privileges which it has secured to believers.
The privilege of a human priesthood, which existed under the
law, is abolished under the Gospel; or rather, in its spirit and
substance, the privilege is enlarged and extended to all believers
under the New Testament Church. It was the peculiar and
distinctive prerogative of the priests under the law, that they alone
of all the worshippers drew near to God without a human mediator. That prerogative is common to all the royal priesthood of
believers under the Gospel.

III. The existence of an earthly priesthood as a standing
ordinance of the Christian Church is inconsistent with the one
office of Christ as the Priest and Mediator of His people.

Earthly priest the New Testament Church has none. The
very name is blotted out from the inspired history of the Church
under the Gospel in its application to any office-bearer within its
pale; and it is found, in so far as it can now be found on earth,
only in connection with that spiritual and universal priesthood
which belongs alike to all true believers, who have equally the
privilege of free approach to God, equally the anointing which
makes them His people, and equally the consecration that sets
them apart for His service. In any other sense than this, there
is no priest in the Christian Church on earth. The material
sacrifice made by men has ceased, the incense kindled by men
no longer burns, the atonement presented by men is no more
offered up. The Gospel is a religion without a priest on earth,
without a sacrifice, and without an altar. And yet there is a
priesthood that belongs to the Christian Church still; and there
is a Priest who yet discharges that office on behalf of His people.
" We have a great High Priest that hath passed into the heavens
for us,"—not a mortal and dying man, but one " of whom it is
witnessed that He liveth for ever,"[1]—not a priest who offers, as
did the sons of Aaron of old, the typical sacrifices of blood, or,
as the ministers of Rome do now, the pretended sacrifices of an
unbloody offering of bread and wine,—but one who, once for all,
offered up a Divine yet human sacrifice for men,—not an intercessor, who, like the high priest under the law, entered into
God's presence with the blood of bulls and goats, nor yet like the
priest of the Papacy with a consecrated wafer,—but an Intercessor,

[1] Heb. iv. 14, vii. 8.

who, with His own precious and more than mortal blood, has
passed into the presence of God,—an Intercessor, the Son of
God, presenting the offering of Himself without spot or blemish,
and pleading for us on the ground of His meritorious sacrifice.
And this office which the Son of God now discharges in heaven
for His Church passes not from Him to any other (ἀπαρα-
βατον ἔχει την ἱερωσυνην.)[1] His is an unchangeable and undying
Priesthood; and He ever liveth to make intercession for His
people. The office which He sustains and discharges in heaven
is His own incommunicable office, which none save Himself has
either the right or the power to discharge. The *one* Priest that has
made the sacrifice and offered it to God for the sins of many,—
there was none that could share with Him in that mighty and
mysterious work. The *one* Priest to stand between God and a
sinful world,—there was none but the Son that could undertake
so to approach unto the Most High. The *one* Priest to intercede
with an offended God for the guilty,—there was none but the equal
of the Father that could so plead. The *one* Priest to dispense
unto men throughout all ages the blessings of redemption and
grace,—there is none equal to the task but He " in whom dwelleth
all the fulness of the Godhead bodily." Alone in His office as in
His nature, unapproachable in His work as in His greatness, " He
abideth a Priest for ever," — the ever-present and ever-living
Mediator, who has no fellow to share in His priestly functions,
and whose glory as Mediator He will not give unto another.

And what shall we say of those Church systems, Romanist
and semi-Romanist, that give to mortal men that office of Priest
which none can bear but the Son of God, and constitute sinners
mediators on earth between their fellow-sinners and the Almighty?
Such an encroachment upon His incommunicable office touches
very nearly the honour of Christ. The assumption by men of
His personal and inalienable prerogatives, inseparable from Himself as Mediator, is a dishonour done to Him in that very character in which He stands forth supreme and alone before the eyes
of the universe. The very title of Mediator belongs in the
Christian Church to none but One, and *He* the only-begotten
Son of the Father. Our lips are now forbidden to name another
Priest but Jesus. Even in the Old Testament Church, the name
and the office of the Priest had something in them of awful and

---

[1] Heb. vii. 24.

mysterious import, typical as they were of the fulness of the
Gospel day, and of the greatness of the Gospel Mediator, and
fenced about, as we know them to have been, with the solemn
and irrevocable sentence of death upon those who should unwar-
rantably assume or encroach upon them. And still more awful
are that name and office of Priest, now that in these latter days
they have been sustained by the Son of God Incarnate, and
mysteriously sanctified by the shedding of that more than mortal
blood which was poured out on Calvary, and which He still day
by day presents in heaven, as He continually pleads with the
Father there. To stand between God and man, as Christ once
stood amid the darkness of Calvary, was a work which none but
He could do. To stand between God and man, as Christ now
stands, a Priest in heaven no less than on earth, is a work which
none but He can accomplish. To bear the burden of such an
office now is as little competent to mortal man as it was to bear
the burden of it in the Garden, or at the Cross. The name of
Priest between God and man is Christ's inalienable and incommunicable name,—whether He bears the anger of an offended Judge,
or pleads with the compassion of a reconciled Father,—whether
He makes, as He *once* did, atonement by sacrifice, or makes, as He
now does, intercession by prayer. It is the sin above others of the
Church of Rome, that it has assumed to itself that name of Priest,
which none in heaven or in earth is worthy to bear but the Son of
God, and that its ministers pretend to stand between the creature
and the Creator in the exercise of His priestly office among men.[1]

SECTION IV.—THE SACRIFICE OF THE MASS, AND OTHER FORMS
OF THE SACRIFICIAL THEORY.

The claim to the possession of a real priesthood, and to the
power of making and presenting to God a real propitiatory sacrifice, is fundamental to the theory of the Church of Rome, and is

---

[1] Litton, *Church of Christ*, Lond. 1851, pp. 599–657. Garbett, *Bampton
Lectures*, 1842, vol. i. pp. 169–228. [See also Luther's vigorous and comprehensive treatment of the question of the universal priesthood of believers,
which is a very favourite subject with him, in his three great works of the
year 1520,—his Letter, " An den christlichen Adel deutscher Nation," his " De
Captivitate Babylonicâ," and " De Libertate Christianâ." Calvin, *Inst.* lib.
iv. cap. xviii. 13–17. Owen, *Works*, Goold's ed. vol. xiii. pp. 19–28, vol. xix.
pp. 3–259. Gerhard, *Loci Theolog.* loc. xxiii. cap. i. 14–16. Arnold, *Fragment on the Church*, 2d ed. pp. 15–46. Goode, *Rule of Faith*, Lond. 1842, vol.
ii. pp. 166–170.]

one of the great pillars on which its spiritual strength leans. The right to stand between God and man in the character of mediator, to exercise the priest's office in place of Christ on the earth, to negotiate as man's intercessor with God, and to arrange the terms of his acceptance or condemnation, to make and offer the sacrifice which alone can avail unto justification of life, to retain or remit sin, to give or withhold saving grace,—in short, the claim to the *sacerdotal* office lies at the very foundation of the Popish system. This one principle of a priestly power existing in her ministry, accompanying all their administrations, and sanctifying all their acts, runs through the whole details of the Church system of Rome, and is the grand secret of very much of its success. We see it fully and conspicuously developed in connection with the Romish doctrine of the Supper, and as the foundation of the sacrifice of the mass. But it is not confined to that one department of the Popish Church system. The sacerdotal principle pervades it, more or less, throughout its entire range; and the Church of Rome has thus added to its many sins the one emphatic sin of usurping the place of Him who has an unchangeable priesthood in heaven and on earth, and of seizing out of *His* hands the powers that He wields as " Priest for ever." But great and awful though the sin be of arrogating the place and prerogatives of the one High Priest of His people, it is yet a sin which pays its price to the Church that commits it, in the spiritual prestige that it confers, and the spiritual authority that it brings along with it. A sense of the need of some mediator between the sinner and an offended God, a feeling of the absolute necessity of a priest and intercessor for a fallen creature, to negotiate the terms of his pardon and acceptance, can hardly ever be rooted out from the guilty conscience. And the Church of Rome, when it ventures to arrogate to itself on earth that very office which guilty nature needs, and succeeds in its perilous claim to be regarded as the only priest and intercessor between sinners and God, establishes for itself a spiritual dominion over the souls of its victims, greater and more absolute than any other dominion in this world.[1] And hence the tenacity with which the Romish Church clings to the claim of a

---

[1] [" Then that feast of free grace and adoption to which Christ invited His disciples to sit as brethren and co-heirs of the happy covenant, which at that table was to be sealed to them, even that feast of love and heavenly-admitted fellowship, the seal of filial grace, became the subject of horror and

priestly or sacerdotal office, inseparably connected as it is with some of the most monstrous and incredible pretensions, with the dogma of transubstantiation, with the claim to forgive sin, which none but God can do, with the pretence of making and present-ing a Divine and propitiatory sacrifice to the Almighty.

In spite of the explicit abrogation of the office with the abro-gation of the Old Testament dispensation ; in spite of the palpable inconsistency of the office with the spirit of the Gospel, and the privileges of believers ; and, worse still, in spite of the inconsist-ency of the office with the sole priesthood of Christ, the Church of Rome ordains each one of her ministers to be a *priest*, and in-vests him with the power and authority of an earthly priesthood. It needs must be that a priest have a sacrifice to present unto God. " This man must of necessity have somewhat to offer." And having ordained, as she alleges, a real priest, the Church of Rome proceeds to put into his hands a real sacrifice, and gives him warrant to offer it to God for the sins of the living and the dead.

The doctrine of the Church of Rome on this vital point is laid down in such a manner in her authorized formularies that it is impossible to explain it away. The Council of Trent has defined it in such terms, that the attempts made by more modern Romanists to soften down the atrocious dogma of the real offering-up of the sacrifice of the Lord, body and blood, soul and Divinity, in the Sacrament by the priest, are in vain.[1] Speaking of " the institution of the most holy sacrifice of the mass," the Council declares that it is " a visible sacrifice, as the nature of man requires, by which

glouting adoration, pageanted about like a dreadful idol ; which sometimes deceives well-meaning men, and beguiles them of their reward by their volun-tary humility, which indeed is fleshly pride, preferring a foolish sacrifice and the rudiments of this world, as St. Paul to the Colossians explaineth, before a savoury obedience to Christ's example. Such was Peter's unseasonable humility, as then his knowledge was small, when Christ came to wash his feet, who at an impertinent time would needs strain courtesy with his Master, and falling troublesomely upon the lowly, all-wise, and unexaminable intention of Christ, in what He went with resolution to do, so provoked by his inter-ruption the meek Lord, that He threatened to exclude him from his heavenly portion, unless he could be content to be less arrogant and stiff-necked in his humility."—Milton, *Prose Works*, Lond. 1753, vol. i. p. 2.]

[1] [" The mass is the great Diana of the Popish priests, the craft by which mainly they have their living, and they will never renounce it ; but some Papists have shown a great desire to explain away the doctrine of the Council of Trent upon this point. Bossuet, in his *Exposition*, ch. xiv. (*Doct. Cath. Expositio*, Antwerpiæ 1680, p. 145), explains the sacrifice of the mass in such a way as to exclude the idea of its being a propitiatory sacrifice, and in substance resolves it into the intercession of Christ personally present on the altar under

that bloody one, once to be accomplished on the Cross, might be represented, and the memory of it remain even unto the end of the world." And with this statement, expressive of the representative or commemorative character of the ordinance, the apologists of the Church of Rome, whose desire is to conceal the real doctrine held by her on this subject, very often terminate their quotation, as if the Council of Trent held it to be no more than a symbolical sacrifice in memory of Christ's. But that this is not the case, the words of the Council's definition leave us no room to doubt. It proceeds : "For after the celebration of the old passover, which the multitude of the children of Israel sacrificed in memory of their departure from Egypt, Christ instituted a new passover, even Himself, to be sacrificed by the Church through the priests under visible signs (Seipsum ab Ecclesiâ per sacerdotes sub signis visibilibus immolandum), in memory of His departure out of this world unto the Father, when by the shedding of His

the appearances of bread and wine. He says that ' it wants nothing to be a true sacrifice,'—a statement sufficiently cautious, but which, in the first or suppressed edition of his work, was thus expressed : ' it may be very reasonably *called* a sacrifice.' He swore at his ordination that it was not only a true, but a proper and propitiatory sacrifice. . . . Another attempt has been made by Popish controversialists to escape from the doctrine to which they are all sworn, thus betraying a consciousness that that doctrine is, in its plain honest meaning, incapable of defence. It is set forth in Prof. Brown's *Supplement to the Downside Discussion*, 1836, p. 44 f., as affording a conclusive answer to Protestant objections. It is in substance this, that a sacrifice may be called propitiatory in two different senses : first, as being actually satisfactory to Divine justice, and paying the price of our redemption ; and second, as making application to us of the benefits purchased by Christ. In the first sense, the death of Christ on the Cross is the only propitiatory sacrifice, and it is only in the second sense that the mass is called by that name. But this is evidently a mere evasion. To say that the benefits of one sacrifice are applied to us by means of another sacrifice of a different kind, is surely very like nonsense. A propitiatory sacrifice, in the fair and honest meaning of the words, can be nothing else than a sacrifice which expiates sin, by satisfying Divine justice and paying the price of our redemption. If the Council of Trent taught merely that the Lord's Supper is one of those means of grace by which the benefits purchased by Christ's propitiatory sacrifice are applied to men individually, no Protestant would object to it ; but if this had been their meaning, they would never have defined the mass to be a propitiatory sacrifice, which, according to the established use of language, ascribes to it a far higher efficacy. The great body of Popish writers are in the habit of asserting, in accordance with the decrees of the Council of Trent, that the sacrifices of the Cross and of the mass are one and the same sacrifice ; but if it be true, as the pretence which we are exposing implies, that the sacrifice of the Cross is a propitiatory sacrifice in one sense, and that the sacrifice of the mass is not a propitiatory sacrifice in the same, but only in a different sense, then surely they cannot possibly be one and the same sacrifice."—Cunningham, in *Notes on Stillingfleet's Doct. and Pract. of the Church of Rome*, p. 213 ff.]

blood He redeemed us and snatched us from the power of darkness, and translated us into His kingdom." "And since in this
Divine sacrifice, which is performed in the mass, that same Christ
is contained and immolated in an unbloody manner, who on the
altar of the Cross once offered Himself with blood, the holy
Synod teaches that that sacrifice is, and becomes of itself, truly
propitiatory; so that if with a true heart and right faith, with fear
and reverence, we approach to God, contrite and penitent, we may
obtain mercy and find grace to help in time of need. Wherefore the Lord, being appeased by the offering of this, and granting grace and the gift of repentance, remits crimes and sins, even
great ones. For it is one and the same victim,—He who then
offered Himself on the Cross being the same Person who now
offers through the ministry of the priests, the only difference being
in the manner of offering (Una enim eademque est hostia, idem
nunc offerens sacerdotum ministerio, qui Seipsum tunc in cruce
obtulit, sola offerendi ratione diversa)." And, once more : "If any
shall say that the sacrifice of the mass is only one of praise and
thanksgiving, or a bare commemoration of the sacrifice which was
made upon the Cross, but not propitiatory ; or that it only profits
him who receives it, and ought not to be offered for the living
and the dead, for sins, pains, satisfactions, and other necessities,
—let him be accursed."[1]

There are two things in regard to the doctrine of the Church
of Rome put beyond all dispute or cavil by these statements.
First, it is Christ Himself transubstantiated into the elements, and
corporeally present in the Sacrament, that is offered up by the
priest as a real sacrifice. It is utterly impossible for Romanists
to escape from this dogma so long as the language of Trent remains uncancelled. No attempt can succeed to give it a mystical
or symbolical meaning, and soften down the authoritative assertion of the Council, that in the Supper there is a real sacrifice
of Christ Himself by the priest. Romish controversialists may
indeed adopt different modes of explaining how the sacrifice of
the mass stands related to the sacrifice of the Cross. Some of
them, like Harding the Jesuit, in his reply to Bishop Jewel,
may plainly and unhesitatingly assert "that Christ offered and
sacrificed His body and blood twice,—first in that holy Supper,

---

[1] *Concil. Trident. Canones et Decreta,* Sess. xxii. ; *De Inst. SS. Missæ
Sacrificii,* cap. i. ii. can. iii.

unbloodily, when He took bread in His hands and brake it, and afterwards on the Cross with shedding of His blood."[1] Others of them, like Möhler, in his *Symbolism*, with a view to make the doctrine less palpably inconsistent with Scripture, may assert another form of it, and maintain that there are not two sacrifices, but one, and that the sacrifice of the Supper constitutes a part of that sacrifice which Christ offered on the Cross; or, to use Möhler's own language, "Christ's ministry and sufferings, as well as His perpetual condescension to our infirmity in the Eucharist, constitute one great sacrificial act, one mighty action undertaken out of love for us, and expiatory of our sins, consisting, indeed, of various individual parts, yet so that none by itself is, strictly speaking, *the* sacrifice." "The will of Christ to manifest His gracious condescension to us in the Eucharist, forms no less an integral part of His great work than all besides, and in a way so necessary, indeed, that whilst we here find the whole scheme of redemption reflected, without it the other parts would not have sufficed for our complete atonement."[2] But however Romanists may choose to explain it,—whether as a repetition of the sacrifice of the Cross, or a continuation of it,—the Supper is unquestionably, according to the doctrine of the Church of Rome, a *real* sacrifice, made up of Christ's body and blood. And *second*, this real sacrifice is truly propitiatory in its nature, having virtue in it to satisfy Divine justice, and to constitute a proper atonement for sin. These two doctrinal positions are clearly and undeniably laid down by the Council of Trent, and in such a manner that Romanists cannot evade them. And it is certainly one cause of thankfulness, and no small one, that the Council of Trent was overruled by Divine Providence to put this and other of the monstrous tenets of Romanism into such a dogmatic and articulate form, that it is now utterly impossible for the Church of Rome to deny or escape from them.

What, then, are we to say to the real sacrifice asserted by the Church of Rome, a true propitiation to God for sin, repeated day after day by countless priests who have authority and power to make and offer it?

[1] Jewel, *A Replie unto M. Hardinge's Answear*, Lond. 1565, p. 564. [For some of the methods of evading the legitimate consequences of the sacrificial theory, which have been in use from Harding's time to our own, see the same work, art. xx. pp. 593–598. Cf. Goode, *Rule of Faith*, vol. ii. pp. 173 ff.]
[2] Möhler, *Symbolism*, Robertson's Transl. 2d ed. vol. i. p. 337. [*Symbolik*, 6te Aufl. p. 307.]

I. The doctrine of the Church of Rome is in direct contradiction to the doctrine of Scripture, which declares that there is one Priest, and no more than one under the Gospel.

"Sacrifice and priesthood," say the Fathers of the Council of Trent, " are so joined together by the ordinance of God, that they existed under every dispensation."[1] There can be no doubt that the statement is correct in this sense, that wherever there is a sacrifice, there must be a priest to offer it, and wherever there is a priest, he must of necessity have a sacrifice to offer.[2] And hence, as part of the sacrificial theory of the Supper and essential to it, the ordination by which the Church of Rome sets apart persons for the work of the ministry includes, as its main and characteristic feature, a commission not to preach the Gospel and to dispense its ordinances, but to make and offer sacrifices to God for the souls of men. Hers is mainly and distinctively an order of priests, and not an order of ministers,—a succession from age to age of sacrificers and intercessors, and not of preachers. And thus her system is distinctively opposed to the system of Scripture, which points to *one* Priest, and forbids our lips to name a second in the Gospel Church. The argument of the last section might be sufficient, without further illustration, to establish this. But the point is so vital, and it is brought out with such power and effect by the Apostle Paul, that I cannot help adverting to his statements on this subject.

The grand design of that magnificent exposition of the doctrine of Christ's office and nature and work in the Epistle to the Hebrews, is to prove that, far above and beyond the mediators and priests under the law, Christ was the *one* Son and the *one* Priest of God, in a way and manner altogether exclusive and peculiar, and such as to contrast Him with all others who ever, in any secondary sense, bore these names. In regard to the priesthood more especially, there were under former dispensations two orders of priests, with one of which the apostle *compares* our Lord, with the other of which the apostle *contrasts* Him; and

---

[1] Sess. xxiii. cap. 1.

[2] ["If we deny," says Dr. Jolly, "that there is any proper material sacrifice in the Christian Church, we pull down proper priesthood, and open a door to Socinianism . . . While the Church of England retains the Christian priesthood, she retains by implication the Christian sacrifice ; for every priest must have somewhat to offer, sacrifice and priesthood being correlative terms; they stand or fall together."—*The Christ. Sac. in the Euch.* 2d ed. p. 139.]

both the comparison and the contrast serve to bring out more
distinctly the singular and exclusive character that He bears as
the Priest of God, who has neither partner nor successor in the
office. There was, according to the apostle, a priesthood after
the order of Melchisedec, and there was a priesthood after the
order of Aaron. With the priesthood after the order of Melchisedec our Lord is compared. There was room in that order for
but one Priest, and no more than one; and for this reason, as
stated by the apostle, " He abideth a Priest continually." In the
office that he held He had no predecessor, and He had no successor. Melchisedec stood alone in the typical order that bears
his name; and the more surely and distinctly to mark out this
singularity of his position, we are told, with respect to his office,
that he was "fatherless, motherless, ungenealogied, having neither
beginning of days nor end of life" (ἀπατωρ, ἀμητωρ, ἀγενεαλο-
γητος, μητε ἀρχην ἡμερων μητε ζωης τελος ἐχων).[1] And such
as the type was, so is the Antitype. The Lord Jesus Christ
was "made a Priest after the order of Melchisedec;" and, like
that of His type, His office is singular and exclusive; He knows
neither predecessor nor successor in it; having not only in His
Divine nature, but in His mediatorial character, "neither beginning of days nor end of life." None went before, and none shall
come after this Priest; or, as the apostle expresses it, His office is
one "that passeth not from Him to any other."[2] The comparison
instituted between our Lord's priesthood and that of Melchisedec
demonstrates that He is the *one* Priest, with none to go before or
succeed Him in that character.

But again, with the priesthood of Aaron that of our Lord is
contrasted by the apostle; and the contrast serves to bring out
in like manner the very same grand doctrine. In that priesthood
there were not *one*, but many priests, following each other in
rapid succession. The mortal and dying men who inherited the
blood and the office of Aaron " were not," as the apostle tells us,
" suffered to continue by reason of death."[3] One after another
passed away in swift succession, so that in the not lengthened
period of the Aaronic Church there were truly " *many priests*,"
following each other rapidly in office, as ever and anon death
removed them from beside the altar where they sacrificed and
interceded. With them our Lord is contrasted, and not com-

[1] Heb. vii. 3.   [2] Heb. vii. 24.   [3] Heb. vii. 23.

pared in this respect. "This man, because He continueth ever, hath an unchangeable priesthood." "He is consecrated for evermore." He is endued with "the power of an endless life," and "ever liveth to make intercession for His people."[1] Compared with the order of Melchisedec, and contrasted with the order of Aaron, our Lord is emphatically marked out as the one Priest of God, who can have none to follow, even as He had none to go before Him in His office. And the many priests, anointed day by day continually, and succeeding each other in rapid succession in the Church of Rome, are most decisively declared to be inconsistent with His *one* glorious priesthood.

II. The Popish theory of the Lord's Supper is in direct opposition to the doctrine of Scripture, which declares that there is one sacrifice, and no more than one, under the Gospel.

This argument is likewise brought out with commanding force and effect—as if by way of anticipation of the very error of the Papacy—in Paul's Epistle to the Hebrews. He exhibits the contrast between the many priests under the law and the one Priest of God under the Gospel, immortal, and living ever to discharge that office of priesthood in which He had no predecessor and can have no follower, and in which, like Melchisedec, He stood alone. But in close relation with this, he exhibits the contrast also between the many sacrifices under the law with their ceaseless repetition, and the *one* sacrifice of the Lord Jesus Christ, which never was, and never could be, repeated. The argument by which the apostle demonstrates the unspeakable superiority of the sacrifice of Christ over the sacrifices offered by the sons of Aaron, is a brief and decisive one. The very fact of the repetition of the one, and the non-repetition of the other, was the conclusive evidence of that superiority. The sacrifices under the law were repeated day by day continually; the priest had never done with offering, and the altar never ceased to be wet with the blood of the victims. What was done to-day had to be repeated to-morrow ; and the sacrifice was never so completely made and finished but that it had to be repeated afresh, and renewed times without number. And why? The reason was obvious. They were essentially imperfect. They could never so accomplish the great object of atoning for sin but that their renewal was necessary ; and what was done on one day had to

[1] Heb. vii. 16, 24, 25, 28.

be supplemented by what was to be done on the next. " The law," says the apostle, " having a shadow of good things to come, and not the very image of the things, can never with those sacrifices which they offered year by year continually make the comers thereunto perfect. For then would they not have ceased to be offered? because that the worshippers once purged should have had no more conscience of sins. But in those sacrifices there is a remembrance again made of sins every year."[1] The fact of their ceaseless repetition was the evidence of their essential imperfection. But in contrast with this, and as an evidence of its sufficiency, the apostle urges the consideration that the sacrifice made by Christ was offered up *once*, and no more than once. It stood alone, as an offering made once for all, and never again to be repeated,—a sacrifice so complete in its single presentation that it admits of no repetition or renewal. Christ cannot die a second time upon the Cross, as if His first death were incomplete in its efficacy or its merits ; for " by one offering He has perfected for ever them that are sanctified " or atoned for. Again and again the apostle renews his argument, and his assertion of the fact on which the argument is founded. " Christ was *once* offered to bear the sins of many." " Nor yet that He should offer Himself *often* as the high priest." "For then must He *often* have suffered since the foundation of the world." " He entered in *once* into the holy place ;" and " we are sanctified through the offering of the body of Jesus Christ *once* for all." " By *one* offering He hath perfected for ever them that are sanctified."[2] The argument is decisive. The perfection of Christ's sacrifice, and the non-repetition of Christ's sacrifice, are inseparable. If that sacrifice needs to be repeated, then it cannot be perfect.

And the reasoning of the apostle is conclusive, as if by anticipation, against the many sacrifices of the Church of Rome in the Supper, whatever explanation may be adopted by its advocates to explain away the contradiction between their practice and the doctrine of Scripture. Let the sacrifice of the mass be a repetition of the sacrifice of Christ upon the Cross, as some Romanist controversialists hold it to be,—and their explanation plainly and undeniably means, that the sacrifice of the Cross needs to be repeated day by day, in order to accomplish the salvation of sinners. Or, let the sacrifice of the mass be a continuation of the

[1] Heb. x. 1–3.   [2] Heb. ix. 12, 25 f., 28, x. 10, 12, 14.

sacrifice of Christ on the Cross, and a part of the same atonement, as other Romanists expound it,—and this explanation plainly and undeniably means, that the sacrifice of the Cross was not finished when Christ bowed His head and gave up the ghost. Explain the connection as you will between the sacrifice of the mass and the atonement made upon the Cross, it is utterly inconsistent with the argument of the apostle by which he proves the unapproachable perfection of Christ's work, from its being that one offering which never can be repeated or followed by another.[1]

III. What is essential to the very nature of a true propitiatory sacrifice is awanting in the pretended sacrifice of the mass.

What was offered on the altar in former times could be no propitiatory sacrifice to God unless it was dedicated to Him by death. Believing sacrifice itself to be a positive institution of God, we must look for the nature and import of the observance only in His Word, and in the practice sanctioned by His appointment. And taking the case of the Old Testament sacrifices, we are warranted in saying that they were uniformly dedicated to God by death, and that " without shedding of blood there could be no remission."[2] There were, indeed, offerings under the law not connected with the shedding of blood, and not accompanied by the destruction of life; but these were not propitiatory. In every case of a propitiatory offering the victim was slain, and the atonement made through the shedding of blood. Expiation and the death of the offering—atonement and shedding of blood— were so inseparably connected, that there could be no real sacrifice of a propitiatory nature when the sacrifice was not dedicated to God by death. From the very earliest times blood was accounted a holy thing, not to be eaten or made use of for common purposes; and the very terms of the prohibition explain the reason of it : " For the life of the flesh is in the blood, and I have given it to you upon the altar to make an atonement for your soul ; for it is the blood that maketh atonement for the soul."[3] Without blood shed there could be no expiation. And here lies one difficulty of the Romish dogma of the sacrifice of the mass. It is a propitiation for the sins of the living and the dead ; it is no bare

---

[1] [Comp. the *seven* senses in which the Church of England, according to Dr. Wordsworth's interpretation of her sentiments, holds that there is a sacrifice in the Lord's Supper. *Theoph. Angl.* ed. 1863, p. 220.]
[2] Heb. ix. 22.   [3] Lev. xvii. 11.

commemoration of a sacrifice, but itself a sacrifice, with virtue to satisfy Divine justice and atone for sin; it is an offering of expiation offered wherever there .is a priest to consecrate the ordinance and present it to God.   It is a sacrifice of Christ, offered up in propitiation of His Father's righteous displeasure, and efficacious for the remission of sin.   But yet we are assured by the apostle that "Christ dieth no more; death hath no more dominion over Him.   For in that He died, He died unto sin *once*: but in that He liveth, He liveth unto God."[1]   The Lord Jesus Christ, in His glorified human nature, has long since passed away from the scene of His suffering and humiliation; seated at the Father's right hand, He has rested Him from His work of sorrow and blood, and can repeat no more the agony of the Garden or of the Cross.   He does bear with Him indeed in heaven, impressed for ever on His human flesh, the tokens of suffering and crucifixion; "as a lamb that has been slain," He appears on high in the sight of His Father and His angels, marked with the visible evidence of sacrifice and death.   But He repeats the sacrifice no more; His blood is not afresh poured out. The proofs of His once finished sacrifice which He carries about in His person are enough; and with these silent but eloquent witnesses to make good His cause, He pleads the virtue of that sacrifice, and never pleads in vain.   His uninterrupted and continual advocacy, founded on the merits of His one sacrifice, all-sufficient and complete, supersedes the necessity of its repetition; He needs to die no more for the many sins of His people, which they daily renew, because He once died a death enough for them all, and now lives a life of everlasting intercession, based upon that death, for His people.   Without shedding of blood, without atoning suffering, without life rendered as expiation for life, the pretended sacrifice of the mass is inconsistent with the scriptural idea of sacrifice dedicated to God by death.[2]

Upon such grounds as these we are warranted to say that the sacrificial theory of the Church of Rome, more fully developed in her dogma of the mass, but running throughout her whole spiritual system, is entirely opposed to the doctrine of the Word

---

[1] Rom. vi. 9 f.
[2] Bellarm. *Disput. de Euch.* lib. v. cap. ii. etc. Ames. *Bellarm. Enerv.* tom. iii. lib. iv. cap. ix. [Stillingfleet, *Doct. and Pract. of the Church of Rome*, Cunningham's ed. pp. 197-221; with the copious references to the literature of this subject given by the Editor, p. 220 f.]

of God, which asserts, as fundamental to the Gospel, that as there is but one Priest, so there is but *one* sacrifice known in the New Testament Church. But there are various modifications of this sacrificial theory which, avoiding the extreme doctrine of the Papacy, are held by many semi-Romanists, and still assert that the Lord's Supper is a sacrifice. There are two of these held very commonly by High Churchmen in the English Establishment, to which I would very briefly advert.

1*st*, In a sense very different from the Romish, it was held by not a few of the Christian Fathers in the early centuries,—and the doctrine has been revived in more recent times in the Church of England,—that the elements of bread and wine were a true material sacrifice, not indeed propitiatory, but eucharistic ; very much in the same way as the first fruits laid upon the altar by appointment of the Mosaic law, were a thank-offering to God for the overflowing of His bounties to His creatures. According to this view, the elements of bread and wine, offered to God in the Supper as a material sacrifice without blood, are the fulfilment of the prophecy of Malachi, in which he foretells, in regard to Gospel times, that " a pure offering," as contradistinguished from the bloody sacrifice of the law, should then be offered into God's name. " From the rising of the sun to the going down of the same, Thy name shall be great among the Gentiles ; and in every place incense shall be offered unto Thy name, and a pure offering."[1] This sacrificial theory of the Supper is certainly free from the vital and most fundamental error of the Church of Rome, when it ascribes to the sacrifice in the ordinance a propitiatory character ; but it is open to insurmountable objections.

First, a material sacrifice, in the sense of a thank-offering to God for the bounties of His providence, has not the slightest countenance in any of those passages of the New Testament which describe the nature and design of the Supper. It is hardly anything else than a conceit, gratuitously invented by those who saw that it was impossible to regard the Supper as a propitiation for sin, but who were anxious, in conformity with the unguarded language of the patristic writers on the subject, to devise some plausible excuse for applying the term " sacrifice" to the Supper.[2] Second, the theory is entirely inconsistent with

---

[1] Mal. ii. 11.

[2] [" Equidem quum pium atque orthodoxum de toto hoc mysterio sensum

the first and primary characteristic of the Supper, as clearly laid
down in Scripture, namely, that it is an ordinance commemorative of the propitiatory sacrifice of Christ. Third, the theory of
a material sacrifice in the Supper, in the sense of a thank-offering
of bread and wine for the bounties of Providence, is repugnant
to the spiritual nature of the Gospel dispensation, which stands
opposed to typical worship.

2d, There is another sacrificial theory of the Supper, much
more common than the one now mentioned, and indeed, with
various but unimportant modifications, the prevalent theory among
those High Churchmen of the English Establishment who reject
the extreme views of Popery, as asserted in the doctrine of the
mass, but who hold that in the Supper there is a real propitiatory
sacrifice, and a real sacrificing priest. According to this view,
the elements of bread and wine, not transubstantiated, but remaining unchanged, become, by the words of institution and the consecration of the priest, the body and blood of Christ symbolically
and mystically ; in consequence of the sacramental union between
the sign and the thing signified in the Sacrament, the elements
are both to God and to us equivalent to and of the same value
with Christ Himself ; and the offering up to God of the elements,
thus both representing a crucified Saviour, and not inferior in
virtue or worth to the Saviour Himself, becomes a true propitiatory sacrifice made to the Almighty for sin.[1] Upon this

retinuisse eos (some of the Fathers who used sacrificial language about the
Supper) videam, neque deprehendam voluisse unico Domini sacrificio vel
minimum derogare, ullius impietatis damnare eos non sustineo ; excusari
tamen non posse arbitror quin aliquid in actionis modo peccaverint. Imitati
sunt enim propius Judaicam sacrificandi morem quam aut ordinaverit Christus,
aut Evangelii ratio ferebat. Sola igitur est præpostera illa anagoge in quâ
merito eos quis redarguat, quod non contenti simplici ac germanâ Christi
institutione, ad Legis umbras nimis deflexerunt. . . . . Sacerdotes Levitici,
quod peracturus erat Christus, sacrificium jubebantur figurare ; sistebatur
hostia quæ vicem ipsius Christi subiret ; erat altare in quo immolaretur ; sic
denique gerebantur omnia, ut ob oculos poneretur sacrificii effigies, quod Deo
in expiationem offerendum erat. At peracto sacrificio, aliam nobis rationem
Dominus instituit, nempe ut fructum oblati sibi a Filio sacrificii ad populum
fidelem transmittat. *Mensam* ergo nobis dedit, in quâ epulemur, non *altare*
super quod offeratur victima ; non *sacerdotes* consecravit qui immolent, sed
ministros qui sacrum epulum distribuant."—Calvin, *Inst.* lib. iv. cap. xviii.
11, 12. Cf. Waterland, *Review of the Doct. of the Euch.* Camb. 1737, pp.
467-534. Arnold, *Fragment on the Church*, 2d ed. pp. 111 ff. 126-132.]

[1] " I conclude that, though the eucharistical elements are not the substantial Body and Blood,—nay, they are the figurative and representative
symbols of them,—yet they are somewhat more too : they are the *mysterious*

theory of the Supper, the office of priest in the Christian Church is similar to that of priest under the law: both offer to God real, although symbolical sacrifices, equally pointing to Christ,— there being this difference, that the Aaronic priesthood offered a sacrifice of blood in the prospect of the Saviour's sacrifice to come; while the Christian priesthood offers an unbloody sacrifice in memory of the Saviour's sacrifice now past; and *also*, that the sacrifices presented now in the Supper, in consequence of their sacramental union with Christ, are infinitely more precious than the sacrifices of the former economy. Such, briefly, and so far as I am able to understand it, is the prevalent doctrine among the majority of the High Church party in the Church of England at the present day, who are not yet prepared, as an extreme section of them appear to be, to accept the Tridentine definitions of the nature and efficacy of the Sacrament of the Lord's Supper. It is maintained and expounded at length in a work recently re-published in the Anglo-Catholic Library, entitled, *The Unbloody Sacrifice and Altar Unveiled and Supported*, by Johnson.

This theory, while excluding the dogma of transubstantiation, which Romanists feel to be necessary to give consistency and foundation to their doctrine of the Supper, approaches in other essential respects very closely to that doctrine, asserting, as it does, a real sacrificing priest and a real propitiatory sacrifice in the Supper.[1] The principles already laid down in opposition to the Popish theory of the Supper are almost all equally available against the now mentioned modification of it. It is subversive of the whole doctrine and character of the Gospel. Under the Christian dispensation there is no priest but *One*, and He is in heaven. It is His incommunicable name, which none in heaven or on earth may bear but Himself. There is no sacrifice or propitiation but *one*, and that was finished on the Cross erected

Body and Blood of our ever blessed Redeemer. By the *mysterious* Body and Blood, the reader will easily perceive I mean *neither substantial nor yet merely figurative, but the middle between these extremes,* viz. the Bread and Wine made the Body and Blood of Christ by the secret power of the Spirit; and apprehended to be so, not by our senses, but by our faith, directed and influenced by the same Holy Spirit, and made the Body and Blood in such a manner as human reason cannot perfectly comprehend."—Johnson, *The Unbloody Sacrifice,* Oxf. 1847, vol. i. p. 323. Cf. pp. 265 ff.

[1] [" The Eucharist, after Baptism, is the *only* mean of the forgiveness of our sins."—Jolly, *Christ. Sacrifice in the Euch.* 2d ed. p. 155. Goode, *The Case as it is;* a Reply to Dr. Pusey's Letter to the Archbishop of Canterbury, 3d ed. pp. 17–20.]

upon Calvary, looking back, as it does, for thousands of years over the long array of bloody offerings, which were but the types that pointed towards it, not yet come; and looking forward, as it does, over the long array of ordinances in the Christian Church, commemorative of it, now that it is past. Neither type beforehand, nor commemoration afterhand, could share in its character as an expiatory sacrifice for sin. There is now no dedication of victims to God by death,—life given for life, and blood exchanged for blood,—in order to make a propitiation. The tragedy of the Cross cannot now be renewed, nor atoning blood be shed afresh; and yet " without the shedding of blood there is no remission" in Sacrament or in sacrifice. Under whatever form or modification the sacramental theory be held, which asserts in the Supper a real sacrifice, and a true propitiation for sin, it is a dishonour done to the Lamb of God, who " by the one offering of Himself has perfected for ever them that are sanctified," and who, in virtue of that one Divine offering, now " liveth for ever to make intercession for His people."[1]

[1] Johnson, *The Unbloody Sacrifice and Altar Unveiled and Supported*, Oxf. 1847, vol. i. pp. 265-433, vol. ii. p. 30, etc. Garbett, *Bampton Lecture*, 1842, vol. i. pp. 231-354. Wilberforce, *Doct. of the Holy Eucharist*, 3d ed. pp. 299-338. Goode, *Nat. of Christ's Pres. in the Euch.* Lond. 1856, vol. i. pp. 11-28, etc., vol. ii. pp. 973-978. *Rule of Faith*, Lond. 1842, vol. ii. pp. 135-190. [" Q. What institution hath Christ appointed for the preserving and nourishing in us this Divine principle or spiritual life, communicated to us in Baptism and Confirmation?—A. The Christian Sacrifice of the Holy Eucharist. Q. Did He not offer the sacrifice of Himself upon the Cross?—A. No. It was slain upon the Cross; but it was offered at the institution of the Eucharist. .... Q. What is the consequence of that privilege (the priest's repeating our Lord's 'powerful words')?—A. They (the bread and wine) are in a capacity to be offered up to God as the great Christian sacrifice. Q. Is this done?—A. Yes. The priest immediately after makes a solemn oblation of them. Q. Does God accept of this sacrifice?—A. Yes; and returns it to us again to feast upon. Q. How do the bread and cup become capable of conferring all the benefits of our Saviour's death and passion?—A. By the priest praying to God the Father to send His Holy Spirit upon them. Q. Are they not changed?—A. Yes; in their qualities."—Catechism of Bishop Innes of Brechin, 1841, as quoted in *Peculiarities of the Scottish Episcopal Church, taken from authentic sources*, Aberdeen 1847, p. 2. Bishop Jolly laments that this " primitive doctrine" is " so dimly seen" in the present Communion Service of the Church of England. "The words require some stretch of thought to make them speak the meaning and produce the effect of the former" more ancient liturgies. He thinks, however, that Bishop Andrews and others " must have *understood* the English Office to have implied the eucharistic sacrifice, however lamelike the form was."—*Christ. Sacrifice in the Euch.* 2d ed. pp. 93, 99. Cf. pp. 81 ff. 129-136.]

DIVISION III.

CHURCH POWER EXERCISED IN REGARD TO DISCIPLINE.

———◆———

CHAPTER I.

NATURE, DESIGN, AND LIMITS OF THE DISCIPLINE OF THE CHRISTIAN CHURCH.

THE Church power that is employed in the way of discipline, or that exercise of authority which is implied in inflicting and removing ecclesiastical censures, in judicially admitting to the communion of the Christian society and excluding from it, has been distinguished by the name of the "potestas διακριτικη."

It is not, at this stage of our discussions, necessary to fall back upon the argument which vindicated for the Church a certain ecclesiastical power, distinct in its nature and objects from that belonging to the civil magistrate,—having its source in the gift and appointment of its Divine Head, and having for its general aim the accomplishments of the grand ends for which a Church has been established on the earth. One branch of that power, we have already seen, has reference to doctrine, and embraces those exercises of spiritual authority by which the Church discharges her duty as the teacher and witness for the Word and truth of Christ. A second branch of that power, we have also seen, has reference to ordinances, and comprehends that use of spiritual authority by which the Church, as the organ of Christ for the purpose, maintains and administers His ordinances for the edification of His people. A third branch of this same power remains for our consideration, and consists in that exercise of ecclesiastical authority by which the Church seeks to enforce the observance of Christ's laws by the judicial infliction and removal of His spiritual censures in the case of its members.

The limits imposed upon us make it needful to compress our discussion of this subject within a somewhat narrow compass.

The " potestas διακριτικη," or that exercise of Church authority which respects discipline, may be held to be directed to two grand objects, which are essentially necessary for the order and well-being of the Christian society. In the first place, its aim is to carry into effect the institutions of Christ in regard to the admission and exclusion of members in connection with the Christian society. There are certain principles laid down in His Word which sufficiently indicate the terms of membership which Christ has enacted for His Church, and the character and qualifications of those entitled to be received into the Christian society, or to remain in it as its members. And the first object which that particular branch of Church authority which respects discipline contemplates, is to execute the laws of Christ in the admission to Church membership of those entitled to the privilege, and in the exclusion of those who are not. In the second place, its aim is to carry into effect the instructions of Christ in regard to those who belong to the Church as its members, in the way of securing their obedience to His laws, and of promoting their spiritual edification. There are certain laws which Christ has appointed, not only for the admission and exclusion of members, but also for the regulation of the conduct of those within the Church,—prescribing to them the duties to be done, and the order to be observed by them, as members of the Christian society. And, accordingly, the second object which this branch of Church power contemplates is to promote and secure both the obedience and the edification of the members of the Church, by the restraints of ecclesiastical authority imposed upon them ; by the inflictions of the penalties of censure and rebuke, and deprivation of the privileges of the society, when these have been merited; and by the operation of a system of spiritual rewards and punishments, calculated to promote the order and profit of the Christian community. Speaking generally, these are the two grand aims of that exercise of spiritual authority in the Church which relates to discipline. It provides for the execution of the laws of Christ as these have been revealed in connection with, first, the admission of parties into, or their exclusion from, the Christian society ; and second, the obedience and edification of Church members.

Such being the general nature and design of that power of discipline claimed by the Church, the question that meets us at the outset of the discussion is, as to the ground on which this claim rests. It will not be difficult to show that the right to exercise such a power is one that belongs to the Christian Church, both by the law of nature, as evinced by reason, and by the law of Christ, as revealed in His Word.

I. The power to regulate the matter of the admission and the exclusion of members, as well as their conduct while they continue members of the society, belongs to the Church by the light of nature itself. It is an inherent right vested in every voluntary association of whatever nature it may be, and necessary to its existence and wellbeing as an orderly society.

The very conditions necessary to the subsistence of an organized body of men, and the order implied in combined operations, obviously require that they shall agree on some fixed principles both of union and action,—a compliance with which forms the terms of their admission into and continuance in the society as members, and a departure from which must entail the forfeiture of the privileges of membership. No society created for a common end, and requiring a common action, could possibly subsist upon the principle of being compelled to admit, or to continue to regard as its members, those who transgressed its regulations, or set themselves in opposition to the ends for which it is established. There must be in every voluntary association a right to impose its own laws on its members,—a power to refuse admission to such as give no guarantee for their conformity with the rules and ends of the society,—and, when no other remedy is sufficient, authority to deprive of its privileges and expel from its fellowship those who perseveringly and systematically depart from the order and obligations of the institution. If a society be a lawful association at all, it must have this right to exercise the power of order and authority over its members which is necessary to the very ends for which it is instituted. The existence of the right as belonging to the Church, in common with every other lawful society of men, is clearly demonstrated from the light of nature itself.

And from the same source it is not difficult to gather a proof, not only of the justice of such a claim, on the part of the Christian society, but also of the limits that are justly appointed to the right. In regulating the order of the society and the conduct of the members, and in exercising the right of admission and expulsion in conformity with its fixed principles, there are two limitations plainly set to the power so used. *First*, no society has a right of this kind beyond the circle of its own members, or of those who have voluntarily come under the rules and obligations of the society. The right of order and authority exercised by it does not extend to those beyond the association. And *second*, in enforcing its regulations even upon its own members, it can award, in the case of transgressions, no other kind or amount of penalty than the deprivation of some or all of the rights or advantages which the society itself has conferred. When it has deprived the offender of the privileges he enjoyed in communion with the society, and expelled him from its membership, it has exhausted all its rightful authority and its legitimate power in the way of punishment. And these two limitations, which are plainly set to the powers of any voluntary society over its members, restrict also the exercise by the Christian Church of its powers of discipline. By the very law of nature, applicable to the Christian society as well as any other, it may lawfully assert a right to regulate the admission and expulsion of its members, and their conduct while they continue members within it. But *first*, the Church has no power of discipline or authority over those who have not sought or adopted its communion; and *second*, the Church has no penalties in its storehouse of authority beyond the forfeiture it may award to offenders of the privileges which they have received from its communion. And when the sentence of expulsion from these is pronounced, in the case of the last extremity, its authority is then and there exhausted and at an end.

II. The power of discipline is a right conferred on the Church by positive Divine appointment.

The right which the Christian Church, in common with every voluntary and lawful society, has to appoint and enforce its own terms of admission, and to carry out, in the instance of its members, its own internal regulations, by no means comes up to the full idea of the " potestas διακριτικη " claimed and exercised by it. There is a spiritual efficacy in this power of discipline, and there are spiritual results flowing from it, which no mere natural right belonging to any society can confer, and which nothing but the authority and virtue of a Divine institution can give. It binds the conscience with an obligation, and carries with it a supernatural blessing or judgment, which no power or act of any voluntary human society can confer, and which can only be explained on the principle of an authority and virtue bound up in the ordinance by the positive appointment of God. Over and above, then, the mere right which every lawful society must have in the way of authority and regulation in the case of its members, the power of discipline exercised by the Christian Church is one of direct Divine institution. That ecclesiastical discipline is an ordinance of God, may be established by three distinct lines of proof : by the positive appointment of it which we find in Scripture, by the examples recorded of apostolic practice, and by the directions given in regard to the mode of its exercise.

1st, We have the direct institution of Church discipline and ecclesiastical censures by Christ Himself.

I do not stop to inquire into the nature and exercise of this ordinance under the Old Testament Church, as it would require a lengthened discussion in order to do justice to the subject. But this I may say, that nothing seems more certainly susceptible of proof than that, apart from any exercise of civil authority on the side of the state, there was also an exercise of ecclesiastical authority in the Jewish Church, in the way of depriving transgressors of the privileges of the Church, and excluding them from the congregation in Divine worship. The subject is discussed with great learning and force of argument in Gillespie's *Aaron's Rod Blossoming*.[1] But, passing by the case of the Jewish Church, we have abundant evidence that the ordinance of discipline was the institution of Christ Himself in the New Testament Church.

There are three occasions more especially on which we find our Lord intimating the grant of such power to His Church. First, on the occasion of the remarkable confession made by Peter, our Saviour declares to him : " I say unto thee, that thou art Peter, and upon this rock I will build my Church ; and the gates of hell shall not prevail against it. And I will give unto thee

---

[1] Gillespie, *Aaron's Rod Blossoming*, B. i. ch. iv.–xiii. B. iii. ch. ii. iii. *Miscell. Quest.* ch. xix. Rutherford, *Divine Right of Church Government and Excommunication*, Lond. 1646, pp. 241 ff. 270–275, etc. Beza, *Tractat. de verâ Excommun. et Christ. Presbyterio*, Genevæ 1590, pp. 37–49, 55–63, 83–92.

the keys of the kingdom of heaven : and whatsoever thou shalt
bind on earth shall be bound in heaven ; and whatsoever thou
shalt loose on earth shall be loosed in heaven."[1] Next, when
speaking of the treatment of offences, our Lord, on another occasion, declares to all the Apostles : " If thy brother trespass against
thee, go and tell him his fault between thee and him alone : if he
shall hear thee, thou hast gained thy brother. But if he will not
hear thee, then take with thee one or two more, that in the mouth
of two or three witnesses every word may be established. And
if he shall neglect to hear them, then tell it unto the Church :
but if he neglect to hear the Church, let him be unto thee as an
heathen man and a publican. Verily I say unto you, Whatsoever
ye shall bind on earth shall be bound in heaven ; and whatsoever
ye shall loose on earth shall be loosed in heaven."[2] A third time,
and after His resurrection, we find our Lord conferring on His
Apostles the same authority in connection with their commission
as Apostles : " Then said Jesus to them again, Peace be unto you :
as my Father hath sent me, even so send I you. And when He
had said this, He breathed on them, and saith unto them, Receive
ye the Holy Ghost. Whose soever sins ye remit, they are remitted unto them ; and whose soever sins ye retain, they are
retained."[3]

It is not necessary for our present argument to inquire as to
the particular party or parties in the Church to whom this special
authority was committed by Christ, and who, in consequence of
His grant, are warranted, rather than others, to administer it.
This inquiry falls under the important question to be discussed
afterwards, of the parties in whom the exercise of Church power
generally is vested. But, postponing this question for the present,
it is plain, on an examination and comparison of these statements
of Scripture, that our Lord did in them convey to His Church a
permanent gift of authority and power in the way of discipline
that was long to outlast the ministry of the Apostles. The passages
I have quoted are evidently parallel, and each helps to interpret
the other. The phrase, "the keys of the kingdom of heaven,"
occurring in the first passage, is parallel to the power of "binding and loosing," spoken of in the second ; and each of these two
is equivalent to the authority to "remit and retain sins," mentioned in the third passage. The expression, " the kingdom of

[1] Matt. xvi. 18 f.   [2] Matt. xviii. 15–18.   [3] John xx. 21–23.

heaven," made use of in the grant to Peter of "the keys," is, according to a very common New Testament use of the words, to be understood of the visible Church of Christ; and the power of the keys is the power of opening or closing the door of that Church, in the case of parties seeking admission or meriting exclusion. Exactly equivalent to this power of the keys is the authority to bind and to loose; or the authority to bind upon men their sins, so that they shall be shut out from the Church, or to loose them from their sins, so that they shall be entitled to admission. And in the same sense, and to the same effect, are we to understand the third form of expression, used by our Lord to the representatives of His Church when He gave them right to "retain and remit sin,"—language not to be interpreted literally, as a power from Christ to forgive guilt, or to visit it with everlasting condemnation, vested in His Church, but to be understood as conferring authority on the Church only in reference to those external privileges and punishments of transgression, which, as a visible society, it has a title to award and to remove. The three passages in which our Lord commits to the Church this remarkable power are to be interpreted in connection with each other; and while they afford, when rightly understood, no countenance to the idea of a power to pardon sin or absolve from its eternal consequences, they furnish a most satisfactory proof of the authority of the Church to exercise a power of discipline in judicially inflicting and removing ecclesiastical censures in the case of its members.[1]

2d, That the power of discipline is a Divine appointment in the Church, may be gathered also from the distinct intimations that we have in Scripture of the apostolic practice on the subject.

The remarkable case of the incestuous person connected with the Church of Corinth is an example of apostolic practice in the use of judicial discipline that affords an authoritative precedent in the matter. In the first letter addressed to the Corinthian believers, we find distinctly laid down the occasion that demands such an exercise of judicial authority in a Christian Church,— the object or end to be attained by the use of it, both as respects

---

[1] Gillespie, *Aaron's Rod Blossoming*, B. iii. ch. ii.–vi. Rutherford, *Divine Right of Church Gov.* Lond. 1646, pp. 226–239, 308–316. *Jus Div. Reg. Eccles.* Lond. 1646, pp. 181–183. Cunningham, *Works*, vol. iv. pp. 235–246.

the purity of Church communion and the edification of the offender,—and the authority for such proceedings, as done in the name of Christ.[1] And in the second epistle to the same Church we find the apostle, in reference to the same person, justifying or commending the sentence of excommunication inflicted, declaring the beneficial effect which the punishment had produced on the offender, and instructing the Corinthian Church in the principles on which, in consequence of his repentance, they ought to proceed to absolve and receive him again into fellowship.[2] Another striking example of the practice of the Apostles in this matter is referred to in the First Epistle to Timothy, when Paul speaks of certain persons who had "made shipwreck of the faith," and adds, "of whom is Hymenæus and Alexander; whom I have delivered unto Satan, that they may learn not to blaspheme."[3] Even in the case of the primitive Church, while yet in the furnace of persecution, it was necessary, by the exercise of judicial authority, to purge out the offence and the offender, that the Christian society might be preserved pure.[4]

3d, The authority of discipline as a Divine ordinance in the Church may be very distinctly demonstrated also by the directions given in Scripture for the manner of its exercise.

These directions, often of a merely incidental sort, scattered up and down the pages of Scripture, plainly take for granted the ordinance of discipline as a standing and authoritative institute in the Church. "Them," says the Apostle Paul, "that sin, rebuke before all, that others also may fear." "And others," says the Apostle Jude, "save with fear, pulling them out of the fire; hating even the garment spotted by the flesh." "A man that is an heretic, after the first and second admonition, reject." "Now we command you, brethren, in the name of our Lord Jesus Christ, that ye withdraw yourselves from every brother that walketh disorderly, and not after the tradition which he received of us." "And if any man obey not our word by this epistle, note that man, and have no company with him, that he may be ashamed. Yet count him not as an enemy, but admonish him as a brother."[5] These, and various other passages that might be

---

[1] 1 Cor. iv. 18–21, v. 1–13.

[2] 2 Cor. ii. 1–10, vii. 8–12, x. 2–8, xiii. 2–10.   [3] 1 Tim. i. 19 f.

[4] Rutherford, *ut supra*, pp. 238–240, 316–344.   Gillespie, *Aaron's Rod*, B. iii. ch. vii.

[5] 1 Tim. v. 20; Jude 23; Tit. iii. 10; 2 Thess. iii. 6–14 f.

quoted, embodying the inspired instructions of the Apostles as to the manner and spirit in which ecclesiastical discipline was to be exercised, afford the most satisfactory proof of the existence of the practice as a standing ordinance in the Christian Church. Added to the example of the Apostles, and the express appointment and commission of Christ, they furnish very abundant and conclusive evidence that the power of discipline is a Divine institution in the Christian Church.[1]

Such are the grounds on which it may be argued that Christ has given a power of discipline to the office-bearers of the Christian society. "The Lord Jesus," says the Confession of Faith, " as King and Head of His Church, hath therein appointed a government in the hand of Church officers, distinct from the civil magistrate. To these officers the keys of the kingdom of heaven are committed, by virtue whereof they have power respectively to retain and remit sins, to shut that kingdom against the impenitent, both by the Word and censures, and to open it unto penitent sinners by the ministry of the Gospel, and by absolution from censures, as occasion shall require."[2] But while there is abundant proof from Scripture of the existence of such an authority in the Christian Church, it is no less certain that there are strict and well-defined limits set in the Word of God to its extent and its operations. It is of much importance to advert to the limits appointed to Church power in this department of its exercise.

In the first place, then, the judicial power of the Church is limited by a regard to the authority of Christ as the source of it.

The power of the keys was usually divided by the old theologians into these two,—the key of doctrine, and the key of discipline. The key of doctrine implies the right and authority of the Church, with the Word of God in its hand, to apply its statements regarding sin to the case of the sinner individually,—to employ its threatenings to deter, its warnings to admonish, its authority to restrain the guilty ; and also to bring to bear its promises and encouragements for the restoration of the penitent, on repentance, specially addressing and accommodating Scripture declarations to each particular case, according to the nature of the offence and the demerits of the offender. The key of discipline implies the right and authority of the Church to exercise the office of admitting into the communion of the Christian society, and of excluding

---

[1] [Gillespie, *Aaron's Rod*, B. ii. ch. ix.]   [2] Conf. c. xxx.

from it; to judge of the qualifications of candidates for membership; and, in the case of transgressors among its members, to
proceed against the offending party by suspension from Church
privileges for a time, or by finally cutting him off by the sentence
of excommunication.[1] In the instance of the exercise by the
Church of the key of doctrine, its right and power are to interpret
and apply, according to its understanding of it, the sentence already
pronounced by the Word of God upon the offence with which it
has to deal; exhibiting before the eyes of the offender, and applying to his case, the judgment of the Scripture as to the future
and eternal consequences of his sin. In the instance of the exercise by the Church of the key of discipline, its right and power
are, by its own judicial act, to exclude the offender for a time, or
permanently, from the outward privileges of the Church.

But beyond this, the Church has no authority and no power.
In the case of the key of doctrine, the office and duty of the
Church are simply declarative, and no more,—having power to
announce what, according to its own understanding of them, are
the decisions of the Word of God, as applicable to the case in the
way of absolving the repentant, and condemning the impenitent
sinner; but having no power itself, and apart from the Divine
sentence, to absolve or condemn. In the case of the key of discipline, the office and duty of the Church are simply ministerial,—
having power to admit to or exclude from the outward privileges
of the Christian society, according as it believes that Christ in
His Word has admitted or excluded; but having no power itself
to open or shut the door of the invisible Church, or to give or
withhold admission to the favour of God. In these respects, the
right of discipline exercised by the Church is limited by the
authority of Christ as the source of it. In pronouncing absolution or condemnation, the Church is simply declaring the sentence of Christ in the matter, according to its own interpretation

---

[1] " The ordinance of excommunication is added, as divines say, to confirm
God's threatenings, as Sacraments do seal the promises. . . . No censure
should be blindly or implicitly made use of, but, both in reference to the party
and others, there should be instruction, exhortation, conviction, etc., by the
Word going before or alongst with the same. In which respect, though *improperly*, censures may be some way looked upon as Sacraments, in a large
sense, in these particular cases, because there is in them both some signifying
and confirming use,—they being considered with respect to the end wherefor
they are appointed."—Durham, *Treatise concerning Scandal*, Glasg. 1720, pp.
55, 62.

of that sentence; it has no independent or mysterious authority itself to absolve from guilt, or to condemn to future punishment. In excluding from or admitting to the fellowship of the Christian society, the Church is merely acting according to its views of how Christ would in the circumstances act; and the effect of its sentence can carry with it no more than the giving or withdrawing of outward privileges. In either case, the sentence of the Church may be wrong and unwarrantable. In declaring the sentence of absolution or condemnation, the Church may have erred, and interpreted the mind of Christ amiss; and if so, the sentence will carry with it no spiritual blessing or judgment. In the ministerial act of admitting to or cutting off from the outward privileges and membership of the Church, it may have erred also, having misapplied the law of Christ; and if so, the act done, although it may wrongfully give or withhold outward privileges, has no spiritual efficacy or virtue to throw open or to close the door of saving privilege. The authority of Christ in heaven, and His power to give or withhold grace, are not to be set aside by the erroneous act of His Church on earth. The Church makes no Popish or semi-Popish claim to absolve or condemn, to admit to or exclude from grace, independently of Christ.[1]

In the second place, the judicial power of the Church in the way of discipline is limited by the Word of God as the rule of its exercise.

Beyond the warrant of that rule, the Church has no right of discipline, and no authority to enforce it. Unto the Christian Church has been given a provision of outward ordinances and privileges, unspeakably precious even as external means, and no more than means, of grace; and in the enjoyment and use of these, her members have advantages of a very important kind, which those not her members do not possess, and the forfeiture of which infers no light or inconsiderable penalty. Such a penalty, but no more, Scripture gives authority to the Church, in the exercise of its judicial powers, to impose upon offenders. The rights and privileges and advantages which the Church gives when it gives a title to its membership, it can also for cause shown take away. But beyond the forfeiture of the outward privileges which itself

---

[1] Durham, *ut supra,* pp. 93–97. [Voetius, *Polit. Eccles.* tom. iv. lib. iv. Tract. ii. c. i.–iii., Tract. iv. cap. iii. Stillingfleet, *Doct. and Pract. of the Church of Rome,* Cunningham's ed. pp. 85–107.

conferred, the Church cannot go in the way of inflicting penalties. In this respect, it is strictly limited by the authority of Scripture as its rule. The temporary suspension or the permanent exclusion of the offender from the outward privileges of the Christian society, is the only discipline or judicial punishment competent for the Church to inflict. The arbitrary and unauthorized discipline which the Church of Rome asserts a right to impose,—its outward penances and inflictions, affecting the person and the estate of the victims, its fleshly mortifications, its forfeiture of civil rights and social advantages, its system of punishment and pilgrimage, of bodily austerity and asceticism,—all these and such like impositions, whether voluntary or compulsory, are inconsistent with the Scripture limits of ecclesiastical discipline, and in opposition to the Word of God as its rule.[1]

In the third place, the power of the Church in the way of discipline is limited by the nature of it, as exclusively a spiritual power.

When the instrumentalities of warning, and counsel, and admonition, and rebuke, and censure, as these are enjoined in the Word of God, have been employed, the key of doctrine gives warrant to go no farther. When first suspension for a season from Church privilege and fellowship, and ultimately the sentence of permanent excommunication, have been resorted to, the powers implied in the key of discipline come to an end. The authority

---

[1] ["In the evangelical and reformed use of this sacred censure, it seeks not to bereave or destroy the body ; it seeks to save the soul by humbling the body, not by imprisonment or pecuniary mulct, much less by stripes or bonds or disinheritance, but, by fatherly admonishment and Christian rebuke, to cast it into a godly sorrow, whose end is joy and ingenuous bashfulness to sin. If that cannot be wrought, then as a tender mother takes her child and holds it over the pit with scaring words, that it may learn to fear where danger is,—so doth excommunication as dearly and as freely, without money, use her wholesome and saving terrors : she is instant ; she beseeches ; by all the dear and sweet promises of salvation, she entices and woos; by all the threatenings and thunders of the Law and rejected Gospel, she charges and adjures : this is all her armoury, her munition, her artillery ; then she awaits with long-suffering, and yet ardent zeal. In brief, there is no act in all the errand of God's ministers to mankind wherein passes more lover-like contestation between Christ and the soul of a regenerate man lapsing, than before, and in, and after the sentence of excommunication. As for the fogging proctorage of money, with such an eye as strook Gehazi with leprosy, and Simon Magus with a curse, so does she look, and so threaten her fiery whip against that banking den of thieves, that dare thus baffle, and buy and sell the awful and majestic wrinkles of her brow."—Milton, *Of Reformation in England,* B. ii. Prose Works, Lond. 1753, p. 28.]

of the Church is purely spiritual, and in these spiritual acts its discipline is exhausted. The theory and practice of the Church of Rome as to the necessity and use of outward satisfactions and bodily mortifications, as a penance rendered for sin, are inconsistent with the nature of discipline as a purely spiritual ordinance. Much more, the gross perversion of the doctrine of excommunication, as directly or indirectly carrying with it civil penalties affecting the person or estate, or even life of the excommunicated party, is plainly opposed to the true and essential character of the institution.[1]

In the fourth place, the power of the Church in the way of discipline is limited by a regard to the liberties and edification of its members.

The exercise of authority by the Church in the way of inflicting and removing ecclesiastical censures, proceeds upon the idea that the parties offending have still a right to be regarded as members of the Christian society, although for a time, it may be, judicially deprived of its privileges, or suspended from its fellowship. It is intended for those who are within the Church, not for them that are without its pale,—for the man that is " called a brother," and not for that other man who has never been " called a brother" at all, or who, in consequence of his excommunication from the Church, is thereafter to be regarded as a " heathen man and a publican." Until the final sentence of excommunication is pronounced, the party offending is to be dealt with, in all the exercises of discipline, as a brother, although, it may be, an erring one; and the procedure of the Church in inflicting censure is to be regulated by a regard to his rights and edification as a brother.[2] Discipline in all its uses, short of

---

[1] [Stillingfleet, *Doct. and Pract. of the Church of Rome,* Cunningham's ed. pp. 183–196.]

[2] " The order and manner," says Durham in that part of his excellent work, already referred to, which treats " Of Scandals as they are the object of Church Censures,"—" the order and manner to be observed in the following of public scandals are not easily determinable, there being such variety of cases in which the Lord exerciseth the prudence and wisdom of His Church officers. And, indeed, the gift of government, to speak so, doth especially kyth in the right managing of discipline, in reference to the several humours and constitutions, to say so, which men have to do with. For as in bodily diseases the same cure is not for the same disease in all constitutions and seasons, and as ministers in their doctrine are to press the same thing in divers manners upon divers auditories, so this cure of discipline is not to be applied equally unto all persons, nay, not to such as are in the same offences;

the sentence of excommunication, is to be regarded, as respects the party offending, as *remedial* rather than *punitive*,—a means adapted by sharp and severe remedies to promote, not the destruction, but the edification of the offender. His rights and best interests as a brother, although a fallen one, set bounds in this way to the exercise of Church discipline, and restrict it to the use of such means of a spiritual kind as shall not hinder but help the good of his soul. A regard to the liberties and edification of the brother upon whom discipline is exercised, must plainly limit the exercise of an authority which is intended to work " for the destruction of the flesh, that the spirit may be saved in the day of the Lord Jesus."[1] " Church censures," says the Confession of Faith, " are necessary for the reclaiming and gaining of offending brethren ; for deterring others from the like offences ; for purging out of that leaven which might infect the whole lump; for vindicating the honour of Christ, and the holy profession of the Gospel ; and for preventing the wrath of God, which might justly fall upon the Church, if they should suffer His covenant, and the seals thereof, to be profaned by notorious and obstinate

for that which would scarce humble one, may crush another, and that which might edify one, might be stumbling to another of another temper. Therefore we suppose there is no peremptory determining of rules for cases here, but necessarily the manner of procedure in the application of rules is to be left to the prudence and conscientiousness of Church officers, according to the particular circumstantiate case. . . . When I speak of *edifying*, I do not speak of pleasing the persons, for that may often be destructive to them and others also ; but this is intended, that it is to be weighed in Christian prudence, whether, considering the time and place we live in, the nature of the person we have to do with, and of those also among whom we live, it be more fit to follow this way with such a person at such a time, or another way. And accordingly, as it seemeth probable that this way will honour God most, more fully vindicate His ordinances, gain the person from sin to holiness, or at least to a regular walk, and edify others most, so accordingly ought Church judicatories to take the way that leadeth most probably to that end ; and therefore it ought not always to be accounted partiality when such difference in Church procedure is observed."—(Pp. 55-58.)

[1] Durham, *Treatise concerning Scandal*, Glasg. 1720, pp. 50–216, 232–243, 358–370. [Calvin, *Inst.* lib. iv. cap. xii. Turrettin, *Op.* tom. iii. loc. xviii. qu. xxxii. Voetius, *Polit. Eccles.* tom. iv. lib. iv. Tract. ii.–iv. Apollonii, *Jus Majest. circa Sacra*, Pars ii. cap. i. Gillespie, *CXI. Propositions*, 8–15, 19–31, 63, 70–74. Milton, *Reason of Church Government*, B. ii. ch. iii. Köstlin, *Luther's Lehre von der Kirche*, Stuttgart 1853, pp. 26–46. Schenkel, Art. Kirche in Herzog's *Real Encyclopädie*, pp. 588 ff. In the symbolical books of several of the Reformed Churches,—among the rest, in the Homilies of the Church of England,—the exercise of discipline is added to a sound faith and right administration of the Sacraments, as the third essential mark of a true Church.]

offenders. For the better attaining of these ends, the officers of the Church are to proceed by admonition, suspension from the Sacrament of the Lord's Supper for a season, and by excommunication from the Church, according to the nature of the crime and demerit of the person."

PART IV.—PARTIES IN WHOM THE RIGHT TO EXERCISE CHURCH POWER IS VESTED.

CHAPTER I.

DIVINE APPOINTMENT OF A FORM OF CHURCH GOVERNMENT.

WE now enter upon the fourth and last of the grand departments of our subject, in which, under the general head of the " parties in whom Church power is vested for its ordinary administration," it will be our endeavour to discuss the main points connected with the constitution, government, and office-bearers of the Christian society. The subject is an interesting and important one; and the discussion of it is surrounded with more than ordinary difficulty, in consequence of the very different views and systems of Church polity which have been adopted and maintained in various quarters, with all the advantages of learning and talent on the part of their respective adherents. To do anything like justice to the argument, would require the devotion to it of a space which it is not possible for us now to give. All that we can pretend to attempt is, to give an outline of the general discussion, referring you to other and easily accessible sources of information for the materials to enable you to prosecute the subject in detail.

In proceeding to consider the merits of the several systems of ecclesiastical polity that have been commonly maintained, perhaps the first question which it is natural to ask is, whether or not any authoritative form of Church government has been appointed in Scripture at all. Very opposite opinions on this point have been entertained. Not a few have maintained the doctrine, that no Divine pattern of government for the Christian Church has been exhibited in Scripture, or enjoined upon Christians; and that the Word of God contains no materials sufficient to form a fixed o.

determinate rule for the order and arrangement of the ecclesiastical society. The alleged silence of Scripture on the point is said to be a fact significant of the mind of Christ, indicating His willingness or intention that the form of government for His Church should be left to the discretion and judgment of its members, and should be adjusted by them to suit the circumstances of the age, or country, or civil government with which they stand connected. According to this theory, there is no scriptural model of Church government set up for the imitation of Christians at all times, nor any particular form of it universally binding. Christianity is a living principle, rather than a fixed institution ; and the religious system of the Gospel is able and intended to assume and adapt itself to the particular shape which the necessities of its outward position may impose, or the development from within of its spiritual principles may favour and suggest. The advocates of this doctrine assert that the Church of Christ, as regards her external constitution and organization, has been left very much at freedom ; the inner spiritual life expressing itself in that outward form which best suits the age and country and condition in which she may find herself placed. Upon this view, Christian expediency, guided by a discriminating regard to the advantage and necessities of the Church at the moment, is the only rule to determine its outward organization, and the only directory for Church government.

The theory which denies the existence of a Divine and authoritative form of Church polity, and leaves the whole matter to be regulated by Christian expediency, or merely human arrangement, is one which has found favour with Churchmen inclined either to latitudinarian or Erastian views of the Church ; although it has been held by others also. The mode in which the Reformation was conducted in England, and the undue interference by the State with the Church in that country, had a very marked tendency to develop this theory of ecclesiastical government.[1] We

---

[1] ["The original defenders of the Prelacy of the Church of England," observes Dr. Cunningham, " took on this subject much the same ground as they did in vindicating the rites and ceremonies which they retained,—namely, that there was nothing unlawful or sinful about it, and that, when it was established by the concurrence of the civil and ecclesiastical authorities, it was right to submit to it." This position of theirs, viewed in the light of the history of the times, was a very natural one. The feelings of kindred, and the sense of a great cause to be fought out in common, were still strong throughout all Protestant Christendom. No English theologian could forget that his

find, accordingly, that it was held by very many of the divines of the English Church, more especially shortly after the Reformation. In defending Episcopacy, they did so on the lower ground of expediency, and not on the higher ground of Scripture institution, which was afterwards adopted by the school of Laud, and has remained almost exclusively distinctive of it. Such was the view of Cranmer, Jewel, Whitgift, and many others of the early English theologians. At a later period it was elaborately argued by Stillingfleet in his *Irenicum*. And among ourselves, similar opinions as to the absence of any Divine or authoritative model for the government of the Church have been maintained by Dr. Campbell.

There is another theory, however, very different from that first mentioned, which asserts that the form and arrangements of ecclesiastical government have not been left to be fixed by the wisdom of man, nor reduced to the level of a question of mere

Church was but one member of a fair sisterhood of Churches, holding the same faith, and owning the same origin; and in that wide circle she stood alone in retaining Prelacy. All the leaders of the Reformation throughout Europe, in seeking, to use John Knox's words, "that the reverend face of the primitive and apostolic Kirk should be reduced again to the eyes and memory of men," had been led, without exception, like Wickliffe and others of their predecessors, by their independent study of Scripture, to reject the essential principles of Prelacy, and to adopt those of Presbyterianism. Their conclusions stood embodied in almost every Reformed Confession of Faith that treated of Church government at all. They were constantly urged by the Reforming party in the Church of England. Hence the defensive attitude and semi-apologetic tone of the first generation of English Protestant divines who wrote on Church polity; and hence the ambiguous language of the Ordinal. It needed some time before even the necessities of their position, the strong instincts of English conservatism, and the growing isolation from the influences of foreign thought, could do away with the impression of the contrast between the free choice of Reformed Christendom and the compromise in worship and government which adverse circumstances, mainly political, had forced upon the English Church in spite of the efforts of Hooper and Jewel, and many of her most gifted sons (see esp. the *Zurich Letters, passim*). To Dr. Bancroft is usually assigned the unenviable distinction of being "the first to break the peace of the Reformed Churches" on the question of Church government, by his sermon at St. Paul's Cross in 1588, and his *Pretended Holy Discipline* in 1593. The very general reprobation he met with at the time from the highest authorities, and the tone of the answer of Dr. Reynolds, then commonly held to be the most learned divine of the English Church, plainly show the feeling of the day. Not until later did any number of English Churchmen begin to find an occasion of pride in the very defects which their greatest Reformers had mourned over, and even, by a curious reversal of the facts of the case, to bestow a good deal of compassion upon Luther and Calvin for the distress they must have felt at not being able to establish Prelacy. Cunningham, *Works*, vol. iii. pp. 516–533. Goode, *Non-Episcopal Orders*, Lond. 1852. Harrison, *Whose are the Fathers*, 1867. M'Crie, *Life of Knox*, 5th ed. notes R. and S.]

Christian expediency, but have been determined by Divine authority, and are sufficiently exhibited in Scripture. The advocates
of this view believe that, in respect of its government and organization, as well as in respect of its doctrine and ordinances, the
Church is of God, and not of man; and that Scripture, rightly
interpreted and understood, affords sufficient materials for determining what the constitution and order of the Christian society
were intended by its Divine Founder to be. In express Scripture
precept, in apostolic example, in the precedent of the primitive
Churches while under inspired direction, and in general principles
embodied in the New Testament, they believe that it is possible to
find the main and essential features of a system of Church
government which is of Divine authority and universal obligation.
They believe that the Word of God embodies the general principles and outline of an ecclesiastical polity, fitted to be an authoritative model for all Churches, capable of adapting itself to the
exigencies of all different times and countries, and, notwithstanding, exhibiting a unity of character and arrangement in harmony
with the Scripture pattern. Church government, according to this
view, is not a product of Christian discretion, nor a development
of the Christian consciousness; it has been shaped and settled, not
by the wisdom of man, but by that of the Church's Head. It does
not rest upon a ground of human expediency, but of Divine appointment.

The parties who maintain the "*Jus Divinum*," as respects the
constitution and government of the Christian society, may indeed
differ among themselves as to the extent to which warrant or precedent is to be found in Scripture for the lesser details involved
in the order or polity of the Church. In the question of the constitution and government of the Church, just as in the question of
the rites and ordinances of the Church, there is room, as respects
the details, for that principle embodied in the apostolic canon: "Let
all things be done decently and in order." There is a certain
discretion granted, not as regards the essentials, but as regards the
circumstantials, in the order and arrangements of ecclesiastical
polity, for the introduction and application of the law of nature
and right reason, to regulate what is common to the Christian
society with any other society, and must therefore fall under such
regulation. And men who hold in common the principle that a
form of Church government is appointed in Scripture, may differ

to some extent as to where the line is to be drawn which shall separate between what is authoritatively fixed in the Word of God, and therefore binding on all believers in every age, and what is not fixed there, but left to the determination and decision of nature and of right reason. The real point in debate, however, between the opposite systems now adverted to is in general terms this: Does the Word of God afford us a model, more or less detailed, of ecclesiastical polity and organization, which it is the duty of Christians at all times and in all circumstances to imitate; or is there no authoritative delineation or exhibition of Church government at all, so that it is left to be regulated entirely by the dictates of human expediency or Christian prudence?

I. The view which denies a Divine and positive warrant for any form of Church government, and leaves the whole question open to the determination of human judgment, according to times and circumstances, can be fairly argued and maintained only upon one or other of two principles. First, it could be asserted upon the assumption that the Church of Christ was no more than a human and voluntary society; the members of which were competent, both as respects authority and as respects knowledge, to appoint their own office-bearers, and regulate the form of the association. Or, secondly, it could be asserted, on the assumption that the Christian Church, although not a mere voluntary society, had its origin in nature; and that the law of nature and right reason gave both the authority and the knowledge to select the administrators of the society, and to determine their place and functions. On either of these two grounds, it might be fairly and logically argued that the form of polity and organization needful for the Church was not a matter for positive appointment in Scripture, but rightly fell to be regulated by considerations of human expediency, and to be ordered by the decisions of human wisdom. That neither of these assumptions is correct, it is hardly necessary, at this stage of our discussions, to stop to prove at length.

In the first place, it is not true that the Church is simply a voluntary society, the members of which must possess in themselves both the right and the power to frame its constitution, and appoint the administrators of it. The Christian society, as an ordinance Divine and not human, does not fall under the regulation of such a principle. It does not exist by voluntary compact; its authority is not founded on the consent or delegation of the members; they did not create the Christian association at first, nor do its order and organization wait upon their permission or appointment. The source of its life and authority is from without, not from within ; and the Church of Christ confers upon its members, but does not receive from them—as in the instance of any mere voluntary association—the privileges peculiar to it as a society. In the case of any voluntary association, its character, its powers, its authority, are delegated and conferred by the members, who have the inherent right, acting themselves or through their organs, to give to it the form and organization that please them. In the case of the Church of Christ, the same thing would hold good were it a voluntary association also. That it is not a voluntary society, but one associated upon a Divine warrant, and constituted by a Divine appointment, is a circumstance which excludes the right and competency of its members to frame its polity or to regulate its arrangements according to their own views of expediency or right.

In the second place, it is not true that the Church is a society wholly originating in nature ; or that the law of nature and right reason is sufficient to authorize or enable its members to appoint the form of its constitution, and determine the functions of its office-bearers. If this second assumption were correct, it would afford no small countenance to the idea that the character of its polity and organization was a matter for human wisdom to fix and regulate. If the Church were, like the State, a society founded in nature alone, and arising exclusively out of the natural relations of man as a social being, there might be some ground for the assertion that the law of nature and right reason was sufficient to warrant and enable men, as in the case of civil government, to determine for themselves its rules and constitution. As the creature of nature, it would fall to be regulated as to its organization by the principles of nature. But if, on the contrary, all that is essential and peculiar to the Christian Church is of Divine, and not natural origin, there are no powers within the compass of nature equal to the task of determining its constitution or the form of its development. No doubt, the duty of men associating together for social worship in society is a duty suggested and required by the dictates of nature ; and to this extent it is true that the Church has a foundation in natural principles. And if there had been no peculiar revelation, or if that revelation had not laid anew the foundations of the Christian society in positive Divine appointment, we must have sought in the principles of nature for the form and ordinances of the Church, and been regulated by reason in determining, however imperfectly, the character and functions of the religious society. These principles, had there been nothing else to guide us, must have left the question of the constitution of the Church very much an open one, which might be settled differently in different circumstances. That this supposition, however, is not true,—that the Church of God is not a society wholly or chiefly arising out of the natural relation of man to God,—is a circumstance which forbids the idea that the law of nature or mere reason can determine its character and organization, or that these have been left as a question which it was competent or possible for reason and nature to decide.

II. The theory which denies a Divine warrant for any system of Church government, and hands over the question to be settled by considerations of human expediency, is contradicted by the fact, which can be clearly established from Scripture, that the Church of Christ, in its essential and peculiar character, is a positive institution of God.

This principle is applicable to the Church in all its aspects : to its doctrine, and its ordinances; to its constitution, and its faith ; to its inward life, and its outward organization ; to the spiritual grace which it imparts, and the external form which it bears. All is equally and alike of positive appointment by God, being, in the strict sense of the terms, a Divine institution, not owing its origin or virtue to man, and not amenable to his views of expediency, or determined by his arrangements. Looking at the Church of Christ as an express and positive ordinance of God, it is clear that man is neither warranted nor competent to judge of its organization.

The very consideration that lies at the foundation of all our conceptions of the Christian Church,—the fact that it is not simply a voluntary society, and not wholly an ordinance derived from nature, but properly an institution of God, of positive appointment in His Word,—seems very plainly to militate against the idea of the competency or the ability of man, left to his own discretion, to determine its character and constitution from considerations of expediency alone. At all events, the presumption is strongly against the notion that Church government is a matter of human arrangement and determination solely; and nothing but a very express and plain declaration of Scripture to that effect would justify us in making such an assertion. Admitting that the Christian Church is, in all its essential parts, a positive institution of Divine origin, and grafted upon man's natural capacity for religion, it may not indeed be a conclusion, *necessarily* following from this fact, that man has no part in framing the constitution or determining the character of the ordinance. But the *onus probandi* certainly lies upon those who assert that this task has been actually assigned to him; and nothing but a very direct statement of Scripture, handing over to human wisdom and decision the right and competency to constitute and regulate the polity of the Church of Christ, would justify us in acquiescing in the assertion.

In addition to the positive nature of the institution, there are two considerations of a very cogent nature that seem to fortify the conclusion that the Church of Christ, as an express institution of God, has not been left to receive its form and organization from the hands of man.

First, the separation between man and God, occasioned by sin, more especially excludes the idea that man is competent, by the aid of reason, to devise or to regulate the constitution of the Church. The terms of a sinner's approach to God in worship, the manner of it, the ordinances to be observed, the forms of religious service, are more peculiarly matters which both his judicial exclusion from intercourse with God in his natural state, and his moral inability to renew that intercourse of himself, render him incompetent to deal with. And to the terms and manner of his restored fellowship with God in acceptable worship, must we add the constitutions and regulations of the worshipping society, as a point more especially beyond the power or competency of a sinner to determine. Neither in regard to the services and ordinances of worship, nor in regard to the constitution and order of the Church, are we justified in saying that these are lawful matters for human arrangement or decision.

Second, not only is the Church set forth in Scripture as a society of positive institution by God, but, in addition to this, it is represented in the very peculiar light of a visible kingdom, of which Christ is the living Head or King. It is not only a kingdom diverse from the kingdoms of the world, but, in addition to this, it is a kingdom in which Christ is personally present, as the Administrator as well as the Founder of it,—the Ruler now, as much as the Originator at first of the spiritual society. Such a personal dispensation by Christ Himself of the ordinances and laws and authority of His visible kingdom, seems very decidedly to shut out the idea that its constitution is a matter of human discretion, and its regulations the result of human arrangement. As the present Head and continual Administrator of the Christian society, Christ has left no room in it for the interference of man as His partner in the work. Man is not the lawgiver of the Christian Church; nor has it been left open to him to frame its constitution or its form of administration. His place in it is that of minister or servant of Him who is the Head.

Upon such grounds as these, then, we seem warranted in saying that the government of the Church of Christ is not a matter of human arrangement or expediency, but rather is a positive appointment of Christ, and that Scripture will be found a sufficient and authoritative guide in regard to the outward constitution of the Christian society, no less than in regard to its doctrines, its worship, and its ordinances. There are two remarks, however, which it is important to make in connection with this matter, in order to avoid misapprehension.

1st, Although the Word of God contains a sufficient directory for our guidance in regard to the constitution and order of the Christian society, yet we are not to look for a systematic delineation of Church government, or a scientific compendium of ecclesiastical law, in Scripture. A system of Church law, or a model constitution for the Christian society, would have been out of place in the Word of God, and inconsistent with the great principles on which revelation is framed. We have no scientific exhibition of doctrine drawn up in a logical system in Scripture; and just as little have we any scientific digest or institutes of Church law. The Bible was not framed upon the model of a Confession of Faith, nor yet upon the pattern of a code of ecclesiastical jurisprudence. The Church must, in these latter days, seek for her directory of government and law, as well as of faith, not in formal or scientific statements on either subject, but in those general principles which can be educed from Scripture as applicable to the case; in apostolical example, as well as precept; in the precedents afforded by the primitive Churches

while under inspired direction ; and in the incidental information
to be gathered from the New Testament as to the arrangements
and institutions of the early believers during the lifetime of the
Apostles. It is in entire accordance with the general structure
and usage of Scripture that we should be sent for information on
the subject to such incidental intimations of the mind of God,
rather than to a formal treatise on ecclesiastical government.
And proceeding upon such a principle in the mode of communicating its information, we must be prepared to find in the Bible,
in reference to the form and order of the Church, not a little
that belonged to primitive times, and is not applicable to ours,
some regulations which were called for by the exigencies of
early Christianity, but were not intended to be permanent or
binding upon all Christians. In the extraordinary circumstances
of the early Church, we must be prepared to find something that
was extraordinary and peculiar, and only suited to the temporary
and incomplete condition of the infant Church. There is some
difficulty occasionally in separating between what was extraordinary in the case of the early Christians, and what was ordinary,
and fitted and intended to be a precedent for us. But, notwithstanding of this difficulty, there are ample materials to be found
in Scripture to constitute a sufficient and authoritative model of
Church government binding upon us.

2d, Although the Word of God be a sufficient guide in matters
pertaining to the constitution and government of the Christian
Church, yet there is a distinction to be drawn between what is of
the substance of the ecclesiastical organization, and what is no
more than circumstantial. The Scripture was intended to exhibit
a model of ecclesiastical arrangement, complete in so far as the
Church is a society peculiar and different from other societies ;
that is to say, in so far as regards its essential structure and
form as a Church. But Scripture was not intended to exhibit a
pattern of ecclesiastical order, in so far as the Church is a society,
identical in its character with other societies, or in so far as
regards not its essential, but merely its circumstantial features.
What is common in order and polity to the Christian society with
any other society is left to be regulated by the light of nature
and reason, and is not authoritatively fixed in Scripture. In
short, very much the same distinction between what is of the
substance, and what belongs to the circumstances of the insti-

tution, which we found to be applicable in regard to the matter of Church rites and ceremonies, is also applicable in the case of Church polity and government. Whatever is proper to its essential and distinctive character as a positive institution of God, and so belongs to those points which separate it from other societies, has been authoritatively determined in Scripture, and is universally binding. Whatever is not essential to it as a positive institution of God, but common to its order and arrangements with those of any other society, is left open to be adjusted by reason, in accordance with its own views of what is "in good form and according to order" (εὐσχημόνως καὶ κατὰ τάξιν). The three marks laid down by George Gillespie in the parallel case of Church rites and ceremonies may serve also to indicate what, in the matter of Church government, is left to the determination of reason according to its views of Christian expediency. First, it must be a matter belonging not to the substance of ecclesiastical organization, but only to the circumstances of it. Second, it must be a matter not determinable from Scripture; and Third, it must be a matter to be decided in one way or other; and for the decision of which in *this* particular manner, rather than in a different, a good reason can be assigned.[1] With the help of these tests, it will not often be a difficult matter in practice to say what in the order and arrangements of the ecclesiastical society is, or is not, left free to be determined by human wisdom.

Such, then, are the conclusions in which we seem to be justified in acquiescing with respect to the question, whether or not any authoritative form of Church government has been appointed in Scripture. And if these conclusions are sound, they serve to settle by anticipation another question of no small importance in this discussion, in regard to the standard of appeal by which we are bound to judge of the different forms of Church polity that demand our attention. If the views already indicated are correct, then it unavoidably follows that the Word of God is the standard by which the controversy is to be determined, and not any appeal to the voice of the Church, or the sentiments and opinions of ecclesiastical antiquity. If the form and order of the Christian society be matters of positive appointment by God, then

---

[1] See above, vol. i. p. 355. Gillespie, *Engl. Popish Ceremonies*, Part iii. ch. vii. 5-7.

it is plain that in His Word alone can we expect to find the
materials for judging as to what that appointment actually is.
From tne very nature of the case, a positive institution must have
express warrant in the Word of God, else it cannot be authoritative or binding. The evidence of the post-apostolic age, even
although it could be proved to be valid and satisfactory in itself
in favour of any form of Church government, would not compen-
sate for the absence of the express authority of Scripture. Evidence extra-scriptural, however conclusive it might be, could not
supply the want of the positive testimony of the Word of God.
Even supposing it could be demonstrated by the testimony of
antiquity that a certain form of ecclesiastical polity prevailed in
apostolic times, and had even been set up by inspired men, this
would not avail, if Scripture withheld its testimony. The fact
might be true; but the silence of Scripture would show that
it was a fact not intended by God to be a precedent binding
upon us. The omission of the fact in the sacred volume, and
the silence of the inspired writers, would prove that the form
of polity was one lawful, it might be, or required in the circumstances of the apostolic Church, but not meant to be a
model for the imitation of subsequent ages. It is most important
to understand this aright, as there has been no small misapprehension in regard to it. Very many of the advocates of Episcopacy, for example, have abandoned the scriptural ground altogether, and have endeavoured, by extra-scriptural evidence, to
prove that that form of polity prevailed in the apostolic times.[1]
We may answer such an argument by calling in question the
testimony adduced, and showing, as can be conclusively done,

---

[1] Thus Mr. Litton, in his very interesting and able work on the Church,
while holding Episcopacy to be an apostolic institution, and entitled to the
weight of such—although that, according to his view, does not make it universally binding—frankly gives up the attempt to prove it to be so from
Scripture. "There is every reason to believe," he thinks, "that it is an
apostolic appointment; meanwhile it cannot be denied that Scripture alone
furnishes but slender data for our pronouncing it to be so. And this, be it
observed, may be admitted *without weakening the evidence for its apostolicity.*
Timothy and Titus may have been bishops of Ephesus and Crete respectively,
and yet it may be impossible to prove from Scripture alone that they were so.
. . . As long as the advocates for Episcopacy are content to rest their cause
upon post-apostolic testimony, their position is impregnable : it is only when
they attempt to prove it from Scripture alone that the argument fails to
convince. Better at once to acknowledge that the institution is traceable to
the Apostles chiefly through the channel of uninspired men, than by insisting
upon insufficient scriptural evidence to bring discredit upon the whole argu-

that it is not sufficient to demonstrate the fact asserted of the establishment of Prelacy in apostolic times or by inspired men. But we may answer the argument in a second way, and one no less conclusive. Even admitting for a moment the fact to be as it is asserted,—admitting that examples of diocesan Episcopacy could be proved to have existed, or to have been sanctioned in apostolic times,—the silence of Scripture, and the total absence, to say nothing more, of Scripture evidence in support of it, would nullify the fact as authority for the binding obligation of that form of Church polity upon future ages. It is not only that we must have better and more conclusive evidence for the fact than the corrupted and unsatisfactory testimony of ecclesiastical tradition. But even though the fact were established, we must, in addition to this, have Scripture authority for the fact, before we can be called upon to regard it as a Divine precedent intended to lay an authoritative obligation upon Christians in subsequent generations.[1]

ment."—*Church of Christ*, Lond. 1851, pp. 411, 436. Mr. Litton, accordingly, claims no more scriptural authority for prelates than a few possible "hints." "If the 'angels' of the Apocalypse and Diotrephes were not of this order, it is more than probable that the New Testament does not present us with any instance of a formal bishop." Of the two, he seems inclined to think that there is most to be made of Diotrephes (pp. 425 f.)—a conclusion in which, I believe, most Presbyterians will agree with him.

[1] *Jus Div. Reg. Eccles.* Lond. 1646, pp. 1-35, etc. Cunningham, *Works*, vol. i. pp. 27–45 ; vol. ii. pp. 64–78. Rutherford, *Divine Right of Church Gov.* Lond. 1646, pp. 26–82. [*Answer to Questions propounded by the Parliament to the Assembly of Divines touching Jus Divinum in matter of Church Government*, Lond. 1646, pp. 10–20. Seigwich (of Farnham), *Scripture a Perfect Rule for Church Government.* Forrester, *Review and Consideration*, Edin. 1706, pp. 27 ff. 343-352. Milton, *Reason of Church Gov.* B. i. ch. i. ii. Brown, *Apologetical Relation*, 1665, pp. 213-243 (in reply to Stillingfleet).]

CHAPTER II.

THE EXTRAORDINARY OFFICE-BEARERS OF THE CHRISTIAN CHURCH.

In discussing the question of the kind of Church government delineated and appointed in Scripture, it is a matter of some importance to fix the date when the Christian Church was formally organized or set up. It is plain that this is a question of considerable moment in the discussion; for, by a mistake as to the date of its formal establishment, we may be led to confound the extraordinary circumstances of its transition state with the ordinary circumstances of its normal and permanent condition. Now, a very slight consideration will be sufficient to satisfy us that the Christian Church was not properly or formally founded until after our Lord's resurrection from the dead. From the day of His resurrection we date the commencement of Christianity itself, as a fully established and developed system of faith, founded, as it was, upon the truth of that great fact. And from the same epoch we date the formal commencement of the Christian Church, as a society which owed its establishment and formal existence among men to the same event. Our Lord's sojourn on earth was a period of time devoted to the work of preparing for a new dispensation and Church, rather than exhibiting the commencement of it. It was an interval of transition, in which the foundations of the ancient Church were in course of being removed, rather than a new one established. The members of God's true Church had not yet been summoned to come out of the earlier society, and to enter into the communion of the later. Christ Himself, during all the period of His abode on earth, remained a member of the Jewish Church, waiting on its ordinances, submitting to its distinctive rites, and frequenting the solemnities of the Temple worship. And those who believed on His name during His own lifetime were neither commanded nor encouraged to depart from the established institutions of the ancient Church, or to incorporate themselves into a new fellowship distinct from the former. The worshippers of the Father were still required to worship Him in His house of prayer at Jerusalem; and the day did not arrive which witnessed the formal abolition of the Jewish Church and the public inauguration of the Christian, until the resurrection of Christ openly declared that a new faith had been developed, and a new order of spiritual things begun. From the date of the resurrection of our Lord the Old Testament economy ceased to be binding, and the Old Testament Church was formally at an end. From the same date the foundation of the New Testament Church was laid; and the people of God came under an obligation to join themselves to it as members.[1]

Such plainly being the period when the Church of God ceased to be moulded after the Mosaic type, and came to be shaped after the pattern of the Christian, the inference to be drawn from this consideration is of no small value in our inquiry as to the authoritative precedent for Church government. We must look for that precedent, not during the transition period of the Church, when it was putting off its Jewish features and putting on the Christian, but after that transition had been fairly accomplished, and the Christian society had settled down into its permanent and normal condition. That fixed condition was not attained, indeed, until some time *after* the resurrection of our Lord. It was the special work which He gave His Apostles to accomplish, to complete in its full and perfect order the Christian society of which He had Himself, after His resurrection, only laid the foundations. And He gave them extraordinary powers and gifts for that object, commensurate with the extraordinary work to be performed by them. Around the Apostles, as the special instruments for developing and completing both the system of Christian faith and the structure and organization of the Christian Church, their Master made to gather all those gifts and endowments demanded by such an emergency, and sufficient for such a task. They formed no part of the ordinary equipment of the Church of Christ, or the ordinary staff of office-bearers by which its affairs were to be administered. Their use and function ceased when the Church of Christ, through their instru-

[1] Ayton, *Original Constitution of the Christ. Church*, Edin. 1730, pp. 13-20.

mentality, had been firmly settled and fully organized, and when it had attained to the condition of its ordinary and permanent development. There was an extraordinary instrumentality necessary to prepare for laying the foundations of the Christian Church; there was also an extraordinary instrumentality necessary, after that, for completing the superstructure. It would be a mistake of no small moment to identify these extraordinary provisions on either occasion, with the ordinary equipment of the Christian Church,—to identify its transition character with its permanent organization. Before the Christian society was formally established, the instrumentality of John the Baptist, the personal ministry of our Lord Himself, the commission granted by Him, first to the twelve, and afterwards to the seventy disciples during his lifetime, were the extraordinary means adopted to usher in that state of things in which the foundation of a Christian Church could be laid. Subsequently to that event, the extraordinary commission and endowments granted to apostles and prophets and evangelists at the outset of Christianity, formed the special instrumentality employed to build up and complete the New Testament Church, and to perfect both its outward and inward organization. Both before and after our Saviour's resurrection, extraordinary and temporary measures were resorted to, suitable to the emergency, first, of laying the foundation; and, secondly, of perfecting the superstructure of the ecclesiastical society. And it is of much importance in the subsequent argument, that we be able to discriminate between what was extraordinary and temporary, and what was ordinary and permanent, in the condition and equipment of the Christian Church.

That the Christian Church was not, and could not be, founded at all until Christ rose from the grave, is a position which is very generally admitted by opposite parties in this controversy, and cannot, with any show of reason, be denied. And the conclusion resulting from this consideration, namely, that no precedent or model of Church polity is to be sought for in the history of our Lord's personal ministry, or in the commission granted by Him in His lifetime to the twelve or the seventy disciples, is an inference which, although sometimes overlooked in argument, can hardly be deliberately impugned. But that after the resurrection of Christ, and in order to complete and build up the Church then founded, a similar extraordinary instrumentality was employed, and that we are equally forbidden to regard such instrumentality as belonging to the normal condition of the Church, or as furnishing any precedent to rule its ordinary form of polity, are propositions which, by not a few controversialists, are openly contradicted. The extraordinary mission of apostles and evangelists, necessary and adapted to the emergency of a Church *to be* established, has been often appealed to as the rule or model for the proper and permanent condition of the Christian society. The temporary and exceptional circumstances of a Church passing through the crisis of its birth and infancy have been mistaken for the pattern binding on a Church in its natural and perfect state. In the language of the old divines, the " Ecclesia constituenda " has been made to give law to the " Ecclesia constituta." [1] It will to a great extent clear the way for our future discussions, if we seek at the outset to separate between the extraordinary and the ordinary office-bearers in the Christian society,—between those adapted to the emergency of its infant condition, and destined to pass away, and those adapted to its permanent and fixed condition, and entitled to a standing place in the external arrangements of Christ for His people.

SEC. I. OFFICE OF APOSTLES.

Let us, in the first instance, direct our attention to the case of the Apostles, and inquire whether the office held by them in the earliest times of the Church was extraordinary and temporary, or ordinary and permanent, in the Christian society. It will not be difficult to show that the peculiarities of the apostolic office are such as to prove that the former alternative is the correct one.

I. One peculiarity—perhaps the primary one—of the apos-

---

[1] [" Versetzen wir uns in Gedanken auf den Zeitpunkt wo der letzte Apostel gestorben ist, und fragen ; wo ist nun das Apostolat?—so antwortet der Katholicismus : es ist in den lebendigen Nachfolgern der Apostel, als den Inhabern der wahren Tradition, in den Bischöfen, den Concilien, dem Papste, in welcher Repräsentation sie die Fortsetzung der apostolischen Inspiration erkennt. Die evangelische Kirche dagegen antwortet, dass sie den vollgültigen Ausdruck für das Apostolat nur in der heiligen Schrift findet, welche die bleibende Stimme der Apostel in der Kirche ist. Während der Katholicismus eine fortgesetzte Inspiration durch alle Zeiten hindurch annimmt, führt der Protestantismus dieselbe nur auf die Stiftung der Kirche zurück."— Martensen, *Dogmatik*, 4te Aufl. p. 296. Litton, *Church of Christ*, Lond. 1851, pp. 410 f.]

tolic office, distinguishing it from other offices in the Christian
Church, was, that the Apostles were separated to be the *witnesses*
of our Lord's ministry, and more particularly of His resurrection
from the dead.

This is very often referred to, both by our Lord and by the
Apostles themselves, as the grand object of their appointment to
the office.   When our Saviour gave to the eleven their final
instructions before He ascended up to heaven, He very distinctly
indicated the purpose for which they had been selected and set
apart: " And He said unto them, Thus it is written, and thus it
behoved Christ to suffer, and to rise from the dead the third day,
and that repentance and remission of sins should be preached in
His name among all nations, beginning at Jerusalem.   And *ye
are witnesses* of these things." [1]   The same thing is still more
pointedly brought out in the election of Matthias to the place
among the Apostles, made vacant by the apostasy of Judas.
The purpose of the apostolic office, as furnishing a personal
witness for Christ, is put beyond all reasonable controversy by
the express language of Peter on that occasion : " Wherefore of
these men which have companied with us all the time that the
Lord Jesus went in and out among us, beginning from the baptism of John, unto that same day that He was taken up from us,
must one be ordained *to be a witness with us of His resurrection*." [2]
The case of Paul, who was *not* among the number of those who
had companied with Christ, and seen Him in the days of His
flesh, although at first sight an exception to the rule, furnishes
in reality a strong confirmation of the same conclusion as to the
design and peculiarity of the apostolic office.   Paul was not
qualified to bear testimony to Christ from personal knowledge
of Him before and after His resurrection, in the same manner
as the other apostles, who had been eye-witnesses, were qualified ;
but, to fit him for the office to which he was called, the Lord
appeared to him on the way to Damascus, and the risen Saviour
was seen of him also " as of one born out of due time." [3]   We have
more than one distinct relation of the conversion and appointment
to the apostleship of Paul, in which reference is made to the object
and design of his extraordinary call, and the heavenly vision
through which it was accomplished.   " The God of our fathers,"
said Ananias to the astonished Saul, " hath chosen thee, that thou

[1] Luke xxiv. 46-48.   [2] Acts i. 21 f.   [3] 1 Cor. xv. 8.

shouldst know His will, and *see* that Just One, and shouldst *hear* the voice of His mouth. For thou shalt be a *witness* to all men *of what thou hast seen and heard.*[1] In the original call granted to the apostle, Christ Himself is represented as thus addressing him : " I have *appeared* unto thee *for this purpose*, to make thee a minister and a *witness*, both of those things which thou hast seen, and of those things in the which I will appear unto thee." [2] Such passages as these can be interpreted in no other way than as a declaration that the supernatural appearance of Christ, when He was seen and heard by Paul, was made in order to remove the disqualification, under which Paul laboured, of having not seen Christ after the flesh; and that the design of the office, to which he was in this extraordinary manner called, was to furnish an eye-witness to the fact of a risen Saviour among men. And the whole character of the life and preaching both of Paul and the other apostles, goes to establish the same conclusion. They constantly felt and declared that their peculiar office or mission was to be witnesses for Christ and His resurrection. " We were eye-witnesses of His majesty," says Peter. " That which we have seen and heard, declare we unto you," says John. " He was seen of James; then of all the apostles; and last of all, He was seen of me also," says Paul. " This Jesus hath God raised up, whereof we all are witnesses," says the Apostle Peter in the name of his brethren. " And we are witnesses of all that He did," says the same apostle on another occasion. " Him God raised up the third day, and shewed Him openly, not to all the people, but unto witnesses, chosen before of God, even unto us." [3] So very express and abundant is the evidence to prove that one peculiarity, perhaps the chief one, which distinguishes apostles from other office-bearers in the Christian Church, was the distinctive qualification—not of course enjoyed by any that came after them—that they were the selected witnesses for Christ and His resurrection.

II. Another peculiarity, marking out the apostolic office from others of an ordinary kind, was the call and commission to it given by Christ Himself.

The twelve were immediately sent forth to their work by

---

[1] Acts xxii. 14 f.   [2] Acts xxvi. 16.
[3] 2 Pet. i. 16; 1 John i. 3 ; 1 Cor. xv. 7 f. ; Acts ii. 32, iii. 15, iv. 20, v. 32, x. 39–41.

Christ, without the intervention of man. Their commission was direct and peculiar, being independent of any earthly authority, and resting immediately on the call of Christ. " As my Father hath sent me, even so send I you," [1] were the words of our Lord addressed to them,—forming the sole and all-sufficient authority by which they ministered as His Apostles. When the vacancy among the Twelve Apostles had to be filled up by the election of Matthias, the choice was referred directly to God. When yet another was to be added in the person of Saul of Tarsus, the addition was made by an extraordinary call from heaven. Indeed it is a fact of great significance in regard to the nature and design of the apostolic office, that the name which, in the primary meaning, was proper to the Son of God, as *The Sent* of God, the *Apostle* of the Father,[2] should have been specially given by Him to the twelve whom He selected as His immediate witnesses and messengers to the world. "And of them He chose twelve," says the narrative of their selection to the office ; " whom also He named apostles." [3]   In the same sense in which the Son was the Apostle, or *The Sent* of the Father, so were these twelve the apostles or the *sent* of Christ. As He came not of Himself, but was commissioned directly by the Father, so they who occupied the foremost place among the office-bearers of His Church were specially commissioned and delegated by Him. In the Gospel by John, when our Lord speaks of the authority granted Him for His work and office as Mediator, the special description of Himself that He gives more frequently almost than any other, is that He is *The Sent* of God, or the Apostle of the Father, who had sent Him into the world.[4]   And the assignation of that description or title to the twelve by Christ Himself marks very emphatically the peculiar investiture which they, as apostles, received. So nearly resembling the very mission of the Son by the Father was the delegation they received from Christ, that He appropriates to it the same name, and tells them, moreover, in reference to their extraordinary vocation : " He that receiveth you, receiveth me ; and he that receiveth me, receiveth Him that sent me." [5]   As regards this direct and extraordinary commission,

---

[1] John xx. 21.

[2] ὁ Ἀπόστολος, Heb. iii. 1. [On the kindred words and phrases in Hebrew, Arabic, etc., see Voetius, *Polit. Eccles.* tom. iii. lib. ii. Tract ii. ch. ii. 1.]

[3] Luke vi. 13.   [4] John iv. 34, v. 23, 30, 36 f., vi. 29, 39, etc.

[5] Matt. x. 40 ; John xiii. 20.

the Apostles stood alone and without succession in the Christian Church.

III. Another peculiarity of the apostolic office was the supernatural power which they possessed to qualify them for their extraordinary mission.

As the founders of the faith and of the Church of Christ, the Apostles received extraordinary gifts, proportioned to the extraordinary emergency which they were called upon to meet. It was required of them, not only to declare the doctrine of their Master, but to complete for the use of the Church and the world the revelation of truth, which, in regard to many things He had to tell, was left incomplete by our Lord at the close of His personal ministry, because, as He Himself said, "they were not *then* able to bear it;"[1] and for this purpose it was necessary that the Apostles should receive the extraordinary inspiration of God, to enable them, by word and writing, to fill up the measure of Divine revelation to men. Again, it was required of the Apostles that they should be not only the teachers of infallible truth, but the witnesses to accredit it in the face of an unbelieving world; and for the purpose of enabling them to accredit it, they went forth among men endowed with miraculous powers, "preaching the Word everywhere, with signs following." Further still, it was required of the Apostles that they should publish the Gospel to every creature, so that men of other languages and nations might be brought into the Church of God; and for this purpose the day of Pentecost beheld them possessed with the extraordinary gift of tongues, so that each one of the strangers out of divers countries "heard them speak in his own language the wonderful works of God." The powers of inspiration, of miracles, and of tongues are spoken of by Paul as "the signs of an apostle" (τα σημεια του αποστολου),[2]—marking out the authority and the special character of his office. This power was indeed bestowed on others besides the Apostles; although there is no reason to think that others possessed it in the same degree with the Apostles. And even with respect to other believers who possessed and exercised miraculous gifts, there seems to be some ground in Scripture for holding that, in ordinary cases, they received such gifts only through the intervention of the Apostles, and in consequence of the imposition of the Apostles' hands. But whether there be

[1] John xvi. 12.   [2] 2 Cor. xii. 12.

sufficient ground in Scripture for that assertion or not, of this there seems to be no doubt, that it was the peculiar office of apostles, by imposition of hands, to confer supernatural endowments; and that this power of imparting and transmitting to others extraordinary gifts was confined to them alone. Here, then, we have another characteristic of the apostle's office, marking it out as temporary, and not permanent.

IV. Another peculiarity which marked the Apostles, was the universal commission and unlimited authority which were conferred on them as Christ's representatives on earth.

There were no bounds set either to the extent of this commission, as embracing the whole world, or to the measure of their authority, as supreme over all Churches and all office-bearers in the Church. In the very terms of their original appointment we read the universal commission which distinguished them as the apostles of the world, and not of any one nation or Church. We see the same unlimited vocation in the " catholic epistles " which they sent forth, not to one Church, or one society of believers, but to the universal Church of Christ. We have evidence of the same unrestricted ministry in the history of their life and conduct. We see them preaching the Gospel wherever they found themselves situated, and reaching forth unto the regions beyond, planting Churches and ordaining office-bearers in every city. And so likewise in regard to the supreme and absolute authority which they possessed, not only over some, but over all the Churches of Christ. We see the proof of this authority in the manner in which, both personally and by writing, they assumed the direction and regulated the affairs of the universal Christian Church in all its departments. We see a distinct intimation of it in the power committed to them by our Lord, when, in the terms of their call to the apostleship, they received warrant to bind and to loose on earth and in heaven. And not less distinct is the evidence of a supreme authority exercised by them, when we see them in their writings, and by their personal interference and control, laying down the whole platform of the New Testament Church,—appointing its office-bearers and its form of government, enunciating its maxims of worship, and prescribing the exercises of its discipline, inflicting and removing censures in the case of its members, and authoritatively overruling the procedure in ecclesiastical matters, both of individuals and of

Churches.[1] Such a supreme jurisdiction and universal ministry were competent only to apostles, and form another distinguishing characteristic of their office as singular and not permanent in the Church of Christ.

Such marks and distinctions as these we can easily gather from Scripture as belonging to the apostolic office, and separating it broadly from other offices in the Christian Church. And all of them go very directly to show that the office was of a temporary kind, suited to the transitional and incomplete state of the Church of Christ in its infancy, but forming no part of its ordinary or permanent organization. The apostleship was the Divine expedient to meet the emergencies of the Church at its first establishment and outset in the world, and not the method appointed for its ordinary administration; and the peculiarities distinctive of the office, to which I have now referred, could not, from their very nature, be repeated in the case of their successors, or be transmitted as a permanent feature in the Christian Church. They could have no successors as personal eye-witnesses of a risen Saviour,—as delegates whom His own hands had immediately invested with office,—as the depositaries and dispensers of His supernatural powers,—as the administrators of His own universal commission and infallible and supreme authority in the Christian society. In these respects, the apostolic power was, so to speak, a delegation to them of the same power that Christ Himself exer-

---

[1] [" L'église fut le fruit du ministère extraordinaire des Apôtres, et des Evangelistes; ce ministère la produisit au commencement, et non seulement il la produisit, mais il luy a toûjours servy de moyen ou de source pour sa subsistance, et l'on peut dire avec verité qu'il la produit encore, et qu'il la produira jusqu' à la fin du monde; car c'est la foy qui fait et qui fera toûjours l'église, et c'est le ministère des Apôtres qui fait et qui fera toûjours la foy. C'est leur voix qui les convoque encore aujourdhuy, c'est leur parole qui les assemble, et leur enseignement qui les lie. Il est certain que le ministère des Apôtres fut unique, c'est à dire uniquement attaché à leurs personnes sans succession, sans communication, sans propagation, mais il ne faut pas croire aussi que c'est esté un ministère passager, comme celuy des autres hommes, car il est perpetuel à l'église; la mort ne leur a pas fermé la bouche, comme elle l'a fermée aux autres, ils parlent, ils instruisent, ils répandent sans cesse la foy, la pieté, la sainteté dans l'ame des Chrétiens . . . . Si l'on nous demande, quelle est cette voix perpetuelle que nous leur attribuons? Nous répondons que c'est la doctrine du Nouveau Testament, ou ils ont rassemblé toute l'efficace de leur ministère, et toute la vertu de cette parole qui fait l'église. C'est là qu'est leur veritable chaire, et leur siége apostolique, le centre de l'unité Chrétienne, c'est de là qu'ils appellent sans cesse les hommes, et qu'ils les joignent en societé."—Claude, *Défense de la Réformation*, 4me Partie, ch. iii. 6. Nitzsch, *prot. Beant.* Hamburg 1855, pp. 224–235.]

cised when on earth; and, from the nature of the case, and the circumstances of the Church, it could not continue as a permanent ordinance on earth. "It was expedient" that even Christ Himself, the infallible Teacher and the supreme authority in the Christian society, "should go away," and the Church be left to the ordinary ministration of the fallible word and erring authority of men. And for the same reason, the apostolic office, exercising, as it also did, an absolute authority and invested with an infallible power to teach, was likewise inconsistent with the normal state and organization of the Church. It was to cease with the lives of those originally appointed to it, as incompatible with the ordinary and permanent condition of the Church of Christ.[1]

Now there are two objections, and no more than two, that are at all deserving of notice, which have been brought against the argument intended to prove that the office of the apostleship was a temporary one, and that the Apostles had no successors in it.

1st, The case of Matthias has been referred to as favouring the idea of a succession in the apostleship. It has been argued that the act of the eleven in transferring to him the same apostolic power which they had received themselves indicates an intention to perpetuate the office, and furnishes a precedent for the appointment of successors to the Apostles in all subsequent times. The difficulty interposed by this objection to our argument is not a very formidable one, and may be removed by a very slight consideration of the circumstances of the case.

In the first place, the election of Matthias was an extraordinary one for the purpose of supplying the place of Judas, and completing the number of the apostolic college, and forms no precedent for an ordinary and unlimited succession of apostles in

---

[1] [It has been more than once remarked that a confirmation of this view of the office of the Apostles may be seen in the language they themselves employ in their latest epistles, at a time when the well-nigh completed organization of the Churches began to make the existence of a rank of officebearers above the ordinary and permanent ones unnecessary. "The presbyter to the elect lady and her children." "The presbyter to the well-beloved Gaius." "The presbyters among you I exhort, who am a fellow-presbyter (συμπρεσβύτερος)." We may be reminded—to use the fine comparison of Milton—of those noble patricians of Rome, who hastened, as soon as the crisis was safely passed, to lay down the temporary dictatorship that spoke of the dangers and confusion of some great emergency, rejoicing to take a lowlier place once more in the settled ranks of the state, and leaving only the record of their deeds to uphold their name and honour among their fellow-citizens.]

the Church.   The number *twelve* was originally appointed as the
full staff of the apostles, the representatives of the Christian
Church, in designed reference to the number of the twelve tribes
of Israel, as the types of the visible Church of God in former
times, — a parallelism which can be made out distinctly from
various passages of Scripture.   The argument of Peter from the
69th Psalm plainly indicates that there was a necessity that this
number should be kept up, and that the vacancy caused by the
apostasy and death of Judas should be supplied by the election of
another with that special object in view.   Both the vacancy and
the supply of that vacancy had been matters indicated before in
the volume of prophecy as what must take place.   " For it is
written," says Peter, " in the book of Psalms, Let his habitation be
desolate, let no man dwell therein : and his bishopric let another
take.   Wherefore," concludes the apostle, " of these men which
have companied with us all the time that the Lord Jesus went in
and out among us, *must* one be ordained to be a witness with us of
His resurrection."[1]   The default in the number of the apostles,
and the necessity of remedying it by another election to the office,
were both indicated by the authority of inspiration.   The step
which the disciples were called to take on this occasion was thus
in every respect a special and extraordinary one, necessary in
order to the fulfilment of prophecy, and in order to keep up the
parallelism between the number of the apostles and the number of
the tribes of that nation which typified or represented the visible
Church of God in former days, but not furnishing any precedent
for a perpetual order of apostles, and an unlimited addition to
their numbers.   Accordingly, we find that when James, the brother
of John, was killed with the sword at the command of Herod, no
proposal was ever made to elect another as his successor among
the twelve, and so to perpetuate the office of the apostleship.

In the second place, whether we have regard to the part
which the disciples took in the appointment of Matthias, or to the
appeal made to the intervention of God, it is equally impossible
to reconcile the transaction with the theory of those who hold
that it was but one ordinary example out of many of the Apostles
conferring the office they themselves enjoyed on another.   If we
look at the disciples, or ordinary members of the Church, giving
forth their lot for the election of Matthias to the office, then they

[1] Acts i. 20-22.

could not confer apostolic powers, as they themselves had not
these powers to give. If, on the other hand, we look at the
appeal made to God to vouchsafe His intervention in the selection
of the apostle, then the case was one extraordinary, and not an
ordinary precedent for future ages.

2d, An objection to our general argument, much insisted on
by those who hold a succession in the apostolic office, is drawn
from the consideration that the name "apostle" in some few
cases is applied to others than the persons commonly known
under that designation; that it is not restricted in Scripture to
the twelve, but is given to different individuals who, it is alleged,
succeeded or shared with the twelve in their peculiar office.
Now the general fact on which this objection rests is perfectly
true. The name "apostle" is applied, in a few instances, to individuals not belonging to the restricted number to whom, as we
assert, the office of the apostleship was limited. In *one* instance
in the New Testament it is given to Barnabas.[1] In another
instance, also *singular*, it is applied to certain brethren sent by
Paul along with Titus to Corinth, as "the apostles," or, as it is
rendered in our translation, "the messengers of the Churches."[2]
In a third case—no less standing alone—it is applied to Epaphroditus, who was sent from the Church of Philippi to Rome, to
carry money to supply the necessities of Paul, and who is spoken
of as "their apostle," or, as in our translation, "their messenger."[3]
And in a fourth instance, in the Gospel by John, it is used in
a very general manner, as expressive of "one sent:" "The servant is not greater than his lord; neither he that is sent—(the
apostle)—greater than he that sent him."[4] There are no more
than these four cases in the New Testament in which the term
"apostle" is applied without doubt to any person beyond the
circle of those to whom we believe the original office was given.
There are two or three passages, in addition, in which the term
may be held as applied in that manner, but in which it is not
necessarily, or without doubt, so employed. Upon the slender
foundation of these instances, then, the whole objection rests.

Now in reply I say, *first*, that the primary sense of the word
"apostle," *i.e. one sent*, or a *messenger* of whatever kind, is sufficient to explain any and all of the very few cases in which it is

---

[1] Acts xiv. 14.   [2] 2 Cor. viii. 23.
[3] Phil. ii. 25.   [4] John xiii. 16.

applied, not in its technical sense of denoting the special office which, by Divine appointment as we assert, was restricted to the twelve, and in which they had no ordinary successors. It is perfectly natural, and in accordance both with the known laws of language, and with the usage of the New Testament in particular, that a word, which had come to have a distinctively technical sense, should yet in two or three instances appear in its primary and etymological signification. This leads to no misunderstanding in other cases;[1] nor is there the slightest reason that it should do so in this. The fact that the term in question occurs three or four times in the New Testament in its primary and general meaning of messenger, does not in the least interfere with the other fact, that, in its proper and restricted sense, the term was used by our Lord and His followers to denote only the twelve disciples, " whom also He *named* apostles."

Second, It is very easy, in all these cases quoted, to understand the special occasion on which the name of apostle was extended beyond its technical and general New Testament sense, to apply to the parties mentioned. In the instance of Barnabas, it was given almost immediately after his being set apart by prayer and imposition of hands, along with Paul, to the first mission to the Gentiles. Whether or not this transaction, as recorded in the fourteenth chapter of Acts, was a regular ordination, I do not

---

[1] [Almost all parties, *e.g.*, agree that πρεσβυτερος and διακονος have a technical meaning in the N. T. as denoting two distinct classes of Church office-bearers; and no doubt is thought to be thrown on this by the circumstance that both words occur several times in their primary sense of " an aged person " and a " minister " or " servant " of any sort. The word διαβολος is used three times in the Pastoral Epistles to signify " a slanderer," and שָׂטָן in the O. T. occurs repeatedly in the general sense of " an adversary." Yet few will account the favourite Universalist argument from that fact against the personality of the Evil One, to be anything more than a wanton attempt to perplex the minds of English readers of Scripture. In like manner, some of the sectaries of the sixteenth and seventeenth centuries sought to prove, from the facts alluded to above, that the language of the N. T. was so loose on the subject of ecclesiastical office-bearers that no conclusions in favour of distinct offices in the Church could be drawn from it at all, but that any man who chose to minister in holy things was a " deacon," and any one sent by the inward light an " apostle," in the full scriptural sense. In order to get rid of the argument, that because the words " bishop " and " presbyter " in their technical sense are always used interchangeably in Scripture, therefore the offices referred to were the same,—as well as to prove that the office of apostle was not restricted to the twelve,—some Episcopalians have adopted a similar line of argument, without apparently seeing how far it would logically lead.]

now stop to inquire.   All that is necessary for our present purpose
is to notice the very obvious and natural connection between his
being set apart solemnly, and sent forth, along with Paul, to the
Gentile mission, and his receiving the name, for the time, of the
" messenger" or " apostle " of the Church; and it is a fact very
significant, that never subsequently, in the New Testament, is he
spoken of as an apostle.   In the second instance—that of the
brethren sent by Paul along with Titus to Corinth—they received
the name of apostles, from their special delegation on that occasion from the one Church to the other; and hence our translators
have with perfect correctness rendered it by the general term,
" messengers."   In the third instance—of Epaphroditus—he was
in like manner the special messenger from Philippi to Rome,
to carry the bounty of the Church at Philippi to the apostle in
his necessity and his bonds in the Roman capital.   And in the
fourth example, the very same kind of explanation is to be given
when, in a general manner, our Lord declares " that the servant
is not greater than his lord, neither he that is sent—(or the
apostle)—greater than he that sent him."

The circumstance that in a few instances the name of apostle
is applied to other men, will not therefore suffice to overturn the
general argument, which demonstrates that the office was one
that did not pass by succession or transmission to ordinary office-
bearers in the Christian Church.[1]

SECTION II.—OFFICES OF PROPHETS AND EVANGELISTS.

In handling the subject of the office-bearers, extraordinary
and ordinary, appointed for the New Testament Church at the
outset, there are two passages of Scripture that may be especially
referred to as throwing light upon the question.   In the fourth
chapter of Ephesians, the Apostle Paul, speaking of the provision
made for the Church by the ascended Saviour, says : " And He

---

[1] Voetius, *Polit. Eccles.* tom. iii. lib. ii. Tract ii. cap. ii.   Bucer, *Dissert.
de Gubernatione Ecclesiæ,* Middelburgi Zeland. 1618, pp. 472–481.   Forrester,
The Hierarchical Bishops' Claim to a Divine Right, Edin. 1799, pp. 85–124.
Ayton, *Orig. Const. of the Christian Church,* Edin. 1730, pp. 20–35.   *Essays on
the Prim. Church Offices* (by Dr. J. A. Alexander), New York 1851, pp. 68–
100.   [Barnes, *Inquiry into the Organ. and Gov. of the Apostolic Church,* Lond.
1845, pp. 43–94.   Smyth, *The Prelat. Doc. of Apost. Succession Examined,*
Boston 1841, pp. 229–255 ; *Presbytery the Script. and Prim. Polity,* Boston
1843, pp. 28–42.   King, *Expos. and Def. of the Presbyt. Form of Church Gov.*
Edin. 1853, pp. 182–209.]

gave some apostles, and some prophets, and some evangelists, and some pastors and teachers, for the perfecting of the saints, for the work of the ministry, for the edifying of the body of Christ."[1] In this statement by the apostle we have plainly an intimation of the staff of officers, ordinary and extraordinary, appointed by Christ, for the work of establishing, organizing, building up, and ministering to the Christian Church. That the enumeration of office-bearers is not complete, appears from the fact that no mention is made of the *deacon,* of the institution of whose office we have an express account in the Acts of the Apostles, and who is admitted by all parties, Romanist and Protestant, Episcopalian, Presbyterian, and Congregationalist, to be an ordinary and standing office-bearer in the ecclesiastical society. In the passage now referred to, however, we have a list of office-bearers, which, although not exhaustive, yet includes the majority of those invested with formal office in the apostolic Church. In the twelfth chapter of the First Epistle to the Corinthians, when speaking of " spiritual gifts" in the Church of his day, the same apostle tells us: " To one is given by the Spirit the word of wisdom; to another the word of knowledge by the same Spirit; to another faith by the same Spirit; to another the gifts of healing by the same Spirit; to another the working of miracles; to another prophecy; to another discernment of spirits; to another divers kinds of tongues; to another the interpretation of tongues." And further on in the same chapter we are told: " God hath set some in the Church, first, apostles; secondarily, prophets; thirdly, teachers; after that miracles; then gifts of healings, helps, governments, diversities of tongues. Are all apostles? are all prophets? are all teachers? are all workers of miracles? have all the gifts of healing? do all speak with tongues? do all interpret?"[2] Now in this passage we have an enumeration, not of the offices, but of the gifts that prevailed in the primitive Church. In writing to the Ephesians, the apostle ranks and enumerates the office-bearers according to their formal offices; in writing to the Corinthians, he classifies them according to their special gifts.

There is a most important distinction to be marked between a formal office and a special gift or endowment. One man might receive and exercise many gifts, while at the same time he held and exercised no more than one office in the Church. The dif-

[1] Eph. iv. 11 f.   [2] 1 Cor. xii. 8–10, 28–30.

ferent and many gifts—χαρίσματα—of miracles, of healing, of tongues, of discernment of spirits, etc., which abounded in the apostolic Church, might in some cases meet in the person of one individual, and be all exercised by him, while at the same time, as a formal office-bearer in the Christian society, he was invested only with one office. In dealing with the question of the form of polity of the New Testament Church, we must take special care not to confound the different χαρίσματα, or gifts, enumerated in the Epistle to the Corinthians with the distinct offices enumerated in the Epistle to the Ephesians, or to assume that because the same individual exercised different endowments or powers for the edification of the Church, he therefore is to be held as invested with different offices, ordinary or extraordinary, in the Christian society. It is with the offices, and not with the gifts of the apostolic Church, that we have at present to do,—the former, or the offices, marking out the form or constitution of the ecclesiastical society; the latter, or the gifts, only marking out the endowments conferred on the persons belonging to it.

Referring, then, to the enumeration of office-bearers in the Epistle to the Ephesians, we find that there are five mentioned as pertaining to the apostolic Church. Three of these we believe to have been special and extraordinary, and two to have been ordinary and permanent office-bearers. We have apostles, prophets, evangelists, belonging to the special emergency and need of the Christian Church at the time; and we have pastors and teachers belonging to the ordinary and permanent equipment of the ecclesiastical body.[1] We have already dealt at some length with the question of the extraordinary office of the apostleship : we shall now proceed to consider the offices of prophets and evan-

---

[1] [*Vide* Calvin *in loc. et Inst.* lib. iv. cap. iii. 4, 5. " Albeit the Kirk of God," says the *Second Book of Discipline*, sanctioned by the Assembly of 1578, " be rulit and governit by Jesus Christ, who is the onlie King, High Priest, and Head thereof, yet He useth the ministry of men as the most necessar middis for this purpose. For so He hath from tyme to tyme, before the Law, under the Law, and in the tyme of the Evangel, for our great comfort, raisit up men indewit withthe gift is of His Spirit, for the spiritual government of His Kirk, exercising by them His own power through His Spirit and Word to the building of the same. And, to take away all occasion of tyrannie, He willis that they suld rule with mutual consent of Brethren, and equality of power, every one according to their functions. In the New Testament and tyme of the Evangel, He hath usit the Ministry of the Apostles, Prophets, Evangelists, Pastors, and Doctors in the administration of the Word,—the Eldership for gude Order and the administration of Discipline ; the Deacon-

gelists. There seems to be warrant from Scripture, as in the
instance of apostles, to say that these offices were special and
extraordinary. Let us, in the first instance, then, direct our
attention to the case of the New Testament prophets, as enumerated among the office-bearers of the early Church. There is no
great difference of opinion among controversialists in regard to
the temporary and exceptional character of their office.

The prophets of the apostolic Church are plainly to be distinguished from the apostles on the one hand, and from the
evangelists on the other, among the extraordinary office-bearers,
and also from both pastors and teachers among the ordinary
office-bearers of the Christian society. The terms *prophecy* and
prophet, when descriptive of this office, are plainly to be understood in the primary and more enlarged meaning of the words,
as referring to an authoritative proclamation of the mind of
God, whether in the shape of a revelation of Divine truth generally, or a revelation more especially of future events. There
seems to be distinct enough ground for saying that the office of
the prophet in the early Church comprehended both the prophecy
or declaration of the Divine mind as to future events, and also
the prophecy or declaration of the Divine mind as to moral or
spiritual truth generally, without reference to the future.

In the first place, the order of prophets in the New Testament Church had the same distinctive power which belonged
to their brethren during the ancient dispensation,—that, namely,
of foreseeing and predicting the future.

That this was the case, appears plainly both from the promise
of Christ given to His disciples before His death, and also from
the intimations of the exercise of such a power in the inspired

ship to have the cure of the ecclesiastical gudis. Some of thir ecclesiastical
functions ar ordinar, and sum extraordinar or temporarie. There be three
extraordinar functions,—the office of the Apostle, of the Evangelist, and of the
Prophet,—quhilkis are not perpetual, and now have ceisit in the Kirk of God,
except quhen it pleisit God extraordinarily for a tyme to steir some of them
up again. There are four ordinar functions or offices in the Kirk of God,—the
office of the Pastor, Minister, or Bishop ; the Doctor ; the Presbyter or Elder ;
and the Deacon. Thir offices are ordinar, and ought to continue perpetually
in the Kirk, as necessar for the government and policie of the same ; and no
moe offices ought to be receivit or sufferit in the true Kirk of God establishit
according to His Word. Therefore all the ambitious titles inventit in the
kingdom of Antichrist, and in his usurpit hierarchie, quhilkis are not of ane
of these four sorts, together with the offices depending thereupon, in ane word,
ought all-utterlie to be rejectit."—Ch. ii.]

history of the apostolic Church. In His farewell address to His disciples before His passion, our Lord distinctly promised: "When He, the Spirit of truth, is come, He will guide you into all truth; *and He will show you things to come.*"[1] There is no good ground for asserting that this promise was confined to the apostles alone. They indeed shared more largely than their brethren in the supernatural gifts of that early age of miracle and inspiration, but they did not monopolize them; and in the ample dowry conferred on the Church in the morning of her espousals by her Lord, we are to recognise the gift of prophecy in the restricted meaning of the term, as the prediction of things to come. Of the order of men who enjoyed and exercised this power, we read more than once in the Acts of the Apostles. "And in these days," says the inspired historian in the eleventh chapter of the Acts, "came prophets from Jerusalem unto Antioch. And there stood up one of them, named Agabus, and signified by the Spirit that there should be great dearth throughout all the world: which came to pass in the days of Claudius Cæsar." In consequence of this prophetic intimation given of the approaching scarcity, the narrative goes on to tell us: "Then the disciples, every man according to his ability, determined to send relief unto the brethren which dwelt in Judea: which also they did, and sent it to the elders by the hands of Barnabas and Saul."[2] The same prophet, in virtue of his extraordinary gift of prediction, shortly afterwards foretold the imprisonment of the Apostle Paul at Jerusalem, accompanying the prediction—precisely as Old Testament prophets had been wont to do—with the significant action of binding his own hands and feet with the apostle's girdle. Nor did he stand alone in giving intimation to Paul of his approaching sufferings; for the apostle told the elders at Ephesus of manifold Divine forewarnings given him of the same event: "And now, behold, I go bound in the spirit unto Jerusalem, not knowing the things which shall befall me there, save that the Holy Ghost in *every city* witnesseth, saying that bonds and afflictions abide me."[3] In short, side by side with the power of working miracles and of speaking with tongues, the gift of prophecy, or insight into the future, was given to the apostolic Church, as a witness to its Divine origin, and an instrument for securing its establishment on earth.

[1] John xvi. 13.　　　[2] Acts xi. 27–30.　　　[3] Acts xx. 22 f.

In the second place, the order of prophets in the New Testament Church had the power of declaring the mind of God generally, and without reference to the future, being inspired to preach or proclaim Divine truth, as it was revealed to them, in an extraordinary manner by the Spirit.

They were infallible interpreters of the Old Testament Scriptures and inspired preachers of Divine truth, declaring the Word of God for the conversion of sinners and the profit of the Church. The difference between the prophets and the ordinary pastors or teachers of the early Church was, that the one were inspired preachers of the Gospel, and the other not inspired. The prophesying or preaching of the first was the fruit of immediate extraordinary revelation at the moment; the prophesying or preaching of the second was the fruit of their own unaided study of the Old Testament Scriptures, and personal understanding of Divine truth. That this was the case, is apparent from the instructions given by the Apostle Paul in the fourteenth chapter of First Corinthians in regard to the use of the supernatural gifts conferred on that Church. "Let the prophets speak two or three, and let the other judge. If anything *be revealed* (ἀποκαλυφθῇ) to another that sitteth by, let the first hold his peace." [1] The prophesying or preaching of this order of office-bearers in the primitive Church was identical with the "*revelations*" given to certain of the early believers for the purpose of edifying the rest.

And it is not difficult to see the foundation laid in the circumstances of the apostolic Church for the necessity and the use of this special class of office-bearers. Our Lord had Himself told His disciples shortly before His death, that He had many things to tell them, which at that moment they were not able to bear.[2] The revelation of His mind and truth was left by Him incomplete when He departed from this world to the Father. It remained incomplete until the canon of Scripture was closed, and the entire revelation of God, as we now have it, was committed to writing. The earliest of the canonical books of the New Testament was not written until some years after the ascension of Christ; and the latest of them was not added until probably a generation had well-nigh passed away after that event. In the interval, the revelation of God remained unfinished; while from

[1] 1 Cor. xiv. 29 f.   [2] John xiv. 25 f., xvi. 12-14.

the difficulty of transcribing and disseminating in manuscript the
copies of the books that partially made up the New Testament
volume, before its completion there must have been, in many
Churches of the early Christians, a want felt of any authoritative
record of the Divine mind and will.   The living Word of prophets, inspired by God to declare His truth, was the instrumentality employed by Him to supply that want in the apostolic
Church.   The Apostles indeed had the same word of revelation
that the prophets enjoyed.   The prophesying of the Apostles
supplied for a time, to the extent to which their personal presence could reach, the want of the written and inspired standard
before the canon was closed.   But the number of the apostles
admitted of no increase, while in the rapid spread and prevalence
of early Christianity there were multitudes added to the Church
daily of such as should be saved.   And hence the necessity of
another order of office-bearers, suited to the extraordinary emergency, and to the transition state of the Christian Church, who
should, by means of personal revelation granted to them, and
personal prophesyings emitted by them, become the teachers of
the early converts, when they had no other adequate source of
information and instruction in Divine things.   The necessity for
such extraordinary instrumentality ceased when the canon of
Scripture was closed.   The written Word in the hands of the
Christian Churches superseded the need of revelations and
prophets.   Both in their character of foretellers of future events,
and in their character of inspired preachers of Divine truth, the
order of New Testament prophets was temporary, and did not
outlive the apostolic age.[1]

But next let us inquire into the case of the third class of
office-bearers mentioned in the list given by the apostle in his
Epistle to the Ephesians.   In that list we have, first, *apostles*,
who undoubtedly were extraordinary office-bearers ; and second,
prophets, who were also a temporary order in the Christian
Church.   After these we find mentioned *evangelists ;* and the
question that arises is, whether or not the nature of their office
and functions constitutes them fixed and standing officers in the

[1] Voetius, *Polit. Eccles.* Pars ii. lib. ii. Tract ii. cap. iii. sec. 3.   Ayton,
Orig. Constit. of the Christ. Church, pp. 35–39.   [Cf. Stanley, *Sermons and
Essays on the Apostolical Age,* 2d ed. pp. 53–61 ; Ewald, *Geschichte des
Volkes Israel,* Bd. vi. 2te Ausg. pp. 168 ff.   Hofmann, *heilige Schrift.* 2ten
Th. 2te Abth. pp. 301–309.]

ecclesiastical body. There seems to be reason from Scripture to assert that they, like the apostles and prophets, were extraordinary office-bearers in the primitive Church. The discussion in connection with the order of evangelists is a somewhat important and fundamental one in attempting to determine the form and polity of the Christian society in apostolic times.

Our information in regard to the order of evangelists, and the nature of the duties attached to their office, is mainly to be gathered from what Scripture has enabled us to learn in connection with Timothy and Titus, the fellow-labourers of Paul in his evangelistic journeys. To Timothy the name of evangelist is expressly given, and in such a manner as to prove that it was an office distinct from other offices in the early Church, and that it belonged to him as his peculiar function.[1] And although the same title is nowhere expressly appropriated to Titus in Scripture, yet the duties he discharged, and the manner in which he is spoken of, leave no doubt that he belonged to the same order, and laboured in the same office as Timothy. There are several others mentioned in the sacred volume that are plainly to be classed in the same rank of ecclesiastical office-bearers, although of their history and labours less is known. But the narrative of the Acts and the Epistles of Paul afford sufficient materials, in the references we find there to Timothy and Titus, for judging of the order of evangelist, separated as it was from the extraordinary offices of apostles and prophets on the one side, and from the permanent and standing office of pastor on the other. It is hardly necessary to say that by evangelists, in the sense of ecclesiastical office-bearers, is not meant the inspired historians of our Lord's life in the Gospels. They are exhibited to us in the Scripture narrative rather as the attendants upon the Apostles in their journeys, and their assistants in planting and establishing the Churches, acting under them as their delegates, and carrying out their instructions. If the contributions of one Church were to be carried to another to supply its more urgent need, it was an evangelist that was selected as the messenger of the Church.[2] If an inspired letter was to be conveyed to the Christian community to whom an apostle had addressed it, an evangelist was the bearer of the precious record.[3] If an apostle had converted

---

[1] 2 Tim. iv. 5.   [2] 1 Cor. xvi. 3 ; 2 Cor. viii. 4–23 ; Phil. ii. 25, iv. 18.
[3] 1 Cor. xvi. 10 ; 2 Cor. vii. 6–8; Eph. vi. 21 f.

many to the faith of Christ in one particular locality, and hastened on to other labours and triumphs, an evangelist was left behind to organize the infant Church.[1] If, in the absence of an apostle, contentions had arisen, or false doctrine had found entrance within a Christian society which he had founded, the apostolic method of applying a remedy was by the errand of an evangelist.[2] We know from him who was not behind the chiefest of the Apostles, that he counted it as his special mission, " not to baptize, but to preach the Gospel ; "[3] or, in other words, that he held it to be a higher department of the apostolic office to convert sinners to Christ, and to edify His people, than to establish and arrange the outward government and ordinances of grace of a standing visible Church.   And accordingly, in the ardour of his zeal that Christ might be preached, he himself passed on to declare the Gospel in other regions, " not building on another man's foundation," and left behind Timothy, or Titus, or some other evangelist, to organize the outward polity of the Church, to which he had been the means of communicating the gift, more precious still, of inward life.[4]   As an apostle, Paul felt that he had higher work on hand than the arrangement of the external polity of the Church or the regulation of its outward affairs; and therefore he gave commission to his assistants from time to time, as occasion demanded it, in their capacity of evangelists, to complete the organization of the infant Churches he had planted, to superintend the settlement of regular pastors and office-bearers among them, to rectify the disorders of their discipline, or their departures from sound doctrine, and to do his occasional errands of affection or authority in those Christian societies where his bodily presence was denied.   Such, generally, in so far as we can gather from the inspired record, seems to have been the work and duty of the evangelist, as these are more especially delineated in the references to the history of Timothy and Titus.   And the question is : Were these evangelists the standing and permanent, or the occasional and extraordinary office-bearers of the Christian Church ?

Those controversialists who assert the formal and permanent

---

[1] 1 Tim. i. 3 f. ; 2 Tim. iv. 9–13 ; Tit. i. 5, iii. 12.
[2] 1 Cor. iv. 17 ; 2 Cor. vii. 6 f. 15 ; Col. i. 7 f., cf. iv. 12 f.
[3] 1 Cor. i. 17.
[4] [Huther, *Pastoralbriefe*, p. 52, in Meyer's *Kommentar*, 11te Abth.]

character of the office vested in the persons of Timothy and Titus, in order to make out this conclusion, endeavour to prove that they sustained a fixed and standing relation, each to a particular Church, as the bishop or overseer of it. It is asserted that Timothy held the permanent position of diocesan bishop in the Church at Ephesus, and that Titus stood in a similar relation to the Church at Crete. The question, then, comes very much to this : Was the office that these evangelists sustained of a special kind, being simply a commission from the Apostles to exercise, at Ephesus and Crete, certain powers given them for a particular purpose ? or, Was that office of a permanent kind, implying a fixed and ordinary relationship to these Churches? We shall find in Scripture abundant reason to conclude that the position of Timothy and Titus was not a fixed and permanent one, and that their relation and powers in reference to the Ephesian and Cretan Churches were special and extraordinary.

In entering upon the argument, it is hardly necessary to say that the subscriptions at the close of the apostolic letters addressed to Timothy and Titus, which speak of them as " bishops," are of no authority at all, being, as is now universally admitted, uninspired additions of a much later date than the Epistles. Confining ourselves to Scripture evidence, let us take the case of Timothy first, and inquire into the nature of his connection with the Church at Ephesus.

1st, At the date of Paul's address to the elders of the Church at Ephesus, whom he summoned to meet him at Miletus, mentioned in the twentieth chapter of the Acts, it is evident that Timothy had no place or office in connection with that Church. The absence of all reference to him by Paul, and the whole tenor of the apostle's address to the elders as the proper bishops or overseers of the Church there,[1] sufficiently establish these two points: first, that at that time Timothy was not at Ephesus, having no connection of an official kind with the Church at that place ; and second, that there was a Church there fully organized and complete without him.

2d, The first, and indeed the only, express intimation in Scripture of the presence of Timothy at Ephesus, is contained in

---

[1] " Take heed to yourselves and to the whole flock over which the Holy Ghost hath set you as bishops" (ἐν ᾧ ὑμας το Πνευμα το ἁγιον ἐθετο ἐπισκοτους).
—Acts xx. 28.   [Cf. Alford in loc.]

the first epistle addressed to him by Paul, in a passage which
shows that he was present there only for a special purpose, and
not in consequence of any fixed connection with the Church of
an official kind. It appears that Paul, and Timothy as his attendant, had been labouring at Ephesus together, when the apostle
had occasion to leave it for Macedonia. In his parting charge
given at Miletus to the elders of Ephesus, Paul had forewarned
them : " After my departure shall grievous wolves enter in among
you, not sparing the flock. Also of your own selves shall men
arise, speaking perverse things, to draw away disciples after
them."[1] Whether this warning was given before or after the
date of Paul's leaving Timothy at Ephesus, has been disputed,
and it is not of material consequence to the argument. It is
undoubted, that about that time dangers of false doctrine assailed
the Church at Ephesus ; and, to counteract the danger, Timothy
was left there by the apostle. This was the special reason of
Timothy's presence at Ephesus, and not his fixed relation to the
Church there. " As I besought thee," says Paul in his letter to
Timothy, " to abide still at Ephesus, when I went into Macedonia,
that thou mightest charge some that they teach no other doctrine,
neither give heed to fables and endless genealogies, which minister
questions, rather than godly edifying which is in faith : so do."[2]
The object of Timothy's being left by the apostle at Ephesus was
not that he might enter upon a permanent connection of an
official kind with the Ephesian Church, but simply in order that
he might accomplish the specific end of meeting the crisis occasioned by the disorders among the Ephesian converts.

3d, The commission granted to Timothy for this special object
was plainly intended to be a temporary, and not a permanent
one. The words of the apostle already quoted seem obviously
to imply this. " *I besought thee* ($\pi a \rho \epsilon \kappa a \lambda \epsilon \sigma a \ \sigma \epsilon$) *to abide still at
Ephesus,*" is not like the language of an apostle conferring a per-
manent appointment, or referring to a fixed connection between
Timothy and the Church of the Ephesians, but the very opposite,
implying, as it clearly does, a mere temporary residence and duty
there.[3] It was a commission granted by Paul to Timothy as his
delegate for certain specific purposes during his absence ; and
was to come to an end, either when the apostle once more per-

---

[1] Acts xx. 29 f.   [2] 1 Tim. i. 3 f.
[3] [Daillé, *Expos. de la prem. Epître à Tim.* Genève 1661, Serm. i.]

sonally resumed the work at Ephesus, or when the occasion which
demanded the intervention of the evangelist had passed away,
and he should be sent on a similar errand to other Churches.
That Paul had the expectation of returning to Ephesus and
relieving Timothy from his special superintendence there, is manifest from such language as we find in the first epistle: " These
things write I unto thee, hoping to come unto thee shortly: but
if I tarry long, that thou mightest know how to behave thyself in
the house of God." "Till I come, give attendance to reading,
to exhortation, to doctrine."[1] That Timothy, after this, actually
left Ephesus to undertake other duty, seems capable of proof from
the second epistle addressed to him. Writing in that epistle from
Rome, Paul enjoins upon Timothy : " Do thy diligence to come
shortly unto me;" and again : " Do thy diligence to come before
winter:"[2] And we cannot doubt that the command of the apostle
was obeyed, and that Timothy actually proceeded to Rome. That
his presence at Rome was required, not for any personal attendance on Paul, at that time a prisoner in bonds, but for the service
of the Church, is rendered probable, in the first place, by the
Christian disinterestedness of the apostle, who would have been
the last man to have asked from Timothy the sacrifice of public
duty for the sake of his own private and personal gratification.
But this is made all but certain by the reason which Paul gives
for requesting the presence of Timothy at Rome,—namely, that
the other companions of his missionary labours were absent; and
also by the request to bring Mark along with him to Rome,
because he was profitable for the ministerial work. " Do thy
diligence to come shortly unto me: for Demas hath forsaken me,
having loved this present world, and is departed unto Thessalonica; Crescens unto Galatia; Titus to Dalmatia. Only Luke
is with me. Take Mark, and bring him with thee : *for he is profitable to me for the ministry.*"[3] Add to this, that by implication
at least, if not by positive assertion, it may be pretty satisfactorily
proved that Timothy was not even at Ephesus when the second
epistle was addressed to him, summoning him to Rome. In the
twelfth verse of the fourth chapter, Paul gives a piece of information not consistent with the idea that Timothy was at Ephesus at
the time : " And Tychicus," says the apostle, " have I sent to
Ephesus." And the conclusion is confirmed by the subsequent

[1] 1 Tim. iii. 14 f., iv. 13.   [2] 2 Tim. iv. 9, 21.   [3] 2 Tim. iv. 9–11.

verse, which seems to take for granted that Timothy was actually
at that moment at Troas : " The cloak which I left at Troas
with Carpus, when thou comest, bring with thee." So strong
and clear is the evidence, that when Timothy was left behind by
Paul at Ephesus, his stay was no more than temporary, and his
connection with the Church there not a permanent office in it,
but the reverse.

But let us next take the case of Titus, and inquire whether
his commission to Crete gave him a permanent connection with
the Church there, or rather was of a special and extraordinary
nature. In this instance also, it can be made out no less clearly
than in the instance of Timothy, that the purpose of the evangelist's presence in this particular field of labour, and his actual
stay there, were both of a temporary kind.

First, The object of Titus' presence in the Church at Crete
was of a special kind, and not requiring or implying a permanent
connection with it. The Apostle Paul had himself been labouring there, and had laid the foundation of a Christian society ;
but, acting upon the general principle, which he seems to have
adopted, of preaching the Gospel himself, and handing over to
his assistants the task of arranging the ecclesiastical polity of the
society he had called into spiritual life, he appoints Titus for this
object. " For this cause left I thee in Crete, that thou shouldest
set in order the things that are wanting, and ordain ($\kappa\alpha\tau\alpha\sigma\tau\eta\sigma\eta s$,
constitute, or settle) elders in every city as I appointed thee."[1]
The nature of the object to be accomplished implies that the
commission was a special and temporary one, involving no fixed
or official relationship on the part of Titus to Crete. The evangelist was left in the island to complete the work begun, but left
unfinished by the apostle ; and this no more involved, on the part

[1] [" Sed videtur nimium Tito permittere, dum jubet eum præficere omnibus Ecclesiis ministros. Hæc enim fere regia esset potestas ; deinde hoc modo
et singulis Ecclesiis jus eligendi, et Pastorum Collegio judicium tollitur, id
vero esset totam sacram Ecclesiæ administrationem profanare. Verum responsio facilis est, non permitti arbitrio Titi ut unus possit omnia, et quos
voluerit Episcopos Ecclesiis imponat ; sed tantum jubet ut electionibus præsit
tanquam moderator, sicuti necesse est. Hæc loquutio satis trita est. Sic
dicitur Consul, aut Interrex, aut Dictator Consules *creasse*, qui comitia eligen-
dis illis habuit. Sic quoque de Paulo et Barnaba loquitur in Actis Lucas
(Acts xiv. 23) ($\chi\epsilon\iota\rho\sigma\tau\sigma\nu\eta\sigma\alpha\nu\tau\epsilon s$ $\alpha\dot{\upsilon}\tau\sigma\iota s$ $\pi\rho\epsilon\sigma\beta\upsilon\tau\epsilon\rho\sigma\upsilon s$), non quod soli præficerent,
quasi pro imperio, Pastores Ecclesiis nec probatos nec cognitos : sed quia
idoneos homines, qui a populo electi vel expetiti fuerant, ordinarent."—Calvin
in loc.]

of Titus, a permanent connection with the Church of Crete than it did on the part of Paul.

Second, That the stay of Titus in Crete was no more than temporary, and that he soon left it, is sufficiently proved in the same epistle. Paul evidently contemplated, at the time he wrote to Titus, relieving him immediately from his duties at Crete by sending another of the apostle's companions and fellow-labourers in his place; and Titus is told that, on the arrival of this substitute, he was himself forthwith to join Paul: "When I shall send Artemas unto thee, or Tychicus, be diligent to come unto me to Nicopolis; for I have determined there to winter."[1] That Titus actually left Crete and joined Paul at Nicopolis, we cannot doubt; and there is no evidence whatever in Scripture that he ever returned to Crete, to resume the duties from which the apostle thus relieved him; on the contrary, our latest information regarding Titus, contained in the Second Epistle to Timothy, which is almost universally held to be the last in date of the Pastoral Epistles, shows him engaged in labour in Dalmatia.[2]

Both as regards Timothy and Titus, then, there seems sufficient ground in Scripture for saying that the commission which they bore in connection with Ephesus and Crete respectively was a special one; that the object of their presence in these Churches involved no fixed or permanent relationship to them; and that their actual residence in these places was but short, and not, so far as we know from Scripture, at any time resumed.

But besides the special lines of proof already referred to with respect to Timothy and Titus, there is one general kind of Scripture evidence of much weight in the argument in support of the extraordinary character of their office as evangelists, and against its involving any standing or permanent connection with any particular Church. I refer to the evidence arising out of the relation which they sustained to the Apostle Paul,—a relation incompatible with the notion of their holding or exercising the functions of any fixed office in any one ecclesiastical society. Timothy and Titus were, in their character as evangelists, the almost constant attendants upon the apostle, and his companions in his missionary journeys,—were at his side, and ready to do

---

[1] Titus iii. 12.
[2] 2 Tim. iv. 10.   [Cf. Alford's *Prolegomena to the Pastoral Epistles.*]

his errands among the Churches, when he could not himself be present, or to complete the work which he had begun, but could not personally overtake. In the wide range of duty which his apostolic labours embraced, and in " the burden which came upon him daily, the care of all the Churches," Paul had no means of supplying the necessary limitation of his own exertions, and his own often unavoidable absence from the scene, where guidance and counsel were especially required, except by delegating to others his powers, in so far as the occasion demanded. And there was a little band whose hearts the Lord had touched, and who were drawn to the apostle by the power of that strong personal attachment, and love, and admiration, which the character of Paul was so fitted to call forth among the young, who followed him as the companions of his ministry and labours, and were at hand to bear his special commissions to whatever new quarter called for his interposition, or needed his peculiar care,—his representatives to the Churches in organizing their polity, in rectifying their disorders, in conveying to them his apostolic instructions, and in carrying out his apostolic decisions.

As the companions or delegates of Paul, we find the names of not a few who seem to have received the office of evangelist under his commission ; as, for example, " Tychicus, a beloved brother, and faithful minister in the Lord ; " " Epaphroditus, my brother and companion in labour ; " " Mark, who is profitable to me for the ministry ; " " Luke, who only is with me." But conspicuous in that little circle of youthful and zealous labourers are Timothy and Titus, both in their personal attendance on the apostle, and in the frequency with which they bore his commission as his representatives to the Churches. We find Timothy the companion of Paul at Rome during his first imprisonment there ; we find his name honourably linked to that of the apostle in his letters to the Churches of Corinth, of Thessalonica, of Philippi, and of Colosse, and to Philemon ; he is spoken of in the Epistle to the Romans as Paul's fellow-worker at Corinth ; we find Paul rejoicing over his recent deliverance from imprisonment in the Epistle to the Hebrews ; we see him the joint labourer with Paul in the Church at Ephesus, and left behind with special instructions to complete the work of the apostle, who had departed ; and we witness him summoned by the apostle to Rome toward the close of his life, and in the near prospect of his martyrdom.[1] In like manner we find Titus the very frequent attendant on the apostle, and the bearer of his commission to the Church. At Troas, Paul "found no rest in his spirit, because he found not Titus his brother;" at Philippi he was joined with the apostle in his active labours there; to Corinth he was sent on a special mission in connection with the collection for the poor saints at Jerusalem; in Crete he was left behind by Paul to complete what the apostle's hands had not been able to overtake; and from Rome we find Paul sending him on a special mission to Dalmatia.[2]

These labourers, ever at Paul's side, and ever ready to carry his instructions to distant Churches, were not, and could not be, attached to any particular Church as holding a fixed and permanent office among its members. Their office was extraordinary; their commission had its origin and its close in apostolic times; the position of the evangelists, like the positions of the apostle and the prophet, must be reckoned among those provisional arrangements of the primitive Church, which formed the transition to its permanent and settled condition. There is no evidence from Scripture that the office of evangelist was a fixed and standing office in the Christian society; on the contrary, there is every evidence that it was extraordinary and temporary.[3]

---

[1] Rom. xvi. 21; 1 Cor. xvi. 10; 2 Cor. i. 1, 19; Phil. ii. 19; 1 Thess. iii. 2; Heb. xiii. 23; 1 Tim. i. 2, etc.; 2 Tim. i. 2, etc.

[2] 2 Cor. ii. 13, vii. 6, 13, 14, viii. 6–23, xii. 18; Gal. ii. 1; Titus i. 5, etc.; 2 Tim. iv. 10.

[3] Voetius, *Polit. Eccles.* tom. iii. lib. iii. Tract. ii. cap. iii. Ayton, *Orig. Constit. of the Christ. Church*, Edin. 1730, pp. 40-48, 435–439, Append. 22–28. Litton, *Church of Christ*, Lond. 1851, pp. 416–424. Cunningham, *Works*, vol. ii. pp. 241–244. [Prynne, *The Unbishoping of Timothy and Titus*, Lond. 1661 (1st ed. 1836). Forrester, *Rectius Instruendum*, 1684, pp. 127–167. Brown, *Letters on Puseyite Episcopacy*, Edin. 1842, pp. 189–217; *Plea of Presbytery*, Glasg. 1840, pp. 206–232. Köstlin, *Das Wesen der Kirche*, Stuttgart 1854, p. 84 f. Rothe, *Anfänge der christl. Kirche*, Wittenberg 1837, pp. 259–263, 305 ff. For an account of the functions of the Scottish "superintendents," and the "visitors" or "commissioners of provinces," whose duties were somewhat analogous to those of evangelists during the time when the Reformed Church of Scotland was in process of organization, see the *First Book of Discipline*, ch. vii. Cf. *Second Book of Discipline*, ch. ii. vii. xi. 9–14; Dunlop's *Collection*, vol. ii. pp. 538–546, 614–616, 792 f.; Alex. Henderson, *Government and Order of the Church of Scotland*, Lond. 1641, pp. 1–5; Calderwood, *Hieron. Philadelphi de Regim. Scotican Ecclesiæ Epistola*, and his *Epistolæ Philadelphi Vindiciæ*, published along with the *Altare Damascenum*, Lugduni, Batav. 1708; Voetius, *Polit. Eccles.* Pars i. lib. i. cap. vi. § 17, Pars ii. lib. iv. Tract. i. cap. iv.; M'Crie, *Life of Knox*, 5th ed. vol. ii. pp. 283–286. The difference between the superintendents of

our Church and diocesan bishops has been briefly summed up by Dr. M'Crie, *Miscell. Works*, Edin. 1841, pp. 178 f. : "They were not episcopally ordained; they derived all their authority from the Church; the exercise of their power was bounded and regulated by the General Assembly, to which they were accountable, and gave an account of their conduct at every meeting; they were not acknowledged as holding any distinct or permanent office in the Church, but merely as persons to whom a provisional superintendency was committed from reasons of expediency at that period.   Even Archbishop Spottiswood, in attempting to evade these facts, has been betrayed into a glaring corruption of the original document. (Comp. Spottiswood's *Historie*, pp. 152-158, with the head 'Of Superintendents' in *First Book of Discipline*.)" "The bishops who embraced the Reformation were not admitted to exercise any ecclesiastical authority as bishops; and when some of them wished to be employed as superintendents, they were rejected for want of requisite qualifications."]

CHAPTER III.

THE POPISH SYSTEM OF CHURCH POLITY.

THOSE preliminary discussions in which we have dealt with the question of the extraordinary office-bearers in the apostolic Church, have to some extent cleared our way to the main subject before us. In separating between what was characteristic of the period of transition, and what belonged to the permanent state of the early Church, we have taken an important step towards ascertaining its ordinary and normal condition; and besides this, we have been enabled to lay down certain general positions, which will be of use in our subsequent argument. In addressing ourselves to the discussion, there are four leading systems of Church government that present themselves to our view, and claim attention,—the Romanist, the Episcopalian, the Independent, and the Presbyterian. A brief and general review of the principles involved in these systems, and the positions maintained by their adherents, will enable us to discuss the whole subject of Church government, or the question of the parties by whom Church power is administered. We shall begin by taking into consideration the particular scheme of ecclesiastical polity advocated by the adherents of the Church of Rome.

The doctrine of the Popish Church in regard to the constitution and government of the Christian society, is briefly set forth in the decree of the Council of Florence, A.D. 1438-39,—one of those councils held by Romanists to be œcumenical and authoritative: "Also we decree that the Holy Apostolic See and the Roman Pontiff have a primacy over the whole world; and that the Roman Pontiff himself is the successor of St. Peter, the prince of the apostles, and is the true vicar of Christ, and head of the whole Church, and the father and teacher of all Christians; and that to him, in the person of the blessed Peter, our Lord

Jesus Christ has committed full power of feeding, ruling, and governing the universal Church."[1]

There are at least three bold and comprehensive positions asserted in this authoritative statement of the views of the Church of Rome as to the form and constitution of the ecclesiastical society. First, it is asserted that Peter was invested by our Lord with such a superiority over the other apostles as to be their official head, and in an exclusive and peculiar sense the depositary of his Master's Divine power and authority over the Church. Second, it is asserted that this primacy of Peter, being not personal but official, was transmitted by him, along with all the powers and prerogatives that belonged to it, to his successors in office,—those successors being the Roman Pontiffs. And third, it is asserted that this ecclesiastical supremacy conferred on Peter, and by him transmitted to his successors at Rome, is of such a nature and amount as to constitute them, in the proper sense of the term, the *vicars* of Christ, holding and administering vicariously His spiritual authority over the Church,—the Roman Pontiff for the time being as much the head of the ecclesiastical body as the Saviour once was on earth, with full powers to feed, order, and rule the universal Christian society. These three general positions are plainly involved in the decree of the Council of Florence, and are exemplified in the system of ecclesiastical polity set up and administered in the Romish Church. The subordinate office-bearers in the Popish Church hold their place and authority in dependence upon the sovereign Pontiff, who is invested both with infallible authority and with supreme and unlimited power. He has the right to enact laws binding upon all the members of the Church, to determine controversies of faith without appeal, to impose and remove spiritual judgments at his own pleasure. The functions of the whole college of apostles are vested in the chair of St. Peter at Rome, or rather, the whole delegated power of their Master is conferred on him who is the earthly vicar of Christ; and throughout the Christian Church, and among the whole body of those who have ever been baptized, the opinions, actions, and persons of all are under the control of the Pope, without any limitation affixed to his jurisdiction, or any appeal open from his decision.

[1] Concil. Florent. Sess. xxv. Perceval, *The Roman Schism*, Lond. 1836, p. 153 f.

The remarkable combination of comprehensiveness and unity in this scheme of ecclesiastical autocracy is obvious. From one centre of infallible and universal authority, the order, government, discipline, and doctrine of the entire Church system of Rome are developed. In that centre there sits the *vicar* of the Lord Jesus Christ on earth, with world-wide jurisdiction and unchallengeable infallibility, and the persons, actions, sentiments and beliefs of every member of the Christian society, all the outward authority and inward grace of the universal Church, are in his hands, and subject to his disposal and control. Such are the fruits of the Romish doctrine of the supremacy of the Pope,—the rich inheritance of that primacy alleged to have been left to Peter by our Lord.[1]

There can be little doubt that the system just delineated is the true exhibition of the Popish theory of ecclesiastical polity; it is countenanced by the public confessions of the Church of Rome, as well as by the works of her most eminent theologians. At the same time, considerable difference of opinion prevails among Romanists as to some points in the Romish scheme of Church power. With some, as Thomas Aquinas and Baronius, the supremacy of the Pope involves directly an absolute sovereignty both in spiritual and in temporal things; while, according to others, as Bellarmine, the Papal supremacy includes a sovereignty in temporal things, not directly, but indirectly. With others still, as Bossuet and the assertors of the Gallican Liberties, it is a supremacy limited to spiritual matters, and allowing of an appeal from the Pope to a General Council.[2] This latter point,

---

[1] ["About what," says Bellarmine at the commencement of the Preface to his five books, *De Summo Pontifice*,—"about what is the controversy when we debate concerning the primacy of the Pontiff? I may answer in one word: About the sum and substance of Christianity (de summâ rei Christianæ). For the question is, whether the Church ought to stand any longer, or whether it should be dissolved and fall. For what is the difference between asking if the foundation ought to be removed from the building, the shepherd from the flock, the general from the army, the sun from the stars, the head from the body, and asking if the building ought to fall, the flock to be scattered, the army to be dispersed, the stars to be darkened, the body to lie dead? . . . The Catholic faith teaches us that every virtue is good, every vice bad; but if the Pope were to err and to enjoin vices or prohibit virtues, the Church would be bound to believe the vices to be good and the virtues to be bad, unless she were willing to sin against conscience."—Lib. iv. cap. v. De Maistre, *The Pope*, Dawson's Transl. Lond. 1850, pp. xvi. xxv. 11, etc. Manning, *Engl. and Christendom*, Lond. 1867, pp. 206 ff.]

[2] Amesius, *Bellarm. Enerv.* lib. iii. cap. ix. Cunningham, *Works*, vol. i. pp. 82 ff. 101-132. [Edgar, *Variations of Popery*, 2d ed. ch. iii. pp. 124-132.]

indeed, or the question of the inferiority of the Pontiff to a General Council, and of the restriction of his power to spiritual matters, is the main difference between the Ultramontane and Cismontane parties in the Romish communion. But these differences of opinion, found within the bosom of the Church itself, as to what more or less is involved in the supremacy of the Pope, do not affect the general theory of Church government which rests upon that dogma. The structure and administration of the Church as an ecclesiastical system would be the same upon the Romish theory, even taking up the lowest view of the Papal supremacy entertained by any Romanist, even supposing it were shorn of all temporal authority whatsoever, and also made subordinate to a General Council. Let us endeavour to understand what grounds in reason or Scripture are to be found to support the superstructure of such a system of Church polity.

I. There are certain general considerations connected with the unity of the Church which are relied upon by many Romanists, as apart from express Scripture authority, sanctioning this system of ecclesiastical polity. It is the natural, or rather inevitable result of the Romish doctrine of Church unity, as belonging, in its highest character, not to the invisible, but to the visible Church of Christ.

The dogma of the Papal supremacy is so unlike the Scripture representations of the fisherman of Galilee and the thrice fallen apostle, that not a few, more especially of *modern* defenders of the dogma, have been contented to abandon, or to pass by in silence, the Scripture argument altogether, and to rest the system upon extra-scriptural evidence. The favourite resource of such controversialists is the necessity of the doctrine of the Papal supremacy to maintain and to represent the essential unity of the Christian Church. And in the Romish sense of unity, the necessity of a visible head and centre of the ecclesiastical system is apparent. The doctrine of the *oneness* of the Christian society is very strongly and explicitly laid down in Scripture. "There is *one* body and *one* spirit," says the apostle in the Epistle to the Ephesians, "even as ye are called in *one* hope of your calling; *one* Lord, *one* faith, *one* baptism." The ordinary figure under which Scripture represents the oneness belonging to the Christian Church is that of the human body with its many members, but its essential unity embracing them all.[1] Romanism adopts this idea, which Scripture suggests, of an organic unity as essential to the Christian society, and transfers it from the invisible to the visible Church; making this oneness to consist, not in the spiritual connection of all its members with an invisible Head in heaven, but in their political or ecclesiastical connection with a visible head on earth. The Papal unity, so far as it exists, is the thorough and perfect realization of the unity attributed in Scripture to the Christian Church; with this difference—and a most fundamental one—that it is a merely outward and ecclesiastical unity, and not an inward and spiritual one. If the unity of the Church could be completely realized according to the Romanist theory of it, we should have a huge, carnal, and political system the exact external counterfeit of the true inward and invisible union which actually belongs to the mystical body of Christ. Under one visible head are arranged, according to their rank and place in the society, both office-bearers and members; all equally connected with the supreme source of authority and order, holding their position from him, and in this connection with a common centre, finding a common connection with each other. The Pope is the centre of unity in the Romish theory of the Church; by his universal and supreme authority binding into one visible corporation the whole members of the Christian Church, and reducing to a certain outward uniformity in faith, and worship, and order, all the parts of the ecclesiastical society. A more perfect and imposing system of external unity than that presented by the Church of Rome the world has not seen; exhibiting as it does a vast corporation with its office-bearers and members alike under subjection to one visible head, and each holding his place in relation to every other in the body ecclesiastical, in virtue of his subordination to the common source of unity and power. Setting out from the fundamental idea of an organic unity, to be realized, not in an invisible Church, but in a visible ecclesiastical society, it must be admitted that the complete development of that idea is found in the primacy of the Roman Pontiff. This theory is the only one, proceeding on such an assumption, that is consistent with itself, and complete.[2] Any attempt to stop short of one visible society

---

[1] Eph. iv. 4, 12–16, v. 23, 29–32 ; Col. i. 18–24 ; 1 Cor. xii. 12–27.

[2] [Hence the numerous attempts among English High Churchmen to make out an abstract unity among all bishops,—" cujus a singulis in solidum pars

subject to one Head, the only fountain of authority within it, and therefore the only source of order and union, leaves the Church, considered as a visible association, a broken and disjointed thing, made up of a number of independent bodies, differing from each other in forms of government and faith and worship, but not constituting, in the highest sense of the term, one communion and one Church. Absolute organic unity, if it can be attributed to a visible Church, is only realized in the so-called Catholic Church and in the primacy of the Roman Pontiff.

It is on this ground that the dogma of the supremacy of the Pope has, by not a few, been argued and defended. Abandoning, or but faintly appealing to, the evidence which Scripture can be brought to exhibit directly in favour of such a system, they represent the supremacy of the Pope as the necessary result and expression of that organic unity which they believe belongs to the outward or visible Church. Such is the ground taken up, more especially in modern times, by those defenders of the Papal supremacy who belong to the philosophical school of Romanists; as for example, Möhler, De Maistre, and others. With them, the Papal supremacy is essentially the legitimate consummation and development of the unity of the Christian Church.[1]

Now, the fundamental error in such an argument is the assumption with which it sets out. The oneness of the Christian Church is not an ecclesiastical union, but a spiritual one; organic unity belongs to it, not as a visible system, but an invisible. That unity is realized, not in the outward connection of all

tenetur"—and by means of this "one visible abstract bishop" to break the force of those passages in the Fathers, asserting analogies between the Jewish hierarchy and the Christian ministry, which have always done such good service in the argument for the Papal supremacy. Others content themselves with the fact that the Fathers of the fourth and fifth centuries did not themselves draw the same practical inference from their own similes which their successors did. "That which Aaron and his sons and the Levites," says Jerome in his epistle to Evangelus, "were in the Temple, the same let the Bishops, Presbyters, and Deacons claim to be in the Church." On which Dr. Wordsworth remarks : " He does not say ' The Bishop,' as if there were to be only one,—a Pope. This, *therefore*, is no argument (as some have objected) in favour of Popery, that is, of one universal Bishop."—Synodal Address, 1864, Edin. 1867, p. 20. Cf. Bellarm. *de Rom. Pontif.* lib. i. cap. ix. etc. Litton, *Church of Christ*, pp. 680 ff.]

[1] [This line of reasoning has been very powerfully pressed by Möhler in his work on *Unity in the Church.* On the Cyprianic and Pseudo-Ignatian theory of the Church, his argument seems not only able, but perfectly unanswerable. *Die Einheit in der Kirche*, 2te Aufl. 2te Abth. ; see esp. pp. 236-252.]

Christians with one visible head on earth, but in the inward connection of all Christians with one unseen Head in heaven. The difference between the Romanist and Protestant systems on this subject may be traced back to the fundamental difference in their views of what is the true and normal idea of the Church of Christ. With Romanists, the initial idea of the Church is that of an outward institute; with Protestants, the initial idea of the Church is that of an inward and spiritual influence. With the former, the visible Church is the primary and fundamental conception; with the latter, the invisible Church is the normal conception of the Christian society. And hence the different manner in which they interpret and apply those passages of Scripture which declare the unity or oneness of the Christian Church,— the Romanist asserting a unity which shall be of an outward and visible kind, realized in the ecclesiastical connection of all Christians with an earthly head; the Protestant maintaining a unity of a spiritual kind, realized in the saving connection of all Christians with their glorified Head in heaven. The Romanist theory of the Church, which makes its essence to consist in external characteristics, necessarily leads to the notion of a unity external, and palpable also; no other kind of oneness is consistent with the Church system peculiar to Popery. And that external unity is only realized in a way at once consistent and complete, when it is expressed in the shape of a society, one in outward organization and fellowship, all the members and office-bearers of which hold of the same visible head, and are in subjection to the same central authority.[1]

There seems to be no intermediate system tenable between an organic unity wholly visible, and resulting in one catholic ecclesiastical corporation under subordination to the same supreme head on earth, and an organic unity wholly spiritual, and resulting in one universal spiritual Church in invisible communion with one unseen Head in heaven. The theory of semi-Romanists and Protestant High Churchmen is inconsistent with itself, and incomplete. With them, the Bishop is the fountain of authority and centre of union in the Christian Church; and the primacy of the episcopal office in each diocese is substituted for the primacy of the Pope in the universal Church. The Bishop, the representative of the apostolic office, or the representative of Christ,

---

[1] Litton, *Church of Christ*, Lond. 1851, pp. 383-398, 447-487. [See above, vol. i. pp. 29-40.]

within his own diocese, is the bond of life and order and unity in the Christian society. Such is the idea first formally, perhaps, exhibited in the so-called Epistles of Ignatius,[1] and more fully brought out in the writings of Cyprian. But in this shape the theory is manifestly inconsistent and incomplete. The outward unity, resulting from the episcopate within the limits of any one diocese, did not come up to the idea of the unity of the universal Church. From such a theory, there could result nothing beyond the aggregation of many dioceses or communities—each a distinct ecclesiastical corporation, and each independent of any and all the rest—into one combination; connected merely by a similarity of governments, and not by one government,—forming many societies linked together by a fragile tie, but not properly *one* society and community of Christians. Such a loose and disjointed alliance of independent unities did not, and never could, realize the proper idea of *one* society and one visible organization.[2] The Pseudo-Ignatian and Cyprianic theory of the Church could

[1] [On these celebrated epistles, which have always been the stronghold of controversialists on the Prelatic side, but which have dwindled by degrees in their hands from fifteen to eight, from eight to seven, from seven to six, and from six to three, see Cunningham, *Works*, vol. ii. pp. 108–120.]

[2] "It seems difficult," observes Mr. Litton, "to refuse assent to the following observations of one who at one time was a zealous maintainer of Cyprian's doctrine of unity, but who subsequently became sensible of its incompleteness, except when viewed as a stage of transition to the Papacy :—' It may possibly be suggested that this universality which the Fathers ascribe to the Catholic Church lay in its apostolical descent, or again in its Episcopacy ; and that it was one, not as being one kingdom or *civitas*, "at unity with itself," with one and the same intelligence in every part, one sympathy, one ruling principle, one organization, one communion, but because, though consisting of a number of independent communities, at variance (if so be) with each other, even to a breach of communion, nevertheless all these were possessed of a legitimate succession of clergy, or all governed by Bishops, Priests, and Deacons. But who will in seriousness maintain that relationship or that resemblance makes two bodies one ? England and Prussia are both monarchies ; are they, therefore, one kingdom ? England and the United States are from one stock ; can they, therefore, be called one state ? England and Ireland are peopled by different races ; yet are they not one kingdom still ? If unity lies in the apostolical succession, an act of schism is, from the nature of the case, impossible ; for as no one can reverse his parentage, so no Church can undo the fact that its clergy have come by lineal descent from the Apostles. Either there is no such sin as schism, or unity does not lie in the Episcopal form or in Episcopal ordination.'—Newman, *On the Development of Christ. Doctrine*, 2d ed. pp. 258 f. De Maistre has expressed the same thought more concisely : ' Soutenir qu'une foule d'Eglises independantes forment une Eglise *une et universelle*, c'est soutenir, en d'autres termes, que tous les gouvernements politique de l'Europe ne forment qu'un seul gouvernement *un et universel*.'—*Du Pape*, lib. i. c. 1."

only find its complete and consistent development in the Romish doctrine of one visible catholic society and one supreme head, under which all the inferior societies and authorities of a visible Episcopacy might unite. And hence the doctrine of the hierarchy embodied in the theory of Cyprian, grew, and was developed until it found its only consistent and perfect expression in the system of the Church of Rome.[1]

There is a sense, indeed, in which it may be truly said that the visible Church of Christ on earth is one body, however widely scattered and distinct the local societies included under it may be. They are all one, as included not only in the same profession of faith, but also in the same external covenant relation to Christ as their Head. But the higher relation of a saving and invisible spiritual connection with Christ as the Head, belongs only to the invisible Church, and is nowhere expressed or embodied in an outward and palpable form. The external and visible unity of the Church of Rome, resulting as it does in the Popish claims to catholicity, and in the supremacy of its one head on earth, is inconsistent with the scriptural idea of the unity of the Christian Church in its complete sense ; belonging, as this unity does, not to the visible, but to the invisible and mystical body of Christ. That theory of Church unity upon which the Popish idea of the supremacy of the successors of Peter is made by many of its adherents to rest, has no real foundation in the Word of God.[2]

II. There are certain scriptural intimations bearing upon the position of Peter among his brother apostles, which are adduced by Romanists in support of the doctrine of his official primacy. The scriptural evidence appealed to by the advocates of the Papacy on this point is of the very slenderest kind, and certainly wholly insufficient to support the magnificent superstructure of ecclesiastical polity reared upon it.

1*st*, The precedency of Peter in the college of apostles is argued from his name generally appearing first in any list of them given in Scripture, and from the place he usually occupied

---

[1] Litton, *Church of Christ*, Lond. 1851, pp. 658–695. [Jameson, *Cyprianus Isotimus*, Edin. 1705, pp. 154–198.]

[2] Litton, pp. 487–509. [See above, vol. i. pp. 41–53 ; Jewel, *Defence of the Apologie of the Churche of Englande*, Lond. 1570, 16 Junii, pp. 403–406, 515.]

as leader or representative of the rest, in speaking or acting on
many occasions recorded in the Gospel histories.

Now, in reference to this point, there is a very plain distinction to be drawn between a precedency which is personal and a
precedency which is official,—the one pertaining to the man, and
the other pertaining to the office held by him. That Peter was
in certain respects superior to his brethren in the apostleship, in
natural gifts and energy, or in zeal and devotedness in his
Master's service, may be readily conceded; and that this superiority marked him out on many occasions as the natural leader or
spokesman of the rest, may be no less readily allowed. And this
is all that can fairly be argued from the evangelical narrative as
belonging to him. But this personal precedency or superiority
over the rest is a very different thing from that official superiority claimed for him by the adherents of the Church of Rome,
and necessary to their theory. Such a personal precedency of
one man over others, is what necessarily arises out of the different characters and endowments possessed by the members of
every society in which men meet and act together, and can no
more be transmitted by the individual who enjoys it to another
than he can transfer to him his own personal character or qualifications. Peter, on not a few occasions, took the place or lead
assigned to him by the rest of the twelve; he stood forward as
the leader or spokesman of the Apostles, acting and speaking on
behalf of the others. But there is no evidence in Scripture that
this personal superiority was ever transmuted into an official
superiority, as if, not the man, but the office-bearer, was different
from the rest. That the circumstance of Peter's name appearing
first in the lists of the apostles given in the Gospels is no evidence of official precedent, is apparent from the fact, that in other
passages of Scripture, when Peter and others of the apostles are
mentioned, the order of names, as found in the Gospels, is not
adhered to, but those of some others of the apostles occur first.[1]

2d, The primacy of Peter among the apostles is very generally
made to rest by Romanists upon the words addressed to him by
our Lord, as recorded in the sixteenth chapter of the Gospel by
Matthew: " And Jesus answered and said unto him, Blessed art
thou, Simon Bar-jona: for flesh and blood hath not revealed it
unto thee, but my Father which is in heaven. And I say also

[1] John i. 44 ; 1 Cor. i. 12, iii. 22 ; Gal. ii. 9.

unto thee, That thou art Peter, and upon this rock I will build
my Church; and the gates of hell shall not prevail against it.
And I will give unto thee the keys of the kingdom of heaven:
and whatsoever thou shalt bind on earth shall be bound in
heaven; and whatsoever thou shalt loose on earth shall be loosed
in heaven." [1]

Now, in reference to this passage, it is not necessary to go
into the many different interpretations that have been given of
it, all of them excluding the idea of an official primacy granted
to Peter by our Lord.   Some of these interpretations assert that
" the rock" that was to be the foundation of the Church, as
declared in this passage, is not meant of Peter, but of Christ Himself.   Others of them assert that " the rock " is to be understood
of the previous confession made by Peter when he said, " Thou
art the Christ, the Son of the living God," rather than of the
apostle personally.   I cannot help thinking that the natural
interpretation of the passage does seem to involve the declaration
that, in some sense, and to a certain effect, Peter is to be regarded, in his official character of an apostle, as upholding the
superstructure of the Christian Church.   The allusion in the
passage to the name given to the apostle by our Lord, σὺ εἶ
Πέτρος, καὶ ἐπὶ ταύτῃ τῇ πέτρᾳ οἰκοδομήσω μου τὴν ἐκκλησίαν,
seems naturally to imply that in a certain sense the Church
was to be built upon the apostle, as its support.   But while
admitting this, it can be easily proved that this declaration to
Peter conveyed to him no superiority over the other apostles,
and constituted him the foundation of the Christian society in
no other sense or way than that in which the other apostles are
to be regarded as its foundation also.

In the first place, it is apparent that, in whatever sense Peter
was constituted the foundation of the Church, it can only be in
that inferior and secondary sense in which such an honour is
consistent with the prerogatives of Christ, as the true and proper
foundation of the Church.   Its Divine Author and Head is the
only real rock on which the Christian Church is built; for
" other foundation can no man lay than that is laid, which is
Jesus Christ." [2]

In the second place, there seems to be sufficient ground for
affirming that the declaration and promise made to Peter by our

[1] Matt. xvi. 17-19.   [2] 1 Cor. iii. 11.

Lord were made to him, not individually, but as the representative, on this occasion, of his brother apostles, and that the privilege conferred through him was conferred on all. The occasion on which our Lord's words were spoken, was one on which, not Peter separately, but all the apostles, had been addressed and appealed to by Christ: " When Jesus came into the coasts of Cæsarea Philippi, He asked His disciples, saying, Whom do men say that I the Son of man am ? " And after their reply, stating the opinion of others, our Saviour renews the question, still addressing, not Peter, but all the apostles : " But whom say ye that I am ? " It was in answer to this question that Peter, standing forth as the spokesman of the rest, gave utterance to the confession in their names as well as in his own : " Thou art the Christ, the Son of the living God." And it is hardly possible to believe that the promise of our Lord, granted in answer to this joint confession, was restricted to Peter, and did not include the other apostles in whose behalf, as much as for himself, he had spoken.

In the third place, the special privilege granted to Peter by our Lord's promise, of becoming the foundation or the founder of the Christian Church in a secondary sense, is a privilege which other express declarations of Scripture, made in the same terms, confer equally upon the other apostles. " Ye are built," says the Apostle Paul to the Ephesians, " upon the foundation of the apostles and prophets, Jesus Christ Himself being the chief corner stone." [1]   That new Jerusalem which John saw in the Apocalypse, had, we are told, " twelve foundations, and in them the names of the twelve apostles of the Lamb." [2]   In other words, we are expressly taught that, in the same sense in which Peter was the founder of the Church, the other apostles were the founders of it also.

In the fourth place, the power or authority over the Christian society, conveyed by our Lord to Peter on this occasion, is the very power at other times handed over to the rest of the apostles as rulers of the Church. It is plain that the authority implied in the place assigned to Peter as the foundation of the Church is in this passage to be interpreted by the words that follow : " And I will give unto thee the keys of the kingdom of heaven: and whatsoever thou shalt bind on earth shall be

[1] Eph. ii. 20.   [2] Rev. xxi. 14.

bound in heaven ; and whatsoever thou shalt loose on earth shall be loosed in heaven." This language is obviously explanatory of the power implied in the office or privilege of being the foundation of the Christian Church, assigned to Peter. Now this very power is, in the chapter next but one following, conveyed in the very same terms to all the apostles, when, in connection with the command to cast out the offender who refused to hear the Church, our Lord says, not to Peter, but to all the apostles: " Verily I say unto you, Whatsoever ye shall bind on earth shall be bound in heaven; and whatsoever ye shall loose on earth shall be loosed in heaven." [1] And again, a power of the same nature and amount is conferred once more upon all the apostles, when receiving the authoritative commission from our Lord before His departure : " Whose soever sins ye remit, they are remitted unto them ; and whose soever sins ye retain, they are retained." [2] So very strong and distinct is the evidence, that the privilege conferred upon Peter in the declaration of our Lord, although addressed to him as the representative of the others, was not intended for him alone, but was a privilege to be shared in equally by all the apostles.

3d, The official superiority of Peter among the apostles is sometimes based by Romanists on the commission given to him by our Lord after the resurrection, to feed the lambs and the sheep of Christ. [3]

It is hardly necessary to deal with this argument. The thrice repeated injunction, " Feed my lambs," " Feed my sheep," so pointedly addressed to Peter, might have reminded him, as it was no doubt intended to remind him, of his threefold denial and fall ; but it could hardly by any possibility convey to his mind the idea of superiority over his brethren. The very same injunction to *feed* the flock of Christ—ποιμαίνειν τὴν ἐκκλησίαν—is given more than once to the presbyters or bishops of the Church, as part of their ordinary vocation, and implies no distinctive or superior authority. [4] Indeed, the history of Peter after he received this charge, coupled with that of the other apostles and disciples, as it is to be gathered from the Acts and the Epistles, is a sufficient evidence of the interpretation he himself put upon these words, and of the absence of any attempt to claim or exercise official

---

[1] Matt. xviii. 18.   [2] John xx. 23.
[3] John xxi. 15-17.   [4] Acts xx. 28; 1 Pet. v. 2.

superiority over his brethren. In that history we see him the
same ardent and earnest man, ever foremost among his equals,
but asserting no official precedence over them, and sometimes
frankly confessing his faults and inferiority.[1] In the Acts of
the Apostles he appears on the same level with the rest of the
disciples in council, and in labours in the cause of the Church.
At Antioch he erred in conduct and speech, and was rebuked
sharply by Paul, and submitted to the brotherly censure.[2] In
his own Epistle to the Christian Jews scattered abroad throughout the world, there is not the slightest trace of the high and
paramount authority claimed for him by Romanists,—a silence
on the point not to be accounted for, on the supposition that it
actually belonged to him. In the Epistle to the Romans, addressed
to the Christians in the very place where it is alleged that he had
the seat of his ecclesiastical supremacy, his name and power and
office are nowhere mentioned,—an evidence in itself conclusive
against the Romish dogma of the primacy of Peter. In short,
the whole inspired history of the Church after the ascension of
our Lord, alike by its silence and its express assertions, contradicts
the theory of Peter's absolute and official superiority to the rest
of the apostles.

So much for the first and leading proposition involved in the
Popish theory of Church government, namely, that Christ conferred upon Peter an official supremacy over the other apostles
and over the Church at large. The absence in Scripture of any
evidence for such an assertion, or rather, the positive contradiction which Scripture evidence affords to it, supersedes the
necessity of our entering upon a consideration of the two remaining propositions in the Romanist scheme of ecclesiastical polity,
founded as they are upon the first. The second assumption implied in the Popish theory, or the assertion that Peter transmitted
his official supremacy to his successors, the Roman Pontiffs, is
contradicted by these two considerations: *first*, that the apostolical office, whatever powers or prerogatives belonged to it, was,
as we have already seen, extraordinary, and terminated with the
apostles themselves; and *second*, that there is no evidence in
Scripture, and nothing but the slenderest possible presumption
from ecclesiastical antiquity, to show that Peter was ever at Rome,
far less to show that he was bishop of the Church there. The

---

[1] Acts xi. 8–17; Gal. ii. 11; 2 Pet. iii. 15 f.   [2] Gal. ii. 11–21.

third assumption involved in the Popish theory, or the assertion
that the supremacy of Peter was such in nature and amount as
to constitute him and his successors in office the true vicars of
the Lord Jesus Christ on earth,—ruling with His power and
authority over the universal Church, and administering vicariously
in the Christian society the absolute supremacy and supernatural
infallibility of our Lord,—is contradicted by the whole tenor of
Scripture, which tells us that the office of Christ is peculiar to
Himself, and incommunicable, and that He has not handed over
His place or His glory to any earthly successor. The theory of
the Romish Church involves a daring dishonour to *Christ the
Head.*[1]

[1] Turrettin, *Op.* tom. iii. loc. xviii. qu. xvi.-xx. Amesius, *Bellarm. Enerv.*
lib. iii. Salmasius, *De Primatu Papæ.* Perrone, *Prælect. Theolog.* Parisiis 1842,
tom. ii. pp. 883-1040. Cunningham, *Works,* vol. ii. pp. 168-171, 207-226.
[Calvin, *Inst.* lib. iv. cap. vi. vii. Whitaker, *Prælectiones in Controversiam
de Romano Pontifice.* Barrow, *The Pope's Supremacy.* Stillingfleet, *Doct.
and Pract. of the Church of Rome,* Cunningham's ed. pp. 160-196.]

CHAPTER IV.

THE PRELATIC SYSTEM OF CHURCH POLITY AS OPPOSED TO THE PRESBYTERIAN.

SETTING aside the ecclesiastical theory of the Romish Church, the arguments in favour of which we have already discussed and disposed of, there remain for our consideration three forms of polity, the distinctive peculiarities of which are commonly known under the names of the Episcopalian or Prelatic, the Presbyterian, and the Independent systems. There are certain positions which are common to these three systems of Church government. Beginning with the inferior office, the order of deacon is one recognised under all these three systems as a standing and Divine institution in the Christian Church. Further, the office-bearer known under the name of presbyter or elder, or, from his chief function, pastor, is also acknowledged by the advocates of these three systems to be a standing functionary in the Christian society. There may be, and there are, different views entertained of the duties and powers of these office-bearers by the parties adhering to the different schemes of Church government now referred to. But these two offices, at least, are admitted by all of them to have been Divine appointments, not of a temporary, but of a permanent character, in the ecclesiastical body. The two orders of presbyters and deacons, acknowledged by all the three parties, are held by Presbyterians and Independents to be the *only* ranks of standing office-bearers divinely instituted in the Church; while Episcopalians contend that, in addition to these, there is a *third* order, superior in place and authority to both, and forming part of the permanent arrangements of the ecclesiastical society. In addition to presbyters and deacons, the advocates of Prelacy assert, against the view both of Presbyterians and Independents, that there is an order of bishops or prelates distinct from the former two, and equally of standing authority in the Christian Church. Presbyterians and Independents occupy common ground in combating this distinctive principle of Prelacy, and denying the existence and authority of the order of bishops as apart from elders or presbyters. There are other points in regard to the office of elder or presbyter where the views of Presbyterians and Independents separate. But they agree in repudiating the *three* orders of office-bearers necessary to the Episcopalian theory, and in denying that there is any Scripture warrant for the office of bishop, in the Prelatic sense of the word, as a distinct and superior ordinance in the Christian society.[1]

In proceeding to discuss the question of Church government as between Presbyterians and Independents on the one side, and Episcopalians on the other, it is of great importance that we keep in view what is essential and peculiar to Episcopacy, and what is not. We have no dispute with Prelatists as to the existence and permanent nature of the office of presbyters in the Church, as an order set apart more especially to minister in the Word and Sacraments. We have no dispute with Prelatists as to the existence and standing character of the office of deacon, subordinate to the presbyter; though we may differ somewhat as to the proper duties that belong to the office. The main and essential distinction between Episcopalians and Presbyterians relates to the order of bishops as separate from and superior to both elders and deacons, and vested with peculiar powers and authority not belonging to either of them. According to the Episcopalian theory as commonly held, the distinction between bishops and presbyters is twofold, —a distinction expressed in the language of the old divines as comprehending a difference in regard to the "potestas ordinis" and the "potestas jurisdictionis :" in other words, the difference

---

[1] [The Council of Trent having to deal with the fact that all the Reformers had rejected the Divine right of Prelacy, and that in England, where alone the form of it had been retained, it was only defended as an ancient and lawful ecclesiastical arrangement, is very express in its language on the subject : "Si quis dixerit in Ecclesiâ catholicâ non esse hierarchiam Divinâ ordinatione institutam quæ constat ex episcopis, presbyteris, et ministris : anathema sit. Si quis dixerit episcopos non esse presbyteris superiores, vel non habere potestatem confirmandi et ordinandi ; vel eam quam habent illis esse cum presbyteris communem . . . : anathema sit. Si quis dixerit episcopos qui auctoritate Romani Pontificis assumuntur non esse legitimos et veros episcopos, sed figmentum humanum : anathema sit."—*Concil. Trid. Canones et Decreta*, Sess. **xxiii.**, *De Sacr. Ord.* can. vi.–viii. Cf. *Bellarm. de Clericis*, cap. **xiv. xv.**]

asserted by the Episcopalian theory between the order of bishops and the order of presbyters is exhibited in the right belonging to bishops, and not to presbyters, of ordaining to office in the Church, and further, in the power appertaining to bishops and not to presbyters, of exercising government and administering discipline in the Christian society. This, according to the generally received form of the Episcopalian doctrine, is the proper and essential distinction between the bishop and the presbyter in the Christian Church. The bishop alone has the power of ordination and jurisdiction; the presbyter has no power to ordain or to rule. And the question in debate between Episcopalians and Presbyterians, setting aside what is not essential to the controversy, is simply as to the existence of an order of office-bearers in the Church superior to presbyters, and exclusively possessed of the powers of government and ordination. A bishop supreme in authority and independent in powers within his own diocese, alone having the right of ordination, and ruling singly over the subordinate ranks of the presbyters, deacons, and Church members, embodies, according to the Prelatic theory, the proper ideal of the Episcopal as distinguished from other forms of ecclesiastical polity.

The right of the rulers of the Christian society to meet together regularly in a Church Court for united counsel and action, and to legislate with real authority and effect, not merely for the clergy, but for the whole body of the Church, although in práctice it is almost peculiar to Presbyterianism, is yet, in a certain sense, and for certain limited purposes, admitted or claimed by Episcopalians as competent to their system. Prelacy does not altogether deny the lawfulness of the Church acting through a Court made up of office-bearers under the form of a Synod or Council, although it may seldom seem to act upon the admission to much practical effect; still, in so far it may be said to coincide with the system of Presbyterianism as exhibited in her Church Courts. And on the other side, the lawfulness of conceding a certain precedency, not of permanent office, but as a matter of arrangement and convenience, to certain office-bearers over the rest in the Courts of the Church, or for the sake of more convenient and concentrated ecclesiastical action elsewhere, is not denied by Presbyterians, but, within certain limits, is avowed and acted upon.[1] Presby-

---

[1] [Thus Calvin, speaking of the only primacy, which, for the sake of argument, he is willing to concede to Peter among the apostles, and which he

terianism does not disown the lawfulness of a temporary or even
a constant moderator, appointed over his brethren by their voice,
with a view to expediting business or securing order, but having,
in virtue of this precedency, no superiority of permanent office or
original authority over others. All Presbyterians hold that presbyters met for common action should and must have a president,
by whatever name he may be designated. What precise degree
of authority should be given to such a president, and what the
length and conditions of his tenure of office ought to be, are
matters of detail, to be settled by every Church upon principles of
Christian expediency and common sense, with a reasonable regard
to the exigencies of the time and the lessons of Church history,
though, above all, " in accordance with the general rules of the
Word, which ought always to be observed."[1]   The concession by
Episcopalians within certain restricted limits of the existence and
powers of Church Courts, and the concession by Presbyterians
of the lawfulness of a precedency, not of original rank, but of
occasional appointment, are points on which the two systems
approximate or practically coincide.[2]   But the proper and essential distinction between the two systems is the assertion by Episcopalians, and the denial by Presbyterians, of Scriptural warrant

holds was all that the bishops had among their co-presbyters in the early
centuries, when, as he says, " even although some exception should be taken
to some of their appointments, yet still, seeing that they strove with an honest
purpose to observe what God had instituted, they did not go far astray from
it : " Hoc enim fert natura, hoc hominum ingenium postulat, ut in quovis
coetu, etiamsi æquales sint omnes potestate, unus tamen sit veluti moderator, in quem alii respiciant.   Nulla est curia sine consule, nullus consessus
judicum sine prætore seu quæstore, collegium nullum sine præfecto, nulla sine
magistro societas."   " Quibus docendi munus injunctum erat, eos omnes (in
the early post-apostolic Church) nominabant presbyteros. Illi ex suo numero
in singulis civitatibus unum eligebant, cui specialiter dabant titulum episcopi :
ne ex æqualitate ut fieri solet dissidia nascerentur.   Neque tamen sic honore
et dignitate superior erat episcopus ut dominium in collegas haberet ; sed
quas partes habet consul in senatu, ut referat de negotiis, sententias roget,
consulendo, monendo, hortando, aliis præeat, auctoritate suâ totam actionem
regat, et quod decretum communi consilio fuerit exsequetur, id muneris sus-
tinebat episcopus in presbyterorum coetu.   Atque id ipsum pro temporum
necessitate fuisse humano consensu inductum fatentur ipsi veteres."—Inst.
lib. iv. cap. iv. 2, vi. 8.]
    [1] Cunningham, Works, vol. ii. p. 235.
    [2] [It was upon these points of approximation that Archbishop Usher, ac-
cording to whose view the bishop of the early centuries was just the constant
moderator of the presbytery, differing from his colleagues " gradu tantum, non
ordine," founded his " Reduction of Episcopacie unto the Form of Synodical
Government received in the ancient Church." Lond. 1656 (first proposed in
1641). Cf. Hoornbeek's notes on it, Dissert. de Episcopatu, Utrecht 1661.

for a third order of ordinary and permanent office-bearers in the
Church above presbyters and deacons, having exclusively in their
hands the *potestas ordinis* and the *potestas jurisdictionis*, and
necessary to the existence of a true, or at least of a regularly
constituted, Church.[1]

Such being the distinctive character of the Episcopalian
system, it is not difficult to understand what the kind of Scripture
evidence is that would be relevant and necessary to establish the
truth of it. Sufficient proof might be adduced in one or other
of two ways. *In the first place*, it might be shown by Episcopalians that the office of bishop, as distinct from presbyter, had
been actually instituted by Christ or His inspired followers in the
New Testament Church, and the Scripture proof for the original
institution of the office, without any warrant given us to believe
that it was extraordinary or temporary, would be sufficient evidence of the truth of the Prelatic system. The evidence for the
formal institution of the order of bishop at first by our Lord or
His apostles would settle the controversy. Or, *in the second
place*, in the absence of any evidence for the separate or formal
institution of the Prelatic office at first, still if proof could be
led from Scripture of the exercise of the peculiar and distinctive
powers of the office by a standing order of men, distinct from

---

[1] [" The question is *not*," says Turrettin, "regarding a distinction of arrangement or polity between different ministers of the same Church, in virtue
of which one may rank above the rest and preside in Church Courts (in sacris
Conventibus), whether under the name of bishop or superintendent. We do
not deny that this may be conveniently done with a view to all things proceeding in seemly form and order in the House of God. As is the case in
several Protestant and Reformed Churches, which, with a view to the preservation of good order, have thought it well to have a certain presidency and
superiority (προστασίαν et ὑπεροχήν quandam) among their pastors, and which
have accordingly their bishops, superintendents, prelates, dekans, inspectors, to
whom belongs *jure ecclesiastico* a certain higher dignity and authority than to
the other pastors. [We may possibly question the *expediency* of some of these
arrangements among the Lutheran Churches to which Turrettin alludes; no
one disputes their abstract lawfulness, or their theoretical consistency with the
thoroughly Presbyterian principles of those who founded them.] *But the
question is regarding a distinction of power both as to degree of order*, in virtue of
which the bishop shall be the superior in office and dignity, and the presbyter
the inferior ; *and as to jurisdiction*, in virtue of which the latter shall be subject
to the dominion of the former : this is what our opponents hold, and we deny.
Again, the question is *not regarding an ecclesiastical right* as derived from an
ancient custom which began to prevail not long after the times of the apostles.
We readily grant that this was the case. *But the question is regarding a Divine
right*, as founded on the appointment of Christ and the practice of the
apostles; which we deny."—Loc. xviii. qu. xxi.]

presbyters in the New Testament Church, such proof would be relevant and sufficient to establish the Scriptural truth of the Episcopalian theory. The evidence for the exercise of proper Prelatic powers by a permanent body of men distinguished from presbyters in Scripture, even although no proof could be brought for the formal institution of the office itself at first, would be enough. By one or other of these two methods, the system of Prelacy might be satisfactorily proved from Scripture. But if no evidence satisfactory or sufficient can be brought to establish the fact of the original institution of the office of diocesan bishop by Christ or His apostles, and further, if, in the absence of that, no evidence can be brought to prove the existence and exercise of the proper powers of the episcopate in the Prelatic sense of the term, by a standing body of office-bearers distinct from presbyters, then the proof for the Episcopalian scheme of Church government completely fails. We believe that Scripture affords ample ground and warrant for meeting, with a decided negative, both the propositions now referred to as the only competent or relevant evidence which would suffice to prove the truth of the Episcopalian pretensions. Scripture evidence denies that any such office as that of diocesan bishop was ever instituted by our Lord or His inspired followers. Scripture evidence denies that the distinctive powers of the office were ever held or exercised by ordinary and permanent office-bearers in the New Testament Church, separate from presbyters. The discussion of these two general propositions will enable us to review the question of Church government as between Episcopalians and Presbyterians.

SECTION I.—NO EVIDENCE IN SCRIPTURE, BUT THE REVERSE, FOR THE APPOINTMENT BY OUR LORD OR HIS APOSTLES OF AN ORDER OF BISHOPS, AS DISTINCT FROM PRESBYTERS.

I. Christ, in instituting the office of apostle, did not institute the office of diocesan bishop.

There is very considerable misapprehension as to this point. It is admitted by all parties that the apostles possessed and exercised the powers and prerogatives which, according to the theory of Episcopalians, properly belong to the office of bishop. And hence, when it is demanded of Episcopalians to point out in Scripture the evidence for the institution of the peculiar office of bishop in the Prelatic sense of the word, they almost all with one consent appeal to the institution of the Apostolate as the evidence for the institution of the Episcopate also. It is admitted, and indeed cannot be denied, that there is no passage in the New Testament which records the institution of the office of diocesan bishop as a separate thing from the office either of the apostles, or of the evangelists, or of the presbyters of the apostolic Church. The Prelatic theory denies that in the institution of the office of presbyter we have any record of the institution of that of bishops; for this would be to confess that they were identical, and not two distinct offices. And therefore Episcopalians, having no record of any separate institution of the order of prelates, are forced to seek for it in the recorded institution of the office, either of apostle or evangelist. The great majority of Episcopalians in the present day assert that in the institution of the apostolic office we have also the institution of the office of diocesan bishop.

Now in this assertion there is a fallacy of a very important kind, and one fatal to the Prelatic argument. It involves the mistake of confounding or identifying the χαρίσματα—certain of the gifts or powers which may belong to a man in an office—with the office itself; and the investiture of an individual with such powers with the appointment of the same individual to the formal office in connection with which they may be found. The supereminent commission with which the Twelve were invested, gave them, besides their peculiar prerogatives, the ordinary powers belonging to the inferior and permanent office-bearers in the Church; as apostles, they could do all that bishops or presbyters or deacons could do in the ecclesiastical society. But the possession of such powers by the apostles did not invest them with the *office* of bishop or presbyter or deacon, nor make the apostolic office to be identical with all or any one of these. The apostles exercised all the functions and authority of those offices attached to the names of evangelist, and prophet, and bishop, and presbyter, and deacon, and much more. But they were still apostles, and did not cease to be so, even while occasionally discharging some of those inferior functions which were destined to be permanent in the Christian society. In short, the powers that may be exercised in office are not to be identified with the office itself. These powers may be devolved upon a man for a temporary purpose, and on a special occasion, while the man himself has not been invested with the formal office. So it is in ordinary life, and so it is in the Church. The commander of an army may do the work and take the place of a common soldier in it, when some crisis in the battle may call for such a step ; but he is not on that account to be reckoned a common soldier. The ruler of the state may in some emergency be called upon to discharge the functions of his own minister; but his office has not on that account been changed from that of a king into that of a states-man. And so it is in the case of the apostleship. The powers occasionally exercised by the Twelve in connection with the de-partments of labour or authority, usually appropriated to other and inferior functionaries in the Church, did not invest the apostles with the formal and separate office which such persons possessed. In the course of the inspired history we may see apostles serving tables and ministering to the necessities of the saints ; but they do not on that account become deacons. We may see them preaching, ordaining, dispensing Sacraments, exercising ecclesi-astical discipline ; but that does not make them, in the technical sense of the words, either presbyters or bishops.

The argument, then, of the Episcopalians, when they point to the institution of the apostleship, as also the institution of the Prelatic office, is altogether insufficient and unsound. It pro-ceeds upon the mistaken assumption that the possession and occasional exercise by the apostles of the powers which Pre-latists attribute to the Episcopate, is the same thing as the formal possession by the apostles of the office itself. It is no doubt true that, along with other and far higher powers, the apostles did possess both the "potestas ordinationis" and the "potestas jurisdictionis," proper, according to the Prelatic theory, to the office of a bishop. But the possession of such powers, involved as they were in the supereminent and temporary office of the apostleship, is not the same thing as the investiture of the apostles with the office of diocesan bishop.

It is of very great importance in the discussion, that this point should be cleared from all the misapprehensions that prevail among Episcopalian controversialists in regard to it. Our general position is, that the admitted fact of the possession and exercise of Prelatic functions by apostles, in connection with the extra-ordinary office and powers which they held, is not identical with their investiture with the formal office of prelate or diocesan bishop; and therefore that the institution of the office of the apostleship, which we find in Scripture, is not identical with, and does not imply, the institution of the office of bishop in the Prelatic sense of the word. There are three distinct grounds on which this general proposition may be established.

1st, There is no assertion in the Word of God, and no evidence whatever, to prove that the apostles possessed and exercised the various and different powers that belonged to them in any other character or capacity than as apostles. If there had been any intimation, direct or indirect, given us, that at different times, and in their different proceedings, the apostles appeared in different capacities, at one time as apostles, at another time as bishops, on a third occasion as presbyters, and on a fourth occasion as deacons, there would have been some ground for the assumption of Episcopalians, that they held not the office of apostle alone, but other offices also, involved in, and necessarily connected with, the apostleship. If it could have been proved from Scripture, that when an apostle exercised the powers of government and ordination, it was in his capacity as a bishop; or that when he ministered in the Word and Sacraments, it was in his character of a presbyter; or that when he carried to Jerusalem, and distributed to the poor saints there, the contributions of the Churches, it was in virtue of his office of a deacon,—then indeed something would have been done in the direction of establishing the Episcopalian theory. But if there be no such evidence in Scripture,—and if, on the contrary, there is reason to believe that these various powers were exercised by the apostles, not in virtue of their special ordination to the separate offices of bishop and presbyter and deacon, but in virtue of the general and supereminent power which belonged to the one and undivided office of apostle,—then everything is against the gratuitous assumption of Prelatists. The total want of any evidence to show that they ever acted in any other capacity than as apostles, or in virtue of any other office than the peculiar one belonging to their order, seems to exclude the hypothesis that in the institution of the Apostolate we have the Scripture institution of the Episcopate also.

2d, The separate and distinct mention in Scripture of the institution of the offices of presbyter and deacon apart from the apostleship, and the absence of any mention of the institution of the office of diocesan bishop apart from the apostleship, seem fairly to exclude the Episcopalian assumption, that in the erection of the apostolic office we have the office of diocesan bishop instituted also. There cannot be a doubt that the powers of the presbyter and of the deacon, as much as the powers of the diocesan bishop, were exercised by the apostles, and connected with their office. And if the circumstance that the functions of an office were exercised sometimes by the apostles, proves that the office itself belonged to them, and was instituted along with the apostleship, then the same reasoning must apply to the office of presbyter and deacon that applies to the office of diocesan bishop, and we should have in the original institution of the apostleship the institution also of the Presbyterate and Diaconate, as much as the Episcopate. Upon the Prelatic theory consistently carried out, the offices of presbyter and deacon must have their origin and institution in the erection of the apostleship, as well as the office of diocesan bishop. That this is not the case, is sufficiently proved by the express record in Scripture of the institution of both these offices of presbyter and deacon apart from the apostleship. We read of the separate erection both of the Diaconate and the Presbyterate, subsequently to the origin and establishment of the apostolic office. Without such mention of the formal institution of these offices apart from the apostleship, and of the exercise of the powers appropriate to them by two distinct orders of men not apostles, we should have had no Scripture warrant for saying that the Presbyterate and Diaconate were separate offices in the Church at all. And the fact that there is no such mention of the institution of the office of diocesan bishop apart from the apostleship, and no proof—as we shall see by and by—that the proper powers of the office were exercised by any standing staff of separate office-bearers, must, upon the very same principle, be held as depriving of all Scripture warrant the office and order of prelate in the New Testament Church.[1]

---

[1] " The question now before us is," says an able modern divine of the English Church, dealing with the Tractarian theory of ecclesiastical government : " Did Christ Himself deliver this form of ecclesiastical polity (the Episcopal) as that by which His Church was to be distinguished from other religious societies? Difficult of proof as this may appear, it is in the last resort affirmed ; and the way in which it is made out is as follows : Christ ordained the twelve—or eleven—apostles to be governors and teachers of His Church : in their apostolic commission were comprised three distinct subordinate ones, —the commissions of bishop, presbyter, and deacon,—so that, in fact, though these offices are not found to have been formally instituted by Christ Himself,

3d, The single commission delivered by our Lord to His apostles, proves that it was a single office with which He invested them, and not a plurality of offices involving two, or three, or four distinct and separate orders in His Church. In that one and undivided commission which made them apostles, we have evidence that, whatever were the multitude of separate powers or gifts conferred upon them, their office was one and undivided also. We have not a distinct commission answering to each of the offices alleged to have been conferred,—one for the Diaconate, with power given to them to serve tables ; a second for the Presbyterate, with power given to minister in the Word and ordinances; —a third for the Episcopate, with power conferred on them to ordain and to rule ; and a fourth for the Apostolate, with powers embracing those of all the four, and others besides.

That the Twelve were appointed to the apostleship, we know from the commission delivered to them by Christ ; but that they had an ordination as bishops, presbyters, and deacons separately, is discountenanced very strongly by the silence of Scripture on the subject. If the Episcopalian theory had been the true one,— if under the one name and the one commission given to them as apostles a congeries of different and separate offices had been included, — we must have had some very express statements or even to have been formally in being until the Church had existed for some time in the world, yet they were present implicitly from the first ; each of the apostles having in himself the polity of the Church in all its plenitude, and the apostolic college by degrees shedding the three orders, hitherto enveloped in their own persons, as need required : first, the Diaconate ; then the Presbyterate ; and lastly, the Episcopate. Several difficulties here present themselves to the mind. In what passage of Scripture is Christ recorded to have delivered to the apostles three distinct commissions, with different powers attached to each ? . . . The apostolic office comprised in itself powers much more extensive than those which were afterwards distributed between bishops, priests, and deacons. But we search in vain for the formal union of the three orders in the persons of the apostles. And be it observed, the theory requires such a formal devolution of the orders ; for no one can transmit to another an office with which he has not himself been formally invested. He may create for the first time a new office, or he may empower others to do certain acts,—as, for instance, to preach or to ordain,—which he has heretofore reserved to himself ; but to make over an office to another, requires that the person making it over have been himself, by competent authority, formally invested with it, and empowered by the same authority to transmit it. If we are to believe that the apostles evolved out of themselves, or out of their own commission, the three offices in question, proof must be given of their having themselves been formally invested with the offices. But of this no sufficient proof is offered. That the Twelve were appointed to be apostles of Christ, is declared in Scripture ; but when and where they were ordained bishops, priests, and deacons, nowhere appears."—Litton, *Church of Christ*, p. 245 f.

of Scripture to counterbalance the evidence to the contrary drawn from the one ordination to their office as apostles. We should require very explicit proof to warrant us in believing that beneath the terms of that single commission were comprehended several distinct offices, one of which—the apostleship—was, by the confession of all parties, extraordinary and temporary; and others of which—the Episcopate, Presbyterate, and Diaconate—were to be ordinary and permanent, and yet separated from each other. There is no principle whatever laid down in the commission itself to enable us to separate between the extraordinary and temporary office admittedly held by them, and the ordinary and standing office alleged to have been included under the same commission, or to separate between these latter among themselves. Episcopalians have no directory for this in the terms of the appointment of the apostles by our Lord at first, but stand indebted wholly to their own arbitrary and gratuitous assumption for the ability to divide the apostolic commission into separate parts and parcels, and to assert that one portion of it, giving the right to ordination and government in the Church, belongs to one office, and another portion of it, giving a right to administer Word and Sacrament, to a second office,—both of them being permanent and ordinary in the Church; and that other portions of the commission still, giving special endowments, belonged to yet another office, which was extraordinary and to be abolished. The very terms of the commission indeed show that the office to which the apostles were appointed was one and undivided, alike when they entered upon it, and when with their own lives it came to an end.

Upon such grounds as these, then, we are warranted in asserting that in the institution of the apostleship we have no record of the institution of the Episcopal office, in the Prelatic sense of the term.

II. The apostles, in instituting the office of evaneglist, did not institute the office of diocesan bishop.

The great majority of Episcopalians in the present day appeal to the establishment of the apostleship as the proper evidence for the institution of the office of diocesan bishop; but some of them —and this was perhaps, on the whole, the favourite argument when the notion of the Divine right of Prelacy was first taken up on Protestant ground by the school of Bancroft and Laud

—put the matter in a slightly different shape, and point to the institution of the evangelist's office as the proper origin of the Prelatic. That the evangelists, like the apostles, were possessed of all the powers subsequently attributed to prelates, and, in virtue of their extraordinary office, often acted as prelates might have acted, exercising both the " potestas ordinationis " and the " potestas jurisdictionis " in addition to their extraordinary authority as evangelists, there can be no doubt. In the unsettled and critical state of an infant Church in a heathen land, with few or no regular office-bearers at all, or amid the disorders of false teachers, factions, and heresies arising in a society of young and unstable converts, an ample measure of exceptional and discretionary authority might obviously be needed by the deputies of an apostle.[1] But the very same argument applies to the case of evangelists, when referred to as the source of the Prelatic office, which we have found applicable to the case of apostles when appealed to for the same purpose. It cannot be alleged that the office of evangelist, in its full extent and in all its powers, is identical with what Episcopalians regard as the ordinary office of bishop now. The evangelist was endowed with supereminent authority and supernatural powers, unknown to the ordinary office-bearers of the Church; and to that extent even Episcopalians will allow that their office was extraordinary, and has ceased. And if it be still alleged that under the extraordinary and temporary office

[1] [We have a vivid picture of such disorders in Paul's Epistles to the Corinthians, and in the earliest of the genuine remains of the apostolic Fathers,—the letter of Clemens Romanus to the same Church. It is noteworthy that in neither case is there the slightest hint of the Prelatic remedy for schism. " There is nothing in the epistle of Clement which directly or by implication affords any countenance to the notion that bishops, in the modern sense, then existed or were thought necessary ; while, from the general substance and leading object of the epistle, it is perfectly manifest, that if there had been any bishop at Corinth, or if the see had been vacant at the time, as some ingenious Episcopalians have fancied, or if the idea, which seems afterwards to have prevailed had then entered men's minds—viz. that Prelacy was a good remedy against schism and faction,—something *must*, in the circumstances, have been said which would have proved this. So clear is all this, that the more candid Episcopalians admit it ; and the latest Episcopalian historian, Dr. Waddington, now Dean of Durham, after asserting, without evidence, that all the other Churches were provided with bishops by the apostles, adds : ' The Church of Corinth seems to have been the only exception. Till the date of St. Clement's epistle, its government had been clearly Presbyterial, and we do not learn the exact moment of the change ' (*Hist. of the Church*, Lond. 1833, p. 21). It is rather unfortunate for our Episcopalian friends that the Church of *Corinth* should have been the exception ; for if Prelacy is felt to promote unity, peace, and subordination, and if this consideration was present to the

there was included the ordinary and permanent office of prelate, —if it be asserted, as many Episcopalians do assert, that Timothy and Titus, although extraordinary evangelists, were ordinary diocesan bishops too,—and if the institution of the office of prelate is held to be involved implicitly in the institution of the higher office of evangelist,—then the very same process of reasoning, applicable to the case of the apostolic office, when adduced as the source of Episcopacy, is applicable no less to the evangelistic. *First*, there is no evidence whatever, but the reverse, in the Word of God to prove that evangelists ever acted in the capacity of diocesan bishops, and not in the character or capacity of evangelists. *Second*, the separate institution of the office of presbyter and deacon, while there is no institution of the office of diocesan bishop apart from that of evangelist, goes to show that the prelate's office is not, like the presbyter's, a separate and standing one in the Church of Christ. *Third*, the special and single commission given by the apostles to the office of evangelist shows that it was one office, and not two united together under one name. The application of these general propositions will dispose of the argument of those Episcopalians who seek for the institution of the office of prelate in the institution, not of the apostolic, but of the evangelistic office.

III. The circumstance that the terms bishop and presbyter are invariably used in the New Testament as but different titles

mind of the apostles in establishing it,—and all this they commonly allege,— there is no undue presumption in saying that the Apostle Paul would surely have taken care that, whatever *other* Churches might have been left to the evils and disorders of Presbyterial government, the proud and factious Church of Corinth should have been subjected in good time to the wholesome restraint of Episcopal domination. There is another unfortunate circumstance about this solitary exception. The Church of Corinth happens to be the only one about whose internal condition, with respect to government, we have any very specific or satisfactory evidence applicable to the end of the first century ; and we are expected, it seems, to believe that *all* the other Churches were at this time in *a different* condition in respect to government, from the only one whose condition we have any certain means of knowing. Dr. Waddington admits that the government of the Church of Corinth was at this time ' clearly Presbyterial,' but he says it was the only exception. Well, then, we put this plain question : Will he select *any other* Church he chooses, and undertake to produce evidence *half* as satisfactory that *its* government at this time was Prelatic ? The remains of antiquity afford no sufficient materials for doing so ; and the important fact therefore stands out, that the *only* Church about whose internal condition we have any clear and satisfactory evidence applicable to the first century, had a government ' clearly Presbyterial.' "—Cunningham, *Works*, vol. ii. p. 245.]

for the same ecclesiastical office, demonstrates that there was no institution of the office of bishop separate from that of presbyter.

It is not difficult to recognise the reason for the use of the two terms, πρεσβύτερος and ἐπίσκοπος, as applicable to the same undivided office. The first of these, πρεσβύτερος, was the title appropriated to the office of elder in the Jewish synagogue; and when transferred to the Christian Church to denote a certain class of its office-bearers, it was employed as the term best understood and most familiar in the case of Churches, the members of which belonged, mainly or exclusively, to the Jewish race. The second of these, ἐπίσκοπος, was a word in general use among the Greeks to denote any kind of overseer; and when transferred to the overseers of the Christian society, it was made use of in the case of Gentile Churches especially, in preference to the other term, carrying with it Jewish associations, not understood by Gentile Christians. The general use in the New Testament of these two words seems to be regulated for the most part, although with some exceptions, by a regard to this principle.[1] But that these words were but different titles of the same official personage, is abundantly proved by a variety of passages in the New Testament. The proof indeed is so strong as to be now acknowledged to be conclusive as to the point by the most candid of the Episcopalian controversialists. It is not necessary to do more than advert briefly to the evidence.

1. In the twentieth chapter of the Acts we are told of Paul, that "from Miletus he sent to Ephesus, and called the elders—τοὺς πρεσβυτέρους—of the Church. And when they were come to him, he said unto them, . . . Take heed unto yourselves, and to all the flock over the which the Holy Ghost has made you bishops —ἐπισκόπους—to feed the Church of God, which He hath purchased with His own blood."[2] It is not possible for any inge-

---

[1] [Neander, *Hist. of the Plant. of the Christ. Church*, Ryland's Transl. vol. i. pp. 164–178.]

[2] Acts xx. 17 f., 28. ["This circumstance," says Dean Alford (that, namely, of the Ephesian presbyters being called bishops), "began very early to contradict the growing views of the apostolic institution and necessity of prelatical episcopacy. Thus Irenæus, ii. 14, 2: 'In Mileto convocatis *episcopis et presbyteris* qui erant ab Epheso *et a reliquis proximis civitatibus*.' Here we see, (1) the two, bishops and presbyters, distinguished, as if *both* were sent for, in order that the titles might not seem to belong to the same persons ; and (2) other neighbouring Churches also brought in, in order that there might not seem to be ἐπίσκοποι in one Church only. That neither of these was the case, is clearly shown by the plain words of this verse (ver. 17). . . . So early

nuity—and a good deal has been expended upon this point by some Prelatic writers—to evade the conclusion, that in this passage the two terms are applied indiscriminately to the same persons, as different titles of the one office that they held.

2. In the Epistle to Titus we have similar and equally decisive evidence: " For this cause," says the apostle, " left I thee in Crete, that thou shouldest set in order the things that are wanting, and ordain elders—πρεσβυτέρους—in every city, as I had appointed thee: if any be blameless, the husband of one wife, having faithful children, not accused of riot, or unruly. For a bishop —ἐπίσκοπος—must be blameless, as the steward of God."[1] In this passage we again find the two terms used interchangeably in reference to the same office. More than this, according to the Episcopalian theory, Titus was, at the date of these instructions to him, bishop of Crete, and yet, in total contradiction to that assumption, we find him in this passage told to ordain a plurality of bishops in every city of his diocese.[2]

3. The language of the Apostle Peter is also decisive as to the use of these terms : " The elders—πρεσβυτέρους—which are among you I exhort, who am also an elder — συμπρεσβύτερος —and a witness of the sufferings of Christ, and also a partaker of the glory that shall be revealed: feed the flock of God which is among you, taking the oversight thereof, or doing a bishop's office in it—ἐπισκοποῦντες—not by constraint, but willingly; not for filthy lucre, but of a ready mind ; not as lording it over the (Lord's) heritage—κατακυριεύοντες τῶν κλήρων,—but being ensamples to the flock." [3]

did interested and disingenuous interpretations begin to cloud the light which Scripture might have thrown on ecclesiastical questions. The E. V. has hardly dealt fairly in this case with the sacred text in rendering ἐπισκόπους (ver. 28) ' overseers,' whereas it ought there, as in all other places, to have been ' bishops,' that the fact of elders and bishops having been originally and apostolically synonymous might be apparent to the ordinary English reader, which now it is not."—Alf. in loc. Cf. his essay on the " Union of Christendom in its Home Aspect," Contemp. Rev. Feb. 1868. This passage, in fact, with 1 Pet. v. 1 f., and " Easter " instead of " The Passover " in Acts xii. 4, are perhaps the only instances in which we may trace, in our generally admirable and most impartial version, the shadow of the rising school of Bancroft.]

[1] Tit. i. 5-7.

[2] [This difficulty has been got over by Bishop Taylor and others, by supposing that Titus was an archbishop, and that he was to appoint " one bishop in one city, many in many." " This deduction," however, as Dr. Ellicott remarks, in his commentary on the passage, " is certainly precarious." Cf. Rothe, Anfänge, pp. 181 ff.]   [3] 1 Pet. v. 1-3.

4. By necessary inference, the same fact is established by the opening salutation found in the Epistle to the Philippians: " Paul and Timotheus, the servants of Jesus Christ, to all the saints in Christ Jesus which are at Philippi, with the bishops—ἐπισκόποις —and deacons." [1] Here, as in other cases, we find the inspired writer mentioning a plurality of bishops in one city. He sends his salutations to them, to the deacons, and to the private members of the Church. He omits and makes no mention of the presbyters,—a fact impossible to reconcile with the Episcopalian theory of the existence of such office-bearers, separate from bishops, at Philippi ; and which can only be explained on the Presbyterian view, that they were the same persons, and not distinct and separate office-bearers.

Such is the kind of evidence which is at hand to establish the general fact that the terms bishop and presbyter are employed in the New Testament as titles of the same ecclesiastical office ; and it seems impossible to resist the conclusion that Scripture, in speaking thus, and in uniformly applying the two words to the same office, meant us to understand, not two offices, but one.

[1] Phil. i. 1. [" The combination of the scriptural and extra-scriptural evidence," says Dr. Cunningham, " in regard to the Church at Philippi, has sadly perplexed the Episcopalians. Some of them, such as Dr. Hammond, contend that the bishops of whom Paul speaks, were bishops in the modern sense of the word, i.e. prelates ; but that Philippi was a metropolis, and had an archbishop, the bishops being the suffragans of the province, and the primate or metropolitan himself being either dead or absent when Paul wrote. But the more judicious among them admit that these bishops were just presbyters ; and they add that the bishop, properly so called, in the modern sense, must have been either dead or absent when Paul wrote, or, that a prelate had not yet been appointed, the episcopate being still exercised by the apostle himself. But, unfortunately, it appears from Polycarp's letter, written about seventy years after, when the apostles were all dead, that the Church of Philippi was still under the government of presbyters and deacons, without any trace of a bishop. What is to be done with this difficulty ? Why, we must just try to suppose again, that the bishop was either dead or absent. Bishop Pearson says, and it is literally all he has to say upon the point: ' Sed quis præstabit Episcopum Philippensium tunc in viris fuisse ? Quis præstabit Philippenses ideo a Polycarpo consilium non efflagitasse quod tunc temporis Episcopo ipsi haud potirentur ? ' (Vind. P. ii. p. 168.) Presbyterians are not bound, and certainly will not undertake, to produce proof, as Pearson demands, that the bishop of Philippi was then alive. It is quite enough for us that there is no trace of the existence of any such functionary in the Church of Philippi,—no evidence that they had had, or were again to have, a prelate to govern them ; while it is further manifest, that if the reason why they asked Polycarp's advice was, as Bishop Pearson chooses to imagine, because the see was vacant at the time, it is not within the bounds of possibility that there could have been no hint or trace of this state of things in the letter itself. Philippi surely should be admitted to be another exception. Its

Looking back upon the whole argument, we seem fairly justified in saying that there is no Scripture evidence whatsoever for the institution of an office of diocesan bishop, as separate from that of a presbyter, in the New Testament. It is a most remarkable fact, and one pregnant with meaning, that we have no account in Scripture of the origin of such an office, or of the ordination of any man to it; and that the advocates of the Episcopalian system are compelled to seek for its first institution in the institution of the apostolic or evangelistic offices. We have seen that there is no evidence, but the reverse, for believing that in the recorded origin of the office of apostle or evangelist we are at liberty to date the desiderated origin of the Prelatic office also. And further, we have seen that the use of the terms bishop and presbyter in the New Testament forbid the supposition that these offices had a separate institution or separate existence in the Church.[1] Even were there no additional proof of the soundness of the Presbyterian theory of Church government as opposed to the Episcopalian, the evidence which has already emerged would be amply sufficient to establish it.[2]

government, likewise, was clearly Presbyterial, and this, too, after all the apostles were dead, and consequently after all the arrangements which they sanctioned had been introduced. So far, then, as concerns the *only* two apostolic men, of whom it is generally admitted that we have their remains genuine and uncorrupted, it is evident that their testimony upon this point entirely concurs with that of Scripture, that they furnish no evidence whatever of the existence of Prelacy, and that their testimony runs clearly and decidedly in favour of Presbyterial government; and if so, then this is a blow struck at the root or foundation of the whole alleged Prelatic testimony from antiquity. It cuts off the first and most important link in the chain, and leaves a gap between the apostles and any subsequent Prelacy, which cannot be filled up."—*Works*, vol. ii. p. 247 f.]

[1] See esp. Principal Cunningham's admirable summary of the facts relative to the gradual change in the phraseology employed with respect to ecclesiastical office-bearers from the apostolic and inspired use of the words, which began towards the end of the second century, and culminated with the Papal supremacy, and his comment on the significance of that change. *Works*, vol. ii. pp. 262 ff. [Compare the very similar remarks of Calvin on Phil. i. 1 and Tit. i. 7, *Comment.* ed. Tholuck, vi. pp. 167, 466.]

[2] Turrettin, *Op.* tom. iii. loc. xviii. qu. xxi. Voetius, *Polit. Eccles.* Pars ii. lib. iv. Tract. i. cap. iv. v. Ames. *Bellarm. Enerv.* tom. ii. lib. iii. cap. iv. Beza, *De divers. Ministrorum Gradibus*, Genevæ 1594. *Jus Div. Ministerii Evangelici*, by the Provincial Assembly of London, Lond. 1654, Part ii. ch. iv. vii. Append. 1–8, etc. Clarkson, *No Evidence for Diocesan Churches, —Primitive Episcopacy stated and cleared from the Holy Scriptures and Ancient Records*, in his select works, Wycliffe Soc. ed. Lond. 1846, ii.–iv. Jameson, *Sum of the Episcopal Controversy*, Edin. 1702, ch. i.–iii. [Calvin, *Inst.* lib. iv. cap. iii. 4–9, iv. 1–5, vii. 23, xi. 1, 4, 6, etc. Miller, *Letters concerning the Constit. and Order of the Christ. Ministry*, Philadelphia 1830,

SECTION II.—NO EVIDENCE IN SCRIPTURE, BUT THE REVERSE,
OF THE EXERCISE OF THE POWERS OF A DIOCESAN BISHOP
BY ANY DISTINCT AND PERMANENT ORDER OF OFFICE-
BEARERS, APART FROM THAT OF PRESBYTERS.

As has been already stated, there are two ways, and no more
than two, in which the doctrine of Episcopacy could be fairly
established by Scripture evidence, as against the views of Presbyterians. If it could be proved that the third order of diocesan
bishop had been instituted by Christ or His inspired followers as
an order distinct from any other in the New Testament Church,—
and we had no reason to believe that the office was extraordinary
or temporary,—this evidence of its express institution would be
decisive of the controversy. Or, failing any evidence for its formal
institution, if it could be proved from Scripture that the distinctive powers belonging to the office were usually possessed and
exercised by a distinct and standing order of men in the Church
separate from other office-bearers, this, too, would be enough to
settle the debate. By either of these methods of proof, the doctrine
of Episcopacy might be relevantly and sufficiently established.
We have already seen that, by the first method of proof, the
advocates of Episcopacy have signally failed to make out their
case. They cannot adduce any evidence of a Scripture kind to
show where, or when, or by what authority the office of diocesan
bishop was first instituted in the New Testament Church, as an
office distinct from any other. When the question as to its origin
and institution is put to them, they are forced to have recourse to
the hypothesis of an implicit and not an explicit institution of the
office,—of an origin involved in the origin of the Apostolate, and
not distinct, and by itself.[1] In this respect it furnishes a striking
contrast to the other two permanent and ordinary offices in the
Church. We can tell where and when the office of deacon was

2d ed. pp. 14–79. Rothe, *Anfänge der christl. Kirche*, Wittenberg 1837, pp.
173–221, 239–243, 259–263, 305 ff. Neander, *Church Hist.* Torrey's Transl.
vol. i. pp. 250-275, 302 f. Gieseler, *Eccles. Hist.* Davidson's Transl. vol. i.
pp. 88–93, 105 ff. For further references to works on Church government,
see the Author's notes on the literature of this department, Append. I.]

[1] "This theory," as Mr. Litton justly remarks, "is more fanciful than
solid." . . . "Moreover, it is at variance with the precedent furnished by the
elder dispensation, to which, however, we are directed as the pattern of the
Christian Episcopate; the high priest, priests, and Levites corresponding, it
is said, with the bishops, priests, and deacons. Neither in Moses, the law-

instituted; and that not implicitly or constructively, as involved in some other and different office, but formally and separately by itself. In like manner we can point to the origin of the Presbyterate, and to the express and formal ordination of men to that office, apart from any other in the New Testament Church. But of the origin and institution of the alleged third order of office-bearers, and of the ordination of men to the office of diocesan bishop as a formal office, not implied in or identical with any other, we have no mention in Scripture at all. No candid or intelligent controversialist will contend that this is a fact of small significance in the argument. No man would say that if the history of the institution of the offices of deacon and presbyter, and of the ordination of men to these as formal offices, had been blotted out from the page of Scripture, we could have had the same clear and satisfactory evidence for their standing place in the arrangements of the Church as we now have; or that it would have been reckoned a very satisfactory or conclusive argument for the existence of these offices, to have asserted their constructive or implicit institution, as involved in the institution of the apostolic office. And yet this is the assertion to which the advocates of Prelacy have been compelled to have recourse, in giving an account of the origin of the office of diocesan bishop. The entire absence of all Scripture evidence for its separate institution must be regarded as an argument of very great weight in the discussion.

But this argument will be greatly strengthened, and become absolutely conclusive, if we can add to it the further consideration, that the powers proper to the so-called office of bishop have never been exercised, in so far as Scripture informs us,—and no extra-scriptural evidence, as we have already seen, can be admitted when the question is concerning a Divine right, and not concerning the mere human pedigree of a human institution,[1]—by a

giver of the old covenant, nor in Aaron, the first high priest, was the Mosaic polity embodied, or its offices concentrated to be shed off in succession, as need should seem to require: the whole of that polity was delivered by God to Moses in the form in which it was to remain, the subordinate offices being as distinctly defined and appropriated to certain persons as the high-priest-hood itself was. . . The draft of the ecclesiastical institution proceeded in every part alike directly from God, and the office of the Levites and that of the high priest stood on the same footing of Divine institution."—*Church of Christ*, p. 247.

[1] ["The claim of Episcopacy to be of Divine institution, and therefore obligatory on the Church," says Bishop Onderdonk, "rests fundamentally on the one question : Has it the authority of Scripture? If it has not, it is

standing order of men separate from other office-bearers in the
Church, but, on the contrary, have always been exercised by the
order of presbyters.   It is of much argumentative importance to
know that the *first* method of proof for Episcopacy entirely fails,
and that there is no evidence from Scripture, but the reverse, to
prove that the office of bishop as a distinct office was ever instituted.
But it will add conclusive force to the argument, to show that
the *second* method of proof also fails, and that there is no evidence
from Scripture to prove that the distinctive powers assigned by
Prelatists to the office of bishop were ever exercised by a standing
order of men separate from the other office-bearers in the Church;
and that, on the contrary, there is sufficient evidence to prove that
they were usually and universally exercised by presbyters.   To
this branch of the argument we now address ourselves.

The distinctive peculiarity of the system of Episcopacy, as
opposed to Presbyterianism, lies in the assertion by Episcopalians
of the existence of a third order of office-bearers in the Church,
possessed of powers appropriate to themselves, and denied to the
rest.   These are the " potestas ordinationis," or the right, denied
to presbyters, of ordaining to office in the Church; and the
" potestas jurisdictionis," or the right, also denied to presbyters, of
exercising government and dispensing discipline in the Church.

not necessarily binding . . . This one point should be kept in view in every
discussion of the subject; no argument is worth taking into account that has
not a palpable bearing on the clear and naked topic,—the scriptural evidence
of Episcopacy."—*Episcopacy tested by Scripture*, Lond. 1840, p. 1 (first publ.
in America, 1831).   In this, of course, the author now cited differs from
many High Churchmen, who hold that it is one of the great proofs of the
insufficiency of Scripture, as the *sole* rule of faith, that we cannot establish
Episcopacy from it, but must have recourse for that purpose to the Epistles
of Ignatius,—*e.g.* Newman, *On Development*, 2d ed. p. 107 ; *Tracts for the
Times*, No. 85.   All Presbyterians, however, will gladly hail Dr. Onderdonk's
admission, although it was one which he himself seemed inclined somewhat to
modify at an after-stage in the controversy which his essay excited.   It would
have been well had all Episcopalian writers set as clearly before them the
essential difference between trying to prove that Prelacy is a venerable institution, known and honoured in the early Church, presumably even sanctioned
by the last of the apostles after the canon of Scripture was closed, and trying
to establish a Jus Divinum on post-apostolic opinion and practice.   We wel-
come the testimony of the ancient Church in its proper place, and for the
ends which it is competent to accomplish.   Where it happens to be clear and
decided, it may possibly throw light on some obscure text of Scripture, and
incline us to one interpretation of it rather than another.   But no human
hand, were it of martyr or of saint, can add one stone to the essential structure of the Christian Church, which must stand complete on the foundation
of the apostles and prophets of the New Testament, or not at all.]

According to the Prelatic theory, as explained by almost all who hold it, the power of ordination and the power of ruling are peculiar to bishops, and so characteristic of the office that they cannot be separated from it. Where the right to ordain or to rule can be proved to exist, as belonging to any one in the Church, there the office and presence of a bishop are to be recognised; and where these can be proved to be awanting in the case of any office-bearer, there the functions of a presbyter or deacon, but not of a bishop, are to be acknowledged. Now this principle, necessarily implied in any system of Prelacy, properly so called, affords an easy and certain test to enable us to bring to the bar of Scripture the pretensions put forth by its adherents. Is the twofold right of ordination and of government in the Christian Church one which, according to Scripture, rightfully appertains to a distinct class of men, holding ordinary and permanent office in the Church, and separate from presbyters; or does the right of ordination and government form one commonly and statedly exercised by presbyters? It is vain to appeal to the extraordinary power exercised by apostles and evangelists, who unquestionably both ordained and ruled in the New Testament Church. Such powers formed part of the general and supereminent functions that belonged to them in virtue of their respective offices of apostles and evangelists. But these offices were temporary, and not standing, in the Church: they have ceased; the powers connected with them have ceased with the offices themselves; and the right to ordain and to rule does not now remain in the Church, in consequence of the office of apostle or evangelist remaining. If we adopt the Episcopalian theory, the right of ordination and government survives, only because the distinct and separate office of bishops survives, and would cease were that office to be abolished, and none but presbyters remain in the Church.[1] A relevant and sufficient proof, therefore, that the right to ordain and govern belongs usually to presbyters, and is exercised by them in the New Testament Church, is fatal to the Episcopalian theory. Let us in the first place, then, inquire whether the " potestas ordinationis," the right to ordain to office in the New Testament Church, is one exercised by diocesan bishops alone, or whether, on the

---

[1] Perceval, *Apology for the Doct. of Apost. Succession*, 2d ed. pp. iv. v. etc. Manning, *Unity of the Church*, 2d ed. p. 342. Smyth, *Prelat. Doct. of Apost. Succession*, Boston 1841, pp. 52 f., 105, 111.

contrary, it is one commonly exercised by presbyters. And, in the second place, let us inquire whether the " potestas jurisdictionis," the right to rule and administer discipline, is one belonging to an order separate from that of presbyters, or, on the contrary, appropriate to it. These two questions discussed and settled, will determine whether there is any evidence in Scripture to prove that the distinctive powers or office of a Prelatic bishop were ever exercised by any class of office-bearers separate from presbyters in the New Testament Church.[1]

To begin, then, with the right to ordain, claimed by Episcopalians as one of the exclusive functions belonging to the office of bishop, there is sufficient Scripture evidence to demonstrate that this power was always possessed and exercised by presbyters.

I. The nature of the office conferred upon presbyters implies a right to ordain.

It is admitted on all hands, that presbyters, by Scripture

---

[1] [Next to the direct scriptural evidence for Presbyterianism, one of the strongest arguments in its favour is to be drawn from that form of government which we find in the Jewish synagogue since the time of what was probably its first formal establishment by the hands of the inspired men who led back the exiles from Babylon. That the polity of the Christian Church was framed on the model, not of the temple, but of the synagogue, just as its Sacraments arose out of Jewish ordinances which had no connection with the temple services, is a point on which almost all theologians agree, at least since the date of Vitringa and Selden's great works on the subject. The evidence is of course partly drawn from extra-scriptural sources ; but it is strongly confirmed by many incidental notices in the Old and New Testament. The names of the office-bearers, the general nature of the offices, the powers of discipline in the hands of a consistory of elders, the elements of worship, the imposition of hands in ordination instead of anointing, as in the consecration of priests, are all points in common between the synagogue and the Church. " The ordinary and regular form of government proper to the synagogue," says Mr. Litton, " was on the Presbyterian model ; as indeed there is only one passage of Scripture (Luke xiii. 14) which appears to imply that there existed any other. . . . The names which Christian ministers bear in the New Testament, presbyter or episcopus, and deacon, are all derived from the synagogue ; while never once are they designated by the term ἱερεύς, or priest, the proper title of those who officiated in the temple. The very term itself, synagogue, is, in James ii. 2, applied to a Christian assembly. . . . But as regards Episcopacy, the analogy of the synagogue fails us. While there can be no reasonable doubt respecting the derivation of the presbyters and deacons of a Christian congregation from the corresponding officers of the synagogue, that institution does not, with anything like the same degree of certainty, present us with the historical type of a Christian bishop."—Church of Christ, Lond. 1851, pp. 249–267, 401 ff. Miller, Letters concerning the Constit. and Ord. of the Christ. Min. 2d ed. pp. 36–50, 277–284. Neander, Church Hist. Torrey's Transl. vol. i. pp. 250–266. Vitringa, De Synagoga Vetere, esp. lib. ii. cap. ii. ix.–xii. lib. iii. Pars i., Pars ii. cap. xix.–xxiii. Stillingfleet, Irenicum, 2d ed. pp. 239–287.]

warrant, have authority to preach the Gospel, and to administer the Sacraments. Presbyterians believe that this is the *chief* work given them to do; Episcopalians believe that it is their *only* work. Now, a very slight consideration will satisfy us that the very nature of such an office implies the additional authority to ordain, just as the greater must always include the less. Whether we regard the nature of the work performed by presbyters when they minister unto the Lord in Word and Sacrament, or the instructions given to them for the discharge of this duty, or the conduct in reference to this point of the inspired servants of Christ, it cannot fail to appear that the preaching of the Gospel and administering the means of grace form *the* grand object for which the Church itself, and more especially the office-bearers of the Church, were instituted, and not the work of ordination and government. The right to ordain and govern was a right of an inferior kind, as compared with the right to preach the truth, and to dispense the Sacraments of Christ. The ministerial authority implied in the latter is of a higher order than the ministerial authority implied in the former. That this is the case, is apparent from the terms of the original commission, which gives authority to the Church in express terms to preach the Gospel and administer the Sacraments to every creature, but makes no explicit mention of the power to ordain or govern, because this was a power implied and included under the authority to dispense the Word and ordinances. It is apparent from the conduct of the apostles, who made it the great work and highest aim of their official life, not to organize the outward polity, but to minister to the inward life of the Church. It is apparent from the very nature of the thing itself, inasmuch as the power of ordination and government is but the means to the higher and nobler end of the ministry of the Gospel. It is apparent from the express statement of the Apostle Paul, who enjoins that "the presbyters who labour in word and doctrine be counted worthy of *special* honour," as compared with those office-bearers who only "rule."[1] And such being the case, it is impossible to believe that presbyters, who are invested with the higher ministerial authority of ministering in Word and Sacrament, are excluded from the inferior right of ordaining and governing in the Church. The superior function must include the lower, as necessary to carry out the

[1] 1 Tim. v. 17.

very object for which it has been conferred ; nor is it possible to
believe with Episcopalians, that presbyters, who are authorized to
discharge the highest functions in the Christian Church, are not
themselves the highest order of functionaries.   The powers of
the presbyter being above the powers of any other office-bearer
in the Church, as regards the nature of his duties, the office to
which these powers are permanently attached must be above any
other in the Christian society.

II. We have, in the case of Timothy, an express example of
the act of ordination performed by presbyters.

In writing to Timothy on the subject of his ministerial
functions, the Apostle Paul tells him, in language which can
hardly be misunderstood in its bearing on our present argument :
" Neglect not the gift that is in thee, which was given thee by
prophecy, with the laying on of the hands of the presbytery."[1]
In this passage we have the imposition of hands, the recognised
Scriptural sign, and invariable accompaniment of ordination, and
we have this imposition of hands performed by the court or
council of presbyters.[2]   In short, we have all the elements of
Presbyterian ordination exhibited in a Scripture example, which
it is impossible by any commentary to make more plain or conclusive as a precedent for the right to ordain, as claimed by the
Presbyterian theory for elders or presbyters, and denied to them
by Prelatists.   There are two ways in which Episcopalians have
attempted, although in vain, to get rid of the evidence which
the ordination of Timothy furnishes against their fundamental
dogma that the " potestas ordinationis " is a right which belongs
to diocesan bishops alone.

In the first place, it is alleged by some Episcopalians, that
although the council of presbyters was present, and consenting to
the deed, yet the authoritative act of setting apart Timothy to
the office was performed by Paul alone.   This explanation of the
passage is founded on a text which occurs in Second Timothy, to

---

[1] Μὴ ἀμέλει τοῦ ἐν σοὶ χαρίσματος, ὃ ἐδόθη σοι διὰ προφητείας μετὰ ἐπιθέσεως
τῶν χειρῶν τοῦ πρεσβυτερίου.—1 Tim. iv. 14.

[2] [" An aristocracy and a monarchy," says Dr. Arnold, " are not so precisely
identical that the government of a single bishop can claim to be of Divine
authority, because the apostles appointed in each Church a certain number
of bishops or elders. Nor can it be shown that, if the ordination by bishops,
one or more, be necessary, the consent of the Church, which was no less a
part of the primitive appointments, may be laid aside as a thing wholly indifferent."—*Fragm. on the Church*, 2d ed. p. 72.]

this effect: " Wherefore I put thee in remembrance that thou stir up the gift of God, which is in thee by the putting on of my hands."[1] The two passages of Scripture are held by some to refer to the same investiture with office in the case of Timothy; and the argument of Episcopalians is, that the apostle, in laying on his hands, did authoritatively convey the right, and really ordain; while the presbyters, in laying on their hands, did no more than express their consent to or approbation of the act. Now, in reference to this objection by Episcopalians to the relevancy of the case of Timothy to our argument, I would remark that it takes for granted what is by no means a clear point—namely, that the gift conferred by Paul on his adopted son was the same gift as is spoken of as conveyed with the laying on of the hands of the presbytery. It has been maintained by many commentators, and I think with good reason, that the gift conferred by Paul was one of those extraordinary gifts—χαρίσματα—of the Holy Ghost, spoken of in the Epistle to the Corinthians, such as " the word of wisdom, the word of knowledge, faith," etc.,[2] which were usually bestowed upon evangelists, and conveyed only through the imposition of an apostle's hands, while the gift conferred by the presbytery was in reality the office of the ministry. There are two considerations which countenance this interpretation. *First*, there is an observable difference in the apostle's phraseology when speaking of the two gifts,—the one kind of expression being more appropriate to the case of an office occupied by an individual, as when he says : " Neglect not—μὴ ἀμέλει— the gift that is in thee, or the office belonging to thee, which was conferred by prophecy, with the laying on of the hands of the presbytery;" the other kind of expression being more appropriate to a personal endowment pertaining to an individual, as when he exhorts him to " stir up—ἀναζωπυρεῖν—the gift of God that is in thee by the putting on of my hands. A man may well be called upon " to take heed to," or " not to neglect" his office ; he can hardly be exhorted to " stir it up." *Second*, from the context it is plain that, in referring to the gift given with the laying on of the hands of the presbytery, Paul is speaking of Timothy's official authority and duty in the Church. Both in

---

[1] Δι᾽ ἣν αἰτίαν ἀναμιμνήσκω σὲ ἀναζωπυρεῖν τὸ χάρισμα τοῦ Θεοῦ ὅ ἐστιν ἐν σοὶ διὰ τῆς ἐπιθέσεως τῶν χειρῶν μου.—2 Tim. i. 6.

[2] 1 Cor. xii. 8 ff.

the verses which precede and in those which follow the passage in question, we see the apostle enforcing upon the youthful evangelist various points connected with his public labours in Ephesus : " Be thou an example to the believers in work, in conversation," etc.; " Till I come, give attendance to reading, to exhortation, to doctrine; " These things command and teach," etc. And it is in connection with these precepts for his official actings that Paul bids him not neglect the high and responsible office with which he has been graced in the Church, and strengthens the exhortation by reminding him of the solemn ordination by which he was formally set apart to its duties. On the other hand, when the apostle refers to the gift communicated by himself, it is equally clear from the context, that he is speaking of Timothy's personal and private character and duty, not of his official standing. " When I call to remembrance the unfeigned faith that is in thee, which dwelt first in thy grandmother Lois, and in thy mother Eunice. For that cause I put thee in remembrance that thou stir up the gift of God, etc. For God hath not given us the spirit of fear, but of power, and of love, and of a sound mind. Be not thou therefore ashamed of the testimony of our Lord, nor of me His prisoner." This marked difference between the two passages seems decidedly to favour the idea that the first gift was ordination to office in the Church, while the second had reference to Timothy's personal qualifications and endowments.

But, even granting that the two passages refer to the same transaction, and both speak of Timothy's ordination, as is held by the majority of theologians, it is not difficult to meet the objection of Episcopalians. We know that Paul had the powers which presbyters commonly and permanently exercised, and on no occasion was he more likely to exercise them than in the case of the ordination of " Timothy, his dearly beloved son," to the office of the Gospel ministry. And nothing could be more natural on the part of the apostle, when he was " Paul the aged," and in bonds, or more forcible and affecting, as addressed to the youthful Timothy, than the statement by Paul calling to the remembrance of his spiritual son how he had shared with the presbyters in conferring on him, by imposition of hands, the right and authority of the ministerial office. If the two passages refer to the same transaction, as most theologians, Episcopalian and Presbyterian, believe, then the imposition of hands by Paul,

and the imposition of hands by the presbytery, must have substantially the same significance and meaning. To assert an
essential difference between the two acts, is purely gratuitous.
To affirm that they are so distinct that the one authority conferred
the ministerial office, and the other did not, is a mere hypothesis,
having no ground whatever to rest upon, and contradicted by the
obvious meaning of the passage. And not only so, but the hypothesis will not even serve the purpose of Episcopalians after they
have invented it. If, as is necessarily implied in their theory, the
ordination of Timothy constituted him, not a presbyter, but a
bishop, the fact that the hands of the presbytery concurred in any
sense in the act, is inconsistent with the Episcopalian system.

An attempt has been made by some adherents of Prelacy to
justify their drawing a distinction between the act of Paul and
the act of the presbytery in the ordination of Timothy, rested on
the ground that, in the mention of the one of these, or the imposition of the apostle's hands, the preposition διά is used, while, in
the mention of the other of these, or the imposition of the hands
of the presbytery, the preposition μετά is used, as descriptive of
the connection between those acts and the right Timothy received
to the office. It is argued that the preposition διά joined with
the genitive case always denotes the instrumental cause,—implying in this passage that it was Paul's hands that were the instrument of conferring the title to the ministerial office; and that
the preposition μετά always denotes a concurrent, but not a causal
act,—implying in this passage that the laying on of the hands of
the presbytery merely expressed the consent or concurrence of
that body in respect of the ordination. It is not needful to enter
into the minute and detailed criticism which has been bestowed
upon these two Greek particles in order to make out this proposition. It is enough to say that the New Testament usage in
regard to these words does not justify the restriction of them to the
special meanings upon which Episcopalians would build their argument,—that the preposition διά with the genitive does not always
imply in Scripture the instrumental cause, and that the preposition μετά sometimes does.[1] The meaning of these prepositions

---

[1] [Among the wider meanings of διά with the genitive, Winer gives
"along with," "accompanied with," "bei," "unter," "von der Ausrüstung
Jemandes und von den Umständen und Beziehungen unter denen er etwas
thut," instancing 1 John v. 6, Heb. ix. 12, Rom. ii. 27, iv. 11, xii. 20. He

is a matter to be determined by the construction and nature of the sentence. It seems impossible, by any such attempt, to get rid of the very explicit and conclusive testimony by this passage of Scripture to the ordinary right of presbyters to ordain.

In the second place, another attempt has been made by the advocates of Episcopacy to avoid the force of this passage, by asserting that the word translated presbytery—πρεσβυτέριον—denotes the office, and not the council of the presbyters. According to this translation of the word, the passage would come to be rendered, " neglect not the gift of the presbyterate which is in thee, which was given thee by prophecy with the laying on of hands." Now, in reference to this rendering, and the bearing of it upon the argument, there are three remarks which may be made. First, the word πρεσβυτέριον occurs only three times in the New Testament, being twice in addition to this example of it in Timothy.[1] In both the other cases it *must* be understood in the sense of the council or court or body of the elders, and is, in fact, so rendered in our version. In both cases it applies to the college of elders which made up the Jewish Sanhedrim ; and when, in the passage already quoted from Timothy, it is used in reference to the Christian Church, it plainly must have the same meaning of the council, and not the office, of the presbyters. Second, the translation proposed by Episcopalians does violence to the natural construction of the words, making the term πρεσβυτερίου to be connected with the word χαρίσματος, in contradiction to the obvious syntax of the passage. And third, even granting that the word denoted the office, and not the college of presbyters, it would not serve the purpose of the Prelatic argument, inasmuch as it would confer upon Timothy the office of a presbyter instead of the office of a diocesan bishop, as the theory demands. Upon the whole, we are, I think, warranted in saying that there is no possible way, in consistency with the ordinary principles of Scripture exegesis, of avoiding the conclusion, that this passage contains a

differs from Kypke in thinking that μετά with the genitive " does not denote the instrument as such in good prose" (referring to the text in question as a disputed case, and rendering it " *mit, unter* Handauflegung, *zugleich mit* dem Act der H."), but cites instances in less classic Greek in which it has this meaning, and admits that, in some passages in the New Testament, as Luke xvii. 15, Acts xiii. 17, it approximates to it,—" doch streift es an diese Bedeutung."—*Grammatik des neutestamentl. Sprachidioms,* 6te Aufl. pp. 337, 339. Alexander, *Primitive Church Offices,* New York 1851, pp. 46–49.]

[1] Luke xxii. 66 ; Acts xxii. 5.

distinct precedent for the power of ordination being exercised by presbyters.[1]

III. We have another example of the authority to ordain as exercised, not by diocesan bishops, but by presbyters, recorded in the thirteenth chapter of the Acts of the Apostles. The narrative is to this effect: " Now there were in the Church that was at Antioch certain prophets and teachers; as Barnabas, and Simeon that was called Niger, and Lucius of Cyrene, and Manaen, which had been brought up with Herod the tetrarch, and Saul. As they ministered to the Lord, and fasted, the Holy Ghost said, Separate me Barnabas and Saul for the work whereunto I have called them. And when they had fasted and prayed, and laid their hands on them, they sent them away."[2] Of the parties mentioned in this extract, we know that Saul and Barnabas had been invested with the extraordinary offices—the one of an apostle, the other of an evangelist—previously to the date of this transaction. Further, of the remainder, we are told that some, although it is not mentioned which of them, held the special and temporary office of prophets in the Church at Antioch. But, setting aside these, it appears that there were others who were simply teachers (διδάσκαλοι) or presbyters in the Church. We have here, then, all that is necessary to make up a true ordination,—the authoritative designation to an ecclesiastical work and mission, the imposition of hands as the Scriptural sign of the investiture with office, the accompanying religious service of prayer and fasting, and the result, or the going forth of the parties so ordained to the work to which they were appointed; and we have all this done by presbyters, in conjunction with other parties, combining together equally to perform the ordination. And, to crown all, we have this example of presbyters ordaining sanctioned by the Holy Ghost: " So they, being sent forth by the Holy Ghost, departed."

The only objection worthy of notice brought by Episcopalians against this authority for ordination by presbyters, is the fact, admitted by all parties, that the persons ordained, Paul and Barnabas, had, previously to the date of this transaction, held extra-

---

[1] [Gillespie, *Miscell. Quest.* ch. viii. ; *Assertion of the Gov. of the Church of Scotland*, Edin. 1641, pp. 131–147. Smyth, *Presbytery the Script. and Prim. Polity*, Boston 1843, pp. 186–199. *Plea of Presbytery*, Glasgow 1840, pp. 25–31.]
[2] Acts xiii. 1–3.

ordinary offices in the Church,—the one as an apostle, the other as an evangelist. But, admitting this fact, it must be remembered that the extraordinary offices of apostle and evangelist were not the same thing as, and did not include, the formal office of presbyter or minister, although they comprehended the powers usually exercised by the presbyter or minister. We have already had occasion to argue this point at some length. The exercise of the powers of an office does not necessarily imply the possession of the formal office itself, unless when it can be shown that the exercise of such powers permanently and necessarily belongs to the party as his distinctive function. The Apostle Paul and the evangelist Barnabas had, before the date of the ordination recorded in the thirteenth chapter of the Acts, exercised the powers of ministers or presbyters in preaching and dispensing ordinances; but these powers were not distinctively the functions that belonged to them as apostle or evangelist. The distinctive and essential peculiarity of the office of apostle or evangelist was not the power of preaching the Gospel which they held in common with other office-bearers; so that it would be a mistake to imagine that because they were,.the one an apostle, and the other an evangelist, previously to the date of their ordination to the Gentile mission, they must necessarily have held the formal office of presbyter or minister. There is no evidence, and no reason to believe, that either of them had been invested with the office previously to this time; and when they were solemnly set apart, therefore, by prayer and imposition of hands to the ministry among the Gentiles, it was an instance of true and regular ordination. The presbyters at Antioch, under the immediate instructions of the Holy Ghost, proceeded by ordination to install them into the formal office of the Presbyterate.

Upon the grounds now indicated, we are prepared to argue that the first of those distinctive powers claimed by Episcopalians for diocesan bishops—the "potestas ordinationis"—was not peculiar to them, but, on the contrary, was commonly and statedly exercised by presbyters.[1] A brief discussion of the Scrip-

---

[1] *Jus Div. Minist. Evang.* Lond. 1654, Part i. pp. 181 ff., Part ii. pp. 16-24, 50-61, 88, etc. [Gerhard, *Loci Theolog.* ed. Preuss, tom. vi. pp. 106, 151-159. Miller, *Letters on the Christ. Ministry,* 2d ed. pp. 24-36. King, *Expos. and Def. of the Presbyt. Form of Church Gov.* Glasgow 1853, pp. 239-270. Barnes, *Inquiry into the Organ. and Gov. of the Apostolic Church,* Lond. 1845, pp. 221-246. As regards the apocalyptic angels, to

ture evidence with respect to the second of the distinctive powers claimed by them, will suffice to show that the " potestas jurisdictionis," or the right of government and discipline, did not belong to prelates exclusively, but was enjoyed and exercised by presbyters.

1*st*, The very nature of the office of presbyter implies authority to govern and rule.

The very same argument applies here as in the case of the right to ordain; and it is unnecessary to repeat it. The power of bearing rule and exercising government and discipline in the Church, is undeniably a lower exercise of ministerial authority than the power to preach the Gospel and administer the seals of the covenant of grace. And yet, by the admission of all parties, presbyters are vested with this highest kind of power as their distinctive function,—a circumstance that renders it very difficult to believe that they are excluded from the lower power of ruling in the Church, or that this lower power is one of the two distinctive peculiarities that mark the highest order of office-bearers in

whom some Episcopalian controversialists have recourse in the last resort, although the confessedly metaphorical character of the book may prevent us from being quite certain that we have selected the right interpretation of one of its many symbols from the multitude of renderings which commentators have proposed, yet Stillingfleet's conclusion seems a very reasonable one, and might be confirmed by various exegetical arguments:—" If in the prophetical style an unity may be set down by way of representation of a multitude, what evidence can be brought from the name that by it some one particular person must be understood? And by this means Timothy may avoid being charged with 'leaving his first love,' which he must of necessity be, by those that make him 'the angel of the Church of Ephesus' at the time of writing these Epistles. Neither is this anyways solved by the answer, that the name 'angel' is representative of the whole Church, and so there is no necessity the angel should be personally guilty of it. For, *first*, it seems strange that the whole diffusive body of the Church should be charged with a crime by the name of the angel, and he that is particularly meant by that name should be free from it. As if a Prince should charge the Mayor of a Corporation as guilty of rebellion, and by it should only mean that the Corporation was guilty, but the Mayor himself was innocent. *Secondly*, if many things in the Epistles be directed to the angel, but yet so as to concern the whole body, then of necessity the angel must be taken as representative of the body; and then why may not the word 'angel' be taken only by way of representation of the body itself, either of the whole Church, or, *which is far more probable*, of the Consessus or order of presbyters in that Church? We see what miserably unconcluding arguments those are which are brought for any form of government from metaphorical or ambiguous expressions, or names promiscuously used, which may be interpreted to different senses." —*Iren.* 2d ed. p. 289. Durham, *Comment. on Rev.* Glasg. 1788, pp. 65 ff., 82, 238–249. As to the idea of James being bishop of Jerusalem, see Rothe, *Anfänge*, pp. 263–276; Cunningham, *Works*, vol. ii. pp. 44, 240 f.]

the Church,—that, namely, of diocesan bishop. Even Prelatists have been struck with the contradiction involved in such a doctrine. " Since I look upon the sacramental actions as the *highest* of sacred performances," says Bishop Burnet, " I cannot but acknowledge those who are *empowered for these* must be of the highest office in the Church."[1]

2*d*, There are a number of passages of Scripture which distinctly ascribe to presbyters the office of ruling and governing in the Christian society.

1. We have Paul, in his address to the presbyters of the Church of Ephesus, expressly charging them with the duty and responsibility of governing the Church in which they had a bishop's office. After summoning the elders of Ephesus to Miletus, the apostle tells them : " Take heed, therefore, unto yourselves, and to all the flock, over the which the Holy Ghost hath made you bishops, to feed—$\pi o\iota\mu a\acute{\iota}\nu\epsilon\iota\nu$—the Church of God, which He hath purchased with His own blood." The expression here employed, as descriptive of the kind of charge the presbyters were to take of the Church under them, is one significant of government and authority as well as inspection. The use of the word in Scripture, as well as in profane authors, amply demonstrates this. 2. We find the Apostle Peter laying upon presbyters the very same duty of government in the Church as is referred to by Paul, and in a manner still more express and emphatic, and more directly contradictory of the notion that ruling is the exclusive function of bishops. " The presbyters who are among you I exhort, who am also a presbyter : feed the flock of God which is among you, taking the oversight thereof—$\epsilon\pi\iota\sigma\kappa o\pi o\hat{\upsilon}\nu\tau\epsilon\varsigma$— not by constraint, but willingly." In addition to employing the same word $\pi o\iota\mu a\acute{\iota}\nu\omega$ as descriptive of the charge devolving on presbyters, which was employed by Paul, and which includes the idea of coercive authority, Peter here characterizes the work of presbyters in the way of ruling by the very term $\epsilon\pi\iota\sigma\kappa o\pi o\hat{\upsilon}\nu\tau\epsilon\varsigma$, which denotes episcopal government claimed for prelates as their exclusive function. No declaration could more decisively demonstrate that bishops and presbyters stand on the same level as to ruling authority in the Church. 3. There is one passage in the First Epistle to Timothy which is especially clear and express

---

[1] Burnet, *Vind. of the Church and State of Scotland*, Glasgow 1673, p. 310.

as to the government entrusted to the hands of presbyters. In giving directions as to matters in the Church of Ephesus, the Apostle Paul instructs Timothy in this manner: " Let the presbyters that rule well be counted worthy of double honour."[1] The word here used—προεστῶτες—is undeniably significant of government and ruling authority. Such passages of Scripture as these plainly show that the right to rule was one not confined to diocesan bishops as their exclusive function, but was ordinarily held and exercised by presbyters.

3d, There are many express intimations in Scripture that the power of discipline belonged not to diocesan bishops, but to every particular Church.

The example of the Corinthian Church, and many others that could be referred to, clearly demonstrate this. A case of immorality or public scandal was not a matter to be handed over to the bishop, but to be dealt with by the Churches themselves, or by the body of their office-bearers. So decisive is the testimony of Scripture on this head, that it would be much more easy to argue, with Independents, that the right of discipline belonged to the members of the congregation at large, than to adduce any plausible evidence for its being restricted to the bishop of the diocese. The admitted interference of the apostles authoritatively in the discipline of the primitive Churches, and the oversight taken in the matter by evangelists, are of no avail for the Episcopal argument, unless upon the principle of first begging the question, or of first assuming that the apostles and evangelists were ordinary diocesan bishops. If this is denied, as we have seen that there is good reason for doing, there is not the shadow of proof to show that discipline was the peculiar function of prelates ; on the contrary, there is every evidence to prove that it belonged to the ordinary rulers in the Christian society, that is, to the presbyters.

Upon a review, then, of the whole argument, we are led to the conclusion that there is no Scriptural evidence in support of the only two propositions relevant or sufficient to establish the system of Prelacy, or Diocesan Episcopacy. In the first place, there is no evidence whatever to prove that the office of bishop, as a third order among the office-bearers of the apostolic Church, was ever instituted by Christ or His apostles,—the circumstance of the indiscriminate use by the inspired writers of the terms

[1] 1 Tim. v. 17.

bishop and presbyter[1] combining with the absence of any express evidence on the point in Scripture to show that no such institution is to be acknowledged. And in the second place, failing any evidence of its original institution, there is no proof that the powers alleged to be distinctive and peculiar to the Episcopate, were ever possessed or exercised commonly and as a permanent function by any except presbyters; and there is ample and decisive proof that they were held and exercised by the latter order of office-bearers in the apostolic Church. Upon the ground of these two general propositions, we have reason to say that Prelacy has no warrant in the Word of God.[2]

[1] ["Hic locus," says Calvin, commenting on Tit. i. 5–7, "abunde docet nullum esse Presbyteri et Episcopi discrimen, quia nunc secundo nomine promiscue appellat quos prius vocavit Presbyteros. Imo idem prosequens argumentum utrumque nomen indifferenter eodem sensu usurpat, quemadmodum Hieromymus tum hoc loco, tum in epistola ad Evagrium annotavit. Atque hinc perspicere licet quanto plus delatum hominis placitis fuerit quam decebat, quia abrogato Spiritûs Sancti sermone usus hominum arbitrio inductus prævaluit. Mihi quidem non displicet quod statim ab ecclesiæ primordiis receptum fuit, ut singula Episcoporum collegia unum aliquem moderatorem habeant: verum nomen officii, quod Deus in commune omnibus dederat in unum solum transferri, reliquis spoliatis, et injurium est et absurdum. Deinde sic pervertere Spiritûs Sancti linguam, ut nobis eædem voces aliud quam voluerit significent, nimis profanæ audaciæ est."]

[2] Calderwood, *Altare Damascenum*, cap. iv. Chemnitz, *Examen Concil. Trident.* Pars ii. Loc. xiii. iv. Bucer, *Dissert. de Gubernatione Ecclesiæ.* Forrester, *The Hierarchical Bishops' Claim to Div. Right Examined,* Edin. 1699; *Plea of Presbytery,* Glasg. 1840, pp. 1–299. King, *Expos. and Def. of the Presbyt. Form of Church Gov.* Edin. 1853, pp. 161–270. *Essays on the Prim. Church Offices* (by Dr. J. A. Alexander), New York 1851, Ess. ii.–v. Cunningham, *Works,* vol. ii. pp. 100–119, 164–171, 227–266, 432; vol. iii. pp. 514–533. [For further references to the voluminous literature of this subject, see Appendix I. The argument from mere human authority, although only to be taken up *ex abundanti,* is a very plain one. The only genuine and uncorrupted writings which have come down to us from men who companied with the apostles, are " clearly Presbyterian " in their teaching. The most learned of the Fathers of the fourth century took up precisely the Presbyterian view of the early Church, and defended it by precisely the Presbyterian arguments. Jerome was classed, for that reason, by one of the most eminent Romanist divines of the sixteenth century, along with Ambrose, Augustin, Chrysostom, etc., as holding the same heresy about bishops and presbyters which the Church condemned in Aerius, in the Waldensians, in Wickliffe, and in the Protestants. " Ergo in Hieronymo et Græcis illis patribus olim propter eorum honorem et reverentiam hæc sententia aut dissimulabatur aut tolerabatur in illis ; contra in hæreticis, quod in aliis quoque multis ab Ecclesiâ declinarent, tanquam hæretica semper est damnata " (Michael Medina, quoted by Gerhard, *Loci Theolog.* ed. Preuss, tom. vi. p. 154). To a partial and imperfect consensus of the later Fathers we oppose the unbroken consensus of all the leading Reformers, joined with the anathemas of the Council of Trent and the arguments of Bellarmine against what they justly held to be the Protestant doctrine. To the theory and practice of the fallen and corrupt Churches

of Rome and of the East, we oppose the clear testimony of the symbolical books of all the Churches of the Reformation, not one of which, not even excepting those of the Church of England, asserts the Divine right of Prelacy ; almost all of which, except those of the Church of England, when they treat of Church government at all, assert the Divine authority of the essential principles of Presbyterianism.   We point to the notorious fact that not a single Church in Reformed Christendom, except one confessedly founded on a compromise, adopted the Prelatic system; and we bring reason to show why this solitary exception should have no weight whatever.   A system expressly maintained by the corrupted Church of Rome, and expressly rejected on scriptural grounds by all those great men to whom, under God, we owe our religious freedom and purity of faith and worship, can hardly be conceived to have a more over-whelming weight of presumptive evidence against it.   " After Medina," says one of the most learned and accurate of modern Church historians, " Richerius defended the view of Jerome, and John Morin (de Sacr. Ord.) asserted that the opinion was at least not heretical — ' episcopos non jure Divino esse presbyteris superiores ; ' yet, since the Tridentine Council, the ' institutio Divina ' of the Episcopate and its original distinction from the Presbyterate be-came the general doctrine of the (Roman) Catholic Church, which the English Episcopalians also followed in this particular, while the other Protestant Churches returned to the most ancient doctrine and regulation on the sub-ject."—Gieseler, Eccles. Hist. Davidson's Transl. vol. i. p. 89.   Conf. Bohem. 1535, art. ix.   Conf. Helv. prior, 1536, c. 17, Lat. ed. 18.   Art. Smalc. 1537, P. ii. art. iv. 9, P. iii. art. x.   De Potest. et Jurisd. Episc. 60–68.   Conf. Sax. 1551, art. xi.   Conf. Württ. 1552, art. xx.   Conf. Gall. 1559, art. xxix. xxx. First Book of Discip. 1560, ch. iv. vi. ix. x.   Conf. Belg. 1566, art. xxx. Conf. Helv. post. 1566, c. xviii.   Consens. Polon. 1570-83, in Niemeyer, pp. 562 ff., 575, 576.   Second Book of Discip. 1578, c. ii.-viii.   Form. Concord. 1577, x. 19.   Decl. Thor. 1645, De Ord.   Westminst. Form of Church Gov. 1645.   Cf. Instit. of a Christ. Man, 1537.   Necess. Erud. for a Christ. Man, 1543.   Neal, Hist. of Puritans, Lond. 1837, vol. i. p. 190, vol. iii. pp. 491-500.]

CHAPTER V.

THE INDEPENDENT SYSTEM OF CHURCH POLITY AS OPPOSED
TO THE PRESBYTERIAN.

IF the conclusions to which we have been led by our previous
discussions are correct, they have narrowed to a considerable
extent the question that still remains for our consideration in
connection with the government of the Christian Church. We
have been enabled, through our previous argument, to separate
between what was extraordinary and what is ordinary in the
condition of the ecclesiastical body; assigning to the former department as special and temporary the offices which we find
existing in the primitive Church of the apostle, the evangelist,
and the prophet. These belonged, not to the normal, but to the
transition state of the Christian Church, and have left behind them
no model for general or permanent imitation. Further still, we
have found that the office of bishop, in the Prelatic sense of the
word, as a third order in the Christian Church, possessed of
certain exclusive powers and functions, and separate from the
order of presbyter, has no warrant in the Word of God. Setting aside these, we have nothing remaining in the way of fixed
and ordinary offices in the Church having any distinct foundation
in Scripture, except these two; first, the office signified by the
various names, used indiscriminately, of presbyter, bishop, or
pastor; and second, the office of deacon. These two orders of
office-bearers, as ordinary and permanent appointments in the
Christian society, are acknowledged by all parties, whether Presbyterian, Episcopalian, or Independent, whatever difference of
opinion may be exhibited, theoretically or practically, in con--
nection with the duties belonging to their offices, or the authority
conferred on them. The original institution of these offices in
the New Testament Church, the appointment of distinct men to
exercise the duties of them, and the separate names, commission,

and authority assigned to them, are matters lying so conspicuously and markedly on the surface of Scripture, as to have called forth a very general acknowledgment from all parties of the existence and permanent standing in the Christian Church of two orders of presbyter, or elder, and deacon.

But in addition to the evidence adduced in previous lectures bearing upon the point, there are more especially two passages in the New Testament which serve to demonstrate, not only that the offices of deacon and elder or presbyter are standing offices in the Church, but that they are the *only* standing and ordinary offices in the Christian society, and that we have no Scriptural warrant for any other. This is a point of much importance in regard to our future discussions, and forms a common ground which the Presbyterian and Independent theories of Church government occupy alike, and from which they start. We find these two classes of office-bearers mentioned in such circumstances, and in such a manner, as to exclude the possibility of the doctrine which asserts that there were usually and properly more than these two in the apostolic Church. *First*, in the salutation to the Church at Philippi by the Apostle Paul in his epistle to converts there, we have distinct evidence of two classes of Church officers, and no more than two. " Paul and Timotheus, the servants of Jesus Christ to all the saints in Christ Jesus who are at Philippi, with the bishops and deacons." Here we have a letter from an apostle written to the Church at Philippi, and addressed to the office-bearers and the members conjointly. The members are addressed as " all the saints in Christ Jesus which are at Philippi," and the office-bearers are addressed as " the bishops and deacons there."[1] It is hardly possible to conceive, that if there had been any other office-bearers besides bishops and deacons in the Church at Philippi, they would have been omitted in the apostolic salutation ; and it is just as difficult to conceive that the Church at Philippi, the first fruits of Paul's labours in Europe, over whose spiritual prosperity he so often rejoices, was destitute of any class of office-bearers necessary for or usual in other Churches. The conclusion seems to be irresistible, that the bishop and the deacon were the only office-bearers of an ordinary and permanent kind known in the apostolic Church. *Second*, in the third chapter of the First Epistle to Timothy, the

[1] Phil. i. 1.

Apostle Paul describes at length, for the information and guidance of Timothy in his regulation and ordering of the Church at Ephesus, the qualifications of those who should be appointed to ecclesiastical office. From the first to the eighth verse we have an account of the qualities that ought to characterize a bishop, given with much minuteness and detail. From the eighth to the fifteenth verse we have, with similar particularity, the qualifications of the deacon. And the object of these detailed instructions is stated by the apostle himself to be fully to acquaint Timothy with his duties in organizing the Church where he at that time laboured. " These things write I unto thee, hoping to come unto thee shortly: but if I tarry long, that thou mayest know how thou oughtest to behave thyself in the house of God."[1] The conclusion to be drawn from this passage points very obviously in the same direction as did the former one. In instructing Timothy in the qualifications of the ecclesiastical office-bearers, whom he was to appoint over the Church, we have mention of these two, the bishop and deacon, but of no more than these two, on an occasion when it is hardly possible for us to conceive that Paul would not have referred to others, had others been in existence. Short of a formal declaration that there were two, but not more than two, orders of office-bearers in the Christian Church, which was not, in the circumstances, to be expected in regard to a matter that must have been familiarly known to all Christians at the time, it is not easy to conceive stronger or more satisfactory evidence of an indirect kind to establish the point.[2]

While the Presbyterian and Independent systems thus occupy a common ground against Prelacy, in the acknowledgment of the bishop and deacon as the only two office-bearers recognised in the Church, there is a wide and material difference between the two as to the distribution of power between office-bearers and members, and as to the relations of one Christian society or Church to another. It is important to mark the difference between our

---

[1] 1 Tim. iii. 14 f.

[2] Jameson, *Sum of the Episcopal Controversy*, Edin. 1712, pp. 9–23. As to the scriptural evidence for the office of deacon, and the duties rightly attached to it, see *Jus Div. Reg. Eccles.* Lond. 1646, pp. 175 ff.; Rutherford, *Due Right of Presbyteries*, Lond. 1644, pp. 159–172. [Smyth, *Presbyt. the Script. and Prim. Pol.* Boston 1843, pp. 241–252. King, *Expos. and Def. of the Presbyt. Form of Church Gov.* Glasg. 1853, pp. 21–48. Rothe, *Anfänge*, pp. 166–170.]

views as Presbyterians and the Independent scheme on these two points, namely, the distribution of power within the Church, and the relations between the Church or congregation itself and other Churches. The difference is expressed in the ordinary name by which this system of Church order is known—the name of *Congregational Independency*—referring as it does to the two distinctive peculiarities of the system. There are certain distinctive views which belong to the adherents of that system as Congregationalists, and certain additional peculiarities that belong to them as Independents.

Under the name of *Congregationalism* are included those principles which lead them to assert for all the members of the Church, as well as for the office-bearers, a share in its rule and administration; so that, to use the language of Dr. Wardlaw, "the government in all its parts is to be administered in the pre sence, and with the *authoritative concurrence*, of the Church collectively considered."[1] According to this distribution of power in the Christian society, as asserted on the Congregational principle, the act of the rulers is null and void without the act of the members consenting with it; the authority of the Church is not deposited for its administration in the hands of office-bearers alone, but is divided between them and the members, in such proportions that the deed of the former is not lawful or binding without the consent of the latter. Both parties must equally sanction the proceeding, before it can be authoritative in the proper sense—the only difference between the rulers and the ruled being, that it is the privilege of those in office, and not of others, in ordinary circumstances, to originate and propose measures for the adoption of the rest, and to execute them after they are adopted. "They *propose* to the Church whatever they may think conducive to its well-being," says Dr. Davidson, "making any regulations, in harmony with the genius of Christianity, which they may deem desirable for the Church's guidance, but *always with the concurrence and sanction of the brethren.* . . . . They alone formally pronounce and execute any censure or sentence, in the presence *and with the consent of the Church.*"[2]

Again, under the name of *Independency* are included those principles which lead the denomination now referred to to assert that

---

[1] Wardlaw, *Congregational Independency*, Glasg. 1848, p. 230.
[2] Davidson, *Eccles. Polity of the New Test.* Lond. 1848, p. 275 f.

each worshipping congregation is a Church, *independent* of every other congregation,—being with its office-bearers complete within itself, and having no connection with others as parts of one ecclesiastical system, or united under one ecclesiastical government. According to this view, the government of each congregation is a government separate from that of any other ; and the visible Church in any country, comprehending, it may be, many congregations, is not *one* body ecclesiastical, but many bodies distinct from and independent of each other. "The independency," says Dr. Wardlaw, "for whose Scriptural authority we plead, is the independency of each Church in regard to the execution of the laws of Christ, of every other Church, and of all other human power whatsoever than what is lodged in itself. It is the full competency of every distinct Church to manage without appeal its own affairs."[1]   Theoretically, these two principles, characteristic of Congregational Independency, are distinct from each other, so that the one might be found existing without the other.   But, practically, they are found united in the case of the ecclesiastical body commonly known under the name of Independents.   They constitute the two distinctive peculiarities which separate the system of Independency from the system of Presbyterianism, and in any comparison between the two theories of Church polity, must both be taken into account.

SECTION I.—THE CONGREGATIONAL PRINCIPLE AS OPPOSED
TO PRESBYTERIANISM.

The principle which we have now to consider is that asserted by Independents when they tell us that the office-bearers of the Church "have no power either to make laws or to apply and execute the laws that exist, independently of the concurrence of their brethren," and that "the government of the ecclesiastical body in all its parts is to be administered in the presence and with the authoritative concurrence of the Church collectively considered."[2]   This is the statement of Dr. Wardlaw, and accurately expresses the views of Independents on this point, as maintained by them in opposition to Presbyterianism.   It would be a mistake to suppose that Presbyterianism, in maintaining a differ-

[1] Wardlaw, *Congregational Independency*, p. 231.
[2] Wardlaw, pp. 230, 320.

ent theory on this point, overlooks or undervalues the importance of the consent of the Christian members of the Church in her authoritative proceedings. The system of Presbyterianism requires that every proper means be employed, in the way of explanation, persuasion, and instruction, to secure the concurrence of the members in the acts and proceedings of the rulers of the Christian society. But Presbyterians do not, like Independents, hold that this consent is a condition upon which the lawfulness of the acts of the office-bearers is suspended, or as much a necessary element in any judgment of the ecclesiastical body as the consent of the rulers themselves. On the contrary, the consent of the members is, upon the Presbyterian theory, a consent added to the authoritative decision of the office-bearers, not entering into it as an element necessary to its validity, without which it would be neither lawful nor binding. And the question between Presbyterians and Independents is not whether the concurrence of the members of the Church in the acts and proceedings of the office-bearers is desirable, or in a right state of the Christian society will be almost invariably obtained, but whether, in Dr. Wardlaw's words, this concurrence is " authoritative," or the ingredient which, and not the act of the rulers alone, gives authority to the ecclesiastical decision, and without which it would not be binding.

In discussing this question, we shall have recourse to the same method of argument as we used to test the Scripture authority of the Episcopalian theory of Church government; and we shall find it no less applicable to the purpose of testing the proof offered for Independency against Presbyterianism. On the principle of Presbyterians, we assert that there is in the Church a power of government and administration vested in an order of office-bearers, separate from " the Church collectively considered," and " exercised independently of the concurrence of the members." This general proposition may be established in one or other of two ways. First, we may prove from Scripture that Christ or His apostles *instituted* an office of authority and government in the hands of an order of men, separate from the Church collectively, and independent of the members at large; or, second, we may, without any reference to the express institution of the office, prove that the peculiar powers and authority of such an office have been usually exercised and permanently administered

by a distinct body of men, separate from and independent of the
Church collectively considered.   If we can establish from the
Word of God the original institution of such an office of government and administration, separate from and not dependent on the
members at large, then this will decide the controversy in favour
of Presbyterianism, and against the Independent scheme.   Or if
we can prove from the Word of God that the distinctive powers
of such an office have been exercised commonly and statedly by
presbyters and deacons, and not by the members of the Church,
then this too will no less settle the dispute in the same manner.
We believe that there are materials in Scripture which give warrant for affirming both these conclusions, and which demonstrate,
first, that Christ and His apostles have instituted in the Church
an office of government, attached to a peculiar class of men, and
not to the members at large; and second, that the distinctive
powers belonging to such an office ought always to be exercised
by a standing and separate order of office-bearers, and never,
unless in wholly exceptional circumstances, by the body of the
society.

That an office of government, power, and authority peculiar
to some and not common to all in the Church has actually been
instituted, we have very express evidence from the multitude and
variety of names given in Scripture to a distinctive and separate
order, implying the idea of power as belonging to them, and not
to others.   The presbyters of the New Testament Church are
spoken of as rulers, as pastors, as overseers, as stewards, as govern-
ments ($\kappa \nu \beta \epsilon \rho \nu \acute{\eta} \sigma \epsilon \iota \varsigma$),—words which all, more or less, include the
idea of authority and governing power as distinctive of the office
held by them.   Indeed this point is so very abundantly and
clearly proved from the language of Scripture in regard to it,
that the Divine institution of the office of ruler in the Christian
Church is not denied, but, on the contrary, acknowledged and
maintained by Independents themselves.   " That the elders,
bishops, or pastors," says Dr. Wardlaw in his work on *Congregational Independency*, " are ordained in the Churches of Christ to
' have the rule over them,' to be ' over them in the Lord, and
admonish them,' to 'feed the flock of God, taking the oversight
thereof,'—we maintain as distinctly, and insist upon as firmly, as
our brethren who differ from us."[1]   This admission, which, unless

[1] Wardlaw, p. 310.

at the cost of contradicting the express statements of Scripture, *must* be made even by Independents, may be fairly and legitimately said to involve a surrender of the whole point in dispute. If it be granted that, by Divine institution, there are rulers in the Church of Christ holding a distinct office from the members, then it is impossible to reconcile this proposition with the principle of Independency, which asserts the necessity of the " authoritative concurrence" of all the Church to the validity of their acts of rule. The dogma of an authoritative concurrence on the part of the members necessary to the authoritative acts of the office-bearers, amounts just to a partitioning of the office of government in certain proportions between the two parties,—a division of the power of ruling between the office-bearers and the members, in such a manner that there can be no separate office belonging to the one apart from the other. An office of ruling which is dependent for its authority on the consent of other parties, cannot be a separate office at all ; and the admission which the very express Scripture evidence on the point compels Independents to make of the existence of such a distinct office in the Church, is fatal to the fundamental principle of their system.

The dogma of Congregationalism, which makes the authoritative acts of the rulers of the Church dependent for their authority on the sanction or consent of the ruled, could be asserted and defended consistently only on the hypothesis that the office of presbyter or ruler was not of Divine appointment at all, but a human arrangement, dependent for its existence on the will of the members, and for its power on the extent of authority delegated to it by their voluntary submission. If the office of ruler did not rest on the basis of Divine institution, but was an office created by the votes of the members of the society, and limited in its powers by the extent of permission they conceded to it, then indeed the principle of Congregationalism might be true with respect to the Christian Church. But in such a case the power of government would reside, as in the instance of voluntary and private societies, in the members at large, and not in the rulers as separate from them ; there could be no distinct office of government at all, apart from and independent of the Church in its collective capacity, nor any rulers as an independent order in the Christian society, distinct from the appointment and delegation of the members. Whatever in argument or in theory may be asserted, this is plainly the legitimate issue involved in the principle of Congregationalism. The rulers of the Church admitted in name are denied in effect; and instead of holding an office Divine and independent, are made the mere delegates of the members of the Church, with authority conditioned by their concurrence, and strictly limited by their commission. Upon the Congregational theory, the office-bearers may have, over and above what other members of the Church may possess, *first*, a power of advising the Church to adopt certain measures; and *second*, a power of executing the measure after it is adopted. But so long as it is asserted that their authority is limited by the condition of the members giving or withholding their consent to its acts, they cannot be said to have a power of authority at all, in the proper sense of the word. And this is very much the doctrine which is avowed by Dr. Davidson in his work in defence of Congregational views. In addition to the power of instruction and exhortation conceded to presbyters, Dr. Davidson says that they have the power of "proposing to the Church whatever they may think conducive to its well-being," and further, the power of "formally pronouncing and executing any censure or sentence," but that all that they do must be "always with the concurrence and sanction of the brethren."[1] In these two respects, then, and in these alone, the office-bearers differ from the members as regards rule, —they are the *advisers* of the Church before any authoritative decision is pronounced by the members, and they are the *organs* of the Church in executing its decisions after they are pronounced; but beyond this, they have no separate function of ruling. They have no office of proper authority distinct from the body of the members. In short, the Congregational principle is inconsistent with the Divine institution of an office of rule in the hands of an order of Church officers separate from the ordinary members; and the very explicit evidence which we have in the Word of God for the institution of such an office, admitted as it is by Congregationalists themselves, is sufficient to exclude the fundamental dogma peculiar to their ecclesiastical system.

In the undoubted Scripture evidence, then, which we have for the Divine institution of the office of presbyter, as an order distinct from the members of the Church, and including the idea of power or authority as connected with the office,—an

[1] Davidson, *Eccles. Pol. of New Test.* p. 275 f.

evidence not denied by Independents themselves, — we have a fact which is inconsistent with the fundamental peculiarity of Congregationalism, which implies a partition of authority between the rulers and the ruled. But this evidence is greatly strengthened by the consideration that, included in the general class of presbyter or elder, there is a special kind of presbyter or elder set apart more peculiarly to the exercise of the office of ruling in the Christian Church. The Scriptures seem to point to three sorts of office-bearers, all belonging to the one common order of the eldership, but distinguished from each other by the peculiar functions discharged by them respectively. *First*, there is the preaching elder, so often spoken of in Scripture under the name of " pastor," and other titles, significant of his distinctive work of preaching the Word and dispensing ordinances. *Second*, there is the teaching elder, spoken of under the name of " teacher," and apparently to be distinguished from the pastor in Scripture, as more especially devoted to the duty of teaching or explaining and interpreting the truth of God. And *third*, there is the ruling elder, to be discriminated from both by having it as his peculiar function to administer rule or government in the Church of Christ. Standing upon the same footing, as all belonging to the order of elder, there are these three varieties in the order to be distinguished in Scripture. If, therefore, as Presbyterians hold, there is a class of elders instituted by Christ in His Church who are distinctively devoted to the work of ruling or government, this fact brings out still more forcibly the unscriptural nature of the Congregationalist principle, which divides that government between office-bearers and the members of the Church at large.

It is impossible to do more than merely advert, in the briefest way, to the evidence for the Scriptural institution of the office of ruling elder, as distinguished from those presbyters specially set apart for preaching or teaching. 1. There is a strong presumptive argument in favour of ruling elders, distinct from preaching or teaching elders, from the precedent afforded in the Jewish Church for a similar order in the Christian, founded, as the polity of the New Testament was, upon the model of the Old Testament ecclesiastical government.[1] 2. There seems to

---

[1] Gillespie, *Assertion of the Gov. of the Church of Scotland*, Edin. 1641, ch. iii. ; *Miscell. Quest.* ch. xix. ; *Plea of Presbytery*, Glasg. 1840, pp. 308–325.

be a distinct reference to an office of government in the enumeration of ecclesiastical offices, given by the Apostle Paul in
the twelfth chapter of his Epistle to the Romans. These offices
apparently fall to be ranged under the two general heads of
" prophecy " and " ministry." " Having, then, gifts differing
according to the grace that is given to us, whether prophecy,
let us prophesy according to the proportion of faith; or ministry,
let us wait on our ministering." Then, under the two heads
of prophecy and ministry, the apostle goes on to give the sub-
division—*first*, under the general head of prophecy: " he that
teacheth (ὁ διδάσκων), on teaching,"—or the work of the doctor
or teaching elder ; " he that exhorteth (ὁ παρακαλῶν), on exhortation,"—or the order of pastor or preaching elder ; and *second*,
under the general head of ministry or service : " he that giveth
or distributeth (ὁ μεταδιδούς), let him do it with simplicity,"—or
the order of deacon ; " he that ruleth (ὁ προιστάμενος), with
diligence,"—or the order of ruling elder.[1] Such seems to be the
meaning of this rather difficult passage, pointing as it does to
the ruling elder, as distinct from the teaching or preaching elder.
3. There is another passage in the First Epistle to the Corinthians,
in which likewise allusion is made to the class of ruling elder, as
one of the offices in the apostolic Church : " And God hath set
some in the Church, first apostles, secondarily prophets, thirdly
teachers, after that miracles, then gifts of healings, helps, *governments* (ἀντιλήψεις, κυβερνήσεις), diversities of tongues."[2] In the
catalogue of offices, extraordinary and ordinary, in the apostolic
Church, the *governments* specified· among the rest apparently
ought to be interpreted as referring to an office of ruling in the
Christian society. 4. But the decisive evidence for the office of
ruling elder is to be found in the well-known passage in the First
Epistle to Timothy : " Let the elders that rule well be counted
worthy of double honour, especially they who labour in the word

---

[1] Rom. xii. 6-8. Gillespie, *Assertion of the Gov.* ch. v.   Rutherford, *Due
Right of Presbyt.* Lond. 1644, pp. 156-159.   King, *Expos. and Def. of the
Presbyt. Form of Church Gov.* pp. 94-100.   [*Vide* Calvin *in loc. et Instit.*
lib. iv. cap. iii. 8, 9. Comp. also the *Second Book of Discipl.* ch. ii. : " The
hail polity of the Kirk consisteth in three things, to wit, in Doctrine, Discipline, and Distribution.   With Doctrine is annexit the administration of
Sacramentis.   And according to the pairts of this division ariseth a three-
fauld sort of office-bearers in the Kirk, to wit, of Ministeris or Preachers,
Elderis or Governours, and Deaconis or Distributeris," etc.]
[2] 1 Cor. xii. 28. Gillespie, *Assertion of the Gov.* ch. vi. ; *Jus Div. Reg.
Eccles.* pp. 136-150. King, *Expos. and Def.* pp. 100-106.

and doctrine."[1] A vast deal of minute and laboured criticism has been expended on this passage, in order to make it bear a meaning against its obvious sense. But the very explicit testimony which it bears to two classes of elders, the one of whom ruled exclusively, the other of whom, in addition to ruling, exercised also the ministry of the Word, is so strong and conclusive, that not a few, both among Episcopalians and Independents, have been led to acknowledge the force of it.[2] Nothing but a very dangerous kind of wresting of the plain meaning of the text will suffice to get rid of such an interpretation of it as carries conclusive evidence in favour of the class of ruling, as separate from preaching and teaching elders. The strong fact, then, of the institution of a distinct class of presbyters for the express purpose of government in the Christian society, in addition to the general order of presbyters, who both preach and rule, serves very greatly to confirm the evidence we have from Scripture against the Congregationalist principle of a distribution of the power of government between office-bearers and members in the Church.[3]

---

[1] οἱ καλῶς προεστῶτες πρεσβύτεροι διπλῆς τιμῆς ἀξιούσθωσαν, μάλιστα οἱ κοπιῶντες ἐν λόγῳ καὶ διδασκαλίᾳ.—1 Tim. v. 17.

[2] [So, among Independents, Cotton, Goodwin, Dr. John Owen, etc., *Apol. Narr.* Lond. 1643, p. 8; *Cambridge Platform of Church Discipline*, 1648, ch. vii. With respect to what Gillespie calls " the footsteps of ruling elders in the Church of England," one specimen may suffice. Dean Nowell's *Catechism* was sanctioned by the same Convocation which passed the Thirty-nine Articles, and again ratified in 1571 and in 1603; it may therefore, with Jewel's *Apology*, be held to be of at least semi-symbolical standing in the English Church. The statement of this document on the subject of ruling elders is as follows : " In Ecclesiis bene institutis atque moratis certa, ut antea dixi, ratio atque ordo gubernationis instituebatur atque observabatur. Deligebantur Seniores, id est, magistratus ecclesiastici, qui disciplinam ecclesiasticam tenerent atque colerent. Ad hos autoritas, animadversio, atque castigatio censoria pertinebant : hi, adhibito etiam Pastore, si quos esse cognoverant qui vel opinionibus falsis, vel turbulentis erroribus, vel anilibus superstitionibus vel vitâ vitiosâ flagitiosâque magnam publice offensionem Ecclesiæ Dei adferrent, quique sine Cœnæ Dominicæ profanatione accedere non possent, eos a communione repellebant atque rejiciebant, neque rursum admittebant donec pœnitentiâ publicâ Ecclesiæ satisfecissent."—Ed. 1572, p. 157. To prove the scriptural authority of such a consistory or kirk-session, Dean Nowell refers to 1 Tim. v. 17 and the other texts which Presbyterians are in the habit of adducing for the same purpose.]

[3] On the subject of ruling elders and the ecclesiastical functions and duties rightfully belonging to them, see especially Gillespie's *Assertion of the Government of the Church of Scotland*, Part i. He begins with a statement of the scriptural authority for the term, and a repudiation of "the nickname of 'lay elders,' by which," as he justly observes, " some reproachfully, and others

II. It appears from Scripture, that the proper and distinctive exercises of Church power and authority are uniformly and statedly performed by the office-bearers of the Church, and never by the members generally. Even although we could not have proved the first institution of a separate office of authority and power in the Christian society attached to a distinct order, and not belonging to the Church collectively, yet Scripture evidence of the stated and continual exercise of the peculiar functions of such an office by a particular class, to the invariable exclusion of the members at large, would itself establish the Presbyterian doctrine against the Congregational view. Now such evidence there is in abundance. Church power, in all its various departments, whether exercised about doctrine, ordinances, government, or discipline, is always administered in the New Testament Church by parties in office, and never by the members of the Church generally. That such is the fact, the briefest reference to Scripture will suffice to demonstrate. The *titles* and names expressive of ecclesiastical authority in Scripture are restricted to a certain class, and not given indiscriminately to all the members of the Christian society ; the *qualifications* neces-

ignorantly, call them." See also a brief but very admirable little treatise by Alex. Henderson, published in 1641, *The Government and Order of the Church of Scotland*, pp. 13, 30, 36 ff. ; *Jus Div. Reg. Eccles.* pp. 123-175 ; Voetius, *Polit. Eccles.* Pars ii. lib. ii. Tract. iii. cap iv.-vii. ; Blondel, *De Jure Plebis in Regimine Ecclesiastico.* [Among Lutheran divines, see J. H. Böhmer, *Observat. select. Eccles.*, in his ed. of De Marca's *De Concord. Sacerdot. et Imperii*, Francf. 1708, and Gerhard, *Loci*, ed. Preuss, tom. vi. pp. 17, 149 ff.; King, *Expos. and Def.* Part iv. ; Miller, *Warrant, Nature, and Duties of the Office of Ruling Elder*, Edin. 1842 ; Lorimer, *The Eldership of the Church of Scotland*, Glasg. 1841. For a very interesting account of the steps taken towards the re-establishment of the presbyterate, in its full development, in the various Protestant Churches at the Reformation, see Lechler, *Gesch. der Presbyterial und Synodal Verfassung seit der Reformation*, Leiden 1854, pp. 7 ff., 13 f., 32, 42 ff., 59, 71, etc. : " Die Gründe für Aufstellung von'Aeltesten' neben den Geistlichen, zur Uebung der kirchlichen Zucht, waren in dieser Zeit vor allen Dingen die *Schriftmässigkeit* des Aeltestenamts ; sodann die geschichtliche Ehrwürdigkeit desselben, sofern es in der apostolischen und auch in der nachapostolischen reineren Zeit bestanden hat ; drittens, die sociale Zweckmässigkeit dieser Einrichtung, sofern sie, (a) das Gehässige einer bloss durch die Geistlichkeit geübten Kirchenzucht vermeidet, und mehr Vertrauen und Ansehen geniesst ; (b) sofern durch Aufstellung einer gemischten Behörde der etwaigen Willkühr, Eigenmächtigkeit, und Ungerechtigkeit einer lediglich clerikalen und hierarchischen Verwaltung der Zucht vorgebeugt wird. Mit anderen Worten : der subjective Beweggrund zu Einführung von Aeltesten war, erstlich, Gehorsam gegen Gottes Wort, zweitens, geschichtlicher Sinn und Ehrfurcht vor dem reineren Alterthum, drittens, praktische Weisheit" (p. 47).]

sary for administering Church power are required, not from all, but from a few only; the *instructions* for the due discharge of its functions are addressed to a limited order, and not to the Church collectively; and the *examples* in the Word of God of the performance of the duties attaching to the possession of ecclesiastical authority are always examples of these duties being discharged by men in office, and never by persons without office.

1*st*, The administration of Church power in connection with doctrine is exhibited in Scripture as always belonging to pastors, and never to the people at large. The chief and highest exercise of Church power, to declare the mind of God from His Word, and to preach the Gospel to sinners, is ever represented as the work of presbyters, and never as the duty of the members of the Church. It may be the right of the members of the Church to elect the pastor to preach the Gospel, but it is not the right, in ordinary circumstances, of the members to preach themselves, or even to ordain to the office of preaching. There is no example that can be quoted from Scripture of the private members of the Church either preaching, in the strict sense of the word, or ordaining preachers. The only instance alleged by Congregationalists in support of their theory, that it is the inherent right of every member to preach the Gospel, is the case of the persecuted disciples of Jerusalem, recorded in the eighth chapter of the Acts, where it is said: " They that were scattered abroad went every where preaching the Word." [1] But in reference to the alleged precedent, it cannot, in the first place, be proved that the scattered disciples who preached were not pastors ordained to the work; [2] and in the second place, although it could be proved that they were private members only, the extraordinary emergency of the Church would both explain and justify the departure from ordinary rule. As Presbyterians, we do not hold that, in an extraordinary crisis or unsettled condition of a Church, necessity may not be laid upon Christians not in office both to preach and to ordain, rather than that the ordinance of the ministry should cease. But we affirm that, in the ordinary and normal condition of the Church, there is no Scripture precedent or warrant for the members of the Church generally exercising this peculiar office, but only for pastors or elders. [3]

---

[1] εὐαγγελιζόμενοι τὸν λόγον.—Acts viii. 4.
[2] [See above, vol. i. p. 458.]   [3] [See above, vol. i. pp. 452-466.]

2d, The administration of Church power in connection with ordinances is always exhibited in Scripture as belonging to office-bearers, and never to the members generally. In the case of ordination, it is by the laying on of the hands of those in office before, that office is conferred and transmitted. There is no Scripture example of ordination by the Christian people; and the only attempt to show warrant for the right of the people to ordain, is when Congregationalists confound or identify election with ordination. In the case of the Sacraments, it is by the hands of office-bearers that they are uniformly dispensed in Scripture. There is not the shadow of evidence in the Word of God to prove that private members ever baptized, or dispensed the bread and wine of a Communion Table. The unvarying and stated exercise of this branch of Church power by office-bearers, and the no less unvarying and stated abstinence by members from all actions involving the exercise of it, furnish conclusive evidence that the power belonged to the one, and did not belong to the other.

3d, The administration of Church power in its remaining branch, or in connection with government and discipline, is always represented in Scripture as belonging to persons in office, and not to the members generally. That this is the case, is very satisfactorily demonstrated by those *titles* expressive of ruling, those *instructions* for the proper administration of authority, and those *qualifications* for rightly exercising discipline, which we find so very often in Scripture in connection with the office-bearers, and not with the members of the Church. In these we have distinct Scriptural evidence that the administration of government and discipline formed part of the ordinary work of the former as office-bearers, and was peculiar to their order, and not common to them with all. To office-bearers, and not to members in general, were such directions given as these: "Preach the word; be instant in season, out of season; reprove, rebuke, exhort with all long-suffering and doctrine." "Against an elder receive not an accusation, but before two or three witnesses." "Them that sin rebuke before all, that others also may fear." "A man that is an heretic, after the first and second admonition, reject." "These things speak, and exhort, and rebuke with all authority."[1] To office-bearers, and not to private members, was the commission given, to bind and to loose, to retain and remit sin, to hold and use the keys

[1] 2 Tim. iv. 2; 1 Tim. v. 19 f.; Tit. ii. 15, iii. 10.

of the kingdom of heaven. And the Scripture examples of the actual administration of government and discipline in the apostolic Church are all spoken of with reference to the office-bearers as distinct from the members of the Church. In opposition to this very strong and abundant evidence, there are three passages of Scripture usually appealed to by Congregationalists in support of their theory, that the power of government and discipline belongs to the members of the Church collectively.

The first passage is in the Gospel by Matthew, where our Lord is giving instruction about dealing with the offences of a brother : "If thy brother trespass against thee, go and tell him his fault between thee and him alone : if he shall hear thee, thou hast gained thy brother. But if he will not hear thee, then take with thee one or two more, that in the mouth of two or three witnesses every word may be established. And if he neglect to hear them, tell it to the Church : but if he neglect to hear the Church, let him be to thee as an heathen man and a publican. Verily, I say unto you, Whatsoever ye shall bind on earth shall be bound in heaven ; and whatsoever ye shall loose on earth shall be loosed in heaven."[1] From this passage the Congregationalists argue, that the power of discipline belongs to the Church collectively in its members, and that the offending brother is to be dealt with authoritatively by them, and not by the office-bearers. Now, in regard to this objection, I remark, *in the first place*, that it takes for granted that the word "Church" must mean a particular congregation, and cannot be understood of the Church as represented by her rulers and office-bearers,—an assumption not borne out by the language of Scripture. But, *in the second place*—and this is really decisive of the question—the Christian Church not being in existence at the moment when our Lord so spoke, He must have referred, in the expression He used, to some existing mode of ecclesiastical procedure known to the disciples, if He was to speak intelligibly to them at all. That He did allude, in the expression, "tell the Church," to the Jewish Synagogue, seems to be quite undoubted,—intimating that the procedure with respect to offenders among His disciples was to be similar to what took place among the Jews in their Church courts. The practice of the Synagogue *must* have been the

[1] Matt. xviii. 15–17.

practice suggested to the disciples by the peculiar language of our Lord ; and that practice involved the invariable custom of the Church dealing with offenders through her office-bearers, and not in the meetings of her members generally. The argument from this passage in Matthew, so far from being in favour of Independency, is, on the contrary, conclusive in support of the Presbyterian theory.[1]

The second passage usually referred to by Congregationalists, is in the fifteenth chapter of Acts ; but as I shall have occasion to discuss it in the next section, I postpone for the present any consideration of it.

The third passage usually appealed to is in First Corinthians, and refers to the excommunication of the incestuous person in the Church of Corinth : " For I verily," says the apostle, " as absent in body, but present in spirit, have judged already, as though I were present, him that hath done this deed, in the name of our Lord Jesus Christ, when ye are gathered together, and my spirit, with the power of our Lord Jesus Christ, to deliver such an one unto Satan, for the destruction of the flesh, that the spirit may be saved in the day of the Lord Jesus. . . . Put away from among yourselves that wicked person." [2] And again, on the repentance of the offender, and after suggesting his restoration, the apostle, in Second Corinthians, says : " Sufficient to such a man is this punishment which was inflicted of many." [3]
Now, from this passage, Congregationalists argue, *first*, that inasmuch as the epistle is not addressed to the office-bearers of the Church at Corinth, but to the members at large, the instructions of the apostle to deal with the offender must be understood as addressed to the members also. This argument would imply that every direction in the epistle not specially restricted, must apply equally to all, — a principle of interpretation obviously unsound, and contradicted by the fact of there being a variety of injunctions in this very epistle, although not limited by any express terms, yet plainly requiring to be limited to particular classes by the very nature of the injunctions themselves. Directions, for example, about prophesying are given, without being

---

[1] Gillespie, *Aaron's Rod Blossoming*, B. iii. ch. iii. v.; *Assertion of the Gov. of the Church of Scotland*, Part i. ch. iv. [Wilson, *The Kingdom of our Lord Jesus Christ*, Edin. 1859, pp. 349–431.]
[2] 1 Cor. v. 3–5, 13.
[3] ἡ ἐπιτιμία αὕτη ἡ ὑπὸ τῶν πλειόνων.—2 Cor. ii. 6.

expressly limited to those among the members of the Church at Corinth who were prophets, as they absolutely require, from the very nature of the precepts, to be. And so also directions about the administration of discipline are given, without any express limitation of them to those qualified or authorized to administer discipline, although such a limitation is no less required by the nature of the directions given. But, *second*, from this same passage Congregationalists argue that the sentence was actually executed, not by the office-bearers, but by the members of the Church at large ; as appears from the apostle's statements : " Put away from among yourselves that wicked person; " and again : " Sufficient to such a man is this punishment which was inflicted of many." Now, in reference to this, it is sufficient to remark that the sentence of excommunication, although pronounced by the authority of the rulers, could be practically carried out only by the aid of all the members of the Church co-operating with the rulers, and withdrawing from the society of the person excommunicated. There was a duty lying upon the members of the Church, to put away from their communion the offending person upon whom the sentence had been pronounced ; and this expulsion from the society of the Christian people, following upon the sentence of the rulers, might well be called a punishment inflicted of the many. This principle is quite sufficient to explain the expression of the apostle in the Epistle to the Corinthians, without having recourse to an interpretation at variance with the uniform language of Scripture elsewhere, restricting as it does the power of government and discipline to the office-bearers of the Christian society alone.

Looking back upon the whole argument, we seem to be warranted in laying down these two propositions, subversive as they are of the doctrine peculiar to Congregationalism. First, we have distinct evidence in Scripture for the institution of an office of rule and authority in the hands of office-bearers apart from others, and not an office partitioned or distributed between office-bearers and members. Second, we have distinct evidence in Scripture that the administration of the powers of this office in all the different departments of their exercise was invariably conducted by Church officers, and not by the members of the ecclesiastical body at large. These two propositions, established, as we believe them to be, from the Word of God, are completely

destructive of the fundamental principle implied in the term
" Congregationalism." [1]

SECTION II.—THE INDEPENDENT PRINCIPLE AS OPPOSED TO PRESBYTERIANISM.

The two distinctive peculiarities of the system of Congregational Independency are marked out in the name by which it has
come to be known. The first of these, or the principle of Congregationalism, which maintains that the proper office of ruling
in the Christian Church belongs to the members collectively, or
is partitioned in some manner between the members and office-
bearers, we have already considered at some length, and have
been led to reject it as without foundation in Scripture. The
second of these peculiarities, or the principle of Independency,
remains to be discussed. That principle, as the import of the
name suggests, is to this effect, that every congregation, including its office-bearers, has within itself all the powers necessary for
accomplishing all the objects of a Church of Christ, irrespective
of every other; that it is complete in and by itself, to the exclusion of all connection with other Churches, for the administration
of Word and ordinance, government and discipline ; and that
all association of congregations under one common rule, or subordination to any authority beyond themselves, is inconsistent
with the nature of the Church of Christ, and unscriptural. According to this view, the power of ruling in the Christian Church
is to be exercised within each particular congregation, apart from
every other, and not in the way of the office-bearers of several
congregations meeting for the exercise of a common authority
over them all, each individual society being absolutely independent and separate from the rest in matters of government, discipline, and order.

This independence and absolute separation of each congregation from every other in the exercise of ecclesiastical authority,

---

[1] Gillespie, *Aaron's Rod Blossoming,* B. ii. ch. ix. x.   Wood, *Little Stone,*
etc., *an Exam. and Refut. of Mr. Lockyer's Lecture,* Edin. 1654, pp. 184–281.
Brown, *Vind. of the Presbyt. Form of Church Gov.* Edin. 1805, pp. 11–117.
Whytock, *Vind. of Presbytery,* Edin. 1843, pp. 22–63. *Essays on the Primi-
tive Church Offices* (Alexander), New York 1851, pp. 1–68. Cunningham,
Works, vol. iii. pp. 543–554. [Lechler, *Gesch. der Presbyterial und Synodal
Verfassung seit der Reformation,* Leiden 1854, pp. 78 ff.]

asserted by Congregational Independents, is a very natural and indeed unavoidable consequence of the other distinctive principle maintained by them—namely, that all government is to be exercised by the Church collectively, and not by the office-bearers alone. It is obviously impracticable for two or more different congregations to associate or meet together for the ordinary administration of a common government. If congregations are to meet for ruling in common, it can only be through their office-bearers associating as their representatives for that purpose. And, on the other hand, while the principles of Congregationalism are inconsistent with the idea of association for the exercise of a common government, the principles of Presbyterianism very naturally or unavoidably lead to it. Presbyterians assert that the right of governing is deposited in the hands of the office-bearers of the Christian society, and not in the society itself,—a principle that paves the way for the elders of different congregations meeting together in the discharge of their peculiar functions, and as the representatives of their several Churches, for the exercise of a joint authority over the ecclesiastical societies which they represent. Such meetings of elders or presbyters in greater or smaller numbers, as the case may require or their circumstances permit, may be called Courts, or Councils, or Presbyteries, or Synods, without the name altering or affecting the nature or amount of the ecclesiastical authority competent to them as office-bearers of the Church. If the governing body in a single and separate congregation—whether with Independents you call it the congregational meeting, or whether with Presbyterians you call it the congregational eldership, or consistory, or kirk-session—have a certain power of government within it, the same in nature and amount is the power of government ascribed by Presbyterians to the eldership of many congregations, when they meet for jointly ruling in the affairs of them all. In the meeting of many rulers of different congregations for united counsel and action in the government of them all, there will indeed be certain advantages and an increase in influence and authority gained for their proceedings by the union, not to be found in the case of the eldership of a single congregation. But the kind of authority in both cases is the same. The decision of the congregational eldership, and the decision of the more general council, met under the name of Presbytery or Synod, are in

their binding force precisely the same. Presbyterians demand
no other kind of authority for the proceedings of Presbyteries
or Synods than Independents ascribe to the decisions of their
congregational courts. The only difference is, that in the former
case you have a government comprehending many congregations;
in the latter case you have a government including no more than
one.[1] Setting aside the question of the *parties* in whom the
power of government is lodged, which has already been under
our consideration, the real and essential point remaining for
discussion as between Presbyterians and Independents is, whether
or not it is lawful and right for the governing body of one congregation to unite with the governing body of a second, or third,
or fourth, for the purpose of common counsel and joint authority
in the exercise of rule over all. Presbyterians hold that there is
warrant and precedent for this in the Word of God; Independents hold that it is incompetent and unscriptural.

The right or power of association in the exercise of government
in the case of more than one congregation is, then, the grand
question in debate between the adherents of Presbyterianism and
Congregational Independency. Other things are mere matters
of arrangement not essential to the question. The number, for
example, of rulers, more or fewer, who may meet together in one
body for the joint exercise of counsel and government in matters
affecting the interests of congregations, is a point of detail in no
way fundamental to the argument. Whether these associations
or courts shall be local, or provincial, or national, or œcumenical,
is also apart from the essence of the controversy, and must be
determined by considerations of expediency, or a regard to the
circumstances of congregations, or of the Church generally.
Further still, if it is lawful or Scriptural for the governing bodies
of different neighbouring congregations to associate for common
counsel and the exercise of a joint rule, this necessarily implies
that the members and rulers of each of these congregations singly
are subject to the authority of the whole representative convention.
In other words, such an association implies the subordination of
each congregation, and the rulers of each congregation, to the
common and more general authority of the higher courts. The
principle of subordination, and the right of appeal from the rulers

---

[1] *Answer of the Assembly of Divines to the Reasons of the Dissenting
Brethren*, Lond. 1648, pp. 185–197.

of one congregation to the rulers of many, are involved in the general principle, that it is competent and Scriptural for the governing parties of the Church to associate together beyond the limits of an individual congregation, for the exercise of ecclesiastical authority and power in common. The warrant for Church courts, made up of the office-bearers of several congregations for the purpose of joint government, carries with it the warrant also for the subordination both of individuals and of narrower associations to the more general conventions of rulers.

To a certain extent, the lawfulness of ecclesiastical Councils or Synods has been admitted even by Independents. More especially, the Independents of former times were accustomed to acknowledge the propriety, or even necessity, of the association of the office-bearers of different Churches, with a power of advice, if not of authority, as respects individual congregations. And although modern Independents have considerably narrowed the concessions made by their predecessors, yet many of them do not profess to deny the lawfulness of ecclesiastical Councils for at least consultation on the affairs of the Church, and of one congregation, through its office-bearers, asking advice or aid from the office-bearers of another in matters of difficulty or common concernment.[1] But the real question in debate between the adherents of Independency and those of Presbyterianism is as to the right of elders or presbyters associating together from different congregations, not only for the purpose of mutual consultation and advice, but for the exercise of a common government. If such a right can be established from Scripture, the proof is decisive in favour of Presbyterianism, and against the Independent theory.

I. The lawfulness of association among the office-bearers of the Church for the exercise of common government, may be argued from the unity of the visible Church.

I do not say that this consideration would of itself be deci-

---

[1] *Answer to Reasons of Dissent. Breth.* pp. 135 ff.   Brown, *Vind. of the Presbyt. Form of Church Gov.* Edin. 1805, pp. 193-206.   Wardlaw, *Congreg. Independ.* Glasg. 1848, pp. 346-376. As regards the practicable workableness, or rather unworkableness, of the Independent system in this respect, see the printed correspondence relative to a lengthened controversy between certain Independent Churches in and near Glasgow, which arose about the year 1844. It is referred to by Dr. Alexander in his *Life of Wardlaw*, Edin. 1856, pp. 423-426. [Cf. Edwards, *Antapologia*, Lond. 1644, pp. 135-154.]

sive of the question, but it affords a very strong presumptive
evidence in favour of the right of association for the purposes of
government in the Church, in so far as circumstances make it
practicable. That there is a kind of oneness which belongs to
the visible Church in consequence of the outward covenant relationship in which it stands to Christ, that there is a seen and
external communion kept up by all the members of the visible
Church through means of the observance of the same outward
ordinances, and the enjoyment of the same outward provision of
means of grace, is a point which we have had occasion to consider
and demonstrate at a previous stage in our discussions.[1] The
man who is admitted into the Christian society by the administration of a Baptism common to all branches of it, becomes, in
virtue of his participation in the ordinance, not so much a member of the local congregation or Church where he worships, as a
member of the catholic Church at large, having a right of membership throughout the whole. The man who is ordained to the
office of a pastor or minister in any local Church, becomes, in
virtue of his ordination, a minister of the visible Church throughout the whole world, qualified and entitled to preach the Gospel,
not merely within the bounds of the single congregation over
which he is so set as overseer, but also in any other congregation
where Providence may order his lot. And upon the very same
grounds we are prepared to argue, that an office-bearer, set apart
not only to preach but to rule in any individual congregation, has
his office of ruling not confined to that congregation alone, but is
qualified and entitled to rule throughout the Church universal,
wherever circumstances may permit, or the edification of the body
of Christ may demand it. Every Christian pastor has a certain
relation to the whole body of believers, qualifying and authorizing
him to preach the Word of God wherever throughout the visible
Church he may for a time have his abode, and making him a
minister of the Gospel, not amidst his own flock alone, but amidst
the members of other congregations. And the office of ruling,
to which he was admitted at his ordination as a presbyter, is co-
extensive with the office of preaching that belongs to him. As
one entitled to govern as well as to preach, he has a certain relation, not only to the particular congregation where he ordinarily
rules, but also to the whole visible Church, and is qualified and

[1] [See above, vol. i. pp. 8–11, 14–21, 29–53.]

authorized to use his gifts in that way wherever he may have a
call to act, and wherever the edification of the members of the
Church can be promoted by it.

This is plainly the proper theory of the unity that belongs to
the visible Church of Christ. No doubt, circumstances may prevent, and do prevent, that unity from being practically realized.
The separation of congregations and Churches by distance of
place and difference of language—and, worse than that, their
separation caused by differences of doctrine and government and
worship—may make it impossible for such a system of visible
unity to be completely exhibited in actual fact. But notwithstanding of this, it is unquestionable that the principles of visible
unity upon which Christ constituted and modelled His Church at
first have laid the foundation for the association of rulers and
office-bearers for the exercise of authority in common, and seem
fairly to require that association in so far as in the circumstances
of the Church it is practicable, or for edification. Although it
may be impossible to carry out the plan of an actual communion
in government among the office-bearers of the Church to the
whole extent of the visible society of Christians, yet this is no
reason why it should not be carried out to any extent or realized
at all. A pastor is something more than a pastor within his own
congregation alone; and a ruler in the Church is something
more than a ruler to his own flock alone. In both capacities,
they sustain such a relation to the Church universal as to lay the
foundations for union or association among the office-bearers of
the Church throughout different congregations for joint action,
mutual consultation, and common ruling. And the unity of
the visible Church seems to carry with it the warrant for such
communion in counsel and government to the whole extent to
which the circumstances of particular congregations, or the advantage of the Church at large, may permit or demand. Unless
there were some express prohibition to be found in Scripture
directed against the lawfulness of such association for government, the principles of unity established in the Church of Christ
seem both to countenance and require it.[1]

[1] *Answer to Reasons of Dissent. Breth.* pp. 2-16.   Brown, *Vind. of
Presbyt. Form of Church Gov.* pp. 211-222.   [" The question raised by such
institutions as unions and confederacies among Christian societies," says Dr.
Alexander in reference to a defence by Dr. Wardlaw of the Congregational
Union, " respects not the *desirableness* of union among such societies, nor the

II. The lawfulness of association among the office-bearers throughout the Church for the purpose of common government, may be argued from the examples in Scripture of such union among the rulers of neighbouring congregations. One of the fundamental positions laid down by Independents is, that the word "Church"—ἐκκλησία—is never found in the New Testament save in two significations,—first, as denoting the whole mystical body of Christ, made up of true believers throughout the world; and second, as denoting a single congregation of Christians, who could all assemble together for worship in one place. On the other hand, while not denying that the word ἐκκλησία occurs in these two senses, Presbyterians are prepared to prove that it is frequently used in Scripture to denote a combination of more than one congregation, united together under a common government, administered by one body of elders associated for the purpose. The difference between the adherents of Independency and of Presbytery on this point is a vital and fundamental one, involving the whole merits of the controversy. If it could be proved that the word "Church" in the New Testament always means either the whole body of believers throughout the world, or else a single congregation consisting only of such a number of members as could ordinarily assemble in one place for the exercise of worship, government, and discipline, and that never on any occasion is it used to denote several congregations, united or represented by their office-bearers, then this proof would, without actually settling the controversy in favour of Independency, furnish a very strong argument on its behalf. If, on the other hand, there is evidence that the word is repeatedly employed to denote several congregations, united under and represented by an association of office-bearers, or a Presbytery, then the proof is decisive in favour of Presbyterian views. This latter proposition, I believe, there are sufficient materials in Scripture to establish. We do not deny that the word "Church" sometimes signifies only

importance of giving expression of mutual esteem and confidence in the ways specified by the preacher, but the *legitimacy* of forming such societies into one conjoint body for this purpose. In the case of Independent Churches, this question is further complicated by the question, whether such union of Churches be *possible*, saving the;independency of the Churches,—whether, in other words, to say that a society is independent and complete in itself, and yet is part of another and larger society, be not a contradiction in terms?" —*Life of Wardlaw*, p. 172. Durham, *Comment. on the Revelation*, Glasg. 1788, pp. 120-136.]

a single congregation meeting in one place. We do not deny that the word " Churches," in the plural, is often employed to denote congregations of Christians scattered over an extensive district of country, and remote from each other; as, for example, when we hear of the Churches of Asia, or of Syria, or of Macedonia, or of Galatia, which very probably possessed separate and distinct governing bodies. But we assert that very often the word Church in the singular signifies more than one congregation, united in no other way than as represented and governed by one body of rulers; as, for example, when we read of " the Church of Jerusalem," or " of Antioch," or " of Corinth," in which cities we are prepared to prove that there were different congregations, and one common government. The use of the word Church in this sense I have had occasion to refer to at an earlier stage in our inquiries.[1] But this point is so important, and so decisive of the debate between Independents and Presbyterians, that I must deal with it briefly once more. There are two parts, then, in the general proposition now laid down, and which it is our object to establish. *First,* the word Church is frequently employed in Scripture to denote two or more congregations connected together; and *second,* the different congregations, so included under the word, were united under one common government.

With regard to the first part of the proposition, or that two or more congregations are often spoken of under the one general name of a Church, we have the proof of it in the instance of the Church of Jerusalem, the first established, and the model of all the apostolic Churches. The Christians worshipping there are uniformly spoken of as *one* Church in the New Testament; and yet that there was a plurality of congregations at Jerusalem, may be demonstrated from a variety of circumstances mentioned in Scripture.

1. That the Church at Jerusalem was made up of different congregations, meeting for worship in different places, is evinced by the vast multitude of converts very soon gathered there by the labours of the apostles. We are not informed of the number of converts to the faith which existed at the period of our Lord's ascension, and previously to the outpouring of the Spirit on the day of Pentecost. Besides the one hundred and twenty disciples who met in the upper room at Jerusalem, we know that on one particular occasion, Christ, after His resurrection, was seen of

[1] [See above, vol. i. p. 12 f.]

"above five hundred brethren at once."[1] To these were speedily added on the day of Pentecost three thousand souls, converted by a single sermon, and at one time. After this vast ingathering of converts, it is recorded that " the Lord added *daily* to the Church such as should be saved."[2] Again, on the occasion of a sermon by Peter, it is said: "Many of them who heard the word believed; and the number of the *men* was about five thousand."[3] There is no reason for thinking that in this statement are comprehended the previously mentioned three thousand, converted on the day of Pentecost; the two numbers must therefore be added together in forming an estimate of the membership of the Church of Jerusalem at this early period in its history. Besides, as *men* are especially and exclusively mentioned (ἀριθμὸς τῶν ἀνδρῶν) according to a very common method of Scripture computation,[4] a large addition is further to be made on account of the female converts. Subsequently to this date, we are told that " believers were added to the Lord, multitudes both of men and women." Further still, it is declared, " the Word of God increased, and the number of disciples in Jerusalem multiplied greatly; and a great company of the priests were obedient to the faith."[5] It is utterly impossible, upon any rational theory of interpretation, to maintain that the many thousands of converts thus particularly mentioned in Scripture, as added to the Church at Jerusalem, could have found it practicable to meet together as one worshipping assembly. They constituted, when taken together, a multitude which could not assemble in one congregation for ordinary worship, but must of necessity have constituted several congregations; especially when we consider that the accommodation which they could procure for that purpose was, in all likelihood, nothing better than an upper chamber, with the door shut and barred for fear of the Jews. It may be right to take into account to a certain extent the resort of strangers to Jerusalem at the time of the feast of Pentecost; and on this ground a slight deduction may be made from the number mentioned as converted and joined to the Church. Another deduction of equally small amount may require to be made for the dispersion of disciples arising from the persecution after Stephen's death, although it seems to be pretty certain that it was

[1] 1 Cor. xv. 6. [2] Acts ii. 41, 47. [3] Acts iv. 4.
[4] Compare, for instance, John vi. 10 with Matt. xiv. 21.
[5] Acts v. 14, vi. 7.

against the office-bearers in the Christian society alone that the violence of the persecutors was especially directed on this occasion, and that, accordingly, it was not the members of the Church at large, but their office-bearers, that were " all scattered abroad, except the apostles."[1] But after making every reasonable deduction from the numbers of converts on any such grounds, those remaining at Jerusalem constituted a multitude which no single place of meeting could have held, and which could not at any time, but especially in the circumstances of the early believers, have statedly met together in one assembly for public worship. And years afterwards, when the Church at Jerusalem must have settled down into its normal condition as to numbers, exhibiting only a gradual increase from day to day, we find the Apostle James speaking of it to Paul as comprehending many myriads of converts. " Thou seest, brother, how many myriads—πόσαι μυριάδες—of Jews there are which believe."[2] With such numbers, it is utterly impossible that there could have been no more than a single worshipping assembly at Jerusalem.

2. The very same conclusion which asserts a plurality of congregations at Jerusalem, is established by the fact of the great number of ministers and office-bearers who for a space of many years can be proved to have had the seat of their ministry at Jerusalem. It is believed by most interpreters of Scripture, that the seventy disciples whom Christ Himself commissioned to preach the Gospel, laboured for a period of time at Jerusalem. But apart from this, we know that for several years the twelve apostles were together in that city occupied in the ministry of the Word. At an early period in their ministry, we find them setting apart seven deacons to discharge that department of Church service which their higher duties prevented them from overtaking. In the eleventh chapter of the Acts we have mention made of elders or presbyters, in addition to the apostles, as forming part of the ordinary staff of Church officers at Jerusalem. In the same chapter we learn that, over and above apostles and presbyters, there were also prophets exercising their peculiar office of revelation and exposition of Divine truth among the believers there.[3] And from an examination and comparison of different parts of the narrative in the Acts, it appears that apostles and presbyters and prophets had their ordinary residence at Jerusalem

[1] [See above, vol. i. p. 458.]   [2] Acts xxi. 20.   [3] Acts xi. 27, 30.

for a series of years, busily engaged in the work of preaching the Gospel, and ministering in Word and ordinance. It is utterly impossible to believe that twelve apostles, a plurality of presbyters, and a number of inspired prophets, besides the seven deacons, could for years restrict themselves to Jerusalem, and all for the purpose of labouring in a single congregation that could statedly assemble in one place for worship. There must have been at Jerusalem such a number of office-bearers of different sorts as entirely to exclude the possibility of there being no more than one congregation under their ministerial care.

Other arguments, such as the diversity of language among the dwellers at Jerusalem, might easily be adduced to show that it is impossible to believe that there existed in that city but one congregation of converts, worshipping regularly in one place of meeting. And if the first part of our proposition be established, which asserts that, under the name of "the Church at Jerusalem," there was in fact a plurality of congregations, the second part of it, or that which asserts that these different congregations were united under one common government, may be demonstrated very briefly. The single name under which the several distinct and separate congregations at Jerusalem are spoken of as "the Church" there, is of itself sufficient to prove that they had a common bond of union in their subordination to one ecclesiastical government or polity. There is no other explanation that can account for it. This view of the matter is confirmed by the fact that the office-bearers in the Jewish capital are uniformly spoken of, not as the elders or deacons of this or that congregation belonging to Jerusalem, but as the elders and deacons of *the* Church there. When Paul and Barnabas went up to Jerusalem with a contribution to the poor saints there, it is said to be sent to *the* elders by the hands of the messengers from Antioch. In the sixth chapter of Acts we find the apostles associating together as rulers of the Church for the ordination of deacons at Jerusalem. In the fifteenth chapter we again read of the apostles and elders met together in a Church assembly or court for the regulation of certain ecclesiastical affairs. From first to last, in the accounts we have of the Christians at Jerusalem, divided as they undoubtedly were into many congregations, we still read of *one* Church, of *one* body of office-bearers, of *one* set of apostles and presbyters ruling and ordering the common concerns of all. So very clear and conclusive is the evidence to prove that the different congregations at Jerusalem were united under one ecclesiastical management, and subject to one ordinary government.[1]

It would not be difficult to enlarge to almost any extent the argument which demonstrates that in the New Testament the word Church is frequently used to denote a number of different congregations, united and represented by one Presbytery or body of office-bearers. Upon grounds to a great extent similar, it might be argued, as that in the case of Jerusalem, so also this was exemplified in the Church of Corinth, of Antioch, and of Ephesus. The multitude of converts which can be proved to have existed in these cities, and the great number of office-bearers which were attached to them, demonstrate that these Churches did not consist of single congregations, but of many.[2] And this fact is decisive of the argument between Presbyterians and Independents.

III. We have a very conclusive proof of the lawfulness of Presbyterial association among the rulers of the Church, not merely in the case of the elders of closely neighbouring congregations, but on a larger scale, in the fifteenth chapter of the Acts. The Synod or Council assembled at Jerusalem for deciding the controversy which troubled the apostolic Church about the obligation of the Mosaic law on Gentile converts, is a precedent for the union of the office-bearers of the Church for the purpose of government, which very clearly establishes the lawfulness and authority of Church courts.

Notwithstanding of the declared opinion of Paul and Barnabas, certain Judaizing teachers at Antioch had insisted that, except the Gentile converts kept the law of Moses, they could not be saved. In consequence of the dissensions and dispeace caused at Antioch by these doctrines, the Church there deputed Paul and Barnabas and certain others to take the decision of the apostles and elders at Jerusalem on the point in dispute. We have reason from the subsequent narrative to believe that, besides Paul and Barnabas and other deputies from Antioch, there were also representatives from the Churches of Syria and Cilicia, commissioned to go up to Jerusalem on the same errand. Even without the presence of the parties last mentioned, however, any ecclesiastical assembly or synod in which the whole body of the twelve was

---

[1] *Answer to Reasons of Dissent. Breth.* pp. 17-56.
[2] *Ibid.* pp. 86-112, 151.

included might fairly be held, in virtue of their extraordinary and world-wide commission and authority, as representing the universal Church. On the arrival of the deputies in Jerusalem, "the apostles and elders," as we are told, "came together for to consider of this matter." After considerable consultation, and, as it would appear, some difference of opinion on the subject, they gave forth their judgment, and commissioned certain members of the Council to carry the decision to the Churches of Antioch, Syria, and Cilicia.[1] Now, in this narrative we have all the elements necessary to make up the idea of a supreme ecclesiastical court, with authority over not only the members and office-bearers within the local bounds of the congregations represented, but also the Presbyteries or inferior Church courts included in the same limits. *First*, we have the reference of a question of doctrine and duty by the Presbytery of Antioch to a Council or Synod at Jerusalem; for that the Church of Antioch consisted of various congregations under one Presbytery, can be sufficiently proved in the same manner as in the instance of Jerusalem. *Second*, we have deputies sent from the Churches of Antioch, and also, it would seem, from Syria and Cilicia, to take part in the Council. *Third*, we have these representatives or commissioners meeting with the apostles and elders at Jerusalem, and, after due deliberation and discussion, ministerially declaring the law of Christ on the question in debate, and issuing a decree on the point, not only to the Christians of Jerusalem, but to the brethren in Antioch, Syria, and Cilicia. The precedent recorded in the fifteenth chapter of Acts, gives warrant for more than the association in a joint government of the office-bearers of neighbouring congregations,—it proves, in addition, the lawfulness of a subordination of courts in the Christian Church.

Now, there are three different ways in which attempts have been made by Independents to rid themselves of the evidence for Church courts afforded by this example. To these it may be right very briefly to advert.

1st, It is asserted by some Independents, as, for example, by Dr. Wardlaw,[2] that the reference from Antioch was one made to inspired authority at Jerusalem, and not an example of reference to an ordinary and uninspired convention of Church officers;

---

[1] Acts xv. 1-33, 41, xvi. 4 f.
[2] Wardlaw, *Congregational Independency*, pp. 262 ff.

and in support of this view, they appeal to the language of the letter addressed by the Synod to other Churches : " It seemed good to the Holy Ghost and to us to lay upon you no greater burden."

Now, in answer to this objection, it may be remarked, in the first place, that the language of the letter is the very language appropriate to the case of men who were not decreeing anything by their own authority, but ministerially declaring and interpreting the mind of the Holy Ghost as expressed in Scripture, to the effect that no ceremonial observance of the Mosaic law was necessary to salvation. In giving forth their own decision, they were only making the Holy Ghost to speak upon the point, and to decide the controversy. In the second place, that it could not have been an appeal from the Church at Antioch to the inspired authority of the apostles at Jerusalem, is demonstrated by the fact, that the reference was made, not to the apostles alone, but to "the apostles and elders," on the question. In the third place, the same conclusion is established by the consideration, that if the apostles acted on this occasion by inspiration as apostles, it is impossible to account for the decision of Paul himself, who was "not behind the very chiefest" of them, not having been accepted at Antioch as conclusive of the controversy. In the fourth place, that the apostles in this matter did not act as inspired men, but simply as men endowed with the functions and powers of elders in the Church, is proved by the fact of their joining together with the elders and brethren in the Synod at Jerusalem for consultation on the point, and by the " much disputing" which, we are told, preceded the final deliverance of the assembled office-bearers. These considerations sufficiently disprove the idea that the question in dispute at Antioch was referred to the decision of inspiration.

2d, It is asserted by some Independents, that the Synod at Jerusalem was an example of one Church asking advice of another, and not of any authoritative power exercised by a council of office-bearers over the members of the Christian society.

Now, that the very opposite of this is the case, may be easily evinced. First, the very terms of the decision itself indicate authority, and not merely advice, as implied in it: " It seemed good to the Holy Ghost and to us to lay upon you no greater burden than these necessary things." And second, the conduct of Paul and Silas in regard to the decision, and the manner in which they enforced it, sufficiently prove the light in which they regarded it : " And as they went through the cities, they *delivered them the decrees for to keep that were ordained of the apostles and elders* which were at Jerusalem."

3*d,* It is asserted by another class of Independents, that the members of the Church were present and aiding in the decision which was decreed by the apostles and elders at Jerusalem, and that, but for their concurrence in it, it would not have been authoritative. This assertion is grounded on the expressions, " the whole Church," and " the brethren," employed by the inspired historian, as well as the words " apostles and elders," in reference to the parties present at or sharing in the proceedings of the Council.

Now, in regard to this objection, it may be remarked, *in the first place,* that the appeal or reference from the Church at Antioch was made, not to the members of the Church, but, as is distinctly stated, to " the apostles and elders" at Jerusalem. *In the second place,* the decision of the Council, when pronounced and transmitted to the other Churches, is expressly called the " decrees that were ordained of the apostles and elders which were at Jerusalem." *In the third place,* the use of the phrase " brethren" does not by any means imply that the persons so spoken of were no more than private members of the Church; on the contrary, there seems reason to believe that it referred to official brotherhood, and to persons who were brethren in the office of ruling the Church. *In the fourth place,* when it is said, in reference to the arrangement of sending messengers with Paul and Barnabas to Antioch with the letter of the Council, that " it pleased the apostles and elders, *with the whole Church,* to send chosen men," even although we should concede—which it is not at all necessary to do—that " the whole Church" refers to the private members, yet this concession would not prove the assertion of Independents. That the members of the Church were present as auditors in the Council of Jerusalem during the consideration of the question, and that they unanimously concurred in the decision come to, is a very probable circumstance. And the expression of this concurrence in the language of the inspired narrative, when, it is said, it pleased the whole Church along with the apostles and elders, is not in the least inconsistent with the other fact, so distinctly proved, both by direct statement and by implication, that the decision was " the decree of the apostles and elders," enacted by their authority as office-bearers in the Church.[1]

Such is the evidence afforded by the history of the Synod at Jerusalem for the lawfulness and right of association among the office-bearers of the Church, for determining controversies of faith and matters of government. There are other passages of Scripture which give warrant for the same thing, although furnishing no example so detailed and particular of Synodical association. We have an example of Presbyterial action in the sixth chapter of the Acts, when we are told that the whole college of the apostles—not one or other acting singly and apart, but all the Twelve as a court of office-bearers associated together—took steps for the ordination of deacons in the Church at Jerusalem.[2] We have another example of Presbyterial action in the thirteenth chapter of Acts, when we are told that in the Church at Antioch the office-bearers united together with prayer and fasting, and the imposition of hands, to ordain Paul and Barnabas to the mission among the Gentiles.[3] We have another example of Presbyterial action in the twenty-first chapter of Acts, where it is stated that, on his return from his labours among the Gentiles, Paul went up to Jerusalem, and in a meeting of the presbyters of the Church there, rehearsed what God had wrought among the Gentiles through his ministry, and that they, as a Church court, instructed the apostle to comply with certain Jewish purifications, in order to accommodate himself to the feelings and prejudices of the Jewish converts.[4] In these and other instances we have distinct Scripture warrant for the lawfulness of Presbyterial association, and sufficient proof that the scheme of Independency is irreconcilable with apostolic practice.[5]

Looking back upon the whole argument, and upon the positions which we have been led to adopt in the course of it, we see at last the Presbyterian platform rising to our view in all its Scriptural simplicity and authority. Step by step has the

---

[1] *Answer to Reasons of Dissent. Breth.* Lond. 1648, pp. 57–68, 139 ff., 171–178. Cunningham, *Works*, vol. ii. pp. 43–64.

[2] Acts vi. 2–6.   [3] Acts xiii. 1–3.   [4] Acts xxi. 18–26.

[5] *Jus Div. Reg. Eccles.* Lond. 1646, pp. 205–262. Wood, *Little Stone*, etc., in reply to Lockyer, Edin. 1654, pp. 283–386. Brown, *Vind. of Presbyt. Form of Church Gov.* Edin. 1805, pp. 118–127, 222–324, 335–383. Whytock, *Vind. of Presbytery*, Edin. 1843, pp. 5–21, 63–93. King, *Expos. and Def. of the Presbyt. Form of Church Gov.* Edin. 1853, pp. 282–326. Cunningham, *Works*, vol. iii. pp. 545–556; vol. iv. pp. 382–387.

discussion been narrowed, until at length we are shut up to that scheme of Church polity, the form and principles of which we see exemplified in the constitution of the Church to which we belong. It is not in the arrogant claims of the Romish Church on behalf of her supreme Pontiff to single and uncontrolled dominion over the whole body of the faithful, that we recognise the form of that primitive Church in which Peter was an elder among fellow-elders; it is not in the pretensions of a third order of diocesan bishops, with exclusive right to ordain and to rule, that we acknowledge the successors of the Presbytery at Jerusalem or Antioch; it is not in the Church system—or, rather, no Church system—of Congregational Independency, that we see an approach to the model exhibited for our imitation in the apostolic Church, —but in the fashion and principles of a Church which recognises no pontiff and no hierarchy, but a college of elders equal in honour and in place, owning among themselves only the aristocracy of genius and of piety, of learning and of zeal, in which they shall have rule and leadership whom God has graced with the birthright of high gifts and the better heritage of His Spirit; which asserts an authority without a lordship over God's heritage, and makes the office-bearers, not the slaves of the members, nor yet the members the slaves of the office-bearers in the Christian society,—in a Church which unites Scriptural order with the Scriptural freedom, and where Christian liberty is sheltered beneath the shadow of Christ's Crown, do we willingly acknowledge the successor of the Church of the New Testament age.[1]

[1] [" It is no marvel if that nation stand to the defence of their Reformation. Had the Lord been pleased to bless us (in England) with the like at the time of our Reformation, we would not have been so unwise as to make exchange of it for Prelacy; we would have forsaken all things rather than have forsaken it. It is more strange that any should have been found amongst them at any time to speak or to do against their own Church. ' Sed quum omnia ratione animoque lustraris, omnium societatum nulla est gravior, nulla carior, quam ea quæ cum Republicâ unicuique nostrum est. Cari sunt parentes, cari liberi, propinqui, familiares; sed omnes omnium caritates patria una complexa est; pro quâ quis dubitet mortem oppetere, si ei sit profuturus? Quo est detestabilior istorum immanitas qui lacerarunt omni scelere patriam, et in eâ funditus delendâ occupati sunt et fuerunt' (Cicero, De Offic. lib. i. 57). If a patriot spoke so of his country, a citizen so of his republic, what should the Christian, born, baptized, and bred in Scotland, think and say, if he have been born there, not only to this mortal, but to that immortal and everlasting life? No children on earth have better reason to say, We are not ashamed of our mother. It were to be wished that the saying were reciprocally true." —Preface to Alexander Henderson's *Government and Order of the Church of Scotland*, 1641.]

At this point, and with the form and constitution of the Free Church of Scotland full in view, do we terminate our labours, feeling that we have done something in the course of the studies of the session, if we have traced in any measure to their source in the Word of God those Church principles which are embodied and exhibited in the Christian communion to which we belong. It has been my part to exhibit from Scripture the theory of the apostolic Church. It will be your part very soon, standing as you do on the threshold of professional life, to reduce to practice that theory, and, in accordance with the principles which you have heard expounded from this Chair, to discharge the high and responsible functions of office-bearers in the Christian Church. To your hands will be committed in no small degree the delicate and arduous task of fashioning and forming the Church principles which may hold sway over the thoughts and actings of a coming generation, and that, too, at a time in the history of the world when interests, civil and religious, so deeply momentous, largely depend upon the direction and development which these principles may receive. I shall enjoy more than my reward if I have been instrumental in enabling any of you to understand better than before the Scriptural authority and value of those principles which characterize our own Church, or if I may hope that, through the teaching of this Chair, you have in any small degree been better prepared to enter upon the duties that now await you as its guides and office-bearers.

"Pray for the peace of Jerusalem; they shall prosper that love thee. Peace be within thy walls, and prosperity within thy palaces. For my brethren and companions' sake, I will now say, Peace be within thee. Because of the House of the Lord our God, I will seek thy good."

APPENDIX.

APPENDIX A., Vol. I. p. 48.

EXTRACT FROM SPEECH ON THE UNION QUESTION, JAN. 9, 1867.

BEARING OF SCRIPTURE PRINCIPLES ON THE LAWFULNESS AND DUTY OF UNION BETWEEN SEPARATE CHURCHES.

. . . .

I SAY that it is high time for the Assembly and the Church to consider what are the general principles which ought to rule the question of Union or Not Union—looking both to the stage negotiations have reached, and to the course of argument which in some quarters has been adopted in this matter. Both within our Church and outside of it, the cause of Union has in some quarters been too much represented as in some way or other antagonistic to the cause of strict principle, and the one of these pitted against the other, as if the friends of Union were arranged against the friends of sound constitutional views. This has been apparent in various quarters in which discussions have taken place; it is apparent in the spirit and language in which the motion before us has been conceived and expressed. It is Union *versus* the principles of the Church ; or the principles of the Church *versus* Union. The Assembly are pointedly warned not to sacrifice one jot or tittle of the distinctive testimony of the Church in their zeal for Christian Union. This certainly is not the standpoint from which to look at the question ; it is not the point of view from which the real *status quæstionis* can be understood. On the contrary, it is a misstatement at the very outset of the matter in debate. It is not Union *versus* the distinctive principles of the Free Church ; it is Union *as one* of the distinctive principles of the Free Church. The doctrine and the duty of Christian Union are to be found among the fundamental articles and obligations which the Free Church, and indeed every Christian Church, embodies in its religious profession. Do those who are so fond of setting forth the distinctive principles of the Church, as standing out in opposition to union, remember that there is a chapter in the Confession of Faith, entitled, "Of the Communion of Saints?" I believe that every principle necessary to justify, in point of argument, the present position of the negotiating Churches, may be found embodied in that chapter. The great doctrine of the Union of Christian men, and of Christian societies or Churches, is there set forth as being at the root of all true ideas of the kingdom of Christ, and constituting, not so much the distinctive principle of any one Church, as the fundamental principle of all Churches. We are too apt to shape our ideas and arguments on this matter according to the narrow views and feelings forced upon us by our position as separate and detached Churches. But we must take a wider view of the matter, and endeavour to look at it from a higher position. There are historical traditions and practices, there are men and deeds of other days, that are dear to our memories and hearts. But the Church of Christ is older than the Church of Scotland; and the principles of the Church of Christ rise higher than our traditions. If we would learn the question of Christian Union aright, we must go to the fountain-head, and learn what Scripture says on the point.

In the chapter on the Communion of Saints, the Confession itself may be our guide, when it traces up the union of Christian men with each other to their primary union with their common Saviour "by His Spirit and by faith." Because Christians are one with Christ, they are one with each other; the reality of this inward union they are bound to acknowledge by outward fellowship and communion; "they are united to each other in love, they have communion in each other's gifts and graces, and are obliged to the performance of such duties, public and private, as do conduce to their mutual good, both in the inward and outward man."[1] So much for the doctrine and the duty of union and co-operation between individual Christians. But in the next paragraph, the Confession deals with the union of Christians in a society or a Church communion. "Saints, by profession, are bound to maintain an holy fellowship and communion in the worship of God, and in performing such other spiritual services

[1] Conf. chap. xxvi. 1.

as tend to their mutual edification." The great and mysterious fact of the union to Christ of every Christian man issues, *in the first place*, in the doctrine and duty of the communion and co-operation of Christians with Christians; and then it is still more perfectly realized and developed, *in the second place*, in their union into a visible society, which we call the Church. This, according to the Westminster Confession, is the fundamental idea of Church Union. Nothing but the want of opportunity in the providence of God is set forth as a valid reason or ground for separation among Christians,—a want of opportunity, such as distance of place, or difference of language, or other hindrances that make union practically impossible or unworkable. For the Confession goes on to say: "*which communion*, as God giveth opportunity, is to be extended to all those who, in every place, call upon the name of the Lord Jesus."

"*As God giveth opportunity*," this is the only limitation set to the doctrine of Christian Union—the only qualification put on the performance of the duty. *Where God giveth opportunity*, there a Christian man should acknowledge another Christian man, and unite with him in all good works. *Where God giveth opportunity*, there a Christian society or Church should acknowledge another Church, and unite with it in the worship of God and Christian fellowship. It is a great misapprehension, then, of the whole question at issue, to set Christian principle against Christian union, or to argue as if the one conflicted with the other. The union of all Christian men and Christian Churches, so far as God giveth opportunity, is a doctrine not antagonistic to the distinctive principles of the Free Church, but one of its fundamental articles, common to it with every true Church of Christ. It is a doctrine to be held, and a duty to be prosecuted at all times, and by all Churches; and if in any particular instances, separation, and not union, is advocated, most certainly the *onus probandi* rests upon those who defend or seek to perpetuate separation. Union, and not division, is a Christian axiom, lying at the very root of all our ideas of a Christian Church; and neither individual Christians nor Churches can acquit themselves of sin in their separation from other Christians or Churches where Providence offereth opportunity for union, unless upon one or other of those grounds, either—*first*, that it is impossible to acknowledge them as Christian men or Churches; or, *secondly*, that while acknowledging them as such, it is impossible to work together with them without sin. One or other of these two reasons will alone justify separation, where opportunity of union is given ; less than one or other of these reasons will not exempt from sin the man or the Church that chooses division rather than oneness in Christ Jesus.

Take the case of individual Christians. What are the Scriptural principles which ought to determine the lawfulness or unlawfulness, the duty or the reverse, of Christian fellowship between them ? The question that meets me at the outset is this : " Am I warranted and bound to own such and such a man as a Christian brother, and so award to him the recognition and rights of brotherhood ?" I can judge of this only by having regard to his religious profession and character. If in his profession I recognise the fundamental articles of a Christian's faith, and in his conduct a conformity to the main obligations of a Christian's duty, I do wrong to him and wrong to Christ's command if I refuse to acknowledge him as a brother, entitled to all the rights and privileges which such acknowledgment of his Christianity implies. Non-fundamental defects—minor shortcomings in creed or conduct—will not exempt me from this duty of confessing him before men as a Christian brother. But this is not all. Acknowledgment of him as a Christian man lays upon me the obligation of acting towards him, and acting with him, as a Christian man. If he be a Christian, I am bound to seek to co-operate with him in all those duties and undertakings and aims which, as Christians, we have in common. And now the second question meets me: "Are those methods and principles, according to which alone we can meet and work together, lawful and Scriptural ; or does the co-operation necessitate sacrifice of conscience or sin on either side ?" If we can act in unison without compromise of principle on either side, if we can work together without anything wrong in the way or manner of working, co-operation becomes not only lawful, but also an imperative duty. Where God offereth opportunity, nothing but an allegation that there is something sinful in the mode or necessities of the union, is a sufficient absolution from the duty laid upon Christian men to join in the work of Christ. The teaching of reason and Scripture are at one on this point. Even in secular matters, union is strength, when those who work together are agreed as to the way and rules of working. In Christian efforts and objects, union is a duty, in so far as there is nothing unlawful in the manner or principle of co-operation. The command of Scripture is plain : " Whereunto we have already attained, let us walk by the same rule, let us mind the same things."

Take the case, not of Christian men individually, but of Christian societies or Churches. The very same principles and tests apply to Churches as to individual Christians. *First* comes the question of acknowledgment ; *second* comes the question of union and co-operation. As in the instance of the individual Christian, so in the instance of a Church ; the question at the outset is : Are we bound to recognise such and such a body of professing religionists as a Church of Christ, yea or nay ? And this question is solved very much in the same way as it is solved in reference to the Christian man. If in fundamentals the creed and the practice of a religious society are in accordance with the Word of God, we are not only justified, but bound to acknowledge that society to be a Church of Christ. The Westminster Confession lays down the simple and catholic doctrine, that " the profession of the true religion " is the one test of a Christian Church. It tells us that " the visible Church of Christ consists of all those throughout the world who profess the true religion, together with their children."[1] By the possession of this one feature, a Church of Christ is known ; and however far in matters non-fundamental it may come short of our standard of belief and practice,—however much it may differ from us in non-essential points of creed, or government, or worship,—we are bound to recognise and to deal with it as a Christian Church, and not a synagogue of Satan. The Westminster divines discard the *many notes* of the Church usually laid down by Romish controversialists, the object of which is simply to enable them to build up the better the exclusive pretensions of the Church of Rome, and to unchurch all other religious denominations. The one note of the true Church, according to the Confession of Faith, is the profession of the true religion. And when we witness that feature in the case of any religious society, we are not only warranted, but bound in duty to confess such society to be one branch of the true Church of the Saviour.

But we cannot in duty stop here. The acknowledgment of any religious society as a living branch of the living Vine lays

[1] Conf. ch. xxv. 2.

upon us instantly the duty of treating it as a Church of Christ. When God giveth opportunity, the recognition of any religious body as a Church of Christ, without doubt, lays upon us a *primâ facie* obligation to go forward to union and co-operation, unless it can be made out that union and co-operation are impossible without sin on one side or other. And now comes the second question that meets us in the case of union for common objects between individual Christians, and which equally meets us in the case of union for common objects between Churches : Are the methods of co-operation which such union implies,—are the principles and ways of joint working which are involved in it, lawful or unlawful, scriptural or unscriptural ? Can the Churches, and the members and office-bearers of the Churches, work together in union without the sacrifice of conscience or principle on either side ? This is the only question that remains to be answered, in order to determine the matter of duty as to union in those cases where Providence offereth opportunity, and where Churches equally recognise each other as Churches of Christ. If the way and mode of that joint action which union necessitates be in themselves lawful, the union itself must not only be lawful, but a duty; if there is nothing required by such incorporation in the shape of unscriptural sacrifice, either as to belief or practice, then there is nothing to stand in the way of that duty which we owe to the one body of Christ—the duty, namely, of joining ourselves to those who are *His* members as well as we. If, on the other hand, the necessities of action in common which the union of Churches implies should impose on either party a compromise of creed or duty amounting to what is wrong, then the separation between them, although itself implying sin on one side or other, cannot be lawfully healed by means of a union which would bring along with it other sin. The controversy about union can only be settled by the settlement of this question. Where the first point must be taken for granted, where the Churches, as in the present instance, recognise each other as equally branches of the one Church of the Redeemer, and when this acknowledgment *primâ facie* involves in it the fundamental duty of showing their oneness in Christ by the visible realization of it, nothing can be a lawful or Scriptural bar to union, except the actual proof that the administration of doctrine, worship, and government by Churches in common would impose upon ministers or members the necessity of doing what was unlawful and unscriptural. Less than this cannot stand in the way of the positive obligation lying upon Churches of Christ to confess, and to act on the confession, that those who are one with Christ are also one with each other. Considerations of expediency, of feeling, of advantage on one side or other, cannot be listened to when, first of all, a question of duty must be heard. It is time that we were studying the Word of God and the standards of our Church, in order to ascertain the great principles which must rule and decide this question of duty.

So far as I have been enabled to understand the question, these are the general principles which, sooner or later, must, in their application to the case in hand, determine the duty of union between the negotiating Churches. We are justified in taking for granted, on all hands, the mutual acknowledgment, cordially made and responded to, that the religious bodies now contemplating union are true Churches of Christ, living branches of the one living Vine, living members of the one living body of which Christ is the Head. The only question that can be raised is the second of those to which I have adverted,—namely, whether, admitting them to be true Churches of Christ, there is, or is not, in a common action on the part of these Churches, in such a joint administration of doctrine, worship, and government, as the contemplated union implies, anything that would lay upon you as a minister, or myself as a member, a necessity of doing what we believed to be unlawful and wrong? If union implies such a necessity, it is a sin; if union imposes no such necessity, it is a Scriptural duty. This is really the hinge of the controversy about union. I may admit a religious society to be a true Church of Christ. But that religious society may be acting upon principles, and necessitating its office-bearers and members, so long as they are in communion with it, to act on principles which involve what is unscriptural and wrong. Notwithstanding of its grievous defections and shortcomings, I cannot refuse to acknowledge that the Established Church of Scotland is a Church of Christ. But I would not be a minister of that Church, because, by my tenure of office as a minister, I should feel that I gave my consent to its Erastian compact with the State, and was bound, in consequence, to do and sanction things which to me would appear to be sin. I believe that the Church of England is a Church of Christ; but I could not be a minister of that Church, because my position as such would compel me to own a creed that is wide enough to cover both Romanism and Rationalism, and to act under a form of government which I do not find in the Word of God. I believe that the Congregational body is a true Church of Christ, and I honour it as sound in the great truths of the Gospel. But I would not be a minister of that Church, because, as such, I should be forced to act upon principles of Church government, which to me, as a Presbyterian, cannot be made to consist with those Church principles which I recognise in Scripture. In all these cases, it is not because they are not Churches of Christ that I refuse to unite with them, but because union would put me in a position in which I should be compelled to acknowledge or to do what, with my views, I felt to be unscriptural and wrong. Would any such acknowledgment or action, to which my conscience could not consent, be forced upon me in consequence of union being realized between the negotiating Churches? Would a common administration of Word and ordinance, of worship and government, upon the grounds and according to the principles contemplated in the union, force me to own doctrines I could not conscientiously own, or to act in a way that I felt to be unlawful? This is really the question on which the matter of duty depends. . . . . There are no more than two ways in which a Church can meet and refuse the call of duty that summons them to union with another Church, and demands that they shall show publicly their oneness in Christ by actually being one among themselves. If, first, a Christian Church can say that the party to whom they are called upon to join themselves is not itself a Christian Church, then indeed the summons falls to the ground. This is an answer to the call to union which no one in the present instance will venture to prefer. Or, secondly, if a Christian Church can say, if it can show that union for the joint administration of Word and Sacrament, of government, worship, and discipline, in a Church, lays upon ministers and members the necessity of some compromise of truth, or some surrender of duty, then this too would furnish a sufficient answer, and union, however desirable, would cease to be lawful or Scriptural. And the question substantially comes to this: Can such an allegation be truly pleaded? Is there, *in the first place*, any compromise of truth, any sacrifice of the doctrines we believe and hold, any denial of one article of our faith, demanded or expected in the event of the union that is contemplated? Or is there, *in the second place*, under the restraint of such union, any obligation or necessity laid upon us to adopt a line of practical conduct other than we would take without union, or to act in a way unscriptural, and by a rule we would not sanction, if we continued as a separate Church?

Take the first alternative alleged, that union necessitates or implies a compromise or surrender of some truth or doctrine which we at present hold. Is this the case? The only article of belief, the only doctrine, so far as I know, on which the Churches differ, is the one point of the lawfulness or duty in certain circumstances of the civil magistrate endowing the Church out of the national resources. In regard to this one point there is a difference, and a conspicuous one, between the negotiating Churches; and one which no protracted efforts at negotiation will ever get over. But I speak not rashly nor unadvisedly when I say that I find no express mention of the doctrine in the Confession of Faith; and no formal obligation by my subscription to it has laid upon me the duty to receive and profess the doctrine. The formula which I sign at ordination and licence does not bind me to this article of belief; if by some strange reversal of all my opinions I should come to repudiate the doctrine, I could not be libelled for my disbelief. My adherence to the Claim of Right and Deed of Demission is expressly guarded and limited to an approval of the general principles contained in these documents as to the spiritual independence of the Church; and I might hold, honestly and truly, all the articles of the Confession of Faith, and at the same time hold the unlawfulness of State endowment, and my position would not infer any departure from my allegiance to the Church. I believe it would pass the skill of my friend Dr. Guthrie, even though assisted by Dr. Begg, to frame out of the standards of our Church, to which we have sworn allegiance, a libel that would convict me of heresy in repudiating State endowment. I frankly admit that it is a natural *inference* from the principles laid down in the Confession as to the duty of the civil magistrate about religion; but it is no more than an inference, and constructive heresy will not do in a libel for deposition. The strongest proof that the Church of Scotland holds the doctrine of the lawfulness of endowments, as a proper inference from the doctrine of the duty of the civil magistrate, is the fact that she received them.

The reception of the endowment was the practical testimony to her opinion of the soundness of the inference. But the fact that the Free Church has ceased to receive the endowment, is the best of all proofs that the inference is not a necessary or indestructible, an essential and unchangeable, part of her principles. Much has been said as to the desirableness and undesirableness of open questions in reference to this particular doctrine. My answer to all that sort of reasoning is, that the doctrine of the lawfulness or unlawfulness of endowments is already an open question. It is no part of our terms of ministerial communion. It is no condition of admission to office; no man could be libelled for affirming or denying it.

Take the other alternative alleged, that union necessitates or implies a course of conduct, a practical line of action, different from what we would, in our separate state, adopt, and in itself unscriptural and unlawful. This idea can only refer to the practical working of the contemplated union in connection with State endowments. Of course, no union could fetter my freedom to believe, as I have always believed, the lawfulness of such endowments in certain circumstances. No union such as is proposed could require the surrender or compromise of such a belief, either as held by individual ministers and members, or as an inference drawn by them from the public profession of the Church, according to their understanding of what may be deduced from it. But I frankly admit that union with a Church which denies the lawfulness of endowments—not making the denial a term of communion, but the doctrine being actually held by the great majority of her ministers and people—would, not constitutionally, but practically, go to limit my freedom of action on the point within the united Church. Constitutionally we would be free to accept of endowments, acting upon our belief in their lawfulness, but practically we would have our freedom limited under the obligation of the Christian duty of not laying a stumblingblock in the way of a brother. "I will not eat meat while the world standeth, if it make my brother to offend," said the apostle, even at the very moment that he also said that the eating of meat was lawful according to his conscience, and indifferent to him. And so, if the contemplated union should take place, the acceptance of endowments might still, in certain circumstances, be a matter lawful to my conscience, but, under the law that forbids me to

offend the conscience of a brother, I would feel myself practically
forbidden to accept of them.   It can never be a duty in all circumstances to avail ourselves of a right, or to exercise a privilege
which we believe to be perfectly Scriptural and innocent in itself.
On the contrary, it may be a duty for the sake of a Christian
brother to forbear.

But it is useless arguing this point as a question of casuistry,
however much, as I believe, the argument would go to show that,
in a united Church, it can be no sin, whatever a man's belief in
favour of the lawfulness of endowments may be, to refuse to act
upon it.   No man that looks at the signs of the political heavens
but must see, that amid all the changes there, one thing rises
unchangeable above them all, and that is, the certainty that, until
the coming of those better days when the princes of this world
shall be taught from on high to bring their honour and glory to
the Church of the Redeemer, State endowment will never come
except when offered as the price of Church subjection,—offered
upon terms confessed on all hands to be unlawful.   Let the morrow
take care for the things of itself,—let the future, if ever it should
bring with it the offer of State endowments on terms that are not
sinful, decide the question for itself.   The present only is ours ;
and present duty cannot be determined by future possibilities.

And that duty, the duty of Christian union, if it is not nega-
tived by the allegation of truth surrendered, or practical action in
the cause of Christ prevented by the union, is surely recommended
by many considerations of a very urgent kind.   The memory of
the past, the dangers of the present, the hopes of the future, all
point in the same direction.   We can never forget that the three
bodies now negotiating for union are offshoots from the same
stock, and descended from the same parentage ; and that each
more than another still desires proudly to trace back its lineage
to that common ancestry when they had no distinctive existence
as religious bodies, but when all that separates them now was
merged in the higher unity of the one Reformed Church of Scotland.   Can we not forget the interval that has since elapsed, and
remember only what we once were ?   The image of the common
parent is too deeply impressed upon the features of the children
to permit us to forget that they are kindred, and were cradled in
the same home.   The Church of the Reformation with its struggles
against Popery, the Church of the Covenant with its struggles

against Erastianism, are reproduced in none but those very Churches that, with the secret instinct of a hidden brotherhood, are now drawing together and awakening to the consciousness that they are children of the same womb. The divisions of the past, as well as its agreements, may serve to bind us closer now. If it was against the unscriptural grievance of patronage that the Seceders and Relief entered their protest when they separated from the Establishment, that is a protest in which we shall cordially join with them now. If it was against the toleration of deadly error in the Church of Scotland that they testified when they went out from among us, this is a testimony which we shall gladly display because of the truth. If it was against the laxity of discipline that they contended in vain when they abandoned its pale, this is a contention in which we shall not fail to join them. If it was from the tyranny of Erastianism in the Church that they found no escape except by secession, this, too, is a freedom for which we have paid a great price. The separations, as well as the agreements of the past, have paved a way for union now. Add to this the dangers of the present and the hopes of the future, and they point to the like result. If there is to be safety for the divided bands of the Church of God amid the double assault of Romanism and Rationalism, it can only be when the ranks are closed and joined against the common foe; for the only rational hope that we can have of a coming day of triumph to the Church, in the face of the many influences opposed, is in the strength that union would confer. There is much in the past, there is quite as much in the aspect of the present and the signs of the future, that may well teach the duty of Christian union. And if across the divisions and separations of more than a hundred years, hearts long alienated shall be brought near, there will be found in them the pulse of kindred blood. If the dispersed of Israel shall be once more gathered, and the stick of Ephraim shall be joined to the stick of Judah, we may perhaps experience the fulfilment of the promise : " They shall be *one* in mine hand."

APPENDIX B., Vol. I. p. 136.

LETTER ON THE DOCTRINE OF THE CONFESSION OF FAITH ANENT RECOGNITION AND ENDOWMENT OF THE CHURCH BY THE STATE.

7 CLARENDON CRESCENT, EDINBURGH,
16th March 1868.

To ———

MY DEAR SIR,—I have been unwell, and an invalid off my public work, for some short time; and this must be my excuse for the delay in answering your letter, and the brief and hurried way in which I answer now.

I cannot go into detail, and can, without doing so, only advert to the general principles that underlie the difficulties you allude to in your letter. There are two misunderstandings—and hardly anything more than misunderstandings — about words, round which the whole controversy (regarding union between the non-Established Churches in Scotland) at present revolves. First, as to the meaning of *civil establishments;* and second, as to the meaning of *distinctive principles.*

I. The expression " civil establishments" may be used in two senses materially different, as denoting either a Church or profession of religion recognised and set up as the national profession *without* pecuniary endowment; or a Church or profession recognised and set up as national *with* pecuniary endowment. The distinction is not fanciful, nor fabricated for the occasion of the argument. A Church may be endowed without being established (in the sound or restricted sense of the word), as is Irish Presbyterianism with its *Regium Donum.* A Church may be established (in the same restricted sense) without being endowed, as are some of our colonial bishoprics, supported by voluntary contributions. Admit this distinction, and mark how the history of the contro-

versy has never brought it out,—although it was always a real
distinction,—to any practical effect until the present day, and you
will see both the nature of the misunderstanding and its origin.
Voluntaries use, and have been accustomed to use, the word
" civil or national establishment" in its wider sense, as including
civil or national endowment. We, although accustomed before
to do the same, according to the use and wont of our Church as
at all times in the past endowed, have now been taught, as a lesson
of Disruption times, to use the word in its narrower sense, although
claiming in neither sense to be established. Now, which is the
proper or strict theological meaning? Take the Confession as
the test. There is no such expression as civil or national establishment in it. But there is in it the general doctrine, in very
express terms, that the civil magistrate ought to know, recognise,
and obey the Word of God in all matters connected with religion
and the Church, wherever it is in his power, or expedient for
religion and the Church, to do so.[1] We know that it is not in
his power, and that it would not be expedient, in many cases, to
exercise his right or duty to endow. Is there nothing intentional
in the omission of the doctrine of *endowment*, while the doctrine
of *recognition* is so pointedly brought in? We have the general
principle of the duty of the nation and magistrate to recognise
religion and the Church. And why? Because it is, as I believe,
at all times and in all circumstances incumbent on him to do so.
We have not the special application of the principle in reference
to pecuniary support. And why? Because in many cases it is
not his duty, and in others not in his power, to endow. Does not
this show the sense in which the compilers of the Confession
understood the expression " civil establishment," as something
different from the national recognition of a Church, if the expression even came into their heads? And although during two
hundred years the two things have been conjoined in the actual
history of this Church, and the words have been identified in our
experience, yet ought we not now to unlearn the past, and even
to confess that endowment is not necessary to establishment,
taken in its stricter and proper meaning, and that the controversy
about the word ought not to put us wrong as to the true meaning
of the Confession.

[1] Conf. ch. **xxiii.** 2, 3.

Take analogous cases in the Confession,—such as the Sabbath. The general principle is laid down, but not the application.[1] The duty of the Sabbath being imposed by lawful authority, is enforced in all cases. But *what* lawful authority? The Confession does not make the application of the doctrine to the State. The lawful authority imposing it may be the Church, or the master, or the parent. Our Articles of Agreement go beyond the Confession there. (By the way, is not the Sabbath a strict case of an institution of a religious kind being established, but not endowed,—an example of the difference we plead for? It has been *established* by the State as a national religious day; but not *endowed*, as it might have been, in addition, by the appointment of paid guardians or teachers of the duty of Sabbath observance.)

Take the case of an oath.[2] The lawfulness of oaths is affirmed. The lawfulness of imposing oaths by competent authority is laid down. The duty of observing oaths is asserted; but no mention of the State being competent to impose them. This is an inference left to be drawn. Here, again, our Articles go beyond the Confession.

Take the case of marriage.[3] Its competency and obligations are set forth in general principles, requiring it to be contracted and observed in conformity with the Word of God; but no mention of the duty of the State or its right in the question. Here also our Articles go beyond the Confession.

In all these cases one course is followed,—the Confession lays down the general principle or doctrine, and wisely leaves the application to be made out according to times and circumstances, making the one binding, the other not. Does not all this prove that the doctrine of the Confession on the duty of magistrates and States to religion involves, and intentionally involves, nothing more than the general principle of a duty to own and favour it, and leaves open the many and varied applications of the doctrine, which must differ in different cases, and be open to different opinions by different men? To my mind it clearly proves that the meaning of "civil establishments," in the stricter sense, and not in the looser, favoured by our practice of many years, is the

---

[1] Conf. ch. xxi. 5–8; xx. 4.   [2] Conf. ch. xxii. 1–5.
[3] Conf. ch. xxiv.

meaning of the doctrine of the Confession, where, without mention of the word, the obligation of rulers to religion and the Church is laid down. Because a man condemns " civil establishments " in the wide sense as including endowments, have we a right to say he runs counter to the Confession ? I am willing to admit that the difference in the use and understanding of the expression " civil establishments " still remains between us and some Voluntaries, and gives rise to an apparent ambiguity of expression, but not to the effect of a real difference of meaning. It crops out in one case when the phrase is used in their Distinctive Articles. But a proper exegesis of the passage can explain it, and no wise man would found a charge of difference of things upon a difference of words. Ask one of the old Westminster divines in what sense the phrase " civil establishment " expresses the doctrine laid down in the Confession, and neither falls short of nor goes beyond it, and he would at once answer: In the restricted sense of recognition without endowment.

II. But there is another misunderstanding in connection with the expression " distinctive principles," as if Unionists were willing to surrender something essential to a Church, or at least to our Church. " A distinctive principle " may mean either what is distinctive of the Church, in the sense of being a principle essential to office or membership within it, or, without being necessary to office or membership, what distinguishes it from other Churches. It is in the former sense alone that it can be truly or properly surnamed distinctive, or, in other words, fundamental. The lawfulness of endowment is no term of office, and hence not, properly speaking, distinctive. Nothing, indeed, but what is laid upon me by oath of office can be such, or, in other words, nothing but what I have engaged to believe as doctrine, and to observe as practice, by the conditions of entrance. The doctrine is limited by the bounds of the Confession ; the practice restricted by the obligations of the Formula,—embracing, over and above the doctrine of the Confession, the Directory for Presbyterian government and uniformity of worship. There is much beyond this that, in a loose and popular sense of the word, may be called distinctive of our Church. An Act of Assembly, or a series of Acts, may be called distinctive, but they are not binding on the conscience of one who differs from them ; they are the testimony, for the time being, of the majority, and may be reversed. The history of the Church is distinctive of it in a certain way; but with what exceptions do we receive it, and how few could say Amen to every tittle! Antimillenarianism is distinctive; but we don't libel Dr. ——. The parochial system for hundreds of years was distinctive, and many an Act of Assembly made it imperative as to its provisions; and Dr. Chalmers used to lecture on it as, along with endowment, the distinguishing superiority of the Church of Scotland over Dissent; but we have abandoned both, and no man can rightfully assert that we have abandoned anything essential to our Church. The Confession and the Formula,—these are the tests. Open questions, from the very necessity of the case, must be in every Christian society or Church. Whatever is outside the Confession and Formula must be open. Where no libel would be possible or relevant, *there* is an open question. The declamation we hear as to the abandonment of distinctive principles is a mere misunderstanding as to the meaning of words. Dr. Duncan used to say that the question of Supralapsarianism or Sublapsarianism being the doctrine of the Confession, depended on the position of a comma in one of its sections; and as the points are not binding upon the parties who subscribe, I suppose this remains, as it was I believe intended to be, an open question.

I have written three times as much as I intended in answer to your request. I think you ought to find most, if not all, your difficulties implicitly, if not expressly, touched upon in what I have said.—Yours, etc.,

JAMES BANNERMAN.

[ARTICLES OF AGREEMENT AND DISTINCTIVE ARTICLES OF THE NEGOTIATING CHURCHES, referred to above, as respects the Civil Magistrate.

I. ARTICLES OF AGREEMENT.

I. That civil government is an ordinance of God for His own glory and the public good; that to the Lord Jesus Christ is given all power in heaven and on earth, and that all men in their several places and relations, and therefore civil magistrates in theirs, are under obligations to submit themselves to Christ, and to regulate their conduct by His Word.

II. That the civil magistrate ought himself to embrace and profess the religion of Christ; and though his office is civil and not spiritual, yet, like other Christians in their places and relations, he ought, acting in his public capacity as a magistrate, to further the interests of the religion of the Lord Jesus Christ among his subjects, in every way consistent with its spirit and enactments; and that he ought to be ruled by it in the making of laws, the administration of justice, the swearing of oaths, and other matters of civil jurisdiction.

III. That while the civil magistrate, in legislating as to matters within his own province, may and ought, for his own guidance, to judge what is agreeable to the Word of God, yet, inasmuch as he has no authority in spiritual things, and as in these the employment of force is opposed to the spirit and precepts of Christianity, which disclaim and prohibit all persecution, it is not within his province authoritatively to prescribe to his subjects, or to impose upon them, a creed or form of worship, or to interfere with that government which the Lord Jesus Christ has appointed in His Church in the hands of Church officers, or to invade any of the rights and liberties which Christ has conferred on His Church, and which all powers on earth ought to hold sacred,—it being the exclusive prerogative of the Lord Jesus to rule in matters of faith and worship.

IV. That marriage, the Sabbath, and the appointment of days of national humiliation and thanksgiving, are practical instances to which these principles apply. (1.) In regard to marriage, the civil magistrate may and ought to frame his marriage laws according to the rule of the Divine Word. (2.) In regard to the Sabbath, the civil magistrate, recognising its perpetual obligation according to the rule of the Divine Word, especially as contained in the original institution of the Sabbath, in the Fourth Commandment, and in the teaching and example of our Lord and His apostles, and its inestimable value in many ways to human society, may and ought, in his administration, to respect its sacred character, to legislate in the matter of its outward observance, and to protect the people in the enjoyment of the privilege of resting from their week-day occupations, and devoting the day to the public and private exercises of Divine worship. (3.) The civil magistrate may, and on suitable occasions ought to, appoint days on which his subjects shall be invited to engage in acts of humiliation or of thanksgiving, but without authoritatively prescribing or enforcing any special form of religious service, or otherwise interposing his authority beyond securing to them the opportunity of exercising their free discretion for these purposes.

V. That the Church and the State, being ordinances of God, distinct from each other, are capable of existing without either of them intruding into the proper province of the other, and ought not so to intrude. Erastian supremacy of the State over the Church, and Antichristian domination of the Church over the State, ought to be condemned ; and all schemes of connection involving or tending to either, are therefore to be avoided. The Church has a spiritual authority over such of the subjects and rulers of earthly kingdoms as are in her communion ; and the civil powers have the same secular authority over the members and office-bearers of the Church as over the rest of their subjects. The Church has no power over earthly kingdoms in their collective capacity, nor have they any power over her as a Church. But, although thus distinct, the Church and the State owe mutual duties to each other, and, acting within their respective spheres, may be signally subservient to each other's welfare.

VI. That the Church cannot lawfully surrender or compromise her spiritual independence for any worldly consideration or advantage whatsoever. And further, the Church must ever maintain the essential and perpetual obligation which Christ has laid on all His people to support and extend His Church by freewill offerings.

II. DISTINCTIVE ARTICLES.

Free Church and English Presbyterian Church Committees.	United Presbyterian Church Committee.	Reformed Presbyterian Church Committee.

" As an act of national homage to Christ, the civil magistrate ought, when necessary and expedient, to afford aid from the national resources to the cause of Christ, provided always, that in doing so, while reserving full control over his own gift, he abstain from all authoritative interference in the internal government of the Church. But it must always be a question to be judged of according to times and circumstances, whether or not such aid ought to be given by the civil magistrate, as well as whether or not it ought to be accepted; and the question must, in every instance, be decided by each of the two parties judging for itself on its own responsibility."

" That it is not competent to the civil magistrate to give legislative sanction to any creed in the way of setting up a civil establishment of religion, nor is it within his province to provide for the expense of the ministrations of religion out of the national resources; that Jesus Christ, as the sole King and Head of His Church, has enjoined upon His people to provide for maintaining and extending it by freewill offerings; that this being the ordinance of Christ, it excludes State aid for these purposes, and that adherence to it is the true safeguard of the Church's independence. Moreover, though uniformity of opinion with respect to civil establishments of religion is not a term of communion in the United Presbyterian Church, yet the views on this subject held and universally acted upon, are opposed to these institutions."

" 1. That while friendly alliance ought always to be kept in view as the normal relation of the Church and the State, the question whether, or to what extent, the realization of it, in any given case, ought to be attempted, cannot lawfully or safely be determined without taking into account the circumstances, character, and attainments of both, particularly the degree of unity which the Church has attained, and the extent to which the State has become Christian.

" 2. That while the Church is bound to uphold civil government, founded on right principles, and directed to its appropriate ends, nevertheless, as a public witness for the truth and claims of Christ, it ought to testify against whatever is immoral in the civil constitution, or iniquitous in public policy.

" 3. That when the civil magistrate sets himself in habitual opposition to, and abuses his power for the overturning of religion and the national liberties, he thereby forfeits his right to conscientious allegiance, especially in countries where religion and liberty have been placed under the protection of a righteous constitution.

" 4. That while it is not lawful for the magistrate to grant aid to the Church from national resources merely from motives of political expediency, it is competent to the Church to accept aid from these resources, provided that the terms on which it is given do not involve the Church in approbation of what may be evil in the constitution of the State; but the national resources cannot lawfully be employed for the support of truth and error indiscriminately."

III. STATEMENTS AS TO THE RELATION OF THE SEVERAL NEGO-
TIATING CHURCHES TO THE EXISTING CHURCH ESTAB-
LISHMENT IN SCOTLAND.

By the Free Church and English Presbyterian Church Committees.

By the United Presbyterian Church Committee.

By the Reformed Presbyterian Church Committee.

"It follows, from the preceding articles, that any branch of the Christian Church consenting to be in alliance with the State, and to accept its aid, upon the condition of being subject to the authoritative control of the State or its courts in spiritual matters, or continuing in such connection with the State as involves such subjection, must be held to be so far unfaithful to the Lord Jesus Christ as King and Head of His Church. And upon this ground, in accordance with the history and the constitutional principles of the Church of Scotland, a protest is to be maintained against the present Establishment in Scotland."

"That the United Presbyterian Church, without requiring from her members any approval of the steps of procedure adopted by their fathers, or interfering with the rights of private judgment in reference to them, are united in regarding as still valid the reasons on which they have hitherto maintained their state of secession and separation from the judicatories of the Established Church of Scotland,—as expressed in the authorized documents of the respective bodies of which the United Presbyterian Church is formed,—and in maintaining the lawfulness and obligation of separation from ecclesiastical bodies in which dangerous error is tolerated, or the discipline of the Church, or the rights of her ministry or members are disregarded."

"That the Reformed Presbyterian Church, while not requiring of her members an approval of every step taken by their fathers, yet holds that they had valid reasons for declining to acquiesce in the Revolution Settlement. Accordingly, not merely from the character of the Government as illustrated in its assumption of supremacy over the Church, and its patronage of other ecclesiastical systems, by which dangerous errors are taught and propagated, but from the express terms of the Settlement by which the Scottish Church was established, involving, as they did, a departure in several important particulars from the covenanted Reformation, and a consequent breach of covenant, the Reformed Presbyterian Church is united in regarding as still valid the grounds on which it has hitherto continued in a state of separation from the present Church Establishment in Scotland."

APPENDIX C., Vol. I. p. 148.

NOTE ON THE HISTORY OF VOLUNTARYISM.

The theory now commonly known as Voluntaryism—though the name is by no means a very happily chosen or appropriate one—did not make its appearance in any definite shape before the period of the Reformation, although views of a kindred sort were propounded by some of the Donatists in the fifth century. In Protestant Christendom, doctrines which would now be described as Voluntary were first broached by the Anabaptists in Germany in the sixteenth century. They were taken up largely by the Socinians, the party known as the Libertines in England and Holland, and by many of the sectaries during the Commonwealth. These views were of course contradicted by the positions maintained by all the Reformed Churches with respect to the duty of the civil magistrate to further in all lawful ways the interests of true religion and of the Church of Christ.[1] In England, Voluntaryism was strongly opposed not only by Presbyterians and Episcopalians, but also by Dr. Owen and other eminent Independent writers, as being the opposite extreme from the Erastianism and persecuting tendencies with which they were then called to contend.[2] The former theory, however, gained ground among the Independents after the Restoration, and still

---

[1] [Cunningham, *Works*, vol. iii. pp. 558–569.]

[2] [Thus Owen winds up his discussion on " Toleration and the Duty of the Magistrate about Religion " with two corollaries. " 1. That magistrates have nothing to do in matters of religion, as some unadvisedly affirm, is exceedingly wide from the truth of the thing itself. 2. Corporeal punishments for simple error were found out to help to build the tower of Babel."—*Works*, Goold's ed. vol. viii. p. 206; cf. pp. 381–394, vol. xiii. pp. 509–516. Compare the noble opening of Milton's second Book, *Of Reformation in England:* " It is a work good and prudent to be able to guide one man ; of larger extended virtue to order well one house ; but to govern a nation piously and justly, which only is to say happily, is for a spirit of the greatest size and divinest mettle. . . . Alas, sir, a commonwealth ought to be but as *one huge Christian personage,—one mighty growth and stature of an honest man*," etc.]

prevails very generally in that body, as in most other denominations of English Nonconformists.   In Scotland, in the eighteenth century, Glass and others propounded Voluntary doctrines. They had not, however, much success among Presbyterians until, in the beginning of the present century, they were taken up by the Seceders.   The Voluntary theory has never been embodied in the public standards of any Christian Church.   The history of Voluntaryism in our own country is a somewhat remarkable one.   In 1733 the Secessionists came out on the very highest Establishment principles, believing that they carried these principles with them in a higher and purer form than that in which they were held in the Established Church of Scotland, and seceding on the ground of the abandonment of these principles, along with other acts of defection by that Church.   The immediate *occasion* of the first Secession, as the younger Dr. M'Crie remarks in his Life of his father, was the tyrannical and unjustifiable conduct of the Moderate party which had now risen to power in the Church Courts, and more especially their enforcing of the obnoxious and unconstitutional law of patronage; but the real *object* of Ebenezer Erskine and his associates was to assert and vindicate the ancient constitutional principles of the Scottish Church.   "The Original Seceders identified themselves with the Church of Scotland as she existed in her purer days, particularly during the period of the second Reformation, between 1638 and 1650.   On this era, distinguished as that of the Solemn League and Covenant, they took up their ground, and planted the banner of their testimony.   They not only espoused the principles of the Covenanters during that period, and of the great body of them during the bloody persecution which followed, but were themselves Covenanters, being the only religious body in the country who renewed the national Covenants in a bond suited to their circumstances, and thus practically recognised their obligation as national deeds on posterity.   In short, they appeared as a part of the Church of Scotland, adhering to her reformed constitution, testifying against the injuries it had received, seeking the redress of these, and pleading for the revival of a Reformation attained according to the Word of God in a former period, approved by every authority in the land, and ratified by solemn vows to the Most High."[1]

[1] M'Crie, *Unity of the Church*, Edin. 1821, p. 118.

From this account it will be seen that the characteristic feature of the profession made by Seceders,—that, indeed, which distinguished it from the profession of the Relief, and similar bodies,—was its *nationality*. To say that they were friendly to the principle of national religion, is to say nothing; this was, in fact, the discriminating principle of their association. The whole scheme of reformation for which they contended was in its form national. The moment this principle was abandoned, the main design of the Secession, as an ecclesiastical movement, was lost sight of; when the opposite principle was embraced, that design was reversed.[1]

The first symptoms of hostility to Church Establishments as such began to show themselves among the descendants of the Original Seceders towards the end of the eighteenth century, at a time when the influences of the French Revolution were telling powerfully in many quarters, and wild views of liberty were afloat in the country. Voluntary sentiments took shape gradually in the Secession Church. They came to a head in the early years of the present century. In 1804 the Associate Synod erected into a term of communion a new " Narrative and Testimony," in which their old position as regards national religion and the lawfulness of Church Establishments was abandoned, and those who dissented from it were forbidden, " either from the pulpit or the press, to impugn or oppose the principles stated by the Synod." In 1806, because of their opposition to this change, Dr. M'Crie, Professor Bruce of Whitburn, and Mr. Aitken of Kirriemuir, were deposed from the office of the ministry in the Secession Church. This called forth Dr. M'Crie's *Statement of the Difference between the Profession of the Reformed Church of Scotland as adopted by Seceders, and the Profession contained in the new Testimony and other Acts lately adopted by the General Associate Synod, particularly on the Power of Civil Magistrates respecting Religion, National Reformation, National Churches, and National Covenants,*—a work which may be regarded as, on the whole, the most masterly discussion of the question of civil establishments in existence.[2]

The expulsion of Dr. M'Crie, and those who along with him

[1] *Life of Dr. M'Crie*, Edin. 1840, pp. 42 f. M'Crie, *Statement*, Edin. 1807, pp. 77–108. [Morren, *Annals of the General Assembly*, Edin. 1838, pp. 1–10. Gib, *The Present Truth: a Display of the Secession Testimony*, Edin. 1774.]
[2] *Life of Dr. M'Crie*, pp. 41–146, 438–447.

formed the Constitutional Presbytery, or "Old Light" body, re-moved all check on the spread of the principles, against which they had protested in the Secession Church. Voluntaryism grew apace among Scottish Nonconformists, until at length Wardlaw, Marshall, and others took up the position, that "persecution was involved in the very principle of an establishment," and that "the State, as such, had nothing to do with religion." A notable point in the controversy, excited by these doctrines, is marked by the lectures on Church Establishments, delivered by Dr. Chalmers in the Hanover Square Rooms, London, in the spring of 1838. They were replied to, on the Voluntary side, by Dr. Wardlaw, who read a series of counter lectures on the same subject in Lon-don next year, at the request of the "Three Denominations of Protestant Dissenters in London."

A very general recoil has taken place of late among the ad-herents of the Voluntary theory, from the extreme views put forth by some of its most eminent defenders respecting the civil magistrate's relation to religion and the Church.   Dr. Lindsay Alexander, for example, in his biography of Wardlaw, dissents from his position on this question in a very marked way. "What Dr. Wardlaw has written on the subject of the civil magistrate's office in relation to religion," he says, referring to his lectures in reply to Dr. Chalmers, "is by no means equal to the other parts of this volume. The conclusion at which he arrives is the extreme one of Voluntaryism—viz. that 'the true and legitimate province of the magistrate in regard to religion is *to have no province at all*,'—a conclusion so startling and unwelcome that it had need to be founded on very cogent reasons to command our assent. On what grounds, then, has Dr. Wardlaw rested this conclusion ? In the first instance, on the assertion that Scripture has confined the magistrate's functions within the sphere of civil matters. But has not the lecturer stumbled here at the very threshold ?   If the magistrate have *no* province in regard to religion at all, with what consistency can he be appealed to the Bible, the standard of re-ligious truth and duty, to determine what his proper province is ? Or, if he may be summoned legitimately, as a magistrate, to learn his functions from the Bible, how can it be justly said that he has nothing whatever, as a magistrate, to do with religion ?

"But, waiving this, let us come to the question, What saith the Bible in regard to the functions of the civil magistrate ?   On this point Dr. Wardlaw is far from being explicit. He asserts the *incompetency* of the civil magistrate to decide for his subjects what is religious truth, and constantly affirms that all that is properly religious lies between God and the conscience. I presume that no modern advocate of civil establishments of religion will deny or question either of these positions. All he will plead for is, that the magistrate may lawfully, for the great ends of civil government, provide the means of religiously educating the people—a claim which neither interferes between the conscience of the people and God, nor assumes to determine for the people what is truth in religion. It would not be fair to represent men of Dr. Chalmers's way of thinking on this subject, as if they contended for the right of magistrates to compel men to believe, or pretend to believe, a given set of dogmas, when all they assert is the right of the magistrate to make provision for the religious instruction of the community, leaving it free to all to accept that instruction or not, as they please. On this point, I frankly confess I cannot see how the negative can be maintained, as an abstract general proposition, without reducing the functions of the civil magistrate to those of a mere policeman, set up to enforce the will of the majority. If governments are to proceed on the recognition of moral distinctions, if they are bound to enact only what is consistent with moral truth, if, above all, they are to receive and obey the Bible, and recognise its declarations in their enactments, then they not only have a province in regard to religion, but it very greatly concerns them that their subjects should be instructed in those principles which can alone enable them to appreciate aright such legislation. Moreover, if government is to be regarded in the light of a trust reposed in the hands of the magistrate for the welfare of the community—not merely their protection from robbery and wrong, but their *welfare* in the healthy development of all their faculties of social improvement— it is surely most unreasonable absolutely to forbid the magistrate to use the only means by which such a result can be certainly attained. Of all tyranny, the most exorbitant is that which ties a man to an end, but refuses to him the means by which alone that can be reached—not only commanding him to make bricks without supplying him with straw, but forbidding him to use the straw even when he has managed to procure it. Of this worse than Egyptian tyranny are those, theoretically, guilty, who would bind the magistrate to secure the order and well-being of the community, and yet forbid him, under any circumstances, to provide that education by which alone this end can be effectually secured.

" It is usual with those who take the extreme views adopted by Dr. Wardlaw, to lay stress on the question, Who is to determine what is to be taught for religious truth to the community? There is, no doubt, a difficulty here; but it is one which surely has been immensely exaggerated, both theoretically and practically.   In this country the omniscience of Parliament is as much a principle of government as its omnipotence,—in the modified sense, of course, in which alone such language can be used of any human institution.   We proceed continually on the assumption that there is nothing on which Parliament may not arrive at full and accurate knowledge.   On all questions of science, of art, of business, of diplomacy, of warfare,—on questions of medicine and metallurgy, of engineering and education, of manufacture and painting,—on every subject, in short, that concerns the welfare of the community, Parliament is continually called to pronounce decisions involving the assumption of all but infallible capacity for determining the truth.   It will not be easy to show why a body, in whose powers of ascertaining truth in all other departments of knowledge the community implicitly confides, should be pronounced helplessly incompetent in the department of theological truth.   It is no doubt possible that Parliament may err in the opinions it may authorize to be taught to the people; but the probability of this is not so great as to render it incompetent for Parliament to make the attempt; and if liberty be left to all who choose to dissent from the opinions taught by the Government teachers, every freedom seems to be secured to the community, which, on grounds of general policy, can be required.

"The only secure and consistent line of argument on this subject seems to be that of those who admit that the magistrate, as such, *has* to do with religion ; who, on the ground of this, summon him to the Bible, that he may learn there what true religion is, and what he may legitimately do in regard to its interests; who admit his obligations to provide for the moral and religious education of the community ; but who stipulate that, as in this the Bible is his authority, so he shall scrupulously refrain from infringing upon any of its prescriptions, or on any of the rights conferred by it on the people of Christ, in the scheme and apparatus of religious education he sets to work." [1]

It is evident that there is a very marked and important difference between these views as to the province of the civil magistrate regarding religion, and those which deny him any province at all in that respect, even although Dr. Wardlaw's distinguished biographer still objects to Church Establishments on various grounds. The majority of modern Voluntaries seem in substance to hold Dr. Alexander's position,—a position very much sounder, and in many respects more tenable, than that of Dr. Wardlaw, but one which can hardly be said to be logically compatible with Voluntaryism at all.

[1] Alexander, *Memoirs of Dr. Wardlaw*, Edin. 1856, pp. 383–386.

APPENDIX D., Vol. I. p. 171.

EXTRACTS FROM ARTICLE ON CHURCH AND STATE.

'Connection between Civil and Religious Liberty — Things Civil and
Spiritual known to English Law—Civil Interests affected by Spiritual
Proceedings—Remedy in Cases of Civil Wrong—Independence of the
Church not founded on Contract.'—*North British Review*, No. lxiv. 6.

[After referring to the three great types, to one or other of
which all existing or past examples of the connection between
Church and State may be ultimately reduced,—the Ultramontane, the Erastian, and that which exhibits "a co-ordination of
powers with a mutual subordination of persons,"—the author
proceeds :—]

The notion of the identity of the spiritual and temporal
powers, or at least the practical denial of their separate and
essential independence, has been exemplified in various ways.
In times before the introduction of Christianity, and in our own
day among nations where Christianity is unknown, we very commonly see the king and the priest to be one and the same person ;
and because usually he is much more of the king than the priest,
and because the civil element throughout the nation is more largely
developed than the religious, the temporal power lords it over the
spiritual.   But a similar result may be brought about in a Christian nation by a process somewhat different.   Among a professedly Christian people, where the subjects of the commonwealth
are, to a large extent, numerically identical with the members of
the Church, and where the laws of the State are more or less bor-
rowed from Christianity, there is a danger that the real difference
between Church and State may be overlooked, from the idea that
they are merged into each other, and that the two are become
virtually one.

[The theories of Hooker, Arnold, and Warburton are then
referred to as exemplifying this, and alike proceeding on the

fundamental assumption, " that it is possible, without destroying
the proper idea of the Church on the one hand, or of the State on
the other, more or less to identify them in their nature, functions,
authority, or objects; as if it were competent for the State to do
the work of the Church, or the Church to do the work of the
State."—See above, vol. i. pp. 107-111.]

Nor is the fundamental idea different when the opposite
extreme is asserted, and the State is subordinated to the Church.
The Romanist theory of the supremacy of the spiritual over the
temporal, whether advocated in the shape of a direct authority or
an indirect, ultimately rests upon the same doctrine, that they are
one and not distinct powers, at least in respect of the sphere that
they occupy, and the jurisdiction they possess.   The superiority
claimed by the Church over the State is a superiority in authority
employed about the same matters, and dealing with the same
persons or things; it is the assertion of a right on the part of the
spiritual body to control the civil magistrate in civil functions in the
same way, or to the same effect, that he himself exercises control
over his inferior agents in the State; and it can be logically defended on no other supposition than the pretence that the Church
originally possesses, or subsequently acquires, an office and jurisdiction the same in kind as those which the State exercises in
temporal concerns.   To the extent, then, that such supremacy is
asserted by the Church, it is a claim to the possession of the same
sort of power that belongs to the State, but in higher degree than
the State enjoys it,—the spiritual society thus taking to itself the
office of the political, and borrowing its character when converting spiritual sentences into civil penalties, or giving to excommunication the force and effect of a temporal punishment.   It is not
necessary, on this theory, that the Church, as supreme over all
persons and causes, should employ the same agency for doing its
temporal behests as for doing its religious duties; it may commission civil officers for the one description of work, and ecclesiastical officers for the other; it may have its orders of secular
agents distinct from its orders of religious servants.   But they
are servants equally of the same master.   The duties they perform are done in the name of the one authority that holds in its
hand both the spiritual and the temporal supremacy; and the
departments in which they labour, whether in sacred or secular
offices, are not essentially separate or distinct, but are merged

together under the unity of one common and ultimate jurisdiction. The doctrine of the subordination of the State to the Church, and the opposite extreme of the subordination of the Church to the State, alike proceed on the idea that their peculiar powers and functions may be accounted of the same kind, or in reality identified.

But, can this theory of the essential identity or sameness of Church and State, in their nature and functions, find countenance or support in Scripture principle, or reason, or experience? or is it not expressly and conclusively disowned by them all? Is it possible, on the one hand, without the sacrifice to that extent of the true idea of a Church, to conceive of it borrowing or usurping the compulsory powers that belong to the State, and employing them for the purpose of establishing a particular religious creed, or enforcing the order of Divine worship, or giving to its spiritual decisions command over the conscience and heart? or is it possible, on the other hand, without the sacrifice to that extent of the true idea of a civil government, to imagine it clothing itself with the character of a Church, and using the spiritual machinery of persuasion and instruction and admonition, in order to punish crime and protect property, or to enforce the national arrangements for internal taxation, or for defence against foreign attack? Do the objects contemplated by a Christian Church admit of their being accomplished and secured by any power or authority similar to that which is proper to the State? or do ends which the State has in view suggest or allow the use of authority identical with that which the Church employs, to tell with effect on the understandings and consciences of men in their relation to spiritual things?

We are advocating no narrow theory of civil government, as if it had nothing to do with anything beyond the secular relations of life, and had no interest or office in what concerns man in a higher capacity. We believe that there can be no sound view of political government which restricts it to the care of man's body and bodily wants, and does not assign to it a wider sphere, as charged in a certain sense with the advancement of human well-being, in its moral as well as its material interests. But still there can be no doubt that the State was instituted, in the first instance, for other purposes than that of promoting the Christian and spiritual good of its subjects; and that however much the acts of government, if wisely shaped, may be fitted, and even intended, indirectly to advance that object, yet, in its first and essential character, it is an ordinance for civil, and not for religious objects. As little would we assert that it is necessary to regard the spiritual society as strictly limited to the one object of seeking the Christian well-being of its members, and as sublimely indifferent to all that affects their temporal or social condition. There are blessings even belonging to this life which the Church can scatter in its way, even while we hold that the first and distinctive object for which it was established is to declare to men the promise of the life that is to come. In the case of the State, it may indirectly, and by the use of its proper power as a State, promote to no inconsiderable extent those moral and religious ends which it is the Church's distinctive duty to work out; but still political government is a civil institute, and not a spiritual. In the case of the Church, it may, by the indirect influence which it puts forth upon society, become the right hand of the civil magistrate in repressing wrong, and the best instrument for advancing the temporal prosperity of the State; but still it is a spiritual ordinance, and not a civil. It is impossible for the State to do the work of the Church; nor is this its primary object. It is equally impossible for the Church to do the work of the State; nor can this be alleged to be its design, except in a very secondary and subordinate sense.

In arguing for the original and essential distinction between Church and State in their primary character and functions, we do not feel at all embarrassed in our argument by the position, which we believe to be defensible on grounds both of reason and Scripture, that there can, and ought to be, a friendly connection between the two. It were beside our present purpose to enter upon the question of the lawfulness or unlawfulness of civil establishments of religion. But this much we may say, that no intelligent advocate of the lawfulness of such connection will ever seek to rest his argument on the denial of the original and essential independence of Church and State, or the possibility of a partial surrender of it on either side. On the contrary, the Scriptural alliance of the spiritual and civil powers is possible, only because they are originally and unalterably different. If the Church and State could properly be identified or merged into each other, there could be no such thing as an alliance, rightly so called. It is because they are different in their primary characters, in the provinces that they occupy, in the powers which they administer, in the membership that belongs to them, that they can unite without confusion, and be allied without danger to each other. To use a form of words, better known in the controversies of other days than of our own, there is much which the civil magistrate may do " circa sacra," without involving him in the charge of interfering " in sacris,"—much that he may do, when in friendly alliance with the ecclesiastical society, to promote its spiritual objects, while he is in no way departing from his own sphere as the minister of the State, or assuming the character or powers that belong to the Church. But to whatever extent the State may go in thus aiding the objects and furthering the views of the Church, any alliance between them, when contracted on Scriptural terms, presupposes that the parties to it are, in the first instance, independent and distinct. It is founded on the idea that the two societies that enter into connection are alike possessed previously of powers of separate existence and action,—each complete within itself for its own purposes and objects, and sovereign in the ordering of its affairs ; and each capable of acting apart as well as in concert, and only consenting to be allied on terms that do not compromise, but rather acknowledge, their independence. The advocates of civil establishments of religion, so far from being called upon by the necessity of their argument to admit the essential identity of Church and State, can never truly or rightly state it without laying down the proposition that the two are fundamentally and unchangeably unlike. It is only two societies self-acting and self-governed between whom it is possible that an alliance should be entered into at all ; and it is only two societies having powers unlike, occupying departments unlike, and dealing with matters unlike, between whom it is possible that an alliance should be entered into safely.

The doctrine, then, that the State is bound to promote the general well-being of man, moral as well as material, and that the Church cannot be indifferent, amid the higher interests committed to it, of his civil and social rights, does by no means involve the conclusion of the sameness in nature and function of the civil and spiritual powers. Neither does the further doctrine of the lawfulness of some kind of alliance between the two imply, that in entering into connection, any one of them abandons its own personal or corporate identity, and becomes lost in the other.

But what is the light that Scripture casts on this sameness or diversity of Church and State? Does it afford any justification of the theory, that the Church is nothing other than the State acting in the matter of religion, or the State nothing other than the instrument of the Church, ruling in civil as well as spiritual affairs? Is there any warrant from such a quarter for saying that the Church is no more than one department or organ of the State, limited to a special class of State duties and objects, or that the State is but one amid the orders of ecclesiastical servants, to do the bidding of the Church with a view to Church ends? On the contrary, we have Scriptural authority for asserting that the Church and the State differ in all that can make them two societies, and not one, being fundamentally and unalterably distinct even in a Christian community, and in the case of a friendly alliance. They differ in their origin, in their membership, in their powers, and in the matters with which they have to deal.

They differ in their *origin*,—a truth illustrated historically, in the fact that civil government, in one form or other, has always existed, whether the Christian Church was known or unknown, and has been acknowledged to be valid and lawful among all nations, whether Christian or not; and a truth founded on the general principle, that the one is an ordinance of nature, and the other an ordination of grace,—the one the appointment of God as the universal Sovereign, the other the appointment of God as Mediator, or the special Ruler and Head of His own people. Whether the community be Christianized or not, civil government is a natural ordinance, not dependent for its power or validity on the religion of ruler or subject, and not more binding in a nation of Christians than in one ignorant of Christianity; and hence it is that " difference of religion does not make void the magistrate's office,"—presenting in this respect a contrast to the ruling power in the Christian Church, which is only binding within the circle of those who have voluntarily submitted themselves as professing Christians to its jurisdiction.

They differ in respect of their *members*,—a fact exemplified most palpably in the case of a State ignorant of Christianity, or hostile to it; where the Christian Church consists of a society of individuals, perhaps small in number in comparison with the rest of the nation,—persecuted by the magistrate, or, at best, only tolerated as a necessary evil, detached from the general com-

munity, and acting apart ; but not less really true in the instance
of a Christianized State, within whose borders all, or nearly all,
conform to a profession of the national faith. Even in those
cases in which the Church becomes co-extensive with the commonwealth—and the two may be regarded as almost numerically one
—the distinction between the citizen and the Christian, the member
of the Church and the subject of the State, is never lost, and
cannot be disregarded. The conditions of membership in the
two societies are fundamentally unlike. A man may be an outlaw
from civil society, or suffer for treason to the State, who is yet
welcomed to the privileges of the Church, and reverenced not
only as a member, but as a martyr here ; and a man excommunicated by the spiritual powers may suffer no loss in his rights as a
citizen. It is not in his character as a subject of the common
wealth, but in his capacity as a professing Christian, that a man
becomes a member of the spiritual association ; and his rights
then give him no title to political privileges, and no protection
from the consequences of the legal forfeiture of the status and
immunities of civil life. Two societies constituted upon conditions
of membership so dissimilar, cannot themselves be alike, but must
remain essentially distinct, even when approaching most nearly to
numerical identity.

They differ in respect of the *powers* they possess and employ
to effect their objects. Here, too, there is a contrast between
them that admits of no reconciliation. To the civil government
belongs the power of the sword, or the prerogative of capital
punishment, involving in it a right to employ all those lesser
penalties affecting the person or property or temporal rights of
men which are included under the greater, and which in their
varied measure and severity are all necessary, and not more than
sufficient, to secure the order and peace and well-being of civil
life. To the religious society belong, on the contrary, the weapons
of a warfare, not carnal but spiritual,—the armoury supplied by
truth and right, the obligations of conscience, and the fear of God,
—the power that is found in a sense of duty to be done, and wrong
to be avoided,—the influence that springs from spiritual instruction
and persuasion and censure,—the force that there is in the doctrine
of a world to come,—the command over the understanding and
hearts of men that is given by speaking to them in the name of
Heaven, even under the limitation of speaking nothing but what

Heaven has revealed,—the mighty authority to bind and loose the
springs of life and action in the human heart, by appealing to its
feelings in the word of an ambassador for Christ, even while
rendering to all the liberty which the Bereans claimed of asking
at His own Word, whether these things be so or not. Powers
so different and so strongly contrasted cannot reside in the same
governing body, without neutralizing each other. The one ends
where the other begins; the same hand at the same moment
cannot grasp the twofold prerogative; the Church, without the
sacrifice of its character and influence as a Church, cannot arrogate
the powers of the State, and the State, without foregoing to that
extent its position and action as a State, cannot enter upon the
functions of the Church.

They differ in regard to the *matters* with which they have
to deal. Here, likewise, there is a separation between the body
spiritual and the body political, which forbids approximation.
The objects immediately and directly contemplated by the State,
in the proper exercise of its coercive authority, terminate in the
present life, and are bounded by that earthly range which fences
the territory of the civil ruler when he deals with the administration of justice between man and man, the preservation of peace
and social order, the advancement of public morals, the security
of person and property and temporal right. Whatever indirectly
a Christian government may feel to be within the sphere of its
duty or power when looking upward to higher interests, it is plain
that its first and distinctive office is to make men good subjects,
and not saints; and with that view, to employ all the civil aids
and instruments that secure such an end. On the other hand,
the direct and immediate object of the Church is the salvation of
souls,—the making of men not so much good citizens as true
Christians; and with this aim, it has to deal, not with the lives
and properties, but with the understanding and consciences of its
members, to minister to the inward rather than to the outward man, to regulate the motions and springs of human actions
within, and to turn and sway the heart out of which are the issues
of obedience and life. The truth of God, and the conscience of
man, the claims of Divine law, and the responsibilities of human
guilt, the ruin by sin, and the salvation of the soul by grace,—
these are the things with which the Christian Church is primarily
conversant; and not any of those questions of civil or pecuniary

right, in the determination of which the magistrate of the State is competent to sit as a judge or a divider. The subject-matter in the one case is spiritual, involved in man's relation to God; in the other case it is temporal, belonging to his relation as a citizen or member of the commonwealth.

Such, without doubt, are the grounds in Scripture principles for the necessity of drawing a line of distinction, broad and deep, between Church and State, and for refusing to regard them as either originally one, or as capable of being subsequently identified. The admission of such a total distinctness, when intelligently made and consistently carried out to its logical consequences, reaches much farther than to a condemnation of the extreme views on either side, that would assert that the Church is no more than the religious department of the State, or the State nothing other than the civil servant holding office from the Church. There may be a very general acknowledgment of the Scripture principles, which forbid us to regard the spiritual and temporal societies as the same in themselves, or in the duties to be discharged by them; while, at the same time, the independent power in each, to regulate its own proceedings, to apply its own rules, and to govern its own members, exempt from all foreign control, may not be held as involved in the acknowledgment. And yet the separation between Church and State so strongly asserted in Scripture can be nothing more than nominal and illusory, if it admits of the one party to any extent, however inconsiderable, occupying the province of the other, and stretching forth its hand to control its neighbour's affairs within its neighbour's borders. The distinction between them as to powers and functions must be very much a distinction without a difference, if the authority of the Church is to any visible effect a valid authority with the servants and in the proceedings of the State, or if the commands of the State can carry lawful force and obligations, in however small a degree, with the members of the Church, in the arrangement of spiritual concerns. A line of demarcation between the territory of the spiritual and the temporal is no line at all, if it can be crossed at any point by either party, for the purpose of taking possession of ground fenced off by such boundary, for the exclusive occupation of the other.

There can be no doubt that the principle so plainly laid down in Scripture, of the entire separation between the religious and political societies as to the nature of their powers, and as to the subject-matter of their administrations, legitimately and inevitably carries with it the conclusion, not only that each is complete within itself for its own work and its own objects, but also that each is independent of any control not lodged within itself, and brought to bear from any foreign quarter upon its internal arrangements. To assert that the spiritual rulers can competently exercise power in the department of the State, in the way of depriving kings of their civil estate, and absolving subjects from their civil allegiance, of visiting men, by means of its sentences, with civil pains or the forfeiture of civil rights, is nothing else than to allege that the authority of the Church is of the same kind as that which belongs to the State, and that it rightly deals, not with different, but with identical matters. To assert, on the other hand, that the civil magistrate must have the right of effective interference in the affairs of the Church, in the way of keeping ecclesiastical courts and officers within the line of their duty, and reversing and controlling their proceedings, is, in like manner, nothing else than to affirm that the power of the State is of the same nature with that which the Church administers, and that it belongs to it to judge in the same subject-matter in which the Church is appointed to judge. An exemption on the part of the State from spiritual control in the management of its own affairs, is necessarily implied in the very proposition that the authority which would interfere is spiritual, and that the matter interfered with is not. An exemption, in like manner, on the part of the Church from civil control in managing its own affairs and governing its own members, is necessarily involved in the very idea that the authority pretending to regulate the Church's duties is civil, and that these duties are not.

But the argument may be slightly varied. We have said that, admitting the primary and indelible distinction between them, it is impossible for the Church to assume authority over any department of the State, and, *vice versâ*, impossible for the State to assume authority over any department of the Church; because this, in either case, would amount to an assertion that in so far their powers were not different, but are one and the same. But with no less truth it may be argued, that if it were possible to do so, if it were possible for the civil power to surrender more or less of its proper responsibilities, and for the Church to assume

them, or for the Church to abandon certain classes of its obligations, and for the civil magistrate to take them up, the result
would only be, that to that extent they would deny their own
character, and divest themselves of the peculiar functions which
make them what they are,—as the one the public ordinance of
God for temporal, and the other His public ordinance for spiritual good. By the sacrifice of its proper functions, and the con-
signment of them into the hands of the spiritual rulers, the State
would to that extent forfeit its character as a State, and assume
the mongrel form of a politico-ecclesiastical corporation. And no
less, by divesting itself of its distinctive responsibilities and duties,
and by abandoning them to the civil magistrate, the Church
would in so far renounce its claim to be accounted a Church, and
be contented to take up the equivocal place and character of a
semi-religious and semi-political society. It may be a question of
casuistry, not easily answered, at what time in the process by
which its essential features are lost or obliterated through the
sacrifice, one after another, of its powers of life and action, the
Church and the State must cease to be regarded as such. The
living man may suffer the amputation of limb after limb, and the
paralysis of member after member, from the hand of the surgeon,
or by disease, and live on still ; but however long the process
may be protracted, and the result delayed, in the end it is fatal.
And so it is with the body politic or spiritual. The " States of
the Church," in their unhappy position of incorporation with the
Romish See, would hardly come up to any true definition of the
ordinance of civil government. And there are Churches secu-
larized under the control of an Erastian supremacy which can
hardly be called the body of Christ.

We have dealt with the question as on the footing of the
Scriptural distinction drawn between Church and State. But
this distinction rests on no positive appointment of Scripture,
but on a deeper foundation, apart from Scripture altogether, and
forces itself upon our notice and convictions independently of any
arbitrary definition to be found in the Word of God,—of the ordinance of the Christian Church on the one hand, or of civil government on the other. The argument, then, for the essential difference
and mutual independence of the spiritual and temporal powers may
be placed on a wider basis, and bring out in a manner more
unequivocal still the freedom from foreign control, which neces-

sarily belongs to each when dealing with its own matters, and
ministering within its proper walk of duty. The lines traced
deeply and indelibly between the spiritual and the civil element in
human life, and which divide into two classes, not to be confounded,
what belongs to God and what belongs to Cæsar, appertain to the
very constitution of things. They have been drawn as they are
drawn by the hand of nature; and Christianity does no more
than adopt, as it found, them,—adding the sanction of revealed
authority to the light of nature, and giving clearer expression and
fuller effect to a distinction known before. The independence of
Church and State is no pet theory of divines, drawn from an
artificial system of theology. The difference between the kingdom
of God and the kingdom of the world—between the sacred and
secular element in human affairs—is not due to Christianity at all,
although it stands in bolder relief, and carries with it a more un-
mistakeable obligation in the teachings of Christianity. But the
difference itself is founded in nature; and the universal and undying belief in the distinction, is the instruction of natural religion,
even to the most untutored heart. There are but two elements
necessary to develop this thought in every mind—namely, a God
and a conscience; a belief in a supreme moral Governor over us,
and in our responsibility to Him. The man who knows these
two truths, even though he should know little more, knows that
his relations to that mysterious Being are distinct from his relations to his fellow-men; that his obligations to God belong to a
different order, and involve a different authority from any implied
in what is due to his superiors on earth, and that the civil
allegiance owing to the ruler of the people is not the spiritual
service to be offered to the Ruler of all. Such a man may know
nothing of the theory of a visible Church, and of its relations with
the State; he may know nothing even of Christianity, or of any
teaching beyond that of nature; he may know nothing of what
revelation has declared as to the ordinances or manner of Church
worship; but he knows that he cannot render to God what it is
sufficient to render to Cæsar, and that things spiritual are not the
same as things civil. What is this truth, except the very truth
which Christianity has developed into the doctrine of a visible
Church, in its faith and worship and government, distinct from
the kingdoms of men, and independent of their control? The
essential elements of the distinction are recognised by every human

conscience, even though unenlightened by revelation; the disregard of the distinction, and in consequence the subordination to man of man's relations to God, is felt to be a violation of its rights; and with nothing short of the emancipation of the spiritual element from the fetters of human control can these rights be vindicated. We must go much deeper down than Christianity before we can understand the foundation and warrant of the distinction so universally, in one shape or other, acknowledged even by nations ignorant of the Bible. There are truths that have their root and the source of their authority in the eternal relations between the creature and the Creator. And this is one of them. Christianity teaches it; but it is older than Christianity. It is the truth that grows up unbidden and irresistible in every human heart that knows that there is a God, and knows that man's relations to Him are more than man's relations to his king.[1]

It is not needful, then, to turn over the pages of polemical theology of other days, in order that we may see the meaning and be able to defend the doctrine of " the two kings and the two kingdoms," which the Bible would set up within every Christian commonwealth,—each having subjects and jurisdiction, and each sovereign and free. 'The elements of such a theology are found wherever natural religion teaches that there is a God who claims to be the ruler of the human conscience, and to be the only ruler there, even although the man taught darkly and imperfectly in this school should know religion only as a personal thing between his soul and his Maker, and should never have felt its influence or understood its commands, calling him to unite himself to others in a society gathered out of the community at large, and uniting together apart for the purpose of joint or Church worship. There is a mighty interval between the complete doctrine of a visible Church under Christ its Head, as taught in Scripture, and the rudimentary doctrine of natural religion, which, out of the fundamental relationship of man to' his Creator, educes the necessity and duty of worship; but yet there underlies both the same essential idea of the difference between what is due to the Divine Being

[1] " Neque enim cum hominibus, sed cum uno Deo negotium est conscientiis nostris. Quo pertinet illud vulgare discrimen inter terrenum et conscientiæ forum. Quum totus orbis densissimâ ignorantiæ caligine obvolutus esset, hæc tamen exigua lucis scintilla residua mansit, ut humanis omnibus judiciis superiorem esse hominis conscientiam agnoscerent."—Calvin, Instit. lib. iv. cap. x. 5.

and what is due to the civil superior. In vindicating, then, that distinction, and the consequences involved in it, we can afford to dispense with all those articles of theology, controversial or controverted, by which divines, drawing from Scripture their weapons of defence, have sought to explain and vindicate it. We can dispense with much, if not all, that Scripture has taught as to a rightly organized and fully constituted Church, standing in well-defined relationship to Christ as Head, and contrasted in bold relief with the kingdoms of the world. It is not necessary to summon to our aid the doctrine of the Headship of Christ—the keystone of any right Scripture theory of a Christian Church. It is not necessary to recall the distinction between the Church and the civil power, as the one is founded in grace and the other in nature. It is not necessary to call to our help the difference between the two societies in respect of the conditions of membership in each. All these are Scripture doctrines that directly and conclusively bear on the question of the essential distinction between Church and State, and the inalienable independence that is the prerogative of each. But, passing these, let us seize upon the one idea that underlies them all—the relation of nature as well as of Scripture—the dogma that all Churches take for granted, and which all, whether belonging to Churches or not, believe to be true—the dogma that " God alone is Lord of the conscience," and that into that domain the king cannot enter; and we have in this single truth all that is necessary to enable us to draw the line between what belongs to God and what belongs to Cæsar, and to justify the claim for Churches and for individuals of exemption in spiritual things from civil control. That doctrine can stand firm upon the foundation of natural religion and the universal beliefs of mankind, apart altogether from the authority which it justly claims as a truth of Scripture, and from any confirmation it may receive from the Scripture definition of a Christian Church. And that doctrine, rightly understood and applied, is sufficient to vindicate for Christian societies, not less certainly or less largely than for Christian men, freedom in all that pertains to God from the commandments and authority of the State.

For, after all, is not the doctrine of the independence of the Church in matters spiritual but another form of the ancient doctrine of liberty of conscience and the right of private judgment? And is not the claim on behalf of the Christian society to be free as regards its creed, its worship, and its order, nothing more than a demand for toleration? Upon what grounds and within what limits do we claim liberty of conscience at the hands of the civil magistrate in the case of individuals? We claim it because there is one department of human duty and obligation in which man is primarily responsible to God, and cannot therefore, in the same sense, and at the same moment, be responsible to human authority. We claim it because in these matters his obedience is forestalled, and himself the servant by prior right of another Master; and seeing that he cannot serve two masters in the same walk of duty, and that he must be at liberty to obey God, he ought to be made free from foreign interference or control. Beneath the shelter of his previous responsibility to his Maker, liberty of conscience is secured to the meanest citizen of the commonwealth, not because it is a civil right due to him as a citizen, but because it is a more sacred right due to him as the moral and accountable creature of God. Within the sanctuary set apart for worship and for duty to his Creator he can stand erect before the face of earthly rulers, because the representative of earthly rule may not there intrude; another has taken the seat of authority, and a higher obligation decides the question of obedience; and because he is acknowledged to be, in the first instance, the servant of God, the ministers of the State cannot bind him to their service, but rather must loose him and let him go. This is the ground on which we argue for liberty and right to every man to inquire and believe and act in spiritual matters as his own conscience, and not another's, shall dictate,—a claim acknowledged on all hands to be good and effectual in the case of individuals against civil authority, which by coercive power cannot, and likewise against ecclesiastical authority, when by instruction and persuasion it may not, succeed in changing his conscientious convictions. And is there one word in the plea which does not apply with equal relevancy and undiminished force to the case of Churches as well as individuals? Can the argument be regarded as good for each man, taken apart and by himself, in his claims to liberty of conscience, and as not equally good in the case of men joined together in a Christian society, and acting not in their private capacity as individuals, but in their public and official character as members or officers of a Church? In this latter capacity no less than in the former, as Church members

no less than private men, they have to deal with God; in their
conjunct or public proceedings the element of conscience is equally
brought in; the Church, in all departments of its duty and actings,
has especially, or rather exclusively, to do with those spiritual
matters in which its rulers and members are primarily responsible to God, and not to man. And if conscience is a plea which
not only ennobles the exercise of private judgment in the humblest
individual, but casts over it the shield of right and law to protect
it against the encroachments of human power, is it not also an
argument sufficient to vindicate the claims of a Christian society
to be allowed to frame its own creed, and administer its own worship, and regulate its own spiritual order, without in these articles
being subject to State control?

Were the Christian society dealing with questions of mere
expediency, in which an unlimited discretion were allowed, and
in which conscience, strictly speaking, had no share, it might be
otherwise. Were there no law to which ecclesiastical courts and
officers were amenable beyond their own will,—were their rules
and decisions to be considered right and wrong in no higher sense
than the resolutions of a farmer's club, or the regulations of a
society for mutual improvement in sacred music, or the prospec-
tus and by-laws of a copartnery for the manufacture of lucifer
matches,—were their judgments not matters of conscience, and
their acts not done in the name of God, it might comparatively
be a small matter of complaint that some authority foreign to the
Christian society claimed right to review and reverse them. But
in no aspect of them can the Church and the Church's acts be
regarded as set loose from the authority of conscience, and not
under law to Him who is its Lord. On the contrary, if we take
the Scripture account of the matter, we shall be constrained to
confess that, in its three great departments of doctrine, worship,
and discipline, the Church is brought into a nearer relationship
of responsibility to God than any other society can be; and that
its organs for spiritual action and duty are, in a higher sense of
the words, God's *ministers*, than can possibly be affirmed of the
agent or officers of any civil corporation in civil affairs, or of
private individuals in the duties of private life. In doctrine, the
Church can teach nothing but what God has taught, and as He
has taught it; in worship, it can administer no ordinances but
those He has appointed, and as He has appointed them; in dis-

cipline, it can bind and loose only in His name, and by His authority. There is no room left, then, for the interference of its own or that of others in any of its matters. Its office is simply ministerial, and nothing more, charged as it is with the duty, first of ascertaining, and then of carrying into effect, the will of another. In nothing that the Christian society does in the way of teaching truth, or administering the ordinances of worship, or exercising discipline, is there any place allowed for a capricious power; it is tied up straitly, in all the conduct of its affairs, to the necessity of following out its own conscientious belief of what is the commandment given to it to walk by in the particular matter with which it is appointed to deal. In every case, the Church is bound to carry into effect the law of its Head, and not its own; and the demand for liberty to do so, without interference or constraint from without, is simply a demand to be allowed to perform its duty to God as His law has declared, and conscience has interpreted it, and nothing more.

But we may take a lower position than the Scriptural one, in reference to the Church's duty, and yet the argument remain substantially the same. It is not necessary for us to enter upon the debateable ground of the extent to which Scripture may be regarded as furnishing a law for the proceedings of the Church in all its departments of duty,—in questions, for example, of government and worship and discipline, as well as in questions of doctrine. We can afford to dispense with the help derived from what we may regard as the complete and accurate Bible view of a Church of Christ. We believe that there is no principle that is consistent with itself, or justified by the Word of God, except the Puritan principle, that nothing is lawful within the Christian society but what, directly or indirectly, is contained in Scripture; and that Scripture, in its precepts or principles or precedents, furnishes a full and authoritative directory for all that the Church, in its distinctive character as a Church, is called upon or commanded to do in any one department of duty. It is easy to see how such a doctrine exhibits the courts and office-bearers of the Church, in the very peculiar light of the ministers of God, commissioned and required to carry into effect His written Word, in all that they do in spiritual things; and that therefore, in claiming immunity from civil control in such matters, they are only claiming freedom, in their official character, to administer

His law. But it is not necessary for the argument, to press this view. We can agree to waive it. We can dispense with all positions in regard to which Christian Churches, or even Christian men, may be found to differ. It is enough for our purpose that we are allowed to stand on that common ground occupied by all—namely, that the territory of the Church is a spiritual territory, and its duties spiritual duties; that the administrators of the Christian society have to deal with those things of God in, which pre-eminently the element of conscience prevails, and that in these matters their responsibility is, in the first instance, to God, and only in a secondary and inferior sense to man. The plea of conscience is a plea competent to every Church, in the same way as to every individual, when the question is one between the soul and God; and the argument is effectual against the claims of authority of all, except of Him. It is not necessary for us to ask, in the case of such a Church, whether, according to our standard, its doctrine is orthodox, or its worship uncorrupted, or its discipline pure, before we concede to it the benefit which the plea of conscience carries with it, any more than we require to ask whether an individual holds Scriptural views, before we accord to him the right of private judgment and the advantage of toleration. Conscience may err in the case of the society as well as in the case of the individual; and yet an erring conscience is to be dealt with reverently, because it has rights as against a fellow-creature, although it may have no rights as against God. Whatever may be their standing as to Scriptural purity and attainment, Churches, unless they have renounced their spiritual character, and become mere secular copartneries, are entitled to plead that they deal in their proceedings with matters of conscience; and their demand to be let alone by the civil magistrate, in their ecclesiastical duties, is like the claim of the individual for his religious life,—a demand for nothing more than spiritual freedom.

The plea of spiritual independence as regards the Church, and the plea of liberty of conscience as regards the individual, must stand or fall together. They are but two forms of one and the same principle, and they ultimately rest on the same foundation. Grant the right of private judgment to the individual; throw around his exercises of conscience, in regard to religious truth and worship and service, the fence of toleration; and we cannot conjecture even a plausible reason for denying to him the same privilege when, as a Church member, he forms one of a religious society, constituted for the performance of the same spiritual duties. The difference between his private and official character can make no difference, in the eye of right reason, for a difference in the treatment of him by the State. The, in one sense accidental, circumstance of his acting in concert with others in a religious association, can give the civil magistrate no right of interference or control which he did not possess before. Nay, is not union into society of a spiritual kind similar to a Church,—a *necessity* arising out of the fact of the toleration by the State of individuals holding the same religious faith, observing the same religious worship, and performing the same religious duties,— more especially when one of the articles of the faith in which they are tolerated is just the belief of the duty of joining together as a society, for the social and public worship of God? It is impossible not to see that the right of toleration for the one involves in it the equal right of toleration for the other; and if a society for the worship and service of God is to exist at all, it must of necessity have all those powers and rights which are found to be necessary for the existence of every other society. It must have some principles of order for the regulation of its affairs; it must have some kind of organs to express its views and to conduct its proceedings; it must have the power of admitting and excluding members. Laws, officers, and authority over its own members are essential to the existence of the Christian Church, even as they are essential to the existence of any organized society; and without them, no orderly community could be constituted, or at least continue to act.[1] It is not necessary to fall back on the Scripture command, which makes the joint or public confession of God a duty, and not a matter of option, to Christians. It is not necessary to have recourse to the Bible for the appointment of government and rulers and discipline in the Christian society. All these things arise out of the very notion of a number of men holding the same views of religious doctrine, worship, and duty, and knit together among themselves, and separated from the rest of the nation by their common profession. And the toleration of all these things by the State is involved in the fact of toleration of religious men at all; the right to the

[1] Whately's *Kingdom of Christ*, 4th ed. p. 92.

free possession and use of them by a Church, apart from civil
interference, as well as the existence of a Church itself, rests on
the same footing as does the liberty of conscience for the individual; and the denial of the one would lead to the denial of the
other also.

The intimate and indeed inseparable connection between liberty
of conscience in the case of the individual, and the spiritual independence of Churches, can be more than established by reasoning; it can be illustrated historically. There may be a difference of opinion as to whether the idea of religious liberty, as
applied to the individual in all the walks of spiritual life and
activity, has preceded, in point of time, and practically wrought
out, the idea of the same liberty, as applicable to Churches and
societies; or whether the reverse of the process is true, and the
spiritual independence claimed by the Church has been the har-
binger and origin of individual freedom. If we take counsel of
theory alone, we may be ready to conclude, that the urgent craving
for personal rights in religious matters dictated by conscience,
may have given rise to the desire of the same privileges in ecclesiastical societies, and have, step by step, developed itself in all
the relations in which man is found, and made itself to be felt in
his public and official, no less than in his private and individual
capacity. But if we examine the history of human progress and
civilisation, we shall find that the opposite view perhaps approximates more nearly to the truth, and that the separation of the
spiritual from the temporal society, and the doctrine of the entire
freedom and independence of each within its own sphere, have
been the bulwark of the right of private judgment, and the great
instrument for developing the principle and practically extending
the blessings of liberty of conscience. So at least the philosophic
statesman, who has written the history of European civilisation,
has interpreted its lessons. Unlike to many in the present day,
who can see nothing in the principle of the spiritual freedom of
the Church but an approach to the Popish tenet of the subordination of the civil to the ecclesiastical powers, Guizot can recognise
in it one of the prime agents in the introduction and progress of
liberty and right in modern Europe. Speaking of the violence
to which the Church, as well as society at large, was exposed
from the barbarians after the fall of the Roman empire, he
continues : " For her defence she proclaimed a principle formerly

laid down under the empire, although more vaguely: this was the separation of the spiritual from the temporal power, and their reciprocal independence. It was by the aid of this principle that the Church lived freely in connection with the barbarians. She maintained that force could not act upon the system of creeds, hopes, and religious promises — that the spiritual and the temporal world were entirely distinct. You may at once see the salutary consequence resulting from this principle. Independently of its temporal utility to the Church, it had this inestimable effect of bringing about, on the foundation of right, the separation of powers, and of controlling them by means of each other. Moreover, in maintaining the independence of the intellectual world, as a general thing, in its whole extent, the Church prepared the way for the independence of the individual intellectual world—the independence of thought. The Church said that the system of religious creeds could not fall under the yoke of force; and each individual was led to apply to his own case the language of the Church. The principle of free inquiry, of liberty of individual thought, is exactly the same as that of the independence of general spiritual authority with regard to temporal power." [1]

And so has it ever been found to be in practice. The two ideas have advanced or declined together. Liberty of personal thought and action claimed by the member of the commonwealth in opposition to arbitrary power in the State, and liberty of spiritual thought and life claimed by the Church as against the same, may be separated in theory, but can never be far apart in the world, not of speculation, but of fact. The right of private judgment belonging to the citizen can only be seen in its true value and sacredness, when seen to rest on the same foundation of conscience, which gives force and holiness to the Church's demand for freedom in all that belongs to the relations between itself and God. The plea of liberty of conscience, on the part of the subject of the State, can never be asserted as it ought to be, unless it be demanded as that same *liberty to serve God*, in virtue of man's prior responsibility to Him, which the Church, in its claims of spiritual independence, does nothing more than seek to vindicate for itself. Both pleas rest beneath the same shield; and the security of both is found in the primary and inalienable

[1] Guizot, *History of Civilisation*, Hazlitt's Transl. Lond. 1846, vol. i. p. 99.

right of individuals and societies, of private men and public Churches alike, to be exempted from the authority of the State, in order that they may be free to obey God. And hence the love of civil liberty in the breasts of a people has never burned so ardently as when it has been kindled at the altar. Nations and individuals have been free from the yoke of arbitrary power, and have prized their freedom, very much in proportion as religious liberty has flourished along with it; and where the sacredness of the latter has not been felt, and its claims have been practically disregarded, there the former has never extensively, or for any length of time, prevailed. The history of the long contendings for freedom to the Church, both in England and Scotland, pointedly illustrates this truth. Though no friend to the Puritans, and pretending no sympathy with their religious tenets, Hallam, in his *Constitutional History*, has felt constrained to acknowledge that their struggles and sacrifices in behalf of spiritual independence kept alive the flame of political freedom, at a time when the cause was almost lost in England, and that the Puritan controversy has left its permanent mark on our national polity, in the principles of right and liberty which it impressed. And the same thing may be said with equal, if not greater truth, of the fiercer struggle through which religious freedom was won in Scotland. The actors in that struggle were unable to separate between the two ideas of religious and civil independence; their controversy with the House of Stuart, begun and carried on in the name of spiritual liberty, in reality embraced not less the cause of political freedom; their love to each, springing from the same root of reverence for conscience, became one passion in their hearts; and while they were ready to give all for a free Church, they were prepared to sacrifice only a little less for a free State. "Take away the liberties of assemblies," said Knox, "and take away the liberty of the evangel." But with a kindred and equal ardour, Knox was the foremost to stand up in behalf of the nation's freedom, and not to fear the face of man. And so it was with his successors in the contest. Their banner that they bore in their hands, while there was inscribed upon it, "For Christ's Crown and Covenant," was equally an expression of their hatred of civil misrule. While others conspired or mourned for national liberty in secret, they publicly displayed the symbol which declared that "all that is past is not forgotten, and all

that is in peril is not lost." And that sign, seen upon the moun-
tains of Scotland, from across the sea, told to William that the
hour for the Revolution had come.

Nor, in advocating the doctrine of the virtually fundamental
sameness of the right of private judgment in individuals, and of
the right of spiritual independence in Churches, and of their equal
claim to civil recognition, are we giving a broader meaning or
more extensive application to the principle than the common law
of this country warrants. That law takes under its protection
the principle of conscience, as a principle available in matters of
worship and duty due to God, equally and in common to religious
bodies and to religious men. It acknowledges the distinction between things secular and things sacred, and the right of complete
independence in the latter, both in the case of societies and in that
of individuals, and in the same measure in both. Mr. Hallam has
referred to the famous case of the Corporation of London against
Evans, decided by Lord Mansfield in 1767, as the case which has
finally settled the law of toleration for this country, and fixed its
limits and application ; and to the opinion delivered on the occasion by that eminent lawyer, as giving articulate and lasting expression to the principles of the British constitution on the point.
In the course of his speech, Lord Mansfield lays down the position,
in which all constitutional lawyers will concur, that " it cannot be
shown from the principles of natural and revealed religion, that,
independent of positive law, temporal punishments ought to be
inflicted for mere opinions with respect to particular modes of
worship ;" and that, whatever may have been the number or
severity of the statutes previously directed against religious views
or practices differing from those of the Established Church, " the
case is quite altered since the Act of Toleration," so that, " by that
Act the Dissenters are freed, not only from the pains and penalties
of the laws therein particularly specified, but from all ecclesiastical
censures, and from all penalty and punishment whatsoever, on
account of their nonconformity, which is allowed and protected by
this Act, and is therefore, in the eye of the law, no longer a crime."
And not only does the Act of Toleration refuse to construe as a
crime, and to interfere with as such " mere opinions " or " modes
of worship," but it lends to them positive sanction, as known to
the constitution, and known to be as lawful in the eye of the constitution as the opinions or modes of worship of the Established

Church. "The Toleration Act renders that which was illegal before, now legal; the Dissenters' way of worship is permitted and allowed by this Act; it is not only exempted from punishment, but rendered innocent and lawful; *it is established*, it is put under the protection, and not merely the connivance of the law. In case those who are appointed by law to register Dissenting places of worship refuse on any pretence to do it, we must, upon application, send a mandamus to compel them."[1]

Two things are plain from this judicial opinion of Lord Mansfield. *First*, it is plain that religious bodies, or Churches, stand upon precisely the same footing as individuals with respect to toleration by the State, the law knowing no difference between the two cases. The frequent use of the expression, "*modes of worship*," "*places of worship*," and so on, applicable only to societies, in addition to the expression "*opinions*," applicable to individuals as well, sufficiently establishes this. And *second*, it is no less plain that toleration, in the view of Lord Mansfield, extends, not only to that one department of the Church's affairs which comprehends doctrine, or, as his expression is, "opinions," but also to the departments of worship and order, or, as he words it, the "Dissenters' way of worship." This latter point indeed is manifest from the consideration that, in Lord Mansfield's day, three-fourths of the Dissenters neither asked nor needed toleration for their doctrines, which were identical with those of the Established Church, but only for their worship, government, and discipline, in which they differed. Here, then, we have a judicial recognition by this great constitutional lawyer of the justice of the claim put forth by Churches of all classes and denominations, that they may be tolerated in the same way as individuals in all that belongs to faith, worship, and ecclesiastical order; and that what they shall, in obedience to conscience, do in this department of duty, shall not be considered as unlawful, or interfered with in any way, or declared null and void, because alleged to be so by the civil tribunals.

But the principle on which he founds his interpretation of the Toleration Act is fully as instructive as the interpretation itself. All positive statutes imposing penalties in respect of religious opinions or modes of worship being removed out of the way by

[1] *Parliamentary History of England*—Speech of Lord Mansfield in the case between the City of London and the Dissenters, 1767.

the Act of Toleration, it is necessary, in order to interpret the right and limits of free opinion, to fall back on those original principles of right and wrong anterior to positive statute, and everywhere the same,—the universal practice and common jurisprudence of nations known as *common law.* "The eternal principles of natural religion," says Lord Mansfield, "are part of the common law; the essential principles of revealed religion are part of the common law." So far from it being true, as is sometimes alleged by the warm assertors of the prerogative of the State, that it knows no difference between things temporal and things sacred, between religious societies and civil corporations, between Churches and trading copartneries, between the province that belongs to God and that which belongs to Cæsar, that, according to this eminent authority, the distinction is itself embodied in the common law of England, inasmuch as the principles of natural religion, of which the distinction forms a part, are so embodied; nay, if we are disposed to go beyond what natural religion may teach of the distinction, and take the fundamental principles of the Bible as our key to the understanding of it, we should not travel beyond the limits of the British constitution, or place our plea beyond its ken, for the essential principles of revealed as well as of natural religion, according to the dictum of Lord Mansfield, are part of the common law. It is impossible, then, to argue that the distinction for which we contend cannot be respected in the proceedings of the civil magistrate, because, however it may be known to theologians, it is not known to him. It is impossible to allege that, in the eye of the law, Churches have no other character than have civil societies, and that the spiritual duties about which the former are conversant have no other privilege than belongs to the matters of temporal interest or right with which the latter have to deal. The magistrate of this country knows all that natural religion teaches, for its principles form part and parcel of his own law. He knows much even that revelation teaches, for its essential principles are no less embodied in the constitution of the State. And when we speak of God and man's relation to God, of conscience and the things of conscience, and say that, in regard to these, individuals and societies are not under law to the State, because previously under law to the Creator, we are using no language strange to the constitution, and which is not strictly and expressly sanctioned by the common law of the land, as a

plea applicable for the purposes of toleration to all religious denominations and parties. A toleration founded on such principles
of natural religion as the constitution makes part of itself, embraces
all bodies of men associated together for the worship of God,
whether Christian or not Christian,—not being confined to those
societies who claim an authority flowing from Christ as Head, and
who are constituted on the model of that Church delineated in His
Word. And without repudiating the principles of the constitution, and running counter to common law, such societies must have
freedom in all that concerns their faith, their worship, and their
discipline, to act as their own conscience dictates, apart from civil
interference, unless one or other of two things can be made out,
—either, *first*, that the act done by the society is not *bonâ fide* a
spiritual act ; or, *second*, that the society itself avows principles
and favours practices so hostile to the order and well-being of the
State, that it cannot be tolerated at all.

Either case may possibly occur. A Church favoured by its
spiritual character may indulge in proceedings not spiritual.
Under pretence of declaring for its own purposes what is Scriptural and unscriptural in doctrine, it may gratify private feeling
by branding a man as a heretic. Concealed by the cloak of a
zealous discharge of the duty of Divine worship, it may hold
secret meetings for civil, if not treasonable purposes. Under
colour of discipline, it may maliciously and wrongfully stain a
man's character, and injure both his reputation and his interests
in society. In such cases, the Church can no longer plead its
character as a spiritual body, or its right to toleration, as a bar
against the interference of the civil magistrate in the way of
reviewing its proceedings and granting redress ; for this simple
reason, that its proceedings have changed their character, and
have ceased to be spiritual.

Or a body of religionists, without, in a certain sense of the
words, losing their spiritual character, may hold opinions and in-
culcate practices hostile to public morals or the well-being of the
community : their creed, like that of the Jesuits, may embody
articles subversive of the distinctions of right and wrong; or their
religious observances, like those of the Mormons, may be fatal to
the order and happiness of social life ; and conscience, familiarized to the evil, may teach its members that they are doing God
service. In such extreme cases it must become a question with

the rulers of the State, whether it is possible to extend to them the benefits of toleration at all, or whether it is not rather necessary to fall back on the last resort of nations as of Churches, to expel from among them the offending members. The limits of toleration is a question for rulers, which it is as difficult to solve as the parallel question for the people, of the limits of obedience. But if the right of resistance is one which the people should seldom remember, and which princes should never forget, the right of refusing toleration is also one which Churches cannot question, even although the State ought to be slow in seeking an occasion to exercise it. But short of those extreme cases of so-called religious societies, which by their teaching or by their practice compel the State, in self-defence, to deny to them the right of toleration altogether, there can be no justification for the interference of the civil power with spiritual societies when dealing with spiritual affairs. If the freedom of any Church in Divine worship and discipline ought not to be permitted apart from civil control, the only consistent alternative to assert is, that such a Church ought not to be tolerated at all. The State may consistently put it beyond the pale of the Act of Toleration, if its character or practice so demand; but the State cannot consistently tolerate a Church, and at the same time repudiate it in the exercise of its essential and distinctive functions.

Taking the law as it has been authoritatively interpreted and settled by the decision of Lord Mansfield, there are two points to be inquired into before the civil ruler is at liberty to interfere with alleged wrongs done by a religious body in name of a Church.

He may properly ask: *Is this a Church* coming within the meaning and intention of the State, when, after full consideration of what was safe for itself, or right for its people, it framed the Act which defined what bodies ought and what ought not to be so accounted, and therefore to be recognised and tolerated, or the reverse? It were absurd to allege that any number of men calling themselves a Church, and claiming its privileges, are entitled, without inquiry, to be held to be such. In the provisions of the Act of William and Mary, the State reserves to itself the means and the power of deciding this question as to each individual case, by enacting that every religious body or place of worship that may seek to avail itself of the benefits of toleration

shall be duly registered by parties appointed by law for the purpose, and that the doors of such place of worship shall be open
to the State or its servants. Such provisions were obviously
designed to furnish to the State those means of information with
respect to the character and proceedings of the body tolerated,
as might enable it to decide for its own purposes whether the
privilege should be continued or withdrawn. Independently,
indeed, of positive statute, it seems to be implied in the very
nature of the State, as the ordinance of God for the security and
advancement of the temporal well-being of its subjects, that it
has a right to make itself acquainted with the character of any
society of whatever kind within its borders; and for that end is
entitled to be present at its meetings, and to be cognisant of its
transactions. Secret societies are, in their very nature, dangerous
and unconstitutional; and upon this ground, were there no other,
a public declaration of the faith taught, and the order observed,
and the rights claimed by every religious body, such as creeds and
confessions of faith furnish in the case of Churches, might be
defended as in fact necessary and indispensable, in one shape or
other, for the information of the State and the protection of the
community. But in whatever way or form the information may
be obtained, the civil magistrate has a right to know and be
satisfied that the Church which claims toleration at his hands is
in truth what it imports to be,—a spiritual society in reality, and
not in pretence.

But there is a second question which he may ask, and it is
this: Are the *proceedings* of the Church brought under his notice
properly to be referred to the class of spiritual things, and is the
subject-matter of them such as to place them beyond the cognisance of a civil tribunal? To answer this further question, it
may be necessary for him to inquire, not only into the character
of the body whose proceedings they are, but also into the occasion,
the circumstances, and the nature of the proceedings themselves,
lest, through haste, or passion, or deliberate wrong intention, they
should cover what is in reality, not a spiritual, but a civil wrong.
We put aside as simply childish the argument, that because the
Church or its officers may unintentionally commit a wrong in
proceedings which are *yet truly spiritual,* therefore the wrong
ought to be redressed by the civil courts—as if the fact that the
former are not infallible were any reason for asking redress from

other parties as little infallible as themselves. In all cases of
courts or judges of last resort there must be the probability of
occasional wrong, and the certainty of no attainable human redress.
But when, under the colourable pretence of religious duty, the
Church or its officers are actuated by malice in what they do in
their spiritual proceedings, or when, without any malice or wrong
intention, the act done is, in its proper nature and effects, a civil
injury, then the civil tribunal may be called upon and warranted
to interfere, upon the plain ground, that the malice in the one
case, and the nature of the act in the other, properly bring it
within the range of its jurisdiction. To ascertain whether it is so
or not, the magistrate is entitled to demand, and the Church is
bound to give, all such information as to the history and circumstances of its proceedings as may be necessary to enable him to
construe them aright; and the demand, and the obedience to it,
cannot be regarded as implying supremacy in the one party, or
subordination in the other, as respects spiritual jurisdiction.

These two cases, in which the State may warrantably deny to
professedly religious bodies freedom in their proceedings, do not
form properly any exception to the doctrine of the full toleration
that is to be granted in spiritual matters to societies as much as
to individuals, inasmuch as in both cases the *subject-matter* with
which the State has to deal has ceased to be spiritual,—either
the society, by its doctrines and practices, having forfeited its
character as a Church, and become a conspiracy against the
safety and good of the nation, or the action done, from its motives
or its nature, being truly civil. And they are cases that must be
of very infrequent occurrence. It must be in very rare cases
that the State shall be called upon to judge whether a professedly religious society is a Church, constituted for the worship of
God, and not rather a conspiracy against law and order. And
the instances can hardly be more frequent in which a spiritual
society—under the check both of public opinion from without,
and a sense of duty within to at least as great an extent, if not
to a greater, than in the case of a civil court, and in which a
member continues under its jurisdiction only by his own voluntary act—can be betrayed into the wilful perpetration of a civil
injury. Looking at the restraints under which they act, such
trespasses into a province not their own must be still more rare
than the parallel and opposite error, of the encroachment by

civil courts upon matters spiritual. But however this may be, it can be no denial of spiritual freedom, that a professedly religious society that has become a mere copartnery for treason or immorality, should be dealt with as Jesuit colleges and Mormon churches have been dealt with, or that the incongruous offence of a civil injury done by spiritual authorities, should, like the excommunication by the Pope, deposing princes and absolving subjects from allegiance, be placed under the ban of the law.

Beyond these two exceptional cases, the right to toleration for religious opinion, recognised in common law, covers the whole territory that the independence of Churches requires. No plea that the religious opinions of an individual are in themselves false and unfounded, will set aside his legal right to adopt and hold them, if his conscience so teaches him; and, in like manner, no plea that the proceedings or deliverance of a Church are in substance and upon the merits wrong, will warrant the interference of civil authority, if the Church is acting within its own province, and *in re ecclesiasticâ*.

As little can the right of the civil courts to review or reverse such proceedings be argued on the ground that the Church, although acting within its own sphere of spiritual duty, has acted informally by departing from or violating its own rules of procedure. Of course it cannot be imagined, and is not to be assumed, that a Church will be brought to confess to having acted in any case contrary to its own laws; so that the fact on which the argument is founded must always be a disputed one, and would ultimately come to be a question as to whether the civil court or the Church knows its own laws best. But, independently of this, the plea of informality of procedure, and of a departure from right rule, as a reason for calling in the interference of the civil courts in spiritual matters, plainly amounts to a denial of toleration altogether. Take the case of the individual, and what would be said of the consistency or the justice of the State if it professed to accord to him full freedom in regard to religious opinions, conscientiously arrived at, and yet this freedom was actually granted *only* when his inquiries were conducted according to rules and methods approved by the civil court, and his liberty of conscience was to be denied when any departure from such rules could be established against him? Would the argument be listened to for a moment, which should assert that a man had violated the right forms of reasoning by reasoning wrong, or had violated the compact with the State on which the privilege of free inquiry was granted to him, by conducting his inquiries after his own erroneous fashion, and that therefore the privilege must be withdrawn? Is it not, on the contrary, essential to the very idea of toleration, that, arrive at his conclusions by what road or method he may—though it should be in defiance of all logic, and by a system of fallacies disowned by every logician from Aristotle to Archbishop Whately—he is free to adopt and hold them still? And so it is with religious societies. To concede to them independence in spiritual matters, only on the condition of their deliverances being reached in accordance with their own rules, as those rules are interpreted by others,—to grant them freedom in regulating their proceedings and pronouncing their sentences, only in the event of the forms by which they walk approving themselves to the minds of other parties as regular and appropriate,—is practically the same thing as refusing them the privilege altogether.

Forms, no doubt, are in many instances the safeguards of justice, and in all kinds of judicial procedure have been found more or less necessary to secure its equal and convenient administration. But in order to gain that end, they must be varied and adapted to the nature and the case of the subjects and tribunals, spiritual or civil, in connection with which they are used and applied. The same forms of process will not be equally adapted to both; but, on the contrary, what may be found admirably fitted to promote the ends of practical order and justice and truth in the one, may be wholly unsuited to the other, and, in fact, productive of results very much the reverse. If the ends of justice, then, are to be easily and effectually attained, or indeed attained at all, it must be within the power and duty of each court of independent authority and action to frame, interpret, and apply the rules that are to regulate its own procedure, as, in fact, the only party competent to vary and adapt them to the purposes contemplated; and any interference from without would only tend to defeat the object in view. But more than this. It is plain that a power to set aside or cancel spiritual decisions on the ground of irregularity in form, amounts, in so far as regards the practical results, to a power to set them aside on the merits. It gives to the party in whom such power may be vested the command of the result.

Forms of procedure, and rules for ordering the course of dealing with questions brought before judges for judgment, are so intimately and extensively intermingled with the grounds and elements of the judgment, that it is impossible to separate between them ; and while this consideration is enough to show that it must, from the very nature of the case, be the right of the tribunal who has to decide upon the merits to decide also upon the forms of the cause, it no less demonstrates the impossibility of giving to any party jurisdiction over the latter, without surrendering at the same time a practical power over the former. Perhaps it were too much to assert that forms of process and rules for the order of business even in a spiritual court are to be held in their proper character to be spiritual ; but it is not too much to assert, that in so far as they are necessary and conducive to the attainments of justice, they are essential means towards spiritual ends; and as a right to accomplish the end must always imply a right to employ the means by which it is to be accomplished, the Church's title to judge in spiritual matters without civil control, must involve a title to freely regulate and interpret and apply its own forms for that object.

The Church whose misfortune it is to have the law of its courts or officers, to a large extent, identical with the law of civil tribunals, and to be amenable to their decision in applying it to spiritual things, must be fettered and helpless in the discharge of its proper functions, and liable to be checkmated at every step. In the exercise of its power to declare for its own purposes and members what is Scriptural and unscriptural in doctrine, it may pronounce a man to be a heretic, and, acting on the apostolic rule, may, after a first and second admonition, reject him from its communion, and then be liable to the injury and humiliation of having him restored to office, because of some alleged technical informality in its proceedings, which was no informality at all in its own judgment, or as affecting either the evidence or the amount of guilt, but was only fancied to be so by a civil tribunal, judging by a standard applicable to civil affairs. Or, in the exercise of the powers of discipline, it may cut off some wicked person for public and gross immorality; and because the notice of citation to the offender to answer for his offence was, in the judgment of a civil judge, twenty-four hours shorter than it ought to have been, the Church may be compelled, under the coercion of civil penalties, to receive him back again. The doctrine, that informality of procedure in the conduct of spiritual matters by a spiritual body may make void its authority, when a civil court shall differ from it in opinion as to what is regular or not, is fundamentally subversive of its independence. If it be right and necessary for the State to acknowledge the freedom of religious bodies in judging of the merits of spiritual causes, it must be no less right and necessary for the State to acknowledge the same freedom in judging of the forms, just because the greater includes the less.

Nor, in asserting the incompetency of the civil courts, consistently with the principles of toleration, to declare to be illegal, and to set aside spiritual decisions, on the ground either of the merits or alleged irregularity of procedure, are we forgetful of the close connection that such decisions may have, or rather perhaps must have, with civil interests. The spiritual and the civil element are so nearly and strangely linked together in every department of human affairs, that perhaps it were not possible to name a single proceeding of any man that might not, in some of its aspects or consequences, be regarded as civil, and in others of them as spiritual. The very same fact may thus properly come under the cognisance of both the spiritual and civil courts, according to the view in which it is dealt with. But shall we, because of this close and constant connection between spiritual and civil interests, say that there is no real distinction to be recognised between them, and that both may be regulated and disposed of by one common governing authority residing in the civil ruler or his servants? Not so. The great fact made public to the universe, of the twofold ordinance of God in His Church and in the State—the one to rule the spiritual, and the other to rule the temporal world of human life—is His answer to the question, and His standing assertion of the distinction between the things that belong to Himself, and the things that belong to Cæsar. The universal belief of mankind, whether Christian or heathen, that the duties within the domain of conscience, and that pertain to the relations of the creature with the Creator, are more than the obligations of civil life, is the testimony of humanity to the same effect. And the law of toleration embodying the distinction is a decision of the same import, pronounced by the common jurisprudence of nations. Civil interests may oftentimes be affected by spiritual acts, and, reversing the proposition, spiritual interests may often be affected by acts, in themselves civil; but even when most closely connected, there is a fundamental and indelible distinction between the two. It cannot be said, therefore, that in the performance of spiritual duties, which may in their consequences very nearly affect the temporal interests of men, Churches are to be held as dealing with those interests, and judging of patrimonial rights; or as thereby trespassing beyond their own province, and making their decisions justly amenable to civil review. There can hardly be any proceeding of a religious society, however purely spiritual the act may be, that may not in this way affect the civil interests of parties concerned. But it must not be alleged, on that account, that the proceeding is not spiritual, but civil, and subject to the cognisance of civil tribunals. When the ecclesiastical authorities are pronouncing a man to be guilty of heresy according to the standard which they and he have both consented to abide by, they are not pronouncing any sentence as to his pecuniary interests, although these, as a consequence of the proceeding, may be nearly and greatly affected by it. When the same authorities remove a man from an office in the ministry for public immorality, they are dealing with a question *in re ecclesiasticâ*, and not pretending to judge of his civil right to the emoluments that happen to be connected with the office, although these may be forfeited in consequence. Such indirect and consequential connection between the spiritual act and the civil interests affected by it, does not change the nature or true meaning of the Church's proceedings, nor subject them to civil supervision or control. Could the opposite be truly alleged, it would really amount to the assertion, that no Church can exist in freedom and exercise discipline at all.

Still there are civil results which follow from spiritual proceedings. These proceedings themselves may properly be within the competency of the parties who are responsible for them; they may not, consistently with the principles of toleration, be liable to the review of the civil courts, so as to be declared by them to be illegal; they may be beyond the reach of any authority, not lodged within the Church, to cancel or set aside. But the consequences of these may affect the pecuniary interests or the character and worldly reputation of the parties concerned. Is there no redress, if from any cause these proceedings are wrong? if, from haste or misapprehension, or the involuntary infirmity that marks all human transactions, the ecclesiastical decision is erroneous, and leads by consequence, more or less near, to civil injury? In so far as regards the civil consequences, the party affected by them may obtain redress in one or other of two ways, corresponding to the character of the injury that he has sustained.

First, There may be, and in the case of office-bearers there commonly are, certain pecuniary interests or civil advantages connected with the possession of office or membership in a religious society, and made dependent upon such possession; and as civil courts are the proper guardians of property and other temporal interests, and spiritual courts are not, it must belong to the former, and not to the latter, to consider and judge of the conditions on which such civil privileges are held, and to award them to the party who can make good his legal claim to the possession of them. The same methods competent to any other of the subjects of the State to vindicate his right to patrimonial advantages, are also competent to the members of the Church in respect of pecuniary interests affected by spiritual decisions. In exercising, in these cases, their undoubted powers of jurisdiction, civil courts may be called upon to judge of spiritual acts and sentences in so far as these are conditions on which pecuniary interests depend, and to determine whether in this light they do or do not carry with them civil effects. They may be called upon to say whether the proceedings of Church courts are good, not as spiritual sentences, but good as legal conditions of temporal rights. To deny them such a prerogative, would be to deny them their full and proper jurisdiction. But it is not necessary, in order to explicate that jurisdiction, that they should have a title to judge of spiritual acts for any other purpose or to any other effect: the power to do so—to declare them to be illegal, and to set them aside as null and void—does not belong to courts of the State, and is not required in order to give effect to their proper decisions; the reduction or cancelling of the spiritual sentence is no part of the process, as means to an end, by which redress, in cases of injury to patrimonial interests, is to be afforded; and without taking upon them the incongruous and incompetent task of judging what is Scriptural or unscriptural in doctrine, and what is right or wrong in discipline, the civil courts can do all that is necessary to judge and determine in regard to the civil interests that may be affected by ecclesiastical proceedings.

Or, *second*, apart from pecuniary interests, a man may be affected in his public character, and injury done both to his feelings and his worldly standing, in consequence of the erroneous proceedings of spiritual judges. And as the courts of the State are the guardians of a man's character as well as of any other of his civil rights, they must have the power, no less than in the former case, of granting redress when character is maliciously injured. The same powers in a civil court that would secure for a man compensation for a malignant and unfounded slander perpetrated by a private party, will no less avail for that purpose, although the wrong should be inflicted by a spiritual court in the course of spiritual proceedings. The element of malice, if proved to be present in the doings of a religious body, will take the case out of the protection of the ordinary privilege granted to tolerated Churches in their proper discipline; for it, strictly speaking, changes the character of the transaction, and makes it to be a civil offence, instead of an act of ecclesiastical discipline. But even in this case, when granting to the party injured civil reparation, it is not necessary or competent for the civil court to deal with the ecclesiastical proceedings in their spiritual character, or to judge of their merit or demerit in that respect.

Still more, it is *ultra vires* for the courts of the State to deal with these proceedings when no malice is alleged, and when all that is asserted amounts to this, that by the proper discipline of a Church, acting within its line of duty, the feelings or character of the party interested have suffered. If the power of discipline is to remain with religious bodies at all,—if the simple privilege not denied to any voluntary or private society, however humble, is to be conceded to religious societies, of saying who shall and who shall not be their members and office-bearers,—it is plain that this power cannot be exercised, without in many cases bearing with painful effect upon the feelings and reputation and public standing of those subjected to it. But such indirect and incidental consequences cannot properly be made a ground of action in a civil court, without subjecting the whole spiritual territory of the Church to civil control. In exercising the right of admitting and excluding members and enforcing the terms of membership and office, the Church is acting strictly within the province of its religious duty; and although private individuals can plead no privilege of being exempted from responsibility in what they do if it affect the character of another, yet this is a privilege which must of necessity belong to Churches, if they are to be tolerated in the exercise of discipline at all. In the case of private and voluntary societies, indeed, the right of fixing and enforcing at their will their terms of membership is exercised to an almost unlimited extent, free from any legal responsibility for the consequences which admission or exclusion may infer. A fashionable club, admission to which is a passport to the highest society, may blackball at its pleasure any man without the risk of an action of damages. A scientific society, whose membership confers fame, does not hold itself legally responsible for the injury to feeling and reputation inflicted by the rejection of a candidate for its honours. A banking copartnery may refuse to discount a merchant's bills, and ruin his credit in the market-place, without being held accountable at law. A man may be expelled from the Stock Exchange, and in consequence become a bankrupt in means as well as reputation, and yet may have no redress in a civil court. And if freedom almost unlimited is exercised in this way every day by private societies not privileged by law, much more must a similar freedom be granted to Christian Churches, which, if tolerated at all, must be tolerated in all that is necessary to their duty as Churches.

The law, then, is open; and competent methods of redress are at hand for all who can plead that their civil rights or patrimonial interests have been affected by spiritual proceedings in the way of unjust loss of income or malicious injury to character. But beyond these two classes of cases, raising, as they undoubtedly do, questions civil, and rightly liable to civil review by the courts of the State, this control can properly reach no further; and even in these cases, the spiritual proceedings of the Church cannot be set aside or interfered with, even at the moment that redress for civil wrong arising out of them may be liberally and justly awarded.

The question of the spiritual independence of civil control claimed by religious societies has sometimes been represented as a case of contract between the Church on the one hand, and its office-bearers and members on the other, and as if the terms of the contract necessarily expressed and defined the extent and limits of the Church's freedom. Upon this view, the liberty conceded to spiritual societies is no more than a liberty for the members to unite together under engagement to each other, and to lay down their own rules for the regulation of their affairs, while the power reserved to the civil courts is a power to judge of the precise nature and conditions of the contract thus entered into in the same way as of any other, and to allow freedom to the Church in its spiritual proceedings, so long as these are in accordance with the terms of the contract, and no further and no longer than they are so. We believe that this is a defective and erroneous view of the question. It would allow of any office-bearer or member, cut off by the discipline of the Church, calling in the intervention of the civil courts in every case in which a breach of contract could be alleged; and it would justify the civil courts, upon the grounds of such an allegation, in at once proceeding to review or reverse the spiritual sentences complained of. It is carefully to be noted, that it is not the *form* of the obligation, whether arising out of contract or otherwise, but the *nature* of it as spiritual, which prohibits the office-bearers or members of the Church from appealing against its authority to that of the tribunals of the State. And it is no less carefully to be noted, that it is not because the liberty of the Church may or may not be embodied in the shape of a contract between itself and its own office-bearers and members, but because of the subject-matter in which that liberty is claimed, that the civil courts are forbidden to interfere. It is the nature of the matters as spiritual, and not civil—as requiring to be dealt with by spiritual and not civil authority—that protects the Church in the exclusive jurisdiction claimed in regard to them, and bars the servants of the State from intervention. The accident that in some cases there may be a written, or at least formal, obligation that may be construed as a contract come under by its office-bearers, on their admission to office, to submit to the spiritual authority of the Church in all Church matters, is not the proper ground on which exemption from civil control for these matters may be asserted. Without such contract, the authority of the Church in these things would be equally valid, and the exclusion of the State would be equally absolute. It is the spiritual nature of the proceedings, and not the contract expressed or implied, that gives the authority; it is the same reason that necessitates the exclusion. Whether the proceedings of the Church within its own peculiar province are protected by express and formal contract between itself and its members or not, they are equally removed from the rightful cognisance of the civil tribunals. The deep and everlasting distinction between the things of conscience and the things of the commonwealth is what gives lawful authority to the Church to deal with the former, and not with the latter, and to the servants of the State to deal with the latter, and not with the former; and there is no contract needed either to warrant or protect the freedom of each party from the encroachments of the other. If a contract do exist in any shape that makes it to be a formal or substantial engagement between contracting parties, it must depend upon the nature of it, as spiritual or civil, whether the tribunals of the State are at liberty to judge of its conditions and enforce its terms or not. If it is exclusively spiritual, and having nothing to do with civil matters, the civil courts can have no power to deal with it, or to redress alleged breaches of its conditions. If it be a civil contract, or one of mixed nature, partly civil and partly spiritual, and embracing matters belonging in some measure to the one class, and in some measure to the other, the courts of the State may, to the extent of its properly civil character, be called upon to judge of it.

The obligations under which the Church comes to its own office-bearers and members, and they equally to the Church, which have been called, perhaps improperly, a contract, may embrace matters exclusively spiritual, or embrace matters partly spiritual and partly civil. The authority of the civil tribunals will be different in its bearing on these two cases. The engagement between the Church and the ordinary and private members of the Church is in common cases wholly spiritual, embracing no pecuniary or civil right at all,—implying as it does the duty of the Church to minister to them in doctrine and sacrament, and their duty to be obedient to the Church in word and discipline. Than this nothing can be conceived as a more purely spiritual engagement, or, if it is to be so called, *contract;* and with obedience to the terms of it, or disobedience to them, the courts of the State can have nothing to do. The engagement between the Church on the one hand, and the office-bearers of the Church on the other, may be spiritual likewise. It may amount to nothing more than an obligation on the part of the Church to give them its commission and authority to preach the Gospel and dispense the ordinances of Christ in some particular congregation, leaving it to the State or to the congregation to give the pecuniary support, and an obligation on the part of the ministers so commissioned to subject themselves to the government, discipline, and authority of the Church. In such a case, the "contract" is wholly a spiritual one, of the nature and conditions and fulfilment of which the Church courts, and not the civil, must be the judges. Whatever relates to the pecuniary rights of the party ordained to the office of the ministry, and discharging its duties, is a question between him and the State in the case of a Church endowed by the State, or between him and the congregation, in the case of many non-Established Churches whose ministers derive their support from their flocks.

There may indeed be an engagement between the Church and its office-bearers embracing more than spiritual matters, and of a mixed nature. There may be an engagement in which the Church, in return for the spiritual services of its ministers, comes under an obligation to pay them a certain pecuniary remuneration, drawn out of a common fund under its charge, and contributed for that purpose, in addition to granting them the benefits of its spiritual authority and commission for their work. In this case, exemplified in some non-Established Churches, the contract is partly spiritual and partly civil, comprehending matters that plainly belong to each category. In so far as regards the spiritual matters of the contract—the spiritual commission granted by the Church on the one side, and the spiritual services to be rendered by the minister in return—these are the things which, from their very nature, the civil courts have no jurisdiction in, and no power to enforce, and the Church alone has. In so far as regards the pecuniary arrangements of the contract, and the breach or fulfilment of its terms in respect of them, the civil courts alone are competent to enforce the conditions in the case of a violation of them by either party. But although the contract in this instance may in a certain sense be regarded as a mixed one, giving to the contracting parties certain temporal rights, as well as laying upon them spiritual duties, yet the line of demarcation between the two is plain, and not to be overpassed from either side; the Church, as trustee of certain funds committed to its charge, for the payment of its ministers, may in that character be a civil party, subject to civil control, in the discharge of its pecuniary engagements, while the same Church, as a spiritual body, requiring certain spiritual duties from its ministers, and giving to them its ordination, is altogether free; and the State has no more the right or the ability, in such a case, to attempt to enforce the purely religious engagements between the parties, or to punish the violation of them, than the Church has the right or power to dispose of the temporal rights.

A sort of mixed obligation of this kind, securing certain pecuniary rights or advantages, on condition of a certain spiritual act being done, or a certain spiritual profession being maintained, is not unknown in our legislation, and serves to make plain the distinction between the two. Under the Test and Corporation Acts, now happily repealed, it was unlawful for any man to hold any municipal office who had not, within a year preceding the time of his election, taken the Sacrament, according to the rites of the Church of England. Intolerant as the spirit of the Act was, and unscrupulous as were the courts at the time, it was not in the contemplation of the one or the other, that in the event of some municipal magistrate failing to comply with this condition, it was possible for the civil tribunals to enforce equally the one branch of the alternative as the other, and to compel a man to take the bread and wine of the Communion Table as easily or competently as they could compel him to demit his civil office. Although the holding of office according to the statute implied that a spiritual act was to be performed, yet the illegal disregard of this obligation did not give to the civil courts the power to compel the performance of the spiritual act, but only left them the power of enforcing the civil penalty. In like manner, the holding of the office of Lord Chancellor of England, according to the Emancipation Act, is, in our own day, fettered with the condition that the holder of it make profession of the Protestant faith. If the present eminent lawyer who fills the position were to go over to the Roman Catholic Church, the law, notwithstanding the statutory connection between the office and the spiritual character, would never contemplate the possibility of enforcing, by means of civil authority, his return to a purer religious profession, although it might contemplate the application of its power and authority to the depriving him of his official position. Or, to take a case still more similar in its character to the one under review: A domestic chaplain, hired on the condition of ministering to a family according to the faith and rites of the Established Church, might abjure its doctrine, and yet insist on retaining his salary. In such a case, the aggrieved employer would find it hard to persuade the civil courts to send the offender to prison to unlearn his heterodoxy, although quite easy to induce them to lend their proper authority to deprive him of his salary. The argument is not different with respect to the contract which may be alleged to exist between some non-Established Churches and their ministers, in which the Church gives ordination and pecuniary support as the condition, on its part, of certain spiritual services being rendered on theirs. The civil courts have power to enforce the civil element in the obligation, but not the spiritual: they might, on the one hand, protect the Church in withholding the pecuniary payment, if, in their estimation, the religious duties had not been performed, but they could not compel the performance of these duties; or, on the other hand, they might authorize the minister, when deposed, to exact the payment, if they believed the duties to have been performed, but could not compel the Church to renew or continue the ordination.

It is the line drawn by the finger of God between things spiritual and things civil that must ever limit the power of the Church on the one side, and that of the State on the other. The landmarks between were not set up and adjusted by contract, but of old had their foundations laid deep in the nature of things. Make light of the distinction, and practically disregard it, and there is no length to which this may not lead in the way of spiritual domination on the part of the Church in the concerns of civil life, or Erastian encroachment on the part of the State in the province of religious right and duty. If a power of any kind, direct or indirect, is conceded to the Church of disposing to the smallest extent of temporal matters, there can be no limit set to its encroachments: it may pervade every department of the State with its tyranny, and subject all in turn to its control, creeping like a palsy over a nation's heart, and extinguishing all that is valuable in the civil liberty, the individual independence, and the manly energies of a people. Or if a power, however small, of rightful authority in spiritual things is acknowledged to belong to the State, it will soon come to make itself to be felt as the weightiest and least tolerable part of its sovereignty. If the liberties of religious bodies in the way of discipline or government are denied to them, and handed over to the civil magistrate, it is a concession which can plead for itself no argument not equally available for dealing in the same way with their doctrine: their conscience, when once fettered in its religious actings, can show no cause why it should be free in religious opinions; and with the independence of its courts and officers, the sound faith and the living piety, and the active power for spiritual good of the Church, must die out also. These are not the deductions of reason only, but the lessons of history as well, and lessons which the nations that have not been taught them from the past are learning at the present day. Between the extreme which makes the State to be the slave of the Church, and that other extreme which makes the Church to be the slave of the State, there is no position that is safe or consistent with sound principle, except that which asserts their mutual and equal independence.

APPENDIX E., Vol. I. p. 215.

RELATIVE OBLIGATION OF SCRIPTURE PRECEPT, EXAMPLE,
AND PRINCIPLE.

Are Scripture examples as binding as Scripture precepts? Do
instances of apostolic practice carry with them the same authority
as express apostolic enactments? Do general principles fairly
established from Scripture lay the same obligation on the conscience of Christian men, in every case to which they legitimately
apply, as an explicit command with respect to the same case
would have done? The point brought before us is an important
one. If these questions are to be answered in the negative, it is
obvious that the strength of the argument in favour of the observance of the Lord's day, in behalf of the Presbyterian form of
Church government, in support of the lawfulness and duty of
infant baptism, of female communion, etc., will, to say the least
of it, be greatly shaken.

By many writers in the present day it is denied that a distinct
Scripture proof of the practice of inspired men can in any case be
an absolutely binding precedent for our imitation. " Let it be
supposed," says Mr. Litton, " that it had been distinctly recorded
in Scripture that Episcopacy, like the presbyterate and diaconate,
proceeded from the apostles: could we, even then, at once infer
that it is of Divine institution, and a matter of perpetual obligation?" Mr. Litton holds, that while the latter two offices are
proved to be of apostolic appointment by Scripture evidence, the
former, or the office of bishop as distinct from presbyter, cannot
be established from Scripture, but only by the testimony of ecclesiastical antiquity. But he does not on that account consider the
presbyterate and diaconate, although not rashly or capriciously
to be done away with, to be of Divine right: " He would be a
bold man who should maintain that it is a matter of *indifference*
whether or not we adhere in regulations of polity to Scriptural

precedent. Nevertheless, the remarkable circumstance is to be borne in mind, that not one of the appointments of the apostles in matters of polity have been transmitted to us in Scripture in the form of *legislative enactments*, but simply as *recorded facts*. For example, the inspired history informs us, that, as a matter of fact, the apostles ordained elders for every Church; but no *law* upon the subject, purporting to emanate from the apostles, can be found in Scripture. To their appointments the apostles append no imperative declarations, making them immutably binding upon the Church. Let their mode of proceeding in this respect be compared with the mode in which the law of Moses was delivered, and the difference between the two cases will be apparent. The Mosaic appointments were not only recorded, but *commanded;* the apostolic regulations are recorded, but not made matter of law; the apostles do not absolutely bind the Church of every age to follow the precedents which they set."[1] Mr. Litton then goes on to take a distinction between revealed *doctrines* and revealed or recorded *facts* and *regulations*. The former, or the doctrines, carry with them their own sanction, and are of lasting obligation on the conscience. The latter, or the regulations, are not perpetually binding, unless there be some express statement to that effect in Scripture. The apostolic appointments were no doubt the best for the existing circumstances. But these might change; and a power of discretion was left with the Church to suit its arrangements to the conditions of the emergency in which it found itself placed.

Now, in reply to these statements by Mr Litton — and his position is one very commonly taken, especially in the Church of England—it is to be observed, that Scripture commands, Scripture examples, and Scripture principles, all rest as regards their authority on precisely the same basis, and are subject to precisely the same limitations as respects the demand they make on our obedience. All Scripture commands are not binding on us now, any more than all Scripture examples are binding. It is not the legislative form or the want of it; it is not the use of the Imperative mood in the one case and of the Indicative in the other that makes the difference. A principle of eternal obligation may be conveyed to us with equal clearness and force in a passage which says, " Thus you are to act," and in a passage which simply tells

[1] Litton, *Church of Christ*, Lond. 1851, pp. 439, 441.

us, "Thus inspired and apostolic men acted." The latter mode of revealing truth and duty may be said to be characteristic of the New Testament—the former of the old; but we are equally bound to recognise and reverence and obey the mind of God, in whichever way He may choose to make it known to us. What we learn in both cases alike is just this : Thus and thus the Spirit of God commanded certain men to act in certain circumstances. We learn no more in the case of the precept than in the case of the example. The one is as binding upon us as the other, *provided we be in like circumstances.* The real point of importance in both instances is the expression of the mind and will of God conveyed to us; and the true test of its permanent obligation upon us is simply this : Was this command—whether it reaches us in the form in which it was perhaps first given, or whether it is embodied in the obedience which followed—founded on moral grounds, common to all men at all times, in all circumstances, or on local and temporary grounds, peculiar to certain men in certain circumstances, at some given time? If the grounds or reasons on which it rests be of the former sort, it is as binding on us now as on those who first obeyed it; if of the latter, it is not binding on us at all, except in so far as our circumstances may be akin to those in which it was originally uttered.

The Ten Commandments stand surrounded by the civil and ceremonial precepts of the Jewish law. The latter are abolished, " save in so far as the general equity thereof may require;"[1] the former remain binding for ever, *not* because of the enactive form in which they are couched, but because of the nature of the duty enjoined. The passover and the other sacred feasts, so solemnly pressed upon the obedience of Israel of old, are not obligatory on the nation in the present day, just because the grounds on which these institutions rested were of a local and temporary kind, and the circumstances of the Jews then are not the circumstances of the Jews now.

Take the case of the decree passed by the Council of Jerusalem, that the Gentile converts to Christianity should abstain from meats offered to idols, from things strangled, and from blood. The apostles and presbyters met in synod gave commandment, and the Holy Ghost gave commandment to this effect;[2] but the command is not binding upon us now, simply because it rested on

[1] Conf. ch. xix. 4.   [2] Acts xv. 23, 28 ; xv. 4.

grounds peculiar to the age and country in which it was given, and our circumstances are in this respect essentially different from those of the early Church. But the general principle of which this decree was a particular and local application is still of universal obligation,—namely, that no man has a right so to use his Christian liberty as needlessly to offend the consciences of his brethren : " Let all things be done unto edification," and " Let all your things be done with charity."

Take the case of the Lord's Supper. There we have both example and precept combined. We have the record of what our Lord did, and the record of His command to do as He had done, in remembrance of Him and of His death. The ordinance itself is of perpetual and universal obligation in the Christian Church ; but some of the features of its first celebration are not so. The partakers in the Sacrament at its original institution were men only. . But females are not to be excluded from the communion table on that account. The ordinance was celebrated in the evening, and in a private house ; but neither the time nor the place can be regarded as furnishing a binding precedent for us. The elements of the Supper were the unleavened bread and the paschal cup of thanksgiving employed by the Jews ; and for the use of these might be pleaded both the example of Christ and His express command : " *This* do." But neither do these peculiar observances rest on moral grounds common to all times, and therefore they are not universally binding.

Many other instances might be given. The Apostle Paul's instructions with respect to marriage given to the Corinthians are a case in point. It was good, he told them, in his judgment, for a man not to marry ; but his reason was founded on " the present distress " (διὰ τὴν ἐνεστῶσαν ἀνάγκην), and his wish that they should be " without fretting anxiety" (ἀμερίμνους).[1] So of the community of goods in the early Church at Jerusalem, etc.

Revealed doctrines, to recur to the distinction which Mr. Litton seeks to establish, generally commend themselves at once to our minds and consciences as founded on moral grounds of universal application, and therefore permanently binding. But this is by no means always the case. The Council of Jerusalem laid down the doctrine, as " a *necessary* thing," that it was the duty of Gentile Christians to abstain from blood, etc., just as decidedly

[1] 1 Cor. vii. 26, 32.

as they enunciated their command upon the subject.   But neither the doctrine nor the precept rested on grounds common to all men at all times, and therefore neither are universally obligatory.

Scripture precepts, then, whether doctrinal or practical, Scripture examples, and Scripture principles, all rest on the same foundation of authority, and are to be interpreted and obeyed according to the same rule.   As regards all of them alike, the same exception is to be made with respect to points which can be already shown to depend on the peculiar circumstances of a given age or country. But with this single necessary deduction or limitation, the practice of apostles, as recorded in Scripture, is just as obligatory as any of their precepts handed down to us in the Acts or the Epistles, and for precisely the same reason, that both alike embody the will of Christ to His Church.   It does not in the slightest degree take from the binding force of any information regarding the constitution, government, worship, and discipline of the Christian society given us in the New Testament, that part of it may reach us in the shape of apostolic commands, and part of it in the shape of apostolic actions.   In fact, there is much about what may be said to be the characteristics of the Gospel dispensation which makes it likely, *primâ facie*, that under it, Christians, as in the manhood of the Church, should be called to guide themselves quite as much by what the apostles *did* in executing their Master's commission, as by what they *said*, and that general principles should be given us, from which we were trusted and intended to draw the right inferences.   The evidence relevant and sufficient to establish the general form of government and administration, which our Lord designed His Church on earth to adopt, will certainly not meet us in Scripture in scientific shape and system, any more than the evidence of Christian doctrine does.   But whatever indications of the mind and will of Christ in any department of the Church's work and duty we do find in the Word of God, whether in the form of direct statement, or positive command, or general principle, or ordinary apostolic practice, we are alike bound reverently and thankfully to accept and to act upon them.[1]

[1] *Jus Div. Reg. Eccles.* Lond. 1646, pp. 11-35.   Brown, *Apologetical Relation*, 1665, pp. 213-248.   Cunningham, *Works*, vol. ii. pp. 64-73.

APPENDIX F., Vol. I. p. 312.

SCRIPTURE CONSEQUENCES.

" The whole counsel of God," says the Confession of Faith,
" concerning all things necessary for His own glory, man's salvation, faith, and life, is either expressly set down in Scriptnre, *or,
by good and necessary consequence, may be deduced from Scripture;*
unto which nothing at any time is to be added,—whether by new
revelations of the Spirit, or traditions of men." [1]

A right understanding of the truths contained in this weighty
sentence may be said to form the basis of all sound and Scriptural Theology, and of all lawful and orthodox Confessions of
Faith. The challenge has been thrown down again and again by
heretics in all ages : " Give us an express text of Scripture contradicting our views, and asserting yours. We refuse to submit
to mere human inferences in place of Scripture statement."

It was on this ground that the Arians of the fourth century
built their favourite and most plausible arguments against the
Nicene definition of the ὁμοούσιον. It was on this ground that
the Macedonians denied the Divinity of the Holy Spirit, and the
Apollinarians and Monophysites the true and distinct humanity
of Christ. In like manner, after the Reformation, the Socinian
party opposed all the leading doctrines held by the Protestant
Churches, on the score of their being based on Scripture consequences, and not on Scripture texts. In fact, in almost every
case in which any show of reverence for the Word of God has
been preserved at all, the errors of false teachers—from Uni-
tarianism to transubstantiation—have been covered by an appeal
to the *letter* of Scripture, while the real sense and meaning of it
have been evaded or denied.[2]

The importance of the question may be illustrated by an

---

[1] Conf. ch. i. 6.
[2] Cumming, *Grounds of the Present Differences among the London Ministers*,
Lond. 1720, pp. 4–9.

example. Take the first verse of the first chapter of Genesis: "In the beginning God created the heaven and the earth." What conclusions may be drawn "by good and necessary consequence" from these words? In the first place, this, that God and nature are essentially distinct and different, as against the various forms of Pantheism. In the second place,—although the passage does not fix the antiquity of the present order of things upon the earth, and does not hinder us from believing, if the fact should be established by other evidence, that an indefinite series of ages may have elapsed between the events recorded in the first verse of this chapter and those recorded in the second,—yet these words prove that, at some far-off date in the past eternity, matter had its beginning, that God only is from everlasting to everlasting, and that the eternity of matter is a fiction of the Materialists. In the third place, these words teach us that matter was at the first created out of nothing by God, as against the various theories of Emanation. "By faith we understand that the worlds were framed by the Word of God, so that things which are seen were not made of things which do appear."

Again, take such verses as, "The Word was made flesh," "The man Christ Jesus." [1] From these words of Scripture we learn, "by good and necessary consequence," *first*, that our Lord Jesus Christ had a true body, as against the speculations of the early Gnostics; *second*, that He had a reasonable soul and a human will, as against the Monothelites; and *third*, that He united in His person a Divine and a human nature, as against the Socinians.

The chief grounds on which the authority of Scripture consequences depend are the following:—

I. These consequences are really *contained in* Scripture, and therefore they are "good." They are contained, not in the *words* of the inspired writers, but in the relations of these words to each other, and in the meaning conveyed by the statement as a whole; and therefore they are equally of Divine origin with the letter of Scripture, and equally binding upon us as an expression of the mind of God. He is not bound to one way only of conveying His will to us. Many important purposes may be served in the case of His moral and intelligent creatures by the discipline involved in an indirect as well as a direct communication of His messages

[1] John i. 14; 1 Tim. ii. 5.

to them. And we are equally bound to give heed to and obey the will and the truth of God, in whatever shape and way they reach us in His Word.

It is no valid objection to this, that an act or process of fallible human reason is employed in drawing consequences from the Scripture words, and that therefore the conclusion arrived at must be a merely human and fallible one. For, 1st, The consequences referred to are not only "good," but "necessary consequences." They might be the former without being the latter. But in order that a Scripture consequence shall come up to the definition of our Confession, it must not only be "good,"—that is to say, really contained in Scripture, really a part of Divine truth revealed there,—but "necessary" as well; that is to say, one which forces itself upon any reasonable and unprejudiced mind as inevitable, plainly contained in the statements of the Word of God, not needing to be established by any remote process of refined argument. 2d, The very same act or process of the fallible human understanding is involved in any interpretation or intelligent reading of Scripture whatsoever. The objection, therefore, if admitted, would equally avail to disprove the Divine authority and obligation of every recorded communication of truth from the mind of God to the mind of man.[1] 3d, Scripture and merely human writings differ in this very essential respect, that the consequences to be lawfully drawn from God's words were all foreseen and intended by Him; the consequences which might be fairly enough drawn from the words of men are very often not foreseen and not intended by them. In the former case, therefore, "good and necessary consequences" are as fully expressive of the mind of the Author of Scripture, and as binding upon us, as any direct statements of His could be. In the latter case, it may neither be safe nor warrantable to argue as to the personal intention of the writer from inferences really contained in his words, and fairly deduced from them.[2]

II. Scripture evidence respecting the procedure of our Lord

---

[1] Cumming, *Grounds of Pres. Diff.* pp. 81–85, 90–98.

[2] ["If we say that necessary consequences from Scripture prove not a *jus Divinum*, we say that which is inconsistent with the infinite wisdom of God. For although necessary consequences may be drawn from a man's word which do not agree with his mind and intention, and so men are oftentimes ensnared by their words, yet (as Camero well noteth, *De Verbo Dei*, cap. 17, 18), God being infinitely wise, it were a blasphemous opinion to hold that anything can be drawn

and His inspired followers very distinctly warrants the principle and practice of drawing consequences from the Word of God, as of equal authority with express Scripture statements. " Do ye not err," said our Lord to the Sadducees, " *not knowing the Scriptures,* neither the power of God ? . . . As touching the dead, that they rise, have ye not read in the book of Moses, in the chapter on the bush, how God spake unto him, saying, I am the God of Abraham, and the God of Isaac, and the God of Jacob? He is not the God of the dead, but the God of the living : ye therefore do greatly err."[1] In this passage, our Saviour's argument for the doctrine of the resurrection consists of an indirect inference from the words of God to Moses,—an inference the force of which it may be fairly said to require a certain amount of thought and spiritual insight fully to perceive. Yet the Sadducees are charged by Christ with sin, with a culpable ignorance of the Scriptures (μὴ εἰδότες τὰς γραφάς), because they had failed to draw that consequence from the words addressed to Moses, and, on the ground of it, to accept the doctrine of the resurrection as one just as really and authoritatively taught in the Old Testament, as if it had been propounded there in express terms.

Again, when our Lord was reasoning with the two disciples on the road to Emmaus, who were dismayed at the crucifixion of the Messiah, and uncertain of the fact of His resurrection, He said to them, " O fools, and slow of heart to believe *all that the prophets have spoken ! Ought* not (οὐχὶ ἔδει) Christ to have suffered these things, and to enter into His glory? And beginning at Moses and all the prophets, He *expounded* unto them in all the Scriptures the things concerning Himself."[2] Here,

by a certain and necessary consequence from His holy Word which is not His will. This were to make ' the only wise God ' as foolish as man, who cannot foresee all things which will follow from his words. Therefore we must needs hold it is the mind of God which necessarily followeth from the Word of God..

" Divers other great absurdities must follow, if this truth be not admitted. How can it be proved that women may partake of the Sacrament of the Lord's Supper, unless we prove it by necessary consequence from Scripture ? How can it be proved that this or that Church is a true Church, and the ministry thereof a true ministry, and the baptism administered therein a true baptism? Sure no express Scripture will prove it, but necessary consequence will. How shall this or that individual believer collect from Scripture that to him, even to him, the covenant of grace and the promises thereof belong ? Will Scripture prove this otherwise than by necessary consequence ? " etc.—Gillespie, *Miscell. Quest.* ch. xx. arg. 3.]

[1] Mark xii. 24-27.   [2] Luke xxiv. 25-27.

again, we find Christ blaming men for not having drawn certain consequences from Scripture statements, and accepted the conclusions thus arrived at as equally binding on their faith and conscience with direct and explicit Divine announcements. So also, to refer to one other illustration of this truth, all through the Epistle to the Hebrews we see with what freedom and effect the apostle uses the privilege of drawing inferences from the inspired language of the Old Testament, and founding upon these as equally decisive in his argument, and equally of Divine authority with express Scripture statements. "From this we may learn," says Dr. Owen, referring to an instance of this sort in Heb. i. 5, "that it is lawful to draw consequences from Scripture assertions; and such consequences, rightly deduced, are infallibly true, and *de fide*. Thus, from the name given unto Christ, the apostle deduceth by just consequence His exaltation and pre-eminence above angels. Nothing will rightly follow from truth but what is so also, and that of the same nature with the truth from whence it is derived. So that whatever by just consequence is drawn from the Word of God, is itself also the Word of God, and truth infallible. And to deprive the Church of this liberty in the interpretation of the Word, is to deprive it of the chiefest benefit intended by it. This is that on which the whole ordinance of preaching is founded ; which makes that which is derived out of the Word to have the power, authority, and efficacy of the Word accompanying it. Thus, though it be the proper work and effect of the Word of God to quicken, regenerate, sanctify, and purify the elect—and the Word primarily and directly is only that which is written in the Scriptures —yet we find all these effects produced in and by the preaching of the Word, when perhaps not one sentence of the Scripture is verbatim repeated. And the reason hereof is, because whatsoever is directly deduced and delivered according to the mind and appointment of God from the Word, is the Word of God, and hath the power, authority, and efficacy of the Word accompanying it."[1]

[1] Owen, *Works*, Goold's ed. vol. xx. p. 147. Cumming, *Grounds of the Present Differences*—Part i. "Concerning the Authority of Scripture Consequences in Matters of Faith," Lond. 1720, pp. 3-178. Dunlop, *The Uses of Creeds and Confessions of Faith*, Buchanan's ed. Lond. 1857, pp. 129 ff. [Turrettin, *Instit. Theol. Elenct.* loc. i. qu. xii. Gillespie, *Miscell. Quest.* ch. xx.]

APPENDIX G., Vol. I. p. 389.

THE BOOK OF COMMON ORDER.

The earliest edition of this work bears the title : *The Forme of Prayers and Ministration of the Sacraments, etc., used in the Englishe Congregation at Geneva, and approved by the famous and godly learned man, John Calvyn.* Geneva 1556. It was first drawn up about a year before that date by John Knox, Whittingham, Gilby, Fox, and Cole for the use of the English congregation at Frankfurt, where some purer form of service than that furnished by the English Book of Common Prayer was then desired.[1] "Our agreement," says Knox,—referring, however, to a form of service somewhat altered from its original shape, in deference to the feelings and associations of some of the English brethren,—"was signified to the congregation, accepted, and allowed by the same to take place to the last day of April; and then, if any contention should arise, that the matter should be referred to the determination of five learned men (Calvin, Musculus, Peter Martyr, Bullinger, and Viret), as a writing made upon this agreement doth testify. Herewith all men seemed to be pleased; no man did speak against it; thanks were given to God, the Lord's Supper was ministered, the Order by us appointed was used, well liked by many, and by none reproved; till some of those who after came amongst us, before they desired to be admitted of the Church, did begin to break the Order, whereof they were by the seniors and others admonished, but no amendment appeared. For they were admonished not to murmur aloud when the minister prayed; but they would not give place, but quarrelled, and said, ' They would do as they had done in England, and their Church should have an English face.' The

---

[1] [Compare Calvin's letter to them on the subject; Knox's *Works*, Laing's ed. vol. iv. pp. 28–30, 51 ff. As to Knox's own opinion of the English Liturgy, see vol. iv. pp. 43 f., vol. vi. pp. 11 ff.]

Lord grant it to have the face of Christ's Church, which is the only matter that I sought, God is my record ; and therefore I would have had it agreeable in outward rites and ceremonies with Christian Churches reformed." [1]

The form of service drawn up by Knox and the other office-bearers in the congregation at Frankfurt was adopted, in its original shape, shortly after in the English Church at Geneva, in which both he and Whittingham were for some time pastors. It seems to have been almost immediately received into general use in Scotland, being probably introduced here by Knox himself during his visit to this country in the autumn of 1555 ; for we find the First Book of Discipline, framed in 1560, speaking familiarly of " our Book of Common Order," " the Book of our Common Order, callit the Order of Geneva," [2] as a work already of recognised standing, and generally employed in the Church.

The need for some such authorized guide and model for the use of Churches suddenly called upon, in a time of great social and political disorder, and amid prevailing ignorance, both to organize their ecclesiastical polity and to settle their form of worship, must be obvious to every one in the slightest degree familiar with the history of the period. The congregations in Scotland, as in all the other countries of Europe, under the sway of Roman Catholicism, had been wont to look on at the mass, independently celebrated by the priests in an unknown tongue,

---

[1] Knox, *Works*, vol. iv. p. 41. A *Brief Discourse of the Troubles begun at Frankeford*, ann. *Dom.* 1554 (written probably by Whittingham, afterwards Dean of Durham), Lond. 1642, pp. 23–42, etc. [in Knox's *Works*, vol. iv. pp. 21-40]. M'Crie, *Life of Knox*, 5th ed. vol. i. pp. 140-159.

[2] *First Book of Discipline*, ch. vii. 1, xi. 3, in Knox's *Works*, vol. ii. pp. 210, 230. [An attempt has been made by Sage, and some other Episcopalian writers, to prove that the English Prayer Book was for some years in regular use in Scotland at the time of the Reformation. Their arguments are mainly founded on a sentence in a letter of Kirkaldy of Grange, repeated by Cecil, and a similar statement by Knox and Calderwood in their histories, to the effect that at an early period, before the establishment of the Reformation in Scotland, the Lords of the Congregation agreed that, when the parish Churches were cleansed from Popery, " Common Prayers should be read in them on the Sunday, with the Lessons of the New and Old Testament, conform to the Order of the Book of Common Prayers." On this point, see the remarks of the learned editor of Knox's *Works*, vol. vi. pp. 277 ff. " These arrangements," he concludes, after adverting to the facts of the case, " were merely prospective, to suit the exigencies of the time ; and if we admit that the English Liturgy was actually adopted, it could only have been to a partial extent, and of no long continuance. But this, after all, is a question of very little importance, although it has been keenly disputed ; for it is well to

much as they might have looked on at a play, only with less understanding of the meaning of the performance. The Bible had long been a sealed book in Scotland. Ignorance of Divine things characterized all classes of the community to an almost incredible extent. They did not know what God's worship ought to be, or on what principles it should be conducted. Those from among whom the office-bearers of the Church must be drawn, for the most part needed instruction and guidance as to their duties, quite as much as the great body of the membership as to theirs. Accordingly, the aim of John Knox and others, who drew up this work and introduced it into our country, was that it should be a *Book of Church Order*—a guide to ministers, elders, deacons, and members in their respective duties and functions; and for this purpose every position advanced has the proofs of it from Scripture attached at the foot of the page. " We," say the authors of the preface to the book, " not as the greatest clerks of all, but as the least able of many, do present unto you which desire the increase of God's glory, and the pure simplicity of His Word, *a Form and Order of a reformed Church limite within the compass of God's Word*, which our Saviour hath left unto us as only sufficient to govern all our actions by; so that whatsoever is added to this Word by man's device, seem it never so good, holy, or beautiful, yet before our God, who is jealous, and cannot admit any companion or counseller, it is evil, wicked, and abominable. . . . The which considerations, dear brethren, when we weighed with

remember that at this period there were no settled parish Churches, and as there were no special congregations either in Edinburgh or in any of the principal towns throughout the country, no ministers had been appointed. The Lords of the Congregation and their adherents were much too seriously concerned in defending themselves from the Queen Regent and her French auxiliaries, and more intent for that purpose in endeavouring to obtain the necessary aid from England, than to be at all concerned about points of ritual observance. In the following year, when the French troops were expelled from Scotland, and the Protestant cause was ultimately triumphant, we may conjecture that, in some measure swayed by the avowed dislike of Knox to the English Service Book (as expressed in his letter to Mrs. Lock in April 1559), the preference was given to the Forms of Geneva. We hear at least no more word of the English Prayer Book ; and in the Book of Discipline, prepared in December 1560, the only form mentioned is ' Our Buke of Common Ordour,' and ' The Buke of our Common Ordour, callit the Ordour of Geneva.' At the meeting of General Assembly, held on the last day of December 1562, is this Act : ' It is concludit that ane uniforme Ordour sal be taken and keipit in the Administratioun of the Sacraments, Solemnization of Marriages, and Burial of the Dead, according to the Booke of Geneva.' " Cf. Anderson, *The Countryman's Letter to the Curate*, 1711, pp. 35-40, 60-94.]

reverent fear and humbleness, and also knowing that negligence in reforming that religion which was begun in England was not the least cause of God's rod laid upon us, having now obtained, by the mercifull Providence of our heavenly Father, a free Church for all our nation in this most worthy city of Geneva, we presented to the judgment of the famous man, John Calvin, and others learned in these parts, the Order which we minded to use in our Church, who approving it as sufficient for a Christian congregation, we put the same in execution, nothing doubting but all godly men shall be much edified thereby."[1]

The first chapter in the Book of Common Order treats of the ministers or pastors of the Christian Church, the qualifications needed for the office, the duties to be discharged by them, the proper manner of their election, examination, and induction into office—all being supported by Scriptural proof. In chap. ii. are discussed the office, duties, qualifications, and election of ruling elders. Chap. iii. takes up the subject of deacons, the requisites for the office, and the duties properly belonging to it—very different from those discharged by the deacons of the Romish Church. Chap. iv. defines the nature and duties of the teaching elder, or doctor, as set apart more especially for the exposition of the Word of God, and urges strongly the need of general as well as theological education throughout the country. "Because men cannot so well profit in that knowledge (of Divine things) except they be first instructed in the tongues and humane sciences—for now God worketh not commonlie by miracles—it is necessary that seed be sown for the time to come, to the intent that the Church be not left barren and waste to our posteritie, and that Schools also be erected and Colleges maintained with just and sufficient stipends, wherein youth may be trained in the knowledge and fear of God, that in their ripe age they may prove worthie members of our Lord Jesus Christ, whether it be to rule in civil policie or to serve in the spiritual ministrie, or else to live in godly reverence and subjection."[2] It is well known to every reader of the history of Scotland how the efforts of our Church to carry into

---

[1] Preface to first Geneva ed. of *Book of Common Order*, 10th Feb. 1556, Dunlop's Collection, vol. ii. p. 389 f.

[2] Dunlop's Collection, vol. ii. p. 410. [Cf. *First Book of Discipline*, ch. vii. ; M'Crie, *Life of Knox*, 5th ed. vol. ii. pp. 10 ff. ; *Life of Melville*, 2d ed. vol. i. p. 156 f., vol. ii. pp. 336–448.]

full effect the noble design of our Reformers in this respect were withstood and frustrated by the avarice of the nobility, the despotism of the Court, and the confusions and persecutions which accompanied the repeated and long-continued attempts to force the Prelatic system upon the nation. Chap. v. states the object of "the weekly Assembly of the Ministers, Elders, and Deacons;" in other words, the regular meeting of the Presbytery or Kirk-session and Deacons' Court. Chap. vi. describes a sort of congregational fellowship meeting for the exposition of Scripture and orderly discussion of some Scriptural subject; and chap. vii. deals at some length with the question of "The Order of the Ecclesiastical Discipline."[1]

Next follows "The Order of Public Worship,"[2] showing what are the legitimate parts of the public services, and how each is severally to be conducted, giving a sort of outline or skeleton of the order of worship, with examples of forms of prayer and benediction, confessions of sin, and intercessions, which, "or such like," the minister is to use. Then come the "Order of Baptism," and the "Manner of the Administration of the Lord's Supper," in which the nature and design of the two Sacraments are explained, and the manner in which they are to be dispensed is appointed. Here also examples of suitable exhortations and thanksgivings are supplied; and the officiating minister is directed to "use either the words following, or like in effect."[3] In like manner are given a form of marriage, directions for the visitation of the sick, and, lastly, for the burial of the dead. On the very same principle are constructed two little works which form a sort of supplement to the Book of Common Order: " *The Ordour and Doctrine of the General Fast, appointed by the General Assembly of the Church of Scotland, halden at Edinburgh the 25th day of December* 1565: *set down by John Knox and John Craig at the appointment of the Assemblie; The Ordour of Excommunication and of Public Repentance used in the Church of Scotland, and commanded to be printed by the General Assemblie of the same* (drawn up by Knox), 1569."[4]

It must be perfectly clear to any man who reads the Book of Common Order with any attention, that to call it a *Liturgy* in the strict and technical sense of that term, is a mere misuse of

[1] [This chapter is in great part literally taken from Calvin, *Instit.* lib. iv. cap. xii.]
[2] Dunlop, vol. ii. p. 417. [3] *Ibid.* p. 450.
[4] *Ibid.* pp. 645–747. [Knox's *Works*, Laing's ed. vol. vi. pp. 381–470.]

words. It was intended to furnish to a community, in general
ignorance on the whole subject, a model or outline of what a New
Testament Church ought to be, as respects its office-bearers, its
congregational Church Courts, its membership, discipline, ordinances, and modes of worship. No fixed and unalterable forms
of prayer are prescribed or imposed. On the contrary, the true
and Scriptural principle of Church worship, as propounded by
Calvin, and afterwards embodied in the standards of our Church,
is laid down in the Preface to the Book of Common Order; and
all unauthorized ceremonies, especially when interfering with the
liberties of Christ's people, are emphatically denounced. Even
where a model or example of public prayer is given, the use of
it is only allowed or recommended, not commanded. Thus, for
instance : " The minister useth one of these two confessions, *or
like in effect*, exhorting the people diligently to examine themselves, following in their hearts the tenor of his words." " The
minister, after sermon, useth this prayer following, *or such like*."
"It shall not be necessary for the minister daily to repeat all
these things before mentioned, but beginning with *some manner
of confession*, to proceed to the sermon ; which ended, he *either*
useth the ' Prayer for all Estates' before mentioned, *or else
prayeth as the Spirit of God shall move his heart, framing the
same according to the time and manner which he hath entreated of*,"
etc. " The minister, exhorting the people to pray, saith in this
manner, *or such like*." " Certain psalms and certain histories are
to be distinctly read (which are then specified as being for a particular occasion of public fasting) ; exhortation to be conceived
thereupon, and prayers likewise, *as God shall instruct and inspire
the minister or reader*." " This ordour may be enlarged or contracted as the wisdom of the discreit minister shall think expedient ;
*for we rather show the way to the ignorant than prescribe order to
the learned, that cannot be amended*." [1]

It is one proof among many of the sound judgment and insight into Scriptural principles which marked the fathers of our
Church, that even in an age when the standard of ministerial
acquirements was at first so low, and the means of a thorough
training for the ecclesiastical office were so hard to be obtained,[2]

[1] Dunlop, vol. ii. pp. 417, 421, 426, 694, 746.

[2] M'Crie, *Life of Knox*, 5th ed. vol. i. pp. 14–26; *Life of Melville*, 2d ed.
vol. ii. ch. xi. ; *Miscell. of the Wodrow Society*, Edin. 1844, pp. 321–328.
Knox's *Works*, vol. vi. p. 388, etc.

they yet carefully refrained from imposing a stated Liturgy on the Church; and while giving models of prayer, and forms which might be employed where desirable, left it to the Presbyteries and other Church Courts to prescribe the use of forms in any individual cases, as circumstances, in their view of them, might demand.

APPENDIX H, Vol. I. p. 469.

IMPOSITION OF HANDS IN ORDINATION.

The laying on of hands, or the action which usually accompanies ordination, is no essential part of it. Ordination essentially consists in the solemn setting apart of a man to the regular discharge of certain ecclesiastical functions, and his formal investiture with office by the Church in the name of Christ. The act of the Church in thus ordaining to office is not rendered null and void by the absence of the accessory or accompaniment of the laying on of hands by the parties who conduct the ordination. For, *in the first place*, there is no Scriptural warrant for believing that the imposition of hands in the New Testament Church conveyed any supernatural gift or grace, except when the action was performed by an apostle for that purpose. There is no evidence whatever, but the reverse, for the assertion, that in the ordinary case of a man's being ordained to office by fasting and prayer, with the laying on of the hands of the presbytery, as we know was the custom in the apostolic Church, any supernatural gifts were communicated by the action or gesture now referred to. Far less is there any ground for maintaining that the special promises of grace and blessing connected with the entrance upon the ministerial office, and with the subsequent discharge of its duties, are made to depend, in all ages and in every case, upon this ceremony of the laying on of hands. And, *in the second place*, imposition of hands in ordination is no significant part of the institution, no teaching sign like the water in Baptism, or the bread and wine in the Lord's Supper. On this ground the Reformers and their successors used to prove against the Romanists, that Orders could not lawfully be reckoned among the Sacraments. They pointed out that, with respect to all the five spurious Sacraments of the Romish Church, there was no significant and Divinely instituted sign answering to the thing signified, as in the case of the two genuine Sacraments of the New Testament.[1]

In the apostolic Church, indeed, imposition of hands seems always to have accompanied ordination to office in the Church; and their recorded practice in this respect gives sufficient warrant for our following their example, as has been done in almost all the Protestant Churches. We lay on hands in ordaining to ecclesiastical office very much as we raise our hands in public benediction in the Church. It is a suitable and Scriptural accompaniment of our then and there imploring the Divine blessing on the person ordained, and of his solemn designation to office and consecration to the work of the Lord, which all take place at that time. But it does not enter as an essential part into the ordination, as if that would be invalidated by the absence of the imposition of hands.

In the First Book of Discipline, drawn up in 1560, after stating that ordinary vocation to the pastoral office involves three things, — election by the people, examination " before men of soundest judgment " in the ministry, and admission by the Presbytery in the presence and with the consent of the congregation, — the authors of the work proceed : " We judge it expedient that the admission of ministers be in open audience, and that some special minister make a sermon touching the duty and office of ministers, touching their manners, conversation, and life ; as also touching the obedience which the Church oweth to their ministers. Commandment should be given as well to the minister as to the people, both being present; to wit, that he with all careful diligence attend upon the flock of Christ Jesus, over which he is appointed pastor ; that he walk in the presence of God so sincerely that the graces of the Holy Spirit may be multiplied unto him, and in the presence of men so soberly and uprightly, that his life may confirm in the eyes of men that which by tongue and word he persuaded unto others. The people should be exhorted to reverence and honour their ministers chosen, as the servants and ambassadors of the Lord Jesus, obeying the commandments which they pronounce from God's Word, even as they would obey God Himself. . . . Other ceremony than the public approbation of the people, and the declaration of the chief minister, that the person there

---

[1] Chemnitz, *Examen Concil. Trident.*, Pars. ii. loc. xiii. sect. iii. 2–4. Turrettin, *Instit. Theol. Elenct.*, loc. xix. qu. xxxi.

presented is appointed to serve the Church, we cannot approve; for albeit the apostles used imposition of hands, yet seeing *the miracle* is ceased, the using of the ceremony we judge *not necessary.*" [1] This opinion with regard to the imposition of hands in ordination—which is, however, by no means expressed in a very decided manner—was evidently founded, in the minds of the authors of the First Book of Discipline, mainly on the flagrant abuse of the rite in the Church of Rome,—where it was considered to be a sign and condition of the invariable communication of the supernatural grace and "character" of the priesthood,—but partly also, perhaps, on a failure to distinguish clearly between those cases in the New Testament in which laying on of hands was connected with the miraculous gifts and endowments conveyed to others by the apostles, and those in which the action simply accompanied an ordinary investiture with office in the Church.

In the Second Book of Discipline, which was drawn up in 1578, with much more deliberation and care than there had been an opportunity of bestowing upon the First, we have the following statements on this point : " Ordination is the separation and sanctifying of the person appointed to God and His Kirk, after he be weil tryit and fund qualifiet. The ceremonies of ordination are, fasting, earnest prayer, and imposition of hands of the eldership." [2]

" Although," says George Gillespie, " (1) I hold the imposition of the hands of the presbytery to be no Sacrament, nor efficacious and operative for giving of the Holy Ghost, as the laying on of the apostles' hands was ; nor (2) necessary to ordination, *necessitate medii vel finis,* as if ordination were void, and no ordination without it, or as if they who were not ordained with the laying on of the hands of the presbytery were therefore to be thought unordained or unministeriated ; although, likewise, (3) I do not hold the laying on of hands to be the substantial act or part of ordination, which I have before proved to be essential to the calling of a minister, but only the ritual part in ordination ; and although (4) I hold the laying on of hands to be a rite whereunto we ought to be very sparing to ascribe mysterious significations, wherein some have gone too far, and taken too much liberty ; yet I hold, with the generality of Protestant writers, and

---

[1] *First Book of Discipline,* ch. iv. 3.   Dunlop's Collection, vol. ii. p. 529.
[2] *Second Book of Discipline,* ch. iii. 6.   Dunlop, vol. ii. p. 768.

with the best Reformed Churches, that the laying on of hands is to be still retained in ordination. I hold also, that this laying on of hands is an ordinance of the New Testament,—and so our dissenting brethren of the Independent way hold also,—and that it is necessary, by the necessity of precept and institution, and in point of duty. ' For although there is no certain precept extant concerning the laying on of hands, yet because we see the apostles did always use it, their so accurate observing of it ought to be unto us instead of a precept,'—saith Calvin, *Instit.* lib. iv. cap. iii. 16. For the example of the apostles or apostolic Churches in approved things, which have a standing reason, are binding, and instead of institutions. The laying on of the hands of the apostles, in so far as the Holy Ghost was given thereby, was extraordinary, and ceased with themselves; yet in so far as the apostles, yea, and the presbytery too, laid on hands in their ordaining of ministers, there is a standing reason why we should do in like manner; the laying on of hands being a rite properly belonging to the praying over those whom we bless in the name of the Lord, as is manifest by those examples of laying on of hands, in Jacob's blessing of Ephraim and Manasseh, and in Christ's blessing and praying over the little children.[1]

"Looking thus upon laying on of hands, *first*, as a rite in blessing and prayer over,[2] *second*, as a rite for public designation and solemn setting apart of such a person,[3] and if you will, *third*, as a rite of giving up, dedicating, and offering unto the Lord,— of which use of laying on of hands there are divers examples in the books of Moses,[4]—in these respects, and under these considerations, we use laying on of hands in ordination, and ought to do so in regard of the primitive pattern."[5]

---

[1] Gen. xlviii. 14 ; Matt. xix. 15 ; Mark x. 16.
[2] Lev. ix. 22 ; Luke xxiv. 50.
[3] Num. viii. 10, xxvii. 18, 23 ; Deut. xxxiv. 9.
[4] Lev. i. 4, iii. 2, iv. 24, etc., xvi. 21, xxiv. 14 ; Deut. xiii. 9, xvii. 7.
[5] Gillespie, " Miscell. Quest.," ch. viii. in *Presbt. Armoury,* vol. ii. p. 46 ; cf. pp. 14 f., 26. " Dispute against the Engl.-Popish Ceremonies," Part iii. ch. viii. digr. i. in *Presbt. Armoury,* vol. i. p. 165.

APPENDIX I, Vol. II. pp. 278, 294.

NOTES ON THE LITERATURE OF THE SUBJECT OF THIS
TREATISE.

The following works are worthy of being consulted in connection with the various departments of our subject. I mention
them in order, according to the different divisions and heads under
which we have been led to arrange the topics discussed. And, in
the first place, I name two works of primary importance and value,
both of which cover, to a certain extent, almost the whole ground
which we are called upon to traverse : the Fourth Book of Calvin's
' Institutes,' taken along with his ' Tracts on the Sacraments,' and
the Third Part of Turrettin's ' Institutio Theologiæ Elencticæ.'
I. The Fourth Book of Calvin's ' Institutes ' is entitled, ' De
externis Mediis vel Adminiculis, quibus Deus in Christi Societatem
nos invitat, et in eâ retinet.' It consists of three parts : 1. ' De
Ecclesiâ ; ' 2. ' De Sacramentis ; ' 3. ' De Politicâ Administra-
tione.' Under the 1st head, or the Church, we have four divisions,
each comprising several chapters. *First*, the Notes of the Church ;
second, the Government of the Church, and more especially, the
corruptions of and departures from its primitive constitution under
the Papacy ; *third*, the Power of the Church as to matters of
faith, legislation, and jurisdiction ; *fourth*, the Discipline of the
Church in its uses and abuses. Under the 2d head, the Sacraments, we have three divisions. *First*, the Nature and Import of
the Sacraments in general ; *second*, Baptism, as administered to
infants and adults, and the Lord's Supper, with a discussion of
the Romish corruptions of both ordinances ; *third*, the five spurious
Sacraments of the Popish system. Under the 3d head, or Political
Administration, the subject of civil government is considered under
its various aspects, more especially as regards the relation between
the State or the Magistrate and the Church.
Two general deficiencies, arising from the circumstances of the

writer, may be observed in Calvin's masterly, and in some respects unrivalled, work. In the first place, it is very largely a polemic against Popery; and, secondly, more modern theories of the Church, such as the Independent and the High Church Episcopalian, are of course not discussed, since they had not yet been propounded among the Reformed Churches.

II. Calvin's ' Tracts on the Sacrament' comprise :

(1.) A short Treatise on the Lord's Supper, 1540.

(2.) The ' Consensus Tigurinus,' or Mutual Consent regarding the Sacraments between the Churches of Zurich and Geneva, 1549.

(3.) Exposition of the Heads of Agreement, 1554.

(4.) Second Defence of the Pious and Orthodox Faith concerning the Sacraments, in answer to Westphal, 1556.

(5.) Last Admonition to Westphal, 1557.

(6.) The true Partaking of the Flesh and Blood of Christ in the Holy Supper, in reply to Heshusius, 1560.

(7.) The best Method of obtaining Concord on the Sacraments, 1560.

III. The Third Part of Turrettin's ' Institutio Theologicæ Elencticæ ' may be divided into four heads :

(1.) The Nature of the Church, loc. xviii. qu. i.–xv.

(2.) The Government of the Church, qu. xvi.–xxviii.

(3.) The Power of the Church, qu. xxix.–xxxiv.

(4.) The Sacraments, loc. xix.

Under (1) we have such subjects discussed as the Scriptural definition of the Church, its membership, unity, invisibility, perpetuity, infallibility, the true notes of the Church, etc. Under (2) we have a discussion of such points as the Scriptural form of Church government, the primacy of the Pope, whether there ought to be any distinction between bishops and presbyters, the necessity of the ministerial office, the call to it, the call of the first Reformers, the immunities of the clergy, etc. Under (3) are considered such questions as, what kind and amount of power belongs to the Church, whether that power is distinct from the civil, how exercised about matters of faith and creeds and confessions, whether the Church has the power of making new laws, properly so called, ecclesiastical discipline and excommunication, the origin and authority of Councils, the power of the civil magistrate *circa sacra*. Under (4) the subject of the Sacraments is taken up very fully, and handled with masterly power and clearness. Beginning with the general nature of the New Testament Sacraments, the author discusses their nature, necessity; the sacramental sign, word, union between the sign and thing signified ; the intention of the minister, the " character" alleged to be communicated by some of the Popish Sacraments, the efficacy of Sacraments, the difference between those of the Old and those of the New Testament. Then, coming on to particular Sacraments, Turrettin takes up the subject of Baptism, its nature, necessity, by whom administered, the baptismal formula, Romish Baptism, the efficacy of Baptism, and on what grounds it is to be administered to infants. Next, the topics connected with the Lord's Supper are discussed,—the nature and design of the ordinance, the consecration of the elements, the breaking of bread, communion under both kinds, the sacramental words, transubstantiation, the real presence, the sacrifice of the mass, the five false Sacraments of the Romish Church.

One or other of these two books I strongly recommend for careful study in connection with our whole subject. If choice must be made between the two, Turrettin is, on the whole, to be preferred, as furnishing the more complete, scientific, and thoroughly well considered discussion of the various departments of the doctrine of the Church. The best edition of his works is the Edinburgh one, published in 1847. I may also refer you to the third volume of Principal Hill's ' Lectures on Divinity,' where the subjects of the Sacraments, Church government, Church power as to doctrine, ordinances, and discipline, are ably, though more briefly treated.[1] Some of the works next to be mentioned profess also to deal more or less with the general subject, as well as with particular branches of it. It may, however, be more convenient to arrange them under the different divisions of the course, although the classification may be of a somewhat rough and general sort.

---

[1] Hill, *Lectures on Divinity*, 2d ed. Edin. 1825, vol. iii. pp. 268–545. [Cf. his *Theological Institutes*, Edin. 1803, Parts ii. and iii. The editions mentioned here and elsewhere in this part of the Appendix are those commonly used by Dr. Bannerman.]

PART I.—NATURE OF THE CHURCH.

Under this head may be named :

Mastricht, 'Theologia Theoretico-practica,' Trajecti ad Rhenum, 1715. A work of much ability and learning. The seventh book takes up the doctrine of the Church under the following divisions: 1. The Nature of the Church; 2. The Ministers of the Church; 3. The Sacraments; 4. Discipline and Government.

Field, ' Of the Church, five bookes,' 2d ed. Oxford 1628.—This is a learned, able, and comprehensive book, and has always been regarded as a standard work in the Church of England. Book i. treats of the Name, Nature, and Definition of the Church; Book ii. of the Notes of the Church; Book iii. discusses which is the true Church as tested by those notes; Book iv. the Privileges of the Church; Book v. the different degrees, orders, and callings of those to whom the government of the Church is committed.

Mestrezat, ' Traitté de l'Eglise,' Genève 1649. A valuable work, by a minister of the French Reformed Church at Charenton.

Bishop Jewel's ' Apology for the Church of England,' and his ' Defence of the Apology.' Jewel was perhaps the first really great theologian of the Reformed Church of England. His works now referred to, deal of course with the doctrinal as well as the ecclesiastical points in dispute between Protestants and Romanists.

Hooker, ' Of the Laws of Ecclesiastical Polity,' eight books, ' Works,' Oxford 1845.—This famous work of Hooker's was written to meet the objections of the Puritans to the defective reformation of the English Church. It exhibits very great ability, eloquence, and learning; but it is by no means fair in the representation often given of the views of opponents, nor happy in the ground which it adopts in its defence of the exist-ing state of ecclesiastical matters in England. Hooker does not attempt to vindicate the Prelacy of the Church of England against the Scriptural arguments of his Presbyterian opponents on the ground of any Divine right supposed to attach to it. He maintains, on the contrary, that no universally binding form of government has been appointed for the Christian Church at all, and seeks to defend the royal supremacy in the English Establish-ment, and the consequences which have resulted from its exercise, on the footing of the king's being " the highest uncommanded commander," who in a Christian country has proper jurisdiction within the Church, as really but another department of the commonwealth. Palmer, ' Treatise on the Church of Christ,' Lond. 1838.— The author belongs to the extreme High Church party in the English Establishment, but to that section of it which still seeks to vindicate a position against the Church of Rome with its own weapons. The literature of the subject is very fully given in the way of reference and quotation.

Archbishop Whately, ' The Kingdom of Christ,' 4th ed. Lond. 1845.—This is a very able, candid, aḋd valuable work. Its chief defect is that of regarding the Church too exclusively from the merely human point of view. The author does not hold the Divine appointment of any one form of Church government; although, as regards the New Testament Church, he gives up almost all the Episcopalian, and adopts many of the Presbyterian positions. Hence he seeks to prove that all the powers and privileges of the Church may be traced up to the powers and privileges inherent in a mere human and voluntary society. His arguments are very generally sound and valuable so far as they go ; but he stops short too soon. The characteristics of Dr. Whately's mind eminently fitted him for dealing with the Tractarian system. Those parts of his work which take up the theory of Apostolical Succession and some kindred points are especially able and effective.

Maurice, ' The Kingdom of Christ,' 2d ed. Lond. 1842.—This work is greatly inferior to Archbishop Whately's in clearness, vigour, and accuracy of statement ; but it agrees with it in contemplating the Church almost exclusively from the human standpoint.

' Jus Divinum Regiminis Ecclesiastici ; or, The Divine Right of Church Government asserted and evidenced by the Holy Scriptures. By sundry Ministers of Christ within the City of London.' Lond. 1646.—This work contains an extremely able, thorough, and satisfactory discussion of most of the points relating to the nature of Church government as a Divine institution, and to the power or authority of the Church, its seat and exercise. Several of the authors of this treatise were members of the Westminster Assembly.

Claude, ' Défense de la Réformation contre le livre [par Pierre Nicole], intitulé Préjugéz légitimes contre les Calvinistes,' Amsterdam 1683.—This celebrated book was written by Claude, minister of the French Protestant Church at Charenton. It contains a masterly discussion of the topics, doctrinal and historical, which naturally arise out of a thorough answer to the favourite question of Romanists to Protestants : " Where was your Church before Luther?" The fourth part is especially worthy of careful study. An English translation of this work was published in London in the year 1683, under the title, ' An Historical Defence of the Reformation, in answer to a book intituled " Just Prejudices against the Calvinists" . . .; translated by T. B. M. A.'

Ayton, ' The Original Constitution of the Christian Church,' Edin. 1730.—This is an able and valuable work. Its author was minister of our Church at Alyth.

Killen, ' The Ancient Church : its History, Doctrine, Worship, and Constitution, traced for the first three hundred years.' Lond. 1859.

Litton, ' The Church of Christ in its Idea, Attributes, and Ministry,' Lond. 1851. In this very interesting and able work, the author brings out with great effect some of the fundamental differences between the Protestant theory of the Church on the one hand, and that of Romanists and semi-Romanists on the other. Mr. Litton, like most other moderate English Churchmen, builds his main arguments in support of Prelacy on expediency and ancient ecclesiastical custom. The Scripture argument in its behalf he very frankly gives up, admitting that there is no evidence in the New Testament that any other order of office-bearers was established in the Christian society by our Lord or His inspired followers besides those of presbyters or bishops and deacons, and that the analogy of the Jewish synagogue upon which the Christian Church was founded, while it furnishes the model of the Presbyterian system, fails us with respect to the Prelatic.

Principal Cunningham, ' Historical Theology,' vol. i. ch. i. xiii., ' Works,' Edin. 1863, vol. ii. pp. 9–42, 390–412. ' Discussions on Church Principles,' ch. vi. viii., ' Works,' vol. iv. pp. 164–234. Of the standing and value of the writings of Principal Cunningham, it is unnecessary that I should say anything.

Jonathan Edwards, ' Inquiry concerning the Qualifications for Communions,' ' Works,' vol. i. Lond. 1834, pp. 434–531.—

This treatise is well worthy of consultation in connection with the subject of the membership of the visible Church.

Knox, ' Answer to a Letter written by James Tyrie, a Scottish Jesuit,' 1572, ' Works,' Laing's ed. vol. vi. pp. 486-512.—This was John Knox's latest work, and deals with great vigour with the question of the visible and invisible Church. M'Crie, ' Statement,' Edin. 1807.—This work comprises about the ablest discussion of the questions of national religion, the relation of Church and State, etc., with which I am acquainted. See also the same author's ' Discourses on the Unity of the Church,' Edin. 1821.

As specimens of works on the Church by divines of the Church of Rome, I name four,—the authors of the first two being representatives of the more rigid and traditional class of Romanists, while those of the second two belong to the modern and philosophic school. Bellarmine, 'De Ecclesia Disputationes,' tom. ii. Ingolstadii 1605.   Perrone, ' Prælectiones Theologicæ,' tom. ii. Parisiis 1842.   Möhler, ' Symbolism,' Robertson's Transl. 2d ed. Lond. 1847, vol. i. pp. 286-361, vol. ii. pp. 1-148. [Symbolik, 6te Ausgabe, Mainz. 1843.]   De Maistre, ' The Pope,' Dawson's Transl. Lond. 1850.—Möhler is by far the ablest of modern defenders of the Church of Rome.   His work is an admirable specimen of what can be done by a thoroughly efficient and dextrous controversialist in the way of omission, modification, plausible explanation, and defence, to maintain the cause of the Papacy.   To any one wishing an excuse for going over to Rome, this is a book to be strongly recommended.   [The best answer to Möhler is probably Nitzsch's ' Protestantische Beantwortung der Symbolik Dr. Möhler's,' which first appeared in the ' Studien und Kritiken,' and was afterwards published separately at Hamburg, 1835.   For further specimens of the views of modern Romanists of the more Ultramontane school, regarding the Church among other subjects, see ' Essays on Religion and Literature by various writers,' edited by Dr. Manning, 1st series, Lond. 1865 ; 2d series, Lond. 1867.]

PART II.—POWER OF THE CHURCH.

Voetius, 'Politica Ecclesiastica,' Amstelodami 1663–1676, in four volumes.—Gisbert Voets or Voetius was Professor of Theology and Oriental Languages at Utrecht. He was a man of extraordinary learning, of very great ability, and of the highest standing among the theologians of the Church of Holland, who at that time were among the first in Europe. This work of his is an exceedingly important one, displaying immense theological research, as well as intellectual power. It discusses, in a very able, elaborate, and exhaustive way, almost all the points connected with the power of the Church and the matters about which that power is exercised, as well as the question of Church government, which is taken up very fully in the third volume. The period was one fruitful to an unparalleled extent in works on Church polity, the sphere of the civil magistrate, etc.; and nowhere are references to the contemporary literature and to the controversies in England and the Continent given more abundantly than in Voetius.

Apollonii, 'Jus Magistratis circa Sacra; sive, Tractatus Theologicus de Jure Magistratûs circa Res Ecclesiasticas,' Medioburgi Zelandorum 1642.—Apollonii, or Apollonius, as in this country he is more commonly called, was a minister of the Dutch Church at Middelburg, in Holland, and contemporary with Voetius. This work of his displays very high ability, sound judgment, and mastery over his subject. It has always been regarded as a standard in the Erastian controversy. Another valuable treatise by the same author, which deals with the question of Church power among other topics, was addressed to the Westminster Assembly. It is entitled 'Consideratio quarundam Controversiarum ad Regimen Ecclesiæ Dei spectantium, quæ in Angliæ Regno hodie agitantur,' Lond. 1644. An English translation of it was published in London in the following year: 'A Consideration of certaine Controversies,' etc.

George Gillespie, 'Aaron's Rod Blossoming; or, The Divine Ordinances of Church Government Vindicated.' Lond. 1846.—This famous treatise is unquestionably the most able, learned, systematic, and complete work on the Erastian controversy in existence. It deserves, and will repay, the most careful study.

The author's 'Treatise of Miscellany Questions,' Edin. 1639, is also an exceedingly important and useful book, discussing a wide range of topics connected with ecclesiastical theology. The whole of Gillespie's works, along with a memoir of his life, are included in the first two volumes of the 'Presbyterian Armoury,' edited by Dr. Hetherington, Edin. 1846.

Samuel Rutherford, 'The Divine Right of Church Government and Excommunication,' Lond. 1846. 'The Due Right of Presbyteries; or, A Peaceable Plea for the Government of the Church of Scotland,' Lond. 1644. These works take up kindred topics with those discussed by Gillespie; the last-named deals especially with the Independent theory of Church power. They are valuable and learned, but somewhat wanting in the clearness and method which characterize all Gillespie's productions.

Cunningham, 'Works,' vol. ii. ch. ii., vol. iv. ch. iii.–vi. ix. x.

PART III.—MATTERS IN REGARD TO WHICH CHURCH POWER IS EXERCISED.

Div. i.—*Church Power exercised in regard to Doctrine.*

Whitaker, 'Disputation on Holy Scripture against the Papists, especially Bellarmine and Stapleton,' Parker Soc. ed. Cambridge 1849.

Tillotson, 'The Rule of Faith' (in reply to Sergeant), Lond. 1666.

Chillingworth, 'The Religion of Protestants,' 4th ed. Lond. 1674.

Goode, 'The Divine Rule of Faith and Practice,' Lond. 1842.—This treatise was written with a special view to the Tractarian heresies. It is a very elaborate, able, and useful book, and has deservedly become a standard on the subject with which it deals.

Newman, 'Essay on the Development of Christian Doctrine,' 2d ed. Lond. 1846.—This remarkable and interesting book was written by Mr. Newman on the eve of his joining the Church of Rome. It embodies an ingenious method—which, if not absolutely new, is at least put in a novel and effective shape—of meeting the Protestant doctrine of the sufficiency and sole supremacy of Scripture as the rule of faith, and our objections on that ground to

the corruptions of the Romish Church. Newman's 'Essay' was
answered with much ability by Professor Archer Butler, in his
'Letters on the Development of Christian Doctrine,' which first
appeared in the pages of the 'Irish Ecclesiastical Journal,' but
were published separately in Dublin in 1850. Professor Butler
does not confine himself to a reply to Newman's theory, but takes
up many points connected with the general question of progress
in theology, and the place of creeds and confessions. Compare
also Principal Cunningham's review of Newman's 'Essay' in his
'Discussions on Church Principles,' ch. ii., 'Works,' vol. iv. pp.
35-77.

Dunlop, 'The Uses of Creeds and Confessions of Faith.'—
The production of this very useful work, along with the larger
compilation to which it was originally attached, forms but one
of the many services for which the Church of Scotland stands
indebted to the illustrious family to which the author belonged,
—services, of which not the least memorable or important have
been rendered in our own day. The little treatise now referred
to was written by Professor Dunlop of Edinburgh, son of the
well-known Principal Dunlop of Glasgow, who lived at the end
of the seventeenth century. It first appeared in the shape of a
Preface to a very valuable 'Collection of Confessions of Faith,
Catechisms, Directories, Books of Discipline, etc., of Public
Authority in the Church of Scotland,' Edin. 1719,—a book
which has now become somewhat scarce and high priced.
Dunlop's Preface was republished a few years ago in a separate
form, under the editorship of my respected friend and colleague,
Dr. James Buchanan. [Lond. 1857. Cf. Blackburne, 'The
Confessional: A Full and Free Inquiry into the Right of Estab-
lishing Confessions of Faith in Protestant Churches,' 1767;
Wardlaw, 'Systematic Theology,' Edin. 1856, vol. i. pp. 46-74.
Dr. Wardlaw admits the abstract lawfulness of creeds and confessions, both as public testimonies to truth, and as tests of fitness
for membership and office in the Church ; but he objects to them
on the ground of practical expediency, p. 55 f.]

Div. ii.—*Church Power exercised in regard to Ordinances.*

'Jus Divinum Ministerii Evangelici; or, The Divine Right
of the Gospel Ministry.' Published by the Provincial Assembly

of London, Lond. 1654. A very able and useful work, dealing especially with the views of the Independents and sectaries of the day. In the Second Part of it, ' Jus Divinum Ministerii Anglicani; or, The Divine Right of the Ministry of England,' the argument from Scripture and antiquity in favour of the Presbyterian system of Church polity is taken up.

Gillespie, ' Dispute against the English-Popish Ceremonies obtruded upon the Church of Scotland,' Edin. 1637.—This was Gillespie's first work, and it may be truly said to have settled the controversy which called it forth, so far as argument was concerned. No answer to it was ever attempted by the Prelatic party; and no answer was possible. It displays singular acuteness, learning, and force of reasoning; and the thoroughness of the discussion is as remarkable as the power with which it is conducted.

Ames, ' Suit against Human Ceremonies in Divine Worship,' 1633. By the celebrated author of the ' Medulla SS. Theologiæ,' and of ' Bellarminus Enervatus.'

Bradshaw, ' Several Treatises of Worship and Ceremonies,' Lond. 1660.—This is a collection of pamphlets written during the Puritan controversy.

Owen, ' A Discourse concerning Liturgies, and their Imposition,' Works, Goold's ed. vol. xv.; giving the Scriptural argument against the Imposition of Liturgies as well as of other humanly devised elements in Divine worship, with great clearness and force. Along with this work may be named one by Clarkson, Owen's colleague in the ministry: ' A Discourse concerning Liturgies,' Lond. 1689. It is published also, together with some valuable works against Diocesan Episcopacy, in Clarkson's ' Select Works,' published by the Wycliffe Society, Lond. 1846, pp. 247–374. In this treatise the argument against Liturgies, from their non-existence in the early Church, and from the history of their gradual introduction and prevalence afterwards, is given with very great learning and effect.

Robinson, ' A Review of the Case of Liturgies and their Imposition,' Lond. 1710.

Sir Peter King (afterwards Lord Chancellor), ' An Enquiry into the Constitution, Discipline, Unity, and Worship of the Primitive Church,' Lond. 1691.

Riddle, ' Manual of Christian Antiquities; or, An Account

of the Constitution, Ministers, Worship, Discipline, and Customs of the Ancient Church,' 2d ed. Lond. 1843.

Seaman, 'Vindication of the Judgment of the Reformed Churches concerning Ordination, and Laying on of Hands,' Lond. 1647.

Courayer, 'Dissertation on the Validity of the Ordinations of the English, and of the Succession of the Bishops of the Anglican Church,' Oxford 1844.—This work is translated from the French. It contains a very elaborate, but by no means very satisfactory or conclusive argument in favour of the validity—from a Roman Catholic point of view—of the Orders of the English Church. [The singularity of a Romanist coming forward to defend a position denounced by the general voice of his Church is lessened by the consideration that Courayer, at the time of writing this book, was unsound on various articles of Roman Catholic belief, besides those involved in the 'Gallican Liberties' (see *e.g.* pp. 148, 150, 219 ff.). Before the close of his life he seems to have fallen into very serious doctrinal errors on many points, pp. lviii.-lxi.]

Calderwood, 'Altare Damascenum,' Lugduni Batavoruni 1708. This is a very learned, able, and comprehensive work. Chap. ix. deals at great length with the question of humanly invented and imposed ceremonies in the worship of God, with special reference to the controversies on that subject in Scotland and England in the early part of the seventeenth century. See also, by the same author, 'The Perth Assembly,' 1619; 'Re-Examination of the Five Articles of Perth,' 1636. [As specimens of works by divines of the Lutheran Church on Ordination, the Ministerial Office, etc., may be named, Gerhard, 'Loci Theologici,' xxiii., 'De Ministerio Ecclesiastico,' ed. Preuss, tom. vi.; Harless, 'Kirche und Amt nach lutherischer Lehre,' Stuttgart 1853; Köstlin, 'Luther's Lehre von der Kirche,' Stuttgart 1853, §§ 2-4, 6, etc.; Nitzsch, 'Praktische Theologie, Gottesdienst,' 2te Aufl., Bonn 1863.]

On the important subject of the Sacraments, the following books are worthy of consultation :

Calvin's 'Tracts on the Sacraments,' and Turrettin, loc. xix., as before mentioned. Bellarmine, in his 'Disputationes,' tom. iii. Ingolstadii 1605, gives a very full and exact statement of the Romish doctrine on the subject.

Archbishop Tillotson, ' On Transubstantiation.'

Waterland, ' Review of the Doctrine of the Eucharist, as laid down in Scripture and Antiquity,' Cambridge 1737.

Bishop Cosin, ' History of Popish Transubstantiation,' Lond. 1676.

Hospinian, ' Historia Sacramentaria,' Tiguri 1602.

Johnson, ' The Unbloody Sacrifice and Altar Unvailed and Supported,' Lond. 1724.—This work was republished by the Tractarian party at Oxford in 1847.

Hoadly (successively Bishop of Bangor, Hereford, Salisbury, and Winchester), ' Plain Account of the Nature and End of the Sacrament of the Lord's Supper,' 2d ed. Lond. 1735. The view of the ordinance advocated by Hoadly is, in substance, that of the Socinian body.

One of the most recent defences of the Romish doctrine of transubstantiation, and that by a plausible and dextrous, if not very profound controversialist, is to be found in Cardinal Wiseman's ' Lectures on the Real Presence of the Body and Blood of our Lord Jesus Christ in the Blessed Eucharist,' published in 1836. The same subject was discussed by him in the second volume of his ' Lectures on the Principal Doctrines and Practices of the Catholic Church,' which also appeared in 1836. His arguments were replied to by Dr. Turton, then Regius Professor of Divinity in Cambridge, and Dean of Peterborough, in his ' Roman Catholic Doctrine of the Eucharist Considered,' Camb. 1837. Dr. Wiseman responded by ' A Reply to Dr. Turton's Roman Catholic Doctrine of the Eucharist Considered,' Lond. 1839 ; to which Dr. Turton again rejoined in some ' Observations on the Rev. Dr. Wiseman's Reply,' Camb. 1839. The controversy was also taken up by Mr. Stanley Faber, in a work entitled ' Christ's Discourse at Capernaum fatal to the Doctrine of Transubstantiation,' Lond. 1840.

Wilberforce, ' The Doctrine of the Holy Eucharist,' 3d ed. Lond. 1854.—The writer advocates the extreme High Church view of the Sacrament; but his book displays a good deal both of learning and ingenuity. The doctrines propounded on this subject by Wilberforce, Pusey, and others of the Tractarian party, were met and refuted with great ability and success by Mr. Goode, afterwards Dean of Ripon, in a very valuable work, ' The Nature of Christ's Presence in the Eucharist ; or, the True

Doctrine of the Real Presence Vindicated,' Lond. 1856. I would also strongly recommend, in this connection, an admirable essay by Dr. Hodge of Princeton upon 'The Doctrine of the Reformed Church on the Lord's Supper,' which is published among his 'Essays and Reviews,' New York 1857. See also Dr. Cunningham's discussion of the subject, 'Works,' vol. i. pp. 225–291, vol. ii. pp. 201–207, vol. iii. pp. 121–143.

Dr. Halley's work on 'The Sacraments,' published as the Congregational Lecture for 1844, marks an era in the history of the English Independents as regards the views which it advocated with respect to indiscriminate Baptism,—views which had been spreading widely for some time among the denomination to which the writer belonged, but which, when publicly maintained by him as their representative, took many by surprise.[1] Apart from this, however, the book is an important and valuable one for its often very effective refutation of the High Church doctrines of Baptism and the Lord's Supper, as well as for the great ability and general scholarship displayed throughout it. [Dr. Halley defended his position as to indiscriminate Baptism against Dr. Wardlaw and other critics, in a work entitled ' Baptism, the Designation of the Catechumens, not the Symbol of the Members of the Christian Church,' Lond. 1847.]

Goode, 'Doctrine of the Church of England as to the Effects of Baptism in the case of Infants,' 2d ed. Lond. 1850. The main object of the author is to vindicate the position and teaching of the evangelical party with respect to Baptism, from the standards of the English Church. With this in view, Mr. Goode proves most conclusively, as indeed had been done before by Hickman, Toplady, and others, that the Reformers of the Church of England, and those who drew up her Articles, were Calvinists in doctrine.[2] Having established this point, he then argues from it, that they, as Calvinists, could not have consistently held the doctrine of baptismal regeneration, and therefore could not have meant to teach it in the Baptismal Service or the Church Catechism ; and therefore that he and other evangelical members of the Church of England who do not believe in baptismal regeneration, need have no scruple in using these formularies and interpreting their expressions about the effects of Baptism in a sound sense,—a kind of argument which, in the case of a Church

[1 See above, p. 54 of this vol.]   [2] Goode, pp. 38–142.

notoriously founded on a compromise, is not perhaps very conclusive.[1] In itself, however, like all the writings of this author,
the book displays much learning, talent, and soundness of view.

Booth, ' Pædobaptism Examined,' Lond. 1829, in three
volumes, first published in 1787.—This work used to be the
standard among Antipædobaptists, before the appearance of
Dr. Carson's writings on the subject. It was replied to with
great ability by Dr. Williams, in his ' Antipædobaptism Examined,' Shrewsbury 1789. Dr. Williams was a theologian of
high standing. He is the author of an ' Essay on the Equity of
Divine Government and the Sovereignty of Divine Grace,' and
of a ' Defence of Modern Calvinism,' in reply to Bishop Tomline,
both of which are very valuable books.

Wardlaw, ' Dissertation on the Scriptural Authority, Nature,
and Uses of Infant. Baptism,' 3d ed. Glasg. 1846.—This is an
acute and masterly discussion of the question of Infant Baptism.
In an Appendix, the author controverts the views of Dr. Halley
and the English Independents as to indiscriminate Baptism.

Carson, ' Baptism in its Mode and Subjects,' Lond. 1844.—
This is the ablest book which has appeared in recent times on the
Antipædobaptist side. Among other replies to it, may be men-
tioned that by Professor Wilson of Belfast: ' Infant Baptism a
Scriptural Service,' Lond. 1848.

Beecher, ' Baptism with reference to its Import and Modes,'
New York 1849. A singularly clear, logical, and scholarly discussion of the Scriptural meaning of the word ' Baptism,' and
the modes in which the rite may be lawfully performed. [Cf.
Princeton Essays, 2d Series, Ess. xvi.] With respect to the
practice of the early post-apostolic Church as to Infant Baptism,
see Wall, ' History of Infant Baptism,' 3d ed. Lond. 1720. It
is a very thorough and reliable book.

Cunningham, ' Works,' vol. iii. pp. 144-154.

[Among the numerous works on the Sacraments by German
theologians, both of the Reformed and the Lutheran Churches,
may be mentioned : Ebrard, ' Dogma vom heiligen Abendmahl,'
Frankf. 1845 ; Jul. Müller, ' Lutheri et Calvini sententiæ de sacrâ
Coenâ,' Halis 1851 ; Harnack, ' der christliche Gemeindegottes-
dienst im apostlischen und altkatholischen Zeitalter,' Erlangen
1854 ; Höfling, ' das Sakrament der Taufe,' Erlangen 1846 ;

[1 Cf. Cunningham, *Works*, vol. i. pp. 176 ff.]

Kahnis, 'die Lehre vom Abendmahl,' Leipzig 1851. The two
last named are very learned and elaborate works, written from
the High Lutheran confessional standpoint.]

DIV. III.—*Church Power exercised in regard to Discipline.*

Durham, 'Treatise concerning Scandal,' Glasg. 1740; see
esp. Part ii. This is a very excellent and useful work. There is
a great deal of practical Christian wisdom and sound judgment
shown, both in the principles which the writer lays down with
respect to the exercise of ecclesiastical discipline, and the applications which he makes of them. [Compare the same author's
'Commentary on the Revelation,' Glasg. 1788, pp. 179–190.]

Voetius, 'Politica Ecclesiastica,' tom. iii. lib. iv. Tract ii.–iv.,
Amstel. 1676.

'Book of Common Order,' ch. vii. Dunlop's Collection, vol.
ii. pp. 413–417. [This chapter is little else than an abridged
translation of Calvin, 'Instit.' lib. iv. cap. xii. Besides the works
referred to on pp. 190, 199 of this vol., see Wilson, 'The Kingdom of our Lord Jesus Christ,' Edin. 1859, pp. 349–431; 'Essay
on Sacerdotal Absolution,' Princeton Essays, 1st Series, No. xv.]

PART IV.—THE PARTIES IN WHOM THE RIGHT TO EXERCISE
CHURCH POWER IS VESTED.

The question of Church government did not come up for any
very formal and detailed discussion until the Reformation, the
monarchical system of ecclesiastical polity which had grown up in
Europe along with the Papacy being generally acquiesced in,
save among the Vaudois, and in a few other such exceptional
cases. "We have, however," as Dr. Cunningham has remarked,
"a pretty full and formal statement of the argument in favour of
the two systems of Episcopacy and Presbytery as early as the
fourth century, of the Scriptural argument in favour of Presbytery by Jerome, usually regarded as the most learned of the
Fathers, and of the argument in favour of Prelacy by Epiphanius in reply to Aerius. And it may be worth while to observe in passing, that Jerome's Scriptural argument for Presbytery
is still generally regarded by Presbyterians as a conclusive and
unanswerable defence of their cause; while the earliest defence
of Prelacy by Epiphanius has been admitted by some of the ablest

defenders of Prelacy—such as Cardinal Bellarmine, De Dominis, Archbishop of Spalatro, and Hooker—to be weak and unsatisfactory, though they have not, I think, been able to devise anything that was greatly superior to it." [1]

Calvin, ' Inst.' lib. iv. cap. iii.–v.

Turrettin, loc. xviii. qu. xvi.–xxi.

Beza, ' Responsio ad Tractationem de Ministrorum Evangelii Gradibus ab Hadriano Saraviâ editam,' 1592 ; ' De diversis Ministrorum Gradibus contra Saraviam,' Genevæ 1594.

Bucer, ' Dissertatio de Gubernatione Ecclesiæ,' Middelburgi Zelandorum 1618.

Voetius, ' Politica Ecclesiastica,' tom. iii. lib. ii. Tract ii.–iv., lib. iv. Tract i.–iii.

Salmasius, ' De Primatu Papæ,' Lugdun. Batav. 1645.—This is a standard book for the views of the Fathers on the subject of the Papal supremacy.

Salmasius, ' De Episcopis et Presbyteris,' Lugdun. Batav. 1641, published under the assumed name of ' Walo Messalinus.'

Blondel, ' Apologia pro sententia Hieronymi de Episcopis et Presbyteris ;' taking up especially the argument from antiquity with extraordinary learning, and in great detail.

Vitringa, ' De Synagogâ Vetere.' A book of immense learning and research, the object being to prove that the government of the synagogue was the model on which that of the Church was founded. The main fault of the work is a tendency to strain likenesses in matters of detail; its general design is very successfully accomplished. As regards the remarkable unanimity with which all the leading Reformers arrived at from Scripture, and maintained in their writings the essential principles of Presbyterianism, see, besides the treatises on Church government of several of them already referred to : Dr. Cunningham's ' Works,' vol. iii. pp. 514–533 ; Miller, ' Letters concerning the Constitution and Order of the Christian Ministry,' 2d ed. Philadelphia 1830, pp. 351–406. [See also Luther, ' sämtliche Schriften,' ed. Walch, Th. xiv. pp. 139 f., 362 ff., Th. xix. pp. 877–886, etc.; Melanchthon, ' Opera,' in the ' Corpus Reformatorum,' vol. xxi. Brunsvigiæ 1854, pp. 834 ff., 1100, vol. xxii. pp. 515–524, etc.]

A rather curious illustration of the difficulty of getting any show of authority from the Reformers in favour of Prelacy, even

[1] Cunningham, *Works*, vol. iii. p. 549.

by the method of isolated quotation, may be seen in Dr. Words-worth's 'Theophilus Anglicanus,' a book which has gone through many editions, and is commonly used as a text-book for students. The author has collected together (ed. 1863, p. 105 f.) most of the passages handed down by Anglican tradition from the days of Bancroft and Durel, with a view to prove that the Reformers were forced into Presbyterianism against their real convictions of the Scriptural authority of Prelacy. I take those which he has thought worthy of being printed at full length; two or three more, given in reference, are even less relevant. The first is the well-known passage from Melanchthon's 'Apology for the Augsburg Confession' (art. vii. 24), in which he states: "We are exceedingly anxious to preserve the ecclesiastical polity and the orders in the Church, *although appointed by human authority.* For we know that this Church polity was *established by the Fathers* in the way that the ancient Canons describe, *with a good and useful design.*" He then goes on to throw the responsibility of the dissolution of this established order of things upon the Romish party, seeing that the other side were willing to yield the bishops their jurisdiction, "if only they would cease to rage against our Churches." Melanchthon was at this time almost overwhelmed by a sense of the dangers that threatened to crush the Protes-tant cause altogether. His very interesting correspondence with Luther, who was unable to be present at the Diet, shows him willing to give up almost anything, if only the light of the Gospel might be spared them. He constantly appeals to Luther to tell him what further concessions he might make to the Romanists. This passage accordingly shows his willingness to yield the bishops their place and jurisdiction, both being regarded simply as of human appointment, for the sake of peace; just as, a few years after this, when signing a decided declaration of the Scripture authority of Presbyterianism drawn up by Luther (art. Schmalc. De Potest. et Jurisd. Episc.), he added to his signature a state-ment that, the Gospel safe, he would, "propter pacem et com-munem tranquillitatem," concede—not only to the bishops but—to the Pope himself, his present supremacy over the Church, "*jure humano.*" This particular concession of his in the Apology ex-posed him, as he tell us, to reproaches from many of his friends; and even Luther, with all his wish to spare Melanchthon's sen-sitiveness to blame from himself, wrote to him: "I have received

your Apology, and wonder what you mean by wishing to know
what and how much you may yield to the Papists.   For my part,
I hold that there is only too much yielded to them already in the
Apology.   (Für meine Person ist ihnen allzuviel nachgegeben
in der Apologia.)" Walch, Th. xvi. p. 1070.   Cf. pp. 1101,
1695, 1756, 1794, etc.

The defects of the German Reformation on several points—
e.g. the place given to the civil power in Church affairs—arose
from a failure on the part of the leading Reformers to insist in
practice upon the Scriptural principles clearly perceived in theory.
Eight years at least before the Diet of Augsburg, Luther had
discovered that no order of Church office-bearers above presbyters
had any warrant in Scripture, and announced his convictions on
the point to the world with his usual emphasis, anticipating Beza's
distinction between "a Divine, a human, and a Satanical Episcopacy."   " Es soll Jedermann wissen," he says in a work written
against the Pope and " the order of bishops, falsely so called,"
" dass die Bischöffe, die jetzt über viele Städte regieren, nicht
christliche Bischöffe nach gottlicher Ordnung sind, sondern aus
teuflischer Ordnung und menschlichem Frevel, sind auch gewiss-
lich des Teufels Boten und Statthalter.   Das will ich redlich und
wohl beweisen, dass weder sie selbst, noch Jemand soll leugnen
können."   He then proceeds to prove the Divine authority of the
Presbyterian system by the usual Scripture arguments.   Walch,
Th. xix. p. 877, etc.

After the extract from Melanchthon's Apology, Dr. Wordsworth gives three short and wholly detached sentences from
Calvin, and one from Beza.   The first is from Calvin's letter to
Cardinal Sadolet in 1539 : " Disciplinam, qualem habuit vetus
Ecclesia nobis deesse non diffitemur ; sed cujus erit æquitatis nos
eversæ disciplinæ ab iis accusari, qui [et] eam soli penitus sustulerunt, [*et quum postliminio reducere conaremur nobis hactenus
obstiterunt?*"]   Now, any one who had read the context could
not fail to be aware that this passage has nothing whatever to
do with Church government, strictly so-called.   " Disciplina " has
just its ordinary meaning, as distinct from " regimen," and refers
to that famous system of Church censures which Calvin was then
striving to establish at Geneva—that same " godly discipline of
the primitive Church," in short, for the restoration of which the
Church of England still utters an annual longing in the Commi-

nation Service. The Genevese Reformer had not yet succeeded in his attempt; he was, in fact, in banishment at that very moment, because of the opposition encountered in it. He could not but admit, therefore, that as yet "the discipline of the ancient Church is wanting to us." It was not until about two years after this that he could write to Myconius: "*Nunc* habemus qualecunque presbyterorum judicium, et formam *disciplinœ*, qualem ferebat temporum infirmitas." If Dr. Wordsworth had given the last clause of the sentence quoted, the true meaning of the first would have been suggested. He has not done so. On the contrary, he has put a full stop after "sustulerunt," and printed immediately after it another short sentence—which does not even occur in the letter to Sadolet—beginning with "Episcopatus," without the slightest break or indication that that is not the next word in the original. The impression left on the mind of the reader is, of course, that the "discipline" referred to was Episcopacy.

The Prelatic value of the other three sentences is simply this, that they happen to contain the word "Episcopus" or "Episcopate." They contain nothing which any Presbyterian in the present day would not heartily agree to, understanding the words, as Calvin and Beza did, in their Scriptural sense. "In that I call those who rule the Churches," says Calvin, when formally discussing the subject, "bishops, presbyters, pastors, and ministers indifferently, I do so according to the usage of Scripture, which employs these terms as synonymous, giving the title of bishop to all who discharge the ministry of the Word" (*Inst.* lib. iv. cap. iii. 8). And this is the evidence by which the authors of the 'Ordonnances ecclésiastiques de Genève' and the 'De *Triplici* Episcopatu' are to be proved favourers of Prelacy!

'Vindication of the Presbyterial Government and Ministry.' By the Provincial Assembly of London. Lond. 1649. 'Reasons presented by the Dissenting Brethren against certain Propositions concerning Presbyterial Government, with the Answers of the Assembly of Divines to the reasons of Dissent,' Lond. 1648. The representatives of Independency in the Westminster Assembly, although few in number, were men of much ability and learning. We have here the arguments urged by them in behalf of the Independent theory of the Church, with a careful and thorough answer to these by the divines who drew up the standards of our Church.

Alexander Henderson, 'The Government and Order of the Church of Scotland,' 1641.

Gillespie, 'Assertion of the Government of the Church of Scotland,' Edin. 1641 ; especially full and valuable in connection with the office and duties of the ruling elder.

Rutherford, 'The Due Right of Presbyteries; or, a Peaceable Plea for the Government of the Church of Scotland,' Lond. 1644. —This is a very learned and elaborate treatise, chiefly directed against the views of the Independents. By the same author is, 'A peaceable and temperate Plea for Paul's Presbyterie in Scotland,' Lond. 1642 ; also dealing mainly with the Independent theory. Principal Baillie's 'Dissuasive from the Errors of the Times,' Lond. 1645, discusses, likewise, the principles of the Independents among those of the other sects of the day. A second part or continuation of the 'Dissuasive' appeared in 1647, taking up the special subject of 'Anabaptism.'

Calderwood, 'Altare Damascenum.'—A sort of first sketch or outline of this celebrated and important work was published by the author in 1621. It is in English ; and the title-page—as is the case with many other of Calderwood's works—exhibits neither the author's name nor the place of publication, this being a precaution very necessary in his case, in order to avoid the persecuting measures of the Court and the Prelatic party in Scotland. The title of the little volume referred to is, 'The Altar of Damascus, or the Pattern of the English Hierarchie and Church Policie obtruded upon the Church of Scotland,'—the allusion being to the incident recorded in 2 Kings xvi. 10, 11. The first edition of the work in its completed form appeared in Latin in 1623, and immediately established the fame of the writer in the theological world, both at home and abroad. It is constantly quoted as an authority by Voetius and other eminent Continental divines of the seventeenth and eighteenth centuries. It contains an exceedingly elaborate, able, and learned discussion of all the main points relating to Church government and worship then in dispute between Prelatists and Presbyterians, beginning with the royal supremacy in the Church of England.[1]

In 1640, Bishop Hall, the author of the 'Contemplations,' at the request of Archbishop Laud, wrote a book called 'Episcopacie

[1] [See the "Life of Calderwood" appended to the last volume of his *History of the Kirk of Scotland*, Wodrow Soc. ed. Edin. 1849.]

by Divine Right, asserted by J. H.,' Lond. 1640. In the same
year, seeing that applications were being largely made to Parliament for the abolition of Diocesan Episcopacy, and the establishment of the Presbyterian system in its place, Bishop Hall came
forward again to oppose this movement in a work published anony-
mously : ' An Humble Remonstrance to the High Court of Parliament by a dutiful Son of the Church.' This called forth a
very able treatise, ' An Answer to a Book entitled " An Humble
Remonstrance," in which the Parity of Bishops and Presbyters in
Scripture is demonstrated, the occasion of their Imparity in Antiquity discovered, the Disparity of the ancient and our modern
Bishops manifested, the Antiquity of Ruling Elders in the Church
vindicated, and the Prelatical Church bounded. By Smectymnuus.' 1641. This work was reprinted from the 5th ed. in
Edinburgh, 1708. The authors were five eminent ministers of
the Puritan party : Stephen Marshall, Edmund Calamy, Thomas
Young, Matthew Newcomen, and William Spurstowe, whose
united initials make up the word Smectymnuus. Bishop Hall
replied in a ' Defence of the Humble Remonstrance against the
frivolous and false exceptions of Smectymnuus, wherein the right
of Leiturgie and Episcopacie is clearly vindicated from the vain
cavils and challenges of the Answerer,' Lond. 1641. In reply
to this appeared ' A Vindication of the Answer to the Humble
Remonstrance from the unjust imputations of frivolousness and
falsehood, wherein the cause of Liturgy and Episcopacy is further
debated,' by the same Smectymnuus, Lond. 1641. Bishop Hall
rejoined in ' A short Answer to the tedious Vindication of
Smectymnuus,' Lond. 1641. The controversy was also taken up
by Milton in his ' Animadversions upon the Remonstrant's Defence against Smectymnuus,' Lond. 1641, and ' An Apology for
Smectymnuus,' Lond. 1642. These works of Milton's, as well as
two others which he published about the same time, ' Of Reformation in England,' and ' The Reason of Church Government
urged against Prelaty,' are very vigorously written, often highly
eloquent, and thoroughly Presbyterian in principle.

With respect to the views of the earlier generation of English
Puritans, I may refer you to the works of one of their ablest
representatives, Thomas Cartwright : ' A full and plaine Declaration of Ecclesiastical Discipline out of the Word of God, and
of the declining of the Church of England from the same,' 1574.

This was drawn up originally in Latin by Travers, but further elaborated and translated by Cartwright.[1] 'A Replie to an Answere made of M. Doctor Whitgifte againste the Admonition to the Parliament.' 'Second Replie agaynst Maister Doctor Whitgifte's Second Answer touching the Church Discipline.' 1575. The second part of this appeared in 1577. See also ' A Defence of the Ecclesiastical Discipline ordayned of God to be used in His Church, 1588' (in reply to Bridges).

One of the most learned and elaborate works on the opposite side is that of Bilson, ' The Perpetual Government of Christ's Church,' Oxf. 1842, first published in 1593. It is still commonly regarded as a standard authority in the Church of England.

Dodwell, ' Separation of Churches from Episcopal Government, as practised by the present Nonconformists, proved schismatical,' 1679.—The author was an extreme and consistent High Churchman. He was replied to by Baxter, in ' A Treatise of Episcopacy,' Lond. 1681 ; and by an eminent Lutheran divine, Buddeus, in his ' Exercitatio de Origine et Potestate Episcoporum,' Jenæ 1705. As among the ablest writers on the same side with Dodwell, may be further named, Cave, ' Dissertation concerning the Government of the Ancient Church,' Lond. 1683 ; and Thorndike, ' Two Discourses ; the one of the primitive Government of the Churches, the other of the Service of God at the Assemblies of the Church,' Cambridge 1650.

Stillingfleet, in his ' Irenicum,' 2d ed. 1662, abandoned the attempt to prove a *Jus Divinum* for Diocesan Episcopacy, as the school of Laud had sought to do, resting his argument for it solely on considerations of expediency, and urging the Nonconformists to union on the ground that no form of Church polity had been specially appointed in Scripture. His book is a remarkably able, and in many respects a very fair and candid one.

Baxter, ' Five Disputations of Church Government and Worship,' Lond. 1659.

Owen, ' An Inquiry into the Original Nature, Institution, Power, Order, and Communion of Evangelical Churches,' ' Works,' Goold's ed. vol. xv. ; ' True Nature of a Gospel Church,' vol. xvi. The first of these two treatises appeared in 1681, in answer to an attack on the Nonconformist position by Stillingfleet, in his ' Unreasonablenss of Separation ; ' the second of them was pub-

[1] [Neal, *Hist. of Puritans*, ed. 1837, vol. i. p. 292.]

lished in 1689, a few years after the death of the author. These
two works, exhibiting as they do the matured opinions on Church
government of the greatest English theologian of that age, are
exceedingly interesting and important. Like all the writings of
Owen, they display great force of argument, and much learning,
wielded by sound judgment. In them the writer maintains very
powerfully all the great leading principles of Presbyterianism,
the Scripture authority for the office of ruling elder, courts of
review, etc. It would be well if the position of modern Independents on the question of Church polity were no further removed
from our own than that which is marked by the illustrious name
of Owen.

I have already referred to the works of Owen's colleague,
David Clarkson, on the subject of Presbyterianism and Prelacy.
They are especially able and valuable in connection with the
argument for the Presbyterian system, which is to be drawn from
the views and practice of the early post-apostolic Church. See
Clarkson's 'Select Works,' Wycliffe Soc. ed. Lond. 1846. As
useful books in the same department of the discussion, I may
mention further, Chauncy's 'Complete View of Episcopacy, as
exhibited from the Fathers of the Christian Church until the close
of the Second Century,' Boston 1721; Boyse's 'Clear Account
of the Ancient Episcopacy, proving it to have been Parochial,
and not Diocesan,' Lond. 1712; and Lauder of Mordentoun's
'Ancient Bishops, considered both with respect to the extent of
their Jurisdiction and the nature of their Power, in answer to
Mr. Chillingworth and others,' Edin. 1707.

Principal Rule, 'The Good Old Way Defended,' Edin. 1697
(in reply to Monro and Sage, two Episcopalian writers of the
day); 'A Vindication of the Church of Scotland,' 1691. The
author published also a 'Second Vindication,' and finally a
'Defence of the Vindication,' in 1694.

Anderson, 'A Defence of the Church Government, Faith,
Worship, and Spirit of the Presbyterians,' Edin. 1820.—This work
was first published in 1714. The author was minister of our
Church at Dumbarton, and took part to a considerable extent in
the controversies of the time. This treatise of his is a remarkably
acute and vigorously written book. I would also strongly recommend the works on this subject of a contemporary of Anderson
and Rule's, Professor Jameson of Glasgow, especially his 'Cypri-

anus Isotimus,' Edin. 1705 ; and his ' Sum of the Episcopal Con troversy,' Edin. 1712. Several very able treatises on Church government were also published about the same time by Principal Forrester of St. Mary's College, St. Andrews ; such as, ' Rectius Instruendum,' in 1684, ' The Hierarchical Bishop's Claim to a Divine Right, tried at the Scripture bar,' in 1699, ' A Review and Consideration of two late Pamphlets,' and ' Causa Episcopatûs hierarchici lucifuga' (in reply to Sage), in 1706.

To come down to more recent works on Church government, I may mention Dr. Mitchell of Kemnay's ' Presbyterian Letters,' Lond. 1809, addressed to Dr. Skinner, a bishop of the Scotch Episcopal body at Aberdeen, who had attacked some of the statements in Dr. Campbell's 'Lectures on Ecclesiastical History,' when published after the author's death.[1] Both Dr. Campbell and his vindicator, in defending Presbyterianism, agree in so far with Mr. Litton and others, that they hold that apostolic practice, even when proved in favour of one particular form of Church polity, will not avail to establish a *Jus Divinum*, and that a proved and fundamental departure from apostolic precedent does not affect the inherent lawfulness of any system of ecclesiastical government.

Dr. Brown of Langton, ' The exclusive Claims of Puseyite Episcopalians to the Christian Ministry Indefensible ; with an Inquiry into the Divine Right of Episcopacy and the Apostolical Succession :' in a series of Letters to Dr. Pusey. Edin. 1842. This is an able, learned, and useful book. Along with it I may name two treatises by an American divine, Dr. Smyth of Charleston : ' The Prelatical Doctrine of Apostolical Succession Examined,' Boston 1841 ; and ' Presbytery, not Prelacy, the Scriptural and Primitive Polity,' Boston 1843. Both of these works are especially valuable for the great collection which they furnish of literary material and references bearing on the subjects discussed.

Mason of New York, ' The claims of Diocesan Episcopacy Refuted,' Lond. 1838.

King, ' Exposition and Defence of the Presbyterian From of Church Government,' Edin. 1853. This is a very useful little volume, comprising in small space a good statement of the main arguments in favour of Presbyterianism as against both Indepen-

---

[1] [Campbell, *Lect. on Eccles. Hist.*, 3d ed. p. 202 f. M'Crie, *Miscell. Works*, Edin. 1841, pp. 67-69. Mitchell, *Presbyt. Letters*, pp. 274-377.]

dency and Prelacy. The same may be said of the 'Manual of Presbytery,' 2d ed. Edin. 1847, by Dr. Miller of Princeton, and Dr. Lorimer of Glasgow.

I next name two very excellent works of somewhat wider range, which discuss with much ability the main points in dispute, both as to government and worship, between Presbyterians and Episcopalians. Both of them were published by ministers of the Synod of Ulster: 'Presbyterianism Defended,' Glasg. 1839, and the 'Plea of Presbytery,' 3d ed. Belfast 1843.

With respect more especially to the Independent controversy, the following books may be referred to : A work by Professor Wood of St. Andrews in answer to Lockyer, who was the first to introduce the Independent theory into Scotland, under the quaint title of ' A Little Stone, pretended to be out of the Mountain, tried, and found to be a Counterfeit ; or, an Examination and Refutation of Mr. Lockyer's Lecture preached at Edinburgh, anno 1651,' Edin. 1654.

Whytock, ' Vindication of Presbytery ; with Twelve Essays on the Church,' Edin. 1843.—The author was minister of the Associate Congregation, Dalkeith, and died in 1805, shortly before the deposition of his friend Dr. M'Crie, whose views he shared, from office in the Secession Church.

Brown (of Gartmore, and afterwards of Langton), ' Vindication of the Presbyterian Form of Church Government, as professed in the Standards of the Church of Scotland,' Edin. 1805. —This is a very acute, vigorous, and thorough discussion of the points at issue between Presbyterians and Independents.

Dr. Cunningham, ' Works,' vol. ii. pp. 43–64, vol. iii. pp. 545–556.

As expressing the views of modern Independents may be named, Wardlaw, ' Congregational Independency,' Glasg. 1848 ; and Davidson, ' Ecclesiastical Polity of the New Testament,' Lond. 1848.

INDEX.

[The Italic *n* indicates that the reference is to the Notes.]

THE END.

CPSIA information can be obtained at www.ICGtesting.com
Printed in the USA
243084LV00005B/7/P